PASSION FOR TRUTH

PASSION FOR TRUTH

From Finding JFK's Single Bullet
to Questioning Anita Hill
to Impeaching Clinton

SENATOR ARLEN SPECTER

with Charles Robbins

Perennial

An Imprint of HarperCollins*Publishers*

A hardcover edition of this book was published in 2000 by
William Morrow, an imprint of HarperCollins Publishers.

PASSION FOR TRUTH. Copyright © 2001, 2000 by Senator Arlen Specter with Charles Robbins.
All rights reserved. Printed in the United States of America. No part of this
book may be used or reproduced in any manner whatsoever without
written permission except in the case of brief quotations embodied
in critical articles and reviews. For information address
HarperCollins Publishers Inc., 10 East 53rd Street,
New York, NY 10022.

HarperCollins books may be purchased for educational, business, or sales promotional use.
For information please write: Special Markets Department,
HarperCollins Publishers Inc., 10 East 53rd Street, New York, NY 10022.

First Perennial edition published 2001.

Designed by Debbie Glasserman

Library of Congress Cataloging-in-Publication Data is available.

ISBN 0-06-095810-3

01   02   03   04   05   WB/RRD   10   9   8   7   6   5   4   3   2   1

To my children,
their children, and
their children, and their children,
in perpetuity.

CONTENTS

PART THREE

PART FOUR

WITH THANKS!

My first acknowledgment is to my parents, Harry and Lillie Specter, who gave me life, values, and motivation. As a child, I heard my father's bitter complaint that the U.S. government had broken its promise to pay bonuses to World War I veterans after he nearly gave his life in the Argonne Forest. Figuratively, I have been on my way to Washington ever since to get my father's bonus, and I have had a lot of help along the way.

In my intermittent legal career, I have benefited from the training and role models of the best of the "Philadelphia lawyers" and beyond. My associates and assistants in the district attorney's office were indispensable in my developing investigative, trial, appellate, and administrative skills.

My colleagues in the political world provided special insights into serving the public, working with governmental agencies, and learning the "art of the possible."

It has been a great privilege to spend two decades in the U.S. Senate; to associate with a remarkable group of intellectual, practical legislators; to interact with presidents, jurists, and foreign leaders; and to serve 12 million Pennsylvanians.

For their love, encouragement, patience, and endurance, I most of all praise my wife, Joan; our sons, Shanin and Steve; Shanin's wife, Tracey; and their beautiful daughters, Silvi, Perri, Lilli, and Hatti, for joining me in literally hundreds of campaign stops, public appearances, and smiling holiday-greeting photos.

I thank the eighty-four friends who are too numerous to name here, who all figure prominently in this book, for refreshing or correcting my recollections of decades past. I especially thank the thoughtful, collegial professionalism of our executive editor, Claire Wachtel, and our able agent, Deborah Grosvenor.

This book has been a labor of love in which I relived my seventy years by reminiscing with Charles Robbins and a tape recorder. In my precarious profession, every effort must be made to make this book totally accurate because my potential adversaries will read it with a microscope. Only time will tell.

"Whom the gods would destroy, they first make angry." The corollary may be "those whom the electorate would reject first tempt to write a book."

My main reason for writing this book is to tell my children and their children something of my generation as a benchmark for them to surpass. To know where you came from may provide some insight on where you may go.

Arlen Specter
Philadelphia, July 2000

PROLOGUE:
THE SINGLE-BULLET CONCLUSION

═══════════

Billionaire industrialist and Reform Party founder H. Ross Perot organized a weekend conference in July 1995 to get President Clinton and his nine Republican challengers, including me, on record about our visions for the presidency in the twenty-first century. And, of course, to put the national spotlight on Perot. It was a blistering summer afternoon and, despite the air conditioning, only a little cooler under the klieg lights at the Dallas Convention Center, as I climbed onto the stage to face a battery of cameras for my "media availability." The reporters fired the usual questions about a balanced budget, universal health care, Social Security cuts, nuclear proliferation, and other public policy issues. In my case, they also asked how a moderate Jewish Northeastern senator could possibly win the Republican nomination.

Then one newspaper reporter hollered a question, an accusation really, that stilled the others. "Cynicism in America," the reporter said, "all began with your Single-Bullet Theory and was fanned by Watergate."

It was a heavy charge. I had developed the Single-Bullet Theory more than thirty years earlier as a staff lawyer on the President's Commission on the Assassination of President John F. Kennedy, more commonly known as the Warren Commission. I now call it the Single-Bullet Conclusion. It began as a theory, but when a theory is established by the facts, it deserves to be called a conclusion. The conclusion is that the same bullet sliced through President John F. Kennedy's neck and then tore through Texas Governor John Connally's chest and wrist, finally lodging in the governor's thigh, as the presidential motorcade wound through downtown Dallas on November 22, 1963. The Warren Commission adopted the Single-Bullet Conclusion as its official explanation. Essentially, the reporter was accusing me of bringing cynicism to American government, with Richard Nixon as an accomplice years after the fact.

I put aside the balanced-budget amendment and my flat-tax chart and explained the Single-Bullet Conclusion to the reporter. I gave him the same basic discourse I had given to Chief Justice Earl Warren several blocks away at the Texas School Book Depository Building on an equally torrid Dallas day thirty-one years earlier. I do not know how much my explanation impressed the journalists at the Perot presidential forum in July 1995. But the reporter who raised the issue about cynicism in government struck a raw nerve, far more important to the public dialogue than any budget blueprint or crime-control formula.

A central problem in America today is distrust of government. It goes beyond cynicism. Many Americans believe that their elected representatives are for sale and that their government lies to them. When momentous historical events occur, such as the assassination of President Kennedy, the popular reaction is that the government deceives and covers up through an explanation like the Single-Bullet Theory.

When Professor Anita Hill came forward to challenge President Bush's nomination of Judge Clarence Thomas to the U.S. Supreme Court, 38 percent of the American people grew in a year to 55 percent who thought the Senate Judiciary Committee had abused the accuser and given life tenure to a liar and sexual harasser. Government did not help itself when the CIA concealed key facts on the murder of a U.S. citizen in Guatemala, knowingly gave the president Soviet-tainted data, and was infiltrated by Soviet mole Aldrich Ames. After deadly blunders by the Bureau of Alcohol, Tobacco and Firearms and the FBI at Ruby Ridge, Idaho, and Waco, Texas, Americans flocked to militias to protect themselves from their government. In the three decades since President Kennedy's assassination, voter participation has plummeted, threatening our democratic process; militias have sprouted in more than forty states; and public confidence in America's institutions has gone into a free fall.

Part of the cure demands that Americans move off the sidelines and onto the playing field. Democracy, after all, is not a spectator sport. But our political and social health also rests on government's doggedly following facts to find truth and then acting on that truth to create public policy. Generally, when people can agree on the facts, on what is true, they can agree on what should be done in a just society.

My own efforts at truth-seeking began right out of college, as a second lieutenant in the Air Force Office of Special Investigations stateside during the Korean War. I continued my work in Philadelphia through several major investigations and trials, first as an assistant and later as district attorney, and through the Warren Commission. Later, as a U.S. senator, I ran investigations on the killings at Ruby Ridge, the terrorist bombing of Khobar Towers in Saudi Arabia, and Gulf War syndrome, and I participated actively in other probes, on such matters as campaign fund-raising abuses and allegations of Chinese espionage on military secrets.

This book contains my suggestions for combating distrust in America by showing how congressional and other governmental inquiries can reveal the truth, how Senate hearings on Supreme Court appointments can answer important public questions on nominees' fitness, and how the Congress responds to international crises. Interwoven with these substantive topics are my own background, experiences, and values, leading to my fetish for facts.

The idea for the book began when my press secretary, Charlie Robbins, decided, after my 1995 campaign for the Republican presidential nomination, to leave to write a novel. That project shifted to a nonfiction collaboration on the Damon Runyon–esque characters I had prosecuted during my DA days, and broadened to include my role on the Warren Commission and my Senate career.

No matter how studious the effort at avoidance, this book may suffer from "hero stories." As a young lawyer, I observed senior attorneys whom I called "chests of vests" recount their "heroic" trial experiences. Despite these potential pitfalls, I decided to proceed.

I believe it is particularly important for staff counsel of the Warren Commission to tell their experiences, especially as to the procedures and integrity of the investigation. We have seen, in the thirty-five years since the assassination, an almost morbid obsession about it. The assassination of John Kennedy is the single most investigated event in world history, with the possible exception of the crucifixion of Christ. And the challenges, the skepticism, and the questions only seem to grow. As soon as the commission legal staff was hired, the chief justice called us together and stressed that our mission was to find the truth and report it. That is what we tried to do. "Your client is the truth," he told us.

During my extensive travel throughout Pennsylvania and the nation, in open-house town meetings and in high school auditoriums, hardly a gathering occurs without questions about the Warren Commission, the Single-Bullet Theory, and the role I played in the investigation. I often answer that truth is stranger than fiction. Generally, I get nods of agreement. I also often point out that questions still linger about the assassination of Abraham Lincoln.

My former law partner Mark Klugheit once said that my career has been marked by my believing a theory most people doubted (the Single Bullet) and doubting a woman most people believed (Anita Hill). The Bible says, "The truth shall make you free." Keats said, "Beauty is truth, truth beauty." Everyone is entitled to his own opinion, but not to his own facts. At the very least, truth is the indisputable foundation for a decent, just, and civilized society.

PART ONE

"IT'S HARD
TO MAKE A LIVING"

My father did not have the money in 1932, at the depth of the Depression, to travel to Washington with his fellow World War I combat veterans to lobby the federal government for payment of their promised bonus. And he was not about to load his wife and four children into boxcars, as thousands of penniless veterans had done, to set up camp in dumps, parks, or anywhere else they could find in the nation's capital. But Harry Specter followed reports in the *Wichita Beacon*, our Kansas hometown paper, and on the radio, soaking up what he could.

The thousand-dollar bonuses were not scheduled to be paid until 1945. But the House of Representatives had authorized immediate payment of five hundred dollars per person, and the veterans came to press Congress and President Herbert Hoover to pass the bill and pay the money. My father had little more than his small disability pension to feed his wife and four children. A five-hundred-dollar bonus would have made a big difference.

Beginning in May 1932, twenty-five thousand World War I combat veterans, some from my father's 355th Infantry Company, many with their families, descended on Washington, D.C. They called themselves "The Bonus Expeditionary Force" and became known as "The Bonus Army." They built shacks and staked tents at Anacostia Flats across the Potomac River from Washington, and they moved into half-razed warehouses and market stalls on Pennsylvania Avenue, where the East Wing of the National Gallery of Art now stands.

President Hoover refused to meet with the veterans. By July 28, at the peak of a sweltering summer, Hoover's patience had ended. When the former soldiers refused to leave Pennsylvania Avenue, police with nightsticks began clearing them off. Veterans from Anacostia Flats arrived and threw rocks at the police. The officers shot four veterans, killing two. Hoover ordered his Army chief of staff, General Douglas MacArthur, to clear the veterans. On his staff, MacArthur had a major, Dwight D. Eisenhower.

At MacArthur's command, Major George S. Patton and his Third Cavalry rode down Pennsylvania Avenue with sabers drawn, followed by infantry with bayonets fixed, mounted machine gunners, troops with tear gas, and six tanks. Patton charged the unarmed veterans. Three thousand tear-gas bombs draped Pennsylvania Avenue in a toxic haze.

"Where were you in the Argonne, buddy?" the veterans hollered at the troops, referring to the bloody French battleground.

The Bonus Army fled toward Anacostia. MacArthur, never impressed by presidential decrees, ignored Hoover's orders to stop at the Potomac. Instead, the Army chased the veterans and burned their makeshift villages. Hundreds of veterans were injured, and two infants died, suffocated by tear gas. It was all over by midnight. Hoover explained to the nation that the Bonus Army was mostly Communist agitators threatening national security, nothing more than "ordinary trespassers."

My father grew up in Batchkurina, a village 160 miles from Kiev in the heart of Ukraine. The date of his birth cannot be fixed because no birth records were maintained in Batchkurina. My father said he was born in the "pear season," which he estimated to be around July 15. His citizenship papers list 1892 as the year of his birth, but he recalled writing that he was ten years old in the year 1903, which could have put his year of birth a year later.

Harry Specter lived in a one-room, dirt-floored hut that he shared with his parents, seven brothers, and one sister. He never received any formal education. With nine children, his parents could not afford school for him. As the only Jewish family in town, they were a convenient target for the villagers' slurs and the Cossacks' sport. At the age of eighteen, determined to avoid the czar's heel and conscription in Siberia, and equally determined to seek freedom and opportunity, my father saved a few rubles and walked across the entire

European continent, alone, uneducated, and destitute, to sail steerage to America.

When he landed in New York, a teeming city of almost 5 million, my father had no address for his brother, his only contact in the New World, but he knew the name and street corner of his brother's bank from a check received by the family in Batchkurina. On a Sunday morning, he went to that street corner with the hope that his brother might live nearby and pass the bank.

After several hours, he saw his brother walk by. He ran up to him and shouted, *"Yussel, Yussel, ich bin dein bruder Aaron,"* Yiddish for "Joseph, Joseph, I am your brother Harry." My father had changed considerably in the seven years since Joseph had last seen his eleven-year-old kid brother. Looking at this stranger, Uncle Joe said, *"Oyb du bist mein bruder Aaron, kum mit mir,"* Yiddish for "If you are my brother Harry, come with me." And so began my father's life in America.

Moving to Philadelphia, Harry Specter worked for a tailor in a sweatshop at Fourth and Lombard streets. Determined to improve his lot, he saved his money, bought a Model-T Ford, and traveled West to learn English and see America. In the Midwest my father told a man he was Jewish. The man expressed surprise that my father did not have horns.

When buying blankets and dry goods at a supply store in St. Joseph, Missouri, in 1916, he struck up a conversation with a woman named Freida Shanin. Harry Specter asked Freida Shanin if she had a daughter.

Mrs. Shanin replied that she did, but that her daughter was too young for him. Actually, Freida Shanin had four daughters and three sons. Her oldest, Lillie, was sixteen, and her youngest was two. Freida Shanin's husband, Mordecai, had died of a heart attack in his mid-forties a year earlier. He had sold fish on the streets of St. Joseph and repaired Singer sewing machines. Widowed, with seven children, Freida Shanin maintained her pride and independence. Her children helped support the family. Lillie had left school after the eighth grade to work in a tablet factory.

Despite Freida Shanin's reservations, Harry Specter courted her beautiful red-headed daughter Lillie. They fell in love.

The romance of Harry Specter and Lillian Shanin was interrupted in 1917 by World War I. Next to his family, my father was proudest of his service in the American Expeditionary Force in France, where he rose

9

to the rank of buck private. He joined Company I of the 355th Infantry on May 6, 1918, and sailed from the United States for France on June 4. Harry Specter was given twenty-nine days to be trained and transported. He was placed in the front lines. Fortunately, he was too proud to realize he was cannon fodder. My father survived—thankfully for my brother, Morton; my two sisters, Hilda and Shirley; and me.

When Harry Specter left, Lillie gave him a photograph of her, inscribed on the back:

> *The French girls may be pretty,*
> *The French girls may be kind,*
> *But don't forget*
> *The girl you left so far behind.*

My father's twenty-nine days aboard ship offered little time for training. One hundred days after he shipped out, he was seriously wounded. He convalesced and returned to the United States on January 5, 1919. On crutches, he returned to St. Joe to marry the slender redhead who would become my mother.

During the course of the next forty-five years, Harry and Lillie Specter moved back and forth between the East Coast and the Midwest, searching for ways to support the family. He often said, *"Schver tsu machen a lebn,"* Yiddish for "It's hard to make a living." That was certainly true for him.

Harry Specter became a peddler. He rose before dawn and worked past dusk, earning a living any way and anywhere he could. He drove a truck in the Scranton coal fields, sold blankets to farmers in the winter in Nebraska, and peddled cantaloupes door-to-door in small Midwestern towns in the summer.

I do not know all of the family's travels, but I know that my brother, Morton, was born in 1920 in St. Joseph and my sister Hilda in 1921 in Philadelphia. My mother recounted living in Camden, New Jersey, and watching a workman fall from the Benjamin Franklin Bridge, which was under construction for several years before opening on June 30, 1926. The family was back in the Midwest when my sister Shirley was born in St. Joe in 1927, and three years later, when I was born in Wichita, Kansas, in February 1930.

I was two in July 1932, when the Army routed my father's fellow World War I veterans. I can only imagine his horror when his comrades-in-arms, who had survived enemy fire in the French forest, were cut down by American troops on the main boulevard of America's capital. In a figurative sense, I have been on my way to Washington ever since to collect my father's bonus—to push government to treat its citizens, the millions of hardworking Harry Specters, justly.

Two years after the bonus march, I had an experience that I think bolstered my confidence to tackle such a tough job. Psychologists now stress the importance of experiences from birth to age five. When I was four, my father took me to see the Wichita sheriff, who asked me what I would like to see or do in his office. I replied I'd like to hold the pistol I saw in his holster. No, he said, but he would make me a deputy sheriff, and he pinned his badge to my overalls for a picture in the spot where mug shots were taken. My proud father sent the photo to "Ripley's Believe It or Not." On June 18, 1934, Ripley's carried my picture with the caption that I was the youngest deputy sheriff in history. Over the years, I saw my father take that clipping from his wallet again and again to proudly show it to his friends, until it literally disintegrated in his hands from the folding and handling. While there is no easy formula for parents to instill pride or a sense of self-worth in every child, these experiences instilled in me, I think, a spirit of confidence and optimism.

My commitment to public service began in 1959 as a Philadelphia assistant district attorney. In 1959, Harry and Lillie Specter were graying grandparents. Eisenhower was president. America was prosperous and optimistic. The Cadillac Eldorado came out with a double-decker grille and swooping tail fins, arguably the gaudiest car ever to roll off an American assembly line. *Ben-Hur* won the Academy Award. Popular songs included "Everything's Coming Up Roses" and "High Hopes." The Soviet Union launched a rocket with two monkeys aboard. Fidel Castro became president of Cuba. Charles De Gaulle became president of France. Hawaii became the fiftieth state. And in Philadelphia, machine politics rolled on as it had since the Civil War.

LEAVING THE WALL-TO-WALL LIFE

Barnes, Dechert, Price, Myers and Rhoads, the Philadelphia law firm I joined after graduating from law school, had wall-to-wall carpeting throughout the office at a time when most firms still had area rugs. Seeing the carpeting, I knew it what wall-to-wall meant: It was the big law firm's equivalent of cradle-to-grave. It was law school graduation to the farm on retirement.

To that point, my career had been conventional. I met a beautiful blonde, Joan Lois Levy, at a dance when I was a college sophomore and she was still in high school. Four years later, in 1953, we married, months before I entered Yale Law School. I joined Dechert upon graduating in 1956. Joan and I moved from our Quonset hut in New Haven to my parents' Philadelphia home on Stirling Street for the summer of 1956 while I studied for and passed the bar exam and then in September to a newly decorated apartment on Pine Street. In 1957, with our first son, Shanin, on the way, we were ready to move again, to a tidy redbrick Center City town house on Latimer Street. We shared a garden with the Colonial Dames of America next door. The Dames, an exclusive club in the Social Register, had retained one row house on the edge of their property to protect their garden after knocking down half a block to build a beautiful clubhouse. Joan and I passed muster from their interviewing committee to rent their house, which was probably tougher than gaining membership.

At Dechert, every Friday morning our twenty-member trial team gathered around the firm's glistening oak conference table to discuss the week's work and often to complain about judges or laws we found unjust. The firm elders were not willing to get into politics to run for state court or for the state legislature. That was beneath them, and it would reduce their income and leisure hours. I decided to leave Barnes, Dechert and the wall-to-wall life of a big-city law firm in October 1959. I wanted to perform public service, gain trial experience, and get involved in politics. I was going to become an assistant Philadelphia district attorney. I was twenty-nine years old. A senior partner at the firm, Owen Rhoads, tried to talk me out of becoming a prosecutor. Rhoads warned me that I would be disillusioned and miserable, and I was throwing away a bright future at the firm.

But I had made my decision. Inheriting my parents' politics, I had become a Democratic committeeman, the lowest rung on the political ladder. My territory was the sixth division of the eighth ward in Center City, Philadelphia. My job was to get residents to register Democratic and then to vote. Twice, I had climbed four flights of stairs in a converted apartment building on Spruce Street to urge a man to register. Finally, I climbed the stairs again and dragged the man out. Annoyed, he registered Republican.

At the district attorney's office, Paul Chalfin, the first assistant, handled day-to-day operations, including hiring. That freed District Attorney Victor Hugo Blanc to attend Kiwanis lunches and the like. At my interview, Chalfin wanted to know why a guy who had been Phi Beta Kappa at Penn and had helped edit the law journal at Yale wanted to leave a top firm to become an assistant DA. My academic background was a rarity at the Philadelphia DA's office.

My application was forwarded to the Democratic City Committee, which was the way the system worked back then. My ward leader, State Senator Ben Donolow, blackballed my appointment, perhaps because he wanted to keep me as a committeeman. Vic Blanc wound up hiring me as a favor to Bob Dechert, the senior partner in my firm, with whom he had gone to law school.

When I arrived at the district attorney's sumptuous office for my interview with Blanc, the DA was being grilled by a television reporter. As klieg lights bathed Blanc's face and cameras rolled, the reporter demanded to know why Blanc had, in effect, sabotaged the prosecution of a massive racketeering case against the Teamsters union. Robert F. Kennedy had been overseeing the case in Washington and was personally pressing Blanc to prosecute. I sat in a corner and watched. When my turn with the district attorney finally arrived, Vic Blanc didn't ask about my record. He didn't ask why I wanted to leave a top firm to become one of his assistants. He had no interest in me. All

Vic Blanc needed to know was that he was doing somebody a favor. He hired me.

The next day, October 21, 1959, I was sworn in as an assistant Philadelphia district attorney. My two-year-old son made his first courtroom appearance, leaping from his mother's arms and running to the front of the chamber crying, "Daddy! Daddy!" Shanin's oratory would improve over the next four decades as he became one of the premier trial lawyers in America. After the ceremony, I moved my books across the street to my new desk on the fifth floor of City Hall and began a new chapter of my life.

My new boss, Vic Blanc, took the part-time approach to government about as far as it would go. He had a special telephone installed on the inside of his City Hall desk that ran directly to the switchboard of his law firm, so he could conduct his private business from his public office.

Philadelphia had probably been running on patronage and favors since William Penn founded the commonwealth in 1682. "Behind all this stood the most quiet and crudely wasteful city government in the United States," wrote urban planner Jeanne R. Lowe in her authoritative 1967 work, *Cities in a Race with Time*.[1] Comedian W. C. Fields may have made the ultimate statement when he proposed as an inscription for his tombstone: ON THE WHOLE, I'D RATHER BE IN PHILADELPHIA.

Victor Blanc let his assistants moonlight, working part-time for full-time pay. Some prosecutors used their titles to develop their private practices. One assistant DA even sent notices about his private practice to the jurors who served on cases he prosecuted. Shortly after I joined the DA's office, Marvin Halbert, chief of the Obscenity Division, asked me to make a presentation for him at a synagogue men's club. Prosecutors made these appearances to drum up business. Halbert had arranged to speak about pornography. He gave me fifty pornographic magazines, to show the audience the kind of smut that was circulating. I made a speech and passed out my fifty exhibits. I got six of the magazines back.

My prosecutor's starting salary was $4,520 a year, a cut of more than 40 percent from my $7,700 Barnes Dechert pay. To supplement my income, I opened a law office with Marvin Katz, my friend from college and law school. Marvin and I, competing as a team for Penn, had won the Boston University National Invitational Debate Tournament in 1951. A brilliant lawyer who could instantly grasp the most complex situations, Marvin had put in a few years after Yale Law as an associate at Wolf Block, a major Philadelphia firm. By the spring of 1959, he had also grown restless and tired of the wall-to-wall big-firm life.

"Spectator," Marvin said, using his nickname for me, "I'm going to go to my own office either now or never." Marvin, his wife, and their infant son went to France for six weeks. When he returned, we set up shop. We opened a "half-bay" office at the Philadelphia Savings Fund Society Building, with just enough room for a small inner office and two chairs in a tiny reception area adjacent to a secretary's desk. The ten-by-twelve cubbyhole at 2237 PSFS cost us $115 a month. Marvin wanted to take space in the PSFS building because his college fine arts textbook hailed the tower as an architectural triumph.

A few blocks away from our half-bay cubbyhole, at Philadelphia City Hall, Victor Blanc's large, elegant sixth-floor office mirrored his life. The paneled walls displayed membership certificates and awards from almost every fraternity, club, and organization in the city. Blanc and the Philadelphia taxpayers paid a high price for those trophies. Each plaque represented groups with hundreds of members who asked lots of favors. And Vic Blanc could not say no.

He walked the courtrooms and corridors of City Hall like a broken-field runner, bouncing from one person to the next. Everybody wanted to touch Blanc and ask him for something. If you asked Vic Blanc, you might get your case fixed. Attorney General Nicholas Katzenbach said in the mid-1960s that in Philadelphia, "half the people are on the take."

THE CRUSADING
KENNEDY BROTHERS

Philadelphia DA Victor Hugo Blanc came under fire repeatedly for sins of both omission and commission. But Blanc drew the most heat, by far, when he let the calendar run until the last day before the statute of limitations expired in September 1959 on a corruption case built by Robert F. Kennedy, then chief counsel for the Senate McClellan Committee, against the Teamsters Local 107, the biggest labor union in the Delaware Valley.

The crusading Kennedy brothers, looking for meaningful national issues in 1957 and 1958, had dug into corruption and political protection in the Teamsters Union. Five years earlier, Robert Kennedy, fresh from law school, had been assistant counsel to Senator Joe McCarthy's notorious Permanent Subcommittee on Investigations. Bobby Kennedy had learned the value of high-profile hearings. Eventually he had resigned from McCarthy's witch-hunt, but he returned to the subcommittee as chief counsel when stentorian Arkansas Senator John McClellan took over. The subcommittee grew into the Senate Select Committee on Improper Activities in the Labor or Management Field, better known as the McClellan Committee. Robert Kennedy applied his theater lessons during the committee's two years of public hearings. The stage was the Senate Caucus Room, a sumptuous crimson and marble Parthenon.

The McClellan Committee hearings also provided a forum for Bobby's brother Jack, a young senator who wanted to move down Pennsylvania Avenue. Robert Kennedy fed Jack material to make him shine. Jack Kennedy would later announce his bid for president in the Caucus Room. The Kennedy brothers knew how to play the public relations tune to advance their political fortunes, but they also added the right lyrics to perform a real public service.

In addition to young John F. Kennedy, a daunting array of senators regularly came into camera range at the McClellan Committee's nationally publicized hearings, including Barry Goldwater, Karl Mundt, Irving Ives, and Sam Ervin. The committee subpoenaed International Teamsters president Jimmy Hoffa and his lieutenants for weeks at a stretch. Hoffa sparred with the Kennedys and occasionally addressed the chief committee counsel as "Bob."

By 1957, the International Brotherhood of Teamsters was the largest, richest, and mightiest labor union in the nation. Under Hoffa's command, the union controlled transportation across the country—or at least had the power to disrupt or disable it.

James Riddle Hoffa deserved his star billing. Short and stocky, with slicked-back brown hair, Hoffa, forty-four, was given to violent verbal and physical outbursts. Raised in Brazil, Indiana, he had begun his career as a dockworker and had organized his first union at age nineteen. Hoffa rose to become one of nine Teamster national vice presidents. He was elected union president two days after the McClellan Committee ended its hearings on him. A few weeks later, the AFL-CIO ejected the Teamsters, saying that the union was dominated by racketeers. Hoffa had built his empire by courting and swallowing a host of other unions, including gas station operators, airline pilots, airline stewards and stewardesses, airport workers, seafarers, jukebox workers, and New York City police. Some of the takeovers were friendly. Some were not.

Teamster leaders at all levels lined their pockets and built their muscle by raiding the union's pension and health and welfare funds. The money ultimately came from firms that had to pay higher rates to union drivers, and from the drivers' twenty-five-dollar annual union dues. Congress had been investigating corruption and racketeering in the Teamsters since the Kefauver Committee in the early 1950s. But no probe had yet nabbed the union leaders.

Hoffa, a courtroom master, testified before the McClellan Committee in periodic bursts for two years. He instructed other witnesses to take the Fifth Amendment, sometimes flashing them an open hand—five fingers—in the Caucus Room. Hoffa often denied that particular testimony had been given, forcing prolonged hunts through the transcript. He often announced that he had to dash for a plane to make an urgent meeting halfway across the country. One of his favorite tactics was "forgettery," as Senator Ives called it.

The committee ended its hearings in 1958 with McClellan charging Hoffa with eighty-two crimes, including misuse of union funds, obstruction of justice, and association with racketeers. The McClellan Committee report warned that Hoffa threatened the nation's survival:

> The Committee is convinced that if Hoffa remains unchecked he will successfully destroy the decent labor movement in the United States. Further than that, because of the tremendous economic power of the Teamsters, it will place the underworld in a position to dominate American economic life in a period when the vitality of the American economy is necessary to this country's preservation in an era of world crisis.[1]

The Hoffa–Robert Kennedy feud came to obsess both men. Hoffa threw the Teamsters' weight behind Richard Nixon in the 1960 presidential election. The union leader even discussed planting a plastic bomb in Robert Kennedy's car or home. "I've got to do something about that son of a bitch Bobby Kennedy," Hoffa told Cincinnati union leader Edward Partin. "He's got to go."[2]

The most notorious chapter in the Teamster epic may have been written on the Bobby Kennedy–Jimmy Hoffa feud. But the Philadelphia story had some even more intriguing overtones. The same Philadelphia politicians who would give Jack Kennedy a decisive majority in the 1960 presidential race were pulling every trick in the late 1950s to whitewash corruption that the Kennedy brothers uncovered in the Philadelphia Teamsters.

The Philadelphia Teamsters had come to power by running a rival union faction out of town and plundering the union treasury. The Philadelphia boss was Raymond Cohen, a Hoffa favorite. Cohen held the title of secretary-treasurer, but Local 107 president Joseph Grace did Cohen's bidding. Cohen had quickly risen from truck driver to business agent to secretary-treasurer and de facto chief. At the 1957 national Teamster convention in Miami, Cohen was elected a trustee of the International on Hoffa's slate.

When Cohen and his crew were in Washington for the McClellan Committee hearings, they often had morning coffee at the Teamsters' elegant new national headquarters on Capitol Hill. Hoffa always made time to shake hands with Cohen's team. "Anything that Ray needed that was Hoffa's to provide, he did,"[3] recalled John Rogers Carroll, who represented the Teamsters before the committee.

Cohen stood about five feet six and was stocky, with a thick chest and long arms. He clothed his muscular physique in dapper dark suits and white shirts. The overall effect made him look like movie tough guy George Raft. "He was obviously physically tough; he looked it and he talked it," Carroll said recently. "He was a labor leader of the old school. He grew up as a labor leader. He thought that people representing management were the enemy. There was very little compromise where Ray was concerned."

Ben Lapensohn was Cohen's man Friday. Lapensohn, known as "Mr. Fix-It," had been fired by the previous Philadelphia Teamsters regime. He joined the incoming clique early, signing on as Cohen's financial adviser in 1953. Once in office, Cohen, Lapensohn, and company bought off or beat up their rivals and replaced them with loyal lieutenants. Cohen would brook no dissent. Ed Walker, as recording secretary, scribbled the minutes of the monthly Local 107 meetings in a school composition book, sometimes in pencil. Joseph Hartsough would then type Walker's notes, adding any edits from Cohen. If Ray Cohen had lost a vote on the floor, he won it in the minutes.

The battle between the Kennedy brothers and the Philadelphia Teamsters began in September 1957, when Cohen was subpoenaed to appear before the McClellan Committee. When Ray Cohen testified on April 16, 1958, he wore a three-hundred-dollar suit and a ten-dollar silk tie and waved manicured hands. But he looked every inch the alley fighter. Before McClellan knew what was happening, Ray Cohen had denounced the committee, accusing the senators of "outrageous conduct." "I don't feel I have been treated decently by the Committee or by your counsel, Mr. Kennedy," Cohen blared in the Caucus Room.[4] McClellan, in turn, rebuked Cohen for his "belligerent attitude." The chairman said he would have made Cohen submit his statement in writing if he had known Cohen would "show such contempt for the committee."

As the Cohen hearings progressed, Senator John F. Kennedy took a leading role. Kennedy pressed Cohen to explain where $250,000 of union money had gone. Kennedy noted the union's phony files and tampered-with reports. Looking Cohen in the eye, Kennedy said, "I don't think you should hold office. . . . I don't think you are a responsible labor leader. I think you should resign."

19

The Kennedy brothers pressed Cohen to explain $31,000 in union funds spent for the labor leader's "personal purposes," including undershirts, suits, ties, socks, his wife's annual trips to Florida, and the $2,000 yearly rent for Cohen's Florida home. Cohen took the Fifth Amendment on each question.

Robert Kennedy pressed. "Didn't Raymond Cohen use $17,000 of union funds to buy a yacht? Didn't Cohen and his cohorts pilfer the union treasury by taking some $31,500 on the pretext of spending that money at a Florida convention? In fact, weren't there more than $250,000 worth of union checks made out to cash and diverted to Cohen and company?"

The session ended with Cohen promising to produce all his personal records at a later date. When he returned before the committee a month later, he reneged on his promise. Meanwhile, Ben Lapensohn was out of the country ducking a Senate subpoena. When the McClellan Committee investigation began in May 1957, Mr. Fix-It left for Europe, saying he would return in September. Lapensohn's family did return in September, but Lapensohn stayed in Montreal. A Senate subpoena could be served only within U.S. territorial boundaries.

Bobby Kennedy assembled a devastating case against Cohen, Lapensohn, and other Philadelphia Teamster leaders. The evidence showed that Ray Cohen had used a goon squad led by Ed Walker, his recording secretary, to seize power. The rival leaders and their families were beaten and threatened until they left town.

But even a flush union of fourteen thousand members could not bankroll Ray Cohen's yachts, suits, and trips. So Cohen expanded Teamster 107 operations by muscling main line firms. He moved against Horn & Hardart, Philadelphia's premier restaurant chain, without much success, and then against Giant supermarkets. Teamster trucks delivered stock, including perishables, for Penn Fruit, Food Fair, A&P, and other chains. Food Fair executives bent to Cohen's pressure and paid for industrial peace. Part of the payoff came in special stock options and benefits to Cohen and Lapensohn.

Bobby Kennedy put most of these pieces together and served them up to Philadelphia DA Vic Blanc. But he could not get Blanc to act. On November 15, 1958, he wrote to Blanc, warning that the statute of limitations on criminal prosecution was about to expire on substantial check forgeries by Local 107.

Kennedy's letter had little effect. Blanc faced pressures he found more compelling than Bobby Kennedy's corruption case. Labor was a powerful bloc in the new Democratic coalition, and Vic Blanc did not want to upset it. Blanc's sponsor was Democratic city Committee Finance chairman Jim Clark, who owned Clark Transfer, a major area trucking firm that depended on Local 107 drivers. And the Teamsters had strength beyond their numbers. A union strike could strangle the city's food supply within hours.

Bobby Kennedy, facing big stakes of his own, pressed Vic Blanc. Philadelphia newspapers took up the crusade, hammering at the DA's refusal to charge the Teamsters. Finally, Blanc acted. He ordered a report. When the pressure grew even heavier, he opened an investigation. Blanc then went so far as to petition for a special grand jury investigation. As Blanc expected, the Pennsylvania supreme court ruled that a grand jury probe was inappropriate for the Teamsters case.

STORMING PAYOLA PALACE

The day before the statute of limitations expired on the Teamsters, September 18, 1959, Vic Blanc staged what seemed one last ploy: He brought the case before the city's September grand jury.

Arguing that there was not enough time to hold a preliminary hearing before the clock ran out on the case, Blanc obtained Judge Vincent Carroll's permission to seek a district attorney's bill of indictment, a rare procedure usually reserved for fugitives who could not be found and brought to preliminary hearings. Instead of a bundle of indictments for the hundreds of individual acts of criminal fraud, Blanc wanted a single indictment that simply charged Cohen, Lapensohn, and five other Philadelphia Teamsters with conspiracy to loot the union treasury. The jury deliberated for five minutes and gave it to him.

October 21, 1959, the day I was sworn in as an assistant district attorney, City Hall was buzzing over the Teamsters case. Vic Blanc was a genius, the gossips crowed. He had done his job by bringing the indictment. But Blanc's emergency charges would certainly be knocked out, so he had also satisfied the political demands.

As the only unassigned assistant in the district attorney's office, I was immediately drafted for legal research on the Teamsters case. Assistant DA Bill Suckle had written two massive reports running some two hundred pages, and he knew the case cold. I trailed along, lugging the law books and memoranda.

At the hearing on Blanc's emergency indictment, the Teamsters' lawyers argued that the indictments were illegal and asked the judge to dismiss the charges. The district attorney could not create his own emergency and then use it as an excuse to deny the defendants their right to a preliminary hearing, the Teamsters' lawyers said.

Vic Blanc took the stand to explain his decision. He would be inter-rogated by Morton Witkin, the top gun in the Teamsters' legal arsenal. At sixty-eight, Mort Witkin was Philadelphia's finest defense lawyer. There were other top criminal lawyers in town, including Witkin's co-counsel Sam Dash, a former district attorney. But no other lawyer could match Witkin's experience, shrewdness, and competitive drive. Witkin had been trying cases for more than forty years. In the 1920s, he had won several sensational murder trials. Witkin was equally accom-plished in the political wars. He had been the first Jewish minority leader of the Pennsylvania State House of Representatives. Afterward, he ran a meticulously honest county commissioner's office. The Clark-Dilworth Democratic reformers had routed the old-guard Republicans in the early 1950s, freeing Witkin to devote himself entirely to trial work.

In City Hall Courtroom 602, Morton Witkin's cross-examination of Victor Blanc was rough and tough, but fair. In a sense, that approach captures the essence of the American trial system. The basic theory of the adversary system is that the clash of opposite interests will produce the truth. The keystone is cross-examination, in which the witness is forced by his opponent's lawyer to justify his position. Mort Witkin aimed, characteristically, for the gut.

As the session began, Witkin rose and shuffled his papers. At full height, Mort Witkin stood no more than five feet four. His figure was not imposing, but his pile of papers suggested exacting preparation. And his expression, as he turned toward Blanc, said he had come for bear and not for bull.

Vic Blanc looked composed, sitting in the witness chair. But Vic Blanc always looked composed. In fact, Vic Blanc could say the most incredible things, looking entirely sincere and composed. Sometimes I almost had to shut my eyes and measure Blanc's words to know what was really going on.

In his cross-examination, Witkin pressed Blanc to explain why he had sat on the case since 1958. It was complex, Blanc said. And the news stories were hearsay.

But didn't Blanc have the facts, from the McClellan Committee notes and from two hundred pages of reports from his own assistant? "Some additional things had been learned," Blanc said. He could not name a single one.

Couldn't you have given the Teamsters a hearing during a five-day interval in September 1959? Witkin asked. No, Blanc said, there was not time. Pressed, Blanc could not name a single hearing that had taken more than five days.

"Didn't you really sit on your hands and nearly allow the statute of limitations to expire due to your own negligence?" Witkin asked.

Blanc squirmed. Finally, he murmured, "No, I had acted as fast as I could."

Witkin had spared Blanc the questions about telephone calls from politicians demanding he lay off the case. He didn't have to ask them. Witkin knew that Blanc owed his job to Jim Clark and the Democratic City Committee. Judge Joseph Gold, presiding, knew it. Gold himself owed his job to the Democratic machine. There was a code that placed questions about the political fix out of bounds, even for the toughest cross-examiner in town, even for the former leader of the rival political camp.

After the session, Witkin left the courtroom first, then waited for his old friend Blanc to come out. Thrusting out his hand, Witkin said, "I'm sorry, Vic, I had to do it."

Blanc reflexively but sincerely shook Witkin's hand. Without a trace of rancor, Blanc said, "You were just doing your job."

Standing nearby, Ray Cohen, Ben Lapensohn, and the other Teamsters were smirking.

The Teamsters had not beaten the rap, at least not yet. They had good reason to be cocky, based on the hearing. But there was a broader issue in the case, the interests of the people of Pennsylvania in seeing the prosecution proceed, even if Blanc's gaffes had deprived the defendants of some of their rights.

Judge Gold, a former ward leader who had climbed the political ladder to the bench, was no more eager than Vic Blanc to jam the Democratic machine. Gold, then newly installed on the bench, was infatuated with his new position. He had reached the apex through brains and hard work. But the debris on the political ladder had stuck to him, and he owed the ladder's owners. Gold had sat on his bench like a king on his throne, glowering down. When Gloria Gold, the judge's wife, visited him one day in the courtroom wearing a massive hat, Gold pontificated about the majesty of the court.

Gold sat on the Teamster case for a year, wanting to put in the political fix and throw out the case, but not daring to. Finally, in the summer of 1960, facing heavy pressure from the public and the newspapers, Gold denied the Teamsters' petition and ordered them to stand trial. He figured they would have adequate opportunities to beat the case at a later stage.

The Teamsters stalled. By the end of 1962, their strategy had worked perfectly, except for one detail: The Kennedy brothers had risen to national power. Jack Kennedy was president. Robert Kennedy was attorney general, and he had not forgotten Ray Cohen's insults.

I saw the determination in Robert Kennedy's eyes when we discussed the Teamster case in August 1962 at the District Attorney National Convention in Philadelphia. Bobby Kennedy was the featured speaker. Before his speech, he took me aside to question me about the Teamster case.

It was my first contact with Robert Kennedy. He seemed very small and slight, with a matching shyness. He hardly looked the tiger who had snarled and clawed through his brother's campaign two years earlier. But there was also a quiet determination in Bobby Kennedy's voice. When was the case coming up for trial? he wanted to know. Why was it taking so long? What did I think about the evidence against the Philadelphia Teamsters? Would there be convictions?

I answered all of Kennedy's questions conservatively. I told him the defendants had used every trick to delay the trial. I said the case had problems because it was so old, and the evidence was largely circumstantial. I was not about to predict convictions, and I told him so.

Bobby Kennedy didn't challenge my answers, but it was clear he didn't believe them either. I felt he distrusted the entire Philadelphia scene. He knew a lot about Philadelphia politics. The same factors that had let the Philadelphia Democratic machine rack up a crushing 332,000-vote majority for his brother Jack made it tough to prosecute politically powerful labor leaders.

When our short conversation ended, Kennedy said, "We'll be in touch." He did not say, "We'll be watching you," but that was clearly what he meant.

I shared Bobby Kennedy's cynicism about the Philadelphia Teamster prosecution. I also shared his determination. I had fallen heir to the Teamsters 107 case. I was the natural choice, because everyone else working on the case had left the district attorney's office, and because none of the remaining assistant DAs wanted the case, which would interfere with their private practices and threaten their political for-

25

tunes. I had been serving as chief of the appeals division since October 1960. Finally, I would lead the kind of courtroom battle that had drawn me to the DA's office.

When "big cases" arose that would put a prosecutor's name in the newspapers, assistant DAs jockeyed for the assignment. Even for the few prosecutors not pushing their private practices, a little publicity didn't hurt the ego. With equal effort, assistant DAs avoided the tough cases.

As celebrated as the Teamsters case was, no prosecutor wanted to go near it. Just as the case had given then-DA Vic Blanc so much grief, it was unlikely to endear the trial prosecutor, whoever he was, to Philadelphia's Democratic leaders, who would probably have a great influence on the assistant DA's future. The Teamsters were part of the Democratic political machine, controlling votes and contributions.

Jim Clark, Congressman Bill Green, and their Democratic Committee ran Philadelphia in the 1960s with seeming impunity. In 1963, a special-investigation grand jury would find "a sinister connection" between the sale of zoning legislation and the Democratic City Committee. The grand jury could not find anyone to indict, and it merely stated what everybody in the city already knew.

With proceeds from their various sources, Clark and Green bought a choice building on the 1400 block of Walnut Street, across from the stately Bellevue-Stratford Hotel, for the Democratic City Committee's permanent headquarters. The building's gilded hue suggested that gold ran through the entire structure. Instantly, it was dubbed "Payola Palace."

Bill Green was supposedly very close to President John Kennedy. Green had sponsored JFK's nomination among the Pennsylvania delegates when other factions were pushing Adlai Stevenson, and he had delivered Philadelphia for Kennedy on election day. Green sat in Kennedy's personal box at the inaugural ball. Then there was the photograph. Green had been invited to fly to New York City with President Kennedy. The president, who was attending a major dinner in New York, wore white tie and tails. Green, who was making the trip to meet with New York Democratic leader Carmine DeSapio about a political concern, wore a business suit. The president and the congressman were photographed together after they landed. Kennedy wrote on the photo, "I always dress up to have my picture taken with Bill Green."

Despite the puppets and puppeteers, I thought we had a fair chance

26

at the trial, although it would be an uphill fight. By mid-1962, Robert Kennedy was hounding national Teamster boss Jimmy Hoffa. After more motions and skirmishes, the case was listed for trial in March 1963. I read and reread both Kennedys' questioning of the Philadelphia Teamsters at the 1957 McClellan Committee hearings. Prosecuting Cohen and his cronies was worth a try. That's what a "trial" means, after all. I admired Bob Kennedy's tenacity in the fight, and this was a slice of it in my city. So I was prepared to go to the mat.

THE TILTING COURTROOM

At long last, on March 25, 1963, the Philadelphia Teamsters came to trial. By that time the DA's office had a stale case. Delay invariably aids defendants. Witnesses die or move away. Their memories dim. Their interests wane. Sometimes they are intimidated. By the time the Teamsters reached the docket, Joseph Grace, president of Local 107, had been dead eighteen months.

But the Teamster case also had its bright spots. In addition to masterful briefs and reports, I inherited two dutiful investigators: John Flanagan, a tenacious U.S. Department of Labor agent who had helped Bobby Kennedy during the McClellan Committee probe, and DA Detective Joe Maex. Maex had a barrel chest, beefy arms, and a Dick Tracy profile. He was nervous about Teamster strong-arm tactics and hovered over me constantly.

We all wondered how the Teamsters would respond to a tough prosecution. Would Ray Cohen send out Ed Walker and his goon squad? There was a lot of hand-wringing around City Hall. My next-door neighbor moved out, fearing that the wrong house—his—would be bombed. There had been several threats. "In those days, you didn't know what 107 would do," recalled Anthony LaRosa, a DA's detective who guarded the Teamster files daily from 4:00 P.M. to midnight.

One day, a rough-hewn man in an open-necked shirt walked up to me outside the downtown Horn & Hardart "automat" cafeteria. "You're Specter, ain't ya?" he asked. Joan and I often wheeled our infant son, Shanin, in his stroller into that Horn & Hardart automat, where we all ate dinner for a dollar. Joan's platter came with three vegetables for forty cents, my beef pot pie sold for forty cents, and a fruit cup for

Shanin cost fifteen cents. The state sales tax took the last nickel. We called that automat "Chicky's Club," after Shanin's nickname.

"You're trying the Teamsters case," the man said.

"Yes," I replied.

"Big case," he said.

"Yes," I said. "Why do you ask?"

"I just wondered," he said. "You know, there are two hundred and fifty big ones in it for you if you did the right thing."

I said, "What do you mean?"

"What do you mean, 'What do I mean?' " he said.

"What's your name?" I asked.

"Get lost, bud," he said, hurrying away.

A couple of years later I would get some pertinent advice from the premier racket-buster, former New York Governor Thomas E. Dewey. I was running for district attorney on the Republican line in 1965, and Pennsylvania Governor William Scranton arranged for me to meet Dewey for a discussion on campaign strategy. Dewey had run for New York district attorney under somewhat similar circumstances in 1937 as a Republican on a fusion ticket battling organized crime.

I visited Dewey at his law office in a Wall Street skyscraper. Dewey was sixty-three then, but looked ten years younger. It was hard to believe this vigorous man had run against Franklin Roosevelt for the presidency twenty-one years earlier. Dewey also seemed like a regular guy, not a wedding-cake caricature. I had prepared for a cool reception from an autocrat in his throne room. Instead I got a warm reception from a friend in his den. Dewey seemed most interested in discussing Philadelphia law enforcement in 1965. But we talked about his radio speeches, his sound trucks, and his problems bucking the organization, and then I asked him about the dangers of prosecuting Murder Incorporated in the 1930s.

Dewey said he had naturally been concerned, but he'd decided early in his investigation that the risks were low. The mob wouldn't target the prosecutor, because an attack would arouse public ire. And another prosecutor would just take his place anyway. Dewey reminisced about one contract to kill him. The hit was quickly canceled by Lucky Luciano, who reasoned that an assassination would do the mob more harm than good. Rough stuff has rarely been used against judges, prosecutors, or law enforcement officers, Dewey noted. Anyway, there's not much you can do about it if you want to take on high-risk assignments.

The Philadelphia Teamsters trial was a massive affair, lasting ten weeks and a day, with the notes of testimony running 4,661 pages. I called 98 witnesses and presented 1,116 documents. But the real production was put on by the defense. No fewer than eight defense lawyers crammed their courtroom table at any given time, and sometimes as many as fourteen. Each of the six Teamsters defendants had at least two lawyers. I chose to sit alone at the prosecution table. I had plenty of help in the wings, but I functioned best in court by myself.

We lined up on the trial's opening day with nine defense lawyers on one side and me on the other, prompting one reporter to write that it appeared the courtroom might tilt to one side. The judge was David L. Ullman, a mild-mannered, bespectacled jurist with receding, graying hair and sagging jowls. Ullman wore stiff three-piece suits, sometimes with a carnation in his lapel.

The defense lawyers were superb. Any one of them handling the case alone might have won it. Together, however, they were bumping into each other. The natural lead fell to Morton Witkin, representing Ben Lapensohn. The defense strategy from the start was to stall the case and try to derail it. The battery of defense lawyers, usually in sequence like an artillery barrage, raised every objection imaginable, no matter how trivial or groundless—they demanded a mistrial because Ullman smiled during questioning of a juror, for instance. Such tactics stretched jury selection two weeks. Once the case was under way, the Teamsters lawyers taunted Ullman, trying to provoke the judge to erupt or to make a rash ruling. They told Ullman that his instructions were unclear, that he had botched jury selection, that he had put them in a poor light. Hundreds of times the Teamsters lawyers demanded a mistrial.

But Ullman withstood their fire, staying poised throughout the seventy-one-day attack. Ullman also sequestered the jury, the first time a Philadelphia jury had been locked up in any case short of first-degree murder. Ullman took the precaution because of attempts to threaten and bribe jurors who had sat on Hoffa's 1962 trial in Nashville, and because of an upcoming election to determine whether the Teamsters or the AFL-CIO would represent Local 107.

Jurors were confined to the Essex Hotel, across the street from City Hall, when they were not in court. Some jurors' relatives came to court just to sit in the same room with their loved ones. One juror's daughter sat regularly in the front row, and mother and daughter gazed at each other. The wife of one male juror wanted him home. She complained in letters, first to her husband and later to the judge. Ullman politely but firmly refused to release the man. The juror, for his part, was delighted with the judge's decision. That was one point where the prosecution and defense agreed: The fellow was better off being locked up at the Essex than at home with his wife.

As the trial raged, Hoffa and some of his lieutenants moved to Philadelphia to try to put down a revolt by dissidents within the Philadelphia Teamsters. As the *Inquirer* put it, "James R. Hoffa, Teamsters Union president, has set up headquarters in the Warwick Hotel and intends to personally lead a fight with the dissident Voice of Teamsters in a representation election." On April 1, the NBC-TV show *David Brinkley's Journal* ran a piece called "Inside Jimmy Hoffa." In the segment, Hoffa gave a live interview from Philadelphia, railing against Robert Kennedy, whom he called "a spoiled young millionaire" on a taxpayer-financed vendetta. The show also featured an interview with Ray Cohen, who denied he had ever sicced any "goons" on the rebels. Hoffa crushed the Teamster dissidents almost two to one in a second election. The only remaining bulwark against Ray Cohen and his goons was our corruption case.

Our case consisted of reams of documents and very few live witnesses, who could testify only about peripheral matters. We had nobody to take the stand and swear he had actually seen Ray Cohen or Ben Lapensohn or any of the other Teamsters taking money or committing some other crime. The closest we got were witnesses such as former Local 107 business agent William Kelleher, who testified that he resigned "to get rid of the harassment that my wife and I were going through."[1]

Our evidence was technical and complex. I wondered how much the jury understood about the forged and predated checks and bogus insurance premiums. I had made a brief opening statement because I did not want to start off by boring the jury. I wanted to establish a rapport with the nine women, three men, and two alternates who would decide the Teamsters' fate and, to an extent, my own.

The Teamsters' lawyers, in an odd way, gave me occasional openings to build my case. When the defense lawyers made a motion for a mistrial, they generally made a speech along with it. They were trying to impress the jury. But they also gave me a chance to reply. In my rebuttals, I wove in the evidence, trying to make some sense of the disjointed stream of documents.

The courtroom had been packed at the beginning of the trial. But as witness after witness testified about document after document, the crowd shrank. A band of two dozen courthouse regulars stayed with the trial, ranging from natty retired businessmen to grubby drunks. Some unidentified men also sat in the courtroom. Rumor had it that Robert Kennedy had planted observers to report to him daily. The word was that Kennedy expected the case to be fixed. His experience with Vic Blanc had left him with little confidence in the Philadelphia criminal courts. And Kennedy also had experience with Jimmy Hoffa and Ray Cohen.

A favorite Teamster defense tactic was to line the defense bench with celebrities. In a Nashville courtroom, boxing champ Joe Louis had put his arm around Hoffa. In Philadelphia, Cecil Moore, a flamboyant African-American civil rights activist and lawyer who would soon become president of the city's NAACP chapter, sat in the Cohen-Lapensohn corner.

As the trial wore on, the jurors seemed polite toward me. I thought I saw them flash me occasional half smiles. The jurors seemed indifferent, bored, or even impatient with the Teamster lawyers as they tried to bait Ullman into a mistrial.

One key element in the Cohen-Lapensohn conspiracy was trailer drops, in which a truck driver leaves his trailer at a supermarket rather than making the store clerks scramble to unload it. A trailer drop saved a supermarket time and space, and at the time one was worth $18 to $25. Ray Cohen and Food Fair president Louis Stein had made a secret deal in 1954 to give Food Fair 283 trailer drops, which gave the company a $300,000 to $400,000 competitive advantage. In return, Cohen and Lapensohn got thousands of dollars of Food Fair stock at a quarter of market value. The Food Fair trailer-drop deal involved many of Philadelphia's heavy hitters. Bernard G. Segal, onetime president of the American Bar Association, came to talk to me to press me to eliminate the trailer-drop aspect of the case. I think he was trying to save some of the pillars of the legal and business community from embarrassment. Segal mentioned the name of his good friend Bobby Kennedy. I ignored his comments about Attorney General Kennedy and went about my business. I insisted politely but firmly that the Food Fair transaction would be a significant part of the case.

I scheduled the trailer-drop subpoenas to go out Thursday afternoon before Easter weekend, for Monday court. Then I took Joan and our boys—our second son, Stephen, had been born in 1960—away for the weekend. When we got back Sunday night and opened our front door, the phone was ringing. It was a ranking assistant from the district attorney's office, ordering me to withdraw the subpoenas. I said no.

In court Monday, Food Fair president Stein was represented by Harry Shapiro, a big-wheel defense lawyer and former state senator. Shapiro was brilliant and experienced, but not sensitive. At a meeting in Judge Ullman's chambers, Shapiro pressed the judge to quash the subpoenas. "Look," Shapiro told Ullman, "you don't have to be Brandeis to understand this." Instinctively, Ullman reached for his Phi Beta Kappa key, which he wore religiously, and stroked it. I knew that my position was secure. On the stand Louis Stein admitted that Food Fair had sold its stock to the Teamsters at a fraction of its value, but he claimed the bargain was an investment in goodwill.

A real break in the trial came near the end, when Marjorie Battisfore surfaced. Battisfore, secretary for deceased Philadelphia Teamsters president Joe Grace, had avoided testifying for years. She'd dodged subpoenas from the McClellan Committee and had refused to testify in our case. Everybody figured that Battisfore knew where the bodies were buried, at least figuratively. Battisfore lived in New Jersey, which put her outside the reach of a Pennsylvania subpoena. Although I had written to her many times asking her to come in, she had never responded. For technical reasons we were unable to issue compulsory process through the Interstate Witness Subpoena Act. With the trial well under way, I'd given up hope that we would see her as a witness.

To my surprise and delight, one morning in the middle of the trial, shortly before 9:00 A.M., my secretary walked into my office and said, "Marjorie Battisfore is in the outer office and wants to see you." Sure enough, in walked Marjorie Battisfore, a striking woman of about forty-two, all made up and wearing a sharp suit and an enormous hat. When I saw Battisfore, I didn't know quite what to do with her. I was due in court shortly to continue the trial, and I knew I had to keep her occupied until the luncheon break, when I would have a chance to talk to her, to see if in fact she could be put on the witness stand. I wanted Battisfore to testify that afternoon, because I didn't know when or if I would ever get another chance.

I called in my assistants to talk to Battisfore during the morning hours. Then I phoned Joan and asked her to come for lunch, so that I could have as sociable a meeting as possible with Battisfore. During lunch recess, Joan and I walked across the street to Wanamaker's and up to the store's ninth-floor dining room. Our lunch proved not too private, but ultimately successful. When the defendants learned that Battisfore was in Philadelphia and scheduled to testify, they went berserk. The morning was consumed with defense motions about why Battisfore could not testify to this, that, and the other thing.

In the afternoon I put Battisfore on the stand. I asked her about twenty-three union checks issued to Joe Grace for trips to Chicago, San Francisco, New York, Washington, and other places. She said Grace had never made any of those trips. She testified that she had personally heard Ray Cohen tell Joe Hartsough, the recording secretary, how Cohen wanted the meeting minutes doctored. Battisfore described how Cohen and Hartsough would take Local 107's blank checks to Grace and have Grace sign them in advance, and then how Cohen would fill out the checks, often for huge sums.

When I finished questioning Battisfore, Mort Witkin took the first round of cross-examination. Witkin wanted to impeach Battisfore's credibility and impugn her integrity. As usual, he went for the jugular. Witkin asked Battisfore a series of questions about her relationship with Joe Grace. He asked her about the frequency of their contacts.

Witkin implied that Marjorie Battisfore had been Joe Grace's mistress and was therefore an immoral woman who lacked credibility. This was 1963, and a woman who lived with a man "in sin" carried a stigma. At a critical point in her testimony, Marjorie Battisfore opened her purse and whipped out a document. It was a marriage certificate showing that she and Joe Grace were husband and wife. Nobody had known. Joe Grace had never told anybody. Witkin blanched. At that moment I understood why Marjorie Battisfore had decided to come in to testify. During her years with Joe Grace, when he had insisted on keeping their marriage a secret, Battisfore had felt the social sting. This was the occasion for her to establish her legitimacy.

Marjorie Battisfore had not finished testifying by the time Judge Ullman adjourned for the day, so we scheduled her to return the next morning. When Battisfore left the courtroom, she noticed a man following her down the hall. The man was nabbed by a county detective and brought to Ullman's chambers. He refused to identify himself or reveal the purpose of his activities. We later found out he was an inves-

34

tigator for a private detective agency hired by the Teamsters lawyers to shadow Battisfore. Marjorie Battisfore would not be intimidated. She returned in the morning and drove more spikes into the Teamsters' case.

The defendants didn't take the stand and didn't present any evidence, to gain the tactical advantage of making the last speech. Under Pennsylvania procedure, if the defendants put on evidence, the commonwealth attorney makes the first closing statement, followed by the defense, with rebuttal by the commonwealth attorney. But if the defendant has brought no evidence—as the Teamsters chose to do—the defense lawyer gets the last speech.

The closing arguments and Judge Ullman's instructions took three full days. At 8:00 P.M. on the third day, the jury was excused for an hour and a half while Witkin and the other defense lawyers lodged countless exceptions to Ullman's charge to the jury. The jurors returned at 9:30 P.M. and voted unanimously to begin deliberating immediately, rather than retire to the Essex and wait until morning. With the jury out, all the lawyers and the judge suddenly became friends. There was nothing more to argue about. Several Teamsters lawyers, Ullman, and I were sitting in a small room behind Courtroom 285. The alternate jurors, who had been excused, came in. Ullman thanked them for their service, and they left. We were all dying to know how the alternates would have voted but were afraid to ask. The court officers were more sophisticated in these matters. A bailiff pulled me aside and whispered into my ear, "Both alternates would have voted to convict everyone."

At about 11:30 P.M., the telephone in the small back room rang. A court officer picked it up, then handed it to me. "Hello, Arlen. How're you doing?" It was Walter Sheridan, Bobby Kennedy's gumshoe.

"How in the world did you find me here, Walter?" I asked.

"Never mind that," Sheridan said, every bit the federal investigator. "What's happening in the case?"

"The jury is out deliberating."

"I know that," Sheridan said. "But what's going on?"

"There's nothing more to be said until the jury comes back," I said.

"Call me as soon as they return," Sheridan instructed.

"Okay, providing it's not too late."

"Never mind what time it is," he said. "Be sure to call."

"Well, I will, Walter. But this jury may not be back in until two or three in the morning or later, and I have a lot of exhibits to gather in, so it may be the middle of the night."

35

Finally Sheridan said, "I don't care what time it is. I have to let the boss know immediately, so promise you'll call."

No sooner had I put down the phone than a court officer burst into the room. "The jury's back!" he exclaimed. "They've got a verdict!" We returned to the courtroom. It was 11:38 P.M. The jury had been out two minutes shy of two hours. Ullman was standing. So were all the defense lawyers. The Teamsters stood behind them, shifting their weight, fidgeting their hands, their eyes finding no place to rest. I stood by the prosecution table, closest to the jury box. I studied each juror in turn as he or she filed into the courtroom. I looked for some telltale sign but could find none.

"Has the jury reached a verdict?" the chief court crier intoned. The jury foreman, an engineer, rose. "We have," he said. Ullman asked the foreman for the jury's verdict on each of the six defendants. Standing in his crisp white shirt and dark suit, Ray Cohen rubbed his nose with his right hand and tightened his lips as he waited to hear his fate.

To each name Ullman called, the foreman answered, "Guilty as charged." The courtroom froze as the word "guilty" sank in. I sighed and loosened. But in an instant the Teamsters' lawyers were on their feet, demanding that the jurors be polled. They wanted each juror to announce his individual verdict for each defendant. There is always a chance a juror will volunteer some doubt, or misspeak, creating an opening for a mistrial. The long process began. It took twenty minutes for the jurors to answer "guilty" seventy-two times. When they had finished, the trial was over. For the first time, labor racketeers targeted by the McClellan Committee's massive two-year investigation had been convicted.

The courtroom clock said 1:15 A.M. By the time I'd gathered all my exhibits and returned to my fifth-floor office, it was past 3:00 A.M. A crowd of jubilant detectives clattered around my desk. "Hold on, fellows, I've got to make a telephone call," I said. "Then I'll buy you all as much as you can drink, provided we can find an open bar."

I dialed Walter Sheridan's direct line in the Washington suburbs. The telephone gave half a ring before Walter's voice snapped, "What happened?"

"Guilty as to all defendants," I said. The word "Great" was cut in half by a click as Walter's finger punched the disconnect button. He had a more important phone call to make.

Philadelphia had closed by the time we left City Hall, but the detectives and I found a small open restaurant. I couldn't sleep much that night anyway, so I arrived at the office about 9:00 A.M. I began to fiddle with my morning mail. The *Inquirer* ran a front-page piece on the verdict, but we lost the banner headline to the death of Pope John XXIII.

My secretary burst into the room. "Attorney General Kennedy is on the telephone," she announced, breathless. I picked up the receiver. "Congratulations," a Massachusetts tenor lilted into my ear. "I hear you won a marvelous victory." Kennedy wanted to know all about the case. What was the high point of the trial? What evidence really sewed it up? How did Cohen and Lapensohn and the others take the verdict? What was the next step in the proceedings? When would the judge impose sentence? What were the chances of holding the case on appeal? Was there any real error in the trial record? We seemed to talk forever.

"Would you be good enough to come down to Washington and visit with me about the case?" Kennedy asked. When I hesitated, thinking about my packed schedule, Kennedy insisted. I told him I would do my best to come down sometime during the following week.

When I reported the conversation to District Attorney Crumlish, he practically pushed me out the door to go to Washington and sing to Kennedy about the triumphs of the Philadelphia DA's office. A visit with the attorney general of the United States was too good for a husband alone, my wife decided, so Joan accompanied me to Robert Kennedy's office. The appointment was set for Tuesday, June 11, at 9:00 A.M. We drove to Washington on Monday, arriving in midafternoon on a hot, sunny day. We checked into the International Inn, which had rooms for twelve dollars a day, and swam at the hotel pool.

Tuesday turned out to be historic for the Department of Justice, although not because of the Specter's visit. That was the day Bobby Kennedy sent Deputy Attorney General Nicholas Katzenbach with federal troops to confront Alabama Governor George Wallace over Wallace's refusal to admit two African-American students to the state university at Tuscaloosa. In the end, Wallace stepped aside, and the students registered.

When Joan and I arrived a few minutes before nine, the day's events had not yet begun to unfold. We were escorted into an office that seemed half a block long and several stories high. Paintings commissioned during the Works Progress Administration covered the walls, below a vaulted ceiling. This was the suite where Bobby Kennedy and Byron "Whizzer" White, the Pittsburgh Steelers star turned Supreme Court justice, had tossed footballs a couple of years earlier when White was deputy attorney general.

Bobby Kennedy was sitting behind a large desk in front of a massive window that overlooked Constitution Avenue. He had one child on his lap and another at his side. When he saw us, he immediately put the sitting child on the floor and walked over to greet us. He was formal and proper. Kennedy seemed even smaller than when I had seen him at the DA's convention.

As soon as we had exchanged pleasantries, Kennedy told his children, "Okay, kids, it's time to go." The children skipped outside, leaving chocolate-milk bottles and stains on the attorney general's desk. Our boys also spilled wherever they went, and I said something about the milk. Kennedy smiled and pointed to some crayon drawings that were taped to deep-grained paneling, several feet beneath the hanging oils. "The kids have made up for it by supplying the artwork for the office." Kennedy sometimes brought the family's giant black Newfoundland, Brumis, to the office with his children, sparking complaints from a bureaucrat who cited a regulation prohibiting dogs in the building. But Brumis had stayed home this day.

Kennedy led Joan and me to a corner of his office-barn, where he had created a sitting area with a coffee table surrounded by a couch and some easy chairs. He launched into detailed questions about the Teamster prosecution.

We were soon joined by Herbert "Jack" Miller, Jr., the assistant attorney general in charge of the Criminal Division. Miller, while a partner at a top Washington law firm, had served as counsel to the Board of Monitors that oversaw the Teamsters International. In 1961, Robert Kennedy had lured Miller to the Justice Department. Jack Miller was so eager to discuss the Philadelphia Teamsters case that he missed Kennedy's introduction of Joan.

"Say hello to the lady," Kennedy said to Miller, who appeared not to hear him. Raising his voice slightly, Kennedy repeated, "Say hello to the lady." But Miller was still so absorbed in the case that he again did not hear his boss. Finally, Kennedy hollered, "Say hello to the lady, Jack!" Jack Miller finally said hello to Joan.

Kennedy was fascinated to hear the procedures we had used in sequestering the jury. The Justice Department had just had a rough time prosecuting Hoffa in Nashville. The case would ultimately lead to Hoffa's first conviction, and an eight-year sentence for jury tampering. Kennedy also wanted to know about any strong-arm attacks or threats by the union thugs. I told him we had been concerned, but nothing had happened. The attorney general particularly wanted to know whether Ray Cohen, Ben Lapensohn, and the four other convicted Philadelphia Teamsters would go to jail. I told him that I intended to press for a jail sentence for every one of them. Kennedy seemed delighted.

I assured Kennedy that we would do everything in our power to get the appeals over as soon as possible. I told him that Judge Ullman had been very cooperative in setting an early date for arguments on post-trial motions, already listed for mid-July.

During the course of our talk in Kennedy's sitting area, there were constant interruptions, several over the Tuscaloosa showdown. Occasionally Kennedy hiked to his desk to talk on the telephone. Sometimes he left his massive office to go to a small outer office. The attorney general's office had been turned into a war room, monitoring locations of marshals and troops, dispatching and relaying messages. "We were very worried about Nick's [Katzenbach's] safety, as a matter of fact," Miller told me recently.

Before we left the attorney general's office, Kennedy invited me to join the Justice Department team prosecuting Jimmy Hoffa. At that time there were several prosecutions pending against the Teamsters boss. I thanked Kennedy for the offer but said I wanted to stay in Philadelphia for both personal and professional reasons. Among them, I said, much work remained on the Cohen-Lapensohn prosecution, including motions to be argued in the trial court and the fight against the Teamsters' appeal. I also did not want to get lost in a Washington bureaucracy, though I kept this reservation to myself.

Later that day in Miller's office, Miller again pressed me at greater length to join the Justice Department staff. To turn the screws, he brought in Howard Willens, a law-school classmate of mine. Miller and Willens had worked together at a Washington firm, and Miller had taken Willens with him to the Justice Department in 1961. I again said thanks but no thanks.

Walter Sheridan tracked the progress of the Philadelphia Teamsters case. On July 15, Sheridan had good news to report: The Teamsters' post-trial motions were dismissed, and all six defendants were sentenced to prison.

PART TWO

THE WARREN COMMISSION

On New Year's Eve in 1963 I was at my desk in the Philadelphia district attorney's office, trying to concoct an excuse for arriving home so late. Joan had made social plans and expected me to be on time. At about 5:30 P.M., the telephone rang. It was my law school classmate Howard Willens, Robert Kennedy's deputy at the Department of Justice.

Howard asked if I was interested in joining the staff of a commission, to be chaired by Chief Justice Earl Warren, that would investigate the assassination of President John F. Kennedy. Willens was recruiting staff, especially young lawyers, for the assassination probe. He was seeking interested people across the country and forwarding promising résumés to former Solicitor General J. Lee Rankin, general counsel for the investigation.

I gave Howard the same answer I had given him, Robert Kennedy, and Jack Miller six months earlier, when I declined their offer to join the Justice team prosecuting Jimmy Hoffa. I didn't see how I could undertake such a job. I had unfinished business on the Teamsters 107 case, which was pending in the superior court. After that decision, there would be a battle to fight in Pennsylvania Supreme Court and then in the federal courts. I also told Howard I did not want to leave Philadelphia for personal reasons, that an absence would be tough on my family. He asked me to think it over. I said I would. At least I had a good excuse to offer Joan for my tardiness that evening.

That night some of our closest friends came over to our house for a New Year's Eve party, and I mentioned Willens's call, sparking a long discussion. My friends urged me to take the job, saying I would be a fool to pass it up. Marvin Katz, my law partner, said if I didn't want the job, he'd like it, a statement out of character for him. District Attorney

Jim Crumlish, who had seen my earlier audience with Robert Kennedy as an opportunity to promote the Philadelphia DA's office, saw the Warren Commission as another chance for good publicity for his office.

I finally decided to accept. I figured I could get back to Philadelphia from Washington any night I had to, and certainly on weekends. The investigation offered a good reason to leave the DA's office. I had always thought four years was about the right tour of duty. I never wanted to stay past a training period or to become dependent on a prosecutor's job and lifestyle. In October 1963 I had marked four years in the DA's office. I probably would have left several months earlier, if not for finishing up the appeals on the Teamsters case.

I had one other misgiving: a possible run for the state senate. Redistricting had carved a new state senate seat out of five wards, including mine. One of the ward leaders backed me for the Democratic nomination. I had been intrigued by politics since childhood, long before I became a committeeman and scaled Spruce Street row houses to roust out unregistered neighbors. My boyhood home rang with my father's constant talk of government and politics. He relied mostly on the *Tog*, the Yiddish daily paper, and on columnists Walter Lippmann and Dorothy Thompson in the *Wichita Beacon*. My father's obsession with politics and my own youthful addiction to baseball combined to instill in me a sense of history. For hours I would pore over Ty Cobb's batting records and other Hall of Fame statistics. Since I could not hit or field but was born on Lincoln's birthday, I gravitated toward politics.

I ultimately decided that I could keep my hat in the state senate ring and still join the commission in Washington. At Willens's request I sent a brief letter with biographical data. A few days later, on January 8, I got a telegram from J. Lee Rankin, general counsel of the President's Commission on the Assassination of President John F. Kennedy, formally requesting that I join the staff. I accepted.

I had great admiration for John F. Kennedy as our nation's vibrant young leader, and for Jackie and their two small children. I was caught up in the swell of Camelot, like so many Americans. Even though the president was older, our two boys were about the same ages as Caroline and John Jr. In fact, our younger son, Stephen, was born just a few days before John. In November 1960, when I was an assistant DA in a Democratic city administration, my colleagues and I had been required to buy hundred-dollar tickets to the annual Democratic dinner, where presidential nominee Kennedy was scheduled to speak. Joan and I sat in a distant section commensurate with my party status. Joan, then eight and three-quarters months pregnant with Steve, stood on her tiptoes on a folding chair to glimpse the handsome nominee.

Both Rankin and Willens wanted me to begin work as soon as possible. The commission had already hired several attorneys for their senior lawyer ranks. They needed young lawyers to work with them. The seven members of the commission, I had heard, had already been in and out of the Veterans of Foreign Wars Building, where the commission had its offices, for several weeks. They included the chief justice, leaders from both sides of the aisle in the House and the Senate, and a former CIA chief and World Bank president. During my stint with the Warren Commission, I would technically be on leave of absence from the district attorney's office, drawing pay for the specific days I worked in Philadelphia on the Teamsters appeal.

I made my first trip to Washington on Monday, January 13. It had snowed heavily over the weekend and again on that day. The snow was so deep that it blocked the side entrance to the new Senate office building, which would have put me near the front door of the VFW Building. When I reported, most of the main commission staff members were not yet on the job. Howard Willens greeted me and introduced me to Rankin. A former U.S. solicitor general, Rankin was then on leave as New York City's corporation counsel, the equivalent of the city solicitor. About five feet eight, slender and unruffled, Rankin was paternal and soft-spoken, with a light humor. He was also, I would find, meticulous and driven. At our initial meeting, Rankin asked me for details on my background and explained the commission's approach.

The commission had divided the investigation into six major areas. At that time the senior lawyers had been assigned to areas, but the younger lawyers had not. As one of the first junior lawyers to check in, if not *the* first, I found that the field was pretty much open. Area 1 covered President Kennedy's activities from his departure by helicopter from the White House lawn on November 21, 1963, to his body's return to the White House early in the morning of November 23, after the autopsy. Area 2 covered the identity of the assassin. The Area 2 team would treat it as an open question, despite Oswald's arrest. Area 3 covered the life and background of Lee Harvey Oswald, except for his foreign travel and his activities on the day of Kennedy's assassination. Area 4 picked up Oswald's foreign travel. Area 5 covered the background and activities of Jack Ruby, who shot Oswald to death in the basement of Dallas Police Headquarters on Sunday morning, November 24, 1963, two days after the Kennedy assassination. Area 6 covered presidential protection for the future.

In my preliminary discussions with Rankin and Willens, we eliminated Areas 2 and 4 as possible assignments for me. They didn't want to assign me to Area 2 because my background as an assistant DA suggested I might be too prosecution-oriented to tackle the question of the assassin's identity objectively. They didn't want to assign me to Area 4 because Bill Coleman, a partner at the Philadelphia-based Dilworth firm, had been assigned as the senior lawyer in Area 4, and they didn't want two lawyers from the same city working in one area. I immediately agreed that I should avoid Areas 2 and 4.

After some thought and discussion with Marvin Katz, I chose Area 1, the president's activities. It seemed the most compelling. Obviously, John F. Kennedy was the focal point of the entire event. I had no idea at that point of the turns the medical evidence would take or where Area 1 would lead. Lee Rankin said that placing me in Area 1 would work well from the commission's point of view, and he made the assignment.

The senior lawyer in Area 1 was Francis W. H. Adams, a former New York City police commissioner who was then a senior partner at a major New York firm. As police commissioner from 1954 to 1955, Adams had handled security for many motorcades that wound around Manhattan's skyscrapers, much as President Kennedy rode through Dallas on November 22. New York City Mayor Robert F. Wagner, Jr., was supposed to have touted Adams to Chief Justice Warren when they both attended the funeral of Herbert Lehman, the former New York senator and governor. I didn't know Frank Adams, but I assumed we would spend much of our time in Washington together. After all, both of us lived in easily reached cities, and it made sense that the two men assigned to the same area should arrange to be in Washington at the same time. Lawyers from more remote places would have tougher scheduling.

I crammed my briefcase with material and headed for Union Station to catch a train back to Philadelphia on Monday afternoon, January 13, 1964. The paperwork would keep me busy for much of the week ahead. I also had a lot of matters to wrap up in the district attorney's office. I told Rankin I would try to report for work full-time the following Monday.

On the train to Philadelphia I was able to get a coach seat without a neighbor so I could read some of the material, taking care to shield it from other passengers. I was drawn immediately to the autopsy report. Two bullets had passed through President Kennedy. One had entered his back and exited through his throat. The other, the head shot, had blown out 70 percent of the right hemisphere of his brain. As I read through the grisly details of the president's wounds, I felt nauseated and depressed. Others on the Warren Commission also found the investigation personally wrenching. Congressman Hale Boggs, a commission member, had become "very close" with John Kennedy beginning when they served together in the House in 1947, his wife, former Congresswoman Lindy Boggs, told me in May 1999. Hale found the whole investigation "emotionally very draining."[1] Reading the gruesome findings of the autopsy surgeons, it was hard to accept that an assassin could bring down the most powerful man in the world and the nation's idyllic dream of Camelot. I would have a similar reaction every time I saw the amateur film by Abraham Zapruder. In frame 313 the film graphically and in vivid color shows the right front side of the president's head explode. That film and especially that frame would haunt America forever.

For the balance of that week I reviewed the two volumes of Secret Service reports, the five-volume summary of the FBI reports, and the many other reports that had been forwarded to the commission. The Secret Service and FBI reports had come out soon after the shooting. The FBI report by Agents O'Neal and Siebert concluded that there had been three shots: The first bullet hit Kennedy's neck, the second hit Connally, and the third hit the president's head. That theory would remain doctrine for months.

The commission had hired a team of lawyers from around the country, accomplished but with limited courtroom and investigative experience. The commission deliberately chose a geographically diverse team with limited government connections to avoid any appearance of a whitewash. We lawyers used to laugh that many documents we were given were marked "Top Secret," even though we would not get our security clearances for more than a month.

Norman Redlich would be Lee Rankin's assistant, the report editor, and traffic cop. He would function as a de facto executive director of the investigation. Redlich, thin and serious, his dark hair combed straight back, had graduated at the top of his class at Yale Law School in 1950. He was a professor at New York University Law School, where he would later become dean. Redlich had served as Rankin's executive director when Rankin was corporate counsel for the City of New York. The two had grown close by the time they teamed up on the Warren Commission.

House Minority Whip Gerald Ford, a commission member, initially balked at Redlich's appointment. Ford complained that in the 1950s, Redlich had belonged to the National Lawyers Guild, a committee Ford found politically unsavory. This was 1964, long past the McCarthy era, and Chief Justice Warren told Ford, "Fine, file a complaint." That was the end of the issue.

Ford told me in June 1997 that his reservations about Redlich were prompted by members of his caucus.[2] "There were three or four people in the House of Representatives, I would say, extreme right-wing Republicans," Ford said. "One of them was H. R. Gross from Iowa, who used to give me hell because Redlich was alleged to be an extreme liberal and he had been associated with some organizations that were liberal and left-wing. And H. R. Gross and two or three others used to give me a hard time on the floor of the House: 'Well, how can you have a good investigation when you've got these left-wing people doing the work?' etcetera, etcetera. Well, I never had any personal reservations, but I did feel obligated to find out more, or all that I could, about his background. And when I had an opportunity to get into it in greater depth, I was assured that he was no communist, as H. R. Gross and the others would allege. Sure, he had liberal leanings, and that was as far as it went." Redlich was on board, although it took longer for him to get his security clearance.

I was assigned to a small room that had two desks and a large window offering a view of the Capitol dome. By January 20 there were already heaps of reports to read from the FBI, the Secret Service, the Dallas Police Department, and the office of the attorney general of the state of Texas. Although the paperwork was mounting, only a few of the lawyers were at work when I reported for duty. Some were on their way, either driving cross-country or gathering their property and their families for several months in Washington, while others were wrapping up work at their law firms.

A day or two after I arrived, Frank Adams came in. Adams was the picture of the high-powered Wall Street lawyer. He stood a bit over six feet but seemed taller. He looked all of his fifty-nine years. Many of Adams's sentences began with "Of course . . . ," as though he were patiently instructing a junior. I liked Frank Adams immediately, although our relationship was difficult. Adams seemed uncomfortable, as though he didn't know how much authority he had over me. I think he was also unused to working on a prolonged project with only one junior associate, and especially with a junior so young. Frank gave the impression he was used to directing a team of four or five veteran aides.

For my part, I was delighted to be Adams's assistant. He had substantial experience, and I learned something from him almost every time he spoke. Adams looked down at the great piles of reports on his desk, the same materials I had received. After chatting for a bit, we both turned to our reading. With my back to him, I could hear the rustle as Adams thumbed stacks of sheets. After a few moments he called his New York office and issued a series of instructions to his secretary, then talked to a couple of his associates. He hung up and turned to talk with me. It was almost lunchtime, and Adams seemed relieved that some event would save him from diving into that pack of papers.

If Adams had lost the drive for detailed work, his thoughts on our material remained insightful. He constantly referred to his experience as police commissioner of New York City, protecting visiting presidents. In his early contacts with Rankin and other staff lawyers, Adams objected to the commission's approach, suggesting that it was too microscopic. Early on, the *New York Post* quoted him as calling the Kennedy assassination "just another first-degree murder case." Adams thought the commission should conduct an incisive, piercing investigation, wrap up the matter, and file its report.

I do not know what Adams had been told about the length of the investigation. I had been told that our work should last three months but that it could go on, depending on developments, for six months. Adams told me right off that he had to start a trial on a major antitrust case by mid-February, five weeks after we began the Kennedy probe. He implied that he expected to finish our work by then, at least in the main.

From the start, Frank Adams did not appear at commission headquarters on many consecutive days, and his sporadic appearances were brief. Adams's law firm—Satterlee, Warfield and Stephen—had a Washington office, and he coordinated his work from there, with periodic visits to commission headquarters. When Adams showed up, he chatted briefly, fingered some files, and phoned his New York office before finding some reason to leave.

One evening he and I dined alone and then made the rounds of a number of his clubs. Adams had a zest for the nightlife, and I begged off long before he was ready to quit. Our conversations ranged broadly over reform politics in New York City, opportunities in the law, public service, how to charge clients. Another evening, after I made a vain attempt to pick up a tab, Frank reminded me that his daily charge for trial work was $2,500. He then compared the impact of the evening's bill, which was substantial, on my personal funds and on his firm's charge account. His aggressiveness, more than his logic, persuaded me.

I did pick up the bill one day at lunch a few weeks later at a fancy French restaurant (Frank Adams did not dine at any other kind of restaurant), when Frank left the table to make a telephone call. He admonished me, but mildly, because he was less forceful at lunch without his scotch and because the tab was only eight or ten dollars.

I defended Adams in many conversations with other staff members—he was not popular at the commission. I didn't mind Adams's absences. From our first meeting I could see that much of our time together would be spent talking rather than working. I believe the basic proposition that one man can move faster and more effectively than a committee, even a committee of two. I was reconciled, really satisfied, to have the office and the work to myself, the same way I had sat alone at the prosecution table during the Philadelphia Teamsters trial.

Early on, the lawyers in each area were asked to prepare outlines. Adams showed up the day the assignment came down, reviewed my proposal, and made some valuable observations. We staff lawyers were then instructed to prepare preliminary memos detailing the evidence. The final section of each memo was to include an outline of the investigation to be conducted and a list of witnesses to be questioned. To write our memos, we had to sift the mountain of reports from federal and state agencies. The commission would not only review every fact gathered by other agencies but also delve more deeply into the salient ones and investigate other issues. Digesting the reports was a herculean task under any circumstances, but it was particularly arduous in the days before computers.

"There was a whole file room—it was endless—of FBI reports," J. Wesley Liebeler, the Area 3 lawyer, told me recently. "We started going through these reports, focusing on matters we were supposed to concern ourselves with. I went through them, hour after hour. There were no computers then. I was doing card files and trying to get control of the files."[3] The commission decided not to hire its own investigators.

Beyond the question of cost, we faced the problem of finding and recruiting investigators. Years later, as a senator, I would use FBI investigators for the Governmental Affairs Committee investigation of campaign finances, for the same reasons.

I prepared the memo for Area 1 by myself. I sent it to Lee Rankin from Francis W. H. Adams and Arlen Specter, with a cover note that Adams hadn't had a chance to review because he was not in the office shortly before the February 18 deadline. Frank's appearances at the commission grew even rarer in late February. He wasn't around at all when plans were made for questioning the Secret Service agents in the motorcade and the witnesses near the assassination scene. On Monday, March 9, 1964, I questioned the four Secret Service agents who had ridden with the president and vice president in the motorcade. The next day Frank was again absent, and I questioned four other witnesses at the scene.

By mid-March, Adams seemed to feel removed from the commission's activities. He came less frequently and was even less engaged than before. He seemed troubled by his situation but unable to change it. He didn't have the patience to do the background work required for detailed interrogation, and it wasn't practical for me to prepare questions for him, as an assistant might for a senior counsel in a high-powered private litigation case, because there were many nuances to follow-up questions that would have eluded him, given his lack of familiarity with the details of the case. Adams also disagreed with the commission's fundamental approach of covering matters in minute detail. The parade was passing him by.

The autopsy surgeons were scheduled to testify on Monday, March 16. I made arrangements to visit with the pathologists at Bethesda Naval Hospital the Friday before, for preliminary interviews. When Adams wasn't available, I asked Joe Ball, another commission lawyer, to join me. On March 16 the commission met at 2:00 P.M. Before the record was opened, I introduced Chief Justice Warren to the autopsy surgeons. I said, "This is Dr. Humes."

"Good afternoon, Dr. Humes," the chief justice said.

"This is Dr. Boswell."

"Hello, Dr. Boswell."

"This is Dr. Finck."

"Hello, Dr. Finck."

Frank Adams walked in during these introductions, just a few moments late. "Good afternoon, Doctor," Warren said to Adams. That was the last we saw of Frank Adams.

David Belin, the Area 2 junior lawyer, wrote in his first book on the Warren Commission:

> One of the best-kept secrets inside the Commission was that Francis W. H. Adams, one of the two lawyers assigned to Area I, performed virtually no work. He should have been asked to resign when it first became apparent that he was not going to undertake his responsibilities, but because of some mistaken fear that this might in some way embarrass the commission, Mr. Adams was kept on in name only and the entire burden of Area I fell upon Arlen Specter. Fortunately for the Commission, Arlen Specter was able to carry the entire weight of Area I on his own shoulders. Nevertheless, it is indicative of the nature of investigations by governmental Commissions that the need for a second lawyer in Area I was outweighed by a political decision. The ramifications of the fact that this decision was made by the Chief Justice of the United States are indeed chilling.[4]

As for my own distractions from the investigation, it turned out I would not have to juggle a run for Pennsylvania state senate with the commission's work. The Democratic ward leaders voted 3–2 to nominate my opponent, Lou Johanson, who went on to win the state senate seat. He later was arrested in the ABSCAM sting, convicted, and jailed.

TRUTH IS THE CLIENT

The Warren Commission's duty, as set forth in the presidential executive order forming the investigation of the Kennedy assassination, was to "evaluate all the facts and circumstances concerning such assassination." Despite the media frenzy and the publicized FBI findings on Oswald, we did our utmost to approach the investigation with open minds. We all had enough experience to know that news reports and the preliminary conclusions did not end the need for a thorough investigation.

Chief Justice Warren delivered our charge at an early staff meeting. All the lawyers gathered around the conference table in the commission hearing room to receive an indoctrination message from the chief justice. Earl Warren had tremendous presence, but even more so on this occasion, when he spoke of duty. His stature derived largely from his position as chief justice and the moral tone he had set for America, but he also radiated great strength as a man.

At the outset of his indoctrination talk, the chief justice explained his reasons for serving on the commission. He addressed the question that had troubled many, about the propriety of a Supreme Court justice's undertaking such an assignment. Justice Robert Jackson had drawn heavy criticism for serving as a prosecutor in the Nuremberg War Crimes Trials following World War II. Likewise, Justice Owen J. Roberts had drawn objections for his work on the commission that had investigated the Pearl Harbor attack. The Kennedy assassination probe was an especially sensitive subject, since the Supreme Court might one day have to review the prosecution then pending against Jack Ruby, or other matters arising from the assassination.

The chief justice told us he had taken on the commission job very reluctantly. "Archibald Cox, the solicitor general, came to see me and said, 'Mr. Chief Justice, I've been instructed to ask you to be chairman of the commission to investigate the assassination of President Kennedy.' " And Warren said, "I told Archibald Cox no. Then Deputy Attorney General Nicholas Katzenbach came to talk to me. And I similarly told him no."

Attorney General Robert Kennedy did not come to talk to the chief justice. The next call came from the White House, less than two hours later. "And then President Johnson asked me to come to the Oval Office, and asked me to do it," Warren said, "and I said no." The chief justice again declined, on the ground that he should not be involved in any such task, given his responsibility to the Supreme Court. The president persisted. He told Chief Justice Warren that only he could lend the credibility the country and the world so desperately needed as the people tried to understand why their heroic young president had been slain. Conspiracy theories involving communists, the U.S.S.R., Cuba, the military-industrial complex, and even the new president were already swirling. The Kennedy assassination could lead America into a nuclear war that could kill 40 million people, the president warned. President Johnson stressed that it was crucial to have men of prestige and ability to reassure the people that the whole truth was being aired. "Then the president said to me, 'Chief Justice Warren, would you refuse to put on the uniform of your country in time of national emergency, if requested by the commander in chief?' "

"Of course not," the chief justice said. Well, the president said, that was the situation they now faced. "I could hardly refuse that," Warren told us. "So I accepted."

Ford told me at our June 1997 meeting that then-President Johnson had told him the same thing. "I was resisting as strongly as I could being a part of it," Ford recalled. "He [Johnson] called on a Sunday night, gave me the big pitch. I said, 'I'm sorry, Mr. President, I'm senior member on the Defense Appropriations Committee, and senior Republican on the overall committee. I've got a lot of special responsibilities. I don't have the time.' Well, you know Lyndon, Arlen. 'It's your patriotic duty, you owe it to the country,' all the lingo. I understand he did that virtually with everybody, from the chief justice on down."[1] The approach worked on Warren, Ford, and all the others.

At the staff meeting, Warren stressed that our mission, and our obligation, was to find the truth and report it. From the very start, the commission understood that we should not be advocates out to prove a case but must act as independent, disinterested professionals with a duty to find and disclose all the facts, regardless of their implications. "Your client is the truth," the chief justice told us. As part of his strength, the chief justice also stubbornly demanded prompt performance. Push through the details and get the job finished. Sure, get it done right, but get it done. The chief justice demonstrated his impatience as I questioned some witnesses.

Apart from the commission's charge, working with Chief Justice Earl Warren was a thrill. All the commission lawyers revered him. When we were in the same room with Earl Warren, we felt we were in the presence of history. Aside from Franklin D. Roosevelt, a deity in my Depression-racked boyhood home, I thought Warren had made the greatest contribution in U.S. history to the quality of life. Earl Warren brought decency to America through constitutional interpretation. Warren had been on the court for eleven years by 1964, when he undertook the assassination probe, and he'd already done some of his greatest work. The strength of America's constitutional government has been providing the framework for justice in our country. Neither the legislatures nor the chief executives, at either the state or the federal level, could deal with the problem of segregation. But the Supreme Court did, through Warren's leadership. The court had been badly divided over the watershed 1954 case, *Brown* v. *Board of Education*, a great case in our constitutional history. Warren was able to use his skills as a lawyer, a politician, and a conciliator to unite the court.

Warren also brought to criminal law a sense of decency and respect for individual dignity. The landmark defendants'-rights cases in the early 1960s demonstrate his approach. *Mapp* v. *Ohio* came down in 1961, holding that the due process clause of the Fourteenth Amendment prohibited the states from obtaining evidence through unreasonable search and seizure. In 1963, in *Gideon* v. *Wainwright,* the Court ruled that a criminal defendant has a right to a lawyer. Today it's hard to imagine a society that would not make sure that a defendant in a criminal case, facing jail, had a lawyer. But that's how cases were tried until 1963. *Escobedo* v. *Illinois* and *Miranda* v. *Arizona,* following shortly after *Gideon,* required that defendants receive warnings about these rights. Taken as a whole, the decisions amounted to an enforced code of decency. Earl Warren took the lead in establishing the national moral conscience.

Chief Justice Warren was also a brusque boss who demanded prompt administration. Ford, for one, found him authoritarian. "He [Warren] was quite well disciplined," Ford told me recently. "He knew he was chairman. In fact, he made a number of decisions that, at least in the original few months, were unilateral.

"And that upset some of the commission members, who thought he had delegated to himself too much control and authority. . . . There grew up some tension between the commission members and the chairman because of some of the actions we thought should have been reviewed by and acted on by the commission as a whole. Now, the situation improved as we went along."

I told Ford it was tough to get Warren to listen to staff arguments. The chief justice must have been more deferential to Ford and the other commissioners, I suggested.

"Not much," Ford answered. "Not much. He was pretty categorical in his views. . . . There was no deviation from his schedule and his scenario. He treated us as though we were on the team, but he was the captain and the quarterback.

"He was never impolite," Ford added. "That was not his nature. But you knew what he wanted done, and that's the way it was going to be— that way."

The initial staff meeting with Chief Justice Warren was the only such session ever held. After that, individual staff members had extensive contacts with the commissioners and with each other, but we were never again called for a general session.

There was too much to be done to permit the luxury of a formal staff meeting, and no pressing need for another one. We lawyers exchanged views informally throughout the day, carrying problems next door to discuss them with each other and to lunch, which we often ate in groups of four, five, or six in the cafeteria at the Methodist Building, two blocks from the VFW Building.

Most of the staff skull sessions took place over long dinners. An ordinary weekday involved working at commission headquarters until about six-thirty and then heading off in a group of from three to eight to a Washington restaurant. Our expense accounts were limited to twenty-five dollars a day for junior lawyers and thirty-five dollars a day for senior lawyers. The distinction between junior and senior lawyers was eventually dropped, and all lawyers were classified as "assistant counsel" when it became clear that there was no connection between age and contribution. Still, the two-tiered expense accounts remained. I usually stayed for twelve dollars a night at the International Inn at 14th Street and Massachusetts Avenue, to squeeze my expenses within the twenty-five-dollar limit.

We didn't drink, partly because of our tight budgets, and also because we were more interested in keeping our heads clear to talk about the case. But our dinners were interesting—sometimes hilarious—finales to arduous days. One night we ate at the Mayflower Hotel restaurant, where an inverted vat of wine hung over our table, with a tray of glasses inverted on a rack that surrounded the wine spout. Norman Redlich, in an exception to our abstinence, drank a lot of wine that night, assuming that it was free for the taking. When the meal ended, the waiter announced, "That's a dollar a glass. Would you please tell me how many glasses you had?" That was the only time I saw Redlich really surprised.

Jim Liebeler, the young Area 3 lawyer, was volatile. Liebeler boasts that he has a plaque from the Warren Commission mounted on his office wall at UCLA, where he now teaches law. The award acclaims Liebeler as the Most Obnoxious Lawyer on the Commission. I don't recall Liebeler receiving any such plaque during his tenure at the commission. Since it apparently pleased him, I wouldn't disagree with Jim's conclusion that he merited it.

The older lawyers had little contact among themselves and little interplay with the younger lawyers. "The older guys, so far as I could tell, had virtually no interrelationship with each other," recalled Burt Griffin, the junior lawyer in Area 5, and now a judge in Cleveland. "The older guys really dropped out of this thing by April."[2] The exception was Joseph A. Ball, the senior lawyer in Area 2. Joe Ball, of Long Beach, California, was a close friend of the chief justice, who had personally asked him to serve on the investigation. Ball was a former president of the California Bar Association and a partner in a Long Beach firm. He taught criminal law and procedure at the University of Southern California and was a noted legal author. Cherubic, with a twinkle in his eye, Ball made women swoon, even at sixty-two.

I had been out of law school for years, and I missed the bull sessions, where we hashed out legal questions at length. Practicing lawyers have much less time for that luxury. The commission work offered us a unique opportunity to immerse ourselves in a single case with a single client. I found the staff dinners exhilarating.

Other elements of the commission work could be stressful. Many of us were upset over a leaked transcript of Jack Ruby's testimony, which ran in newspapers across the country in July 1964 under Dorothy Kilgallen's byline. That leak triggered an investigation of the commission, by the commission itself. I was questioned by two FBI agents, who came to my Philadelphia office. I described my access to the Ruby transcript, told them that I had guarded it and kept it confidential, and said that I had no knowledge as to how Kilgallen got it. After the interview, I heard nothing more about the leaked Ruby transcript. I felt very uncomfortable being interviewed by the FBI.

We were troubled at the outset about the appropriate procedures for a commission. As lawyers, we were all used to representing a client on one side of a case, facing an opposing lawyer on the other side, and dealing with contested issues of fact or law. For a while there was some uncertainty as to how the commission would function. Many after-dinner speeches were delivered on the subject. A key commission procedure was established over a request—or, more accurately, a demand—from lawyer Mark Lane to represent the late Lee Harvey Oswald before the commission. The commission brass turned Lane down. Oswald wasn't alive, so technically there was no one to represent in the capacity of the defendant. When Lane testified before us on March 4, 1964, he again pressed to represent Oswald, and again was rejected.

The matter had already been decided, as Lane knew, Warren replied. "Now, this is not for any discussion. We are not going to argue it. You have had your say, and I will just answer." Warren's exchange with Mark Lane was the only time Gerald Ford saw the chief justice incensed. "The one time I saw him get irritated, and I mean really irritated, at a witness, was Mark Lane," Ford recalled. "Because, as you know, Mark Lane interjected himself, representing Marina. And he kept demanding more participation, more flexibility. The chief justice was so irritated with his tactics, raising questions and so forth, the chief justice insisted Mark Lane come before the commission and testify under oath. He would not give any leeway to Mark Lane. It was a clash."[3]

Whatever his motives, Lane did a service by asking the commission for a public hearing, thereby indirectly raising the issue of whether the commission should give the public and press access to its proceedings. The commission wisely granted Lane an open session. We also wound up taking the testimony of lead-off witness Marina Oswald, widow of the alleged assassin, in public because her lawyer insisted on it.

When Chief Justice Warren walked to the VFW Building from the Supreme Court to preside at the questioning of Mrs. Oswald, he stepped into a lobby packed with reporters. They asked Warren, as they might ask the chairman of any congressional committee, what his lead-off witness was going to testify to. But Chief Justice Warren did not know what Mrs. Oswald was going to testify to, because he had come to listen and find out. Warren became flustered. Instead of answering that he didn't know, or "Let's see what she testifies to," or "I'd rather not discuss her testimony in advance," the chief justice blurted, "There may be some things we won't know during our life-times."

That was Warren's spontaneous way of avoiding the question. But it cast a pall over everything the commission did. Because of that remark, and because all the sessions were closed, the staff protested when it learned that the commission had voted not to publish the notes of testimony from the public sessions and depositions. While no reason was given for not publishing, the reason apparently was the cost.

The staff contacted the members of Congress serving as commissioners who had not been present at the vote on publication. Those commissioners took action to see that the record was published. The legislators' experience with publishing proceedings in the *Congressional Record* apparently influenced them. Members of Congress are often not too selective about what they put in the *Congressional Record*. Once Senator Bob Dole, making a sweeping gesture with his left hand across his body, quipped that it was easy to clean off his desk: "I just put it all in the *Congressional Record*."

In the end we would publish seventeen thousand pages of Warren Commission proceedings in twenty-six volumes. While those seventeen thousand pages provided grist for critical books' mills, they also showed our willingness to put the evidence and exhibits on the public record. Years later, in 1992, I co-sponsored legislation to declassify and publish as much as possible.

The Warren Commission was unique in that it was an investigation conducted entirely on the record, documented as it went along. I know of no other comparable investigation before or since. In most judicial or quasi-judicial proceedings, such as court trials, evidence is presented systematically, to support a given argument. After a piece of evidence is introduced, other material may be presented to dispute earlier contentions. In a trial most evidence is available in advance. Some prosecutors will not take any written statements until they have all the facts and have assembled the entire picture, because they do not want a written statement that may conflict with what they find out later. An investigation is intended to determine the facts. No one knew exactly where the Warren Commission investigation would lead, and that was just as it should have been.

Ford, for one, favored taking testimony in private. "I really think we did a much better job by having the witnesses testify as we arranged it," he told me recently. "If we'd had open hearings, we would have had something like the O. J. Simpson trial. Witnesses would be on exhibition. You can imagine Oswald's mother, who was about the screwiest person . . . And Marina was a bit of a show-off. So I think by having it the way we did, we got the business done better."[4]

Still, many of us on staff remained troubled by Chief Justice Warren's remark about "some things we will never know," and about the commission's lack of public hearings, despite our unique, on-the-record investigation. If we had held public hearings, covered by the press, the public could have followed the developments as they unfolded, which would have inspired much more confidence in the investigation. Our policy, in the end, was not to hold a public hearing unless the witness requested one, as Marina Oswald did through her lawyer.

When the time came to take testimony, a battle erupted among the staff lawyers as to whether we should interview witnesses in advance. Joe Ball, by far the most experienced trial lawyer on staff, Dave Belin, and I argued that we had to. Norman Redlich led the opposition.

Redlich said we might be accused of leading witnesses one way or another if we talked to them before they testified. Ball, Belin, and I countered that the witnesses had already been interviewed by other agencies, that they were adults, and that we would have to be trusted not to push them. We also argued that it was necessary to talk to witnesses before they testified, to get a general idea of what they would say. Otherwise it would be almost impossible to present their testimony in any orderly way.

The logical lead-off witnesses for my area were the people closest to the president when he was shot. Former first lady Jacqueline Kennedy would have made an appropriate beginning. But the commission resisted questioning her. The chief justice had taken a protective stance toward Mrs. Kennedy. It was, of course, natural for him to want to spare the widow the anguish of reliving her husband's murder. Perhaps Warren's attitude drew from the natural protective posture of a man with daughters, or from his old-fashioned courtliness. The chief justice showed the same protective attitude toward Marina Oswald. My efforts to bring Mrs. Kennedy to testify before the commission were unsuccessful.

I also wanted to question President Johnson, who would under other circumstances have been considered a prime suspect. I had been asked to prepare a list of questions for the new president. I composed seventy-eight questions, including many alternatives, depending on how the president responded to a previous question. I didn't think Lyndon Johnson was complicit in the assassination, but no self-respecting investigator would omit a thorough investigation of the slain president's successor. I strenuously objected when the commission would not question Johnson either, letting him submit a seven-page affidavit instead. "It was very important to have Johnson questioned, to the extent there were rumors," agreed fellow commission lawyer David Belin. "Also, he was a witness. He was in the mototcade."[5] Belin also dismissed Johnson's abridged, seven-page affidavit, which the president sent us several months before his 1964 election. President Johnson was not asked to expand that brief affidavit, and on the verge of the election he obviously was not inclined to say more than required.

The investigation had plodded along until early March, as we sifted mountains of reports. We were delayed by Jack Ruby's trial in Texas for murdering Oswald in the basement of Dallas police headquarters two days after the Kennedy assassination. The commission had decided that none of its representatives would travel to Texas while Ruby's trial was in progress, because the trial had received enough publicity without adding an element of potential prejudice. FBI and Secret Service agents, however, continued to investigate in Dallas, just as they had been doing since the day of the assassination.

I did interview Senator Ralph Yarborough, the Texas Democrat who had been riding in the follow-up car with then–Vice President Johnson. Kennedy had gone to Texas partly to soften the intra-Democratic spat between the Yarborough liberal faction and the Johnson conservative faction. Kennedy was reportedly annoyed that Johnson had not worked out the problem and saved him at least that portion of the trip. After the shooting, Yarborough told the *Washington Post* that he had smelled the gunpowder.

Lee Rankin called me in and told me, "We don't want to bring Senator Yarborough before the commission, but we do want to find out what he has to say, especially after his extensive interview in the *Washington Post*." Rankin did not say that Yarborough was eccentric, but that was the implication. "Arlen," Rankin said, "you go over and get an affidavit from him." Yarborough fell under Area 1, my domain.

I walked two blocks from the VFW Building on Constitution Avenue to the old Senate office building, later renamed the Russell Senate Building, where Yarborough had his office. I listened attentively to the senator but didn't take notes. When we finished, I returned to the commission headquarters, where I prepared an affidavit. The next day I returned to Yarborough's office to secure his signature to the affidavit. The senator read the document and erupted. I had come into his office with a tape recorder without telling him, he raged. I said, "No, Senator, I didn't, but thank you very much for the compliment."

He said, "Well, this is exactly what I said." I didn't consider it too complicated to interview a witness, walk a couple of blocks, and prepare an accurate affidavit. Yarborough remained incensed, but he signed the affidavit.

Yarborough's volatility was demonstrated about this time by an encounter with South Carolina Senator Strom Thurmond during Judiciary Committee proceedings on the 1964 Civil Rights Bill. Strom was standing outside the Judiciary Committee room, not entering because he didn't want to make a quorum to allow the Judiciary Committee to proceed with its business, but he wanted to be able to make an immediate entry to participate if enough senators arrived to make a quorum. Yarborough urged Thurmond to come in, and Thurmond refused. Yarborough told Thurmond, "I'm going to pull you in," and he grabbed hold of the former Army general. "You can try, if you're man enough to do it," Thurmond said.

Yarborough tugged. Thurmond threw the Texas senator to the floor outside the Judiciary Committee room and clamped a body scissors on him. Thurmond wouldn't let up until Yarborough promised not to go into the committee room himself. But when Yarborough got up, he went back into the room, breaking his pledge.

QUICK REFLEXES

T here were many Secret Service agents involved in the activities the day of Kennedy's assassination who could have been called as witnesses. There were agents in the lead car that preceded the presidential limousine, in the president's follow-up car, with the vice presidential limousine, and in the car that followed the vice presidential limousine. Statements had been obtained from each of the agents and were included in the Secret Service report. The two agents who demanded attention, in addition to Roy Kellerman and William Greer, who had been riding in Kennedy's Lincoln, were Clint Hill and Rufus Youngblood.

Hill had jumped from the left running board of the president's follow-up car after the shooting and caught up with the Lincoln. I was amazed every time I watched the Zapruder film and saw Hill dash to the limousine, barely grasp the handle on the left rear fender and leap on the small running board at the left rear just as the car accelerated. Hill was one of the agents who went out on the town the night before the assassination. According to his own signed statement, Hill left his hotel shortly before 1:30 A.M., drank a Scotch and water at the Press Club of Fort Worth, then had part of a nonalcoholic fruit drink at a nightspot called The Cellar, leaving about 2:45 A.M. to return to his hotel. But Clint Hill's reflexes could hardly have been quicker later that day.[1]

In the instant after the assassination, Clint Hill saved Jacqueline Kennedy's life. The first lady had inexplicably climbed onto the trunk of the moving limousine. Clint Hill pushed her back into the car. If he had not, Mrs. Kennedy would have tumbled into the street when the Lincoln accelerated, into the path of the speeding backup car.

We speculated about why Jacqueline Kennedy climbed onto the trunk. Perhaps she was trying to retrieve part of the president's head.

She might have instinctively thought that if she retrieved chunks of it, they might be reattached, as severed fingers or limbs sometimes are. Some surmised that Mrs. Kennedy jumped onto the trunk out of fright. I doubt that. Her strength and composure shortly afterward at Parkland Hospital, by all accounts, were extraordinary. Also, it would make little sense to leave the back seat in search of protection on the trunk of a moving car. It would make more sense to crouch lower into the limousine's hold. Still another theory held that Mrs. Kennedy simply wanted to get away from the blood, carnage, and terror of her husband's wounds. I doubt that also, given that she later cradled the president's mangled head and wore her blood-soaked dress the rest of the day.

Mrs. Kennedy may not have been thinking rationally under such extreme circumstances. But all we have is speculation. Mrs. Kennedy later said she did not remember anything about her climb onto the trunk of the limousine. During her brief testimony she volunteered one reference to the incident: "You know, then, there were pictures later on of me climbing out the back, but I do not remember that at all." Lee Rankin then asked Mrs. Kennedy, "Do you remember Mr. Hill coming to try to help on the car?"

"I do not remember anything," Mrs. Kennedy replied.

I did interview Secret Service Agent Rufus Youngblood. According to preliminary reports, "Rufe" Youngblood had scrambled to protect the life of Vice President Johnson. Youngblood was sitting on the right front seat of the vice presidential limousine. Johnson was sitting in the rear on the extreme right, Mrs. Johnson was in the center of the rear, and Senator Yarborough was on the left. It had been difficult to get Johnson and Yarborough to sit in the same car. Those seating arrangements were made only with President Kennedy's intervention.

When I spoke briefly with Youngblood before he was called to testify formally before the commission, he was sheepish about his speed in bounding from the front seat to the vice president. At the time of the shooting, Youngblood had jumped over the front seat and shielded the vice president with his own body. Johnson had said Youngblood was on top of him after the first shot and before the second. Youngblood deferred to President Johnson's version, for at least two obvious reasons: First, who wants to contradict his boss? And, second, it would not harm Youngblood's reputation to be considered so quick.

In reconstructing the assassination, it seemed unlikely that Youngblood could have moved fast enough to vault the front seat and land on

Johnson between the first and second shots. But it sounded great. Some of the commission lawyers, jesting among ourselves, made it an even more spectacular story: Shortly *before* the first shot, Youngblood leaped over the front seat to shield the vice president with his own body. Several lawyers thought that sequence was almost as plausible as Johnson's version.

When Hill and Youngblood testified, they were in much better spirits than Kellerman and Greer, the other two Secret Service agents we interviewed early. Hill and Youngblood could emerge from the assassination as heroes, or at least with praise for their swift action. The other two could not. Kellerman acted blasé, perhaps covering a sense of guilt for not having done more to protect the president's life. Kellerman looked like a casting model for the role of special agent in charge. He stood six feet four, weighed well over two hundred pounds, and was muscular and handsome. In the informal session Kellerman talked about all the presidents he had worked with. He did not seem to share the other agents' attachment to Kennedy.

In hindsight, if the agent in the Lincoln's right front seat was expected to move quickly to protect the president in an assassination attempt, Kellerman was the wrong man for the job. He was forty-eight years old, big, and his reflexes were not very quick. But it is probable that the agent in Kellerman's seat wasn't expected to shield the president with his body. Kellerman was too far from Kennedy to do that, and there were too many obstacles in his way, even if he had Youngblood's feline reflexes. The president's custom-designed 1961 Lincoln convertible limousine had collapsible jump seats between the front and rear seats. A metal frame extended across the breadth of the car, fifteen inches above the back of the front seat. The bar had four handles for riders to grasp while standing during parades.

As the Lincoln drove down Elm Street on that November day, Kellerman was separated from Kennedy by the front seat, by the metal frame that added at least fifteen inches to the necessary hurdle, and by Governor Connally, who was sitting in the jump seat in front of the president. The Lincoln was designed to give several Secret Service agents easy access to the president. At the rear of each side was a small running board designed to carry an agent and a metal handle for him to hold. But only a few days before the assassination, in Tampa, Florida, Kennedy had objected to the agents riding on those running boards.

Agents on running boards would obstruct the president and make him look defensive and afraid.

In general, I believe that a president should have less authority to direct his own security detail. Constitutionally, it's tough to say that the commander in chief may not give instructions. But when the issue is his own safety, I think he should defer. When Ronald Reagan was shot in the chest in March 1981, I introduced legislation to change presidential protection policies to restrict a president's authority, along the lines of preventing Kennedy from pulling agents off the running boards.

Presidential protection, never foolproof, was relatively slack in the early 1960s. "Processes for protection in those days were pretty ineffective," said Sam Stern, the commission junior lawyer in charge of presidential protection. "The president was terribly vulnerable."[2]

Notwithstanding those obstacles, Kellerman insisted that neither the bar nor the governor would have prevented him from protecting the president. But I had the distinct impression he was paying more attention to the weather in Dallas than to the possibility of an assassination.

In his informal interview, Secret Service Agent William Greer seemed shaken by the shooting. He clearly felt deep affection for Kennedy, which I sensed had been reciprocal. Greer was fifty-four when he testified before the commission, on March 9, 1964. He had immigrated to the United States when he was twenty, after growing up in Ireland. That background may have established a bond between him and Kennedy, who was also of Irish descent. Greer told a touching story that he later repeated in part in his formal testimony before the commission.

I was interested to know whether President Kennedy wore an undershirt, because his clothes could indicate the direction and location of the bullet. Fibers from the back of the president's jacket and shirt had been pressed forward, indicating that the bullet had come from the rear. The president's garments were also important, given the controversy over the location of the hole in his body versus the locations of the holes in his clothing. Some critics have seized on the locations of the holes in the suit jacket and shirt to argue that the hole was lower on the president's back than the reports asserted. This concern has been aggravated by the withholding of the autopsy photographs and X rays.

President Kennedy's activities, dress, and physique indicate that his shirt and jacket rode up on his body. During the ride from Love Field to downtown Dallas, the president had twice ordered the limousine stopped so he could stand up and greet watchers. When Kennedy sat down in an open convertible, his contact with the seat would tend to move his clothing up. Waving with his right hand, as shown on the Zapruder film, would also tend to lift the president's jacket and shirt on his body. Kennedy's back brace and muscular build would further hike up his garments.

To nail down both the direction and the location of the bullet that struck the president's back, we wanted all possible indicators. One of those was an undershirt, if in fact Kennedy had been wearing one that day. The simplest approach would have been to ask Mrs. Kennedy, but the commission was reluctant to make that inquiry. Instead I asked every witness I questioned whether the president was wearing an undershirt in Dallas. Generally, I got nowhere. Then, to my surprise, Agent Greer said, "Oh, no, he wasn't wearing an undershirt."

"Well, how do you know, Mr. Greer?" I asked.

"Well, because he came to your town [Philadelphia] the year before for the Army-Navy game," Greer said, "and it was a chilly day, and I said to him, 'Mr. President, you need your topcoat,' and he said, 'No, Bill, I don't need my topcoat, I've got my undershirt on.'

"So when the president wore an undershirt instead of a topcoat on a chilly day, I knew he wouldn't be wearing an undershirt in Dallas on that balmy warm day." Greer's point, simply, was that Kennedy would wear an undershirt only as a substitute for a topcoat on a cold day.

When Secret Service agents Kellerman, Greer, Hill, and Youngblood testified, I questioned them about minute details of the assassination. I knew they could not give precise answers to all my questions, but I believed that those questions should be asked. To draw a composite picture of the shooting, we needed to gather and weigh evidence from all the vantage points. So I asked each witness for his best estimate of the number of seconds between shots or other noises that he heard and the distance the motorcade traveled during those intervals. I also asked the witnesses to mark a map showing their best recollection of the Lincoln's location when the shots were heard.

Most of the commissioners were patient with my efforts, but not the chief justice. When I questioned witnesses, Warren frequently tapped his fingers. His annoyance at my prolonged questioning was obvious.

The day the Secret Service agents testified, we began at 9:10 A.M. and didn't finish until 6:20 P.M. Shortly after the morning session began, Warren left to sit with the Supreme Court. He returned for the afternoon session, when the questioning of Agent Kellerman continued. At one point during my questioning, when the chief justice's finger-tapping reached a crescendo, he took me aside and asked me to speed it up. He said it was unrealistic to expect meaningful answers to questions about the elapsed time between the first and second shots and between the second and third shots, or about the distance traveled between the first and second shots or the speed of the car at the time of the first shot, at the time of the second shot, and at the time of the third shot.

I said I thought the questions were essential. I knew it was difficult for witnesses to give precise answers, I told the chief justice, but I thought we had to ask those questions and get the most precise answers possible—this might produce some valuable information that would otherwise elude us. And people would read and reread this record for years, if not decades or perhaps even centuries. Even at that stage, on the basis of my experience reading records on appeals cases, I was concerned that the commission record be as professional as possible. The chief justice appeared dissatisfied with my answer, but he didn't order me to change my approach. Aside from drumming his fingers, Warren did not interfere with the examination.

Several days before John Connally was scheduled to arrive in Washington, Rankin told me that the chief justice had ordered him to take the governor's testimony. Connally, riding in front of the president, fell into my area. But I understood. Warren had great confidence in Rankin, and it was appropriate that the general counsel handle the most important witnesses. And I knew that the chief justice found my detailed queries tedious.

Lee Rankin asked me how he should approach the questioning of Governor Connally. In order to get all the information from the governor, I replied, it was necessary to correlate the medical findings, including the tests done at Edgewater and the X rays, with the velocity of the bullet and the path it followed. I pointed out to Rankin that the bullet had a muzzle velocity of approximately 2,200 feet per second; that by the time it reached the president, the bullet's speed was about 2,000 feet per second; and that, on the basis of the tests at Edgewater with a gelatin solution and compressed goat meat, the bullet would have had an exit velocity of about 1,900 feet per second. The velocity decreased as the bullet entered slightly to the left of the governor's right armpit, exited beneath his right nipple, leaving a large exit wound, and entered the dorsal aspect of his wrist and exited the volar aspect, finally lodging in

69

his thigh. I presented a longer sequence to Rankin, taking in the path of the Lincoln limousine, the seating arrangements in the car, and other factors.

By the time I had finished, Rankin, knowing he had little time to immerse himself in such detail, shook his head in despair. "You'll have to question Connally," he said.

I hadn't intended to discourage Rankin and displace him as Connally's questioner. But I wouldn't say I regretted it either.

GOVERNOR CONNALLY

Watching Governor John Connally watch himself get shot in the Zapruder film was fascinating. I had already seen the historic amateur movie hundreds of times, so I was primarily interested in the reactions of the governor and Mrs. Connally as they viewed the film for the first time. The governor gaped as the garment manufacturer's movie showed the few seconds that Connally had doubtless relived in his mind countless times during the previous five months.

We showed the film to the governor, Mrs. Connally, and Texas Attorney General Waggoner Carr, who had accompanied them to the commission offices, as a preliminary to the governor's testimony on the afternoon of April 22, 1964.

Even before Connally testified, it was clear he had his mind set about the events of November 22. As far as I know, no investigator from the commission or any other federal agency had interviewed John Connally before his appearance in Washington. But I knew that the governor had discussed the shooting with others.

The doctors who had treated Connally at Parkland tried to reconstruct the shooting in the operating room to figure the bullet's trajectory. Later, they followed up with Connally. Dr. Robert Shaw, the thoracic surgeon who had operated on Connally's chest at Parkland Hospital, testified that he and the governor had talked more than once about the sequence of events in the shooting. Dr. George T. Shires, who operated on the governor's thigh, testified that he and Connally had talked over the assassination events periodically during the governor's convalescence. Shires said he first discussed the governor's injuries with Mrs. Connally late in the afternoon on November 22, right after Connally's surgery.

According to Shires, Mrs. Connally said the governor had turned to his right after the first shot. Connally told Shires that he had turned after the first shot to see what had happened, and was then hit. Shires insisted that Connally "definitely remembers turning after hearing the first shot, before he was struck with the bullet."

Shires's first conversation with Connally took place four or five days after the shooting. When I asked what the occasion was, Shires replied, "In part of his routine care one morning, he was reconstructing his memory of events, because his memory was quite hazy, since he had a sucking wound of the chest and came in here relatively in anoxia—he had some cyanosis, as you know." Shires added that the governor's memory was accurate for events leading up to the time he fell over in the car.

During the viewing of the Zapruder film, I chatted with Connally, to see whether he could identify the frame in which he was hit. When the camera was running on the day of the assassination, slightly more than eighteen frames flicked by in a second, and the action was over quickly. But when the Zapruder film was shown frame by frame, it suggested a long sequence of events between the time President Kennedy was obscured from the gunman's view behind a tree from frames 167 to 210 and the time his head exploded in frame 313.

At one point while viewing the film, Connally and his wife argued over whether the governor had fallen into his wife's lap or she had pulled him into her lap. Connally insisted that he had fallen. Mrs. Connally insisted that she had pulled him. "No, Nellie," "No, John," they shot back and forth, several times. Eventually Mrs. Connally had the film halted and took Connally and Carr out to the hall for a conference. When they returned shortly, Nellie Connally and the governor were in agreement—on Mrs. Connally's version.

Of course, I didn't know what they said outside. But considering I was trying to gather a witness's own account of the shooting, the Connally summit was not comforting. Later that afternoon, when the governor testified, he said, "So I merely doubled up, and then turned to my right again and began to—just sat there, and Mrs. Connally pulled me over to her lap." His wife's words.

Mrs. Connally, for her part, was bitter about the reception her husband had received at Parkland when he arrived bleeding and unconscious. She complained that Secret Service agents and other officials rushed to the president, lifting Connally out of the car only because they had to move him to reach Kennedy. Mrs. Connally also criticized

72

the hospital staff, who swarmed around the president, ignoring their wounded governor.

Governor Connally had been closer to President Kennedy than anybody except Mrs. Kennedy when the shots were fired. His testimony, scheduled for 2 P.M., stirred the most excitement at the VFW Building since Marina Oswald's lead-off deposition. The entire Commission assembled. It was the first and last time I saw Senator Richard Russell at any proceeding where testimony was taken. Russell expressed impatience that Connally's testimony didn't begin on time. Russell had made a special point of attending the appearance of an important Southern governor. Russell himself had once been a Southern governor, of Georgia from 1931 to 1933.

Connally arrived at the VFW Building a few minutes after 2 P.M. in a large black Cadillac that had unmistakable signs of being the presidential limousine. Earlier in the day Connally had told Rankin and me he had a luncheon date with a friend. He had not identified the friend. Clearly, Connally's unnamed luncheon date had been the president. Fellow Texans John Connally and Lyndon Johnson had been friends for years.

One subject that had intrigued the younger staff was the purpose of Kennedy's visit to Texas. The media had speculated that the trip was politically motivated, and several young commission lawyers thought Connally should be asked about that explicitly. We considered it important to put this on the record. I guessed that the chief justice might not like my exploring this background issue. To get the governor's candid response on a subject he had not expected—and to explore the area before the chief justice could preempt me—I led off with that question. According to Connally, the trip had been a combination of political fund-raising, presidential flag-waving, and general fact-finding, taking the pulse of the people toward the end of Kennedy's first term. Connally said he had initially objected to a Dallas motorcade because of time limitations but dropped his objection when the Austin leg of the trip was shuffled.

Connally's testimony would generally follow the outline we had discussed at our brief morning meeting. I thought the governor should know about some additional facts and testimony the commission had gathered, so he could weigh them along with his own experience. In the morning I had told Connally of factors that suggested he might have been struck by the same bullet that had first passed through Kennedy's neck. Connally summarily, emphatically rejected that possibility. "It is not conceivable to me that I could have been hit by the first bullet," he testified. Connally reasoned that he heard the first shot, did not hear the second, which he assumed struck him, and was in his wife's lap when he heard the third shot strike the president's head.

When we got to the assassination itself, Connally's testimony was among the most graphic and detailed we heard. "What is the best estimate you have," I asked the governor, "as to the time span between the sound of the first shot and the feeling of someone hitting you in the back which you just described?"

"A very, very brief span of time," Connally answered. ". . . I knew I had been hit, and I immediately assumed, because of the amount of blood and, in fact, that it had obviously passed through my chest, that I had probably been fatally hit. . . . And then, of course, the third shot sounded, and I heard the shot very clearly. I heard it hit him. I heard the shot hit something, and I assumed again—it never entered my mind that it hit anybody but the president. I heard it hit. It was a very loud noise, just that audible, very clear. Immediately I could see on my clothes, my clothing, I could see on the interior of the car—which, as I recall, was a pale blue—brain tissue, which I immediately recognized, and I recall very well, on my trousers there was one chunk of brain tissue as big as almost my thumb, and again, I did not see the president at any time either after the first, second, or third shots. . . ."

Toward the end of his testimony, I asked Connally, "What was the nature of the exit wound on the front side of your chest, Governor?"

"If the committee would be interested," Connally said, "I would just as soon you look at it. Is there any objection to any of you looking at it?" There was no objection, and Connally took off his shirt to show a large, ugly, four-inch-diameter scar under his right nipple, from the exit wound. While Connally's shirt was off, Lee Rankin's secretary, Julie Eide, came in. Seeing the governor bare-chested, she gasped and walked out.

As I was questioning Connally, I noticed Chief Justice Warren's impatience. When I finished, Warren left no doubt, on the record. Before swearing in Mrs. Connally, he said, "Mrs. Connally, would you mind telling the story of this affair as you heard it, and we will be brief and will start right with the shooting itself, and Mr. Specter will also examine you. . . ." Without the inflection, those words do not jump out.

But Warren's tone left no room for doubt. "We *will* be brief," he stressed. His statement that "we will start right with the shooting itself" made clear that he did not want me to explore any of the background. Having covered the background and a reasonable amount of detail with the governor, I tried to comply with the chief justice's interdiction.

BULLET 399

The line between Area 1, the activities of President Kennedy, and Area 2, the identity of the assassin, had not been sharply drawn. Since the moment of the assassination brought together the president and his killer, the witnesses at the scene could have been placed in either area. There would always be some overlap.

In early March, I worked out an agreement with the Area 2 team of Joe Ball and Dave Belin for dividing the witnesses: They would handle all witnesses at the assassination scene except for those in the presidential motorcade, whom I would handle. Even that split could not be made precisely. The wounds on the president's body naturally fell into Area 1, Kennedy's activities, but the source of the shots fell into Area 2, the assassin's identity. We decided that the bullet in flight was the dividing point between Areas 1 and 2. Before the bullet left the rifle barrel, it was the responsibility of Ball and Belin. After striking the president, it was my responsibility. Ball, Belin, and I continued to work closely and never fought over turf.

Beginning in early March, the commission stepped up the pace for hearing testimony. By the second week in March, Jack Ruby's murder trial in Dallas seemed to be nearing its end. But the ban held on commission staff traveling to Texas, and it forced us to shuffle our schedule. It would have made more sense to investigate the activities at Parkland Hospital, where Kennedy and Connally were treated, before taking testimony from the autopsy surgeons, who had worked on Kennedy's body after it left Texas. Rather than wait, we scheduled the autopsy evidence for Monday, March 16.

I had studied the autopsy report that was signed by Navy Commanders J. J. Humes and J. Thornton Boswell and by Army Lieut. Col. Pierre A. Finck. Kennedy's body had arrived at Bethesda Naval Hospital at about 7:35 P.M. on November 22, seven hours after he was shot. The autopsy had begun about 8 P.M. and ended three hours later, about 11 P.M. The procedure was rushed, because Robert and Jacqueline Kennedy waited outside the chamber, pressing the doctors to finish. The surgeons skipped some steps, such as tracing the bullet paths.

I wanted to talk to the autopsy surgeons in advance to prepare an orderly presentation of their testimony. Redlich's ban on pre-testimony interviews was also still in effect, so I got authorization from Rankin. An interview was set for Friday, March 13. Frank Adams was not in Washington that day, so I asked Joe Ball to come with me to Bethesda Naval Hospital, just north of Washington, where Humes and Boswell were based. Ball was the most experienced trial lawyer on the commission. And that Friday afternoon, Ball was the only other lawyer around.

Kennedy had been taken to Bethesda, rather than to the better autopsy facilities at the Army's nearby Walter Reed Hospital, because Mrs. Kennedy wanted her husband, a Navy man, taken to the Navy hospital. But Humes and his team had never handled this type of case.

Joe Ball and I arrived at the hospital early in the afternoon. Humes and Boswell were asked to join us. Humes, thirty-nine, the lead autopsy surgeon, was director of labs at the Navy medical school at Bethesda. Boswell, forty-one, was the school's director of pathology. Finck, the Army doctor, had been brought in for his expertise on bullet wounds.

After the introductions, Humes wanted proof that we were really with the Warren Commission. I figured he had been besieged by people claiming various affiliations. The only credentials Ball and I could produce were our passes to the VFW Building. My building pass didn't look very official to begin with, even less so because the typeface used for my name didn't match the print on the rest of the card. Humes's doubts were eased more by the admiral's orders than by our papers. "Humes was scared to death," Ball recalled recently. "Humes came in there and he didn't want to talk to us, and the admiral ordered him to, after he saw our identification."[1] Ball said he still has his VFW Building pass framed on his wall, more than thirty years later.

We began the interview by reviewing the autopsy reports and the general procedures the doctors had used. We couldn't go over the surgeons' notes because Dr. Humes had burned them in his fireplace. Some have suggested that Humes was trying to hide his mistakes, or worse. Humes had responded to an extraordinary situation, with FBI agents in the middle of his autopsy room and the president's wife and brother sitting outside waiting for him to finish. I concluded that he was inexperienced and naive, not realizing how many people would be looking over his shoulder, but not at all malicious.

Nearly thirty-five years after the Kennedy autopsy, Humes told me why he had burned his notes. He, Dr. Boswell, and I spoke over lunch in Washington in May 1998. Retired at seventy-five and teaching part-time in Jacksonville, Florida, Humes had grown frail in his six-foot-four frame, but he still spoke with gusto. He had never publicly told the story about his notes. One of my aides suggested taping our luncheon conversation with Humes and Boswell, but I rejected the idea, thinking that it would be too inhibiting. As my aide walked Humes to the train station after lunch, he asked the surgeon to repeat his explanation on tape, and Humes did:

A couple of years previous to the president's death, I had a responsi-bility for touring foreign naval officers, [taking] physicians from foreign navies various places. One of the places I took them to was Detroit, so they could see industrial medicine, on our way to Great Lakes, where they could see medicine at a Naval training center, and we took them to Greenfield Village, which is right outside of Detroit in Dearborn, Michi-gan, where they have any number of exhibits that Henry Ford brought there from all around the country.

And one of them was a courthouse allegedly from Illinois or Indiana or someplace where President Lincoln served as a traveling judge. And in that building were just a bench for the judge and some places for the witnesses and so forth, a very plain, simple building. But they also had a chair, sort of a rocking chair, which they alleged was the chair in which Lincoln was seated when he was assassinated at Ford's Theater. Whether that's true or not, I don't know.

But they pointed out the stains on the back of the chair, which they said was President Lincoln's blood. And I thought this was repulsive, that they were displaying this, and so forth.

And this was on my mind when I got some of the notes we took at the Kennedy autopsy, which were stained with his blood.

And I was bound and determined that they weren't going to be a pub-lic display like this chair in this courthouse.

It turned out later, by the way—whether that was his chair or not is sort of immaterial—the stains were not blood but were a substance called "Macassar." Eighteenth-century [sic] gentlemen often used this material, I don't know what it comes from, as a pomade for their hair. And many young people probably never heard of an antimacassar, but my grandmother had these doilies on the back of her fine furniture so nobody's head stained with Macassar or anything else would stain her lovely furniture. And that's the derivation of the term "antimacassar." It's a poor day when you don't learn something.[2]

At Bethesda, Ball and I tried to clear up some confusion over how far the bullet that struck Kennedy's neck had traveled through his body. The now-famous preliminary report of FBI agents O'Neill and Sibert, filed in December 1963, stated that one bullet entered Kennedy's body "just below his shoulder to the right of the spinal column at an angle of 45 to 60 degrees downward, that there was no point of exit, and that the bullet was not in the body." An FBI report in January said the bullet "penetrated to a distance of less than a finger's length."

The Bethesda doctors, while performing the autopsy, knew that the Parkland team had given Kennedy external heart massage. They also knew that a whole bullet had been found on a Parkland stretcher. Initially they surmised that the bullet on the stretcher might have been pushed out the back of Kennedy's neck by the massage. When I later questioned FBI agents Sibert and O'Neill, they told me that they had overheard the autopsy surgeon's hypotheses during the examination and used them as the basis of their report.

As the autopsy progressed, the surgeons realized that the bullet had passed farther through the president's neck. They saw that the muscles in the front of the neck had been damaged at about the same time the wound was inflicted on the top of the chest cavity. Both wounds indicated that Kennedy's heart and lungs were working when they were inflicted, unlike the incisions made at Parkland after the president's circulation had weakened.

The morning after the autopsy, Humes had called Dr. Malcolm Perry, one of the Parkland team, to ask about Kennedy's neck. They talked for about half an hour. Perry told Humes that he'd had to perform a tracheotomy on Kennedy to insert a breathing tube. There was no bullet hole in Kennedy's throat because Perry had performed the "trache" there, obliterating any evidence of that wound. When all the facts came in, it became clear that the neck shot had exited Kennedy's throat. The simple, innocent explanation would not stop the cynics. A host of books, beginning with Edward Jay Epstein's *Inquest*, charged that the autopsy doctors had falsified their report and that the bullet never exited Kennedy's throat.

Our Friday interview with Humes and Boswell produced a revelation: The bullet that passed through Kennedy's neck proceeded in a straight line, struck nothing solid, and exited with great velocity. The doctors had not mentioned this in their autopsy report. "The missile struck no bony structures in traversing the body of the late president," Humes testified when I questioned him the following Monday. "Therefore, I believe it was moving at its exit from the president's body at only very slightly less than that velocity, so it was still traveling at great speed."

Humes then referred to Commission Exhibit 398, a frame of the Zapruder film that showed Kennedy raising his hands to his neck, presumably after being shot there. "I believe in looking at Exhibit 398, which purports to be at approximately the time the president was struck," Humes said, "I see that Governor Connally is sitting directly in front of the late president, and suggest the possibility that this missile, having traversed the low neck of the late president, in fact traversed the chest of Governor Connally."

During Humes's testimony, the commission was introduced to its most famous exhibit. I affixed a tab marked "Commission Exhibit No. 399" to the small plastic container that held the bullet believed to have come from Connally's stretcher. By commission procedure, the lawyer who did the questioning tagged the exhibits as he went along. We began each day with a sheet of exhibit numbers that were typed on self-adhesive tabs. It was random as to which number would wind up on any given piece of evidence. When I marked the bullet as Commission Exhibit 399, I added, "May I say now that, subject to later proof, this is the missile which has been taken from the stretcher which the evidence now indicates was the stretcher occupied by Governor Connally."

At one point Allen Dulles asked Humes a question about the stretcher on which the bullet was found. "He [Dr. Humes] was not there," Warren interjected. "He does not know anything about it."

"Yes," Dulles said, "I wonder if there is other evidence of this."

"We shall produce later, subject to sequential proof," I promised, "evidence that the stretcher on which this bullet was found was the stretcher of Governor Connally."

There was a real question whether Humes should be asked at all about matters beyond his immediate personal knowledge, such as his view on the trajectory of the bullets or the metallic flakes in Governor Connally's wrist. Under the technical rules of evidence that apply in court, such testimony might be barred. But the commission made the commonsense decision to ask Humes and other witnesses for their views, impressions, and opinions on a variety of issues. Questions about outside subjects might produce more answers about inside subjects. For example, by asking Humes—who had never examined Connally—about damage Connally might have suffered, we were probing at the same time about resistance the bullet met in passing through Kennedy's neck, an area within Humes's sphere. From this freewheeling questioning, the Single-Bullet Conclusion developed naturally.

Humes saw Bullet 399, which was almost pristine, for the first time the day he testified. When I showed him photographs of the positions that Kennedy and Connally had occupied in the Lincoln, Humes suggested that the same bullet might have exited Kennedy's neck and then passed through Connally's chest.

I asked Humes whether he thought Bullet 399 could have caused Connally's other wounds, to the right wrist and left thigh. Humes could rely only on the Parkland Hospital records to answer. "I think that extremely unlikely," he replied. "The reports, again Exhibit 392 from Parkland, tell of an entrance wound on the lower midthigh of the governor, and X rays taken there are described as showing metallic fragments in the bone, which apparently by this report were not removed and are still in Governor Connally's thigh. I can't conceive of where they came from this missile."

Humes also did not think Bullet 399 had caused the wounds to Connally's wrist, because of metallic fragments found in that wound. "The reason I believe it most unlikely that this missile could have inflicted either of these wounds is that this missile is basically intact; its jacket appears to me to be intact, and I do not understand how it could possibly have left fragments in either of these locations." At this point, then, there was no Single-Bullet Theory. Humes had given us vital information indicating that the bullet had exited from Kennedy's throat at high speed. The theory that the bullet then went through Connally's chest and wrist and lodged in the governor's thigh would have to be checked out against his X rays, a suggestion Humes made. The key lay in the size and weight of the metal fragments.

We would later prove that Bullet 399 could indeed have passed through the president and then inflicted all of the governor's wounds. We would make the case partly by weighing Bullet 399 and the metal fragments taken from Connally's body. Together, the nearly whole bullet and the fragments weighed no more than an ordinary bullet.

Affirmation came initially during my questioning of Dr. Charles Gregory, the orthopedist who had treated Connally's wrist. I asked Gregory about the size and weight of the metal fragments. "They would represent in lay terms flakes, flakes of metal," he said. I asked the orthopedist to estimate the fragments' weight. "It is something less than the weight of a postage stamp," he said. Gregory, in answer to my questions, said it was indeed possible that Bullet 399 had passed through the governor's wrist and lodged in his thigh. Humes had never consulted Gregory about the fragments' minuscule weight.

I have been credited, or condemned, as the author of the Single-Bullet Conclusion ever since Epstein published *Inquest,* the earliest of the conspiracy books. Gerald Ford, for one, sends his Single-Bullet Theory queries my way. "Anytime I've had an opportunity, or if I'm asked about the Single-Bullet Theory," Ford told me recently, "I respectfully say, 'You ought to talk to the author of it. He knows more about it than I.' "

While I later put the pieces together, Humes laid them out, even if he did not think the bullet went through Connally's wrist. I have always been willing to take on the mantle of authorship that Epstein first thrust upon me, mostly because I have always been confident that the Single-Bullet Conclusion is correct. I have also had a sense that if the conclusion turned out to be incorrect, that would be okay, too, because it was an honest, good-faith, soundly reasoned judgment. Let the chips fall where they may.*

---

*One author recently asserted that there has been resistance to accepting the Single-Bullet Conclusion because of collateral disagreement with me. "The fact that the 'single bullet theory' was initially proposed by now-Senator Arlen Specter, considered by some to be exceedingly arrogant, has made it harder for some to accept," wrote Gus Russo in *Live by the Sword.* "It is a classic example of the maxim that sometimes one must accept the message, in spite of one's feelings about the messenger. (No one is more upset than the author over the fact that Anita Hill's basher-in-chief was correct about the single bullet, but in fact he was.)"

Continuing to question Humes about matters outside his sphere, I also asked about the president's clothing. The FBI found that the bullet had entered the back of Kennedy's suit jacket and exited through the front of his shirt, by his tie. The tie showed a mark where it had been nicked. The caliber of the bullet could not be gauged from the holes in the jacket or shirt. But those holes were consistent with damage from a 6.5-millimeter slug.

Kennedy's jacket contained traces of copper around the hole margins. On the back of his shirt, the fibers surrounding the bullet hole were pressed inward, indicating an entrance hole. That meant that the bullet had passed from back to front. The ragged slit on the front of the shirt showed that the bullet had exited from the front, but the irregular nature of the slit ruled out a firm conclusion that it was a bullet hole.

The president's clothing had been cut off at Parkland in order to let the doctors work. Following emergency procedure, Kennedy's tie was cut at the loop, immediately to the left of the knot. The knot, as a result, stayed in its original condition. As Humes was discussing the tie, former CIA Director Allen Dulles entered the hearing room and took a seat behind me and to my right. I was sitting at one end of the conference table, Humes at the other end, in the usual positions of witness and commission questioner. I had marked the president's tie as Commission Exhibit 395, and I asked Humes to identify it. Humes held up the exhibit, with its knot showing and its loop curving behind, and said it was the necktie purportedly worn by President Kennedy on the day of the assassination. He said that the tie was still in its knotted state and that the portion of the tie that looped around the neck had been cut by scissors or some other sharp instrument.

Dulles may have been distracted, or maybe he'd dozed off. When Humes held up the tie, Dulles remarked, "By Jove, the fellow wore a ready-made tie." When we later discussed the day's events, we all found it funny that anyone, even for a moment during a warm afternoon, could think that President John F. Kennedy would wear a ready-made tie.

At another point in the hearings, while the commission discussed the two metal fragments that had been removed from Kennedy's head, Dulles, who regularly attended the sessions, examined the vials that held the metal fragments. The former spymaster announced that there were four metal fragments, not two. An FBI agent raced from one end of the table to the other to inspect the contents of the vials. The agent took two of the fragments and crushed them between his fingers. "No, Mr. Dulles," the agent said. "These are two flakes of tobacco that fell out of your pipe."

Allen Dulles may have withheld vital information from the commission, the type of vital information we were counting on him to supply. Dulles, for example, did not tell other commission members about CIA plots against Cuban leader Fidel Castro. Attorney General Katzenbach later testified before the House in 1978 that he was "astounded" by the omission. Dulles had been tapped for the commission largely to get some insights from an investigator, and to find out what the CIA knew. Still, the fact that Dulles had been head of the CIA didn't necessarily mean he knew all about the agency's activities. I have learned that lesson all too well as a U.S. senator, chairing the Intelligence Committee that oversees the CIA.

The commissioners and staff had keen interest in the president's clothes. As with other evidence of the assassination, there was a morbid element to the clothing. There was also great human interest in what the late president wore, especially on the last day of his life. John F. Kennedy had been wearing a blue patterned Dior tie, obviously expensive. His dapper gray suit bore no label and clearly had been tailor-made. His shirt, white with subtle milk-colored stripes, bore the label "Charles Dillon, 444 Park Avenue."

Not too long after the commission report was released, I was in New York City. Joan and I had taken my parents to board the liner *Shalom* for passage to Le Havre on October 9, and we spent the rest of the day traipsing around Manhattan. At one point I happened to find myself at the entrance of Charles Dillon, Shirtmaker, at 444 Park Avenue. Recalling Kennedy's shirt label, I went inside. Bolts of cloth lay around the store. I searched for the milk-striped bolt from which the president's shirt had been made. I found the exact bolt just as a salesman approached and asked if he could help me.

How much would it cost to have a shirt made from the bolt? I asked. The salesman said it would cost $26.95. I was shocked (that would be about $150 today). And I was ambivalent, in any case, about having a shirt of that particular cloth. Such a garment would have been interesting to own, but it would have been a macabre reminder of the tragedy.

As the salesman glanced at me expectantly, I said, "Wasn't President Kennedy one of your customers?"

The salesman looked askance. "We never discuss our clients," he said. Recovering his composure, he asked, "How did you know?"

"Well," I answered, "I never disclose my sources of information." That was my exit line.

THE BIGGEST MISTAKE

The Warren Commission has been attacked—and rightly so—for not examining the X rays and autopsy photographs of President Kennedy in its investigation. A number of us on staff felt strongly that we should see the fifteen to twenty photographs and ten to twelve X rays that had been made before and during the autopsy. We did not doubt the autopsy surgeons' testimony about the wounds. But we thought all the evidence should be presented. Repeatedly, Ball, Belin, Redlich, or I urged that the photographs and X rays be examined.

"It was a disastrous decision," Belin wrote in his first book, *November 22, 1963.* "It was a decision with which Joe Ball and I, as well as Arlen Specter, disagreed. It was a decision that gave rise to wild speculation and rumor. It was a decision that violated basic elementary rules of evidence familiar to every law student in America that when a person testifies he should have the 'best evidence' available."[1]

As hard as we pressed for the materials, Rankin consistently refused. We were told that the Kennedy family opposed having the photographs and X rays made available. They were worried that those ghastly images might reach the public. They feared that the American people would then remember John F. Kennedy as a mutilated corpse with half his head blown away, rather than as the dashing young president.

We brushed off that concern. We could have included an analysis of the autopsy materials in the commission report without including the images as a commission exhibit. That approach should have satisfied the Kennedy family. Beyond the Kennedys' natural interest in privacy, it seemed that the family wanted to preserve the late president's image in part for the future political benefit of family members. Younger Kennedy brothers Robert and Edward both closely resembled the late president. Any damage to John Kennedy's image could harm them. The Kennedy clan's concern about the photos and X rays was understandable. It is fair to wonder, though, how successful they would have been at preventing access if Robert Kennedy had not been the attorney general of the United States.

Belin recently called the commission's decision on the autopsy materials "the biggest mistake." "My argument was, if Officer Tippit's widow wanted to keep photos and X rays of her husband private, she would not [get her way], so why should President Kennedy be treated any different?"[2] Oswald, shortly after slaying the president, shot J. D. Tippit four times with a revolver when the police officer approached him on a Dallas street. "One of the basic lessons of the Warren Commission investigation is the ramifications that arise when special treatment is given to a favored few," Belin wrote in *November 22, 1963*. "The reverberations from the decision to withhold publication of the autopsy photographs and X rays will be felt for many decades as a part of the overall diminution of the confidence that the American people have in the integrity of their elected officials."[3]

Any investigator likes to have all the facts before drawing conclusions. That applies to corroborative evidence, such as photographs and X rays, as well as to general testimony. A picture is usually worth a thousand words. The photographs and X rays could have gone a long way toward resolving the controversy over the direction and location of the shots.

It turned out that Chief Justice Warren, alone among the commissioners, had reportedly seen the autopsy materials. I heard that long after the commission report was filed. Warren never told me or, I believe, any of the others associated with the commission. The fact that the chief justice saw the materials does not give any real comfort. Warren should have had the evidence examined in the regular course of business by the staff and commissioners.

I complained about the photographs and X rays, maybe more than I realized at the time. One staff lawyer was quoted in a national magazine as saying that I left a meeting with tears in my eyes after unsuccessfully insisting that the photographs and X rays be released. I recall long, bitter arguments on the subject, but no tears.

When Belin and I had dinner together shortly after the commission nixed the photos and X rays, he suggested resigning from the probe. "It was discussed," he told me in April 1996. "I don't think that either one of us thought about doing it." In the end I submitted a memo to the commission on April 30, 1964, saying that the photos and X rays were indispensable to our investigation.

Tom Kelley, the Secret Service liaison officer to the commission, tried to ease my concern about the photos. In May, Kelley and I, among others, traveled to Dallas to conduct our on-site tests at the assassination scene. When Kelley and I were alone in a hotel room, he showed me a small picture of the back of a man's body, with a bullet hole in the base of the neck, just where the autopsy surgeons said Kennedy had been shot. I was eager, of course, to examine the picture. My trust in Tom Kelley led me personally to accept his assurance that he was showing me a photograph of Kennedy's body. But an unauthenticated photo was no way to establish facts for the record. I never mentioned it officially.

I finally saw the original autopsy photographs and X rays, along with recent computer-enhanced images, at a branch of the National Archives in April 1999. I took the occasion to reexamine the once-elegant suit, shirt, and tie the president had been wearing that day, which had been reduced to bloodied rags. The Kennedy family turned over the materials to the archives in 1966, but access remains highly restricted.

The photos are gruesome. John F. Kennedy is lying on an autopsy table, his handsome face discolored and distorted by the gaping bullet wound in his head. As I looked at the slain president, I was struck again by the same waves of nausea that had hit me when I first read the medical reports thirty-five years earlier. I was also struck by the president's clearly robust physical condition, which somehow made the photographs even more ghastly. Kennedy, at forty-seven, had well-defined, muscular shoulders and arms, a flat stomach, and a full head of brown hair.

Dr. Boswell, who lived near the archives center, came over to help me interpret the materials during my two-hour inspection. The bullet wounds, as shown on the photographs, were consistent with the Single-Bullet Conclusion. The entrance wound on the neck was about an inch below the shoulder line in the president's back. The exit wound, at the site of the tracheotomy in his throat, was lower. The massive head wound was also consistent with a shot from above and behind.

When the autopsy surgeons testified before the commission in 1964, they didn't know whether the photographs and X rays would ever be made available as a check against their testimony. They put their hands on the Bible and swore to tell the truth, subject to stiff penalties for perjury. My contacts with Humes, Boswell, and Finck convinced me that they were telling the truth. When Joe Ball and I talked to Humes and Boswell, in Bethesda on the Friday before they testified, we told them that they would be testifying without the aid of photographs and X rays. Humes asked if it would be helpful to have some sketches made of the president's body. Most helpful, I said.

When the doctors came to commission headquarters on Monday, March 16, they brought with them three drawings made by a hospital corpsman who was an illustrator at the Naval Medical School. The drawings showed Kennedy's body and head from various angles, with the wounds and bullet holes marked. Humes pointed out that the sketches had been made in just two days, without access to the photos or X rays. They were made from the autopsy surgeons' verbal descriptions, with Humes supervising.

I asked Humes a number of questions when he testified before the commission to suggest the benefits of making the actual photographs and X rays available to the commission. "Would it be helpful to the artist, in redefining the drawings if that should become necessary, to have available to him the photographs or X rays of the president?" I asked at one point.

"If it were necessary to have them absolutely true to scale," Humes said, "I think it would be virtually impossible for him to do this without the photographs."

"And what is the reason for the necessity for having the photographs?" I asked.

"I think that it is most difficult to transmit into physical measurements the—by word—the exact situation as it was seen to the naked eye," Humes replied. "I cannot transmit completely to the illustrator where they were situated." Responding to another of my questions, Humes said, "The pictures would show more accurately and in more detail the character of the wounds. . . . They would also perhaps give the commissioners a better—better is not the best term, but a more graphic picture of the massive defect."

Following that answer, Warren closed the matter with Humes. "Before we get off that," the chief justice said, "may I ask you this, Commander: If we had the pictures here and you could look them over again and restate your opinion, would it cause you to change any of the testimony you have given here?"

"To the best of my recollection, Mr. Chief Justice," Humes said, "it would not." Humes gave that last answer only moments after saying that the "photographs are far superior to my humble verbal description. . . ."

The sketches were rough. If we had it to do all over again, and we knew those sketches would be reproduced in hundreds of books, credited with more precision than was intended, and so closely scrutinized, I would have opposed doing them. But that's twenty-twenty hindsight.

When the autopsy surgeons finished testifying, the chief justice and some of the rest of us stood around discussing our next steps. Humes had raised many questions about the president's treatment at Parkland, such as why he had not been turned over to observe the back of his head and neck, and about the hole which had been obliterated by the tracheotomy. Only two days before, on Saturday, March 14, Jack Ruby's murder trial had ended. There was no longer any reason for the commission to stay out of Dallas.

Warren asked me how soon I could leave for Dallas to question the Parkland staff. I said I thought I could be there in a week or ten days. Warren said he hoped I could leave that afternoon. The chief justice did not let grass grow under anyone's feet. We compromised. I would be in Dallas later that week. Thinking about plans with my family for Passover later that week, I satisfied the chief justice by assuring him I would take depositions at Parkland before the week's end. I reconciled the issues of family, Passover, and depositions by taking Joan and our sons to Kansas early on the morning of Thursday, March 19. I left them with my sister Hilda in Wichita and then caught a plane, arriving in Dallas later the same day.

Ball, Belin, and I had asked Rankin to authorize the lawyers to take sworn depositions, just as lawyers do in pretrial discovery proceedings in civil cases. Belin and I urged Joe Ball to take up the matter with his close friend, the chief justice. When the lawyers submitted their preliminary reports, due February 18, the commission brass saw the number of witnesses we needed to interview. It would have stretched the investigation to bring all those witnesses to the VFW Building. Ball reported back that Warren had agreed to let us take sworn testimony in the field. The chief justice, Ball said, wanted "to get things cleaned up."

THE MAGIC BULLET

Four months after the shooting, the Parkland Hospital staff was still reeling over its hour with the dying president. To the commission, technical questions on location of the bullet and characteristics of the neck wound were crucial. But they were overshadowed by the raw emotion that still shrouded Parkland. Parkland's emotional reaction was also telling for the investigation. It answered a number of questions, such as why the president's body was not turned over in Trauma Room 1 and why it was hard to find some of the tangible evidence.

From reconstructing events at Parkland Hospital on the afternoon of November 22, it was clear that there had been an air of disbelief that it was all really happening. Early in the lunch hour, some of the nurses in the dining hall were chatting about the president's trip to Dallas that day. One remarked that it would be exciting to have the president come to Parkland if he were in an automobile accident. Another replied that he would not come to Parkland because he would be nearer to another hospital.

At 12:33 P.M., Doris Nelson, the emergency room supervising nurse, answered the telephone at the major surgery station. She was told by the operator that President Kennedy had been shot and was en route to the hospital. "Stop kidding me," Nurse Nelson said. When Nelson passed on the news to Dr. Charles Baxter, he reacted the same way. "Yes, what else is new?" As Kennedy was wheeled into Parkland Hospital on a gurney, his eyes were protruding from the intracranial pressure, distorting his face. A hospital attendant saw him and thought the injured man was the president's stand-in, a look-alike who rode in the president's car. Kennedy had no such stand-in, but the attendant couldn't bring himself to believe that the body on the stretcher really was the president of the United States.

In the major surgery area, shortly after the shooting, Dallas mayor Earle Cabell was overheard saying to no one in particular, "It didn't happen, it didn't happen." When the news circulated through Parkland that President John F. Kennedy had died, the staff all just stood around. They didn't believe that the president was really dead.

Dallas officials, chiefly Coroner Earl Rose, tried to stop Secret Service agents from removing Kennedy's casket from Parkland. Rose insisted that the locals had jurisdiction over the president's body, which was evidence in a homicide, and that they would perform an autopsy in Dallas. The agents and presidential aides, backed by the president's personal physician, Admiral George Burkley, would not yield. Eventually the Washington team muscled the casket through the hospital doors, bulling the Dallas suits out of the way. They wheeled the casket to the dock and loaded it into an ambulance. Mrs. Kennedy, Secret Service agents, and presidential aides crammed in. The ambulance drove to the airport, where John F. Kennedy's body was loaded aboard Air Force One. On the flight back to Washington, Lyndon Baines Johnson was sworn in as the thirty-sixth president of the United States.

I dealt with FBI agents continually, regarding physical evidence, polygraphs, and witnesses, and I generally found them competent and helpful. Commission staff members in other areas, such as Oswald's travel, relied far more heavily on the bureau. They generally found the FBI obtuse. "They didn't like college boys taking jobs from professionals," said Joe Ball, summarizing the bureau's attitude toward the Warren Commission. For Ball, the distaste was mutual. "We found out we could not rely on the FBI reports," Ball told me over lunch in 1996. "The FBI got to be a joke for us. . . . They'd have breakfast and decide who they talked to in the morning, have lunch and decide who they talked to next."

Jim Liebeler, who was working on Oswald's life and background, described the commission's relationship with the FBI as "adversarial." At one point, he said, FBI agents told him it would take six years to run down all the prints on the sixth floor of the Book Depository Building. "If you'd started when you should have, it would be down to five and a half years now," Liebeler told the agents, and stalked off.

Bill Coleman also got snagged in the bureau's red tape, beginning with the FBI's demand to have every commission request in writing. "I never knew any time I could just go over there and talk to them and get questions and answers, the way you would if you're really interviewing," Coleman said recently. "Obviously, at the very beginning, there must have been an instance where the FBI and the Secret Service both felt that the investigation might show there was something they didn't do right. And the natural tendency to try to protect your agency, I'm pretty sure that existed. But I can't remember anything we didn't get that we wanted to get."

The FBI was defensive largely because it had been investigating Oswald at the time of the assassination but had failed to sound an alarm about him. Agent James P. Hosty, Jr., in charge of the case, turned up in an entry in Oswald's diary. The FBI didn't tell the Warren Commission about that entry. Hoover, later asked to explain, said he passed only valid leads to the commission and that Hosty's diary appearance was irrelevant because the FBI was obviously not involved in the Kennedy killing. Hoover had acted improperly in withholding the reference to Hosty in Oswald's diary. It was self-protection at its worst. It raised the obvious question of what else was withheld that the commission never found out about. It's doubtful that Attorney General Robert Kennedy could have forced Hoover to cooperate with the commission unless he found some specific act of omission, like the Hosty entry in the Oswald diary. Hoover's intransigence and obsession with control were well-known, despite his being technically subordinate to the attorney general in the chain of command.

There was a basic question about whether it was sound for the commission to farm out investigative work to the FBI, which had a conflict of interest, since it was being investigated itself. There was tension between Hoover and the commission. And Hoover ran the bureau with an iron hand, covering up any unsavory event, such as the Hosty journal entry, as no FBI director could do today.

Of course, the Secret Service also had a conflict. It had fouled up. The president had been killed. On the key parts of the investigation, we commission lawyers went over the evidence independently. We checked all the key facts, such as Oswald's location, locations of cars, the Zapruder film, and all the medical evidence. We disagreed with the initial FBI report, which said two bullets had hit Kennedy and a third had hit Connally, and we wound up supplanting it with the Single-Bullet Conclusion. But we simply did not have the time or resources to recruit and train our own corps of investigators.

After the investigation ended, accusations arose that Gerald Ford had reported to the FBI on commission activities. Ford denied the charges. He recently gave me a lengthy explanation: "I never had any contact with Hoover," the former president told me. Ford said that as a member of the House Appropriations Committee, which he joined during his first term in 1950, he dealt with Hoover's congressional liaison, Cartha D. "Deke" DeLoach, who was the number-three man in Hoover's echelon.

"And by the time this all happened," Ford said, "I had gotten quite a bit of seniority on the Appropriations Committee, and, typical of Hoover, he had his representative up here dropping by people that at some point might be helpful to the FBI with appropriations, or what have you. So Deke DeLoach, before the assassination, would probably drop by my office once every month just to say hello, were there any problems that the FBI had that I could tell him about? Well, when I got on the commission, those visits to my office became once every couple of weeks. I was always suspicious that Deke DeLoach would go back and talk to his boss and expand extensively the information that he found on the Hill, that came from me and, I'm sure, from others. That was his way of justifying his job, impressing his boss, etc.

"Now, when I became a member of the commission, he used to come by more often. And he would ask questions about, is the FBI doing all right in the commission's areas, etc., etc. Well, I was previously suspicious of his role, of his role in portraying what he knew about me, and what he could tell his boss. So I was very very circumspect. Now, after the hearings ended and the report came out, and maybe a year or two later, Deke DeLoach in some publication said in an interview that J. Edgar Hoover had a pipeline to the commission because he had this relationship with me, and I filled him in extensively on what was going on. I always resented it, because I had been very circumspect. And I certainly didn't want any of our commission activities related to the FBI related indirectly behind the scenes to Hoover."[1]

In general, the various intelligence agencies hoarded information rather than sharing it. "It really was set up to the contrary, not to share information but to impose barriers to the attainment of information, one from the other," recalled Sam Stern, who dealt extensively with the agencies on the issue of presidential protection.[2]

At Parkland, C. Jack Price, administrator of the Dallas County Hospital District, gave me a small, stark meeting room in the administrator's

94

suite to use as an office and offered to contact all the hospital staff I wanted to interview. I gave Price a list. I included every staff member even tangentially involved with the procedure or the equipment. Price checked the duty rosters and arranged to have them report so that I could move quickly from one witness to another. But accommodating the staff's schedules made it impossible to take testimony in order on a given subject. Odell Oliver, a federal court reporter who served as my stenographer, worked quickly and cheerfully and was always available, even on March 25, when I interviewed thirteen witnesses back-to-back.

I would begin by introducing myself and then plow through detailed questions for as long as it took. We later brought some of the doctors to Washington to testify before the full commission. I sent the interview transcripts to Warren, who devoured four hundred pages of staff reports every weekend. Commission lawyers called it "feeding the monster." Rumor had it that the chief justice needed lots of reading material to fall asleep. The deposition transcripts and our draft reports fitted the bill.

When I'd introduced the whole bullet at the commission hearing, I had promised, "We shall produce later, subject to sequential proof, evidence that the stretcher on which this bullet was found was the stretcher of Governor Connally." The Parkland depositions would put that evidence on the record.

Shortly after Kennedy was pronounced dead at 1:00 P.M., Commission Exhibit 399—the so-called magic bullet—had rolled off a stretcher on the ground floor at Parkland. Ballistics tests proved that the slug had been fired from Oswald's Mannlicher-Carcano, which was found on the sixth floor of the Book Depository Building. Working backward, we had to determine from whose stretcher Bullet 399 had fallen. To find out, I intended to take the sworn testimony of every doctor, nurse, orderly, and bystander who had been interviewed. I spent my first two days in Dallas on that effort.

I looked first at Connally's stretcher. The governor had been lifted from the limousine at Parkland's emergency entrance, placed on a metal gurney with a rubber pad on top, and wheeled into Trauma Room 2. While the governor was lying on the stretcher in Trauma Room 2, intravenous fluids were hooked up, his clothing was removed, and a sheet was placed over him. No bullet was found while Connally was disrobed and covered.

Connally was rolled down the corridor into the emergency elevator.

He was taken to the second floor, where he was moved from the stretcher to an operating table in the hallway of an operating room suite. Connally's clothes were taken from the bottom of the stretcher and placed in the hallway by the operating table. The governor's clothes, incredibly, were later cleaned, dried, and pressed before they were examined, making them useless as evidence.

Connally was rolled into the operating room. A nurse wheeled the stretcher near a clock and turned it over to R. K. Jimison, a hospital attendant. Jimison pushed the stretcher onto an elevator so the cart could be returned to the emergency area and cleaned. The elevator Jimison used was the only one in the area. Jimison testified that no other stretcher was placed on that elevator during his shift, which ended at three-thirty that afternoon. He said he saw no bullet on the stretcher.

Darrell C. Tomlinson, senior engineer in charge of heating and air conditioning at Parkland, had been called in shortly after the wounded arrived to switch the elevator from automatic to manual operation, so that the car would not stop at each floor. Tomlinson got to the elevator at around 1:00 P.M. and saw a stretcher in the elevator. He wheeled the stretcher off the elevator and put it against the south wall on the ground floor. Another stretcher was resting about two feet from the wall.

"An intern or a doctor, I didn't know which, came to use the men's room there in the elevator lobby," Tomlinson said. "He pushed the stretcher out from the wall to get in, and then when he came out, he just walked off and didn't push the stretcher back up against the wall, so I pushed it out of the way where we would have clear area in front of the elevator."

"Where did you push it to?" I asked.

"I pushed it back up against the wall," Tomlinson said.

"What if anything happened then?" I asked.

"I bumped the wall," Tomlinson said, "and a spent cartridge or bullet rolled out that apparently had been lodged under the edge of the mat."

I was surprised. I had talked to Tomlinson briefly before going on the record, as I did with all the witnesses, to organize the testimony for a more orderly presentation. Not only had Tomlinson told me a short time earlier that the bullet came from the stretcher that he had wheeled off the elevator, but he'd said the same thing to the Secret Service. Now he was saying he wasn't certain whether the bullet came from Connally's stretcher or from the stretcher next to it.

I went out of my way not to lead Tomlinson or put words into his mouth, questioning the engineer as carefully as possible. History was looking over my shoulder. Tomlinson had marked on a diagram the locations of the two stretchers, labeled A and B, and their distances from the elevator. I gently asked, "Now, Mr. Tomlinson, are you sure that it was stretcher A that you took out of the elevator and not stretcher B?" After a lengthy exchange, Tomlinson said, "Well, we talked about taking a stretcher off of the elevator, but then when it comes down on an oath, I wouldn't say for sure. I really don't remember."

I next investigated what had happened to Kennedy's stretcher. As the blood-soaked Lincoln arrived at Parkland, Diana Bowron, a twenty-two-year-old nurse from England, heard an intercom message that carts were needed at the emergency room entrance. She and an orderly grabbed a gurney from Major Surgery and ran down the hall. The stretcher was pushed near the limousine. The president was lying across Mrs. Kennedy's knee. Nurse Bowron tried to lift the president's head, but the first lady pushed her away. Jacqueline Kennedy then lifted the president's head onto the cart. The stretcher was rushed into Trauma Room 1, with Mrs. Kennedy running beside it. Jacqueline Kennedy placed a bouquet of red roses, which she had been given at the airport, on the president's chest as he lay on the stretcher. Her pink pillbox hat, along with the roses, was lying on top of the president when he was wheeled into the emergency room.

Kennedy remained on that stretcher from the time he was wheeled into Trauma Room 1, through the unsuccessful medical treatment, until his body was placed in a casket in the same room. After Kennedy was in his casket, the sheets from his stretcher were gathered and placed in a linen hamper. The stretcher was then wheeled over to Trauma Room 2. Kennedy's stretcher was never near the area where Tomlinson found the bullet.

Commission Exhibit 399 obviously had dropped from the stretcher that had carried either Kennedy or Connally. We proved that the bullet could not have come from Kennedy's stretcher. It also could not have come from an odd stretcher that happened to be resting by Connally's stretcher near the ground-floor men's room. The bullet, the commission concluded, had to have fallen from Connally's stretcher.

Late in the afternoon of Saturday, March 21, I flew from Dallas to Wichita to spend what was left of the weekend with my family. I returned to Dallas early on Monday, March 23, to take testimony on the wounds inflicted on the president and governor.

BEDLAM

In the history of emergency care, probably no procedure was more difficult than that facing the Parkland doctors when President John F. Kennedy, already blue-white, and Governor John Connally were rushed into their emergency room.

Parkland's medical and professional staff were not immune to the drama that swept the hospital. "Certainly, everyone was emotionally affected," said Dr. Charles Carrico, a resident in general surgery who was first to treat the wounded president. From all indications, Parkland's medical effort was superb. "I think, if anything, the emotional aspect made us think faster, work faster and better," Carrico said.

Parkland, on Harry Hines Boulevard, was a rambling, dun-colored, thirteen-story teaching hospital that has produced some leading medical experts. Kennedy was taken to Trauma Room 1, a stark, windowless room walled in gray tile and floored in black rubber. Two nurses cut away Kennedy's clothes and back brace. The president had a full head of hair, which was bloody and matted, making it difficult to find his wounds.

On arrival, Kennedy was alive but moribund. The president had "slow agonal respiration, spasmodic respirations without any coordination," Carrico testified. When Kennedy's shirt was opened, Carrico "listened very briefly to his chest, heard a few sounds which we felt to be heartbeats." "From a medical standpoint," Carrico concluded, "I suppose he was still alive, in that he did have a heartbeat."

Although the president's condition was clearly hopeless, the Parkland doctors made every conceivable, desperate effort to save him. They followed the ABCs of treatment: Airway, Breathing, Circulation. The doctor who took the lead was Malcolm O. Perry, an affable, lanky thirty-four-year-old surgeon. Perry was known to his friends as "Mac," after his grandfather, a country doctor who had raised him and gone by the same nickname. A former Air Force pilot, Perry later became chairman of surgery at the University of Texas Southwestern, after a stint, among others, as chief of vascular surgery at Cornell Medical Center in New York City.

Perry entered Trauma Room 1 just as Carrico had inserted an endotracheal tube, hooked to an automatic respirator. Perry performed a tracheotomy, to create a better airway. He used the bullet hole in the president's throat to gain access, enlarging the hole during the procedure and destroying it as evidence. In order to establish circulation, cuts were made and an intravenous fusion inserted in Kennedy's right leg.

Meanwhile, Dr. William Kemp Clark, who headed the hospital's division of neurological surgery, was examining the president's gaping head wound and the exposed cerebral and cerebellar tissue. The galaxy of specialists who attended Kennedy also included experts in anesthesiology, cardiology, general surgery, neurological surgery, oral surgery, vascular surgery, and urology. The medical team prepared to insert chest tubes to help the president's circulation, but they abandoned the effort, apparently when his heart stopped beating. Perry and Clark then began externally massaging Kennedy's heart, to try to jump-start it. They continued until Clark told Perry that there was no response. "It's no use, Mac," he said.

Since the head wound was the cause of death, it fell to Clark to sign the death certificate. The time of death was approximated at 1:00 P.M. Nobody had been watching the clock.

Connally's medical treatment was almost as swift and obviously more successful. During the few hours following the governor's arrival at Parkland, he underwent major surgery on his torso, an operation on his wrist, and a less serious operation on his thigh.

Even though the massive opening in President Kennedy's skull made it clear he was moribund, the Parkland doctors worked feverishly to try to save his life. They had no choice. After all, he was the president. But the Parkland examination was so cursory that the doctors did not even turn Kennedy over. They never saw the bullet entrance wounds in the back of his head and the back of his neck. The Parkland doctors saw only the exit wounds: the small hole on the front of Kennedy's neck and the large wound on the right side of his head.

Carrico was the only member of the Parkland emergency team who even felt for any back wounds. "Without taking the time to roll him over and look or to wash off the blood and debris, and while his coat and shirt were still on his arms," Carrico said, "I just placed my hands at about his belt line or a little above and, by slowly moving my hands upward, detected that there was no large violation of the pleural cavity." Carrico added that his examination would not detect a small bullet entrance; it would just make sure that there was no "gross injury" to the back.

The Parkland doctors saw the clean, round, quarter-inch hole in the front of the president's neck but didn't know about the wound in the back of his neck. It was a natural first thought, for some of them, that the hole in the president's throat might be an entry wound, since they knew of no other way the bullet might have entered his body. Dr. Ronald Jones's report, filed on the day of the assassination, stated that the hole in the front of the president's neck was "thought to be a bullet entrance wound."

Questions and charges have sprouted over apparent inconsistencies between the Parkland doctors' observations and the autopsy surgeons' findings. If the Parkland doctors had turned Kennedy over and seen the entrance wound, those questions would never have been raised. Once the Parkland doctors were informed of the wounds on the back of the president's head and neck, their findings were consistent with the autopsy report. They all independently concluded that the wound on the front of the president's neck could have been caused by a high-velocity *exiting* bullet. Why, then, did the Parkland doctors not turn the president over when he was in Trauma Room 1 and see for themselves?

While the president was being treated, Secret Service agents buzzed throughout the area. Agents looked after Mrs. Kennedy, guarded the hallway, and, finally, took custody of the president's body. After the president had died, the Parkland doctors felt they had no business making any further examination, especially given the official aura that engulfed Trauma Room 1. The agents asked the Parkland crew to wrap up as quickly as possible and clear the room.

"We felt like we were intruders and left," Dr. Pepper Jenkins said.

There was no further examination after the president was pronounced dead, Carrico testified, because "no one, at that time, I believe, had the heart to examine him." Thirty-three years later, with questions still lingering in the public mind, Carrico told me, "A lot of times we look, for our own education and curiosity, but I make no apologies. I just saw the president die."

In any case, the Parkland doctors had every right to expect that an autopsy would include the thorough examination that was beyond the scope of their work. "The medical examiner . . . would often call the team down and point out to us wounds and how to recognize them, and ask us for information,"[1] Carrico told me in 1997.

That discussion between pathologist and trauma surgeon ultimately played out long-distance when Humes phoned Perry the morning after the autopsy. Humes, in Bethesda, phoned Perry, in Dallas, twice in about thirty minutes, asking why the Parkland crew had performed the tracheotomy and why the chest tubes were inserted.

The media frenzy set off by the president's assassination spurred several organized press conferences on the afternoon of Friday, November 22. There were more press conferences the next day, Saturday, and more on Sunday after Lee Harvey Oswald was shot at police headquarters and died at Parkland Hospital. The news conferences spread confusion and misconceptions. The world wanted to know what had happened—and now!

Reporters stormed Parkland. At the first press conference, Perry and Clark fielded questions. Before one could be answered, another would be fired. Many of the questions called for the doctors to speculate on the direction of the bullets, the number of bullets, and the exact cause of death.

"Unfortunately," Clark told me, "I think nobody was, quote, in charge, which I think led to some of the commotion."[2]

The place was bedlam, as Perry aptly described it. Testifying before the commission, he said:

> There were microphones and cameras and the whole bit, as you know, and during the course of it a lot of these hypothetical situations and questions that were asked to us would often be asked by someone on this side and recorded by someone on this, and I don't know who was recorded and whether they were broadcasting it directly.
>
> There were tape recorders there and there were television cameras with their microphones. I know there were recordings made but who made them, I don't know and, of course, portions of it would be given to this group and questions answered here and, as a result, considerable

102

questions were not answered in their entirety and even some of them that were asked, I am sure were misunderstood.

It was bedlam.

The first Friday press conference at Parkland was held shortly after the president's death, before the doctors there knew about the entrance wounds on Kennedy's back and head and before Perry had spoken with Humes and sorted out the facts. Perry told reporters it was possible that the president's wounds were caused by one bullet. Pressed, Perry said it was conceivable that a bullet had entered Kennedy's throat, hit the spine, changed course, and exited out the top of his skull. "I expressed it as a matter of speculation that this was conceivable," Perry later testified. "But again, Dr. Clark and I emphasized that we had no way of knowing."

Perry told reporters that it was "conceivable or possible" that the wound on the front of the president's neck could have been an entry wound. He made it plain to the reporters that he was merely speculating. His caveat drew little interest.

Perry blames himself for the spread of conspiracy theories. "I did say at the initial press conference that the [exit] wound was small, like an entrance wound. I'm to blame for giving it some credence, for saying it looked small, like an entrance wound. I wish I hadn't said that." Of course, Perry noted, the media jumped on only part of his statement. But he was also frustrated by criticism from medical novices and ignoramuses. "Give me a break," he said recently. "I made an incision big enough to control a wound to the trachea, and big enough to clamp a blood vessel. Anybody that's been in the business would know that."[3]

On Sunday, two days after the first news conference about Kennedy, Perry was called again to make statements to the press, this time about Oswald, who had just died of his gunshot wound, also at Parkland. This time Perry issued a written statement and did not take questions.

Press coverage complicated our work at the commission. I took Dr. Clark's deposition on Saturday, March 21. A few days later Lee Rankin asked me to ask the neurosurgeon more questions, about an article from the French magazine *L'Express*, dated February 20, 1964, that had just come to the commission's attention. *L'Express*, citing a November 27 *New York Times* story, quoted Clark as saying that a bullet had hit President Kennedy "right where the knot of his tie was" and that "this bullet penetrated into his chest and did not come out." The *L'Express* story also quoted Clark as saying that a second wound had been caused by a bullet that hit the right side of Kennedy's head. Clark denied the key portions of the story. He said they were based on either a partial or an incomplete quotation.

Some reports attributed to Parkland personnel referred to wounds of the chest and the left side of the head. The sources of those reports, like those of many other rumors, were never positively identified.

THE SHERIFF'S KITCHEN

For weeks we didn't know whether Jacqueline Kennedy would testify before the commission. The first lady was the closest eyewitness to the president, and the best source on his habits. I urged that she testify comprehensively, because her account could shed light on the sequence of shots, the president's position, the governor's position, and the timing. Until a witness is questioned, there's no way to know how much help he or she can give.

I often asked Lee Rankin about plans to question Mrs. Kennedy. No decision had been reached, he always told me. I was asked to prepare questions for her. I submitted a list of ninety. Preparing questions involves anticipating possible replies and the new lines of inquiry that any given reply can open. Answers to some of my questions might have proved vital. I wanted to know whether there was other noise in the limousine when the shots rang out; exactly when the president was hit; and what all the riders were doing or saying before, during, and after the shooting. I also wanted to ask Mrs. Kennedy whether her husband had unbuttoned his suit jacket. If the jacket had been buttoned, it might not have ridden up as much. I didn't know whether Jacqueline Kennedy would ever answer any of those questions.

On Friday, June 5, we were making final plans to go to Dallas that weekend to take Jack Ruby's testimony. The chief justice would be going. Before interviewing Ruby, Warren had told Rankin, he wanted to get a firsthand look at the assassination scene, covering the Texas School Book Depository Building, the Texas Theater, and the topography on Elm Street. Warren also wanted to interview some of the players, such as Texas Attorney General Waggoner Carr.

Rankin had asked me to escort Warren and Ford through a tour of the assassination landmarks. Several of the commissioners had made an earlier trip to Dallas, but neither Warren nor Ford had been to Texas during the investigation. In the initial planning stage, Rankin gave the chief justice a full week's itinerary, crammed with meetings and inspections. Warren said he was not going to spend a week in Dallas. Rankin came back with a revised plan that had the chief justice leaving Washington at noon Friday after Supreme Court arguments and returning in time for Monday-morning arguments. Warren told Rankin he would not spend much time in Dallas. "I'll give you Sunday." It would be a day trip, then.

In addition to handling some details and escorting Warren and Ford around Dallas, Rankin wanted me to tell the chief justice about the Single-Bullet Theory—right from the assassin's perch on the sixth floor of the Texas School Book Depository Building. At the time the assignment seemed like an imposition. I would have to fly down to Dallas on Sunday, instead of taking the train to Philadelphia to spend the whole weekend with my wife and young sons.

Since I was going to have to return to Washington on Saturday, I was anxious to catch the 4:00 P.M. Friday train to Philadelphia. But I had to coordinate with Rankin before I left for Union Station, and I couldn't find him anywhere. I asked Rankin's secretary, Julie Eide, who told me Lee was due to return shortly. She didn't tell me where he was. I missed the four o'clock train, and then the five.

Rankin returned after five. It was one of the few times I ever saw him visibly distressed. I ran into him in the men's room shortly before 6:00 P.M., when I was getting ready to leave the office, since I at least had to catch the 6:00 P.M. train. Rankin said he'd heard I was looking for him. I said I had the details worked out for Sunday's trip to Dallas. Rankin said he had been at Jacqueline Kennedy's house, taking her testimony. He braced for my response. I didn't say anything. I didn't have to. Rankin knew I was livid.

Unlike other witnesses in Washington, the former first lady had not come to commission headquarters. Instead the commission brass went to her apartment in northwest Washington. The only ones present at Mrs. Kennedy's interview were Warren, Rankin, Robert Kennedy, and a court reporter.

I had been pressing for an interview with Jacqueline Kennedy because she fell into my area and because her deposition would obviously be a key moment in the investigation. Warren had not wanted to subject Mrs. Kennedy to formal questioning before the commission. "The chief justice had a respect bordering on reverence for young John F. Kennedy," recalled Sam Stern, Warren's former clerk. "He really thought he was the personification of young America. . . . Also, Warren's courtliness and family-values orientation made him very, very protective of Mrs. Kennedy, of the Kennedy family, the autopsy photographs—all of that stuff he found personally very difficult to deal with and leaned over far backward."[1]

The word, unconfirmed to this day, was that Commissioner John McCloy confronted Warren and insisted that the commission take Mrs. Kennedy's testimony. The chief justice, reportedly, flatly told McCloy that Mrs. Kennedy's testimony would not be taken. McCloy, the former World Bank president and U.S. military governor of Germany, pressed the chief justice for Mrs. Kennedy's deposition. When discussing the issue, McCloy reportedly addressed Warren as "Mr. Chairman," which was a cutting insult. "She's talking about [the assassination] at all the cocktail parties in Washington," an exasperated McCloy reportedly told Warren. Neither I nor any of the other young lawyers were privy to the allegedly heated conversation between Warren and McCloy, nor did we know whether McCloy was right about the cocktail parties, but the story was circulated so extensively that it came to be accepted.

In the end Warren decided to take Mrs. Kennedy's deposition at her apartment. But he was not going to subject her to my detailed, protracted questioning, which he found so painful. I wound up questioning twenty-eight of the ninety-three witnesses who testified before the commission—but not Jacqueline Kennedy. The record on Mrs. Kennedy's deposition shows an abbreviated, nine-minute session. The interview omitted most of the lines of questioning I had proposed. It was almost worthless.

Even Rankin's mild approach was too much for Warren. After Rankin had been at it for less than ten minutes, he gently asked Mrs. Kennedy, "Can you think of anything more?" The chief justice interrupted. "No, I think not," he said. "I think that is the story and that is what we came for. We thank you very much, Mrs. Kennedy." Extensive questioning of Jacqueline Kennedy would probably not have produced any revelations. But we will never know. I continue to believe that far more questions should have been put to the former first lady.

Rankin, in the men's room that Friday afternoon, griped that he was joining us in Dallas because Warren had insisted on it. "It looks like I'm going to have to have a damn bed in the skies," said the usually unflappable Nebraskan. Rankin commuted regularly between the commission in Washington and the home he and his wife shared in Manhattan.

My hotel was on the way from Warren's home to Andrews Air Force Base, so the chief justice picked me up in a black limousine at the International Inn early in the morning on June 7. We drove out to Andrews and flew to Dallas on an Army JetStar twin-engine plane. The chief justice was in good spirits, which was not always the case. Earl Warren was justly revered for many of his skills and qualities, but his treatment of his staff was not one of them. On the plane we speculated about the Giants-Phillies baseball game that was to be played that afternoon for sole command of first place. The chief justice was from Oakland and I was on leave from Philadelphia, so the battle lines were clear.

Warren, following Rankin's schedule, crammed that Sunday full of activities. On the ground in Dallas, Warren chatted and kidded with a stream of passersby. When he got to the Book Depository Building, the stream turned into a swarm. Warren chatted away. We reconstructed the scene. Oswald had built his nest with cartons of "rolling readers," which were blocks that taught children to follow lines of text. A carton was opened, and Warren took out the rolling readers, signed them, and gave them out them out to the crowd. He even signed one for me, which I still have.

But it was strictly business at about 11:00 A.M. Central Time, as Warren stood with his arms folded across his chest and studied Dealey Plaza. The chief justice and I stood by the sixth-floor window at the southwest corner of the Texas School Book Depository Building, where Lee Harvey Oswald had fired three shots from his Mannlicher-Carcano rifle at President Kennedy. Except for the cheering crowds and the presidential motorcade, our view of Dealey Plaza, Elm Street, and the Triple Underpass matched what Oswald had seen as he crouched at that window six and a half months before. Tall buildings flanked three sides of the small park, and highways rolled under a railroad trestle on the fourth side.

Warren was always in command. He assumed a silent and thoughtful pose at the window, which I knew was my cue to begin. For about eight minutes the chief justice didn't say a word as I summarized the Single-Bullet Conclusion. I opened with the incontrovertible physical evidence: The Mannlicher-Carcano rifle had been found on the sixth floor of the Book Depository Building, not far from the southwest corner window. The evidence proved that the rifle belonged to Lee Harvey

Oswald. A bullet, recovered in Parkland Memorial Hospital from Connally's stretcher, was proved through ballistics tests to have been fired from the Mannlicher-Carcano. The autopsy showed that a bullet had struck Kennedy near the base of his neck on the right side and passed between two large strap muscles in his neck, striking only soft tissue as it continued in a slightly right-to-left, downward, and forward path, exiting from the president's throat, nicking the left side of the knot of his tie.

The bullet's speed, I explained to Warren, was critical, for the missile to have done all the damage we theorized. Tests showed that the muzzle velocity of the Mannlicher-Carcano was 2,200 feet per second. After a flight of 275 feet, the approximate distance between the rifle and Kennedy's neck when the first shot was fired, the muzzle velocity was about 1,975 feet per second. Tests performed on a simulation of the president's neck showed that the velocity of the bullet as it sped past the nicked tie was about 1,875 feet per second.

Where Oswald had pointed his rifle, I pointed my finger to show the bullet's trajectory. Standing at the window, it was clear that the assassin had neither a long shot nor a hard shot, especially with a four-power scope. It was also clear that the assassin could maintain the same line of fire as the president's open limousine rolled along the slightly dipping road before easing to the right and heading for the Triple Underpass.

Quickly, but in as much detail as possible, I drew the picture that emerged from the Zapruder film, backed by our on-site tests, on the positions and reactions of the president and the governor to one of the shots. Like the rest of us, the chief justice had been entranced and horrified by the amateur movie that just happened to catch the critical seconds of the assassination as Abraham Zapruder watched the motorcade through the lens of his camera.

I reminded the chief justice of the sequence in which Kennedy had suddenly raised both hands to his throat, showing an unmistakable reaction to the shot that pierced his neck. I also reviewed Connally's movements, as shown on the film, immediately after the president raised his arms. The governor had turned to the rear and then slumped out of sight, having fallen onto his wife's lap inside the car.

I then shifted to the view of the assassination scene from the perch where Warren and I stood. I reminded Warren of the on-site tests that we had conducted two weeks earlier. Beginning at 5:20 A.M., before dawn broke over Dealey Plaza, we had cordoned off the area and re-created the assassination. We had used the president's follow-up car, a 1959 Cadillac similar to the 1961 Lincoln limousine, which had then been in Detroit undergoing extensive renovations for security. We had adjusted the heights of the Cadillac's backseat and jump seat to match those on the Lincoln on November 22, 1963. Two Secret Service agents who matched the president's and governor's heights sat in their corresponding places.

With the Zapruder film as an absolute reference point, we had placed the Cadillac in the exact spot the Lincoln had occupied when Kennedy first raised his arms. We had photographed the view through the four-power scope on Oswald's rifle, which was mounted where it was believed to have been when the shot was fired.

As I stood at Dealy Plaza on June 7, 1964, with Warren, I told him what the scene had looked like two Sundays before, when I'd held Oswald's rifle and peered through the scope, sighting on the figure in the rear seat. I didn't mention how ill I'd felt aiming the weapon that had killed the president.

Having seen the Zapruder film countless times, having reconstructed the shooting at the scene and then in my own mind so many more times, I could almost see the assassination take place as I described and redescribed it to the chief justice.

It all boiled down to one key fact: When the bullet exited the president's neck, the limousine was in such a position that the bullet had to strike the car's interior or someone in it. Our exhaustive examination of the limousine had shown that no bullet had struck the car's interior. Then there was Connally, sitting right in the line of fire, directly in front of Kennedy, about to collapse from gunshot wounds. Could the president's neck wound and all of the governor's wounds have been caused by a single bullet? Could the whole bullet found on Connally's stretcher have first passed through Kennedy's neck, then penetrated Connally's chest, wrist, and thigh, leaving the trail of metallic fragments? That's where the facts led.

The physical evidence, ballistics experts' analyses, and tests all supported those facts. The president's and governor's clothing offered compelling proof. The president's garments had holes and tears showing that a missile entered the back in the vicinity of his lower neck and exited the front of his shirt immediately behind his tie, nicking the knot of the tie. Traces of copper were found on the hole in the back of the president's suit jacket. The cloth fibers around the margins of the hole in the back of the president's jacket and in a perfectly aligned hole in the back of his shirt were both pressed inward, establishing that the holes were caused by the same entering bullet. The holes on the front of the president's shirt, which were aligned when the shirt was buttoned, had fibers protruding outward, showing they were caused by an exiting bullet. Governor Connally's shirt and suit had holes that matched his wounds.

While the precise size of the bullet could not be determined from the holes in the men's clothing—especially since Governor Connally's garments had been cleaned and pressed before they could be scientifically examined—all the holes could have been caused by a 6.5-millimeter bullet, such as Oswald's Mannlicher-Carcano fired.

The wounds on the president and governor supported the Single-Bullet Conclusion. The first bullet would retain most of its high velocity after passing through two large strap muscles in the back of the president's neck, slicing the pleural cavity, striking nothing solid, and then exiting from the front of his neck, nicking the left side of his tie.

The wound slightly to the left of the governor's right armpit was caused by a bullet with only slight yaw, or wobbling, which was consistent with the status of the bullet traversing the president's neck. The X rays showed that the bullet had grazed Connally's rib, and the wound below his right nipple, roughly two inches in diameter, was evidence that the bullet had tumbled out of his chest. The wound on the back side of the governor's wrist was consistent with a tumbling bullet, which then, having lost virtually all its velocity, punctured his left thigh.

The condition of the whole bullet found on the governor's stretcher suggested that this bullet could have caused all the wounds. The weight of the bullet was 160 to 161 grams prior to firing. Exhibit 399 weighed 158.6 grams, consistent with the loss of very minute fragments left in the governor's wrist and thigh. Critics of the Single-Bullet Conclusion have seized upon the metallic fragments in the governor's wrist, arguing that Exhibit 399 was too perfect to have left such fragments. That assertion overlooks the doctors' testimony that the fragments could be accounted for by the bullet's slight weight loss.

The other major argument against the Single-Bullet Conclusion was that the holes in the president's shirt were so low that the bullet would have had to zig and zag—descend, rise, and then descend again—to cause the wounds. That overlooks the fact that the real issue is where the bullet hit the president, as opposed to the location of the bullet holes in the president's clothing. The lower holes in the clothing were accounted for by the shirt and jacket riding up from Kennedy's back brace, by his getting up and down during the ride, and his constant waving.

When I finished my discourse, the chief justice remained silent. After a moment he turned on his heel and stepped away, still saying nothing. Chief Justice Warren later agreed, and the commission ultimately accepted the Single-Bullet Conclusion.

From the Book Depository Building, the chief justice and I traced Oswald's purported path to the Texas Theater. We went to East 10th Street, where Oswald shot Officer Tippit. Later that day we had lunch with Texas Attorney General Waggoner Carr at Carr's apartment. After lunch we walked out of Carr's apartment into the corridor to find reporters gathered at the end of the hall, by the elevators. Instead of turning left and facing the pack, the chief justice ran down a corridor to the right and down a flight of stairs to avoid talking to them. Warren had no presence with the media, which was shocking considering the public offices he had held, including the governorship of California.

Sam Stern was baffled by Warren's awkwardness with the press. "It is not consistent with the rest of his personality, because he did have the capacity to be an extrovert in public life, although actually he wasn't," the chief justice's former clerk told me. "He was much more an inner-directed, limited-circle, family-committed human being who turned himself into a successful politician, a crowd-pleaser, and so forth. And why he didn't use the press as part of that as much as he could have, I don't know. We had the press all around us."

In the afternoon we were scheduled to take Jack Ruby's testimony. Ruby, a Dallas nightclub owner, had been convicted by a Texas jury of murdering Oswald and sentenced to death. Ruby's testimony before the commission was scheduled to take place in the sheriff's kitchen, because Warren wanted to limit the size of the group. A swarm of Washington and Texas bigwigs had descended on the Dallas Sheriff's Station to hear Ruby. But whom to exclude? Joe Ball was the chief justice's long-standing friend. Texas Attorney General Carr was still in tow and could not be left out. Leon Jaworski, later the celebrated Watergate special prosecutor, was on hand with the Texas attorney general's office and could not be excluded. Sheriff Decker, whose kitchen we were using, wanted to watch.

As the chief justice studied the roster, he found only one person he could exclude: me. So I sat in the sheriff's office watching the Philadel-phia–San Francisco baseball game on national television. At the time I didn't mind too much. In retrospect I should have.

After about an hour, Elmer Moore, a Secret Service agent assigned to the chief justice, barged into the sheriff's office. "They want you upstairs," Moore told me. "Ruby wants a Jew in the room." Ruby was Jewish, and his heritage was important to him. Since childhood, Ruby had often fought and beaten others over perceived anti-Semitic remarks. He felt keenly that Jews were being blamed because he was widely suspected of involvement in the Kennedy assassination.

In the sheriff's kitchen, chairs were spread around the perimeter, but there was no table. I sat in a chair by the door, in front of the court reporter and not far from Jack Ruby. To Ruby's left was the chief jus-tice. Toward the back of the room, Ford was sitting next to Ruby's new lawyer, Joe Tonahill, who was trying to save Ruby's life.

Ruby studied me. Looking straight at me, he mouthed the words. "Are you a Yid [Jew]?" No one could hear him, including me, but I could read his lips.

I sat expressionless. I knew from my experience as an appellate lawyer what it would look like in print if I responded. Again Ruby mouthed the words "Are you a Yid?" Again I sat stone-faced.

Ruby, then fifty-three, was swarthy and intense, with a potbelly. He stood five-foot-nine and weighed 175 pounds. Not big, but scrappy. He mouthed the question again, twice more. And again I didn't flinch or respond in any way.

At about that time the stenographer ran out of paper and had to reload her machine. Ruby jumped up, grabbed the chief justice, who was on his left, and pulled him into a corner. Ruby ordered me into the corner also.

Joe Ball walked up behind us. He figured, If Arlen Specter's in this huddle, why am I not in it? Ruby turned to Joe Ball. "Are you Jewish?" he asked. "No," Ball said. "Well, go away," Ruby snapped. Joe Ball did as he was told.

Ruby turned back to Warren and me. "Chief," he said, "you've got to get me to Washington. They're cutting off the arms and legs of Jewish children in Albuquerque and El Paso."

I was astonished, and I attributed Ruby's remarks to his being out of touch with reality on the matter he had brought up.

"I—I can't do that, Mr. Ruby," Warren stammered.

"Get to Fortas. He'll get the job done," Ruby said, referring to Abe Fortas, the celebrated trial lawyer and presidential adviser who would soon take a seat on the Supreme Court. Fortas was also Jewish. "Get to Fortas. He'll get it worked out."

By this time the stenographer had reloaded her pad. The three of us went back to our chairs and sat down. Ruby saw his lawyer, Tonahill, pass a note to Ford and demanded to see it. The chief justice, the House Republican leader and future president, and assorted other heavy hitters were all in the room, but Jack Ruby was indisputably in command. Ruby got the note, but he couldn't read it. He was farsighted. So the chief justice of the United States removed his eyeglasses and handed them to Jack Ruby, who then read the note.

"You see," Tonahill's note read, "I told you he was crazy." Ruby threw the note away, uninterested. And we went on with the deposition.

It turned out that Jack Ruby had been in charge from the time the deposition began, or even before it began. I didn't know that until I read the transcript of the first part of the deposition. As Ford put it to me recently, Ruby "flaunted his power and presence. He was a strange guy."

His testimony began not with the chief justice formally convening the commission but with Ruby demanding a lie-detector test. "Without a lie-detector test on my testimony, my verbal statements to you, how do you know I am telling the truth?" Ruby asked.

"Don't worry about that, Jack," Tonahill advised his client.

"Just a minute, gentlemen," Ruby said.

Warren still did not call the meeting to order, as he should have. Instead he asked, "You wanted to ask something, did you, Mr. Ruby?"

"I would like to be able to get a lie detector test or truth serum of what motivated me to do what I did at that particular time," Ruby said.

"I will say this to you," Warren said, "that if you and your counsel want any kind of test, I will arrange it for you. I would be glad to do that, if you want it. I wouldn't suggest a lie-detector test to test the truth. We will treat you just same as we do any other witnesses, but if you want such a test, I will arrange it."

"I do want it," Ruby said. "Will you agree to that, Joe?"

"I sure do, Jack," Tonahill said.

I later found out that David Belin, the junior lawyer in Area 2, had put Ruby up to the polygraph, planting the idea through Rabbi Hillel

Silverman, the leader of a Dallas congregation who regularly visited Ruby in jail. "No one found out that I had anything at all to do with it, other than Hillel Silverman," Belin told me recently. "No one found out until I wrote it in my 1973 book, *November 22, 1963*."[2] Belin was apparently trying to provide some basis, through a polygraph, to give weight to the conclusion that Ruby had no connection to Oswald.

In any case, on the flight back from Dallas to Washington that night, Warren was unhappy about having agreed to the polygraph. He and I were alone in the plane. Ford had gone to Michigan, Ball to California. "What are we going to do?" Warren asked me. "I agreed to give Ruby a polygraph."

"Mr. Chief Justice," I said, "you're going to have to do it, unless you can get him to withdraw the request."

"Well, I don't believe in polygraphs!" the chief justice thundered. "I don't believe in Big Brother. Who's going to do the polygraph?"

"Well, we better not have a police agency do it," I said. "We got in a lot of trouble having the Illinois State Police do the ballistics." The ballistics work had drawn a heated complaint. I suggested contracting for the lie-detector test with a private agency.

"Do you know what a polygraph company will make being the one to do this celebrity polygraph?" Warren cried. "Zapruder got $150,000 for the film he made. We don't want the polygraph company getting rich over this." Earl Warren had never made much money during his lifetime of public service. Around this time, a newspaper highlighted the chief justice's thrift by running a photograph of him at a black-tie Washington affair handing his limousine driver a couple of bills. The chief justice was discharging his driver early to avoid paying the full charge, after another guest had offered him a ride home.

Warren, never particularly quick on his feet, could have told Ruby, "Mr. Ruby, we don't place any credence in lie-detector tests." Instead, three times, Warren agreed to give Ruby the test, if Ruby wanted it.

"Mr. Chief Justice," I told Warren, "you promised him a polygraph." It would look awful if the commission reneged on an on-the-record promise. And even if Ruby's lawyer fought Ruby's own request, I said, "You can't take the word of counsel on this, because the Supreme Court just had a case on voir dire on a defendant being questioned, and the court held that only the defendant himself, not counsel, could make a representation to the court on such an important matter. I think that principle will apply here." In other words, I told Warren, his only way out of this promise was to get Ruby, on the record, to withdraw the request for a polygraph.

"If you don't give him a polygraph, having promised him one, unless he asks that it be withdrawn on the record, it will look like— It will be a problem," I continued. At best it would look as though the commission was not exhausting every lead. I didn't use the word "cover-up," but that was my implication. The public believes in lie-detector tests, even if they are inadmissible in court.

The commission then arranged with the FBI to give Ruby a lie-detector test. Questions were drafted and the polygraph scheduled. Then Ruby's lawyers—who changed periodically—and relatives weighed in. They sent mixed signals. Some warned that Ruby's mental state would make the test meaningless. But Joe Tonahill, still Ruby's primary lawyer, told me he wanted the test.

I was sent to meet Ruby at Dallas County Jail on July 18, six weeks after we took his deposition in the sheriff's kitchen. Two of Ruby's lawyers, Tonahill and Clayton Fowler, were with him. The test would be administered by Bell P. Herndon, the polygraph supervisor assigned to the FBI lab in Washington and one of the best polygraph operators in the country.

When most of the players had assembled for the polygraph, Fowler, who had objected to the test, said he wanted to discuss the matter with Ruby one last time. "If he insists on it, I can't and won't hold him back," Fowler told me. He left the room and walked to Ruby's cell. I had the court reporter make a formal record of what was going on. Fowler returned five minutes later. "He says he's going to take the test regardless of his lawyers," Fowler reported.

My first task, as I had arranged with the chief justice, was to ask Ruby if he wanted to withdraw his request. I moved very carefully. It was important, I knew, for the record not to seem as though I were suggesting anything. It had to be Ruby's decision and appear to be his decision. I told him that the choice was entirely his. If he wanted the test, we would have it. If he didn't, we wouldn't.

Jack Ruby wanted the polygraph. He even had prepared his own list of questions he wanted asked. A lie-detector test is supposed to last forty-five minutes. Typically it involves a few control questions to test biological responses and a limited number of real questions going to the heart of the issue. Ruby's polygraph exam lasted from twelve noon until twelve midnight. Everybody had questions he wanted Ruby to answer. And we started with Ruby's own sizable list.

Ruby stuck to his story, that he was outraged and upset over President Kennedy's assassination and acted impulsively to spare Jacqueline Kennedy further pain. "The thought never entered my mind prior to that Sunday morning when I took it upon myself to try to be a martyr or some screwball, you might say," Ruby had testified in the sheriff's kitchen, and essentially repeated during the polygraph. "But I felt very emotional and very carried away for Mrs. Kennedy, that with all the strife she had gone through—I had been following it pretty well—that someone owed it to our beloved president that she shouldn't be expected to come back to face [Oswald's] trial of this heinous crime.

". . . I had the gun in my right hip pocket, and impulsively, if that is the correct word here, I saw him, and that is all I can say. I didn't care what happened to me. I think I used the words 'You killed my president, you rat.' The next thing, I was down on the floor."

After the test finally ended, Tonahill, Bell Herndon, and I went to a famous nearby steak house, Cattleman's, for a midnight dinner. To wash down the beef, they gave us champagne. Whiskey was not sold in Dallas.

I flew from Dallas to Baltimore the next day on American Airlines with Herndon. He said he thought Ruby had passed the test with flying colors and clearly was not involved in the assassination. But J. Edgar Hoover filed a report that Ruby was out of touch with reality and that the polygraph was worthless.

The House of Representatives, in a 1978 probe, also found the Ruby polygraph unreliable. The Assassinations Committee cited four factors: Ruby's earlier extensive questioning by various officials about the Oswald shooting, the time lapse between the shooting and the polygraph, the number of people present at the polygraph, and the lack of control questions. Some of those are valid considerations.

But I believe that the most reliable assessment came from Herndon before he consulted any of his superiors. Herndon, a top polygrapher, not only had Ruby's readings but also could see Ruby's reactions—his frowns, smiles, gestures—as Ruby fielded the questions. I believe that Herndon was correct in accepting the polygraph's validity, and I was surprised when Hoover overruled him. We published the full transcript of the polygraph, so history can decide.

TRUTH AND LIES

The Warren Commission submitted its report and closed its investigation on September 24, 1964, ten months after it had formally convened. We had taken three times as long as the chief justice originally planned and five times as long as Frank Adams figured. It had been a marathon instead of a sprint.

The Report of the President's Commission on the Assassination of President Kennedy runs 888 pages, plus photographs and drawings. The single-volume report was designed for easy—or at least manageable—reading by the press and public. The commission also published 17,000 pages of testimony in twenty-six volumes, containing transcripts of our interviews of all ninety-three witnesses, plus various notes.

We staff lawyers had submitted draft chapters on our areas. The commissioners reviewed our material. The report was edited and assembled by Rankin's assistant, Norman Redlich. Redlich essentially let my work stand, especially the key points about the assassination and the Single-Bullet Conclusion. That material appears in Chapters 2 and 3 in the published volume.

The Single-Bullet Conclusion may have emerged intact from the commissioners' closed meetings and escaped Redlich's pen, but not for lack of debate, I later learned. Ford recently confirmed that at one of their final meetings, some members of the commission balked at my theory. No minutes were taken at those closed, members-only commission sessions.

"There was extensive discussion at the end," Ford told me in June 1997. "The staff presented a suggested draft, and, as I recall, there were two basic issues, where there was dispute: Number one, the staff draft said there was no conspiracy. Categorically, saying there was no conspiracy. And the commission—and I don't recall who raised the issue—said that goes too far. And so we inserted the language, 'The commission found no evidence of a conspiracy.' And once that came up to that point, there was a unanimous vote to have that language, rather than the staff language.

"The other issue was the Single-Bullet Theory. And you were the author of that point of view. There were several, but I can't remember who, who raised questions about it. If my suspicion is right, one of them would have been Dick Russell. I wouldn't swear to that. Dick Russell probably would have influenced John Sherman Cooper. And I don't recall how the vote went, but it was 4–3 or 5–2. But it was an issue that was discussed in some detail and with some vigor."[1]

In my draft, and especially on areas that touched on the Single-Bullet Conclusion, I had gone out of my way to include material that contradicted my conclusion. I described, for example, how Tomlinson, the Parkland engineer who found Bullet 399, had grown confused about which stretcher the bullet had dropped from. I included the hole in the back of the president's jacket and the postage-stamp-weight metal fragments. We were not writing a trial brief, pushing a particular view. We were writing a report of an on-the-record investigation. As a matter of integrity, we included all considerations.

Joe Ball and Dave Belin, the Area 2 team, found the report lacking in style and, somewhat, in substance. Redlich's final version read more like a law-review article than a report, they complained. It omitted too much material from their draft, they said. Belin had pressed for two volumes, in the interest of thoroughness. Belin went on to write two books and countless articles and columns about the commission.

If Ball thought Redlich had not gone far enough, Liebeler thought he went too far. "Redlich wrote it like a brief," Liebeler told me. "A plaintiff's brief. I thought that he claimed more than the evidence would support, as a generally consistent proposition. I got my way on some of those issues." Some thought Redlich had heated the porridge too much; some thought he hadn't heated it enough. I think he did it about right.

I've been hearing about the Warren Commission and its report regularly since 1964. An early complaint came from William Manchester, the historian, author, and former Kennedy aide. Manchester was irate that I had included in the report that Jacqueline Kennedy had a drink in the back of Air Force One while returning to Washington from Dallas. I had learned about Mrs. Kennedy's drink while questioning Kenneth O'Donnell, another Kennedy aide, who later wrote *Johnny, We Hardly Knew Ye*.

By the time I returned to commission headquarters from the White House, where I had interviewed O'Donnell, word of the deposition had already reached Lee Rankin. "Why did you ask O'Donnell about Mrs. Kennedy having a drink on the plane?" Rankin asked me.

"Lee," I said, "I didn't do that." O'Donnell had volunteered that comment without being asked.

"Well, they've already called us," Rankin said, "and they're madder than hell about it."

"It never happened," I said. The transcript confirmed that I had not asked whether Mrs. Kennedy had a drink on the plane. I'd asked O'Donnell some questions about what Mrs. Kennedy had done, and he volunteered the part about the drink.

I almost sued Oliver Stone after his 1991 pseudodocumentary movie *JFK*, which libeled me by name, calling me a liar in reference to the Single-Bullet Conclusion. Stone's film has done more than any other single effort to distort history and the commission's work. In grainy black and white, Stone filmed scenes conveying his own account of the assassination, then inserted them into his Technicolor movie as though they had been lifted from actual newsreel footage. *JFK* reached a whole generation of Americans who rely on the screen, whether television or cinema, for information. And the film, depicting a vast government conspiracy to kill Kennedy, was such a big lie that it almost defied belief. But the lies will be corrected in time. Eventually, Stone's movie will fall largely on its own weight, with help from responses like Walter Cronkite's vehement denunciation of *JFK* and his affirmation of the Warren Commission, David Belin's books and later generations' study of the twenty-six-volume, 17,000-page record.

I consulted ace Philadelphia litigator James Beasley about suing Stone. I had a strong case. The trial would have involved the whole Warren Commission story, which would have been fine with me. But I had too much on my plate at the time, including a 1992 Senate campaign, to pursue the suit. Besides, I didn't need a movie company. In the end I let it go.

Gerald Ford also points to *JFK* as a prime source of distortion about the Kennedy assassination. "Despite all of those well-written, highly documented books, you get Oliver Stone, which was a terrible distortion, an erroneous thing; at one point I was tempted to challenge him to a debate," Ford told me. "Well, I thought that would just help him sell the damned movie.

"I swore, Arlen, I would never see it," Ford insisted. "Get on a plane in New York City going to Los Angeles, I'm a captive audience." The film was showing on the flight.

Did you get a headset? I asked the former president.

"Well, I finally put it on. As long as I didn't have to buy a ticket."

I had to see the movie, because I was asked so many questions about it. The film came out in December 1991, while I was in a primary fight. My opponent circulated leaflets outside theaters throughout Pennsylvania accusing me of misconduct in the Kennedy investigation, based on Oliver Stone's misrepresentations.

Ford said his answer to Stone was to offer a litany of facts, which cannot be disputed. "And Oliver Stone comes up with a new theory: There was another gunman, there was another gun, there were more shots, but he hasn't identified a person, he hasn't identified a gun, he hasn't found a bullet. So it's total speculation, in contrast to the hard facts that the commission came up with. And when you put it in that context, you pretty well destroy the baloney that he puts out."

One good thing did come, at least in part, from Stone's movie: We created the Assassination Review Board in 1992, to expedite disclosure of materials relevant to Kennedy's murder. I co-sponsored the legislation. The review board has transferred some ten thousand documents to the National Archives and Records Administration. The board has worked to disclose as much material as possible that may have been withheld by the FBI, CIA, or Secret Service, or any other federal agency. As I noted in a June 1997 speech on the Senate floor, "The review board serves a vital function of removing some of the uncertainty and speculation about the contents of government files relating to President Kennedy's assassination."

The Warren Commission reported the truth, in as much detail and as precisely as we could. The watchword was integrity. We followed the chief justice's order, at that initial staff meeting, that the truth be our client.

As Bill Coleman notes, Attorney General Robert Kennedy was privy to every bit of information the commission had, through his liaison, Howard Willens. "Certainly, the one guy who wouldn't cover something up is the brother of the president who got assassinated,"[2] Coleman said. As Ford put it, the notion that Earl Warren and Gerald Ford would conspire on anything is preposterous.

No second assassin, and no other plausible theory, has emerged in more than thirty years. But it is hard to prove a negative, to dispel conspiracy theories. And our conclusions—including the Single-Bullet Conclusion; that Oswald acted alone to kill the president; and that Jack Ruby, the CIA, Fidel Castro, and the Soviet Union were all uninvolved in any plot—failed to satisfy. More than two thousand books have been written on the Kennedy assassination, and more continue to roll off the presses, many challenging our conclusions. Why?

Various reasons, perhaps, including some of our own creation. The commission relied on the FBI, a federal agency accused of involvement in the assassination, for some tests and investigation. We never looked at the autopsy photographs and X rays. Lyndon Johnson, a conceivable suspect and a witness, was never interviewed. "I think something about Johnson's personality has an effect on this," Sam Stern said diplomatically.

There was Oswald's role in the Fair Play for Cuba Committee and his move to Russia and marriage to a Russian woman, which tapped passions about the Cold War and the Castro conflict and fed the raging paranoia, even post-McCarthy, about our enemies in the world. And there were the Single-Bullet Conclusion and Jack Ruby's assassination of Oswald, which both seemed too pat.

At a gut level, it felt wrong to so many people. John F. Kennedy was not only the leader of the free world but also king of Camelot. Kennedy was erudite, charming, lucky. How could he be brought down by an insignificant lone assassin? "Fundamentally," Stern observed, "it is dramatically unacceptable that this shining prince could be brought down by such a minuscule twisted little animal. . . . Shakespeare would not have written about Kennedy being brought down by an Oswald. It wouldn't work."

The assassinations of Robert Kennedy and Martin Luther King, Jr., following in 1968, only added to the skepticism. "These are all assaults on our dignity as a people, our pride as a people," Stern said, "and to attribute them to the aberrational acts of twisted little men may not be as satisfying as seeing these as part of the great international Cold War, or wars that were going on, in which we have sustained our position."

All of this passion and circumstance has been churned by obsessed or opportunistic conspiracy theorists, who too often have received airings from irresponsible publishers and reporters.

For a while after we finished the investigation, I did not talk about the Warren Commission. I felt bound by a sense of lawyer-client relationship between commission staff and the commission itself. We had done our talking in the report. It seemed inappropriate for us to talk further. I also had a sense that Chief Justice Warren, whom I deeply respected, would not want us to talk about our work. The best thing to do, when in doubt, was to keep quiet.

I did appear with Bill Coleman at a Philadelphia Bar Association program shortly after the commission filed its report, but that was the exception. Then Edward Jay Epstein came along. Epstein was doing a master's thesis when he came to see me on a Sunday in the summer of 1965, while my family picnicked in our backyard. I talked to Epstein about our work in a removed, almost academic way, sticking to what was in the report.

Epstein published his book *Inquest* in 1966, challenging our findings. Soon after, I got a call from Fletcher Knebel, who was writing an article for *Look*. I didn't realize that Knebel was the acclaimed author of *Seven Days in May* and other political novels. I declined his request for an interview. Then Knebel came back to me and said, "Nobody will talk to me, and I'm not going to have any choice except to give credence to everything Epstein has said."

I thought it over. I decided that as an elected public official—I was then in my first year as Philadelphia DA—I was accountable to the public and should not refuse to comment. I decided to talk to Knebel. He quoted me extensively in his *Look* piece, which turned out to be accurate and fair. Then I received a request from *U.S. News and World Report*. I gave them a three- to four-hour interview in September 1966. They also did a decent job, reporting a lengthy verbatim transcript. David Belin and I traveled to London in January 1967 to debate Mark Lane on the BBC. The program, scheduled from seven to eleven on a Sunday night, was extended until almost midnight.

All of us who played roles in the Warren Commission have been questioned about it all of our lives. I get questions about the Warren Commission at almost every open-house town meeting, high school speech, and political forum I hold.

When will the mania ebb? Dr. Clark, the neurosurgeon, found himself sitting next to the congressional custodian of records when Clark stopped for lunch at a Senate office building during a recent, unrelated trip to Washington. "How long am I going to be getting questions about this?" Clark asked the man. "We get a hundred questions a year about the assassination of President Lincoln," the man answered.

PART THREE

PART THREE

THE NATION'S WORST COURTS

*T*he *Philadelphia Inquirer* waged an old-style newspaper crusade in September 1964 to expose the city's magistrates, who presided over Philadelphia's minor criminal and civil courts, as corrupt and inept. In front-page, two-inch-tall banner headlines, the *Inquirer* blasted the magistrates, who owed their jobs to the political machines, and cried for reform. It was into this maelstrom that I returned to Philadelphia from Washington and the Warren Commission.

I was glad when the Warren Commission finally turned in its final report to President Johnson on September 28, 1964. The investigation, the travel, the long weeks away from home were finally over. I thought the day had finally ended at ten-thirty that night, when I landed in Philadelphia after going to Kansas to visit my brother.

Joan met me at the gate. "Ted Voorhees called," she said, by way of greeting. "He asked that you call him back no matter how late." I knew that Voorhees, as chancellor of the Philadelphia Bar Association, had been working with Vincent Carroll and Joseph Sloane, two top Philadelphia judges, to launch an investigation of the magistrates. Inspired by the *Inquirer* series, Governor William W. Scranton and Walter E. Alessandroni, the state attorney general, were leading the charge. The Scranton administration believed that by exposing Philadelphia's corrupt minor judiciary, it could persuade the public of the need for overall state constitutional reform, which the voters had narrowly rejected in 1963.

Voorhees wanted me to run a full investigation of the magistrates. I would serve as chief counsel, with the rank of special assistant state attorney general. I had worked for Voorhees before, at Barnes Dechert. Voorhees, then a partner at the firm, had chaired the Associates Team of young lawyers. He was meticulous. Those were the days before computer "spell-check" programs, and Voorhees drilled us to read over every word we had written, syllable by syllable, to make sure no imperfect document left the Dechert office. When Voorhees asked me to investigate the magistrates, I told him no, categorically. I'd had enough of investigations for at least a while. Voorhees pressed me, insisting we at least talk about it. I agreed to that.

After I'd had a refreshing night's sleep, the magistrates probe seemed less onerous when I met with Voorhees and Judges Sloane and Carroll. A trip to Harrisburg to confer with Attorney General Alessandroni followed. By the time we finished talking, the project looked very interesting. I accepted.

Before the Warren Commission and the Philadelphia DA's office, I had investigative experience going back to my Air Force days, from 1951 to 1953 as a lieutenant in the Office of Special Investigations. I conducted background investigations on people seeking top-secret security clearances, checking birth and other records and interviewing people who knew them. I also investigated crimes and procurement fraud. For a while I'd thought my military career was going to begin on the front lines. As an ROTC wing commander in 1950, I had gone to Lowery Air Force base for my summer training, which was part of the requirement for a commission. A couple thousand of us, all in khaki, arrived at Lowery on June 25, 1950—the day the Korean War began. We were sure we were going to be sent straight to Korea. But during the course of the summer, the Air Force got a good look at us and decided it wanted to win the war, so we were sent back to our respective colleges. I returned to Penn for my senior year.

Upon our graduation, the brass assigned us to our home areas, because they figured we knew the territory and would do a better job there. I was assigned to OSI District 3, which covered West Virginia and Delaware as well as Pennsylvania. The uniform was suits and ties, like FBI agents, which were supposed to make us blend in. At one point I drove to West Virginia to do a background check on an airman who was up for "top secret." I came to a taproom along the road and asked the bartender if he could help me out, and I named the man I was trying to locate. "Zeke!" the barkeep hollered at a guy at the door. "Will you tell this FBI feller where Lum lives down in the patch?"

The OSI assignment was terrific. I lived at home in Philadelphia, saved my money, checked out people's backgrounds, and investigated crimes and procurement fraud. I was usually able to complete fifteen to twenty interviews a day, with plenty of time left over to meet Joan for lunch at Temple University, where she was going to college, and to serve as the University of Pennsylvania debate coach for the 1952–53 academic year.

Philadelphia's magistrates deserved their national reputation as America's worst, after centuries of selling justice and abusing the poor people brought before them. When Lincoln Steffens described Philadelphia at the turn of the century as "corrupt and contented," the magistrates could have been his Exhibit A. Dealing with far more Philadelphians than any other court, the magistrates always had a great impact. When people see and sense corruption in the only court system they know, they inevitably think all government is the same. That cynicism weakens the moral fiber of the community.

The lay magistrate was a carryover from William Penn's Second Charter of 1691. And complaints about the magistrates were recorded almost that far back. In 1825, Justice Thomas Duncan of the Pennsylvania supreme court referred to extortion by minor judicial officials "which we hear such loud complaints of everywhere. . . ." The Citizens Municipal Reform Association urged the Pennsylvania Constitutional Convention of 1872–73 to abolish the magistrates, arguing, "No greater blot upon our civilization exists than the administration of justice in petty cases as exercised in a great city such as Philadelphia." The new constitution of 1873 did little more than change the title from alderman to magistrate. Reform movements in the twentieth century fared no better. In 274 years, more than thirty magistrates had been indicted, a few had been convicted, and only one had been jailed. And the system rolled on as strong as ever.

I saw my first magistrate's hearing as a student in the dilapidated police station at Paul and Ruan streets. A fat man, smoking a fat cigar, sat on a raised platform. His mood vacillated between bellowing anger and sweet compassion as cases were called before him. His attitude toward the various defendants seemed to have little to do with the facts of their cases. Over the protests of police witnesses, the magistrate dismissed some serious cases. He held other cases for trial, on the same charges with less evidence. After the hearings ended, I learned the magistrate's method from neighborhood residents who had also come to see the show. They talked about cases "blown out." Payoffs, not evidence, determined the cases' outcomes.

I didn't set foot in another magistrates court for ten years, until late 1959, when I became an assistant DA. In my early days as a prosecutor,

131

I began my mornings with a joust in magistrate's court on preliminary hearings in criminal cases. Typically the magistrate arrived at the police-station court by pulling a Cadillac into the premier parking place reserved by a side door. Before the magistrate entered that door, he held a series of parking-lot "conferences" with a swarm of fixers waiting for him. The fixers had to catch the magistrate on the spot, because they wanted to discuss arrests made within the past twenty-four hours, many during the preceding night. They wanted to negotiate with the magistrate before the case came up. Payoffs were legendary, and some magistrates had a sliding scale, depending upon the gravity of the offense. Lawyers and committeemen customarily arranged the fixes.

When a fixer didn't arrive in time to catch the magistrate on his way in, the magistrate would sometimes leave the bench during the session and walk to a corner of the courtroom for a "conference." There were other subtle fixes, such as flashing the "high sign" to the seated magistrate while a particular case was being heard, so he didn't have to break his rhythm. Fees could be negotiated with hand signals, as at an auction.

"I can well remember cases being heard and the magistrate hanging fingers over the bench, signaling, I found out later, one hundred or two hundred or so dollars," said Donald Goldberg, a premier Philadelphia criminal defense lawyer beginning in the 1950s. "It was one finger per hundred-dollar increment. I used to try to get in behind a fix, so if they threw that case out, they'd have to throw mine out, too."[1]

When the first cases I prosecuted were blown out over my objections, I rushed back to the district attorney's office to prepare indignant requests for re-arrests. It was not double jeopardy for the DA to have a new arrest warrant issued, with the case taken to a higher court. Some of my requests were granted; others were not. My more sophisticated seniors were not as outraged as I was. We were, after all, in Vic Blanc's DA's office. When I pressed the point, they conceded that the magistrates' practices were reprehensible. But they said that there was no way to deal with the problem without re-arresting practically every defendant who had been discharged.

Philadelphia's magistrates were mostly ward leaders who had toiled in the political vineyards, done the right favors, and climbed the political ladder. Magistrates were required to give up all political titles and power when they ascended the bench. Generally they bequeathed their ward leaderships to a spouse or friends who would serve as their puppets. The "neighborhood Solomons" remained Philadelphia's most entrenched pols. As magistrates they enjoyed the prestige of the title "judge" and substantial financial rewards not wholly reflected by a $12,500 annual salary. In the early 1960s a candidate needed three hundred signatures to run for state supreme court justice but had to collect three thousand signatures to run for magistrate. Magistrate was regarded as a much better job. Essentially it was a license to steal.

The requirements to be a magistrate were minimal: A candidate had to be thirty-five years old, a natural-born U.S. citizen or naturalized for ten years, a five-year resident of Philadelphia, and a registered voter in the city. Only one of the twenty-eight magistrates was an attorney. Only nine had graduated high school. I knew from personal experience that many magistrates were unqualified to hold the job.

From the outset of the investigation I knew it would be tough to change the magisterial system. Payoffs greased the machinery, and Philadelphia magistrates were the most powerful politicians in the state. As one state official told *Time* magazine, "They do favors for people every day, and state legislators are scared to death of them."[2] I knew it would be hard, maybe even impossible, to document the corruption. The fixes—even those in parking lots—while visible, involved conversations that couldn't be overheard. The magistrates certainly wouldn't admit anything. Their conspirators would be equally loath to confess. And City Hall would wink at the whole exercise.

For decades magistrates had fended off attacks and threats. At a quarterly meeting on October 2, 1963, several gloated about foiling a 1962 attempt at constitutional reform:

MAGISTRATE HARRY ELLICK: I control the 24th ward, and when they come in for their money, they are going to be told I am against it. Malone controls the 25th ward and Eddie Cox here controls his ward and it's a cinch if we give the people instructions that they will follow orders.

MAGISTRATE THOMAS MAROTTA: That's a very good suggestion.

ELLICK: You don't have to go to the street corners with a box. I'll give the committeeman instructions. . . .

MAGISTRATE BENJAMIN SEGAL: I think you ought to cross that out of the minutes and I think you ought to ask anybody if they are against it.

MAGISTRATE JOHN WALSH: They are not available to the public.

MAROTTA: Instruct him to take it out of the minutes.

CHIEF MAGISTRATE DALY: Everything that was discussed regarding this last subject is off the record.

WALSH: Nobody can see the record anyway.

133

DALY: The Governor can examine the minutes. The law says they must be available for the Governor . . . Is anyone against taking it off the record?

(No answer)[3]

Fortunately, the stenographer did not follow the magistrates' orders to strike the record.

One of my deputies on the probe, James McGirr Kelly, later a federal district court judge, confided to me recently that he never thought we would be able to uproot the system. "I thought at best we would have a holding action against some of the abuses, maybe catch a magistrate or two or a court aide, rap their knuckles, and that would be it," Kelly said. Our prospects *were* dim. But I thought we had a chance to change the system because it was so rotten.

It was so widely known that the magistrate courts were corrupt that in May 1964, six months before our investigation began, a magistrate felt compelled to tell a defendant at the end of a preliminary hearing, "Due to the fact there is no case, I am going to discharge you. Don't give anybody any money and don't let anybody say the magistrate wanted so much money or you couldn't be discharged. The only reason you are being discharged is for lack of evidence. . . . Don't pay anybody money on the case. The case was not fixed."[4]

The magistrate was doing the man a favor. In those days courthouse fixers had a wonderful repertoire of ploys not just to fix cases, but to con their clients into paying even for fixes that had not been worked. In sight of his client a defense attorney would throw his arm around an assistant DA as the prosecutor entered the courtroom. The fixer would pull out his wallet, show the prosecutor a photo of his wife and child, and ask, "Aren't they cute?" The prosecutor, naturally, would smile and nod. The fixer would then return to his client and demand payment, saying the client had just seen a payoff being arranged.

My investigation set up shop at the new state office building on Spring Garden Street. The tower, which included a local office for the governor, was a monument to the Keystone State. Our quarters were not so plush. We had a few desks and phones and some mismatched furniture in a cramped room on the seventh floor. Our team began with my assistant counsel, three other eager lawyers in their mid-thirties. For investi-

134

gation and arrests, we had twelve Pennsylvania state troopers, led by Sergeant Keith Dane, who could have posed for a recruiting poster. Dane's troopers were the cream of central Pennsylvania—clean-cut, well-spoken, courteous, intelligent. We also had eight special agents from the state department of justice. And Joe Maex, the barrel-chested former Philadelphia homicide detective who had guarded me during the Teamsters trial, was back, this time as an investigator. Maex had kept his policeman's swagger and shiny black shoes. He began his interrogations by demanding witnesses' addresses. He would ask, "Where do you hide, bum?" Maex always wore a fedora, night and day, indoors and out, topping off his square-jawed Dick Tracy profile. The others took to calling Maex "Old Iron Head." They figured he wore his hat so that if it ever rained, his head wouldn't rust.

I had just come off the Warren Commission, and I modeled the magistrates investigation on the Kennedy probe. We began with mountains of paper, which led us to interviews and suspects. Fact-finding is the most difficult facet of administering justice. Many facts cannot be found or cannot be proved in court. But that was the challenge.

Harry Karafin, the ace *Philadelphia Inquirer* reporter whose September 1964 series on the magistrates had prompted our probe, showed up daily at our office looking for scoops. Karafin was a favorite of *Inquirer* publisher Walter Annenberg, and everybody knew it. Karafin strutted into our offices with his coiffed gray hair, tailored sports coats, and rings. He "sat on my lap" and collected tips, as he once put it. Karafin was under standing orders to produce daily page-one stories on our *Inquirer*-inspired investigation.

On occasion Karafin's purple prose caused me grief, as when he wrote that Specter "drew first blood" while I was struggling to maintain every appearance of fairness. Karafin's motto was "Never let the facts get in the way of a good story." He found that one of our agents had paid a traffic ticket by endorsing over his paycheck, and before one of my deputies could explain, the reporter penned an exposé headlined STATE FUND USED TO PAY TRAFFIC FINES.

My father, visiting Philadelphia when the investigation began, was fascinated by the avalanche of publicity. Every morning he walked a mile to pick up the *Inquirer* at Ridge and Midvale to see the banner headlines. It was the first time my father had ever seen a family member in the media, and he delighted in it. Here he was, a Russian peasant, and all this attention was being paid to his son. Coming to America had been worth it!

State Senator Ben Donolow, on the other hand, was incensed by our investigation. By his reckoning, the upstart who had won an assistant prosecutor's job over Donolow's objection was now hitting too close to home. Donolow took to the senate floor in March to denounce me and my probe, calling me the "kid from Kansas." Short and slight, Donolow wore sharp suits and combed over his thinning black hair. His head continually darted from side to side, ferretlike, as he flailed his long-fingered white hands. Donolow was doing me a favor. His publicized assault lent credibility to our efforts.

During our preliminary talks, Judges Sloane and Carroll had promised me subpoena power, which I considered essential, to force witnesses to testify and to gather documents. But when we began our probe, subpoena power was not included in our charter. The judges, it turned out, talked tougher in private.

Of the seventy-five hundred witnesses we asked to meet with us, nearly a third had ignored or snubbed our written requests by March 1965. Some lost their memory after beatings by goons. I asked the judges on the city's board of common pleas for subpoena power, and they turned me down. It seems the Philadelphia judges found my special state investigation a "usurpation" of their authority, as Karafin reported. The *Inquirer* reporter saw the denial of subpoena power as a crippling, perhaps mortal, blow. He wrote that we might fold our investigation by April 1, some three weeks later. We forged ahead. And we got creative.

The magistrates began to sweat. The mood among the neighborhood Solomons grew "very depressed, apprehensive, but I must say, almost resigned," recalled Ed Becker, later chief judge for the U.S. Third Circuit Court of Appeals, who was the lawyer of the magistrates board. "I think there was a certain inevitability. The corruption had been so entrenched, so long-standing, that so many were resigned that the investigation would lead to their downfall."[5]

Payola Palace was quaking. "The action of the Democratic magistrates was apparently the result of someone pushing the panic button at 1415 Walnut Street, Democratic City Committee headquarters," the *Inquirer* wrote. "Walnut Street is believed fearful of the effect on the fall elections of any prosecution of magistrates." One magistrate, an obese former pharmacist and real estate assessor named Harry Ellick, lost eighty pounds after we began investigating him. Becker asked Ellick how he did it. "Try worrying," Ellick answered.

Ellick was the first magistrate we arrested. We indicted him for extorting money from a bar owner and his bartender, who had been in Ellick's court on charges of serving alcohol to minors. Ellick was renowned for his policy of charging "five hundred dollars for big guys, two hundred dollars for little guys." Ellick checked himself into the Philadelphia Psychiatric Center prior to his hearing. He had more visitors than any other patient at the mental hospital, and he regularly signed official papers brought to him. He had planned to fly to Florida the day before he was indicted. Dane's state troopers wheeled portable fingerprinting and photographic equipment into Ellick's hospital room and the magistrate was "mugged, fingerprinted and booked at bedside," as the *Daily News* described it.

We arrived at the State Office Building by 8:00 A.M., and stayed late. We pored over 50,000 documents. We interviewed 250 witnesses, a small fraction of those we asked to come in, but enough. Hundreds of people signed sworn affidavits that they had paid off magistrates to free them from jail. We disclosed more than 40 cases of payoffs demanded to fix criminal cases. We documented the corrupt magistrate-constable collection racket. We identified thousands of technical violations showing magistrates' incompetence and indifference. We produced the first admissible proof of outright corruption in the 274-year history of the Philadelphia magisterial system. We laid bare the magistrates court to public view.

We put it all into a 515-page report. By mid-1965 I was running for district attorney, but I reserved Saturdays for dictating to my secretary, Mary Perelman, from 8:00 A.M. to 6:00 P.M. Then I would go home and go out with Joan on Saturday night, as we've done throughout our marriage. On Sunday mornings I would go into the office, and Mary would have the previous day's dictation typed, so we would start again.

I sent Mary Perelman's time records to Attorney General Alessandroni for processing and payment. Alessandroni phoned me, for the first and only time during the entire investigation. "Arlen," he said, "there must be some mistake. These papers say she worked a hundred and twenty hours last week, which can't be right. That would be more than seventeen hours a day, seven days a week. There must be a typographical error." I said, "Well, General, have you read my draft report?" Alessandroni said he had not. I said, "Then you should weigh it. The payment invoice is accurate." The attorney general paid it.

I had promised to file the magistrates report by May 1965. I had met many deadlines, including tough ones with the Warren Commission, and I was confident I could meet this one. But despite staffers' strenuous efforts, my own discipline, and Mary's typing skills, the May deadline for the full report proved impossible. I found a way to meet that commitment by publishing the key chapter on summary and conclusions, which comprised the first part of the final report, in May.

"This investigation has shown that a majority of the magistrates are guilty of extortion," the *Inquirer*'s Karafin and Goulden reported in a front-page story under the three-deck headline CITY'S MAGISTERIAL SYSTEM / A CESSPOOL OF CORRUPTION; / ABOLISHMENT IS ADVOCATED.

We filed our full report on August 16. That document, modeled after the Warren Commission report, is the best work I have done in my years of public service. Governor Bill Scranton, now thirty years out of office, still praises the magistrates report. "I have never read a report of a research on a governmental problem that was better done than that one," the former governor told me recently. "It's one of those cases which are rather rare in American government, where an investigation won the victory by being just so excellent that nobody could overcome it with other arguments."[6]

The magistrates were less impressed. "Chief Magistrate John P. Walsh responded with shouted curses . . . to findings of State probers that corruption is rampant among his fellow Neighborhood Solomons," Karafin began his *Inquirer* piece. "His voice trembling with anger, Walsh denounced Special Assistant Attorney General Arlen Specter ('liar'); the bar and civic groups pressing magisterial reform ('ivory tower'); and *The Inquirer* ('half truth, half-fact and half-lies')."

The grand jury returned hundreds of indictments against magistrates, bondsmen, constables, lawyers, and ward leaders. The real object was to abolish the three-hundred-year-old system.

MAN AGAINST MARS

In early January 1965, in the midst of the magistrates probe, U.S. Senator Joseph Clark wrote a letter to the Democratic City Committee that was published in the *Sunday Philadelphia Bulletin* listing five potential district attorney candidates and three potential city controller candidates whom he preferred to the Democratic machine's slate for the 1965 Philadelphia city elections. The second name on Clark's list for DA was mine.

Joe Clark at the time seemed like the last guard of good government. His fellow white knight Richardson Dilworth had resigned as mayor in 1962 to run a second failed race for governor and was out of elective office, though he would later resurface as president of the board of education. Clark and Dilworth were at odds with Payola Palace and were no fans of District Attorney Jim Crumlish. I went to see Clark after his letter appeared in the newspaper.

"Senator, will you help me?" I asked him. "Will you help me raise money?" I figured it would take $250,000 to wage a Democratic primary for DA.

"No, no, I wouldn't do that," Clark said.

"Well, would you come out and publicly support me?"

"No, no, I can't do that," the senator said. "I have to run for reelection in three years myself." But he added, "I will vote for you in the Democratic primary." Clark meant that he would support me publicly if the party followed his recommendation and slated me, but not if I was running against the party choice.

I didn't fare much better with Dilworth. The other white knight told me he would wait and watch what happened. He wanted to see who my opponent was, gauge my strength, and decide where his interest lay.

For years I had thought of running for district attorney. When I confided my ambition to my law partner and friend Marv Katz, he told me it would never happen, that it was just a pipe dream. Still, I felt I could do a better job than Vic Blanc, Jim Crumlish, or any other Payola Palace pol. There was talk about Crumlish's getting a federal judgeship, which meant a possible opening. The Democratic organization was worried about Crumlish's reelection prospects. They weren't worried enough to dump him, but they were worried enough to try to ease him out to pasture, and the federal bench seemed a comfortable corral. But Joe Clark, who served on the Senate Judiciary Committee, wouldn't go along. He thought Crumlish unqualified.

I went to see Francis Smith, chairman of the Democratic City Committee, to see if I had any chance for the Democratic nomination. He wasn't interested. "We don't want another Tom Dewey," he told me. In other words, the machine wanted a DA it could control. The *Philadelphia Bulletin* interviewed me about my encounter with Smith and a few months later ran a page-one Sunday story, quoting me as saying, "I did a slow burn and told Smith, in so many words, that I wouldn't play that game. I told him that in my book a guy had to do his job as he saw it. I realized finally that Smith and his organization demanded nothing less than absolute obedience. . . . So when I left Democratic headquarters, I knew it was all over." A bit purple, but on target.

Shortly after my session with Frank Smith, Billy Meehan, the Philadelphia Republican leader, approached me about running for DA on the Republican line. I had met Meehan through Morton Witkin, the former statehouse Republican leader who had defended Ben Lapensohn at my Philadelphia Teamsters trial in 1963. Witkin had no hard feelings over the Teamsters case and had grown into a sort of father figure for me. On Saturday nights Witkin and I used to go out to dinner with our wives. He also pressed me to run for DA.

In February 1965, several weeks after Meehan popped the question, I was getting a haircut when my secretary forwarded a phone call from Senator Hugh Scott. Scott, a portly and dapper Philadelphian with a mustache, horn-rimmed glasses, and a pipe, was Pennsylvania's most prominent national politico. "Senator Scott's on the phone!" echoed the cries through Bart's Barber Shop. "Senator Scott's calling! Senator Scott! Senator Scott!"

I've since had some experience with senators' phone calls, but that one was overwhelming. I sometimes wonder, as I place my calls from the Senate, whether any has ever produced a Bart's Barber Shop reaction. As I took Scott's call, the barbershop hushed and listened. "Arlen," Scott began, "I hope you'll consider becoming the Republican candidate for district attorney."

"Senator Scott, I'm certainly honored and flattered that you'd call me," I said, "and I'm thinking about it."

"Well, I think you have a great chance to win, Arlen. I know of your record, and I think the time is right. The Democrats have done a terrible job, and they're very vulnerable. And it would be a wonderful thing and a real shot in the arm for Republicans."

"Senator Scott, to what extent would you be willing to help me?"

"Do anything I can for you, Arlen."

I didn't ask Scott for anything. I just left it that I would think about his offer. Scott had called at Meehan's request, but he didn't say that.

Shortly after Scott's call, I ran into Dilworth at a Yale Club function and sounded him out again, this time about the prospect of a Republican run. Dilworth told me not to be affected by the business of party. He also said that if I won, I would have a great political future. But if I ran as a Republican and lost, I would be "dead."

Witkin hosted strategy sessions at his large apartment at South Rittenhouse Square, where he and Meehan pressed me to make the run. The pressure and arguments were an evolving process, like a seduction. Meehan and Witkin knew they had an interested prospect. They were playing on that, and I wasn't denying it. But they were also desperate. They'd been unable to find another candidate for what seemed like a suicide run. So they were willing to make concessions.

They never pressed me, for example, about my decision to remain a registered Democrat while running on the Republican line. In retrospect, they may have seen it as an advantage. Philadelphia was a Democratic town, and they may have figured that my Democratic registration would encourage Democrats to vote for me, hoping I would remain in their party after the election. My registration also lent the appearance of a fusion ticket, which had even wider appeal. I was the first Republican candidate to win backing from Americans for Democratic Action.

I insisted to Meehan and Witkin that there would be no strings attached and no obligations for patronage. We never discussed that they would raise all the money, but that was understood. At one point a wearying Witkin lectured me on patronage: "If they give you a round

141

peg for a round hole, take it. If they give you a square peg for a square hole, take it. If they give you a square peg for a round hole, don't take it."

I was apprehensive about running on the Republican ticket, which was almost like changing my religion. The decision was even tougher because I couldn't consult my father, my lifelong adviser. A few months earlier, in the fall of 1964, my parents had decided to fulfill a lifelong dream of visiting Israel. When I was a youngster, my father had often said he wanted to be buried in Israel. On October 9, Joan and I drove my parents to New York, put a bottle of champagne in their stateroom, and watched them sail on the *Shalom* for Israel.

A few weeks later an envelope arrived from Israel bearing my mother's distinctive handwriting, drawing great excitement. My mother had long been touted as the star family letter-writer, sending long, newsy accounts of her and my father's activities. But this letter caught me short. As gently as she could, she broke the news that my father was in a Tel Aviv hospital, having suffered a serious heart attack. He'd been so excited on his arrival in Israel that he had exerted himself, going too many places too fast to see the marvels of the young country. My father had no history of heart problems, and we prayed for his speedy recovery.

At 5:30 A.M. on Monday, November 2, our telephone rang. It was my mother. When I heard her voice choked by tears, I knew what she was about to say. My father had passed away.

It was 12:30 P.M. in Israel. According to Jewish law, my father would be buried the next day. I hurriedly called my siblings. It was two hours earlier in Denver, where Hilda then lived, so I reached her at 4:00 A.M. We quickly calculated that she could make it to New York City in time for the overnight flight, which she did, although the passport office had to stay open to accommodate her. In Russell, Kansas, where my brother Morton lived, it was impossible to make the connections for an on-time arrival at JFK. Shirley, too, in Phoenix had travel difficulties and had four young children who needed her attention. Monday evening, Hilda and I boarded the El Al flight and arrived in Tel Aviv in the early morning hours of Tuesday, November 3. That happened to be election day in the United States, but the Lyndon Johnson–Barry Goldwater race was far from my mind.

My mother, overwhelmed with grief, was relieved to see Hilda and me arrive to care for her, and for our father for the last time. The funeral setting was austere. The Holon Cemetery was dusty and sparsely settled. My father's body was carried on a horse-drawn cart. I wanted to see my father one last time, but was told no in no uncertain terms by the religious leaders. It was contrary to Jewish law. I later learned it would have been a big mistake to see my father in death, which might be my lasting memory of him, instead of all the good times we'd shared.

My father's body was wrapped in a tallith, a prayer shawl, following religious custom. No coffin. We buried him there in Israel, thousands of miles from his home in America and from the one-room hut in Russia where his journey had begun. In the midst of the sadness I focused on the fact that at least he had gotten his wish: He was buried in Israel. Later I heard about so many American Jews and perhaps Jews from all over the world who wanted to be buried in Israel but were turned away because of the limitations of burial space.

Hilda and I brought our mother back to the United States, and I returned to my crowded agenda. By mid-November the magistrates investigation was in full swing and the DA's race looming. Joan was fully supportive of my running if I wanted to. Morton and Shirley, while encouraging, did not have a great deal to say. My mother preferred me to stay out of politics. Before making my final decision, I consulted with Hilda. Although two years younger than Morton, Hilda had emerged as the family matriarch and was interested in politics. I asked Hilda, as I was wont to do, "What would Dad say?"

My father had frequently spoken with pride about shaking hands with the Democratic nominee for president, Al Smith, at the Wichita train station in 1928. I can just picture my dad at the train station, standing in a crowd with so many other people to touch the candidate. But I'm sure my father was not one of those who said, as many do, that he wouldn't wash his hand after shaking the candidate's. My father, who grew up with his parents and eight siblings in a one-room dirt-floored hut, had a fetish about washing his hands at virtually every opportunity. That's one of his many habits I have inherited.

During the Depression, my family found times tough. President Hoover had promised a car in every garage and a chicken in every pot. The Specters did have a car, because my father had to drive to sell blankets in the winter and cantaloupes in the summer in neighboring towns. But there was no chicken in a pot, and I'm not sure the family even owned a pot. Then Hoover ordered the World War I bonus marchers routed. My father became a devotee of Franklin Roosevelt when FDR launched the New Deal to help the little guys in America.

While I was not a political activist, I had written a supportive letter to Democratic presidential nominee Adlai Stevenson in 1952, and I greatly admired President Kennedy. My warm feelings toward the national Democratic leadership clashed with my distaste for the corrupt Philadelphia Democratic organization. By 1965 I had seen the favoritism and political fixes in the city's criminal courts and contracting procedures. Still ringing in my ears was Attorney General Nick Katzenbach's comment that in Philadelphia, half the people are on the take. I held no allegiance or even sympathy for the local Democratic machine. I had to fight the machine to bring the Teamsters to trial and to subpoena the necessary witnesses who were Democratic bigwigs.

Nonetheless, changing parties involved a high level of trauma. It wasn't like changing religions, but there were elements of arguable disloyalty and opportunism that rubbed me the wrong way. I thought about what my father would say. He had been a staunch FDR Democrat. In his absence I turned to my sister Hilda, eight years my senior.

In the Specter household it had been Hilda, as a college student, who had engaged my father in long discussions about history and politics when I was ten or eleven. She had chastised me on my first seventh-grade report card from Roosevelt Intermediate School in Wichita when I brought home one A and seven B's. Beside the critical "stick," she added the "carrot" of one dollar for every future A. It wasn't so much the money as the criticism that motivated me, although I did cash the check for $266 she and her husband, Arthur Morgenstern, gave me on graduation from high school.

As a youngster, I had admired Hilda's intellect and judgment, observing that she had to wait until 10:00 or 11:00 P.M., once everyone else had gone to bed, before sitting at the table in the quieted dining room to begin her studies. After graduating from Wichita University in 1942 with top grades, she won a scholarship to Syracuse University to study for a master's degree in government. Had she been born fifty years later, she might have become CEO of a major corporation. When she moved to Jerusalem in 1979, I urged her, only partly in jest, to become prime minister. After all, Milwaukee-born Golda Meir had done it. I told Hilda of my aspiration to be president and said, again mostly in jest, that we could negotiate for Israel and the United States as leaders of those two nations.

While studying at Syracuse, Hilda's heart and her preference for "Mrs." won out over her interest in an "M.S." when she caught a train to

San Francisco in April 1943 to marry Arthur, who was about to embark to the South Pacific in the anti-aircraft corps. The two had met when Arthur came to Wichita in 1941 from Fort Riley for Yom Kippur services, immediately noticing the attractive redhead who up to that time had preferred books to boys. After World War II they raised a model family in Russell before moving to Wichita, then to Denver, then to New York City, and finally to Jerusalem to give their four children the best possible Jewish education and life.

Hilda's advice about running on the Republican ticket was forceful: Do it!

So I agreed to run for district attorney as a Republican, maintaining my independence and my status as a registered Democrat. For me, the timing of the run was terrible. In early 1965, even without the run for DA, my hours were staggering. I was in the throes of the magistrates investigation, I was preparing a landmark product-liability case for trial, and I was saying kaddish every day for the year following my father's death.

Witkin, Meehan, and I kept my candidacy a secret while we prepared. It was amazing we were able to keep our plotting quiet so long. The day before my announcement in February 1965, word leaked to the *Philadelphia Daily News*. The paper ran a story that quoted Philadelphia County GOP Chairman Bill Devlin vehemently denying the rumor, saying he would certainly know if any such plan were afoot.

I decided to make the race. The announcement was planned at the Bellevue-Stratford Hotel, the nineteen-story, 556-room Taj Mahal of Philadelphia's political and social scene. I would debut at the maroon and red-leather Hunt Room, one of the restaurants at the French Renaissance palace. A Hunt Room inscription boasted that the Bellevue was a place "to wheel and deal . . . create heroes and defeat enemies . . . and select leaders and create followers." Meehan had arranged for Senator Hugh Scott to introduce me.

On the big day I arrived at the Bellevue early. I was walking down a corridor when I saw Senator Scott, my patron, coming the other way. I slowed my pace and awaited the senator's greeting. Scott breezed past me. He didn't know who I was.

A few minutes later, in a packed chamber, Meehan introduced me to Scott. Jim McDermott, the conservative 1963 mayoral candidate, almost lost his breakfast when I walked into the room and he realized that I, then a Democrat, was Meehan's choice. But McDermott rubber-stamped my candidacy, along with the rest of the nominating commit-tee, and the show went on. When the cameras and reporters had gath-ered, Scott threw his arm around me and proclaimed, "I want to recommend to you for the Republican nomination my old friend Arlen Specter." His old friend for almost a full hour.

I was doing what nobody else was brave—or foolish—enough to do: trying to unseat a party-backed Democratic incumbent in a Democratic town, while running as a Republican. Republicans had not won a DA's race since 1947. Echoing Dilworth's forecast of political doom, some of my closest friends implored me not to run. It wasn't man against machine, they said. It was man against Mars.

I was also fighting an accusation of betrayal. Democrats shouted "Benedict Arlen!" and "Judas!" But I had never taken an oath to the Democratic Party. I *had* taken an oath to the people of Philadelphia. I firmly believed that DA Jim Crumlish had shirked his responsibilities as the city's top law-enforcement officer. He had not cracked down on crime and corruption. I knew that Philadelphia needed tough law enforcement, and I thought I could deliver it.

PEDDLING CANTALOUPES
AND CANDIDACIES

I had never run for public office. Joan suggested Bob Kunzig as campaign manager. Kunzig was Senator Hugh Scott's chief of staff and a player in his own right in the Philadelphia scene and beyond. Kunzig, then forty-five, had been a Nuremberg prosecutor, winning the conviction of a Nazi officer at Buchenwald who supervised the making of lampshades from human skin, among other atrocities. In the Eisenhower administration, Kunzig had served as executive director of the Civil Aeronautics Board. In 1962 he had run for U.S. Senate in Minnesota, against a young man named Walter Mondale. Locally Kunzig had helped try Philadelphia's chief magistrate in 1948, and served from 1949 to 1953 as an assistant Pennsylvania attorney general. In 1964 Kunzig had run Scott's reelection campaign and preserved the moderate Republican against the Goldwater landslide.

I figured that a big Washington wheel like Bob Kunzig would never agree to run my DA campaign. But I indulged Joan, who invited him for dinner. From my point of view Joan and I were Mr. and Mrs. Joe Schnook. I didn't appreciate that the Philadelphia DA's race was a big deal for a lot of players, starting with the local Republican Party—including Hugh Scott, who was climbing toward Senate minority leader and was eager to rack up points by doing anything to strengthen the GOP, in Philadelphia and nationally.

Kunzig accepted Joan's invitation, and she picked him up at the North Philadelphia train station. Kunzig was hard to miss. He stood six-foot-two, weighed almost three hundred pounds, wore small horn-rimmed glasses, and combed his black hair straight back. Kunzig told Joan he was on a diet. Joan, a gourmet cook, served steak and grapefruit.

When it came to serving just the right thing for dinner, Joan had no peers. She studied cooking at the Cordon Bleu in London and at the Culinary Institute of America, ran several cooking schools, and eventually organized and operated a business that sold frozen candied apple walnut and chocolate mousse pies in forty states and wrote a food column for many years for the *Sunday Bulletin*. Early in our marriage she told me I could be fat or bald, but not both. Her wholesome cuisine kept my waistline in check, and my genes kept most of my hair intact.

When I went to Washington, with its notorious cocktail circuit, Joan advised me not to eat standing up, explaining if you took an hors d'oeuvre here and there, you would never realize how much you had eaten, but if you put them on a plate and sat down, you could quantify your consumption. Over the years I've come to agree with another of her original maxims: "We're going to run out of time before we run out of money." So we haven't turned down too many interesting opportunities over worries about funds. Our son Steve credits his mother with giving him especially sound advice when she told him, "I never learned anything when things were going well." While that might not be exactly correct, it is a good antidote to adversity. Some of the best lessons do come from the toughest problems.

Joan's advice on reaching out to Bob Kunzig proved to be a winner. After dinner Joan and I drove Kunzig to the Union League, the drawing room of Philadelphia Republican politics. Sitting in our 1955 Chevrolet convertible on Broad Street outside the Union League, the three of us talked for an hour and a half. It turned out that Kunzig was dying to manage my campaign. His ambition was to be a Philadelphia common pleas court judge, and he would do anything for Meehan, who could put him there. Ultimately Kunzig would do better, becoming a judge on the U.S. court of claims.

Scott agreed to lend me Kunzig and also lent me another of his top aides, his press secretary, Eugene Cowen. Cowen, a veteran newsman, was then forty, five years my senior. He was also quiet, in contrast to the blustery Kunzig.

Kunzig had a set speech for each new staffer who came aboard. "Look, if the candidate needs a widget, you go out and find a widget. If somebody throws up on the floor, you clean it up." The campaign staff followed Kunzig blindly, from a combination of awe and fear. He recruited the best and brightest. One of his gofers, Evan Dobelle, became president of Trinity College. Another, Russell Byers, was a featured columnist who was tragically stabbed to death by a robber in December 1999 outside a Wawa store in Philadelphia.

Meehan teamed me with Jim Cavanaugh, his candidate for city controller. The offices of DA and controller were up every four years, and the candidates often ran as a slate. Meehan needed an active Republican on his citywide ticket to balance me, his Democrat-registered DA candidate. Cavanaugh, thirty-three, fit the bill. He had run well for Congress against overwhelming odds in 1964 and was a Republican committeeman. Tall and trim, with thick, dark hair, Cavanaugh also looked the part. But he would be up against Alexander Hemphill, Philadelphia's tough and popular controller. Cavanaugh said he had no illusions. "I saw it as an opportunity for a young lawyer to run for the second or third highest office in the city."[1]

We printed letterhead and signs, CITIZENS FOR SPECTER & CAVANAUGH. I penned the slogan "Return to Reform" and wrote other slogans that saw less use, such as "Tough Sentences for Tough Criminals" and "Firm but Fair." Someone wrote a campaign jingle to the tune of "When the Saints Go Marching In": Philadelphia needs / A new DA / Philadelphia needs a new DA / And his name . . . is Arlen Specter / Philadelphia needs a new DA.

Billy Meehan constantly told me to simplify my language. In one speech I used the term "de minimis," referring to something I considered minor. "Look, Specter," Meehan said, exasperated, "you've got to start saying, 'It's a fish cake,' not 'de minimis.' "

Our strategy meetings at the Bellevue were serious business. Meehan dominated them. Physically, Bill was unimposing: short, slight, and asthmatic. But he was tough and shrewd. We discussed strategy and tactics, from sound trucks to sound bites. Every once in a while I would bring up public policy, and Meehan would say, "Cut it out, Specter. We don't want to know what you're going to do; we want to win this election." We always ate at Kugler's, on Chestnut Street near the Bellevue. One day I told Meehan we ought to eat someplace else. "We didn't run you to eat," Meehan said. "We ran you to win this election." We continued to eat at Kugler's.

Cavanaugh and I campaigned furiously, putting in far more than a thousand hours on the trail. Even though it was my first political run, I had prepared for a campaign, in a sense, from childhood. When I was five, my father sold cantaloupes door-to-door in the summer in Kansas.

My father, my sister Shirley, and I would pile into the front seat of his four-door Plymouth and drive to the Wichita market at 5:30 A.M. My father had removed the car's backseat, and we loaded the Plymouth with melons up to the rear window. The cantaloupes cost us a dollar a bushel. We sold melons eight inches in diameter three for a quarter. Six-inch melons sold four for a quarter. One day Shirley and I were rolling down the cantaloupes inside the car, having a grand time. My father caught us, and we got spanked. But usually we were serious workers.

We spent the days driving to neighboring towns and peddling our goods. We knocked door to door. For lunch we stopped at a grocery store, bought slices of lunch meat—a pink, processed, Spam-like amalgam—and white bread and made sandwiches. To this day I love lunch meat right off the slicing machine, mostly for the memories. On the road the local people fussed over us kids selling melons and were generally very nice. But the local grocers were not so kindly disposed, since we were taking their sales. They called the constables, who would run us out of town. So we'd climb into the Plymouth and hit the next town.

I got lessons in salesmanship by osmosis from my brother Morton, ten years my senior. Morton was a product of the Depression. He was the hardest worker I have ever seen, and 100 percent honest. On his tombstone I insisted on putting, HONEST, HARD-WORKING. Morton was always trying to make money, usually in nickels and dimes when I was a child. At seventeen, he would go to the Wichita golf course at night and wade the lakes, which were loaded with golf balls. I went with him a couple of times, mostly to swim. We would climb through a barbed-wire fence, trespass across the fairway, disrobe, and feel along the bottom of the ponds with our feet for lost golf balls. Morton would wash the balls and put them in glass jars of peroxide to bleach them brilliant white. He would then sell them at downtown office buildings.

A little over six feet tall and a slender 180 pounds, Morton was strikingly handsome. After graduating from college, he served as a Navy lieutenant in World War II. He found Officers Training School at Great Lakes tough, telling stories of studying after "lights out" by reading textbooks with a flashlight under his blanket when he was supposed to be sleeping.

Returning from the war, Morton sold magazines door to door. In June 1945 I joined him in Sioux Falls, South Dakota, to sell *Cosmopolitan, Good Housekeeping,* and *Liberty.* When he approached one house, a young girl ran excitedly inside shouting, "Mommy, Mommy, here comes Dennis Morgan!" referring to a famous movie actor. My first week, I made $225, which was pretty good for a fifteen-year-old kid more than fifty years ago.

Selling melons or magazines was like running for office, I found. Whether I was selling a product or myself, a lot of it was salesmanship. I knocked on doors all over town and shook endless hands, on trains, in stores, on street corners, and anywhere else I found them. We held street-corner rallies, in the style of Joe Clark and Dick Dilworth. Jim Cavanaugh and I would stand on a flatbed truck at a busy Center City intersection and urge passing pedestrians to support us. At first it was like jumping into an ice-cold pool. But people responded in a good-spirited way, and it almost became fun.

When I told Tom Dewey about the rallies when I visited him in late summer, he was astounded I would do such a thing. Frank Rizzo, the future mayor who was then a deputy police commissioner, used to tell me, "Mr. Specter, I saw your speech today, at Broad and Chestnut. It was really wonderful. You had that crowd in the palm of your hand—until the light changed." Rizzo used to kid me when he was a police captain and I was an assistant DA. He would put his arm around my shoulder and say, "That's a nice suit you have on. Too bad they didn't have one in your size." Or, "That's a nice suit you have on. Where did you get it shined?"

Joan hit the campaign trail with me most of the time. We recruited my mother to look after our sons. Joan softened my hard prosecutor image. People figured I couldn't be so hard if I had such a congenial and beautiful wife.

The May 20 Republican primary was a breeze. I was unopposed. It was hard enough for the Republicans to find someone to run at all, let alone someone to oppose the party choice. At 11:00 P.M. on May 19, the eve of the DA primary, my press secretary, Gene Cowen, phoned to say that if I could get to the polling place by seven the next morning, he could get me in the early edition of the *Philadelphia Bulletin.* Joan and I looked at each other and said simultaneously, "What do we do about the children?" It was too late to arrange for a baby-sitter, so we did the next best thing. We took them with us. Shanin at seven and Stephen at four were a big hit and thereafter a frequent addition to our campaign family. On schedule, we arrived at the polls shortly before 7:00 A.M. We were registered Democrats, but I suggested to Joan that she shouldn't vote in the Democratic primary, lest we be accused of trying to influence it. My recommendation was to vote just on the loan questions.

I went in and voted on the loan questions and also for judges who were on both tickets. Joan voted only on the loans. When she had made her choices, she pulled the lever but couldn't open the voting-booth curtains, no matter how hard she tugged. It turned out the machine had been designed not to open until at least one candidate's lever had been pulled. Voting only on the loans would not activate the exit lever.

Steve was alarmed at seeing his mother trapped in the voting booth. Finally Joan stepped through the gap where the curtains met and we had a happy, smiling family reunion before the newspaper cameras. The newspapers went to press, and by 9:00 A.M. on election day were on the newsstands with a big front-page family picture. By 10:00 A.M., I was in federal court to continue a trial for Pete Thompson, a soldier who'd had over half his body burned in a one-car auto accident. I had a soft spot in my heart for motor-vehicle product-liability cases, from the time a spindle bolt broke on my father's new Chevrolet pickup truck in 1937. The truck had rolled over my father's arm and crushed it. My father got a paltry five-hundred-dollar settlement and a permanently disabled arm. To this day I am livid about the way his lawyer handled the case. The Thompson jurors filed in with newspapers showing a picture of the smiling Specters. The defendants settled the case that day for a hundred thousand dollars, which was a big surprise to me. The smiling photo seemed to be more influential than the courtroom evidence.

Gradually the campaign's momentum grew. In June and July the weather had been hot, but the hands we shook were cold. Now at street corners and shopping centers, eyes that had once stared into shopping bags were making contact. The campaign pace was frenetic. We put in eighteen- and twenty-hour days. Volunteers whisked me from street walks to coffee klatches to speeches to debates. Volunteers and T-shirted "Specter girls" raced into beauty parlors ahead of me, shouting, "Come meet Philadelphia's next DA!"

I refused to write off any group. I wanted to bring out the African-American vote, which was not a traditional part of the Republican coalition. I was still a registered Democrat, which helped. And I had a lot to say to the African-American voter. Meehan said, "Specter, if you pull off a miracle, you'll get four out of ten. Forty percent. And no matter what you do, six are going to vote the other way. So the more you bring out, the more you lose." Meehan might have been right, but I went after every vote anyway.

Jim Cavanaugh and I did countless coffee klatches in living rooms throughout Philadelphia. Usually, we drew about fifteen people. On a good night we might draw twenty-two. Occasionally we got only seven or eight. One night at a Germantown home, only one guest showed. Undaunted, Cavanaugh gave his full forty-minute speech. That Germantown meeting was a milepost in my career, because no matter what has happened, I have never drawn a smaller crowd. To this day, as long as we make the maximum effort to get a crowd, I don't care how many people show up.

The DA race grew nasty at times. At one event I was beaned in the back of the head by a lush, ripe, red tomato that exploded on impact. Paraphrasing the Hallmark slogan, I thanked the man "for caring enough to throw the very best."

There was a heavy overhang of politics, if not worse, in Crumlish's DA's office. Crumlish gave his prosecutors license to handle cases as they liked, including plea-bargaining, dismissing tough cases, allowing continuances, and horse-trading with defense lawyers. Crumlish ran his 1965 campaign out of his DA's office, relying on a stable of part-time public relations men and Payola Palace regulars. At street-corner rallies, I blasted "The James Boys," James Tate and James Crumlish: "The mayor does nothing right, and the district attorney does nothing at all."

Americans for Democratic Action broke ranks and set up a parallel Democrats for Specter campaign. The ADA had spawned the Clark-Dilworth "Young Turks" Democratic reform movement a generation earlier and had never before endorsed a Republican for citywide office.

Our most successful television spot featured my program to crack down on rape. It opened showing a woman's legs walking along a dark city street. The legs walk, walk fast, then faster, faster still, and then break into a frantic run. With a criminal docket that left defendants charged with rape out on bail and on the street for months, the message hit home.

Other top Republicans pitched in. Governor Scranton arranged a brief meeting and photo op with former president Eisenhower. My appointment was at Eisenhower's office in Gettysburg. Eisenhower's aide ushered me in. The former president was at his desk. He was wearing plaid slacks and a plaid jacket, unmatched. His hair was a little whiter and thinner than it had been during his presidency, but otherwise he looked the same as his news photographs. He seemed relaxed and cordial. Even after his aide called him "General," I was still uncertain what to call him.

The aide told Eisenhower that here was a lawyer who could answer a legal question that had been troubling him. Eisenhower proceeded to complain to me about recent Supreme Court decisions that made it more difficult for police officers to question and search suspects. "Why are these goll-darn Supreme Court decisions coming out?" he asked. "Why doesn't Congress pass a law?"

Surprised that the ex-president thought Congress could pass a law to override a court decision on constitutional grounds, I explained that such a reversal would require a constitutional amendment. Eisenhower took it in. Then, still relaxed and chatty, he asked about the work of the Warren Commission and the chief justice's role as chairman. Eisenhower questioned whether it had been proper for Chief Justice Warren to serve on the commission.

Forgetting momentarily that I was speaking to a former president, the one who had appointed Earl Warren to the high court, I related Warren's rationale for taking the job. I went through the various officials who had in turn approached the chief justice, up to President Johnson himself, and detailed Johnson's request to Warren to serve his country in a time of crisis. Eisenhower grew impatient and scowled. "Warren did not have to do that. He is not under the president. If he were, I would have fired Warren a long time ago."

At the end of our talk, as a photographer clicked away, I showed Eisenhower a bound copy of the magistrates investigation report. Innocently, the former president said, "Yeah, this is like the story I read about an investigation of judges in Philadelphia."

For most of the campaign all signs showed I had little chance to topple Crumlish. It wasn't until roughly a month before the election that our polls showed me turning the corner. Presumably Crumlish's polls showed the same. The Saturday before the election, I heard that Senator Joe Clark wanted to talk to me. I was in Cheltenham at the north edge of the city, but I found a phone booth and called the white knight. "Arlen," the senator said, "I think you're going to win the election. Before you do anything after the election, come see me." I knew he meant a possible change in registration. I agreed to talk to him before doing anything.

Clark had promised his vote, but nothing more. Meanwhile, Billy Meehan had strained himself and never asked for anything. Meehan financed my entire campaign. He had raised $550,000, mainly through two dinners. In the spring, for a $25-a-plate affair, Meehan had crammed Convention Hall so full that he had to put the head table on the stage. The *Bulletin* ran a story, "Specters Dine with 4,000 New Friends." In the fall, when I was a better prospect, Meehan had raised the rest of the money through a $100-a-plate banquet.

The race went down to the wire. Some threatened tampering with voting machines, a standard Philadelphia ploy, proved critical. In the closing week of the campaign, we got word that the voting-machine levers were misaligned with the candidates' names. This meant that a voter who wanted to split his ticket, rather than pulling a straight party lever, would wind up voting for a candidate other than the one he intended. As we understood it, the candidate who lost out would be me.

My staff received permission to examine the machines. Kunzig dispatched Bob Moss, my driver and sound-truck man, to photograph the machines. The guard at the warehouse, saying he was following orders, refused to let Moss in. Within an hour I was at the warehouse, surrounded by the press. The guard still would not let us in, even waving his fist in my face, which made a terrific shot on the evening news.

I filed a lawsuit for an injunction, charging that Payola Palace was trying to steal the election for DA. I got heavy coverage during the final six days. The judge assigned to my suit turned out to be David Ullman, who had presided at my 1963 Philadelphia Teamsters trial. On the eve of the election, I presented my case about crooked voting levers to Ullman.

"Well, it is out of line," the judge agreed after inspecting a voting machine, "and the only thing to do is alert the voters." With television crews lined up outside his City Hall chambers, Ullman adjusted his glasses under his long forehead, straightened his three-piece suit, and said into the cameras that he had looked into it and the voting machines were indeed misaligned. But rather than printing all the ballots again, Ullman said, he was just going to advise the voters, if they want to vote for Arlen Specter for district attorney, be sure to look very carefully at Line 23.

Now I had a judge on every Philadelphia TV station telling people the night before the election how to vote for me. Ironically, it turned out

155

that the voting machines were not misaligned after all. When the machines were anchored and opened at the polling places, the levers came down a fraction of an inch, into perfect alignment.

Crumlish, for his final barrage, ran a TV spot of me calling him a good district attorney. I had made the remark on a television show in January, at a time when I was still hoping for the Democratic nod if the party bosses either promoted Crumlish to the federal bench or dumped him. At the time the comment had seemed a safe and simple gesture. Crumlish played that quote heavily in various neighborhoods the weekend before the election. His sound trucks blared, "Listen to what Arlen Specter says! Listen to what Arlen Specter says! Jim Crumlish is a good DA." But all that many people heard was "Listen to Arlen Specter," which drove up my name recognition.

The night before the election, while Judge Ullman was telling Philadelphia how to vote for me, we ran a thirty-minute TV spot on Channel 6. A half-hour spot, oddly, cost only about $3,000 at 7:00 P.M. Frank Gifford, the football star later turned announcer, narrated. We did a rehearsal and two takes. At one point we trotted out my sons, Shanin and Steve, and Cavanaugh's son Mark. In turn each boy was asked what he wanted to be when he grew up. A lawyer, Shanin said. A lawyer, Mark said. "I don't know," Steve said. Steve, then almost five, was displaying an early independent streak. In the second rehearsal, the same thing: "A lawyer." "A lawyer." "I don't know." Finally, on the live round, Steve said, "A lawyer." We all broke up. It was only a momentary lapse. Steve is now a professor with a Ph.D. in nutrition.

When the votes were counted, I beat Crumlish 52.5–47.5 percent. Thousands of Democrats crossed over to vote for me. On election night Senator Scott and I went to the ADA's suite at the Bellevue-Stratford. The portly senator climbed onto a table and gave the ADA much credit for my win. SPECTER BREAKS MACHINE'S HOLD AT HALL, the *Bulletin* screamed in a banner headline.

It was an exhilarating experience to win that election. I felt great. Looking back at the photos, I didn't realize I could smile that broadly. I would have to remember that victory and my 1969 reelection during the following decade-long losing streak.

Shortly after the election I went to see Senator Clark, as I had promised. "I really admire what you've done," Clark said. "I just hope you don't become a Republican."

"Senator Clark," I said, "up until this minute I hadn't made up my

156

mind. But now I have." As ungenerous as Clark had been, it took a lot of nerve to say I shouldn't change parties. Billy Meehan, on the other hand, broke his back for our victory and didn't say anything. Maybe Bill was just smarter about getting his way, knowing my idiosyncrasies.

A month later, in December, after getting the okay from my sister Hilda, I officially changed my party registration to Republican. Clark, Payola Palace, Meehan, and Witkin all played a part in the decision. I also wanted to bring back a second major party to Philadelphia. The city needed it.

GUARDIANS AT THE GATES OF HELL

My shoes clicked against marble, the taps echoing in the vast lobby, as I entered Philadelphia City Hall at 8:30 A.M. on January 3, 1966, three and a half hours before I was to be sworn in as district attorney. On the sixth floor, I passed through a great oak doorway to Room 666, beneath a gold DISTRICT ATTORNEY sign. The complex was deserted. The huge paneled chamber where Richardson Dilworth had plotted his early reforms, where Vic Blanc had hung his service club certificates, where James Crumlish had ruled for almost five years, was now mine. I marveled at the orderly transition of power in a democracy. I thought how much different the transition would be in a dictatorship. But there it was. Crumlish was gone. It was my office. I just walked in and took over.

At noon I was sworn in by Governor Scranton, in a grand ceremony at the office of the city council president. Mayor Tate was in the audience. City Hall had been buzzing with rumors that Tate was going to resign rather than face indictment now that I had been installed as DA. The *Observer* had even run a front-page story on the prospect. While I knew the rumor was untrue, it set a curious tone between the mayor and me on the day I took office.

Joining me on the stage were Joan, in a beautiful red plaid suit and pillbox hat; Scranton; and Attorney General Walter Alessandroni. Scranton had run for president the previous year, losing the Republican nomination to Barry Goldwater. Alessandroni had done nothing to hide his own ambitions for the governor's mansion. He might have made it, if he had not died in a plane crash later that year. One newspaper featured my inauguration in its "Politi-Comics." The four of us were standing on the podium as I took the oath. The other three were all looking at me, with thought clouds above their heads. Scranton's thought cloud said, "If he thinks he's going to be president before me, he's crazy." Alessandroni's cloud said, "If he thinks he's going to be governor before me, he's crazy." Joan's cloud said, "If he thinks he's going to be late for dinner again tonight, he's crazy."

I got no formal transition from Crumlish and needed none. I brought a sense of outrage and urgency to the district attorney's office. Assembling my team was the first order of business. Of Crumlish's fifty-one assistants, I kept about a third, fired or immediately accepted resignations from a third, and eased out the remaining third in a transition over the coming weeks and months. I made it a point to resolve all doubts in favor of his assistants, even when it was difficult and costly. I honored Crumlish's commitment to Emmett Fitzpatrick, his first assistant, for six months of accrued vacation time. If the institution had made a promise to an individual, I felt obliged to honor it. I left Fitzpatrick on the payroll until mid-June, which kept me from hiring my own first assistant until then. Many of Crumlish's assistants eventually became state court judges. The common pleas courts were a refuge for political lawyers.

I hired bright, ambitious young talent. Many went far in the office and far after they left. Three of my assistants have become district attorney themselves: Lynn Abraham, the current DA; Ron Castille, now a Pennsylvania supreme court justice; and Edward Rendell, later a two-term mayor and now chairman of the Democratic National Committee. Oscar Goodman is mayor of Las Vegas. Paul Michel is a U.S. court of appeals judge. Three have become U.S. Attorneys. Two have become university presidents. Many have become state court judges. Legions of my former prosecutors became top private attorneys.

As my first assistant, I named Dick Sprague, the former homicide division chief. Sprague was a courtroom master. He had never lost a first-degree murder case in sixty prosecutions, and he never would. The cops called Sprague "the police department's attorney." They phoned him immediately and incessantly, no matter the hour, about any homicide or for legal advice generally. Sprague had a police radio in his car.

I hired on merit and professionalized the office. No more clearance from ward leaders for jobs. In fact, no questions about political affiliation. Under the new regime all prosecutors worked full-time. I raised their salaries to give them full-time pay for full-time work.

Rendell credits me for bringing "more dramatic and more radical change than Clark and Dilworth brought to overall city government in the 1950s." Rendell recently recalled that in December 1973, when I was leaving the DA's office and Rendell was my chief of homicide, we ran into each other at the elevator one evening. "Eddie, you decided what you're going to do?" I asked him.

"Yeah, Arlen, I'm going to leave the office and open up my own practice. I'm also going to try to get active in politics."

"Great," I said. "I think you'd be a natural for politics. I'd be happy to give Billy Meehan a call for you."

"Thanks very much, Arlen," Rendell said, "but there's only one problem: I'm a Democrat."

Rendell told my aide, "I had served for seven years for the man, held one of the six or seven most important positions in the DA's office, and he never knew what party I was registered in. Never knew."[1]

I also never asked Lynn Abraham about her registration when she came to see me about an assistant DA job in 1966. Lynn was and is a Democrat. I didn't ask about politics, and I didn't weigh personal factors like religion. I knew what it was like to suffer prejudice. My lessons on discrimination had begun in the late 1930s, when my father sat glued to his radio listening to the news. Harry Specter agonized as he heard about the Nazis overrunning Russia, including the Ukrainian village of Batchkurina, where he had grown up and his family still lived. He knew that his relatives, like all other Jews in Hitler's way, would not survive the onslaught. Most of my father's eight siblings died in the Holocaust.

On a 1982 trip to the Soviet Union, I found my father's village. None of the villagers, including the mayor, said they had heard of the Specter family. I asked the mayor to locate the oldest man or woman in Batchkurina. He produced a wizened, eighty-two-year-old hunchback, under five feet tall, wearing thick glasses. I told the man that my grandfather had been a student and that he and my father had picked fruit in the summer.

"No, no, no, I don't know anything about your family," said the man, who obviously didn't want to be bothered. It dawned on me to tell him that my father's family had been the only Jewish family in the village. The man looked up and said, "Oh! Avram the Jew." Avram was my grandfather's name, but I had not mentioned it. That's what it was like being a Jew in Russia. My grandfather had died in the famine of 1922, sixty years earlier, but this man still remembered Avram the Jew.

Growing up Jewish in Kansas in the 1930s and 1940s, I knew I was different. In second and third grades, the school prayers naming Jesus

160

Christ made a deep impression. I wasn't intimidated. My reaction was to assert my Jewishness and to be proud of it. Years later, when the Senate considered a constitutional amendment to reinstate school prayer, I thought of my own experience in grade school and felt that children of different faiths should not be subjected to others' prayers. I told President Reagan of my childhood experiences and my personal views when I was invited to the White House with three other Republican senators as a vote was nearing on the amendment. Reagan, as always, was gracious. He expressed his views in a low-key way. He listened to me and to the other senators and countered by saying that school prayers he had heard growing up in Illinois were a source of strength and aid to him. The amendment vote failed.

The prayer issue came up again in the Senate, where the Wednesday prayer breakfast was a long-standing tradition. Early in my Senate career I attended one of the 8:00 A.M. breakfasts and found no other Jewish senator in attendance. That surprised me, because we had had quite a few Jewish senators. I jokingly refer to our having a *minyan* in the Senate, which means at least ten Jews, the minimum number for a prayer service. From time to time it had been necessary to count Barry Goldwater or Bill Cohen, who were half Jewish, or Dianne Feinstein and Barbara Boxer, even though women don't qualify under some interpretations of Jewish law.

I became a quasi-regular at the prayer breakfasts, with only morning squash standing between me and full-fledged membership in the group. I found the meetings meaningful. Senators would share personal experiences and private feelings in a way unmatched by any other Senate activity and, for that matter, by any other meetings I have ever attended.

When my first turn came to deliver the "sermon," I spoke about biblical passages blaming the Jews for the crucifixion of Jesus and about the bigotry, hatred, and violence those passages have spurred. I told my fellow senators of the many incidents of people citing those passages as they beat up Jewish boys. I told them about my own experience of being called a "Christ killer." My colleagues found the situation hard to believe.

At one prayer breakfast then-Senator Al Gore closed the meeting by reciting a prayer referring to "Our Lord and Savior Jesus Christ." When he had finished, Al walked over to me and said, "When I was giving the prayer referencing Jesus Christ, I just wondered how that made you feel and whether you were in any way offended by it." I replied that I could understand the reason for the reference, but thought it better, in the spirit of ecumenism, to omit the reference in the presence of Jews or others with different religious views. Gore said he understood and would not repeat the reference.

Several months later Gore was again called upon for the concluding prayer. And again he closed in the name of "our Lord and Savior Jesus Christ." When he was nearly done, Gore looked over at me and clapped his hand against his forehead, realizing his repeat faux pas. He then walked over to me and we shook hands, and he again promised never to repeat his mistake. Unfortunately—or perhaps fortunately, certainly for Al Gore—he became vice president, left the Senate, and has never attended another prayer breakfast, at least with me present, so he had no further opportunity for recidivism.

Shortly after coming to Washington in 1981, distinguished biblical scholar Naomi Rosenblatt, whose husband, Peter, attended Yale Law with me, told me there were many Bible-study groups on Capitol Hill, but none on the Old Testament. I said I would be delighted to host an Old Testament Bible class if Naomi would lend her leadership and expertise. She agreed, and we began sessions that have lasted more than a decade. Naomi uses the Old Testament to explore timeless dilemmas and conflicts that confront all of us in our personal and professional lives, including those of us in Washington trying to lead the nation. We've applied the Ten Commandments to such issues as genetic engineering, individual privacy in the age of technology and communication, and the right to die.

Through Naomi's gentle guidance and sometimes firm hand, we learn as much from each other as from her. Our group includes Republicans and Democrats, lawmakers and judges, spouses and children, offering a range of perspectives and insights. Regulars have included Senators Strom Thurmond, David Durenberger, Larry Pressler, Al D'Amato, Howard Metzenbaum, Bill Bennett, and Bill Armstrong. Some Senate wives attended, including Lynda Johnson Robb and Joyce Bennett. Armstrong was a regular until he and Metzenbaum got into a heated exchange. Armstrong said that the Bible should be taken literally. Metzenbaum raised his eyebrows and expressed surprise that anybody could believe that. Perhaps that clash highlights the old warning against discussing religion and politics.

My first confrontation occurred in 1981 when I heard Senator Fritz Hollings call Metzenbaum "the senator from B'nai B'rith" during floor debate. Surprised that Metzenbaum uttered no protest, I walked over to Hollings and gave him notice that I thought his comment was out of line and intended to say so on the Senate floor. I did just that.

Later that day I was asked by Majority Leader Howard Baker to join Metzenbaum and Hollings in agreeing to delete the colloquy from the *Congressional Record*. Only with the agreement of all senators who participated could such an exchange be expunged. Metzenbaum urged me to go along because he was up for reelection in 1982 and did not want publicity that might stir up an anti-Semitic reaction. He attributed a prior defeat to an election-eve TV program that publicized the fact that he was Jewish.

Very reluctantly, I agreed to strike the exchange, but only on the condition that the *Congressional Record* note there had been a deletion without any indication of what it was. Years later, when I joined a floor debate siding with Senator John Danforth, who was in a heated argument with Hollings, Hollings referred to his "senator from B'nai B'rith" remark. I do not believe Senator Hollings intended to be disrespectful to B'nai B'rith or Jews. But from my perspective, it was an inappropriate remark and I told him so to give him my perspective in an effort to influence him not to repeat such comments. Despite these incidents, Hollings and I have had a collegial relationship over the years, co-sponsoring many bills.

If I felt apart as the only Jew at a Senate prayer breakfast, I felt even more apart when I was twelve and our family moved to Russell, Kansas, where we were the only Jewish family in town. While I lived in Russell, from eighth grade through high school and the following three summers, I had only one fistfight, after a slightly drunk schoolmate uttered a religious slur.

When the time came to go to college, there were no Jewish fraternities at the University of Kansas, where my entire clique of close friends went. I enrolled instead at the University of Oklahoma, which did have a Jewish fraternity, Pi Lambda Phi. In the spring of 1948, we Pi Lams were reminded we were Jewish when a huge swastika was painted on our front sidewalk.

I told Penn State football coach Joe Paterno about the swastika incident during my 1998 election cycle when he was my featured speaker at a Pittsburgh fund-raiser. He then told me of an incident involving anti-Semitism when he was an undergrad at Brown at about the same time. A Jewish student who aspired to be in Paterno's fraternity applied for admission after being blackballed twice. Again a single blackball appeared when the basket was passed among the members. At that point Paterno said he jumped up and said, "That's my blackball. I've changed my mind, and I want to withdraw it." Unwilling to face up to his prejudice, the culprit said nothing, and the fraternity had a new member.

Paterno's sense of humor was displayed in 1983 after he testified at a Senate Judiciary Committee hearing on the threat to college football by the signing of Herschel Walker by the New York Generals before he finished his college eligibility at Georgia. Paterno, noted for his coal-black hair, unusual for someone his age, was accompanied by two younger, gray-haired assistant coaches from Penn State. After the hearing I jokingly asked, "Coach, how come your hair is so black and your younger assistants are gray?"

"Well, Senator," he replied, "it's like it was with Vince Lombardi. Everybody around him had ulcers; but not Vince. He was asked a similar question—why everyone around had ulcers, but not him. 'It's simple,' Lombardi explained, 'I'm a carrier.' Same thing with me, Senator," Paterno concluded. "I'm a carrier."

In the fall of 1948 I transferred to Penn because I wanted to live at home, unlike most college students. I wished to spend as much time as possible with my father, who talked a lot about dying. Life in Philadelphia was different. While everyone knew everyone else and everyone else's business in Russell, my family didn't know the neighbors more than three or four doors away in Philadelphia. One of my first impressions was that everyone in Russell was accountable, while almost everyone in Philadelphia was anonymous.

There were, of course, many Jews in the big city of so-called brotherly love. There was a subtle sense of anti-Semitism, but it sort of went with the territory—there was also an aura of bigotry against Catholics and various ethnic groups, especially African-Americans.

As a prelaw student at Penn, I heard how tough it was for young Jewish lawyers to get started in the legal profession. The old-line white-shoe law firms had policies against hiring Jews. There were two big firms that took the cream of the Jewish law school graduates. It was much tougher for African-Americans. Future transportation secretary William Coleman, a top Harvard Law graduate and clerk for Justice Felix Frankfurter, couldn't find a suitable job in Philadelphia and commuted to New York, where he found a position with a major firm.

As an undergraduate at Penn, I was concerned how I would break the ice in this rigid, tough city. In Pennsylvania a law student had to have a "preceptor," an established lawyer to guide him on ethics and protocol. In order to qualify for admission to the bar, the aspiring attorney had to serve a six-month preceptorship after graduating from law school, usually with little or no pay. It was close to involuntary servitude. In the spring of 1951, when I first saw the notice with that requirement posted on the Penn bulletin board, I wondered how I would qualify. I didn't know any lawyers, and neither did my parents. I discussed the matter with my father, who discussed it with his brother, who took it up with the local state senator, Maxwell Rosenfeld, who arranged for his allegedly less busy partner, Hirsch Stalberg, to add me to his list of preceptees. Stalberg made it plain that his law firm was making no commitment to hire me or even to take my services free for six months. When I later told Stalberg I planned to work at a Denver firm the summer before my third year of law school, he said that being almost a "Philadelphia lawyer" would seem prestigious in what he considered the hinterlands. Most Philadelphia lawyers like to think of the term "Philadelphia lawyer" as signifying extraordinary talent, but people beyond the city limits often take a derisive tone when using the expression.

I'm pretty sure it was because I was Jewish that I didn't get a permanent job offer at the Denver law firm, where I worked for thirty-five dollars a week in the summer of 1955. I can't prove it, but the signs were unmistakable. The partners apparently didn't know I was Jewish when they enthusiastically hired me as a summer associate and praised my work. Then they found out and immediately lost interest in me. The firm was expanding and hiring in 1956. My law school record at Yale opened doors just about anywhere. One of the firm's senior partners tried to let me down easy at the end of my summer stint, telling me not to count on getting a permanent job at that firm. Although it was not stated, religion was the obvious reason.

One of the qualifications for admission to the Pennsylvania bar was to establish "good character." I was instructed to make an appointment with the Bar Association's representative, an establishment lawyer named John Archer. That meeting still rankles, nearly fifty years later. Archer essentially wanted to know how a young potentially shyster Jewish lawyer would support himself at the Philadelphia bar without paying runners to drum up business or engaging in other unethical practices. I answered Archer's question more assertively than I've answered

165

any other question before or since. I told him that since I had graduated Phi Beta Kappa at Penn, and was on the law journal and near the top of my class at Yale, I expected no trouble finding a good job such as clerking for a U.S. Supreme Court justice. Somehow I passed Archer's test. I did not seek or get a Supreme Court clerkship, but I have managed a professional career without anyone thinking me—or at least calling me—a "shyster."

During my final year at law school, Yale graduates were in demand. Law firms from all over the country came for interviews. I decided to ask early in each interview whether the firm hired Jews. While none denied it, the absence of a single Jewish lawyer in so many of those forty- or fifty-lawyer firms made the policy clear. When I asked the two representatives of the prestigious Philadelphia firm of Barnes, Dechert, Price, Myers and Rhoads whether the firm hired Jews, they answered simultaneously. One said, "Of course we do." The other said, "We've never considered that." Neither reply was accurate. Dechert had no Jews among its forty lawyers. The firm did hire Norma Levy Shapiro, later a federal judge, and me at about the same time in December 1955. Once I joined the firm, they couldn't have cared less where I attended religious services but were concerned only with my work product.

There would be no ethnic or religious litmus tests in my DA shop. I recruited at the nation's top law schools and at the best local schools. I raided the top Philadelphia law firms for young talent. I asked the senior partners to lend me a junior associate for a couple of years. I would get sharp young go-getters, and in two years the firms would get back their young associates with more trial experience under their belts than the firms' senior trial partners. These young lawyers came to be called "lend-leasers."

I offered my prospects the chance for intensive trial work and public service in an office that emphasized community service and crime prevention, in addition to tough criminal prosecutions. The lure of the DA's office was weakened by our low salaries. At that time the large New York firms raised their starting salaries to $15,000, and Philadelphia firms fell in line with initial packages of $13,500. By contrast, the starting salary in the DA's office was $6,277. I wrote an article for *The Shingle*, the Philadelphia Bar Association magazine, essentially as a help-wanted ad. "To become an assistant district attorney today, it is not a matter of who you know, but what you know," I wrote. "Ability and vigor are the sole qualifications for appointment."

In all, I reviewed more than five hundred résumés to hire some thirty-five assistants. Among my first hires were two honors Harvard Law grads from top Philadelphia firms, Alan Davis and Martin Heckscher. Mike Baylson and Mike Rotko, Penn Law grads, were also among that first group. Both later became distinguished U.S. Attorneys.

It was not always so easy. At Pepper, Hamilton and Sheetz, another top Philadelphia firm, I called on the managing partner, Ernest Scott, and asked for an assistant for my office. Scott said he could not afford to give up anybody. I told Scott, "I'm thirty-five years old, I've just been elected district attorney, the toughest job in town, especially with Jim Tate as mayor. I need one of your young lawyers to help me." Scott insisted that he couldn't spare anybody. I went away empty-handed. Ironically, Scott's son David joined my office a few years later.

I taught a course in prosecution at the University of Pennsylvania Law School, principally to draft law students to help with DA issues. For example, I had one student analyze statutory rape cases. Should it be statutory rape if a man is sixteen years and one day old and has sex with a woman a day shy of sixteen? I was also interested in the power structure. If a thirty-year-old man has sex with a fifteen-year-old girl and uses no force, does the disparity in their power relationship make the act implicitly coercive? Another student reviewed our many cases involving barroom killings in which liquor was a significant factor. I wanted to establish review standards to distinguish genuine manslaughter cases from self-defense to ease the trial load from our five hundred homicides each year. I later taught a seminar at Temple Law School under an arangement with Dean Peter Liacouris, later the university president, who had worked as a special assistant in my office. The students got nine hours of credit, almost a full semester course, to help our limited staff with its heavy caseload in criminal court.

My understanding with Bill Meehan that I would owe no patronage did not preclude Meehan from suggesting people. Generally he sent me good prospects. I hired them when they fit in. For detectives, he sent me a crop of fine young police officers who were prepared to work hard. Once Meehan sent me a prosecutor prospect who had a serious speech defect. It was a tough impediment for a trial lawyer. No, I told Billy. He did not argue. That young man had a great legal career, but not in the courtroom.

Police Captain Clarence Ferguson, the noted and notorious head of the vice squad, wanted to be my chief of detectives. "Fergie" wore a porkpie hat and had lots of contacts. He was rumored to have taken so much graft that he and his men were known as "Ali Baba and the Forty Thieves." I talked with Ferguson and then–Deputy Police Commissioner Frank Rizzo one day at a party in South Philadelphia. Rizzo looked Ferguson in the eye: "Fergie, you're going to die, and before you die, I want to know where it's [the alleged graft] buried. Fergie, just tell me where it's buried." Fergie smiled, said nothing, denied nothing. I did not appoint Clarence Ferguson my chief of detectives.

The DA's office buzzed with optimism, excitement, and hope, guided by a vision of government as an engine of justice. "It was the mid-sixties, and there was a lot of enthusiasm for change, optimism which spilled over from Kennedy's ideas to the Great Society," said Alan Davis, waxing nostalgic recently. The civil rights movement was booming, the Supreme Court had issued a spate of rulings expanding individual rights, and while troop levels were escalating in Vietnam, disillusionment had not yet set in. "There was a feeling of ferment in the criminal justice system. It could be changed, made better, made an engine for social improvement," Davis said. Criminal justice reform was at the nexus of social change, and the Philadelphia district attorney's office was at the forefront of criminal justice reform. My prosecutors came to work excited about prosecuting the crimes on their lists, and excited about contributing to social reform on a grand scale.

"I've often said that Arlen inspired in us the belief that we were the last guardians outside the gates of hell," Rendell said. "And it was on our shoulders that the city of Philadelphia rested. If we didn't do our job, the city was gong to slip right into those gates of hell. That inspired me to tremendous nonstop hours of work, tremendous dedication, and tremendous sense of esprit."

"We felt like young Eliot Nesses," recalled Mike Baylson, a lend-leaser who later became my homicide chief. The day I hired Baylson, a *Daily News* reporter phoned his home, got Mike's father, and asked if Mike was a registered Democrat. Baylson's father said, "Yes, but he'll switch." I told Mike he didn't have to. He didn't.

Among my initial hires, I brought on Paul Dandridge, then thirty-nine, an African-American former schoolteacher and bartender. Dandridge had just passed the bar and was working as an investigator at the Philadelphia Commission of Human Relations, focusing on discrimination in the building trades. Dandridge's interview was not one of my

168

smoothest. I asked him where he had finished in his class, a question I routinely ask job applicants to this day. "At the bottom," Dandridge said. "Where do you think? I was working fifty to sixty hours a week." I asked Dandridge why he wanted to become an assistant DA. He said he wasn't sure he *did* want to become one. Then he became the interviewer and I became the interviewee. I liked that. At the end of our talk, we both said we would think about it. Eventually we decided to give each other a chance. Dandridge had never been in a courtroom. Within three months he was trying and winning rape cases. Within a year he was one of my top deputies.

I reached out vigorously to the African-American community, for both assistant DAs and detectives. Dandridge helped. I wanted greater representation by minorities, to generate confidence in the system. The minority community, often with good reason, felt disenfranchised and isolated. There were so many African-American defendants and so few African-American lawyers, judges, or assistant DAs. I personally phoned many of the approximately five hundred members of the African-American lawyers' association and asked each of them to send me as many prosecutor prospects as they could.

"There was a general sense within the black bar in the late 1960s and [early] seventies, not only could you get a fair opportunity to work in the DA's office, but you had a fair chance once you got there," said H. Patrick Swygert, now president of Howard University, who spent the summer of 1973 as a special assistant DA. "It gave black staff the professional sense you were involved in something, and you did not have to have a particular political pedigree, nor a school pedigree, nor did you have to have a racial pedigree—but you had to be good."[2]

I also hired more women. The *Philadelphia Bulletin* ran a profile on the first female assistant I hired, a Yale Law graduate. The story was headlined, GILLIAN GILHOOL—PRETTY PROSECUTOR. Gilhool's husband, Tom, still kids me that Gillian was my token woman and Dandridge my token African-American, among my first ten hires. "But that was amazing for 1965," Gillian said recently. "There weren't even any tokens back then." As my hiring progressed, our annual photos showed many women and African-Americans.

In that era women were even sentenced differently from men. Women, like the mentally incapacitated, were given indeterminate terms. We changed that in the *Jane Daniels* case, shortly after I took office. Daniels was convicted of robbery in May 1966 and given an indeterminate term in the state prison. Daniels appealed, arguing that her open term made an unconstitutional distinction between men and women. I agreed with her. Along with Alan Davis, I appeared before the superior court to concede an error, which was heresy for a district attorney. But I thought the statute was unconstitutional, and I said so. I took very seriously the legal proposition that I was a quasi-judicial official—part advocate, part judicial—and should not prosecute cases or support rulings I considered unjust.

The judges disagreed with me, and the case was appealed to state supreme court. I notified Israel Packel, state attorney general. There is a strong presumption of the constitutionality of statutes, and the commonwealth's attorney was supposed to defend those statutes. Packel took over the appeal on behalf of the commonwealth and argued to keep indeterminate sentences for women. In its opinion the state supreme court noted, "Philadelphia District Attorney Arlen Specter has filed a candid and persuasive brief in support of the conclusion that the Muncy Act is unconstitutional. He offers the following exerpt from the work of a leading criminologist of fifty years ago to illustrate the philosophy underlying the statute:

> There is little doubt in the minds of those who have had much experience in dealing with women delinquents, that the fundamental fact is that they belong to the class of women who lead sexually immoral lives. . . . [Such a statute] would remove permanently from the community the feeble-minded delinquents who are now generally recognized as a social menace, and would relieve the state from the ever increasing burden of the support of their illegitimate children. Furthermore . . . such a policy, thoroughly carried out, would do more to rid the streets . . . of soliciting, loitering, and public vice than anything that could be devised. There is nothing the common prostitute fears so greatly as to know that if she offends and is caught, she will be subject to the possibility of prolonged confinement.

I found it patently unjust to base indeterminate sentences on that Neanderthal rationale. The state supreme court agreed and abolished the open sentences.

My high-spirited assistants often clashed, occasionally in open court. Richie Phillips, who became the controversial head of the baseball umpires' union, and Ed Rendell, later heralded as "America's mayor" and now chairman of the Democratic National Committee, were involved in an incident in a homicide courtroom one day that almost led to both being fired. Phillips asked a defense lawyer, Milton Leidner, for a loan for lunch money. Rendell, seeing Leidner hand Phillips a twenty-dollar bill in open court, shouted, "Bribe!" A few minutes later my chief deputy burst into my office urging the immediate firing of Rendell. I listened patiently, more amused than concerned, and then commented that they deserved firing about equally. I finally decided that the office should not lose either of those young tigers and kept them both on.

Sometime later I reluctantly came to a different conclusion as to Phillips because of a situation that involved a cardinal rule in the office barring assistants from engaging in the private practice of law. That had been a major problem for my two immediate predecessors, Blanc and Crumlish, and I was determined to avoid it. I extended the prohibition against any outside practice of law to myself as well. Long after the twenty-dollar incident, Phillips told me he wanted to go into private practice and needed to represent athletes as a transition to leaving the DA's office. Notwithstanding my strict policy against moonlighting, we worked out an arrangement where Richie could have private clients as long as he was not an attorney of record. I permitted some flexibility when someone like Richie Phillips intended to return to private practice in the reasonably near future and needed some opportunity for transition. But I did not want him out front as an attorney of record where he might spend too much time and set a bad example for others. One Saturday afternoon I bought the early edition of the *Sunday Bulletin*, as I customarily did, to check for stories I might want to answer for a later edition. I sat in my den and noted a front-page story that Phillips had represented Howard Porter, a famous basketball player, in signing a pro contract. As I was reading the article, the phone rang. It was Phillips. "Hi, boss, how are you?" he asked.

"Okay, Richie, how are you?" I asked. "I'm glad you called. I want to talk to you."

"Well, what's it about, boss?" he asked.

"Well, it's your nickel, Richie."

"No, you go first."

"Okay, Richie, you're fired."

Richie Phillips remains colorful. *Time* magazine featured him in an August 1999 "Winners and Losers" column after his attempt to beat a major league no-strike clause blew up. Phillips had all the umpires submit letters of resignation, which the leagues surprised the umps by accepting. *Time*'s comment: "Umps say their attorney is 'too confrontational'—this from guys used to being spat on." Richie was also a confrontational assistant district attorney, and a good one.

THE SLIDING SCALE OF JUSTICE

Near the top of my agenda as the new district attorney was to prosecute the magistrates I had investigated in 1964 and 1965. I decided to personally try the cases until I convicted a magistrate. Then I would let my staff handle the rest.

By breeding a pervasive disdain for the law, the magistrates had done more to boost crime in Philadelphia than had any criminal brought before them. At best, defendants in magistrates court faced callous rudeness. More often they faced demands for payoffs under threats of serious indictments. Most magistrates preyed on the vulnerable, especially the poor, minorities, and homosexuals. No laws had been written against some of their tactics. The architects of the court system had not imagined such abuses.

I prosecuted the first case against Ruth Marmon, a plump, matronly magistrate, and her clerk, Joseph Bardascino. *Time* magazine called Marmon "an iceberg of corruption."[1] The Marmon-Bardascino case began in August 1963, when police found a slip of paper scribbled with thirty-four illegal lottery plays in a cellar hallway while searching an apartment house. That was more plays than anybody would play on his own. The paper's owner had to be a numbers writer, not a player. A resident, Andrew Crittenden, was arrested. Crittenden's committeeman, John Welsh, who was also a state representative, was enlisted as Crittenden's advocate. Welsh waited for Marmon outside the local police court and pleaded with the magistrate to discharge Crittenden.

"A hundred dollars or a thousand dollars' bail," Marmon said. In other words, either Crittenden could pay her a hundred-dollar bribe on the spot to dismiss the case, or he'd be held for trial on a thousand dollars' bail. If Crittenden chose to fight, he'd have to pay a bondsman a hundred dollars to post a thousand dollars' bail. Welsh relayed Marmon's position to Crittenden. All he and his neighbors could come up with was fifty dollars. Welsh wound up paying Bardascino fifty dollars on the spot and fifty dollars the next Monday. Marmon dismissed the case.

I learned of the episode from a ward leader in whom Welsh had confided. We had to give Welsh immunity to get him to testify. We indicted Marmon and Bardascino on charges of bribery, extortion, and conspiracy. After some legal challenges, including an attempt to have one of my deputies indicted for witness tampering, Marmon and her clerk went to trial in March 1966.

Marmon arrived in court in a black dress with white lace collar and cuffs, leading her nine-year-old daughter by the hand. Looking every bit the widow, she wore no makeup and had her black hair pulled back in a bun. "She is a woman inexperienced in the duties of a magistrate and needed help," Marmon's lawyer told the jury. Shortly after the trial began, as the *Inquirer*'s Karafin described it, "Suddenly Mrs. Marmon's body was racked with sobs. She put a handkerchief to her eyes and cried audibly. Hearing this, Bardascino started to sob. He removed his glasses and dabbed at his streaming eyes with a handkerchief. The emotional display continued for some 10 minutes."

Marmon and Bardascino both testified that they had not known Welsh and had never spoken to him. The entire case rested on Welsh's testimony. The jury had to decide who was telling the truth: Welsh testified under immunity that he had paid Marmon and Bardascino a hundred dollars to blow out the case. The magistrate and her clerk countered by testifying that Welsh had pocketed the hundred dollars and concocted the bribe story after "getting his hand caught in the cookie jar." Judge John McDevitt, in his charge to the jury, told them, "Somebody is lying."

Relying on Welsh, who was at best a reluctant facilitator of a shakedown, was a risky gambit on our part. Most prosecutors would not bring a case that relied on one immunized witness against two witnesses. But conspirators willing to testify against magistrates in corruption cases were hard to find, so we pressed ahead.

The jury deliberated, took lunch, and deliberated some more. Finally the jurors filed into the courtroom. They found Marmon and Bardascino guilty on all counts. The magistrate was sentenced to eleven to twenty-three months in prison. The clerk got three to six months.

Welsh, for his part, said he did not expect his participation in the bribery of a magistrate to have any effect on his political future. "He said he has heard no adverse reaction to his admission, either from voters or from the Democratic Party leadership," the *Bulletin* reported.[2]

Marmon and Bardascino never served their time. In June 1967, more than a year after their trial, the state superior court voted 4–3 to reverse the convictions on procedural grounds. Before the case could be retried, John Welsh died. Without our only witness, Marmon and Bardascino escaped jail, but their convictions were a significant step in reforming the system.

Magistrate Earl Lane was king of the "copy of the charge." Until the fall of 1966, when we created a twenty-four-hour police court, a person arrested even for a minor offense, such as disorderly conduct, punishable by a small fine, had to stay in jail until a magistrate signed a document known as a "copy of the charge." The copy of the charge had developed into a form of currency in the political system. In theory, a magistrate should sign a "copy" only if he had an assurance, or at least good reason to believe, that a defendant would appear in court for his hearing. In practice, magistrates signed copies as favors to other politicians and to power brokers. Politicians could make points by arranging to have constituents sprung from jail in the middle of the night.

The copy of the charge had also become a tool for corruption. Magistrates often demanded payoffs before they would sign. During our investigation hundreds of people swore they had been forced to pay five to twenty-five dollars for a magistrate's signature, even though the law allowed a maximum charge of one dollar as a filing fee. Nineteen of the twenty-eight magistrates were implicated. But Earl Lane stood out: 170 people accused him of gouging them for his signature.

"Early" Lane, as he was known, was sixty-four, small, and pudgy. After dropping out of high school, he had worked as an elevator operator and Pullman porter before becoming a ward leader in 1954. In 1956 he'd been elected a magistrate. The system depended on magistrates' being available to sign copies of the charge. By all accounts Earl Lane was always available. He made a quick and handsome profit on his availability. Lane was signing fifty to a hundred copies a week, at an average charge of ten to fifteen dollars a copy. That came to at least five hundred dollars a week, and probably closer to fifteen hundred. In a year, on "copies" alone, Earl Lane hauled in at least fifty thousand dollars. That did not include what Lane made by blowing out cases.

Lane sold his signature on a sliding scale, depending on the hour of the day and the gravity of the charge. He kept a large sign in his office with a detailed price list. A "copy" during business hours generally ran five dollars. In the middle of the night it rose to twenty-five dollars. Even in the wee hours Lane had a system that limited his discomfort. When awakened by the doorbell at his North Philadelphia home, Lane lowered a cigar box by a cord from his second-floor bedroom window. The caller would place the copy and the cash in the box, which Lane would then raise. If the cigar box held the right amount of cash, Lane would sign the copy and lower it back to the caller. The more interruptions, the sounder Earl Lane slept.

Lane was indicted on fifty-one counts of extortion and receiving illegal compensation. Jack Mason, my deputy from the investigation, handled the trial. Mason found himself opposite Lane and his two lawyers, who were all African-American. It seemed clear to Mason that Lane was trying to play for sympathy to the African-American jurors. So Mason called only African-American witnesses. Seventy of them, in turn, testified about Lane's prices.

Lane, wearing a dark gray summer suit and his trademark bow tie, took the stand to insist that he took only one-dollar fees to sign copies. Where Lane had taken any additional money, he said, it was in tips, volunteered by grateful citizens who told him to buy himself some cigars. "I have done nothing the whole time I have been a magistrate except help people."

Like an interminable drumroll, the jury took twenty-two minutes to declare "guilty" 102 times, twice for each indictment. Earl Lane was sentenced to jail, fined twenty-five thousand dollars, and removed from office. While his case was pending on appeal, he died. Again the publicity from the trial focused public attention on the abuses and helped reform the system.

Magistrate Harry Schwartz may have been the worst of a bad bunch. Among other things, Schwartz exploited gay men. In the early 1960s homosexual acts were a crime in Philadelphia. Most gay men lived in dread of exposure. Once exposed, they would pay anything to avoid prosecution and further notoriety. Schwartz traded on their despair.

Gay men gravitated to the Family Theatre, in the shadow of Philadelphia City Hall, for chance encounters with each other at the all-night movies shown there. Undercover cops from the morals squad went to the Family Theatre to mingle and to make arrests.

George Hubert was a quiet little man who had emigrated to the United States from Germany and still spoke with an accent.[3] He worked as a cafeteria busboy. Every other week Hubert visited the Philadelphia Saving Fund Society to deposit a few dollars he had scrimped from his paycheck. Hubert's bankbook showed a meticulous pattern of depositing $13.50 to $16.50. He was putting away every cent he could.

One night in April 1963, Hubert dropped in at the Family Theatre and sat down beside a blond, blue-eyed man. After about fifteen minutes, Hubert began to take some liberties. He pressed his leg against the blond man's leg. Gathering his courage, Hubert repeated the gesture. When the man didn't object, Hubert reached over and gripped the man's crotch and began to squeeze.

The blond man identified himself as a police officer and arrested George Hubert. Hubert was taken to a nearby police station and locked in a cell. A few minutes later a guard informed Hubert that he was wanted on the telephone. The unidentified caller told Hubert that he had witnessed the arrest and could get Hubert out of jail for twenty dollars. Hubert quickly agreed. A few minutes later a young man arrived at the police station, arranged for Hubert's release through a magistrate, and drove him a few blocks to the office of Joseph Nardello, a bail bondsman.

Hubert told Nardello that he'd been in the same trouble before and that he wanted to talk to the lawyer who'd handled his earlier case. Nardello said it would be hard for Hubert to beat a second rap, but Nardello could "take care of the matter" for one thousand dollars. "I have to pay three or four people to take care of this. I can fix the case and you won't have to go to court." Hubert agreed to pay the thousand dollars.

The next morning Nardello met Hubert near the police station where Hubert's hearing would be held. The bondsman introduced him to a lawyer, Melvin Goldstein, and assured Hubert, "Everything is taken care of. You don't have to worry about a thing."

The hearing before Magistrate Harry Schwartz lasted just a minute and fifteen seconds. "This man has been in the country ten years," Goldstein told the magistrate. "He comes from Germany. He came through a concentration camp. His family was killed in Germany. He worked ten years at H&H. He has a problem, as you can see. He had difficulty in understanding. He will continue to go to a psychologist. The psychologist really cured him one time."

"Take him away," Schwartz said. "Discharged."

Afterward, while he paid the thousand dollars in cash to Nardello, Hubert complained about Goldstein's fabricated story about a concentration camp and murdered relatives. Nardello brushed off these qualms.

Later, when I looked at Hubert's savings book, noted the meticulous small deposits every two weeks, and then saw the giant thousand-dollar withdrawal, I was livid.

Throughout the month of April 1963, while Schwartz sat at the 11th and Winter Streets station, the same scenario played out with nine accused homosexuals. The five who could make hefty payoffs bought their freedom. The four who could not faced bail, jail, and trial. The contrast showed most starkly when two men were arrested ten minutes apart and booked on the same charge, solicitation to commit sodomy. They were locked in the same cell and represented by the same lawyer, James Tracton. But the similarity ended when Tracton demanded his fee. Schwartz discharged the man who could afford to pay and held for trial the man who could not.[4]

Eventually indictments were returned against attorneys Tracton and Goldstein and bail bondsman Nardello. Filing criminal charges against Schwartz was a stickier matter. A prosecution against the magistrate would have been based solely on circumstantial evidence. None of the bondsmen or attorneys involved in the payoff cases would answer questions. The gay men had dealt only with their lawyers and bondsmen, not with the magistrate. We had nobody to testify about Schwartz's motives or the behind-the-scenes moves. In the end we decided not to prosecute Harry Schwartz on these matters. But that was largely because a stronger collection-racket case against him had emerged.

Philadelphia's magistrates handled both civil and criminal cases. The state legislature had limited the magistrates' authority to civil claims of a hundred dollars, reasoning that nonlawyer judges could do little harm on such minor cases. The legislators underestimated the magistrates. The magistrate and his associate, the constable, whose job was serving legal papers and collecting money, found a way to do great harm on minor civil cases, while building personal fortunes. Their vehicle was the collection agency.

A hallmark of our judicial system is the judge's lack of personal interest in the outcome of a case. That principle did not apply in Philadelphia magistrates court. Constables formed collection agencies and dragged debtors to court, where magistrates ruled in the constables' favor. The constables and magistrates then split the profits, which included a host of interest charges and illegal fees they heaped onto the already inflated bills.

Our investigation uncovered an extensive magistrate-constable collection mill. Fourteen constables openly owned and operated collection agencies. All around town their office windows bore the constable's official seal next to their collection agency trade names. A few years earlier, constables had been even bolder. They had advertised in the Yellow Pages, some boasting connections with particular magistrates courts, others declaring simply, "Magistrate Connections—Prompt Service."

Magistrate Harry Schwartz and Constable Abraham Siegel ran a Fortune 500 collection racket, the Active Collection Agency. They fleeced tens of thousands of poor Philadelphians over more than a decade. On Siegel's "Notice to Appear" stationery, the words "Magistrate Court Connections" covered a quarter of the page, despite a standing order from the chief magistrate against such threats.

Schwartz and Siegel hardly looked menacing. Schwartz, sixty-four, was bald, with a round, cherubic face and a florid complexion. A high-school dropout, Schwartz had begun his career as a stenographer, shifted to selling shoes, and become a constable in 1933. He climbed the Democratic political ladder at the same time, from committeeman to ward leader. Along the way, then-Constable Schwartz had formed Active Collection Agency and hired Abraham Siegel, a small mustached man, to help him.

The two men realized that their collection business would improve if Schwartz were on the bench deciding the debt cases himself. Schwartz's wife, Lillian, was named president. One of Active's main clients was the Philadelphia Credit Bureau, which served some of Philadelphia's most prestigious firms. By 1964, Active handled Credit Bureau claims totaling $683,969, and made $79,680 collecting them.

We questioned Schwartz during our investigation about his ongoing role in Active Collection Agency, even after he had become a magistrate. He told us, "Whether it's a violation of the act, the Magistrates Act or not, I don't know. Some say yes, some say no. I handle all this business for one reason. If my wife makes money, I'm going to benefit by it because I have an opportunity to spend some of the money she makes, being the president of the company that employs the constable who handles the work."

We also asked Schwartz about magistrate-constable teams. "I don't think you will find a single constable in the city of Philadelphia who didn't use that word, 'magistrate connections,' " Schwartz told us. Collections moved much quicker when the debtor knew that the constable had ready access to a friendly magistrate, Schwartz confirmed. His testimony would prove costly to him.

Abe Siegel and many other constables were not shy about pressing for payment. When a constable's tough memo did not work, a magistrate's notice often followed. Magistrates routinely sent notices to accused debtors, asking for payment to avoid civil lawsuits. Magistrate Schwartz, in a letter to one debtor, generously offered "a chance to settle this matter by calling Constable Abraham Siegel within five days. Failure to comply will result in added costs to you." So much for due process.

When a debtor still refused to pay, there were other tactics. Often a constable filed a lawsuit against the debtor but did not serve notice. Court rules required the constable to serve legal papers on anybody he was suing, so the person could defend himself. Naturally, a defendant who did not know he had been sued missed his court date. The magistrate then ruled against him by default.

When a defendant did appear in court, the magistrate often didn't bother hearing him. One man, issued a summons from Magistrate Harry Ellick over a dispute about mail-order car seat covers, waited at magistrates court for two hours until Ellick told him to go next door to see his constable. When the man asked for a hearing and tried to show Ellick correspondence and a canceled check to prove he didn't owe money on the seat covers, Ellick said, "I am not going to read that; I am not going to be bothered with it." When the man persisted, Ellick grew angry and told him twice, "I don't care what you say, I am going to give judgment against you."

When other tactics failed, the magistrates issued arrest warrants for the debtors, and the constables executed these warrants. When Ralph Ross fell behind on payments on a television set, Constable D. M. Laken got an arrest warrant for Ross on a charge of "fraudulent conversion." The "fraudulent conversion" theory was that title of the TV had reverted to the appliance store when Ross missed a payment. That made Ross guilty of possessing stolen property, since he no longer owned the set in his home. Laken arrested Ross at Ross's foreman's office, in front of his co-workers, and threatened to "lock him up." Ross pleaded with the constable, who took him instead to a credit company office, where "arrangements" were made. Constable Laken also filed larceny charges against Howard Gordanos, who had fallen behind on furniture payments. Laken and two deputies took Gordanos into custody and began dismantling his furniture and loading it into a truck. They threatened to handcuff Gordanos and drag him to jail. Gordanos promised to pay what he could.[5]

Neither of these debt cases, nor countless others like them, offered any conceivable basis for criminal charges. And if there had been proper cause for arrest, the defendants were entitled to go through the criminal courts instead of being muscled in back rooms.

More than twenty-five thousand civil cases passed through Philadelphia's magistrates courts each year. A review of thousands of those cases showed that the plaintiff won more than 99.5 percent of the time, not even counting payments coerced before cases reached court. The system was purer than Ivory Soap, from the creditor's point of view. It was a multimillion-dollar collection racket.

The city's biggest and most prominent firms brought their claims to magistrates court, including Bell Telephone, Sears Roebuck, Humble Oil, Philadelphia Gas Works, and Florsheim Shoes. Many of the claims were legitimate. But most of the court costs piled on the claims were illegal. Even where debts were owed, the system gave the defendants no hope for due process. These small claims courts convinced thousands of inner-city residents that justice existed only for the rich man.

During our investigation we had reviewed fifteen thousand cases handled by Schwartz, and not found a single case in which Active Collection Agency had not collected. We had stopped at fifteen thousand. "Somewhere there had to be an improper claim," Jim Kelly, my deputy on the probe, said. "There just had to be shoddy merchandise somewhere."

Despite Active's volume, Schwartz and Siegel had not settled merely for the commissions on their collections. Siegel generally added an arbitrary sum, often $5, to any claim. He then piled on phantom fees, including a mileage charge even though he didn't actually serve the paperwork, and charges for notices of levy and inventory of goods. The law permitted fees of $2.50 per case. Siegel generally added $7.50 or $9. He and Schwartz pocketed the padded charges, on top of the commissions.

Prosecution of this misconduct was difficult because there was no criminal law on Pennsylvania's books against constables' dragging their victims before friendly magistrates. Even so, Pennsylvania had kept the doctrine of "common-law" criminal offenses, for outrageous acts that were not specifically barred by other laws. We fashioned a common-law charge called "official oppression" and arrested Schwartz and Siegel.

Dick Sprague prosecuted the case. At the trial a parade of inner-city residents described their travails at the hands of the Active Collection Agency. They told of fabricated debts that grew six- and sevenfold with interest and fees, of four-year-old daughters who were served with legal papers, and of liens placed on their furniture and appliances. None was more compelling than Anna Mayall, a frail seventy-five-year-old widow who could barely see over the witness box. Mayall testified that Siegel had phoned and ordered her to appear in Schwartz's court for failing to pay a $38 fuel bill. "I can't go," Mayall had pleaded with Siegel. "I'm sick. I can't get around." Two weeks later Siegel had sent Mayall a writ raising her debt to $63.60, including interest and other charges.

The jury took seventy-five minutes to convict Schwartz and Siegel of conspiracy and official oppression. Judge McDevitt aptly summed up the defendants' behavior: "A most outrageous and heinous obstruction and perversion of judicial process."

Schwartz and Siegel were each sentenced to eleven to twenty-three months in jail. But that was not the end of them. As Schwartz's lawyer told the *Bulletin* after the convictions, "We have just begun to fight." Schwartz and Siegel applied the same cunning and tenacity to their appeals that they had applied to their collections. They proved equally skilled at both accelerating and slowing the wheels of justice. Where they had pressed in the past for speedy collections, they now pushed for postponements. For four years Schwartz and Siegel filed an endless barrage of motions and appeals, up to the U.S. Supreme Court. In September 1970, Harry Schwartz died, with the appeals process still not completed. For the next two years Abe Siegel filed more appeals and motions. Finally, more than six years after his conviction, his legal options exhausted, Siegel went to jail on April 4, 1973.

Ultimately our investigation netted hundreds of indictments and convictions against magistrates, bondsmen, constables, lawyers, and ward leaders—Democrats and Republicans alike. We had exposed the venal "neighborhood Solomons" and convicted more of them than any other probe in the system's nearly three-hundred-year history. But we had not struck the deathblow. The remaining magistrates fought reform and protected their powers.

Chief Magistrate John Patrick Walsh held a news conference to announce, "I will advise the magistrates to ignore [Specter's] orders. It is apparent that he is a co-conspirator in plotting to destroy the poor peoples' court in Philadelphia."

The poor people's court, as Walsh called it, let poor people sit in jail all night, until a magistrate arrived in the morning and got around to arraigning them. The 1937 Magistrates Act had called for a twenty-four-hour police court, to hold bail hearings around the clock. That statute had been honored in the breach. Almost thirty years later, the length of a suspect's jail stay depended on how many politicians he knew. Working with judges and police brass, my office insisted on activating the twenty-four-hour central police court as required by state law. As part of the new system, magistrates had to hold preliminary arraignments every hour, which they could handle in two to three minutes each.

The magistrates were livid. They couldn't charge ten to twenty-five dollars to sign copies of the charge if a night magistrate would sign for one dollar. Two days before the new central police court was slated to open in October 1966, the Board of Magistrates announced it was boycotting the program. With no judges, there could be no court.

We went ahead anyway. I arrived at Central Police Court at 9:00 A.M. on opening day, along with several of my assistants. I brought along Judge Joseph Sloane, president judge of Common Pleas Court 7. A common pleas judge had the authority to sit as a magistrate, so I had asked Sloane to come to Central Police Court and open the docket, since none of the magistrates would. In the courtroom Sloane and I had a serious talk with Chief Magistrate Walsh. Sloane persuaded Walsh that everybody would be better off if he ordered his "neighborhood Solomons" to do their jobs, which he did.

It was clear that the only way to cleanse Philadelphia's courts was to change the Pennsylvania constitution to abolish the magistrates system. A constitutional convention was convened, and the question came before the state's voters as a referendum on the 1967 primary ballot. It passed. The convention's reforms were adopted in February 1968 and implemented in January 1969. The twenty-eight magistrates courts were abolished, replaced by a six-judge traffic court and a twenty-two-judge municipal court. All the new municipal court judges would be lawyers.

As I look back at my public service, reforming the three-hundred-year-old magisterial system gives me the most satisfaction. The Philadelphia magisterial system had created enormous human urban blight by abusing the city's underclass for centuries.

THE KEYS TO THE JAIL

⎯⎯⎯

The prosecutor's power is paramount in the criminal justice system. While the police can arrest and judges can sentence, the prosecutor decides which cases to prosecute, the scope of the indictments, and the allocation of resources. As the maxim states, "The district attorney has the keys to the jail."

Most of Philadelphia's trial courts ran on schedules designed to please the judges. Some judges put in more time on the golf links than on the bench. Judges were supposed to sit from 10:00 A.M. to 12:30 P.M. and from 2:00 to 4:00 P.M., and also to work several hours in chambers. But in practice, many judges typically arrived shortly before 11:00 A.M., left a little after noon, returned close to 3:00 P.M., and quit by 3:30. I sent my detectives to court to record judges' morning arrivals, lunch breaks, and quitting times.

One common pleas judge held my detective in contempt. I marched down to the courtroom. "Judge," I said, "you can't hold him in contempt of court because he was following my orders. If you're going to hold anybody in contempt of court, it's me. But you can't hold me in contempt because this an open court. Anybody can come here and write down anything he wants. That's a discreet, nondisruptive act." The judge backed down. I went to Chief Justice John Bell of the state supreme court and persuaded him to require judges to sit from 9:30 A.M. to 5:00 P.M. Bell entered the order.

When I found a judge's sentence lacking, I let him know. I sparred with Lewis "Turn 'Em Loose" Mongelluzzo. I also had frequent run-ins with Judge Adrian Bonnelly, president judge of Philadelphia's county court. Bonnelly, a cherubic, white-haired septuagenarian, stood barely five feet tall. He once walked into a magistrate's court, sat on the bench, and asked the presiding magistrate to free a defendant accused of illegal lottery. The defendant's wife nursed Bonnelly's ailing wife. "Bonnelly said later that he merely had served as a character witness," the *Inquirer* reported. "However, Bonnelly was listed with [Magistrate] Dennis on the official transcript as presiding judge. Specter commented at the time, 'I have enough trouble with magistrates blowing out cases without judges being imported to blow them out.' "[1] The next week I had the numbers writer rearrested.

Bonnelly, as president judge of the county court in 1966, assigned cases to the nineteen other judges. He also picked his own cases. When I became DA, I ordered a review of all cases listed before him. Certain lawyers had more cases listed before him than the law of averages allowed. Bonnelly so rarely gave jail time that the *Daily News* wrote that the judge's "personal be-kind-to-criminals program has made him the darling of the defense attorneys."[2] Over the years, the DA's office had tried to keep serious cases out of Bonnelly's court. When asked about his leniency, Bonnelly had a stock reply: "They always bring me the chipmunks. Why don't they bring me the bears, and I would show you what I would do."

In May 1969, a few months after Bonnelly had retired as president judge but was still hearing some cases, his wife came to my office. Mrs. Bonnelly was distraught over newspaper stories reporting accusations that her husband's court clerk took payoffs to fix cases. Mrs. Bonnelly handed me an envelope that the clerk had brought to her home and asked her to give to her husband. There was a small tear at a corner of the envelope, obviously made by a curious Mrs. Bonnelly. Through the tear I could see a thick wad of bills.

Mrs. Bonnelly, who was quiet and shy, said she disliked the clerk. She seemed to be trying to protect her husband from the clerk and also looking for some assurance from me that her husband was clean. She protested the terrible things people were saying about her husband, but through her words floated the music of guilty feelings for having kept silent about the envelope until now. Mrs. Bonnelly told me she wanted her husband exonerated. But she probably knew better when she brought me the envelope.

After exchanging a few words with her, I called for Dick Sprague, my first assistant, to join us. This was the only time I can remember wanting a witness. Both before and after Sprague came up to my office, I told Mrs. Bonnelly that I wanted to give her an opportunity to talk to her husband before we further opened the envelope. No, Mrs. Bonnelly insisted, she didn't want that.

I then phoned Bonnelly at his office at the Philadelphia Saving Fund Building, where he had joined a law firm. I got right to the point: Did Bonnelly want to come to my office before we opened the envelope his wife had brought? No, Bonnelly said, he definitely would not come to my office. I told the judge I would proceed to discuss the matter with his wife and see what was in the envelope. Mustering his strongest voice, Bonnelly said, "Go ahead. Do anything you like." In Sprague's presence I opened the envelope and removed its contents: twenty fifty-dollar bills.

As soon as Mrs. Bonnelly left my office, I again phoned the judge. I wanted to see him right away, I said. I wanted to talk to him before he had a chance to talk to his wife. I offered to go to his office to save him the embarrassment of coming to mine. Sprague and I immediately walked the two blocks from City Hall to the PSFS Building. We gave Bonnelly his Miranda warnings. He said he was willing to talk. I asked Bonnelly about the money. "I don't know anything about it," he maintained. Contacted recently, the clerk told me that the envelope of cash was his repayment of a loan the judge had given him two to three months earlier.

We couldn't force Bonnelly's wife to testify against him because of the husband-wife privilege. The clerk refused to answer any questions and, of course, wouldn't testify against the judge. After talking to Chief Justice Bell, I decided I couldn't prove a criminal case against Bonnelly. I went to the common pleas president, Judge Vincent Carroll, told Carroll what was going on, and made sure that no criminal cases had been assigned to Judge Bonnelly, or would be. I put the twenty fifty-dollar bills into the DA's office safe and on my last day in office in January 1974 filed a petition, with court approval, to turn the one thousand dollars over to the use of the county.

To be sure, Philadelphia did have some good and talented judges. Common Pleas Court 6 was remarkably good, featuring Curtis Bok, Gerald Flood, and Louis Leventhal. Bok was an author and later a distinguished state supreme court justice. His son Derek became president of Harvard University. Common Pleas Court 8 wound up an extraordinary court. When CP8 was being formed, Bar Association chairman

Ted Voorhees asked John McDevitt, a leading trial lawyer, to chair the nominating panel. "Would that preclude my being named?" McDevitt asked. Voorhees was shocked that McDevitt would want a seat on the common pleas bench. When the magistrates prosecutions came up, I asked McDevitt to preside. He tried Marmon, Lane, and Schwartz and Siegel, who were all convicted.

Many Philadelphia judges gave outrageously light sentences to hardened criminals convicted of serious crimes. When I was an assistant DA, the prosecutor's office had no policy on recommending sentences, which left the matter entirely to the judges. When I became district attorney, I changed the policy and insisted on recommending sentences. The judges had ignored my requests for a policy of jail time for anybody caught illegally possessing a gun. Now those requests and others would become formal recommendations, ultimately precursors to mandatory sentencing guidelines. At our daily staff meetings I would go over all facets of cases on the docket, with special emphasis on sentencing.

The judges vehemently opposed my new policy and frequently ignored our sentencing recommendations. But the recommendations gave us a pressure point on the judiciary. When a judge imposed a sentence substantially lighter than the assistant DA had recommended, a newspaper story often followed. If a sentence was way off, I would file a formal petition for reconsideration of the sentence under a statute that gave the trial judge thirty days to reconsider the assigned penalty.

I filed a petition, for example, over the Arnold Marks case. Marks was convicted in 1969 of possessing six ounces of pure uncut heroin worth $280,000. In the common pleas court Judge Fred DiBona sentenced him to six to twenty-three months in jail. I objected. Loudly. When an irate DiBona found me in contempt of court, he might have been right. But on the big issue, Marks's sentence, he was conclusively wrong. After the contempt citation, DiBona called for the sheriff to take me to a cell. The sheriff left me in the courtroom. A few minutes later DiBona said he would release me from contempt if I apologized. "Absolutely not," I said. DiBona left the courtroom. I stayed there, in technical custody. The judge came back twenty minutes later. "We'll exchange mutual apologies," he offered.

"Absolutely not," I said. DiBona again stormed out of the courtroom. Again I sat there. When DiBona returned, he let me go. I personally argued the motion to reconsider Marks's sentence. It was a heated hearing. The Marks case happened to erupt during my 1969 reelection campaign for district attorney, and it drew heavy publicity and strong public support for me. Republican leader Bill Meehan said I made one mistake: I should have gone to jail, to get even more attention and support.

At a public bench-bar conference in 1969, Judge Herbert Levin criticized me for petitioning for reconsideration of one of his sentences. Levin had found a repeat offender guilty of involuntary manslaughter for killing a man while robbing him, and then let him off with probation. I disagreed with Levin before a packed audience. Then the defense lawyer in the case, who was also at the conference, stood and backed me on the facts. The conference provided the forum for many criminal defense lawyers to vent their objections to my reform policies. Joan, in tears when we drove home, said it was her last judicial conference. For me it was just another day of fighting an entrenched system.

Sentencing decisions should be treated like other key court rulings, I argued. Citing three cases in which judges had handed down ludicrously light penalties, including the Marks case, I appealed to the state supreme court for a common-law right to appeal sentences. I then proposed a bill to the state legislature for the right to appeal sentences set by the trial court. "Specter argues that appeals are taken on just about every other judicial act," the *Daily News* opined. "Why not criminal sentences? Why not indeed?"

My bill never got a hearing. The state supreme court even set me back a step, barring me from asking the trial judge for reconsideration of sentence by ruling that reconsideration meant double jeopardy, or unconstitutionally trying a person twice for the same offense. The supreme court was stretching to a fallacious rationale. There had been only one conviction. There was no retrial, so there was no double jeopardy. The only question was on sentencing.

Sometimes, especially in political cases, we never got to the sentencing phase. Judges found the defendants not guilty and blew out the cases. With so many fixes, I sometimes demanded jury trials. That took fact-finding away from the judges, which made them furious. It also required lawyers and judges to work harder, which further riled them, since they plea-bargained cases to spare themselves the work demanded by jury trials. As a result, tough criminals often got soft sentences. No more. During my first two months in office, according to the

Philadelphia Daily News, jury trials increased 50 percent. In my second term the state supreme court, by rule, rescinded the commonwealth's right to jury trials. Some twenty-five years later the DA's right to a jury trial was reinstated through a constitutional amendment. In a sense I had the last word on the matter when I voted for that amendment.

Prosecutors' offices throughout the country generally let the defense take the lead on appeals. As a result, appellate decisions almost always reflect a defense point of view. Defense lawyers could pick cases that would most likely persuade appeals courts to create new rules of law limiting the prosecutor's power and discretion—not only in those extreme cases but in every other case. Largely to counter that bias, we filed more appeals.

The more my assistants and I were attacked by judges and lawyers, the more public support our office got. That's not to say there were no risks. "I never thought about it in those days—that this could hurt a career, that people could get pissed off," Barnett Lotstein, one of my assistants, said recently. "I might think about it today. It was almost like we were white knights, and we were doing right, and right will prevail."

The Warren Court, in the early and mid-1960s, issued a series of seminal rulings protecting defendants' rights and due process. Some veteran judges and lawyers could not adjust to the new regime. In 1961, Judge John Boyle had peered down from the bench in his Philadelphia City Hall courtroom at a nineteen-year-old hoodlum who'd been caught with a loaded revolver. Boyle had been a tough first assistant DA for ten years, and he knew what to do with young punks.

But the defense lawyer was raising a furor about this case for some reason Boyle couldn't figure out. Usually defense lawyers saved their pleas for sentencing. A smooth, experienced criminal lawyer wouldn't risk antagonizing the judge on a point he couldn't win. But here it seemed an old pro was doing just that. Leaning forward on the bench, Boyle said, "The police stopped the defendant's automobile on a 'routine car stop,' and they found a loaded gun. What more is there to be said?"

"But, Judge," the lawyer countered, "you can't consider the loaded gun as evidence because the police picked it up as part of an unconstitutional search and seizure. The Supreme Court of the United States decided last month that the district attorney cannot introduce evidence which is seized in violation of the United States Constitution."

"What case was that?" Boyle asked. The lawyer replied, "*Mapp* v. *Ohio.*" Shifting his papers, the judge said, "Well, that's an Ohio case. It doesn't apply to Pennsylvania. I find the defendant guilty as charged." Evidently Judge Boyle didn't realize that Pennsylvania was part of the United States and that state trial judges must follow the U.S. Supreme Court. Some police officers and even some of my prosecutors had nearly as much trouble grasping the concept.

Mapp v. *Ohio* came down in 1961, when I was chief of the appeals division at the DA's office. For the first time, judges suppressed evidence in pretrial hearings. I structured a common-law right of appeal. Nobody in the Pennsylvania courts had ever taken an appeal from a pretrial suppression order because there never had been such an order. I chose *Commonwealth* v. *Bosurgi* as the test case.

Bosurgi was a professional burglar who'd looted a jewelry store on Snyder Avenue in South Philadelphia. When the police arrested Bosurgi, they found glass in his trouser cuffs from the store's front door, which he had broken. The trial judge had suppressed the evidence. I took an appeal to the superior court, where I argued the case against a young lawyer who lived up the street from me, Dave Savitt, later an excellent common pleas judge.

Judge Chester Rhodes, superior court president, listened to Savitt make his argument, looked down, and said, very much in the spirit of Judge Boyle, "You want this man acquitted and this evidence thrown out? But it was in his cuffs, and it came from the front door of the jewelry store on Snyder Avenue! What are you talking about?" Judge Rhodes had a hard time accepting that conclusive evidence of guilt had to be thrown out because the police officer had blundered.

In the end, I was able to get *Bosurgi* reversed, not by ignoring the new *Mapp* standard, but by showing the evidence to establish probable cause to justify the search and seizure.

The Supreme Court's rulings on defendants' rights brought many vital changes. It is a basic premise today that a criminal defendant cannot have a fair trial without a lawyer. But when I started practicing law, and until *Gideon* in 1963, a criminal defendant on trial for any crime short of murder was not entitled to counsel.

Miranda v. *Arizona* was designed to prevent coerced confessions, a noble purpose. *Miranda* required police to give suspects detailed warnings about four specific constitutional rights before interrogating them: the right to remain silent, the reminder that anything said could be used against the suspect, the right to counsel, and the reminder that a lawyer would be provided to those who could not afford one. The warnings served a dual purpose: When a police officer tells a defendant, "You don't have to talk unless you have a lawyer," the defendant knows he has a right to a lawyer, and he also knows that the police officer knows he has that right.

The line of defendants'-rights cases cascaded down to the city courts. At the DA's office, prosecutors versed in the new rulings taught the others and the police. Training the police was not the prosecutor's job, but if we didn't train them, we wouldn't have competent evidence. So it had to become our job. Every policeman carried a pocket card with the Miranda warnings and the questions to ask suspects to get the required waivers for admissibility of any statements in a criminal prosecution.

My office took on a classroom atmosphere. I wrote a book with my former law partner, Marvin Katz, called *Police Guide to Search and Seizure, Interrogation and Confession*. We also churned out a series of advisory pamphlets for the police. When *Miranda* came down on June 13, 1966, I knew it would set off an upheaval and jeopardize police procedures. I got the fifty-four-page opinion late Monday and turned out the *Miranda* advisory by Friday.

I testified before a congressional committee in August 1966. I produced statistics on cases that were lost because of *Miranda*. Those numbers helped inspire the Omnibus Crime Control Act of 1968, which said that admissibility of confessions would be gauged on the totality of the circumstances.

In May 1966, about six weeks before the Supreme Court issued its *Miranda* decision, a Philadelphia man named Ronald Hickey confessed to murdering a cabdriver. Police went to Hickey's apartment and found a gun, valuables taken from cabdrivers, and other evidence. Officers arrested Hickey and advised him of his rights as required by the law at the time. But when Hickey came to trial, the judge threw out the case because Hickey had not been given his more extensive Miranda warnings.

The crime, the investigation, and the indictment had all occurred before *Miranda* came down on June 13, 1966. But the Supreme Court, in its *Johnson* decision on June 20, 1966, ruled that *Miranda* applied to every case in which the trial began on or after June 13—no matter when the crime and questioning had taken place. The retroactive rule was absurd. Across the land, convictions against confessed murderers and other violent felons were vacated because the police had not read them their rights, even though those rights had not been established when those criminals were arrested and questioned.

I was so irate about *Hickey* that I looked for a similar case we could use to overturn the retroactive decision. I eventually found William Ware's case. Ware had pushed several elderly women down staircases, killing them, and then looted their apartments. Ware had been found incompetent to stand trial and put in an insane asylum in 1963. In 1968, the courts found Ware competent and said he could stand trial. I wanted to prosecute Ware, who obviously had not been given his Miranda warnings, for the burglary-murders. I argued the case, asking the state supreme court how a man arrested and questioned in 1963 could possibly be entitled to Miranda warnings, which were not even established until 1966. The state supreme court ruled against us. *Ware*, even more than *Hickey*, pointed up the absurdity of requiring Miranda warnings retroactively. I thought I had found a powerful case to press the U.S. Supreme Court to review the *Johnson-Miranda* retroactivity rule. The Supreme Court agreed to hear the case.

When the state supreme court found out that the U.S. Supreme Court had granted certiorari, the state court filed an addendum to its opinion, deciding *Ware* on state constitutional grounds. Once a case is decided on that basis, the state supreme court, as the final arbiter of the state constitution, has the last word. The state supreme court justices, who were not eager for me to challenge their decision in the U.S. Supreme Court, had made my appeal moot and prevented me from arguing the Ware case in Washington.

In 1969 I argued *Frazier* v. *Cupp*, an Oregon case, in the U.S. Supreme Court at the request of the National District Attorneys Association. The defendant had been arrested and tried when confessions were governed by *Escobedo*, which required police to warn suspects that they had a right to counsel and a right to remain silent. The Court had instructed counsel to be present on Monday, so I sat through arguments for two and half days by the time my case was finally called on Wednesday afternoon. Throughout all those arguments, Justice William O. Douglas, then the senior associate justice, had sat on the bench with his chin in his right hand, leaning over, appearing uninterested, almost asleep.

When *Frazier* v. *Cupp* was called, Douglas looked up and asked, "How is Philadelphia interested in this case?"

I had not seen Douglas since he presided at the finals of the moot court competition at Yale Law School in May 1954, when I was a first-year student representing the prosecution. At that time we argued a case involving due process. Douglas brought up *Rochin* v. *California*, a 1952 case in which the Supreme Court reversed a conviction for possession of morphine because the defendant's stomach had been pumped against his will. Justice Frankfurter had concluded in that case that the police procedures "shocked the conscience." *Rochin* became a standard of invalidating police conduct that "shocked the conscience."

As the law school argument progressed, Douglas leaned over and posed a critical question: "Counselor, would it shock your conscience if I told you that the police conduct in this case shocked my conscience?"

"No, it wouldn't, Your Honor," I replied, "especially if the judges on your right and left agreed with me." Notwithstanding the sophisticated legal arguments in the case, that one reply drew the most laughs and comment on the evening's argument, and I won the fifty-dollar Harlan Fiske Stone Award for first place. I doubt that Douglas remembered my retort in moot court when I appeared before him on *Frazier*.

My argument in *Frazier* was involved. First, I noted that Congress had recently passed the Omnibus Crime Control Act of 1968, which determined admissibility of a confession or statement on the totality of the circumstances, as opposed to the specific warnings of *Escobedo,* a case on warnings before *Miranda*. Next, I noted that an act of Congress was presumptively constitutional. Then I said that the standards for admissibility in the state case could be no higher than in a federal case, since the limitation on state action was derived from the due-process clause of the Fourteenth Amendment, which incorporated the Sixth Amendment right to counsel and the Fifth Amendment exemption from self-incrimination. Accordingly, I asserted that admissibility in a state court turned on the totality of the circumstances, and therefore the absence of the specific *Escobedo* warnings would not render the statement unconstitutional. Although in the long run police have accommodated to *Miranda*, which curtailed abusive interrogation, I thought the 1968 congressional standard was reasonable.

Chief Justice Earl Warren, presiding, peered down at me incredulously. Warren was then seventy-nine and would retire several months later. "Your argument would require the overruling of *Miranda*," he said.

"With all due respect, Mr. Chief Justice," I responded, as nonchalant as I could be, "I'm concerned here about the *Escobedo* ruling, not *Miranda*. But if *Escobedo* goes and so does *Miranda*, then so be it."

Warren gave me another incredulous look, perhaps recalling some of our discussions during the Warren Commission's work. "Are you authorized to make that argument?" he asked.

"Yes, I am, Mr. Chief Justice," I said. "And I have Mr. Roger Rook from Clackamas County." Rook was the district attorney from the Oregon County where the *Frazier* case had originated. "Mr. Rook, would you confirm that?" I asked. "Would Mr. Rook step forward?" Rook stood, walked to the front of the courtroom, and said I was authorized to make my argument. That was a rare, perhaps unprecedented, calling of a witness before the U.S. Supreme Court. The Court did not consider my novel arguments in reaching its unanimous decision in my favor. I won the case 8–0, but *Escobedo* and *Miranda* remained unaffected. The argument on admissibility on totality of the circumstances, under the 1968 act, lay dormant until 1999, when the Fourth Circuit issued a decision essentially overruling *Miranda*. In June 2000 the Supreme Court reversed the Fourth Circuit and reaffirmed Miranda. That case is pending before the Supreme Court.

My policy against plea-bargaining was overloading the court system. Trials were delayed. So we pressed for, and got, more judges. But many of the new judges were not up to the job, including a number of Crumlish's prosecutors I had fired when I took office. They had become judges through the same political connections that got them into the DA's office.

I pressed my assistants to take on the judges. I showed them it could be far less painful for them to fight poor rulings and light sentences than to explain to me why they did not. One of my instruments was the daily staff meeting. We generally met at 5:30 P.M. and went over all the hundred or more cases from the day's dockets. I called on each prosecutor in turn to review his or her cases and to discuss any decisions or developments that required explanation. Was it tried? Why wasn't it tried? A key witness was gone—Why didn't you send out a police car to bring in that witness? The defense lawyer wasn't there—Why didn't you send for the lawyer? The sentence . . . every last detail. I ran the meetings like workshops, so that each prosecutor could learn from the others' feats and foibles.

Lotstein, now a top prosecutor in Phoenix, recalled afternoons when I was delayed and staff meetings were called by Mike Rotko, my deputy who administered the office. Lotstein said at those times there were mad scrambles as prosecutors begged Rotko to review their cases first, hoping to get critiqued before I arrived and took over the questioning. Rotko later became a U.S. Attorney, and he was no cream puff.

Former Mayor Ed Rendell told an associate recently that he will never forget arriving late for a meeting when he was a new assistant DA. "Arlen had a meeting at 7:30 A.M. in the office," Rendell recalled, "and it was a meeting that I think seven of us were invited to attend, and I showed up at 7:42, twelve minutes late. And Arlen absolutely excoriated me and went through the fact that I had made eleven people wait, and estimated what those eleven people would bill, were they in the private sector, and told me that I had wasted $4,872. I can't ever remember being more frightened in my working career. I'm still perpetually late, but never for Arlen." He is, but that's another matter.

At the time I knew those staff meetings were tough, but I thought they were necessary. I was elected with a mandate to make Philadelphia's criminal courts work for the people. My approach was to make my assistants prefer to take a strong stand to get cases tried and appropriate sentences imposed with recalcitrant judges than to face me in the staff meetings with weak excuses for not getting the job done. A forceful, persistent assistant DA, armed with the facts and the law, can usually prevail with a judge who might otherwise not be disposed to press a defense attorney to trial or to succumb to a plea for an inappropriately lenient sentence. That approach did work.

In retrospect, I should have done it differently. It would have taken more time to deal with each assistant privately and the others would not have benefited from their associates' mistakes, but it would have been preferable as a matter of professional dignity. More than thirty years after those staff meetings, my ex-assistants still talk about them when we occasionally get together. Beyond the shared pride in what our office accomplished, those meetings stand out. Learning from those mistakes, I've tried to mellow on dealing with staff—not always successfully.

The most important subject at staff meetings was sentencing. Judges back then tended to mete out sentences by whim, and I wanted my assistants to know what was appropriate and to fight for it. I once distributed a circular to all the Philadelphia judges asking them to establish a policy to sentence any defendant found with a concealed deadly weapon to a minimum of thirty days. The judges ignored my memo.

I argued that the commonwealth was a party like anybody else and had a right, even a duty, to be heard and to recommend a sentence. The defendant had every right to talk about mitigation and to argue he should be treated leniently. So why shouldn't the DA have the right to talk about aggravating factors and to argue that the defendant should be treated not harshly but justly? My assistants made suggestions on sentences and pressed the judges, even when the judges didn't want to hear them. Lotstein was fined fifty dollars, charged with contempt, and hauled off to a cell when he berated a judge for releasing a heroin peddler without prison time. I held an impromptu news conference to ask why the only ones sent to prison in Philadelphia were my assistants.

We also found a new tactic: bringing victims to sentencing hearings. A defendant often brought his mother and maybe a pregnant wife or girlfriend to his sentencing hearing to work the judge, who was often a sympathetic, people-oriented politician. We brought in the victims to even the emotional seesaw. And it worked. "Defense attorneys are also finding judges a little tougher on their clients, because Specter is standing firm for the sentences he wants," the *Daily News* reported. Our effort was a precursor of victims' rights. Today courts follow an elaborate victims'-rights code, and uniform sentences have been codified nationally. But we were doing all this in the 1960s.

A NATIONAL MODEL

A major innovation in American criminal law began over corned beef sandwiches and coleslaw at a Philadelphia deli in 1968. Alan Davis, chief of my Appeals Division, was having lunch with Leonard Packel, his Harvard Law School classmate and counterpart at the public defender's office. The talk turned to the many people sentenced to probation, mostly first-time offenders convicted of nonviolent crimes. Many of these convictions were eventually expunged, so that a minor criminal record would not bar a person from graduate school or a job.

Davis and Packel had a revelation over their corned beef. If they could select in advance those people likely to get probation, they could put them directly on probation and save the courts and taxpayers the time and expense of trials. That would also free the courts to focus on more serious crimes. "We would eliminate indictment, trial, sentencing, appeals, and the petition to expunge," Davis said. "For the same result."

And the person would have an incentive to stay clean. Those who committed another crime within a year would be prosecuted for both the first and the later offense. Also, by persuading defendants to admit the facts in police reports, we could get them drug and alcohol counseling or other help at an early stage. We could pull them off the criminal ladder before they climbed to higher rungs. Davis wrote a plan, which I approved. Packel got an easy okay from the defender's office. The program would handle only nonviolent, first-time offenders. In each case a prosecutor had to get sign-offs from his or her immediate supervisor and from the arresting officer. I had the final say.

Davis and Packel went to Judge J. Sydney Hoffman of the state superior court to sell their plan. "Hoffman was an imaginative, creative guy, open to ideas, and someone we all liked, on the defense and the prosecution side," Davis said. "We needed somebody with prestige who was trusted by both the prosecution and the defense and had good judgment."

Hoffman sold the "diversion" concept to the other superior court judges. Then Hoffman and I presented our plan to the state supreme court justices in their conference room. At that time, I was arguing three cases seeking a new right for the commonwealth to appeal weak sentences. Before we got to our diversion program, the justices let me know in no uncertain terms that they did not care for my appeals, or for my attitude toward some of their fellow judges. They said I was diminishing the public's respect for judges. I replied that the Philadelphia trial judges were doing that to themselves. When they had finished, they approved our diversion program.

By January 1971 we had funding from the Department of Justice for a pilot program that Hoffman would run called "preindictment probation," later called "Accelerated Rehabilitative Disposition," or ARD. It was applied statewide by the Pennsylvania Rules of Criminal Procedure and became a national model. We cleared a quarter of our caseload through the program, some seven thousand to eight thousand cases a year, as many as eighty cases a day. Hoffman, in business suit and bow tie rather than a black robe, sat at a conference table with the defendant and the lawyers from each side. He explained the program, warned that the deal was off if the defendant was charged with another crime within a year, and collected signatures on a contract.

"It changed the whole theory of trying cases," Hoffman, still on the bench, said shortly before he died in 1998.[1] "It's now used in every state. It had never been used before. Arlen Specter and I worked out the details. It was innovative—nobody ever thought of it before. If it hadn't been for this, the criminal dockets of the whole United States would be so clogged we'd never get out from under."

Officials from across the nation trooped to Philadelphia to see the new program in action, then developed similar programs of their own. Diversion programs are known by a host of names, such as preindictment probation, but they all follow the Philadelphia concept.

Even President Nixon liked our program, as he told his top aide, H. R. Haldeman, in June 1971, after ending a meeting with me, according to recently released Oval Office tapes:

RN: . . . He [Arlen Specter] says he's got this, eh, pre-indictment probation which is what you do when you've got somebody's out for a
joyride, you pick him up, you know, a college kid, you arrest him and
then you bring him in before indictment and you say, "All right, you're
on probation for a year." But *(pause)*

HRH: No official record.

RN: But there'd be no record if you don't break it. But if you break it
then they're going to throw the book at you. Excellent idea.

HRH: I'm for that.

RN: Excellent idea . . . [Attorney General John] Mitchell agrees with
it completely and I said that's very good.[2]

On the sixth floor of City Hall, we were forging the modern prosecutor's office. Robert Kennedy had set some benchmarks as U.S. attorney
general, with backing from his brother the president. Our task as a
county DA's office was tougher. We were tackling the whole system:
political corruption, judges' indifference, a breakdown of the courts.
But I had campaigned on reform, and we felt we had a strong mandate
and strong public backing. We tried to bring judgment, imagination,
and creativity to law enforcement. As I look back, some of our innova-
tions in the Philadelphia DA's office seem obvious. But many were rev-
olutionary at the time.

My office opposed plea-bargaining. Plea-bargaining means probation or short sentences for repeat offenders who should go away for
years. Plea-bargaining also pressures innocent people to plead guilty
and leave with time-in-detention credit, rather than staying in jail and
fighting in court. We made exceptions only in extreme circumstances,
such as a rape case in which the victim had moved to another state and
missed several court dates, and the judge said, "You take probation, or I
will throw out the case." We took probation. That way, if the rapist committed another crime, we could nail him at least for violating probation.

I attacked plea-bargaining as a member of a federal commission in
Washington. As *U.S. News & World Report* put it, "A federal commission looking into the causes and cures of violence has been given an
example of what happens to crime in a city when its officials take a
'tough line.' The city was Philadelphia. . . . Mr. Specter's solution is
'tough sentences for tough criminals.' "[3] The National Commission on
Criminal Justice Standards and Goals, convened in 1972, adopted that
standard to eliminate plea-bargaining. Regrettably, the policy has been

observed more in the breach, because the criminal justice system has not been provided with sufficient resources to try the serious cases.

We took on environmental menaces. We sued polluters under an 1860 Pennsylvania common nuisance statute. Our targets included the city and its SEPTA buses, which billowed black, lung-clogging fumes. In 1971 we forced a construction company to enclose a construction site across the street from City Hall, where much of the asbestos the company sprayed onto steel beams for fireproofing wafted into the downtown Philadelphia air. On a personal note, when the asbestos spraying reached the sixth floor, the same height as my office across the street, we accelerated the case.

Some of our pioneering dated back to efforts before my election. In the fall of 1962 I stepped out of my role as chief of the Appeals Division to try a case to expand the definition of murder in the first degree. Thomas Young had entered a West Philadelphia hardware store to rob it. When Thomas demanded money at gunpoint, the proprietor died of a heart attack. This case established a new principle of first-degree felony murder where no physical contact was made with the victim. Although the conviction was reversed on appeal because of an evidentiary issue, the precedent stands.

My office moved promptly on my campaign promise to crack down on rape. When I became DA, rape was treated like any other crime. Victims generally gave their accounts, including the most lurid personal details, in a crowded police squad room. When rape victims talked, everybody listened, just as in the old E. F. Hutton ads. My office changed procedures to put rape victims in a separate room, where they were interviewed by female detectives. We also brushed for hair follicles and took photos to show the victim's bruises. Before, all that evidence was simply lost or ignored, along with the wounds that healed before trial.

My second year, in 1967, I created a rape-control unit, with an assistant DA available twenty-four hours a day to advise the police. We asked all rape victims to take a physical exam at Philadelphia General Hospital and to forward the results to us. We pushed for heavy prison terms. From 1967 to 1968 the conviction rate for rape jumped from 66 to 74 percent, in part because we were making stronger cases, which in turn gave us leverage to get more guilty pleas without compromises on sentences.

I personally tried our first rape case, on February 9, 1966, five weeks after I took office. A nineteen-year-old Army private, James Fredericks, was charged with raping a woman after burglarizing her apartment. Fredericks claimed he had falsely confessed because he was scared. I was cross-examining him, attacking his alibi, when Judge Theodore Reimel cut me off. "Folks," the judge said, "I have a rather pleasant duty to perform."

My forefinger still pointing, I turned toward the bench. So did the rest of the packed courtroom.

"It's a wedding," Reimel said. "So we will pause briefly." The judge called, "Will the wedding party please step forward?" With that, the bride, groom, and seven attendants came to the front of the courtroom. The judge fumbled through a small black Bible and stepped off the bench. As the *Philadelphia Inquirer* reported it:

> "We are gathered here in the sight of God," Reimel began.
> The jury watched transfixed.
> "Do you, Milton, take Elizabeth as your lawfully wedded wife?"
> The district attorney and defense counsel were open-mouthed. The courtroom spectators, about 100 of them, were pop-eyed. . . . Only Fredericks was unimpressed. Throughout the entire proceeding he remained placidly expressionless. Even his squirming stopped.

The Philadelphia courts did not take rape nearly as seriously as they should. Nonetheless, Fredericks was convicted.

I had also promised to crack down on nuisance taprooms, the rowdy bars that spilled vandals, muggers, robbers, and urinating drunkards onto neighborhood streets. These taprooms ruined entire communities. They were spawning grounds for crime and violence and drove out local merchants, especially laundries, groceries, and clothiers. Residents who had the means would move. Those who did not would suffer.

Our main weapon was the Pennsylvania Liquor Control Act, which allowed the court to close a bawdy bar for a year in an equity proceeding ending with an injunction. To gather evidence, we sent our detectives undercover, posing as bar patrons.

In late January 1966, after only a few weeks on the job, I filed my first padlock petition. Our target was the Wheel Bar, a pit where several people had been stabbed in 1965 and which women were afraid to walk past. Judge Joseph Gold balked at my petition. The Wheel Bar case carried weight beyond its eventual verdict. As the *Inquirer* put it, "The case was the first to enter the courts in Specter's drive against nuisance taverns. If the prosecution is successful, the District Attorney is expected to bring charges against other establishments." The publicity sent a message throughout Philadelphia that City Hall, or at least one agency in it, cared about communities. I fought with Gold for a year. Finally, in June 1967, the state supreme court overruled Gold, finding that we had supplied ample evidence to justify shutting the Wheel Bar and that Gold had "abused his discretion" in keeping the tavern open.

We continued apace for a couple of years. Then, in 1969, I formed a special taproom bureau. We went after ten of the worst dives and closed all of them. At the Wellington Bar, a motorcycle gang hangout, topless and bottomless go-go dancers gyrated while patrons drank until they had to be carried outside. The milieu was completed by a house midget who ran around the bar pinching the female patrons and fondling their breasts. Assistant DA Harvey Steinberg, who ran the taproom bureau in 1969, went undercover at the biker bar for three weekends. "I watched the midget cupping his hands over their breasts," he recalled almost thirty years later. "I saw a mother, a go-go dancer, with her three-year-old daughter in matching costume, dancing at 1:00 A.M."[4] The matching costumes featured tasseled bikinis. The Beefburger Tavern, described by its owner as "an old-time Kensington bar," ran beer-throwing contests that made it dangerous to open the door. In 1970 and 1971, we closed eleven bars. After the fight with Gold, no judge denied a padlock petition, and we never lost a case in court.

In the mid-1960s drug trafficking increased. In 1968 we formed a special unit of police and prosecutors to fight major drug traffickers. Police were ill matched against mid- and upper-level drug dealers. Criminal courts were filled with drug users charged with burglaries and larcenies committed to feed their habits. Long before I introduced drug-court legislation in the Senate in the late 1980s and 1990s, I promoted rehabilitation of users to stop the crime cycle. In 1972, we convened a special investigating grand jury to focus on organized crime's drug operations. Those efforts preceded RICO, the federal statute targeted to fight organized crime.

My office helped create an early residential drug treatment center.

Modeled after Daytop Village in Swan Lake, New York, then the foremost drug program in the country, the program was called "Gaudenzia House," after the mythical Greek horse that fell in the middle of a race, recovered, and went on to win. We took the idea to Governor Ray Shafer, who put up $250,000 in state funds for the rehabilitation center in a Philadelphia suburb. Gaudenzia House has flourished and expanded in the last thirty years. The push had begun when Judge Leo Weinrott of the common pleas court told the president of the Greater Philadelphia Movement, a group of city movers and shakers, that he was concerned about the drug problem. The GPM executive director, Bill Wilcox, wound up steering the effort.

To get personal insights into the rehabilitation process, Joan and I spent a remarkable weekend at Daytop Village in October 1968, at Wilcox's suggestion. We drove up on a Friday morning, and, as Joan put it, they broke us down so they could rebuild us. Staff members walked us around the grounds all day so that we were exhausted by midnight. We then began a twenty-six-hour marathon with ten people, talking about our experiences and problems. The group was led by three ex–drug users and included, among the nonusers, a psychiatrist, a schoolteacher, and a social worker. At that hour, with everyone so weary, discussion was frank and open.

We were so exhausted by the end that we hallucinated. I thought I saw bugs crawling the walls. They brought in our only food, cold-cut sandwiches. We were allowed to leave the room only to use the toilets. At 2:00 A.M. Sunday we adjourned for seven hours of sleep. At nine on Sunday morning we went back into the room for feedback, and we discussed what we had learned about ourselves and the others, until about two the next morning. The marathon sessions demonstrated the similarity of the participants' problems. They showed drug addicts that their problems were shared by everyone else, and could be confronted and solved.

When the courts began to recognize drunkenness as a disease in the mid-1960s, my office pressed to take intoxication out of the criminal courts. We reasoned that if alcoholism was a disease, then public drunkenness was a symptom, and it made no more sense to punish a person for being publicly drunk than to punish a person with a cold for publicly sneezing. Working with the defender's office, we picked two test cases. In one of those cases in August 1967, Judge Weinrott ruled that drunkenness was a disease. Treatment programs for alcoholics were then developed.

The DA's office policy was changed to give suspects a chance to offer a defense before an arrest warrant was issued. This policy seemed wise on several grounds: First and foremost, it was the fair thing to do. Second, hearing a person's defense might help the prosecution's case. Many people are convicted on their own lies. Finally, I wanted to hear a person's response, because that might persuade us that we had no case. We could check out the explanation and maybe save the suspect from an unwarranted prosecution and our office from embarrassment.

The policy proved its worth when one of my top assistants asked for authorization to arrest a federal judge on charges of exposing himself. Two women living across an alley from the judge, in a facing apartment, had told police that the judge was flashing from his window. I asked my assistant what the judge had said when confronted with those facts. When told the judge had not been questioned, I told my assistant to go back and talk to the judge. He came back later in the day to tell me the women had the wrong floor. Obviously, arresting the federal judge would have been a disaster. The judge's reputation would have been damaged, along with our rapport with the judiciary and the public's opinion of our competence.

Among my reforms, I probably took the most criticism for cracking down on police brutality. I believe I was the first DA in the country to systematically prosecute police for brutality. This was twenty-five years before Los Angeles police officers went on trial for beating Rodney King. Brutal police officers, like corrupt judges, send a signal that average citizens cannot count on government for justice or fairness. People, especially minorities and the poor, become distrustful of the police and withdraw, refusing to serve as witnesses in court, further complicating the fight against crime. But my prosecutions of police ran up against the tough-on-crime mood of the times and Philadelphia's law-and-order police commissioner, Frank Rizzo, a flamboyant national figure who later served two terms as mayor. Philadelphia—and America—liked aggressive police, and they liked Rizzo's bare-knuckles style.

Rizzo was often described as "larger than life." The *Philadelphia Daily News* ran his photo on page one without a caption. The entire city recognized the set stare in the meaty face under the thick, graying hair. Frank Rizzo was six-foot-three and 240 pounds, and always well groomed, from his spit-shined oxfords to his tailored suit to his combed cut. The son of a South Philadelphia patrolman, Rizzo had quit school in eleventh grade, put in a few years in the Army and in construction work, then joined the police force. Talented and tough, he had risen quickly through the ranks. Along the way he acquired the nickname "The Cisco Kid." Rizzo gained early fame raiding coffeehouses and rousting out patrons he found undesirable, with little thought for the Constitution.

In 1972, President Nixon came to the Philadelphia Convention Center to speak about education. The president shared the stage with Cardinal Krol, Mayor Rizzo, me as DA, and one or two other local leaders. A heckler shouted continually from the balcony. After a while Rizzo got up, walked to the edge of the stage, and jumped off the platform about six feet to the floor. His landing sounded like an explosion. The beefy mayor went up to the balcony and quieted the heckler. Later he explained his technique. A policeman sits next to a heckler and says, "You blankety so-and-so. You're in real trouble. We're going to teach you a lesson." But the words, too soft to reach any other ears, are spoken through his teeth with a broad grin.

Rizzo and I had a complex relationship. Martin Weinberg, Rizzo's city solicitor, campaign manager, and longtime confidant, and later a candidate for mayor himself, recently told me I was one of only four people of whom Rizzo would never speak ill, even in private. "It was unbelievable. Frank Rizzo would never say anything ever, even in private, that was unfavorable against Arlen. He had this special place in his heart. There was President Nixon, Cardinal Krol, [*Inquirer* publisher] Walter Annenberg, and Arlen Specter," Weinberg said. "Nixon and Annenberg and Krol were all close personal friends of Frank's, so I always understood why Frank always held them in such high esteem."[5]

Why did I enjoy such favor with Rizzo? The best Weinberg could figure, it was because our disagreements rested on sincere and deeply held views. Rizzo liked my taking on the judges, a battle he could not undertake while working his way up the police ranks. From his position as deputy police commissioner, Rizzo couldn't join fights, but he cheered me on from the sidelines. When Rizzo became police commissioner in May 1967, he took off his gloves, showed his brass knuckles, and dominated Philadelphia and, to an extent, the national scene.

Weinberg may have given part of the answer about my complex relationship with Rizzo when he told one of my associates in 1998, "Frank always had a tremendous amount of respect for Arlen and the fact that he was a guy who came in and wanted to do the right thing, and positive things, for law enforcement for Philadelphia." The mutual respect continued, but the honeymoon was short-lived.

Police were tough all over the country, but perhaps a little more so in Philadelphia because of Rizzo. A celebrated photo showed Rizzo with a nightstick wedged in his tuxedo cummerbund, about to race to a police call from a formal dinner. "I guess Frank Rizzo had some subtlety in his nature," said Dan McKenna, my Senate press secretary, who earlier had served as Rizzo's press secretary. "But I never saw it."

"As a general proposition, Frank was a counterpuncher," Weinberg said. "Frank basically was a guy that if somebody took shots at him, he would hit back, and the hitting back was not in proportion to the original attack. A slap in the face was returned with an anvil over the head."

After I had arrested one policeman for brutality, Rizzo said, "Arlen Specter will rue the day that he arrested that police officer." While Rizzo was not exactly right, we never convicted any of the many police officers we prosecuted for brutality. It wasn't that juries doubted there was police brutality. They thought there was not enough of it. The police could hardly be too brutal with criminals, much of the popular thinking went.

Several times, by chance, I authorized the arrest of a police officer around the time a policeman was murdered in the line of duty. I attended all the funerals for police officers killed in the line of duty, and I had some tough days when recently arrested cops walked down church aisles at masses for fallen comrades. It was also problematic to prosecute police officers because our office depended on the department's cooperation. After all, the police were our prime witnesses in most cases.

Rizzo and I had long arguments about police brutality and whether I should arrest a particular officer. I would give him notice about my plans to arrest one of his officers, and he would come to my office, sometimes taking two hours trying to change my mind. Rizzo never talked me out of an arrest, because I never gave him notice until I was sure there was real cause to prosecute. My office brought police brutality cases only when they were clear-cut. Despite those prosecutions, I enjoyed excellent relations with police, since they knew that our policies were fair and my assistants and I were tough on violent crime.

I would tell Rizzo that he shouldn't defend officers when they were wrong. He would reply that anyone could defend them when they were right, and they needed him to defend them when they were wrong. Rizzo routinely made a forceful argument. One day he was particularly effective. "How can you arrest this guy?" he thundered. "There's an eighty-mile-an-hour chase up a one-way street with a stolen car, a guy driving the wrong way, he runs into a telephone poll, the cop chases him, risking his life, the guy jumps out of the car, runs down a dark alley, the cop chases him on foot, the guy whirls, the cop sees the guy, thinks he has a gun in his hand, the cop shoots him and it's fatal, the Supreme Court deliberates seven years, five-to-four decides this was unreasonable, and you want to arrest the guy who has to make a decision in a few seconds." Well-founded prosecutions counterbalanced Rizzo's rhetoric.

Although we didn't get convictions, we did send a message that police abuses would not be tolerated. Our prosecutions also showed concern and respect for the African-American community. African-Americans, almost half of Philadelphia's population, felt victimized by the police and written out of the social contract. Philadelphia was a city divided. To try to bridge the gap, I recruited African-American prosecutors and detectives. Diversifying the staff brought perspective and sensitivity. Paul Dandridge, my first African-American hire, complained to me that many African-Americans were arrested for carrying brown paper bags. I looked into the matter. It turned out the police had decided that African-Americans were breaking the blue laws by buying liquor at speakeasies. I ordered discharges on constitutional grounds, then called the department, and the arrests stopped.

For a time, I held weekly "open house" hours, beginning my first Wednesday as DA. I began with twelve-hour days and later shifted to evening sessions. Anyone could come into my office to discuss any matter. I saw 849 people personally in 1966. On the basis of tips I got during those sessions, we closed two bars, prosecuted consumer fraud cases, and made many assorted arrests. We also sent a message that people at City Hall cared about street-level problems miles away and would fight to solve them. Our efforts and visibility worked to reduce public apathy and hopelessness. I have kept up the practice of constituent contacts in the Senate by regularly holding open-house town meetings in all sixty-seven Pennsylvania counties. Those sessions work better than polls and focus groups to tell me about public sentiment, and they carry a strong message of concern for people.

During one open house we learned about a battle brewing between two rival youth gangs over the killing of a gang member. Gil Branche—the first African-American to be appointed chief of detectives—Dandridge, and I raced to ground zero, the three-way intersection of 6th Street and Diamond and Germantown avenues. The gang members were lined up facing each other with lethal weapons. We were able to head off the battle and get a promise of a truce from the rival gang leaders. But gang warfare continued to rage in Philadelphia and in most other American cities. In 1968 Philadelphia hit a high of thirty reported gang-related murders. In early 1969 I traveled to Washington to ask newly appointed Attorney General John Mitchell for a federal grant for a gang-control project. We proposed one-stop juvenile centers featuring remedial education, recreation, tailored job counseling, and group attitude-adjustment sessions. The Department of Justice gave us $80,000 to open two centers.

We created a riot-control unit during the turbulent Vietnam era. My office wrote a first-in-the-nation response to the report of the Kerner Commission, formally the National Advisory Commission on Civil Disorders. Our pamphlet, "Rights and Limitations on Speech and Assembly," summarized complex Supreme Court decisions in layman's language and instructed police and protesters on how far each could go. The *Philadelphia Bulletin* reprinted the booklet on a full page in its Sunday edition.

Rizzo and I rode the streets on hot summer nights in 1967 and 1968, when parts of the country were burning, including cities in Pennsylvania and neighboring New Jersey. The night in 1968 that Martin Luther King, Jr., was assassinated, cities burned across the country. In Philadelphia that night, the air smelled of a riot. But Philadelphia remained still. A cloudburst helped. Rain, Rizzo said, was the policeman's best friend. We may have contributed to the calm. Riots had ripped Philadelphia in 1964, and it may have been just coincidence, but when I was DA and Rizzo was police commissioner or mayor, Philadelphia did not burn.

MAYOR

I'd been district attorney less than a year in the fall of 1966 when Bill Meehan asked me to run for mayor. The Greater Philadelphia Movement, the community leaders known as the "Movers and Shakers," also weighed in. The civic and business crowds were eager to rid themselves of Mayor James H. J. Tate, who had not carried on the tradition in the Dilworth years of partnership between City Hall and the business community.

The Philadelphia mayor's race carried weight nationally, coming a year before the 1968 presidential election. Philadelphia was the key to Pennsylvania, and Pennsylvania was a key to presidential victory. But I resisted running, for several reasons. I was thirty-six years old and was having a banner first year as DA, a job I loved. I also knew it would look opportunistic to run for mayor so soon after being elected DA. But it was tempting, with an early poll showing me winning 67–33 percent. That survey, by Meehan's pollster John Bucci, was taken on April Fools' Day, 1966. The city also needed new leadership, which my team could provide; and it would be a real accomplishment to bring two-party government to Philadelphia.

The business community ran a quasi-contrived draft. Bill Wilcox, the GPM executive director, placed a full-page ad in the *Inquirer* signed by the city's leading bluebloods, urging me to run for mayor. Meehan, again, would raise all the money, about $1 million this time.

On the Democratic side, Tate faced a primary challenge from Alexander Hemphill, the city controller. Tate found himself an unpopular mayor with an approval rating of 26 percent facing a popular controller who had both a sterling image and the party's support. Tate seemed a sure loser in the primary. But he was crafty and well armed.

The mayor outspent Hemphill six to one. He used his police force to raid taprooms run by Democratic ward leaders, to cool their opposition. On primary election day, Tate edged Hemphill. That made it Jim Tate against me in the general election.

Tate called on me to resign as DA shortly after I challenged him for mayor. The city charter required a city official to resign when running for another office. Hemphill had resigned as controller to challenge Tate in the mayoral primary, and Dilworth had resigned as mayor in 1962 to run for governor. Even some of my strongest supporters urged me to step down as DA. Henry Sawyer, then the ADA chairman, came to my house one morning and implored me to resign, ruining my Sunday breakfast. Meehan, on the other hand, did not want me to resign. By his calculus, keeping the DA's office and the daily headlines it generated was a net plus for my candidacy. I got plenty of press during the campaign when some Philadelphia Teamsters got into a gunfight on Spring Garden Avenue, and I indicted one of their leaders for flashing a signal to start a shoot-out.

I figured I was entitled to stay. I had won the DA's race through sweat and risk, and I wasn't eager to give up the job, nor to run for mayor. I had made it clear, when the party and the GPM brass were pressing me to run, that I wouldn't give up the DA's office for the campaign. I also thought I had legal grounds to stay in office. I argued that I was a state officer, not a city officer, which meant that the city charter and its resignation requirement did not apply to me. As DA, I prosecuted cases in the name of the commonwealth, not the city. The key to my status lay in a test case that was pending at the time, over a subpoena I had issued to a magistrate to inspect his files. My theory was that if I was a city officer, I was entitled to use the subpoena power granted in the city charter to get the magistrates' records. And if I was not a city officer, there shouldn't be civil-service limits on my detectives.

I had personally argued the test case, *Commonwealth ex rel Arlen Specter* v. *Freed,* in the state supreme court. In early 1967 the justices split. Three justices said I was a state officer and therefore did not have subpoena power. Three justices did not really deal with whether I was a city or state officer, but simply said I didn't have subpoena power. Chief Justice John Bell said I was a city officer and had subpoena power. The decision left muddled the question of whether I had to resign. I took the position that I didn't have to. After all, only one justice had said I was a city officer.

Tate stopped my pay. Charles Klein, the distinguished president judge of the Orphans' Court, invited me to his chambers and offered me a $10,000 loan to tide me over. Thanks, but no thanks. I had a wife and two young sons, but I had saved enough to keep us going for a while. Edward Bauer, Tate's city solicitor, offered to restart my pay if I promised to reimburse the city if I ultimately lost the fight. No deal. I sued the Tate administration. The case went to state supreme court, where I won 4–2. Most of the judges said that whether I was a state or city officer, I deserved to be paid. Most Philadelphians seemed to feel the same way. They knew what it meant to cut a person's financial lifeline.

Late in the campaign a third lawsuit was filed to strike my name from the ballot. The suit came before the state supreme court in October 1967. By this time the three Democratic justices had unified, saying I was a city officer and had to resign, with the three Republicans holding that I was a state officer and did not have to resign. Chief Justice Bell was up against it, because he had already ruled in the Freed subpoena case that I was a city officer, and he couldn't change his opinion now. Bell said he still believed I was a city officer, but that it would be "a gross miscarriage of justice" to leave the Republican Party without a candidate a month before the election. So I stayed on the ballot and in the DA's office.

Bill Wilcox, the big thinker and social engineer from the Greater Philadelphia Movement, led the issues team, which toiled all summer, meeting nights, weekends, and during vacations at the New Jersey shore. We churned out a dozen superb papers, which we bound and printed under the title "Blueprints for a Better Philadelphia." We were preparing for a big job.

Two major issues emerged in the campaign: Frank Rizzo and state aid to parochial schools. Together, my views on these issues probably cost me 75,000 votes. Police Commissioner Ed Bell had resigned on primary night in disgust over Tate's raids of Democratic ward leaders' taprooms. That gave Tate an opening to appoint a new commissioner, and he named Frank Rizzo. The Cisco Kid was the hero of the city, after quelling the 1967 riots. Tate, desperate to capture the law-and-order issue, pledged to keep Rizzo as commissioner in his second term. I would make no such pledge. I said I would appoint my cabinet after I was elected, not before. The fact was, I would have kept Rizzo because he was a solid police commissioner. But I wasn't going to go on record and owe my election to Frank Rizzo. I wouldn't want to owe my election to anybody, and especially not to Rizzo. I didn't say anything privately either, about reappointing Rizzo, and I certainly didn't tell him. If you told something to Rizzo, you told it to the world. You might as well call a news conference.

As for state aid to parochial schools, I opposed it on the grounds that it was unconstitutional and that we shouldn't divert funds from public schools. State aid wasn't even an issue for the Philadelphia mayor. It was an issue for the state legislature, which was already debating House Bill 1136 on the subject. I refused to support the bill. The legislature eventually passed HB 1136, and the U.S. Supreme Court eventually ruled that it was unconstitutional. But the Supreme Court's ruling came too late for my campaign.

The Democrats wanted to enlist Robert Kennedy, then seeking the 1968 Democratic presidential nomination, to stump for Tate in Philadelphia. The city, especially its large Irish Catholic bloc, adored the Kennedys. But the former attorney general demurred. I figured he wouldn't campaign against me because of my work prosecuting the Philadelphia Teamsters, and perhaps to a lesser extent because of my work investigating his brother's murder.

Other national figures did lend Tate a hand. Vice President Humphrey phoned the mayor from Rome in late May to urge him to go to Israel, where war was imminent. Tate went, cowered in a bomb shelter, and broadcast live to KYW Radio in Philadelphia during the Six-Day War. When Tate returned, he held a news conference on his front porch, playing the global humanitarian. In August, Archbishop Krol went to Rome to be made a cardinal. Tate went along. The *Bulletin* ran a huge page-one photo of Tate kissing the pope's foot.

A key factor popped up, by chance, days before the election. Stephen Weinstein, who ran a Philadelphia tobacco shop, was arrested for seducing a Penn freshman from Iowa named John Green, drugging him with a hamburger laced with sleeping pills, strangling him, and dumping his body in the river. Weinstein, twenty-nine, was captured in Times Square during a search of sex shops. The grisly crime made banner headlines for days. On the Saturday before the election, Dick Sprague and I drove to New York City to bring Weinstein back. In a holding cell, I read Weinstein his rights. He gave a detailed confession, saying he felt strong attraction to boys in tight pants, and that Green had been wearing tight Levi's. Weinstein waived extradition and agreed to return to Philadelphia. He was eventually tried and sentenced to life in prison. Harold Stassen, who was practicing law in Philadelphia at that time after serving as president of Penn and running for mayor on the Republican ticket in 1959, told me that Green's murder cost me many votes by stirring up blatant anti-Semitism because Weinstein was obviously Jewish.

The race came down to the wire. Some of my aides heard reports that pro-Tate literature was distributed at churches on the Sunday before the election, noting that I opposed aid to parochial schools. On election day, union toughs blocked me from my customary rounds of visiting the polls—at the legal distance, of course. I was the DA, but I couldn't get past ten goons stationed at each polling place wearing huge overcoats adorned with big buttons: PULL LEVER NUMBER 2, VOTE STRAIGHT DEMOCRAT.

On election night, our pollster, John Bucci, analyzed the race for KYW Radio. He had people set up in key districts ready to telephone him immediately after the polls closed at 8:00 P.M. By 8:12 P.M., after getting sample returns at the station, Bucci knew the end result, and he announced it. Our son Shanin, then nine, walked into our bedroom as Joan and I prepared to go to campaign headquarters for what we hoped would be a victory celebration. He said, "John Bucci says you lost, Daddy." It was a shock that Shanin and KYW listeners knew the result before I did.

In the end, Tate edged me by 10,954 votes out of some 700,000 votes cast, the closest margin in a citywide race in Philadelphia history. Cecil Moore, the city's NAACP president, running on a third-party ticket, got 9,018 votes. I lost the race by 1.5 percent. Exit polls showed that 3 percent of the voters cast their ballots for Tate because they wanted me to remain their district attorney.

Interestingly, I lost some of the Jewish vote, from people who worried that any shortcomings on my part would tar Jews at large. I would hear the same reasoning much louder when I ran for president in 1995. Some Jews told me they opposed me because Jews are blamed for Hollywood movies, for Wall Street, for everything. If I were to become president, I would be blamed for anything that went wrong. Michael Halberstam explored such a scenario in his celebrated political novel, *The Wanting of Levine*.

Many people had been counting on my victory to bring back two-

214

party government to Philadelphia and to begin preparation for a major event, the Bicentennial of 1976. The loss took a lot of the wind out of my sails. It was a long election night conceding defeat. There were no recriminations. Tough as that defeat was, I tried—I think success-fully—not to take it personally. I had done my best. I had strong family support and much to look forward to notwithstanding the loss.

I'd learned about losing many years earlier in high school debates. I've never become a "good loser," subscribing to the dictum "Show me a good loser and I'll show you a loser." At Russell High School, my teammates and I suffered some bitter, bruising losses in debates. When you suffer such losses at fifteen or sixteen, you sometimes learn. We lost the state championship in 1946 by a hair and came back to win it decisively the next year.

Scholastic debate involves ferocious competition, joined on all sides with the passion and energy of youth. The whole debate experience was so important to me at a formative age that to this day, more than fifty years later, I can remember who was paired with whom in most tourna-ments, the subjects, and the won-lost records. In 1941, when Bob Dole was a Russell High senior, Russell had a dominant team. Dr. Irwin Luthie, who coached the team, said in 1996 that Dole, who shunned the debate team, preferring to be a basketball star, would have become president if he'd acquired debating skills in high school.

I learned a most poignant lesson on coping with disappointment while working on a farm when I was fourteen. In the summer of 1944 I worked for Clyde Mills, father of my close friend and high school classmate Steve, driving a tractor in the wheat fields. The tractor pulled a combine, which cut the wheat, extracted the grain, and collected it in a large bin. From sunup to sundown I drove around fields of fifteen to twenty acres, cutting fourteen feet of wheat in a square, then driving in another square, cutting down fourteen more feet of wheat, and so on until the entire field was cut.

In my other Kansas summers I worked in my father's junkyard. When the tornadoes ripped through the prairie, they often knocked down hundred-foot oil derricks, which were then fit only for salvage. My brother-in-law, Arthur Morgenstern, a partner with my father and brother in the junkyard, and I would cut the derricks into small pieces with oxygen-acetylene torches. We saved the angle iron for resale as structural steel at $2^3/4$ cents a pound under federal price controls and loaded the unsalvageable junk onto the truck for later shipment to the smelters. We had to be careful. Sparks from the torches singed our clothing in the hundred-plus-degree heat. Cutting the coiled-spring base of a derrick the wrong way could be fatal. We sometimes uncovered rattlesnake nests while pulling scrap iron from the oil fields.

Farming and working the oil fields were great incentives to become a lawyer.

In 1944 heavy rains lasting days at a stretch interrupted the harvest. Wheat could be cut only when it was dry, so the grain could be shaken loose. Each day the rain continued meant substantial losses for Clyde Mills. I knew he needed the year-end wheat profits to meet payments on a heavy mortgage on his farm. Sitting on the porch watching the rain, I asked Mr. Mills how he felt about it. He looked at me and with a soft voice said, "Some years it's good, Arlen, some years it's bad. It all works out in the end. We'll be okay."

Mr. Mills was right. We eventually cut the wheat. Despite that year's losses, somehow he met or refinanced the mortgage and continued farming. I got $10 a day, or $140, for my fourteen days on the tractor, which I put in my bank account. Shortly after the harvest ended, my father had an opportunity to buy a 250-barrel tank, but he lacked the purchase price. He suggested I invest $90 in the tank, which I did. Several months later he sold the tank for a $60 profit. As I look back at the tank transaction some fifty-five years later, I realize how little capital my father had: none. But it all worked out.

The biggest cost of the mayoral race was my "white-knight-on-a-charger" image as a young DA. It had been too soon to run again, and that made me look too "political." "You have the energy and aggressiveness of Arlen, and then you tie in the ambition, and you run for office right away when you're a first-timer, then all of a sudden the hunger becomes the lead thought in people's mind," my longtime political consultant David Garth said recently. "My feeling is, it probably had an aftertaste that lasted a long time."[1]

COFFINS ON WHEELS

After the mayoral election in November 1967, I returned immediately to a full agenda in the DA's office. We looked into prison violence, running what I believe was the first such investigation in the nation by a prosecutor's office. Deputy DA Alan Davis, who had pioneered the pre-indictment probation program, began his 1968 report on rape behind bars with the account of a young, slightly built, mentally disturbed inmate:

> I was lying in my bed when seven or eight inmates came to my bed, pulled the blanket off me, put it on the floor and told me to pull my pants down and lay face down on the blanket. I said, "No" and was punched in the face by one of the inmates. The inmate that punched me stated if I didn't get on the floor the other inmates would gang up on me.
>
> I got on the floor and my pants and shorts were pulled off. Two inmates spread and held my legs apart while two more inmates held my hands in front of me. While I was being buggered from behind, another inmate would make me suck his penis. This continued until all the inmates had attacked me and I heard one of them say it was 1:30 a.m., so let's go to bed. They put me on the bed, covered me with the blanket and one of them patted me on the behind saying, "Good boy, we will see you again tomorrow night."
>
> While I was being molested I was held by the neck and head and threatened with bodily harm if I yelled or screamed. They stated that they would beat my head on the floor if I made any outcry.[1]

This grotesque episode occurred in a prison, and episodes like it probably still occur in prisons nearly everywhere. We found systemic prison rape that was known and tolerated. Our report sounded a national alarm. In the last thirty years, of course, improving prison life has become a vogue, inspired by media exposés and by films such as Robert Redford's *Brubaker*. But back in the turbulent 1960s it was a bold move to stand up for the rights of inmates. Just as much of the public thought there could not be too much police brutality, they also didn't care what happened to inmates. The public, and even the police, had no idea how bad life behind bars could be, or that rape victims often included youths arrested for nonviolent crimes who were awaiting trial. It was important to eliminate this kind of brutality in prisons, both for humanitarian reasons and for public safety.

As a young assistant DA, I used to talk to death-row inmates and to lifers who wanted their sentences commuted. Those interviews gave me a peephole into the world behind bars. I have continued my prison visits as a senator for insights on legislation and for my Judiciary Committee work. I saw that releasing inmates who were functional illiterates without trades or skills just sent them back to lives of crime. We warehoused prisoners. We did not rehabilitate them or give them job or literacy training, to give them a chance. And the brutality and sodomy behind bars that we uncovered in 1968 only made released inmates more hostile and vicious. Society has not yet focused on the basic fact that rehabilitation is not just for the inmate. The recidivist returns to criminal attacks on the innocent.

Our investigation grew out of the 1968 trial of Frank Joseph Mitchell, a nineteen-year-old arrested for killing a fifteen-year-old girl, Doris Shenk, after having sex with her. Mitchell gave us a full account:

> Me and Doris started to walk down Boston Street. We stopped on the vacant lot for about five minutes before we went into the house. After we got inside the house, we sat by the wall and started necking, then we started to lay down on the floor where I removed her coat, then as we continued to neck, I started to remove her Wranglers, then I started to remove her underclothing but after a while she unbuttoned her blouse.
>
> After the blouse was removed, I started to remove her brassiere but I couldn't, then I ripped her brassiere off her, the snaps and all. She was completely nude then but wasn't afraid until after I laid down, then we had sexual intercourse, afterwards when I got up, she said she was going to tell the police that were on the corner.
>
> Then, I got up and I walked around her to where my feet were at her

head, she was still laying on the floor crying. Then, I started to get scared and I put my right foot on her throat, then reached for the chair that was alongside of me.

At that point Mitchell was interrupted and given a cup of coffee. He refused anything more to eat. Ten minutes later, he continued:

> Then, she put her arm up and tried to pull my leg away from her throat, then I put my left leg on her arm to stop her from pulling at my leg while her other arm was scratching at my right leg.
> I kept putting pressure down as I leaned against the chair. Then she fell limp.[2]

Doris Shenk was dead.

I tried the case. After an intense two-week trial, the jury found Mitchell guilty of first-degree murder. He received a life sentence. On his way to prison, other convicts sodomized Mitchell in a sheriff's van. The dark vans, which looked like armored trucks, ferried inmates and defendants from their cells in the Philadelphia suburbs to their hearings at City Hall. The prisoners sat in windowless boxes in the back during the nearly hour-long trips. The guards up front couldn't see or hear them. But the guards must have had some idea what had been going on when they arrived and unloaded their cargo.

When Mike Wallace of the new CBS newsmagazine *60 Minutes* interviewed me in late 1968 about our investigation, I told him about a ride in a sheriff's van like the ride Mitchell had taken:

> This past June there was a 17-year-old boy in this crowded van with more than two dozen people and he was the victim of a very brutal attack. Five or six, or maybe even more men, jumped him, they penetrated his body, they defiled him, they raped him. That 17-year-old boy was a runaway; wasn't even charged with an offense himself but he just happened to be thrown into this "coffin on wheels."
> His body was so bruised and bloodied that he did not have the strength to leave the van without assistance. His pants had been ripped off, and, after the sexual attack, he had been left lying on the floor of the van while the others filed out past him. An investigation was launched into this incident immediately. As a result, six persons were arrested and charged with sodomy for their roles in this sordid crime. They are currently awaiting trial in criminal court.

Frank Mitchell's complaints about his rape in a prison van reached the ears of Judge Alexander Barbieri of the common pleas court, a fine jurist who later became a state supreme court justice. Barbieri, who had been the judge in Mitchell's murder trial, was horrified. He called Alan Davis and, with my concurrence, appointed Davis in July 1968 as a special master to investigate sexual assaults in the Philadelphia prison system and sheriff's vans.

Initially, Davis found little enthusiasm for his prison probe. "No one was really interested in prison reform, with all the priorities on how to spend public funds," he said. "Perhaps rightly so, prisons were at the bottom of the list." Commissioner Rizzo's police and Mayor Tate's bureaucrats were hostile. By their reckoning, Davis was interfering with law enforcement.

"Finally," Davis said, "we convinced the city administration it would be better to do it cooperatively than do it outside, battling them." Rizzo assigned Chief Inspector Joseph O'Neill and a squad of forty cops to work with Davis. Davis found that rape was an accepted part of prison culture. During the twenty-six-month period he investigated, there were an estimated 2,000 gang rapes involving 1,500 victims and 3,500 violators. Among young inmates, rape was not only widespread but almost inevitable.

Nearly every slightly built young man was sexually approached within hours after entering prison, Davis found. "After a young man has been successfully assaulted, he is marked as a sexual victim for the duration of his confinement, and this mark follows him from institution to institution until he returns to the community embittered, degraded and filled with hatred."

After a month-long investigation, Davis filed a 102-page report, which drew enormous publicity, in Philadelphia and around the world, in various languages. The local dailies ran Davis's findings and new charges on their front pages for a month. *60 Minutes* came to Philadelphia to do a piece on the probe. Mike Wallace interviewed Alan Davis and me in a jail cell. The TV newsmagazine broadcast its segment in December 1968, and years later included the Philadelphia piece in a *Best of 60 Minutes* anthology. "This is a new kind of Philadelphia story, but it is not Philadelphia's story alone," Wallace concluded. "It applies to every big city prison system. Only Philadelphia, however, has had the courage to investigate it and publicize it. And what they have found should be a warning to the rest of the country."[3] *Time* also featured the investigation. "Few readers of the document that was made public last week are likely to be prepared for the results,"[4] the magazine wrote.

The community also woke up. As Mike Wallace put it, "Davis appeals to our self-interest." Davis condemned jailhouse rape on several grounds: It offends basic humanity, even behind bars. Putting a man in prison turns him into a finely honed weapon who will be released one day to do more damage. And if anybody has a son who may one day go to jail for joyriding, that parent should move heaven and earth to prevent such abuse.

We went after both inmates and guards. We arrested fifty-one prisoners and former prisoners on charges on sodomy, solicitation to commit sodomy, and conspiracy. We also arrested four prison staffers on charges of extortion, blackmail, and conspiracy, either for joining in the assaults or for ignoring them. We convicted almost all those we arrested.

The investigation brought sweeping reforms to Philadelphia's prison system over the next two years. The sheriff's vans were scrapped, replaced by buses that were manned by guards front and back. Walls and barriers were razed and lighting was added to eliminate dark alcoves. The city hired ninety more prison guards and two supervisors in December 1968. "It's one of the few times I accomplished some real reform," Davis reflected years afterward. "It was very, very satisfying. We made some contribution to changing the culture."

Two years later we investigated grisly behavior behind bars of another sort, after the Holmesburg Prison riot of July 4, 1970. Inmates, dividing largely along racial lines, had butchered and stabbed each other for hours. Like most prisons, Holmesburg was a tinderbox waiting for a spark to erupt. We found overcrowding, lack of security, mismanagement. "Then they took us out of the hallway and put us in the bread room and threatened to kill us," one inmate told us. "We were there about two hours until the police guards came in. I was holding a man's hand on for him because it was chopped off with a meat cleaver." Another inmate told us:

So we managed to make it to the back of the mess hall and hid under the black table. They then started grabbing us three at a time. They were yelling "Three at a time, three at a time," chopping them up with meat cleavers, they were chopping them up. The last three that they took, they picked a kid who was on top of me and a couple more, making three, and they took them out, stabbing them, chopping them. So I started to pray.

I convened a committee on prisons that included prosecutors, NAACP leaders, and assorted experts. In a scathing report, the committee blasted the prison brass for running a closed system with virtually no rehabilitation programs, and recommended building a better, safer prison. Little was done. In 1972 I filed a lawsuit against Mayor Tate on the grounds of cruel and barbarous treatment. The case was taken over by the defender's office after I stepped down as DA in 1974. On July 1, 1974, the state supreme court ruled, in a landmark decision, that treatment behind bars in Philadelphia violated the Eighth Amendment prohibition against cruel and unusual punishment. I believe that was the nation's first such case, although many more followed.

SOUTH PHILADELPHIA TRADITION

A certain camaraderie emerges from all the years of battle. When I spoke at former State Senator Buddy Cianfrani's seventy-fifth birthday party, State Senator Vincent Fumo, a Pennsylvania powerhouse, introduced me as "the man who arrested me and Buddy in 1972."

I rose to slight applause and picked up where Fumo had left off. "Well, Vince is wrong," I said. "I arrested him in '72. Buddy's prosecution was four years earlier."

The Cianfrani saga began on primary election day in April 1968, when I was sitting in my office sorting papers, and my secretary announced, "There's a man here to see you named Jimmy Tayoun. He says he's been beaten up at the polling place by Buddy Brown."

Buddy Brown, I knew, was Buddy Cianfrani, also known as State Senator Henry J. Cianfrani, a Philadelphia political overlord. Cianfrani, protégé of State Senator Ben Donolow, was a powerhouse in Harrisburg, clawing his way up the Appropriations Committee.

"Show him in," I said.

Jimmy Tayoun came into my office. Pale and slight, he had an ugly welt on the right side of his head. He put on his eyeglasses, and the right lens was cracked in a cross. Tayoun, a thirty-seven-year-old restaurateur, was running for a state house seat against the Democratic machine's candidate. "Buddy Brown beat me up at the polling place," he said.

Assault and battery at the polls is a serious charge. A person convicted is banned for life from voting or holding public office. By long-standing protocol in Philadelphia, only the district attorney personally can ask for an arrest warrant on election day, and only the election court judge can issue the warrant. The policy had been set because politicians in the old days had enlisted friendly magistrates, who had locked up their opponents on election day, defeating them by keeping them off the street and unable to get out their vote.

I listened to Tayoun's story and checked it out. It turned out that Cianfrani had indeed mauled Tayoun at the polling place at 13th and Fitzwater streets, as Tayoun claimed. Certainly, Cianfrani was physically capable of the act. The balding, forty-five-year-old state senator was a beefy former athlete who had kept his schoolyard mettle.

"Mr. Tayoun, I'm going to issue a warrant of arrest for State Senator Henry J. Cianfrani," I said. "But I expect you to prosecute."

"On my mother's grave, I'll prosecute," Tayoun swore.

"Because if you don't prosecute," I said, "I'm going to subpoena you, and I'm going to make you prosecute."

"My mother's grave."

So I arrested Buddy Cianfrani on primary day 1968. The state senator, accompanied by his lawyer, formally surrendered. Judge Robert N. C. Nix, Jr., son of a congressman and later Pennsylvania's chief justice, released Cianfrani on one-dollar bail. A hearing was scheduled for June 7.

Tayoun won his election, launching an illustrious political career that has involved, so far, a seat on the Philadelphia City Council, a felony conviction for corruption, a stretch in federal prison, and a book on how to survive in prison. But after his 1968 victory and Cianfrani's arrest, Tayoun lost his hunger to prosecute. He reneged. I subpoenaed him.

Instead of the regular magistrate's hearing, the case was docketed on June 7 in common pleas court. Not just one judge came out, but two: Nix was joined by Judge James T. McDermott, who would also become a state supreme court justice. Tayoun testified that Cianfrani had actually hit him not in the polling place but in the entrance to the polls. The project at 13th and Fitzwater streets was circular, with a hallway that led from a foyer into the rooms where the votes were cast. Tayoun, who had been a watcher at the polling place, testified that he'd greeted Cianfrani when the state senator arrived, and had warned, "You can't go in there. You need a watcher's certificate."

"I don't need any," Cianfrani had told Tayoun, and brushed past him into the voting room, Tayoun testified. On Cianfrani's way out, he took Tayoun aside and said, "You'd better win this election. If you don't, you're finished in this town."

"This sounds like a threat," Tayoun told Cianfrani.

"I'm even getting the Internal Revenue Service to check your business records," Cianfrani said.

"That sounds like a threat, too," Tayoun replied.

"Well, take off your glasses and I'll show you another threat," the senator said.

Tayoun said he took off his glasses, and Cianfrani belted him. Tayoun had changed his story. His cracked lens, which I had personally seen, demonstrated that Tayoun had been wearing his glasses when he was assaulted.

Judges Nix and McDermott threw out the election-code violation charge. They held Cianfrani for simple assault and released him on one-dollar bail. The state senator eventually paid a fine. "I took into consideration the normal tradition in South Philadelphia politics," former Chief Justice Nix told me. "Unless you're born there, nobody can really understand it."[1]

After regaling the crowd with the Cianfrani arrest, I shifted to my arrest of Fumo over alleged election fraud. The Democrats and Republicans made a deal in South Philadelphia in 1972. The Democrats would cede the top of the ticket, Nixon-Agnew, to the Republicans, and the Republicans would give the rest of the ticket to the Democrats. From the GOP viewpoint, Nixon was probably going to coast to reelection over Senator George McGovern anyway, but one never knew. The GOP wanted every last vote. And if some South Philly pols could win a contest legally or illegally, many would choose to win illegally.

To pull off the deal, the pols decided they had to get rid of the McGovern poll watchers. Democratic leaders gave the party's poll-watching certificates—which the McGovern people needed, and to which they were entitled—to Democratic committeemen. But that didn't finish the McGovernites. They got certificates from the Constitutional Party, a third party on the ballot that year.

On election day, Judge Robert Latrone of the common pleas court, a South Philadelphia Democrat, arrived at City Hall at 5:30 A.M., a little early for anyone, especially Latrone. He signed in, as required for anyone coming in before regular office hours. Latrone was scheduled to begin his shift as an election court judge at 2:00 P.M., more than eight hours later. At 7:00 A.M. a lawyer arrived at City Hall and handed Latrone an injunction petition to void all Constitutional Party certificates. The petition had been notarized the day before by the secretary of Democratic boss Buddy Cianfrani. "Latrone and Cianfrani are known

225

to be long-time friends," the *Inquirer* reported, noting that Cianfrani had recently served as master of ceremonies for Latrone's testimonial dinner at Palumbo's restaurant.

The petition claimed that it was illegal for poll watchers to carry certificates of another party. The state court had already ruled the other way. But Latrone signed the order around 9 A.M., barring the McGovern watchers.

Within hours another judge voided Latrone's order. But by then McGovern poll watchers were being chased from polling places throughout South Philadelphia. "Read this and get the hell out of here," a judge's son told a McGovern poll watcher, showing her a copy of Latrone's order. "I'm tired of seeing you."

A complaint came to me as DA, and I investigated. We ended up arresting Latrone; Fumo, then a twenty-nine-year-old Cianfrani protégé; a Republican city councilman; a former city councilman; a former state representative; and three others. Cianfrani narrowly escaped arrest. We were pretty sure the dean of South Philadelphia politics was linked to the plot, but in the absence of sufficient proof, we left his name off the arrest warrants.

The defense lawyers challenged the case on procedural grounds and tied it up for more than a year. With some skill, cases could be tied up for years, as the Philadelphia Teamsters did in the early 1960s. After I left the DA's office in January 1974, my successor dropped the case. Cianfrani, whose own legal troubles and prison term lay ahead of him, was sore over the arrest of his cronies, and said so. One newspaper headline screamed that Buddy vowed to "get" me.

By 1998, at Cianfrani's seventy-fifth birthday party, the earlier battles were largely forgotten, or at least the statutes of limitations had run out. There was a curious collegiality among the old combatants. Nostalgia had overtaken the vote counts and even the arrests.

"THEY'RE YOUNGER, THEY'RE TOUGHER, AND NOBODY OWNS THEM"

I was up for reelection as DA in 1969, and the Democratic machine came up with a candidate widely expected to trounce me: a former bar association chancellor and city solicitor named David Berger. Berger had a dazzling résumé that included creating Philadelphia's SEPTA regional transit system.

My running mate was State Representative Tom Gola, the candidate for city controller. Gola had been an All-American forward in 1952 and probably the best basketball player in the country when he led LaSalle to the NCAA championship one year and to a second-place finish in another, beating San Francisco and its star, Bill Russell. Gola had gone on to make All-Pro in five of his ten seasons with the old Philadelphia Warriors. Then, coaching LaSalle, he ran up a 23–1 record. Tom Gola was a strapping six feet seven, with dark good looks, easy charm, and evident decency. Adding in a degree in accounting, his résumé touched all the bases. In the end we made a powerful team. We ran under the well-received slogan "They're Younger, They're Tougher, and Nobody Owns Them."

Berger proved less daunting than the Democrats had hoped. *The National Observer* wrote:

> Berger, by all accounts, is a better lawyer than a political candidate. During the campaign he generally managed to make the wrong speeches and appeals to precisely the wrong audiences. Nor was his cause helped by a growing land-development scandal involving men intimately connected on a high level with the city's Democratic administration.[1]

Candidate Berger's most lasting moment came during a radio interview about one of his law partners and the land-development scandal over which the partner was indicted. Asked by the press about the scandal, Berger stood silently, not answering, for a full minute, as the cameras and tape recorders rolled. KYW Radio played Berger's "response." KYW-TV played about fifteen seconds of the silence. Anything longer, and viewers would have figured the station had a transmission problem. "It was devastating," said Berger's running mate, Charles Peruto.[2]

On election day it wasn't even close. I beat Berger by 101,000 votes. Tom Gola won his race by 80,000 votes. Berger has gone on to help pioneer class-action and securities law and has earned a fortune in the process.

I asked Chief Justice Earl Warren, my old boss from the Kennedy assassination probe, to administer the oath of office for my second term. Warren had just retired in the spring of 1969. He declined, saying he would be visiting family in California over the Christmas break beyond the January 3 swearing-in date, but he invited me to lunch. We ate at his office in the Supreme Court building.

We had a fascinating conversation, talking much more easily than we had when I was answering his questions about the commission's work. We talked about "one man, one vote," the famous Supreme Court decision that replaced disproportionate representation systems and had come down during Warren's final years. When Warren was governor of California, he had fought "one man, one vote." When he became chief justice, he supported the concept. "It all depends on which side of the mountain you're looking at," he told me. It was inspirational to spend a leisurely lunch with the former chief justice. After the tense Warren Commission assignment, it was also enjoyable to see him relaxed.

Days after the election, President Nixon invited Gola and me to Washington to see him. Gola wasn't interested. But I was eager to meet the new president, who'd been in office less than a year. After passing through White House security and winding along a maze of corridors, my escorts and I reached the Oval Office. The president was standing by a massive desk lit by a curve of windows behind it. I stepped onto the white carpet.

"Hello, how are you doing, Arlen?" Nixon asked, gripping my hand. "It's very nice to see you. Come pose for a picture." The president gestured to a photographer. I had a tough time smiling for a photographer in those days and could not do so even on the president's cue. Nixon, still gripping my right hand in his, poked the fingers of his left hand into the small of my back. I broke out laughing, and the photographer snapped a fine picture.

I was invited again to meet with Nixon two years later, in June 1971. When I said good-bye to my sons as I left for Washington, Shanin, then thirteen, handed me two three-by-five cards. "Dad, if you can, get me the president's autograph," he asked. Shanin had become an autograph collector about that time. He told me that autographs of sitting presidents were worth twenty-five dollars.

"Shanin, I can't do that," I said. "I can't ask the president for his autograph."

"I understand that, Dad," Shanin said. "But put them in your pocket, just in case." Shanin was tenacious about autographs. Around this time Joan and I took our sons to Yankee Stadium for a July 4 game between the Washington Senators, managed by legendary Ted Williams, and the Yankees. It was ball day, so each child got a baseball. Shanin took his ball down to Williams, who was being swarmed over by kids, was able to get his attention, and asked him to autograph the ball. Williams took the ball from Shanin and asked him for a pen. Shanin didn't have a pen. He trudged back, dejected. I gave him a pen, and he went back to Williams. Now there were even more kids around the baseball great. Again Shanin got Williams's attention. He handed Williams the ball and the pen and got his autograph.

Shanin was actually a second-generation autograph hound. When I was a child in Wichita in 1941 and 1942, major league teams came to town to play exhibition games, and I collected autographs. When the Philadelphia Athletics played the Pittsburgh Pirates, I got signatures from A's owner Connie Mack, who wore his trademark black suit and wing collar and signed "Cornelius McGillicuddy," and baseball immortal John "Honus" Wagner, who was then coaching for the Pirates. Wagner was about sixty-five, more bowlegged than ever, and looked very old, at least to me at eleven. Then I saw Frankie Frisch, the "Fordham Flash," who was managing the Pirates after a legendary career at shortstop for John McGraw's Giants and the Cardinals' "Gas House Gang." I rushed up to him and said, "Mr. Frisch, Mr. Frisch, may I have your autograph?" He said, "Later, kid, later," and walked into a lunchroom. I waited outside for about forty-five minutes until Frisch came out. "Mr. Frisch, Mr. Frisch, may I have your autograph?" I pleaded again.

"Later, kid, later," Frisch said, and walked into a barbershop to get a haircut. Again I waited for him. When he came out, I said, "Mr. Frisch, Mr. Frisch—"

"Later, kid," he said. I never got Frisch's autograph. Years later, when Shanin was about twelve and collecting autographs, we visited a Chestnut Street curiosity shop and bought a Frankie Frisch autograph on a three-by-five card for two dollars. I then told Shanin my Frisch story. Shanin wrote Frisch complaining how he had abused his father many years earlier. Frisch wrote back, stating, "Young man, I never in my life denied anyone an autograph." I learned an early lesson to be patient and responsive to anybody looking for an autograph or a moment of my time.

My 1971 meeting with Nixon lasted from noon until 12:50 P.M. Attorney General John Mitchell joined us. We discussed a wide variety of subjects, with heavy attention to the drug problem and the criminal justice system. When the subject of federal habeas corpus procedure came up, I told the president and attorney general of the long delays and serious problems facing law enforcement. Nixon leaned across the desk and told Mitchell, "John, get hold of [Chief Justice Warren] Burger, get that straightened out," as though the chief justice were at Mitchell's beck and call, and a word from the attorney general would resolve that issue.

When our meeting ended, the president went into the drawers of his Oval Office desk and gave me a tie clip, a set of presidential cuff links, a pin for Joan, a golf ball, and a fountain pen. As Nixon was bidding me good-bye and I was heading toward the door, I pulled out Shanin's two three-by-five cards and said, "Mr. President, would you mind signing an autograph for my son?"

Nixon walked back to his desk and pulled out a sheet of letterhead. "What's your son's name?" he asked.

"Shanin," I said, wondering if the president would know our last name. He did. He wrote, "To Shanin Specter, June 4, 1971, Richard M. Nixon." That autograph may be worth even more than twenty-five dollars today.

JUSTICE SPECTER?

H. R. "Bob" Haldeman, President Nixon's chief of staff, wrote in his diary on September 17, 1971, that the president was considering me for an appointment to the U.S. Supreme Court. "The attorney general wants guidance from the P on what he wants to do on a replacement [Supreme Court] appointment. Feels that we've got to really think it through carefully and establish our position on it. The P said to consider Arlen Specter as a Jewish seat."[1] Nixon and Haldeman had discussed my prospects several months earlier, in June 1971, according to recently released Oval Office tapes:[2]

> RN: Mr. Specter, he's a very impressive fellow. Jewish . . . liberal . . .
> hard-line—
> HRH: Hard-line lawyer.
> RN: With good credentials.
> HRH: Which is unusual for a Jew.
> RN: Yeah. Good credentials and he's got a very good communication with the young people and the Blacks and the rest because he's got imaginative procedures like, for example, in the field of drugs, he's got this program that he's against legalizing marijuana which is a position that's exactly right, because the evidence points to that . . . That's the kind of guy, you know, I've been thinking of . . .
> HRH: He could run your thing, couldn't he?
> RN: In Pennsylvania?
> HRH: No, here—your dope thing if you don't get what's-his-name?
> RN: Hmmn, yeah. I don't think he'd do that . . . His future is there . . . We do have some appointments to the Supreme Court. If you go the Jewish route . . . I'm glad we've seen him . . . He's got a great future . . . I will never see him acting an asshole like this [Pennsylvania U.S. Sen.

Richard] Schweiker . . . Man, he's tougher. He's a Jew that's come up like Henry [Kissinger].

Haldeman's diary entry coincides with newspaper reports in the fall of 1971 that the Nixon administration was considering me for the Supreme Court. There were two vacancies. Senator Hugh Scott had been touting two "Arlens" for the Supreme Court: Arlin Adams, then a judge on the Court of Appeals for the Third Circuit, and Arlen Specter.

I was sitting in my office one Friday morning in October when the phone rang and my secretary announced, "Attorney General John Mitchell would like to see you in Washington."

"I'll go down next Thursday," I told my secretary. I figured I'd schedule some business at the same time. She came back and said, "He wants you in his office at nine o'clock Monday morning." I replied, "I'll be there."

I'd had a number of contacts with the attorney general, including giving him advice earlier in 1971 on the First Amendment issue of right to assembly. I had published a pamphlet in 1968 on that issue. A torrent of cases about street-corner crowds was flooding the courts. In Pennsylvania we kept unruly crowds from gathering by relying on an old statute that barred more than twelve people from gathering on a street corner. Where there was clear and present danger and when riots had become a national epidemic, government had a right and a duty to keep unruly crowds from gathering. At that time such crowds did arguably constitute a clear and present danger, so I thought it was appropriate to use the statute under limited, controlled circumstances.

But when John Mitchell had asked for advice, the situation was different. When riots swept Washington in 1971, Mitchell ordered an army of police onto the streets and onto the mall to make wholesale arrests. It was a law-and-order year, and the Nixon administration was exceedingly tough. Mitchell had phoned me, and I had told him he couldn't make those mass arrests on those facts. Mitchell made the arrests anyway. The government wound up paying $10,000 to each of the people taken into custody.

The weekend after Mitchell's call, Joan and I had plans to get away for a few days to a Pocono Mountains resort. We went, but we were preoccupied the whole time. I really didn't want to be on the Supreme Court at forty-one and out of the fray for the rest of my life. But I knew I couldn't turn it down. In my situation it would have been foolish to turn down a seat on the United States Supreme Court. Years earlier I had considered becoming a judge of the common pleas court. When I was thirty-three, a five-year stint had seemed appealing. But not for the duration.

On the following Monday morning at nine, I reported to Justice Department headquarters in Washington. John Mitchell's office was small but impressive. Robert Kennedy's large office, where Kennedy, Jack Miller, and I had discussed the Teamsters prosecutions in 1963, was now a conference room. I was escorted to Mitchell's inner office and shook the attorney general's hand. We sat for twenty to twenty-five minutes. Mitchell talked about the weather. Whatever he'd wanted to discuss with me when he phoned urgently on Friday, he'd changed his mind by Monday.

Mitchell probably changed his mind very late. I've heard that others, including Senator Robert Byrd and Senate Majority Leader Howard Baker, were sounded out about the Supreme Court and asked for a night to think it over, only to find the president uninterested the next day.

Several months later, in late 1971, the media reported President Nixon on the verge of appointing me attorney general. WPVI-TV anchorman Larry Kane cited "unimpeachable sources" who said that I would "imminently" be named head of the Justice Department.

"The last time Arlen Specter was headed for Washington, he was supposed to become an associate justice of the U.S. Supreme Court," the *Philadelphia Daily News* wrote. "This time, there is word that he's going to take Attorney General John Mitchell's place when and if Mitchell resigns to head President Nixon's bid for re-election."[3]

The *Daily News* tracked me down at a Philadelphia fund-raiser for Nixon shortly after Kane's newscast and told me about the anchorman's remarks.

"So I've been appointed by Larry Kane, huh?" the paper reported me as saying. Then, more seriously: "I haven't heard anything about it except the speculation. Fact is, I just don't know."

Alas, Larry Kane's sources proved wrong. And few in the Nixon White House turned out to be "unimpeachable."

"EVEN CARMELLA DOESN'T LIKE THAT"

$\equiv\equiv$

While Richard Nixon was considering me for the Supreme Court, Bill Meehan had other plans for me. I had wanted to run for governor in 1970. I felt ready. And coming out of Philadelphia with a 101,000 majority in the 1969 DA race, I was in great position. As Senator Richard Schweiker put it, I was entitled to a promotion in 1970. But Meehan would not back me for governor. He was saving me for the junior prom, the 1971 mayor's race. Jim Tate was finishing the full second term of his two-term limit, and the top city job would be open in 1971. I balked. I wasn't going to run for mayor in 1971. I'd made a mistake running for mayor in 1967. I'd been galloping along as the new law-and-order DA and been eager to continue riding my white charger. I wouldn't have run for mayor in 1971 in any event, but I was doubly resolved not to run when the city organization and Meehan rejected my interest in the governor's race out of hand.

Meehan applied extreme pressure and got others to help turn the screws. Tom Gola tried to enlist President Nixon in a draft effort. Nixon said he understood that I didn't want to run, and didn't join in. Finally, when they saw it would do no good, they relented.

One Philadelphian who wanted very much to run for mayor in 1971 was Frank Rizzo. In October 1970, Rizzo invited me to lunch at the Ben Franklin Hotel. I anticipated a serious political discussion. "Mr. Specter," Rizzo said, "I would like to see you run for mayor, but if you don't run, then I will run." Rizzo, at the time, addressed me as "Mr. Specter." He did that until he was elected mayor. When Rizzo worked his way up in the police department, even after becoming commissioner, he was the model of deference.

"I'm not going to let Bill Green become mayor and run this city,"

Rizzo said. Rizzo didn't like Congressman Green, son and namesake of the former congressman and Democratic boss. He considered the younger Green a liberal. "But if you run, I won't run," Rizzo continued. "But I want you to tell me whether or not you're going to run."

"I'm not running, Frank," I said.

"I don't want you to tell me you're not running, then change your mind and run," Rizzo said.

"Hey, Frank, if I want to change my mind, I will. I don't owe you anything," I said. "But I'm not going to change my mind. But I'm still not going to give you any guarantees." I didn't waffle by saying it was my present intention not to run. But I wouldn't give Rizzo any further assurances because he wasn't entitled to any.

The race for mayor was a contest of heavyweights, at least physically. The Republican nominee, City Councilman Thacher Longstreth, a former Princeton football end, stood six feet six and weighed a solid 230, a match for the Cisco Kid, who won the Democratic nomination. I supported Longstreth because I thought he was a better prospect for mayor. If I couldn't have supported the Republican in good conscience, I would have kept quiet.

I got caught in the middle of the candidates' verbal fisticuffs. At their only televised debate a few weeks before the election, Longstreth questioned Rizzo's honesty. Rizzo, who was gutsy, replied, "Thacher, ask your campaign manager, Arlen Specter, what kind of police commissioner I was. I'll rise or fall on what Mr. Specter says." When the newsmen caught up with me, I answered candidly that Frank Rizzo had been an honest police commissioner. I wouldn't back up Longstreth when he was wrong. Rizzo was an excellent commissioner except where police brutality was concerned. I wasn't for Rizzo for mayor, but I wasn't going to denigrate him or anybody else falsely.

Rizzo was elected. On election night, to the news media, the mayor-elect described his lunch with me months earlier, disclosing that he wouldn't have run if I had run. It was a curious election-night statement.

Skipping the 1971 election allowed me to focus on running the DA's office. My office prosecuted not only Democrats but Republicans, such as City Councilman Dave Silver, Magistrate Harry Ellick, and Ward Leader Gene Lenart, when there was adequate evidence of corruption. When an arrest rankled a party power, I might get a call from Bill Mee-

han. Meehan would say, "I got a call from somebody asking me to talk to you. Now I've talked to you." That would be it. Meehan never asked me to do anything improper.

I did my part for the party in other ways. In 1972 I was state chairman of President Nixon's reelection campaign in Pennsylvania, a job that took much of my free time. Nixon had won the presidency by an eyelash in 1968 after losing by an eyelash in 1960, and the Committee to Re-elect the President was running the 1972 campaign as though it were headed for a one-half-of-one-percent decision, as 1968 had been. Nixon won the statewide campaign by almost 1 million votes and lost Philadelphia by fewer than 100,000.

On the home front I was concentrating on several major grand jury investigations. In April 1969 the common pleas court gave me permission to investigate urban renewal and land development, after a 7,500-square-foot section of the new Spectrum sports arena blew off during an ice storm, injuring three people. We found bid rigging, bogus inspections, and other fraud at the Spectrum and at then-new Veterans Stadium. We indicted and prosecuted the stadium coordinator. He was convicted but only given probation.

The highlight of that first investigation was the 1500 Market Street project, an $80 million office tower across from City Hall. The grand jury, in a presentment drafted by my diligent deputy Gil Stein, called the $80 million downtown office project a "classic study in corruption . . . including conflict between personal gain and public duty, favoritism, influence in high places, bureaucratic incompetence and outright fraud." Most of our 1500 Market Street indictments were ultimately dismissed on appeal on technicalities. Some of those defendants, widely regarded as the city's elite, wielded enormous power. Several members of the Philadelphia Board of Rabbis came to see me to urge me not to prosecute the head of a Jewish organization. I said no. Whenever a prominent member or any ethnic of religious group was indicted, I heard complaints about discrimination, which I ignored.

While behemoths such as 1500 Market Street, the Spectrum, and Veterans Stadium made headlines, our grand jury probe focused at least as keenly on abuses in housing for the city's poor. The city had won widespread kudos for the "Philadelphia Renaissance," begun in 1951 under reform mayors Clark and Dilworth and orchestrated by a team of urban planning and engineering maestros. But less than two decades

later, after Tate had replaced Dilworth, the city's top talent had fled, and vision had given way to fraud.

Tenants were evicted from decent housing so that their buildings could be "rehabilitated," at major cost, and sold to the city. Developers won approvals by making hefty political donations. Instead of rebuilding unsafe walls, contractors coated them with stucco to hide the defects, pocketed the difference, and paid off the building inspectors. Homes opened without bathroom basins or kitchen floors. Children suffered pneumonia and rat bites.

The grand jury indicted Frank Steinberg, head of the Philadelphia Housing Authority, for steering $2 million in home-refurbishing fees to his brother's development firm and steering $3 million in Housing Authority funds to a small bank where he was a director and shareholder. Even before the grand jury issued its presentment, Steinberg resigned from the Housing Authority. We convicted him on many counts of corruption. By the time of his sentencing, Steinberg was seventy-four and ill. He got probation. We also convicted the deputy commissioner of licenses and inspections on city corruption.

A year into the investigation, *The Wall Street Journal* wrote in a page-one story:

> A special grand jury still in session after 11 months of work has uncovered what it calls "widespread corruption" in renewal, particularly in the area of housing. Forty-seven firms or individuals, including high-ranking officials and civic leaders, have been indicted on a variety of charges. The chairmen of the Housing and Redevelopment Authorities, and another member of the Redevelopment Authority, have resigned under pressure. Programs to house the city's poor are seriously lagging.[1]

The grand jury finished in September 1970, after eighteen months. In all, it issued fifteen presentments recommending a total of 2,464 indictments against 65 individuals and firms. The grand jury produced an unexpected result in the resignation of Judge Joseph Gold, who had sat on the Philadelphia Teamsters case for a year, wanting to put in the fix but not daring to.

"He was a politician first," John Rogers Carroll said. "He was always friendly to everybody that he ever ran into." That friendliness sometimes hid an ulterior motive. Carroll, the feisty criminal defense lawyer who had fought me in the 1963 Teamsters case, had signed on as a special counsel for our 1969–70 grand jury probe. "Joe Gold and I had zero relationship," Carroll said. "He and I had been seeing each other around City Hall for years, but never had a cup of coffee, never more than two-minute conversations. One day I'm walking up 15th Street to City Hall. He comes up beside me, he starts passing the time of day, the weather, and he said, 'You know, John, you ought to get yourself a good personal injury case before me, we can both make some money.' I was just aghast. I wondered how many people he did this with, because I had to be way down the list of co-conspirators."[2]

In 1969 Carroll and his grand jury team were investigating a stock scam at Citizens Bank when they happened on transactions involving Joe Gold. Carroll discovered that Gold had made a stock-buying arrangement with lawyers in which the lawyer would borrow money and buy stock. If the stock went up, the purchase belonged to Gold, who paid off the loan. If the stock dropped, it belonged to the lawyer, who took the loss.

The grand jury was ready to indict Gold for violating the Pennsylvania Securities Act. Gold went to Judge Joseph Sloane, who was presiding over our grand jury, and demanded that Sloane make us ease off. Sloane came to me. Joe Gold was after him, Sloane said. Would I agree to meet with Gold? Sure, I said. I had always been willing to meet with anybody.

I went to Judge Sloane's chambers. The room was dark and book-strewn. The window opened onto an inner courtyard. Gold tried to talk me out of the indictment.

"No, I'm not going to relent, Judge," I said.

Sloane was at the meeting but said nothing. He pressed himself into the farthest corner of the room and stared out at the courtyard, trying to get as far from the conversation as he could.

Gold urged me either to indict the lawyers involved in the scam or say that if I wouldn't indict them, I shouldn't indict Gold either. No deal, I said. I told Gold he was the institutional culprit who had power over the lawyers who had made the loans.

In the end I agreed to let Gold resign quietly. The fact is, Joe Gold would probably never have been convicted of anything in Philadelphia. He would have waived a jury trial and had his case blown out by one of his buddies on the bench. By 1969 the state supreme court had taken away the commonwealth's right to demand a jury trial because of the court's anger over my office's using it to challenge trial judges' integrity. Gold resigned because he didn't want to suffer the shame and publicity of an indictment. And he couldn't be sure that he would be acquitted, and might have faced heavy prison time if convicted.

A second grand jury, convened in January 1971, tackled the city's drug epidemic and led to 140 arrests and 80 convictions of major drug distributors, lieutenants, street ushers, financiers, runners, and testers. I ran a third grand jury in June 1972 to probe official corruption. I shifted that jury's focus to police misconduct shortly after Rizzo became mayor. The *Inquirer*, conducting its own investigation, ran an exposé saying that scores of police officers were taking bribes from gamblers. That grand jury indicted twenty-four people on corruption charges, including the city council's Democratic majority leader, Isadore Bellis, who was ultimately convicted of bribery, and Councilman David Silver. The 1972 grand jury also indicted twelve police officers, three former officers, and assorted state employees. By the end of 1973, forty-five police officers had been arrested and seventeen convicted on corruption charges, with fourteen more awaiting trial.

Mayor Rizzo, barely a year out of the police commissioner's office, didn't care for my police corruption probe. Government was riddled with corruption, Rizzo thundered. Why focus on the police? Well, we targeted officials throughout the city, having convicted the chairman of the Housing Authority, the deputy commissioner of Licenses and Inspections, and the stadium coordinator. But it was obviously a serious problem for police officers to shake down drug dealers, sell dope, and turn a blind eye to drug-pushing.

After Rizzo was elected mayor, our relationship deteriorated substantially. Rizzo dominated Philadelphia in the 1970s, and our paths often collided. Although he had limited formal education, Rizzo was extraordinarily street-smart. When I made a speech on prison conditions, criticizing putting two and three men in a cell, Rizzo phoned me. "My brother Joe and I used to sleep in the same bed," he railed. "It wasn't too big, there was an invisible line down the center, and neither of us crossed it." Frank and his brother Joe, whom he later appointed fire commissioner, were both about six feet three and 240 pounds.

When Rizzo was really mad at me, he would play his trump card and say, "Even Carmella doesn't like that." Rizzo's wife, Carmella, was and is a great lady and ordinarily a supporter of mine. She stood about five feet and handled the Cisco Kid the way a drill sergeant treated a recruit.

Rizzo's own spy squad was a highlight of a 1972 grand jury investigation. As mayor, Rizzo formed a thirty-three-man squad to follow politicians, photograph strikers, and perform other unsavory tasks. Rizzo's agents assembled dossiers on his opponents, real and imagined, and on a variety of players. Then he collected the ammunition and used it to intimidate people.

Rizzo, taking a cue from his idol J. Edgar Hoover, had dossiers on everybody. I heard at the time that Rizzo had put together a file on me. Recently, in researching this book, I found out it was true. Rizzo's code name for me was "Boozy Boy," after a childhood nickname my parents have given me. Max Greenberg, the World War I veteran and family friend, had called his son Danny "Sonny Boy," from the Al Jolson song. So my parents had called me "Boozy Boy." Rizzo apparently used some of my own detectives and assistants to surveil me, with instructions to take no action unless ordered, according to Sal Paolantonio's biography, *Frank Rizzo*. The big concern about me, according to Rizzo's dossier, was that my law partner, Marvin Katz, said I had read "Lanny Budd" novels as a teenager. "This series of novels, known as World's End, was written by an avowed radical socialist, Upton Sinclair," the dossier said. "How deeply the socialistic ideas imbued in the novels infected the subject is not known."[3]

The Lanny Budd books had been recommended to me by my sister Shirley, three years my senior. Reading was Shirley's principal activity in Russell, where she attended high school, because of the limited availability of Jewish boys. In 1948, when Shirley was of marriageable age, my parents moved back to Philadelphia so she could find a nice Jewish boy, which she did. In Russell there was only one Jewish boy: me, her brother. The Lanny Budd series taught me a great deal about world history in the early twentieth century but not much about socialism. I was amused by Rizzo's reference to my early reading habits but not so pleased by some of his other tactics.

Former mayors Dilworth and Tate and City Council President George Schwartz charged that Rizzo was tapping their home phones. Tate also said in a newspaper interview that Rizzo had routinely tapped phones when he was police commissioner. Dilworth thought he also had proof of Rizzo's electronic ears. The white knight said he'd made a statement only on his home phone, and that his remark was later cited, proving that his phone had been tapped. That logic was inconclusive because Dilworth was a notorious gabber—he would stop anybody on the street to chat and gossip.

Rizzo, for his part, angrily denied that he'd ever authorized a wiretap of anyone. "This is their big chance," he told the *Inquirer*. "This is the chance for my opponents to bring me down. Let them have me arrested if they have any evidence I've done anything like that."[4]

I called Dilworth to follow up. He would have nothing to do with an investigation. Dilworth had been DA, and he figured I would make him cool his heels for two days before a grand jury. He erupted over the phone. "Mayor," I said, referring to the office he once held, "I need to talk to you about this, and I don't have any intention of having you cool your heels." I told him, sincerely, that I would never set out to embarrass anybody, especially not somebody who had contributed to Philadelphia what he had.

The fact was, I admired Richardson Dilworth, and still do. I'd been excited, in the late 1950s, to arrange for Dilworth, also a Yale Law graduate, to speak at the Yale Law School Association. Joan and I had driven to Dilworth's 6th Street town house to pick up the mayor and his wife. We crammed them into the backseat of our 1955 Chevrolet and drove them to our house, where we had a reception before Dilworth spoke at the Yale Club.

At any rate, after Dilworth exploded at me over the phone, we went to lunch at the Racquet Club to continue our talk more cordially. I wrote a memo to the file based on the conversation, outlining Dilworth's points but noting that they were vague. I concluded that there was no evidence of wiretapping by Rizzo against Dilworth.

I decided, though, that Tate should appear before a grand jury to air his charges about Rizzo. I explained in a television interview, "As to Mayor Dilworth, I do not believe there is any justification to call him before a grand jury because his charges are of such a general nature. But Mayor Tate is supposed to have said on TV Sunday night that there was wiretapping going on in the police department to his knowledge when he was the mayor. And that we're going to pursue very precisely to see if there is such evidence. And we will act on it accordingly."

I was respectful of the former mayor when I called him to testify and didn't make him wait. I questioned Tate personally before the grand jury. He had nothing of substance to say. But he did seem to appreciate the courtesy. The *Inquirer* ran the headline TATE TESTIFIES ON WIRETAPPING, SAYS SPECTER WAS KIND TO HIM.

Rizzo was ultimately cleared of the wiretap charges. But he lost his spy squad. In August 1973 the mayor ceded control of the unit back to the police department, "in what appears to be a concession to critics who charge the squad has been used to intimidate and investigate his political opponents," as the press described it.

In 1970 my district attorney's office was also fighting another court—a softball team known as The King & His Court in a game at Connie Mack Stadium. The star, Eddie Feigner, pitched so fast that nobody could see the ball, much less hit it. That allowed Feigner to play with only a catcher, a shortstop, and a first baseman. Feigner began pitching conventionally and then shifted to throwing the ball behind his back. Later he would put on a blindfold and repeat his conventional and behind-the-back tosses. I considered my batting against Feigner a great success. I never hit him. He never hit me.

A DUMB MISTAKE IN
A CLASS BY ITSELF

Dick Sprague, my first assistant, walked into my office with a cassette tape in May 1972 and declared that the *Bulletin* had been caught wiretapping. The *Bulletin* and the *Inquirer*, at the time, were investigating Frank Rizzo. Among other things, the papers were looking at the mayor's spy squad. It turned out that *Bulletin* reporter Greg Walter had taped his own phone calls with some sources, mainly a police officer and a go-go dancer, without telling them. Walter's conduct explicitly broke Pennsylvania law, which required both parties' consent to tape a call.

I had just come back from Erie, where I'd participated in hearings as vice chairman of Governor Milton J. Shapp's commission on capital punishment. Earlier in 1972 the U.S. Supreme Court had struck down existing death penalty statutes, forcing states to rewrite their laws in order to retain capital punishment. Shapp, who didn't want to preserve the death penalty, had appointed his attorney general, Israel Packel, to chair the commission. Shapp appointed me as vice chairman. I wrote the minority report, and we ultimately brought back Pennsylvania's death penalty in 1974.

Fresh from battle in Erie, I made a major mistake after Sprague made a pitch to arrest Greg Walter. I approved the warrant, setting off the worst chain of events in my professional and political life. One makes many mistakes in a long career, but arresting Walter ranks in a class by itself. The arrest set off a firestorm. The press closed ranks over this attack on one of its own. Journalists saw me as advancing a Sprague-Rizzo conspiracy. "Arlen incurred the wrath of the media," recalled Dan McKenna, the *Bulletin* reporter who later served as press aide for Rizzo and me. "Not only did he incur the wrath of the *Bulletin*, but the media generally, for making a big deal out of something and pillorying a guy who hadn't really done anything really bad, at least in the media's terms."[1] Reporters noted that the Walter case marked the first time the DA's office had prosecuted under the state's 1957 wiretapping law. The *Inquirer* devoted a full page to the arrest in its Sunday paper and to the transcript of an interview I gave KWY Radio reporter Andrea Mitchell, now a national reporter with NBC-TV.

In court, Sprague prosecuted Walter. The newsman made an improbable villain. Tall and intense, he seemed unable to relax. One former colleague described him as "a trifle neurotic, very nervous." Walter was convicted in September 1972 in municipal court and fined five hundred dollars. He appealed to common pleas court. Fired by the *Bulletin*, Walter was hired by the *Inquirer* and assigned to a city beat. He covered Sprague, me, and others involved in his arrest and prosecution—which I thought was hardly professional. Many said it was outrageous.

The Walter case and the chain of events it set off didn't happen in a vacuum but took place amid battles raging among Governor Shapp, State Attorney General Shane Creamer, State Police Commissioner Rocco Urella, Rizzo, Sprague, and me. I was in the middle of a spat with Creamer over law enforcement in Philadelphia County, which was my jurisdiction. Shapp, who had appointed Creamer, wanted to destroy Rizzo and embarrass me, or perhaps vice versa. We were both after his job. Creamer was threatening to supersede me and my grand jury and launch his own investigation of the Philadelphia police.

At that time in New York, legendary New York DA Frank Hogan was being superseded by Governor Nelson Rockefeller and his attorney general. I advised Hogan not to let the state barge in. I saw Rockefeller when he came to Pennsylvania to speak for Nixon during the 1972 presidential campaign. I urged the governor not to supersede Hogan, and explained to him the DA's role and the attorney general's role. Rockefeller listened sympathetically and seemed to agree with me but didn't change course. I was determined not to let Shapp and Shane Creamer do to me what Rockefeller did to Hogan. Just try, I told Creamer.

Creamer was also locked in a power struggle with Urella, the state police commissioner. The two apparently wiretapped each other. Their fight would soon bring them both down. Urella got fired for bugging

Crime Commission headquarters. Creamer resigned under pressure not long after that. Packel became attorney general.

On another front, Rizzo and I were needling Shapp about possibly running against him when he sought a second term in two years. In June 1972 Rizzo and I had gone to Harrisburg for the first state lottery drawing. We began the trip at the governor's mansion. "Hey, hey," Rizzo said, thundering into the reception room, "I want those drapes changed, this carpet's gotta go, rearrange those couches. And this room, I don't like that at all, that's all got to go." Rizzo wanted everyone to know he was doing advance planning on a takeover.

Shapp wasn't in the room at the time, but I'm sure he heard plenty about Rizzo's pretend takeover. The governor soon came down, and we all piled into his state car, a Chrysler sedan, for the ride to the capitol. Rizzo climbed in on one side, taking up most of the backseat. Shapp sat next to him, and I climbed in the other side, taking my third of the seat. That left the governor with a smidgen of the cushion in his own car. That was the only time Rizzo and I effectively middled Shapp.

Amid the political maneuvering, Sprague was prosecuting Walter and the *Inquirer* was going after Sprague on the ten-year-old Applegate case. The Applegate saga had begun around 1:30 A.M. on March 2, 1963, at a Broad Street bar. John Applegate, a forty-eight-year-old clerk, met Rocco Urella, Jr., the twenty-one-year-old son of then–Police Captain Rocco Urella, and young Urella's college classmate David Scalessa. As Urella and Scalessa later told police, the three went to Applegate's nearby apartment on Applegate's suggestion that they would meet some women and have a drink. Applegate allegedly made a homosexual pass at Scalessa, who punched him in the jaw. Applegate fell, hit his head, and died.

Sprague, who was chief of homicide in 1963, found no crime, determining that Scalessa's punch didn't rise to the level of involuntary manslaughter. Urella Sr. was a good friend of Sprague's. Sprague might have recused himself from the case, but Dick Sprague was not one to recuse himself just to avoid a controversy.

Ten years later, in 1973, while Sprague was prosecuting Greg Walter and Urella Sr. had recently been defrocked as state police commissioner, the *Inquirer* dug up the Applegate story. The newspaper asked me, now custodian of DA office records, to turn over the case file. I reviewed the file and sent the *Inquirer* a short letter saying that Sprague had acted properly in deciding not to prosecute. The paper again

245

demanded to see the Applegate file. I told the *Inquirer* to get it from the police department. But Police Commissioner Joseph O'Neill also turned down the paper.

The *Inquirer* went after me in print. "In forcefully supporting Mr. Sprague," the *Inquirer* editorialized, "Mr. Specter has now assumed substantial responsibility for the decisions made, although he was not originally involved."[2] The paper titled one column MR. SPECTER'S OWN WATERGATE. The *Inquirer* ran dozens of consecutive daily editorials demanding the Applegate file. The pieces were later headlined 29 DAYS, MR. SPECTER, then 30 DAYS, MR. SPECTER, and so on, referring to how long I had refused their request. Each editorial carried the same short text, ending with the one-sentence paragraph "What does Mr. Specter have to hide?"

I had nothing to hide, and I finally gave the paperwork to the state attorney general, Packel. I called on Packel to investigate the case and to clear the cloud from my office. Packel ultimately found that there was insufficient evidence to charge Urella Jr. But he said it was unfortunate that certain clues had not been pursued back in 1963, noting a failure to take fingerprints and to interview more witnesses. Packel also said Sprague's close relationship with Urella Sr. raised a "question."

The *Inquirer,* which finally got the Applegate file, called on me to fire Sprague. The paper ran an editorial headlined, THE APPLEGATE REPORT IS IN; MR. SPRAGUE SHOULD BE OUT. The column declared, "And it becomes equally impossible for him [me] to retain any public confidence in the district attorney's office so long as he allows Mr. Sprague to remain as the second in command there."

Sprague sued the *Inquirer* in April 1973, along with three of its editors and four of its reporters, including Greg Walter. He accused the paper of libeling him in its coverage of the Applegate case as well as its coverage of charges about alleged bugging of the Pennsylvania Crime Commission, which was investigating police corruption in Philadelphia. Sprague's main complaint was over an *Inquirer* story about Applegate that ran on April 1, 1973, under the headline DID SPRAGUE QUASH HOMICIDE CASE AS FAVOR TO URELLA? Sprague called the story a pack of "bald-faced lies." He traded printed insults with *Inquirer* reporters and editors. He refused to speak to *Inquirer* reporters Walter and Kent Pollock. Walter had allegedly said he was "out to get" Sprague and to "smear" him. Such remarks could satisfy the "actual malice" standard for libeling public officials.

At one point Sprague and I met with *Inquirer* editor Gene Roberts to try to settle the matter through a retraction or at least a clarification. I had first met Roberts in 1964, when he was a *New York Times* reporter and visited me in the Philadelphia DA's office. The *Times* was going to do a seven-part series on the Warren Commission, he told me. Roberts came back a few weeks later and said the series had been cut to three parts. He came back again and said the *Times* was going to run a single article. Then he came back and said the paper wasn't going to run anything, that there was nothing further worth writing about the Warren Commission. Apparently the *Times* had initially planned a massive exposé on how the commission had fouled up but dropped the story when it couldn't substantiate the charges.

In 1973 Sprague, Roberts, and I had a long discussion on the Applegate matter. But Roberts refused to issue a retraction or clarification. Sprague's lawsuit finally came up for trial in 1983, based on a 1973 story about a 1963 incident. Sprague won a verdict of $1.5 million in compensatory damages and $3 million in punitive damages. In 1990 the case was reversed on appeal and a new trial ordered.

In 1992, almost thirty years after John Applegate's death, the libel case was retried. *Inquirer* editor Roberts took the stand for seventeen days. Jim Beasley, one of the country's top trial lawyers, representing Sprague, conducted an exhaustive and exhausting cross-examination. When Beasley was done, the jury gave Sprague a verdict of $34 million. The judgment was a benchmark in libel law and a national sensation. That $34 million judgment withstood review all the way through state supreme court, although it was shaved by the superior court to $26 million. While a petition to hear the case was pending before the U.S. Supreme Court, it was resolved for a rumored $16 million, though the precise amount was never disclosed. Sprague now lives in a grand Main Line mansion with a crew of four gardeners to tend his grounds.

In any event, in May 1973, a month after Sprague filed his suit against the *Inquirer*, we were preparing to fight Greg Walter's appeal on his wiretap conviction. Walter's lawyers insisted that Sprague should not represent the commonwealth. For that matter, they wanted me and all my assistants off the case. The trial judge ruled that Sprague had a conflict of interest. Sprague asked to be recused. I agreed, although we could have appealed the judge's ruling. Of course, if the *Inquirer* had taken Walter, who had an obvious conflict of interest, off the case, the whole controversy could have been avoided.

In August 1973 I terminated the Walter wiretap case. The case was an open sore, festering and creating friction between government and the press. Walter was guilty as charged, but I decided, and Walter and the court agreed, to end the case in a way that meant neither admission of guilt nor acquittal. It was a practical end. But the *Inquirer* wasn't finished with me.

In retrospect, I think I erred in prosecuting Walter. While there was a bona fide criminal case against him, the chilling effect on freedom of the press outweighed the seriousness of the charges. The criminal process should be the last resort in the most serious cases on matters touching on First Amendment rights.

"YOU KNOW YOU CAN TRUST THEM. DOESN'T IT MAKE SENSE TO KEEP THEM?"

═══════════

Again in 1973 Bill Meehan pressed me to run for an office I did not want. He wanted me to run for a third term as district attorney. I wanted to finish my second term as DA at the end of 1973 and spend 1974 running for governor. Meehan wanted me on the DA ballot largely to bring in Republican judges on my coattails. Whoever controlled a majority of the Board of Judges controlled significant patronage in Philadelphia. The Democrats had run city government since 1951, but the Board of Judges remained the last bastion of Republican control, and Meehan wanted to keep it that way. Tom Gola and I had carried the entire judicial slate of four judges in 1969. And this time the stakes were much higher, with twenty-nine judicial candidates on the ballot.

On the Democratic side, Rizzo wound up in a feud with the party's city chairman, Peter Camiel, over choosing a DA nominee. Camiel claimed in September that he and Rizzo had struck a candidate-for-patronage deal. Rizzo denied it and offered to take a lie-detector test. The *Daily News* took the mayor up on his challenge. The newspaper flew in an examiner and scheduled tests for both Rizzo and Camiel. Rizzo told reporters, "If this machine says a man lied, he lied." Rizzo flunked the test, and Camiel passed. Rizzo even brought along a deputy mayor who had been at the men's room session, who also flubbed the polygraph. Frank Rizzo was the only man who ever brought along a corroborating liar to a lie-detector test. The next day, the *Daily News* ran perhaps the most famous headline in Philadelphia history: RIZZO LIED, TESTS SHOW.

I implored Rizzo not to endorse Gola and me, because it gave the appearance of undercutting our independence. Given his ebbing political fortunes at the time, I thought Rizzo, despite his claims, wanted to see me fall. Our relationship had soured, and he wanted me out of the picture—he was angry that I was investigating his police. By late 1972, newspapers were running headlines such as RIZZO'S HONEYMOON WITH SPECTER IS FADING. There were occasional eruptions, such as when Rizzo pulled thirty officers I needed to serve warrants, calling my work an outrageous waste of manpower. In a news conference, I called the mayor's objections "a lot of nonsense."

Our biggest clash came in November 1972, when I said that police corruption was "serious and systematic," and Rizzo shot back that I was "incompetent." After several days of banner headlines, we essentially agreed to disagree. The *Inquirer* ran a piece headlined RIZZO, SPECTER "REALLY FRIENDS"; JUST DISAGREE ON A FEW THINGS. But the honeymoon was clearly over. There was heavy speculation that Rizzo and I were at odds because we both wanted to run for governor in 1974. I don't think Rizzo ever wanted to become governor, though he toyed with the idea. Rizzo told me he didn't want to be governor, and I take his word. He didn't want to move out of Philadelphia.

At a Bellevue men's room session with Camiel, Rizzo had pushed for Hillel Levinson, his managing director, who had never prosecuted a case, as DA candidate. But his true first choice was Dick Sprague, who was always one of his favorites. Rizzo publicly said he would like to see Sprague as DA if I sought higher office, meaning the governorship. The *Bulletin* ran a story in November 1972, RIZZO LIKES IDEA OF SPRAGUE AS DA, BUT OPPOSES BID ON 2-PARTY TICKET. A state representative even introduced a bill in November 1972, admittedly tailored for Sprague, to let Philadelphia DA candidates run on more than one line.

Rizzo, Camiel, and other top Democrats repeatedly implored my first assistant to run against me. When Sprague refused out of loyalty, Rizzo and company reminded him that I had run against my boss, Jim Crumlish, in 1965. Why, then, they asked Sprague, would he not run against me in 1973? Sprague replied he would agree to run for district attorney if he had the nominations of both parties. When Rizzo couldn't find a candidate to his liking and opposed Emmett Fitzpatrick, the eventual Democratic nominee, he gave lip service to support my candidacy. Rizzo's pro forma endorsement, while probably not decisive, certainly didn't help.

Fitzpatrick, for his part, rarely missed a chance to tie me to Nixon and Watergate. "I think the public has a right to know how much of the $23 million raised nationally was raised by Specter and how much of it was spent for the Watergate break-in and cover-up," he thumped. The answer was none. I did no fund-raising for Nixon.

Tom Gola and I were way ahead in the polls a week before the election. Hard as it was to believe, the polls showed us winning 75 to 25 percent. That would have translated into a victory of more than 150,000 votes. I lost by 26,000 votes. Pollster John Bucci said we would have won big if a new election had been held the next day when it was not raining—so much for wishful thinking. Gola lost, too. We even lost the judges' races. Gola had been so widely expected to win that Camiel, the Democratic chairman, hadn't even bothered to know his own candidate, Bill Klenk. At the Democrats' election-night victory party, Camiel called on Fitzpatrick for a speech. When Fitzpatrick was done, Camiel called on Klenk. "Now, Bill Klenk, which one is Bill Klenk?" Camiel asked.

Nobody had thought we could lose that race. My undoing lay largely outside Emmett Fitzpatrick's barbs. "I believe to this day," Fitzpatrick said recently, "that it was not so much that I won that election, but that Arlen lost it."[1] For a lot of reasons, 1973 was complicated. It took a confluence of many factors to produce that defeat, given the extraordinary standing Tom Gola and I had in the polls. The main factor was public disillusionment with politics after the Saturday Night Massacre, which took place just nine days before the election, and my participation in President Nixon's 1972 campaign. Nixon wanted Watergate Special Prosecutor Archibald Cox fired. The president's new attorney general, Elliot Richardson, and deputy attorney general, William Ruckelshaus, in turn refused and resigned. Finally Nixon found somebody willing to do the deed: Solicitor General Robert Bork. Republicans stayed home in 1973 and '74, in Philadelphia and across America.

Turnout in our 1973 DA race was 43 percent, down from the normal 61 percent. Generally a low turnout helps the candidate with the best organization, whose regular voters can be expected to follow the party line. In 1973 Philadelphia, that was the Democrats. The turnout was so low that Fitzpatrick, in beating me, drew fewer votes than David Berger had drawn four years earlier in losing to me by 101,000 votes. Some didn't want to brave torrential rains that pounded Philadelphia on election day. Others figured we didn't need their votes. I also had not hidden my interest in running for governor in 1974. The Democrats argued that I was going to resign six or eight weeks into my third DA term just to move up, so why bother voting for me?

The collective weight of all my indictments of powerful political players also pressed hard on me. "I think what happened to Arlen, as I look back on it, was that through the eight years that he'd been in office, he made about as many enemies as he could make," Fitzpatrick said. "Sometimes it looked like he was doing it intentionally."[2] My biggest enemies, Fitzpatrick said, were the pols and power brokers whom I had indicted but not convicted. "And these people all sort of lay there and waited. And this was the opportunity to get back at Arlen, and I really think that was the deciding factor."

Over the years I had upset a lot of powerful people, including the *Philadelphia Inquirer* and other media over the Greg Walter case. The *Inquirer* responded months before the DA election with an incredibly heavy hand, running an eight-part series attacking me, beginning on a Sunday and ending on a Sunday. The paper spent seven months making a massive statistical study of the criminal courts and my office. Their assumptions and conclusions were grossly inaccurate. Since I owned no printing presses, the best I could do was to hold a news conference to reply. I noted many errors, such as the paper's not including guilty pleas in tallying my conviction rate. At the end of my news conference, I issued a line-by-line reply to the series, listing "major errors and distortions." The *Inquirer* did run a page-one story on my response, headlined SPECTER CALLS INQUIRER SERIES "GARBAGE, UNFAIR, INACCURATE." But the damage was done.

In 1973 I received limited support from the Republican organization, other than Bill Meehan. Some GOP leaders had always been lukewarm toward me. They tolerated me because I won but were never enthusiastic. I never played ball with them, and some saw me as a liberal former Democrat. And my Democratic support had weakened. The once-mighty Philadelphia ADA, which had helped me in the past, was defunct by 1973.

Whatever the extenuating circumstances, it was a devastating defeat. The stakes had been higher in losing for mayor, but this was a real shocker. Considering the maxim that death is nature's way of telling a person to slow down, this defeat was the political world's way of telling me to reassess.

PART FOUR

RUNNING

I did not dwell on my loss for a third term as DA. In late 1973 my biggest concern was my mother, whose health was failing. Early in the new year, I felt my real loss when Lillie Shanin Specter died from stomach cancer.

As chairman of the Senate Appropriations subcommittee on Health and Human Services, I have heard many experts testify on self-esteem, character, and confidence-building. I attribute my strengths to the Specter family—brother, sisters, father, and especially my loving mother. Lillie Specter was a perfect mother—always there. In the 1930s, mothers stayed home to care for their children. My mother didn't have to be told about prenatal care or the zero-to-three age group's critical need for touching or holding or kissing or anything else. She never talked about "having children." Her term was "giving birth." Lillie Specter was the consummate homemaker, always in the kitchen preparing the next meal unless she was caring for her children or cleaning the stove. My mother was always at the door seeing her children off to school, waving until we were out of sight, and back at the door to welcome us home for lunch or at the end of the day.

When the Specter children were out of the nest, my parents' attention turned to their grandchildren. When Hilda's husband, Arthur, spent thirty-one months fighting in the South Pacific during World War II, my father and mother welcomed their first grandchild, Judith Morgenstern, to their household. When my two-year-old son, Shanin, fell headfirst off a sliding board at a Philadelphia playground, my father was there to catch him before he hit the concrete. In 1961 my sister Shirley and her husband, Dr. Edwin Kety, settled in Phoenix with their two young children after he served in the Public Health Service at a southern Arizona

Indian reservation. My parents decided they could help out most by moving to Phoenix. After my father died in 1964, my mother returned to Phoenix from Israel to help with the Kety children, now four in number, and to keep the postman busy delivering newsy letters to her children and siblings. She had never driven a car at age sixty-four, but with my father no longer behind the wheel, she learned.

In her early seventies, my mother was diagnosed with stomach cancer. At her children's urging she reluctantly underwent a painful but potentially lifesaving operation. She made a reasonable recovery and returned to live with Shirley, who had moved to Elizabeth, New Jersey. In early 1974 the cancer had returned, and my mother died. She was seventy-three. We didn't consider burying my mother in Israel because we felt she would not have wanted to be transported so far away but would rather be interred, as she had expected, in our family plot in a suburban Philadelphia Jewish cemetery. I have always regretted that my parents couldn't be together in death. But at least my brother, Morton, has lain beside our mother since his death in 1993.

In an era of so much emphasis on family values, there is at least one barometer where the Specter family scores an extraordinary reading: My parents were married forty-five years, Morton and Joyce were married fifty-one years before my brother's death, Hilda and Arthur have been married fifty-six years and are still going strong, Shirley and Edwin were married forty-six years before he passed away in 1996, and Joan and I have been married forty-six years, for a total of 244 years for five couples.

On the work front I also didn't have time to dwell on the 1973 DA election. I soon got a call from Washington asking if I would be interested in representing President Nixon in the looming impeachment proceedings. In a sense it was a natural, since I had a defense team ready to go from my departing assistant DAs who would not serve under Fitzpatrick.

Between election day and Christmas in 1973, I met four times with Alexander Haig, Nixon's chief of staff, who still carried himself like the four-star Army general he had been. At our second meeting a fire crackled in Haig's office hearth, taking a little of the chill out of the despondent White House. Haig, looking to close the deal, at one point suggested we walk down the hall to the Oval Office to see the president. I declined. I didn't know enough about the case and didn't want to be in the position of meeting with the president and telling him that I wasn't prepared to take his case. If I had met with Nixon, he probably would have expected a commitment. Certainly the president would want my commitment before making his own.

Haig and I hit an impasse over Nixon's Oval Office tapes. I insisted on listening to the tapes, because a lawyer cannot represent a client without knowing the evidence against him. Worse, a lawyer risks obstruction-of-justice charges for making false representations about evidence he doesn't know.

On top of the Haig meetings, I had one White House session with several other lawyers, some of them also under consideration for the post of special counsel to the president. The larger meeting was held in the Roosevelt Room, a small, windowless chamber filled on one side with tributes and artifacts related to Theodore Roosevelt and on the other with mementos of Franklin Roosevelt. The other lawyers were chatting away about the case. "I have a real question about the wisdom of our sitting around talking," I told them, "because we're all subject to being witnesses before a grand jury."

"What? What? Who?" they exclaimed. "What! What?"

I said, "The lawyer-client privilege attaches only if the discussion is between a lawyer and his client, or among a number of lawyers who represent the client. But when you have all these third parties as we have here, everything we're saying is subject to subpoena before the grand jury." That killed the mood—and much of the conversation.

Marvin Katz, my ex–law partner and former college debating partner, devised a simple but brilliant potential defense for President Nixon: Nixon should cite the doctrine of separation of powers and respond to neither the courts nor the Congress. The key lay in denying jurisdiction of the courts, so Nixon would have to assert the position from the start. It would be too late for the president to deny the court's jurisdiction once he litigated and lost on Special Prosecutor Jaworski's claim to Nixon's Oval Office tapes.

Nixon was eventually sunk when the tapes disclosed discussion of $1 million in hush money and other criminal acts that his staunchest supporters in the Senate could not defend. Up to that time the conventional wisdom was that more than thirty-four senators would support Nixon in a Senate impeachment trial, ensuring his acquittal.

Absent the tapes, which Nixon could have refused to turn over if he hadn't conceded the Supreme Court's jurisdiction, his indefensible conduct would never have been disclosed. Nixon could have expressed his respect for the Court and the Congress but asserted his coequal authority to maintain the privacy of his presidential conduct.

Over the years I've discussed Katz's proposed defense with many lawyers and a few Senate colleagues, who considered it potentially successful. I had one such discussion with my then-colleague Senator Sam Nunn of Georgia when we were traveling to Geneva as part of the Senate observer team on arms reduction talks with the Soviets. I was reading former vice president Humphrey's autobiography on the Air Force plane when I hit a passage about Nunn. I said, "Hey, Sam, I'm reading Hubert Humphrey's autobiography, and there's a story here about you and him visiting President Nixon in the White House family living quarters in early 1974 when the impeachment issue was hot. How about that?"

It was hard to stir Sam, the Senate's premier military-affairs expert, from reading arms-control literature, but he looked up with interest and said, "Let me see the book, Arlen." We then discussed Katz's defense, and Sam found it intriguing, although he didn't commit on its odds of success. It was always hard to get a firm opinion out of Sam until the Senate clerk called his name at a roll call.

Unable to hear Nixon's tapes in 1974, I was inclined not to take the case. Nixon wound up hiring Boston attorney James St. Clair as his special counsel. I never got a chance to offer Katz's strategy to the president. "When I look at how badly beat up St. Clair was at the end, I realized how right we were not to get involved," said Steve Harmelin, who is now head of the Dilworth law firm and was a would-be member of my Nixon defense team.

Early on, I was much more critical of Richard Nixon than I am today. In the spring of 1967, while running for mayor, I was invited to Washington to meet informally with a group of reporters. By the group's own rules, the session was completely off the record. They asked me whether I could support Nixon for president in 1968. I said no. The next day my comments appeared in the newspapers. Nixon read my remarks and called Bill Meehan. "What's Arlen Specter got against me?" he asked. I just didn't think Nixon was a good prospect for the presidency. I thought he was out of touch with the people, and I didn't like his principles.

In the spring of 1974, at the height of the Watergate fiasco, I wrote four columns about Nixon's plight for the *Philadelphia Bulletin*, at the paper's request. Free of any role in Nixon's defense, I wrote what I thought. Nixon was then the subject of a major criminal investigation, challenging in importance even the Warren Commission inquiry. "Lee Harvey Oswald was only charged with assassinating the president, while Richard Nixon is suspected of assassinating the presidency," I wrote.

"President Nixon's resignation would be a national disaster—worse even than Vice President Agnew's heralded exit in a federal courtroom—not because either is indispensable, or even desirable, but because resignation cheats the American people out of knowing the truth," I wrote. "We can survive without a president doing anything. We cannot survive without knowing what a president has done." The facts and the truth are still seeping out, some twenty-five years later.

My opinion of Nixon improved over the years. He had been an excellent foreign-policy president, which we knew at the time. But I didn't appreciate until later his efforts to start the Environmental Protection Agency and his major advances in civil rights. Nixon's reactionary, retrogressive image was belied by the facts. He wanted to win too much, to win at any cost, which is a common failing among politicians. But most politicians don't record their plots and deliver signed, taped confessions.

Nixon phoned me in late 1991, after Clarence Thomas's Supreme Court confirmation hearing. The former president complimented my questioning of Anita Hill very briefly and then launched into an extended discussion of his interrogation of Alger Hiss before the House Un-American Activities Committee on August 25, 1948. Nixon pointed out that his questioning marked the first-ever televised congressional hearing. I got the transcript. Nixon had done a terrific job questioning Hiss.

A few weeks later Nixon invited me, along with other senators, to meet him on one of his visits to Washington. During the meeting a Senate bell rang for a vote. When votes come up, senators dash for the Senate floor. It doesn't matter what they're doing, even if they're talking to the president. I left Nixon to cast my vote. I should have known better. I had some things I wanted to ask the former president. I wanted to tell him about my strategy for his impeachment defense. I wanted to ask him if there was any truth to rumors that I had been considered for

Supreme Court or attorney general. I never had another chance to meet with him privately.

In early 1974 I returned to my old law firm as a partner. Barnes, Dechert, Price, Meyers and Rhoads had tripled in size, but otherwise things were pretty much the same. I joked that I picked up some of my old files after a fourteen-year absence and found the interrogatories (discovery requests) still unanswered.

At Dechert, I took on complex litigation in Securities Act and antitrust cases and some criminal defense work. In 1975 I represented Frank Perdue, the chicken magnate, in a criminal death case. Perdue had driven onto the Pennsylvania Turnpike at the Valley Forge interchange, not knowing the turnpike was under construction. He gunned around the first car he saw, not realizing that he was swerving into a lane of oncoming traffic. He collided head-on with another car, killing its driver. The chicken king wasn't even scratched. Perdue was arrested for involuntary manslaughter. Confusing road signs gave an avenue for defense. After extensive pretrial proceedings, Perdue was discharged. At the end he wasn't sure my bill was less punitive than a conviction.

In 1977 I represented Dr. C. Everett Koop, later surgeon general, who faced an extraordinarily difficult medical and legal case involving Siamese twins born with a single, shared heart. Without an operation, both would surely die. One had a slim chance to survive with an operation. My legal research disclosed that Koop indeed might face a criminal prosecution under the legal principle that no man can lawfully decide who will live and who will die. In an old case, a ship sank at sea, leaving several people in a lifeboat without enough food and water for all to survive. After lots were drawn, one man who lost refused to go overboard. The ship's captain, a survivor and lottery winner, threw him overboard to his death. The court decided that the captain had to stand trial on homicide charges, because no man could send another to his death, even granting the assumption that all couldn't survive and even with the lottery as a factor. With time rapidly running out, I asked the Philadelphia county court to convene a three-judge panel to hear Koop's dilemma and decide if authorization could be lawfully granted for Koop to perform the operation. The court granted permission. Notwithstanding Koop's great skill as a pediatric surgeon, neither twin survived.

In the mid-1970s I represented Spencer Gifts, an Atlantic City subsidiary of MCA, in a case involving an allegation of willful failure to pay state sales taxes. I reported to media mogul Lew Wasserman, MCA's chief executive. I was convinced that my clients had done nothing wrong and urged them to fight the case. Wasserman expressed chagrin about spending time on a case that could be settled for as little as $250,000.

At one stage the U.S. Attorney for New Jersey inquired about the case. Wasserman asserted that my prominence had piqued the U.S. Attorney's interest. I responded that Wasserman's comment was the highest compliment I'd ever received—that I, not Wasserman, was the cause célèbre. In any event, we didn't have long to discuss the matter, because the U.S. Attorney soon lost interest in our case.

The cases at Dechert generally were not as exciting as the battles at the DA's office. In the midst of my mostly civil trial work, I was asked in 1979 to represent counterculture guru Ira Einhorn, known as "The Unicorn," who was charged with murdering his girlfriend. He was credited with founding Earth Day in Philadelphia in 1970. A self-described "planetary enzyme," Einhorn began by promoting LSD and be-ins. Mostly he promoted himself.

Einhorn was living with Helen "Holly" Maddux, a Bryn Mawr graduate and beautiful former cheerleader from Texas. Maddux, then twenty-seven, disappeared in September 1977. In March 1979 her decomposed body was found in a steamer trunk in a closet at Einhorn's apartment. The inference was that Einhorn had killed Maddux, because they'd been heard arguing and she was threatening to leave him. The Unicorn was madly in love with the blond Texan.

I agreed to handle the case for purposes of the bail hearing. When I talked to Einhorn at the Philadelphia detention center, he insisted he'd been set up by the CIA and that mind control was involved, like the feats performed by spoon bender Uri Geller. I thought Einhorn might have a winning defense: temporary insanity. A person would arguably have to be out of his mind to keep his lover's corpse in a trunk for such a long time. That devotion and attachment might be consistent with a passion killing to stop her from leaving him.

Einhorn's friends produced a long line of Philadelphia's finest to attest to his good reputation and the likelihood of his appearing for trial. The commonwealth requested bail in the amount of $100,000. The judge set bail at $40,000, requiring Einhorn to post $4,000 cash for his pretrial release. A month before he was slated to stand trial in January 1981, the Unicorn jumped bail and fled.

He remained at large for sixteen years, an international cause célèbre, and was finally located in June 1997 in a village in the south of France. In December 1997 a French court set Einhorn free, ruling that extraditing him would violate his civil rights because he had been tried and convicted of first-degree murder in absentia. Recently the French have reconsidered, and Einhorn may yet face punishment.

Although my part in Einhorn's case was limited to the bail hearing, the news media emphasized my role after I was elected to the Senate, to give the case more flavor. The TV clip of Einhorn and a younger Arlen Specter, briefcase in hand, walking down the City Hall corridors to the bail hearing has been replayed countless times. In a news feature on the Einhorn case in February 1998, NBC's *Dateline* showed me speaking on an entirely different issue and made it appear as though I were commenting on the case. In a letter, NBC acknowledged "the clips which you have cited had nothing to do with the Einhorn story. They were used merely to add visual context by showing you in your current position as a United States Senator." Similarly, in a four-hour NBC docudrama on Einhorn in 1999, an actor playing Arlen Specter said things I have never said. When I complained, NBC sent me a letter explaining, "As a dramatization based on fact, the movie didn't purport and was not understood by viewers to confine itself to the presentation of precise documented facts as does a documentary. Rather, like all fact-based dramas, it employed simulated dialog and other techniques intended to dramatize, while still remaining faithful to the facts in source materials." That is absurd on its face. When a person identified as Arlen Specter, an individual known to the public, makes statements in a television program, the obvious conclusion would be that Arlen Specter spoke the lines, not that the public knows better. That was a ridiculous defense rationale by an overreaching network.

My law practice at Dechert was comfortable and lucrative and brought interesting cases, but the wall-to-wall life still left me unfulfilled and restless. I continued my interest in public policy, both foreign and domestic, and decided to run for Senate in 1976. I went to see the incumbent, Senator Hugh Scott, in October 1975. "Senator," I told him, "I want to run." The minority leader said, "Well, that's very interesting. I haven't made up my announcement yet."

"Senator Scott," I said, "I just want to tell you my plans," with the clear implication that they were not contingent on his decision. I thought it was important to get an early start, and I declared my candidacy in news conferences around the state on November 17, 1975. Scott held a big dinner at the Pittsburgh Hilton on December 2, 1975, and announced his retirement. The Pittsburgh paper ran a headline the next day: STAGE SET FOR HEINZ, namely Congressman John Heinz of Pittsburgh, heir to the ketchup and food empire. I wound up in a three-way primary for the GOP Senate nomination with Heinz and former *Philadelphia Bulletin* editor George Packard. Packard, who was once a CIA staffer, had resigned his newspaper post to campaign.

I thought a candidacy against Heinz was financially feasible because the recently passed 1974 federal election law allowed a candidate for Senate to spend a maximum of $35,000 of his own money on his campaign. That was about what I had accumulated, and I was prepared to throw it in. Then, on January 29, 1976, the U.S. Supreme Court ruled in *Buckley* v. *Valeo* that, as a matter of free speech, candidates could spend millions. And John Heinz did. But the federal law, upheld in *Buckley,* limited noncandidates to campaign contributions of $1,000. My brother, Morton, could have financed my campaign and might have, but he was limited to $1,000. Why was John Heinz's speech unlimited, but not Morton Specter's? I have been trying to overturn that ruling for the past twenty years. Senator Ernest Hollings and I regularly press a constitutional amendment to overrule *Buckley.* We have, by now, drawn backing from a daunting cadre of academics and attorneys general. Maybe the firestorm over campaign finance abuses will someday put us over the top.

For my 1976 race I hired Elliot Curson, who had written a Clio-winning radio spot during my run for DA in 1969. We were doing some TV spots when Curson turned to me and exclaimed, "For you, this is just another election. For me, it's important." David Garth had represented both Heinz and me in the past and felt constrained to stay out.

Early in the election cycle, the *Bulletin* ran a front-page, banner-headline Sunday story about a Gulf Oil lobbyist who allegedly gave Heinz $6,000 in cash. This was now 1975, and cash gifts had been banned by 1974 post-Watergate reform laws. The issue would linger and fester. Curson made an effective TV spot with a man holding out a wad of cash.

Late in the campaign, Heinz, Packard, and I debated at the Union League. I had always drawn uneasy support from this bastion of conservative Republicanism. George Packard spoke first, I went second, and John Heinz was scheduled last. Closing my ten-minute speech, I said, "There's been a major controversy in this campaign, as to whether Congressman Heinz accepted or didn't accept a campaign contribution in cash for $6,000.

"And I think it ought to be in or out of this campaign, and I have decided how to handle it, and that is I've prepared an affidavit." I noted that a notary public was sitting in the front row. "And let me just read the affidavit: 'I, H. John Heinz III, being duly sworn according to law, depose and state, under oath, subject to the laws of perjury, five years upon conviction, that I didn't take a cash contribution of $6,000.' And this is it, Congressman Heinz," I said as I left the podium, "sign this and you'll never hear another word from me about it."

Heinz got up. "I want to tell you how much I appreciate being here at the *Urban* League," he said, misstating the Union League's name. Clearly flustered, he ignored my affidavit, and the issue lingered.

On election night, April 27, the early returns from the east all ran my way. I carried Philadelphia 10–1, 64,800 to 6,400 votes. I carried Montgomery and Bucks and Delaware counties, outside Philadelphia, by big numbers. UPI declared me the winner at 1:30 A.M.

Packard had walked across the state during the campaign, following the lead of Lawton Chiles of Florida. But most of George's support came in protest votes against two people: the guy who had reportedly taken $6,000 in cash and the guy who had complained about it. I learned a good lesson in that campaign. Although a factual negative ad will hurt the target, it will also boomerang against the candidate who makes the criticism, no matter how well founded, and will wind up benefiting a third candidate. Packard and I were both from southeastern Pennsylvania, and most of his 160,000 votes, which came from the Philadelphia area, would otherwise have gone my way.

Later in the night the western Pennsylvania returns came in. Heinz's home county, Allegheny, came in 93,000 to 6,000 for the Pittsburgh congressman, almost 16–1. Beaver County came in 19–1. When the last ballot was counted, Heinz was ahead by 26,000 votes out of 1 million cast. Heinz had 366,000 votes, I had 340,000. Packard's vote was clearly the difference.

After the primary I didn't immediately endorse Heinz. Those primary wounds took a while to heal. In early September, Faith Whitlesey, a Delaware County council member, urged me to endorse Heinz at the big post–Labor Day county Republican rally. I did. The media speculation that I would sit out the race gave my endorsement an element of drama. Unlike so many postprimary endorsements, mine was not perfunctory.

In 1978 the governor's office would be on the ballot. And it would be open. Milton Shapp, who had done a surprisingly good job, had served his two-term limit and couldn't run. I'd wanted to run for governor in 1970 and 1974 but had sat out both races, for different reasons. In 1978 I threw my hat into the ring.

The 1978 race would feature an unusual number of top-notch candidates. Five Republicans and three Democrats entered the primaries. On the GOP side, I was one of three former prosecutors. The other two were Richard Thornburgh, who had been an excellent U.S. Attorney in Pittsburgh and an assistant attorney general in the Ford administration; and David Marston, a former U.S. Attorney in Philadelphia.

Marston, thirty-five, had a meteoric political rise. He had been a legislative assistant to Senator Richard Schweiker, who had made him U.S. Attorney in Philadelphia in 1976. Marston had sent several Harrisburg pols to jail and investigated two congressmen. All his targets were Democrats. In January 1978 President Jimmy Carter had fired Marston. It was disclosed that Democratic Congressman Joshua Eilberg, one of the young prosecutor's marks, had called the president two months earlier to urge Marston's ouster. Overnight, Marston had become a national celebrity and a martyr. He jumped into the governor's race just before the filing deadline. The rest of the Republican field included Robert Butera, speaker of the state house of representatives, and Henry Hager, the president pro tempore of the state senate.

I pressed the issues. I wrote and distributed a twenty-four-page booklet titled "A Platform for Pennsylvania." I was the only candidate with a written platform.

In the middle of the campaign I was subpoenaed to testify before the U.S. House Select Committee on Assassinations, which was investigating President Kennedy's murder and the Warren Commission. The committee wanted to question me about the memo I had written in April 1964 urging the commission's general counsel, Lee Rankin, to press for access to the autopsy photos and X rays. I had to break off a campaign day and take a charter plane from Reading to Washington.

Dick Sprague had been the Assassination Committee's chief counsel. But the committee had fired my former first assistant over a vintage Sprague performance. Sprague had walked onto the House floor, something no staffer ever does, and taken over. He had ordered congressmen around, including the committee chairman, Henry Gonzales.

The House committee did a solid job—almost. They were prepared to conclude that one gunman killed Kennedy until acoustics experts listened to an audiotape and heard what they decided were gunshots firing one and a half seconds apart. Two experts testified that the shots occurred at an interval too brief for both shots to have been fired from Oswald's rifle. The committee found a conspiracy. But later tests showed that the House committee's experts had been wrong. The second shot identified by the experts as a rifle report had actually been a noise made by a police motorcycle.

I had known Dick Thornburgh for years before we wound up as rivals in the 1978 gubernatorial primary. We'd met one afternoon in September 1966 in Pittsburgh, when I had come to campaign for Ray Shafer, who was running for governor. I'd gone to Squirrel Hill, the city's Jewish section, to do a "Friends for Ray Shafer" event, which was a euphemism for "Jews for Ray Shafer." I'd done a similar event in Harrisburg. And while I was working Squirrel Hill, I also campaigned for a young lawyer named Richard L. Thornburgh, who ran unsuccessfully for Congress.

After Thornburgh had been appointed U.S. Attorney in 1969, I'd gone out to visit him. I was then the Philadelphia DA, and we had a lot in common. We had lunch at Pittsburgh's Yale-Harvard-Princeton Club and struck up a friendship.

I led Thornburgh in polls before the election. But there were three of us running from the Philadelphia area, and the geography tipped the victory to the lone western candidate, Thornburgh. The Democrats nominated Pete Flaherty, former Pittsburgh mayor and associate U.S. attorney general. Thornburgh beat Flaherty in the November general election and was sworn in as governor in January 1979.

My frequent trips to Atlantic City on the Spencer Gifts case stirred my interest in practicing law there, at least part-time. Casinos were burgeoning, and I could see an interesting, lucrative, regulatory (quasi-criminal) law practice. So, in 1979, with no office to run for at hand, I decided to take the New Jersey bar exam. With New York lawyers to the north and Pennsylvania lawyers to the south, New Jersey didn't allow admission to its bar on reciprocity, so I had to take the bar exam if I wanted to practice law in New Jersey's courts.

I knew it was risky to take the New Jersey test. It would have made news and been embarrassing if I'd failed the exam. But I took my chances. Interestingly, *Frazier* v. *Cupp* , the case I had argued for the National DA's Association in 1969 before the U.S. Supreme Court, came up on a question in the 1979 New Jersey bar exam. Like most multiple-choice questions, this one had four possible answers that could be readily narrowed to two. The situation proved the adage that too much knowledge can be a problem on the bar exam. I had difficulty figuring how much the bar examiner knew about *Frazier* v. *Cupp*, which was important, because one answer was correct from my knowledge of the case, but the other appeared more plausible. I decided to put aside my special knowledge of the case, reject the correct answer, and answer as I thought the bar examiner would. I never did find out whether my answer was judged correct.

Some weeks later I was sitting home on a Sunday night when I got a call from *Philadelphia Bulletin* reporter Dorothy Brown. "Do you know another Arlen Specter?" she asked. I replied, "No, why?"

"We just got the results from the New Jersey bar," she said, "and there's an Arlen Specter who passed the bar exam."

"That's me, kid," I said. I had heard that line a year earlier, while campaigning for governor in Reading, Pennsylvania, I'd run into a grizzled old man, bald and potbellied. Following my usual procedure, as I shook hands at each table, I asked, "What's your name, sir?" He replied, "Whitey Kurowski." The star of the 1942 World Series had the same name, I recalled. But that Whitey Kurowski was a dashing young St. Louis Cardinals third baseman whom I had seen in a newsreel field a wicked grounder, tag out a runner, pirouette, and throw out the batter at first. I told the man, "That's the same name as the famous Cardinal third—" realizing just then that this was that young man thirty-six years later. Before I could shift gears, he said, "Dot's me, kid."

In August 1979, juggling my new Atlantic City law practice with my work at Dechert, I was sitting in my Philadelphia office when Bob Teeter, Ronald Reagan's pollster, came to see me. It was Teeter who reportedly had raised Bob Dole's name during an all-night deliberation at the Kansas City convention over who should be the Republicans' 1976 vice presidential candidate. Teeter wanted to talk to me about the 1980 Pennsylvania Senate race. Senator Richard Schweiker had announced his decision not to run again.

"I came to see you because I think you're one of the three guys who

269

could run and win," he said. Teeter's other two potential winners were Lieutenant Governor William Scranton and retired general Alexander Haig. "I'm polling, and you're known by 60 percent of the people in Pennsylvania, which is a big head start," Teeter told me.

I was interested to hear that I ranked in name recognition alongside the sitting lieutenant governor and Haig, who had drawn tremendous national publicity as the commanding general at NATO and Nixon's chief of staff. I had run in two statewide primaries and had served eight years as district attorney of Philadelphia, with a media market that reached about 40 percent of Pennsylvania's population. The cumulative effect, apparently, put me in a potentially strong position.

Teeter was after me not so much to land a client as to try to help Republicans win the Senate. It was highly unlikely that the GOP could capture the upper chamber, but there was a sense that it was possible. Teeter didn't do a hard sell. He offered an interesting analysis and planted an idea for me to think about. And I thought about it.

I decided to run. I realized that since I had lost my previous three elections, many people might ridicule my candidacy. My own family, in fact, opposed another run. I wouldn't say they were embarrassed, but close. I had never felt rejected. I thought the losses stemmed from factors other than my own ineptitude. I didn't consider those defeats a personal rebuff. But this time, in 1980, it was me against the world. I called Bill Meehan on February 11, 1980, and told him I was going to run for Senate. Later that same afternoon, I found out, Meehan told somebody else that I wouldn't be a candidate. Billy genuinely didn't believe I would undertake another campaign.

John Heinz, three years into his first Senate term, invited me down to Washington for lunch. We had hamburgers in his office. "So you'd like to have an office like this?" he asked me. I said yes. I went in to use Heinz's private lavatory and saw his large Russell Building suite and his large staff working on the nation's toughest and most interesting issues. So this was the U.S. Senate. And I had come within an eyelash of beating Heinz in 1976. I said to myself, why not?

In the Republican primary my chief rival was Harold "Bud" Haabestad, the Republican state chairman and a Delaware County council member, who had been an all-star basketball player at Princeton. Haabestad's slogan was "This Bud's for You." Heinz opposed me. So did Schweiker, on his way out of the Senate, and Thornburgh, now governor. Even Meehan came out for Haabestad. Billy depended on

Thornburgh for many patronage jobs. Meehan and I had a long history, and I understood, sort of, when he lined up against me. After singing my praises in 1965, 1967, 1969, 1973, 1976, and 1978, he couldn't turn around his committeemen, much less the voters, with his own change. I carried Philadelphia by big numbers.

I beat Haabestad 36 to 33 percent. In Pennsylvania a plurality won. There was no runoff. The rest of the votes went to an array of candidates that included State Senator Ed Howard, a gutsy maverick who would become my longtime aide and adviser.

In the general election I would face Pete Flaherty, the former two-term Pittsburgh mayor whose recent losses looked like mine. When Flaherty and I emerged as the candidates, one newspaper ran the headline ONE OF THESE RETREADS WILL BE A SENATOR. David Garth came aboard for the general election. The 1980 general campaign began with Flaherty thirteen points ahead of me. I spent the summer on the campaign trail. Pete mostly did other things. In late August, I was no longer behind by 13 percent. I was behind by 19 percent.

On the issues, Pete Flaherty and I were not far apart. As the *Washington Post* put it, "Although separated by wide gulfs of philosophy and style, both men have made revitalization of the Pennsylvania economy—help for coal and steel and the cities—centerpieces of their campaigns. Both talk of stronger defense and a better shake for Pennsylvania in getting money from Washington."[1] As the campaign progressed, Flaherty made it a practice to agree with me on the issues after I took a stand. I would come out for the B1 bomber, then Flaherty would come out for the B1. I would come for the MX missile, then Flaherty would come out for it. I wondered if Flaherty knew what the MX was. But Flaherty was sitting on a big lead and neutralizing every move I made.

Then, in August, I devised a strategy that has since been so widely copied that it now has a name: The 67 Club. I visited every one of Pennsylvania's sixty-seven counties. Pennsylvania, stretching from the Delaware River and New Jersey border to Ohio and West Virginia, is like six states: Pittsburgh and its blue-collar industry, the south-central farm country, metropolitan Philadelphia, the Allegheny National Forest, Wilkes-Barre and Scranton and their coal mines, and the diverse Lehigh Valley and its high-tech industry. I hit them all.

One August morning, Shanin and I rose at 5:00 A.M., drove to Montrose in Susquehanna County on the northern tier, said "Westward ho," and started an odyssey to the Ohio border. After a while the fun exceeded the fatigue. I really enjoyed meeting the people. I've done it ever since. I don't need polls or focus groups to tell me what Pennsylvanians think and want. And the voters have remembered in my reelection bids.

Philadelphia Inquirer reporter Paul Taylor, who later moved to the *Washington Post*, wrote, "Arlen Specter would shave twice a day." I didn't, but Taylor was taking poetic license. He meant, I suppose, that I was willing to go the extra mile, to rise in the middle of the night, put in long days, and that I looked okay doing it.

I was also helped by my former rival, Senator Heinz. He had become chairman of the Republican Senate Campaign Committee and jump-started my campaign with $525,000.

By November the work paid off. I beat Pete Flaherty 51–48 percent. Republicans, riding partly on Reagan's coattails, captured the Senate. I was sworn in as a U.S. senator in January 1981, as a member of the new majority party.

CENTER STAGE

Washington was buzzing with excitement after the 1980 election. Savoring victory on election night, president-elect Reagan luxuriated in announcing that he would be accompanied into office by a Republican Senate. The seemingly impossible had happened: Sixteen new Republican senators had been elected, giving the GOP control of the Senate for the first time in a quarter century. Slade Gorton accomplished a virtual miracle by ousting Senator Warren Magnuson, chairman of the Appropriations Committee, in the state of Washington. James Abdnor unseated Senator George McGovern, who eight years earlier had been the Democrats' presidential nominee, in South Dakota. Steve Symms beat venerable Frank Church in Idaho. Chuck Grassley, badly beaten in the Iowa debates, at least according to the *Des Moines Register*, replaced John Culver. Handsome Dan Quayle at thirty-three took over from entrenched Birch Bayh. Young Mack Mattingly retired Herman Talmadge, a Georgia institution. Bob Kasten toppled three-term Senator Gaylord Nelson in Wisconsin. Warren Rudman ousted Senator John Durkin in New Hampshire. John East beat Senator Robert Morgan in North Carolina. And so the giants of the Senate fell across America in the Reagan revolution.

The Pennsylvania picture was different. In my race the voting patterns did not reflect a coattail effect. Reagan lost Philadelphia by 225,000 votes, and I won the city by 14,000. He won western Pennsylvania big, which I lost, and our returns in upstate Pennsylvania differed substantially.

Wednesday morning, after spending half the night celebrating my victory, I awakened almost out of a dream, with the sober realization that I was heading to the United States Senate. "Yippee," I said, more to myself than out loud. To think of the opportunity to enter the hallowed chamber where Henry Clay and Daniel Webster struggled to keep the union together, where Robert LaFollette held forth about workers' civil liberties, and where the modern giants, Arthur Vandenberg, Robert Taft, and Jacob Javits, held sway.

The distinguished career of Senator Javits had ended with his loss in the 1980 New York Republican primary. Javits's futile candidacy on the Liberal line enabled Alfonse D'Amato to win a narrow victory over Elizabeth Holtzman in the general election. But even without Javits, there were many Republican senators who shared my position on the political spectrum: Mark Hatfield and Bob Packwood of Oregon, Bob Stafford of Vermont, Lowell Weicker of Connecticut, Bill Cohen of Maine, John Chafee of Rhode Island, Warren Rudman of New Hampshire, Alan Simpson of Wyoming, Jack Danforth of Missouri, Charles Percy of Illinois, Charles Mathias of Maryland, and my colleague from Pennsylvania, John Heinz.

At a party at the home of the new majority leader, Howard Baker, to welcome newly elected senators, Hatfield talked proudly of being a "liberal." That was the first and last time that I heard a Republican senator identify himself as a liberal. When straying from conservatism, most Republican members selected the label "moderate," and my preference was the term "centrist." With Reagan's election, Republican senators started a decisive move to the right that would leave the moderate Wednesday Lunch Club, founded by Javits in the seventies, with only five members by the end of 1999: James Jeffords of Vermont, Olympia Snowe and Susan Collins of Maine, Linc Chafee, who had been appointed to fill his father's unexpired term, and me.

The day after the 1980 election, I was sitting in my den when the phone rang. "Can I speak to senator-elect Specter, please?" a voice drawled. I replied, "This is Arlen Specter."

"This is Strom Thurmond calling, Arlen. How you?" Thurmond, the 1948 Dixiecrat presidential candidate, was a living institution. I said, "I'm fine. It's good to hear from you, Senator Thurmond."

"Well, I wanna congratulate you on being elected to the United States Senate," he said.

"Well, thank you very much, Senator Thurmond."

"And I just wanted to know if you'd be willing to suppot [support] me for president pro tempore?"

Shortly after their arrival from Uganst, Russia, in 1906, Lillie Shanin, Lillie's younger brother, Max, mother, Freida, and father, Mordecai Shanin, pose for a family photograph. (*author's private collection*)

Arlen's father, an immigrant from Russia in 1911, was seriously wounded in the Argonne Forest in World War I. He returned to St. Joe, Missouri, to marry Lillie Shanin in 1919. (*author's private collection*)

Lillie Shanin Specter, Arlen's mother, on her wedding day in March 1919. (*author's private collection*)

Even at two, Arlen sports an elephant on his playsuit, sitting between his brother, Morton, and sister Hilda with his sister Shirley between their parents. (*author's private collection*)

When four-year-old Arlen Specter asked the Wichita sheriff to hold his gun, the sheriff pinned a badge on Arlen, making him the youngest deputy sheriff in history, according to "Ripley's Believe It or Not." (*Ripley Entertainment 2000*)

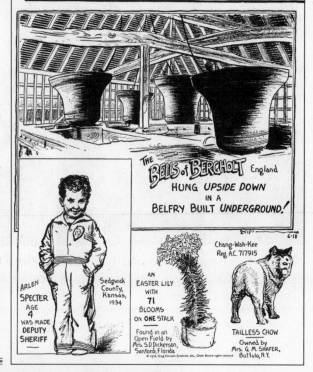

Pictured with Arlen is his brother, Morton Specter, a Navy ensign, in front of the rented family bungalow at 91 South May, Russell, Kansas, in the spring of 1943. (*author's private collection*)

At fifteen, Arlen played second base for the Russell Junior American Legion baseball team, which tied for third in the state tournament. (*author's private collection*)

Though a graduate of Yale Law School and Penn, Arlen's best educational experience was at Russell High School, where he was on the Kansas state championship debate team in 1947. (*author's private collection*)

When he continued debating at the University of Pennsylvania, Arlen Specter's team won the Boston University National Debate Tournament in February 1951. (*author's private collection*)

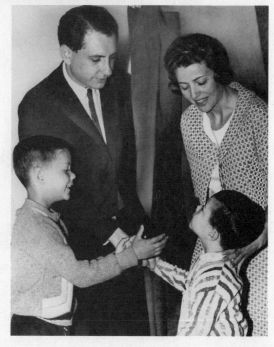

Joan Specter was locked in the voting booth in the May 1965 primary when Arlen ran for district attorney. Her worried sons, Shanin and Steve, burst into smiles when she was extricated. (Philadelphia Inquirer)

The Specter family's 1999 holiday greeting-card photograph was taken on the dunes in Long Beach Island, New Jersey, in August. Arlen, Joan, Tracey, Shanin, Silvi, Peri, and Lilli (*left to right*). (*author's private collection*)

When Arlen Specter told former President Dwight Eisenhower in August 1965 that Chief Justice Earl Warren accepted the chairmanship of the commission because President Lyndon Johnson insisted, Eisenhower scoffed and replied: "The chief justice is not under the president. If he were, I would have fired Warren a long time ago."
(*author's private collection*)

Chief Justice Warren agreed with the Single-Bullet Theory after Arlen Specter detailed the facts while they looked down at Dealey Plaza from the assassin's perch at the Texas School Book Depository Building. (*author's private collection*)

In the reenactment of the Kennedy assassination, with stand-ins in a replica of the president's limousine, Arlen Specter demonstrates the bullet's path through the president's neck and into Governor Connally's back. (*National Archives photograph, Warren Commission Exhibit 903*)

Joan and Arlen flash winning smiles after his stunning upset election to become district attorney in November 1965. Henry Sawyer, president of Americans for Democratic Action, and Barnett Lotstein, now Phoenix first assistant prosecuting attorney, smile in the background. (*author's private collection*)

District attorney candidate Arlen Specter conferred with Dr. Martin Luther King, Jr., in August 1965 on civil rights and a Citizens Advisory Board to investigate charges of police brutality. (*author's private collection*)

In August 1969, Police Commissioner Frank Rizzo (*center*) brokered a rapprochement between Mayor James H. J. Tate and DA Arlen Specter. Tate defeated Specter by 1.5 percent in 1967, the closest mayoralty vote in Philadelphia history. (Philadelphia Bulletin)

In June 1971, President Nixon, Attorney General Mitchell, and District Attorney Arlen Specter discuss law enforcement in the Oval Office. Nixon later considered Specter for both the U.S. Supreme Court and attorney general. (*author's private collection*)

Arlen Specter urges President Reagan to sign the Armed Career Criminal bill in January 1983 in the White House. Facing the camera from left to right: Attorney General William French Smith, Congressman William Hughes, Vice President George Bush, Specter, and Domestic Counsel Ed Meese. With their backs to the camera, from right to left: Senator Joe Biden, Senator Strom Thurmond, and President Reagan. (*author's private collection*)

In 1983 Senator Specter, spokesman for the "Sweet Sixteen" Republicans elected with President Reagan in 1980, thanks the president in the presence of Majority Leader Howard Baker for the president's help, advice, and support on Specter's Armed Criminal bill up until, as Specter put it, the president vetoed the bill earlier that year. The bill was reintroduced and signed into law in 1984.

The Arlen Specter–John Heinz softball teams square off on the Washington mall circa 1983. (*author's private collection*)

After the 6300 block of Philadelphia's Osage Avenue was decimated by incendiary explosives and fire in May 1985, HUD Secretary Sam Pierce, Joan Specter, Arlen Specter, Mayor Wilson Goode, and Senator John Heinz tour the wreckage. (Philadelphia Inquirer)

Pope John Paul II
greets Joan and
Arlen Specter at the
Vatican in 1986.
(*author's private
collection*)

In January 1990, Joan and Arlen Specter pose with Syrian
President Hafez al-Assad in front of his famous crusades
painting during one of the Specters' visits with the Syrian
president. (*author's private collection*)

In a January 1990 meeting in Baghdad, Iraq, Saddam Hussein questioned Senator Richard Shelby (R-Ala.) and Arlen Specter about U.S. policy on sending all Russian Jews to Israel. Specter replied that he favored a choice for Russian-Jewish immigrants, which his father had in 1911. He wanted to be sure Saddam knew he was Jewish. (*author's private collection*)

In the Oval Office on September 25, 1992, President Bush unsuccessfully urged Arlen Specter to vote to sustain the president's veto on the Telecommunications bill. (*author's private collection*)

Steve, Joan, and Arlen Specter happily greet election-night supporters in November 1992 after a narrow victory over Lynn Yeakel. (*author's private collection*)

Former Soviet Premier Mikhail Gorbachev and Senator Specter discussed U.S.-Russian foreign policy in Moscow in June 1994. (*author's private collection*)

Traveling on Air Force One, Senator Specter stresses a point in a discussion with President Clinton, Congressman Ron Klink, and Senator Harris Wofford. (*author's private collection*)

A six-and-a-half-hour dinner meeting in Havana in June 1999 gave Arlen Specter a chance to question Castro about the Cuban missile crisis, human rights, Oswald, and drug interdiction. (*author's private collection*)

In his Senate office, Arlen Specter posed with Palestinian Chairman Yasser Arafat in March 1999 in front of a Clinton-Arafat poster circulated in Bethlehem, Israel, in December 1998. (*author's private collection*)

Arlen Specter and other Senate Appropriations Committee members met with Prime Minister Barak in Jerusalem in January 2000 to discuss U.S. aid to Israel on the Wye Accord and possible assistance on a prospective Israeli-Syria peace treaty. (*author's private collection*)

I said, "Of course I would, Senator Thurmond, although little as I know about the Senate, I thought your designation was automatic, being the senior Republican."

"Well, I just never take any votes for granted," he said. "It's been mighty fine talking with you, and I look forward to serving with you in the Senate and thank you for your suppot."

The first big event for newly elected senators was committee selection. The Finance Committee, which handles taxation and trade, was considered by many to be the most important. It was ruled out for me because John Heinz, my fellow Pennsylvanian, already had a seat there. Next was Appropriations, which directs spending, and I watched the open spots dwindle until my turn came. Members who had been neither governors nor House members were ranked in Senate seniority on the basis of the populations of their states, from highest to lowest. The Republican caucus had adopted a rule of alphabetical order, after giving preference to former governors and House members for seniority on choosing committee seats. The policy was designed to lessen the influence of big-state senators from the Northeast and Midwest and to elevate Southern and Western senators, so with 12 million constituents, I would have my turn after John East of North Carolina, Mattingly of Georgia, Jeremiah Denton of Alabama, and Frank Murkowski of Alaska, whose states ranged in population from 600,000 to 7.5 million. But one seat remained on Appropriations when my turn came, and I grabbed it.

In 1981 there was still some debate as to whether Finance or Appropriations was the more important. When only one seat on the Finance Committee was left, Bob Kasten, who was right behind Chuck Grassley in seniority, told Grassley how much more important Appropriations was than Finance. As Grassley later told the story, "You figure Finance must be the better committee, or why would Kasten be touting Appropriations?" Grassley selected Finance and is in line to chair that committee during the 108th Congress.

In selecting Appropriations, I had bypassed Agriculture, which gave me some pause, because I had made a campaign promise to take Agriculture. Although taking Appropriations first was risky, I could justify doing so because of its importance to Pennsylvania, and I thought I might get Agriculture in the second round, but it was gone when my turn came again. My next best approach was to try for a seat on the Agriculture Subcommittee of Appropriations, but there was no vacancy. I told my colleagues of my campaign promise, and Ted Stevens shifted subcommittees to open a spot for me on the Ag subcommittee.

My keenest interest, arising from my legal background, was Judiciary. In the second round, one opening was left on Judiciary, which Thurmond chaired. As hard as Strom Thurmond tried, he could not find people to fill that Judiciary vacancy before my turn came. He was concerned that I was not sufficiently conservative. With moderate Republican Senator Charles "Mac" Mathias already on the committee, there might not be enough votes to carry some of Strom's issues. To keep me off, Thurmond created two new subcommittees for two new members (Terrorism for Denton and Separation of Powers for East) and funded Grassley's subcommittee generously, as an inducement for them to join the Judiciary Committee. Thurmond was hoping all the committee's spots would be taken by the time my turn came. But there was still one spot left, and I took it.

Before I came to the Senate, my impression of Thurmond was not positive. I didn't like his early record as a segregationist and his opposition to civil rights. His 1948 presidential run, which came close to putting the election in the House of Representatives, threatened the stability of our two-party system. I had heard that over the years he'd moderated his views, so I approached him with an open mind.

From the outset, Thurmond and I had a cordial relationship. It became close. I made it a point to arrive on time for Judiciary Committee executive sessions, which was the exception to the rule. Most senators arrived late, figuring it would take at least fifteen or twenty minutes beyond the convening time for ten of the eighteen Judiciary Committee members to arrive to constitute a quorum. The newly elected senators were more punctual, and I always arrived, if not at the prescribed time, a few minutes before. Strom appreciated that, and we had a few minutes to chat before others arrived.

At a 1982 confirmation hearing for two nominees from Pennsylvania, Strom asked them if they would be "cuteus" (courteous) if confirmed. I thought the question meaningless, because what else would they say but yes? After both responded in the affirmative, Strom said, "The more power a person has, the more cuteus that person should be." I've come to consider that as profound a statement as I've heard in the Senate. On occasions when Thurmond is not present or does not ask that question, I do. Several federal judges, long after their confirmations, have told me that they often reflect on that admonition to be courteous in their judicial duties.

As Strom grows older—at this writing he is nearly ninety-seven—fewer newly arrived senators sit next to him at our Tuesday caucus lunches, because he may not be as easy to talk to as some of their contemporaries. Whenever I can, I sit next to Strom, to hear more of his stories going back to his days as a delegate at the 1932 Democratic convention and serving with President Eisenhower or that "young fella" Jack Kennedy, right through LBJ, Nixon, Carter, and the eighties and nineties.

Many times Strom and I sipped soup in the middle of the night and he told me fascinating stories. When he was governor of South Carolina, Strom and his wife rode in an open car down Pennsylvania Avenue in the Inaugural Parade on January 20, 1949. They passed in front of the White House, and there were President Truman, freshly inaugurated, and Vice President Alben Barkley. Thurmond tipped his hat, and Barkley began to raise his hand. Truman pulled the new vice president's arm down, commanding, "Don't you wave at that SOB."

Former Pennsylvania senator Hugh Scott had a wonderful expression: "Every senator dances on his own center stage." I had an image of the portly, mustached Republican minority leader twirling around, doing pirouettes at the center stage of a theater. Scott, of course, meant that every senator's activities were so important in his or her own mind that each felt he held center stage. Of course, there are times, such as when the president enters a scene or when the majority leader or speaker commandeers a conference, that a senator is bumped off center stage, even in his or her own view.

When I first came to the Senate, watching senators congregate and talk in the well on the floor, I thought of Valhalla, the meeting place of the Norse gods. I watched with some awe prominent senators about whom I'd read for years come in to vote: Barry Goldwater, Scoop Jackson, Bob Dole, Ted Kennedy, John Tower, Joe Biden, Ted Stevens, Nancy Kassebaum, Fritz Hollings, and others. The camaraderie and backslapping, crossing party lines, almost resembled an NFL team after a big play.

Norris Cotton, a distinguished senator from New Hampshire from 1954 to '75, reputedly said that what he loved most about the Senate was the smell of white marble. After two decades I still get a thrill every time I leave the train from Philadelphia, exit Union Station, and see the

Capitol dome. When I leave the Senate chamber and see the Senate pillars lined up directly with the U.S. Supreme Court columns, the scene brings to mind the Senate's confirmation power and its final word in sending nominees to the Court. Other facets of Washington's geometry and symmetry still fascinate me. The distance from the statue of Miss Freedom atop the Capitol dome to the top of the Washington Monument is reported to be exactly one mile. On my first visit to the president's family quarters, I was struck by how the portico columns on the second floor of the White House lined up exactly with the columns on the Jefferson Memorial.

This is not to say the Senate always inspires goose bumps. Senator Dale Bumpers of Arkansas and I used the Senate gym at about the same hour and had long talks in the steam room. One of the earliest bits of advice Bumpers gave me was "Arlen, you're going to spend the first six months wondering how you got here and then you're going to spend the next five and a half years wondering how the other guys got here."

Life in the Senate was like diving into a bottomless pool, or into the ocean. Some of the currents were warm, like the Judiciary Committee, where I had a firm grasp on pending legislation on crime and antitrust issues. Other currents were icy, such as when I watched my newly elected colleagues take their turns presiding over the Senate. That duty is the formal responsibility of the vice president, who appears on the rare occasions when a tie is anticipated so he can cast the decisive vote. The president pro tempore sits as the vice president's first alternative and customarily opens the Senate, then yields to a junior senator. I studied the Senate's complex rules and precedents and wondered how I would handle the job when my turn came to preside in the vice president's chair and make the necessary rulings. I soon found that the job was not hard at all, because the parliamentarian, seated directly in front of the presiding officer, whispered the rulings like Edgar Bergen to Charlie McCarthy. Still, it was quite a heady experience to preside.

Learning the ropes and protocols of the Senate wasn't easy. Shortly after I arrived, the Appropriations Committee was "marking up" or writing the Interior budget bill for the fiscal year beginning October 1, 1981. As a big-city senator, I received a number of calls urging me to support an appropriation for urban gardening. One of the calls came from Hal Haskell, the former Republican mayor of Wilmington,

Delaware. Hal said the modest investment would help beautify and humanize cities across America. I studied the issue and decided he was right. As the lowest-ranking committee member, I voted last. When the vote was taken in our twenty-nine-member committee, all fourteen Democrats voted aye and the other fourteen Republicans voted nay. You could have heard a pin drop or seen twenty-eight jaws drop when I voted "aye." The urban gardening amendment passed 15–14.

Later that day Warren Rudman, who came to the Senate with me and sat next to me on the committee, pulled me aside and said, "Let's take a walk." As we strolled onto the Senate portico, Warren lit one of his ever-present cigarettes and said in his gentlest manner, "You know, Arlen, everyone expects you to vote your conscience, but if you're going to oppose the party's position and vote against the subcommittee chairman, you really ought to let him know in advance so he can deal with it appropriately." Rudman was right. An independent vote is much easier for the party to swallow if it's not a surprise. By the same token, senators often engage in strenuous debate capped by 51–49 or 50–50 votes; this makes each senator's vote as precious as hens' teeth and has spawned the motto "The next vote is the most important one."

I learned many lessons from Senator Henry "Scoop" Jackson, the Washington State Democrat, whom I found easy to talk to. I got to know him fairly well in the gym, which we both frequented late in the afternoon. I had admired Jackson from his early days in the Senate, especially his role in the Army-McCarthy hearings in the summer of 1954. When I got to Washington, I devoured books on the Senate, including the 1972 biography on Jackson, *A Certain Democrat,* published as he was running for president.

I was on an elevator in the Russell Building one day when Jackson got on and said, "Arlen, I've got this resolution on which I've got forty-nine co-sponsors. I'm very anxious to get you to be the fiftieth co-sponsor."

I said, "Well, Scoop, I've got the resolution on my desk, and I'm studying it."

"Why don't you come to my office and let's talk about it?" Jackson replied. "If you know exactly what I have in mind, you may be willing to co-sponsor it." So we went to his office. Jackson, first elected to the Senate in 1952, had a large office filled with furniture inherited, as is customary, from other senators. He said, "See this red couch? This used to be the couch of Senator Warren G. Harding. This is the couch where he reputedly did the dastardly deed," referring to Harding's fathering of a child born shortly before he became president in 1921. Harding's mistress, Nan Britton, claimed she conceived their daughter, Elizabeth Ann, late one night in 1919 in Harding's Senate office. That was quite an introduction to our discussion on Jackson's resolution, which I then agreed to co-sponsor on the spot—on its merits.

I didn't always agree to lend my name or my vote to my colleagues' efforts, even my Republican colleagues. I got my reputation as a centrist—more like a maverick—when I took on William Bradford Reynolds, the heir apparent as Ronald Reagan's attorney general, when Reynolds was nominated for associate attorney general in 1985. While I respected the new president, I didn't feel that I'd reached the Senate on his coattails.

At the outset of President Reagan's first term, with the House of Representatives still under Democratic control, the Republican initiatives fell to the Senate. Majority Leader Baker pushed the Reagan conservative agenda to cut federal spending on social programs and reduce taxes.

Some proposed spending cuts were harsh. One day in the spring of 1981, I approached the Senate chamber to vote on a cost-of-living adjustment for senior citizens on Social Security. Pam Turner, the administration's Senate liaison, was in the lobby handing out a letter to every Republican senator urging us to eliminate the COLA. The letter was signed by Treasury Secretary Donald Regan and Office of Management and Budget Director David Stockman. "What does President Reagan say about this, Pam?" I asked. She replied, "He hasn't taken a position." I handed back the piece of paper and said, "You may need this for somebody else." I was one of four or five Republicans who voted for the cost-of-living increase.

Social Security has become in effect the third rail of politics, with both parties afraid to touch it. Republicans did in 1985, and it may have cost us control of the Senate in the 1986 elections. Senate Majority Leader Dole took a strong party position against the COLA. Four GOP senators—"Mac" Mathias, Paula Hawkins of Florida, D'Amato, and I—had staked out a public position in favor of the COLAs. Mathias, who was not running for reelection in 1986, did not talk about the issue; but Hawkins, D'Amato, and I agonized over breaking ranks with the party. On the afternoon of the vote, the three of us huddled in the rear of the Senate chamber. Paula said she felt duty-bound to vote with Dole.

D'Amato and I inveighed against her for changing her stated position in favor of the COLA.

Paula then walked to the well of the Senate, where we watched an animated discussion between her and Dole, with Dole shaking his head no. Even though the vote was expected to be razor-thin, Dole told Hawkins not to change her position. A few minutes later we found out why. Senator Pete Wilson of California, who'd recently had a serious operation, rolled into the chamber at the end of a vote in a wheelchair with a tube running from an IV pole into to his arm. Wilson mustered the strength to say "aye" to cut the COLA. That made the vote a tie, as Dole had planned, requiring Vice President Bush, Dole's prospective opponent for the 1988 presidential nomination, to cast an unpopular tie-breaking vote against senior citizens.

When I came to the well of Senate to vote on Dale Bumpers's amendment to add $7 million for child immunizations, I felt great pressure to join the other Republicans, but I finally voted for that modest expenditure, remembering my own roots, the polio scare of the mid-1930s, and my own family's limited budget.

In the Senate, party demands could be fierce. Baker ran the chamber with an iron hand when I arrived in 1981. One fellow Republican freshman came in late for a vote to find that almost all of the other fifty-three Republicans had voted aye and I was the only one who had voted nay. He looked at me and asked, "Are we permitted to vote no?"

Bucking the president and the party on such issues as the MX Missile and Robert Bork's nomination to the Supreme Court have fed my centrist or maverick image. In April 1987, Reagan vetoed the highway bill. There were thirty-four votes to sustain his veto, providing North Carolina Democrat Terry Sanford voted to sustain, which he announced publicly he would.

As fate would have it, the president was due to go to Philadelphia that day, and I was to ride up on Air Force One with him. I approached Senator Robert Byrd, who was the majority leader—the Democrats had recaptured control of the Senate in the 1986 elections—and said, "Bob, I need to go with the president, so I hope you'll vote either by eleven or after three."

Responding to my question, Byrd decided to apply a little not-so-subtle pressure: "How are you going to vote on it?"

I said, "I'm going to vote with the bad guys, Bob; I'm going to vote with you." That is, to override the president's veto. So Byrd scheduled the vote for 11:00 A.M. I voted to override. Then I headed for nearby Andrews Air Force Base to board Air Force One.

Sanford, a solid senator with an extraordinary background as president of Duke University, governor of North Carolina, and a candidate for president, ended up voting three ways: yes, no, and present. A senator could change his vote as many times as he liked while the roll was being called. And the vote was not going to be closed down until Byrd, who was working on Sanford, said so. The Senate was thrown into bedlam. I was asked to come back to the floor, so I didn't go with the president to Philadelphia. I was a little relieved. It might not have been a pleasant ride, since I'd just voted against the president's position on a big issue. Then again, consistent with President Reagan's frequent attitude, he might not have said anything about it. Eventually the vote was put over until the next day.

The full contingent of Republican senators, including the thirteen who had voted to override, gathered in the Old Senate chamber for a caucus with President Reagan and Vice President Bush, who were after one more vote to sustain the president's veto.

Steve Symms of Idaho was the principal sponsor of the highway bill. He must have lobbied me fifty times, because the bill increased the national speed limit to sixty-five miles per hour, a major item in his rural state. Senator John Warner, a former secretary of the Navy, stood and said, "Mr. President, I know Steve Symms is a good Marine and when the commander in chief asks him to sustain the veto, I think he will."

Symms rose, spent more time looking at his shoes than at anyone else in the room, and finally said, "Well, Mr. President, I hate not to support you, so I'll tell you what I'll do: If everybody else will change and vote to sustain your veto, so will I."

I anticipated a situation developing where my twelve Republican colleagues who had joined me in voting to override would peel off one by one, leaving the final pressure on me. I decided not to risk that contingency and sought recognition: "Mr. President, I will not change my vote for a number of reasons. First, the highway trust fund has enough money to pay for the bill without going into the general treasury. Second, the highways and bridges across America are in deplorable condition and need to be rebuilt. Third, the bill has many special projects for Pennsylvania. And fourth, the highway bill will consume a great deal of Pennsylvania steel, which will stimulate an industry where Pennsylvanians have lost many jobs. So at the outset I want to make my position clear."

Then Pete Wilson stood and said, "Mr. President, I have to also stay with my vote to override. There's a $5 billion subway project for Los Angeles." Then Larry Pressler of South Dakota stood and said he was going to vote to override the veto.

The full Republican caucus disbanded, and the thirteen who had voted against the president were summoned to an adjacent room for more personalized presidential pressure. No vote was changed, and the highway bill became law. The next day the president's press secretary, Marlin Fitzwater, was quoted as saying, "Arlen Specter rained on our parade."

As the eighties progressed to the nineties, the so-called Senate moderates retired, died, or were defeated. Mathias, Stafford, Danforth, Kassebaum, Cohen, Simpson, and Hatfield all retired, and Packwood preferred resignation to ouster amid a harassment scandal. Weicker and Percy lost reelection bids. John Heinz and John Chafee died.

The Republican move to the right was accentuated in the early 1990s on the issues of health care and crime. To my knowledge, Bill Cohen was the first senator to spot the health-care issue, during his 1990 reelection bid. The next year health care came into full bloom with Democrat Harris Wofford's race against Republican Dick Thornburgh for the Heinz seat. Wofford gave the strongest sound bite that I have ever heard in a commercial when he appeared with a sick patient behind a hospital bed and said, "If criminals have the right to a lawyer, I think working Americans should have the right to a doctor."

Still, centrists continued their efforts. A group of centrists, both Democrats and Republicans, led by Chafee assembled in his hideaway regularly at 8:00 A.M. during 1991 and 1992 to hammer out a health-care proposal, with the explicit blessing of Republican leader Dole. When our group finally produced a centrist legislative package, Dole, whose band of Republicans had shrunk to forty-three, demurred, saying he preferred to be the leader of thirty-seven Republicans, not six.

During my tenure, public scrutiny combined with senatorial timidity led to the removal of many so-called perks. Stung by comments that all Americans should enjoy the same health care given free to members of Congress, we now pay for the availability of medical attention under the Capital dome. Faced by medical emergencies from late-night House and Senate sessions, the attending physician long ago established a policy of keeping medical personnel on duty as long as either body was in session to render emergency treatment. Occasionally, bodies—of a different definition—are brought to the dispensary during those sessions. Similarly, members now pay for using the Senate and House gyms, and the cost of Senate haircuts has risen to approximate market values.

One so-called perk remains: foreign travel. In my opinion, the public gets full value from travel that educates senators and House members on big international issues. When I am asked about foreign travel at my town meetings, I run through an arithmetic lesson on a senator's pro rata appropriations spending. Taking a federal budget of $1.7 trillion, dividing it by two into House and Senate, I hold each body responsible on a pro rata basis for $850 billion in federal spending. Dividing that by a hundred senators leaves $8.5 billion per senator. Figuring fifty weeks per year, sixty hours per week leaves more than $2.8 million per hour of his or her time. Against that background, the cost of foreign travel is minimal, to say nothing of the important substantive issues that are beyond dollars and cents.

Foreign travel has broadened my understanding of international issues, including the important issue of arms control, which has concerned me since my high school days. As a teenager in an oratory contest, I posed the rhetorical issue "The atomic age is here to stay. The question is, are we?" My first opportunity to promote disarmament came in the spring of 1982, when I proposed a sense of the Senate resolution calling for a summit between the leaders of the United States and the Soviet Union. I had heard President Reagan's Saturday radio address, which noted that each superpower had enough of a nuclear arsenal to destroy the other. It seemed obvious to me that a negotiated agreement on arms control was better than relying on the doctrine of mutual assured destruction.

When I called my resolution for a vote on the Department of Defense Authorization Bill, I was sharply challenged by fellow Republican John Tower, then chairman of the Armed Services Committee. Fortunately for me, I had already inspected our Trident submarines outfitted with nuclear weapons in Charleston, South Carolina; the Minuteman missile sites in Grand Forks, North Dakota; and the advance bomber at Edwards Air Force Base, California. Before filing the summit resolution, I had studied our weapons systems and checked my facts very carefully. When Tower questioned my entry into that complex field after a relatively short time in the Senate, I had the facts to buttress my arguments. A few years earlier, one of my senior colleagues had been chided by one of his more senior colleagues: "When the senator is in the waters of foreign affairs up to his ankles, he's in over his head."

Pressing me on the logistics of communicating with submarines during an attack, Tower asked me on the Senate floor, "Is the senator prepared to support that with information for the Record? Is the senator saying that they do not have to trail a wire just beneath the surface?"

"I am saying that it is possible to communicate without being detected, according to the information which has been provided to me," I replied. "I received that briefing last month when I visited the nuclear submarine base in Charleston, South Carolina. But again I come back to the point that the real issue is being obscured here in a grand way by the senator from Texas, because it is not just the senator from Pennsylvania who is suggesting it is realistic to have summit talks . . ."

When the debate ended, Tower was confident his position would prevail. One of the first senators to vote was Paul Laxalt, who walked into the well of the Senate and said, "No." Tower rushed over to Laxalt and pointed out that the vote was on a tabling motion, so an "aye" was needed to oppose my resolution. Laxalt replied that he knew the procedural situation and intended to vote with me. "But," Tower persisted, "Specter's trying to tell the president what to do." "Well, what's wrong with that?" Laxalt said. "Everyone else is, too, but Specter's right." My resolution won 90–8. It didn't produce an immediate result, but it may have given a little impetus for the successful summits a few years later.

During my first four years in the Senate, Majority Leader Howard Baker ran frequent all-night sessions to complete contentious bills. During such a session on the 1982 tax bill, the Reception Room outside the Senate floor was filled with lobbyists, all looking to protect and further their interests. At 11:45 P.M., Baker stood in the well of the Senate and announced that there were sixty-three amendments pending. "Amendments are like mushrooms: They grow in the dark," Baker said, meaning that the staff would write some new ones if they had a chance before morning. Baker continued, "The Chairman of the Finance Committee, Senator Dole, would like to proceed, so we're going to go ahead."

Many of the amendments were withdrawn. Others were accepted with the obvious prospect of being dropped in conference. Still others were defeated by voice vote. Several were debated, requiring roll-call votes. It was amazing how succinct and pointed the debate could be at 3:00 or 4:00 A.M. Some senators caught catnaps on cots in the reading room, but most stayed on the floor. Obviously, there are no conflicting appointments in the middle of the night. If a senator's argument runs a little long at about 3:30 A.M., some senators will shout "Vote!" in the middle of a colleague's argument, which tends to bring the debate to a quick close. At about 6:30 A.M., the tax bill was completed. We emerged at dawn with the feeling that we had accomplished more in the past seven hours than we frequently do in seven days.

Former Majority Leader George Mitchell reminisced about an all-night session shortly after he was appointed to the Senate in 1980 to replace Edmund Muskie, who became secretary of state. Mitchell was stumbling through the Senate reading room, where cots were set up, stepping over one cot and another, feeling a little sorry for himself for having left a cushy federal judgeship to sleep on a cot in a crowded room during an all-night filibuster. Then he stumbled on Senator John Warner and felt better. Warner was obviously sacrificing more than Mitchell, given Warner's alternative nocturnal companion. Warner was married to movie star Elizabeth Taylor.

Elizabeth was a sparkling addition to the Senate family, if only for a short time. She and Warner helped me draw a big crowd for a fund-raiser at Tavern on the Green in New York City when I first ran in 1980. She didn't say anything at the event. She didn't have to. After John Warner and Elizabeth Taylor were divorced, I bumped into her at a Philadelphia restaurant. She asked me if I would deliver a note to Warner. She wrote it in front of me so I saw it without snooping. It was not exactly a love note, but close. The two have a friendly relationship to this day.

My investigative background, from the Air Force through the Dechert office, the Warren Commission, the magistrates probe, and the district attorney's office, has served me well in the Senate, especially on legislative oversight and confirmation hearings. I am occasionally razzed by my colleagues, especially Iowa Senator Chuck Grassley, for being "the Philadelphia lawyer." But Chuck likes my legal background when we work together on technical matters on the Judiciary Committee.

Early on, I developed a simple, direct, three-pronged approach to questioning witnesses: Ask a single question, listen to the answer, follow up. Especially when hearings are televised, senators are tempted to make speeches before letting the witness respond. One common technique is for a senator to spend his or her full allotted five or ten minutes making prefatory statements, concluding just when the red light goes on, so the witness's answer does not take any of the senator's time.

By the time a senator finishes a verbose, multipart question, the witness has many options for a responsive answer. My single-question approach tends to force the witness to focus on the narrow range of inquiry. Listening to a witness's answer is practically a violation of the Senate Rules of Ethics. Much of the time the senator is thinking about the next question or speech, oblivious of the response. When the witness does not respond directly to the question, which is often the case, I try to follow up until the witness does respond to my inquiry.

My background naturally led me to focus on crime control when I arrived in Washington. Carrying forward forty years of effort beginning in 1959 in the Philadelphia DA's office to the present on the Senate Judiciary Committee, I continue to push for a criminal justice system that will impose tough sentences on tough criminals to get career criminals off the streets, and will provide realistic rehabilitation—beginning with job and literacy training—for those, especially juveniles, who will be released from custody.

When I was DA, I identified five hundred career criminals in Philadelphia. A relatively small number of career criminals commit a very large number of the crimes in our country. If we want to reduce crime, we must target these career criminals and keep them off the streets. When I arrived in Washington in 1981, I introduced the Armed Career Criminal bill, which mandated a sentence of fifteen years to life for criminals convicted of three previous enumerated felonies who are found in possession of a firearm. I went to see President Ronald Reagan in the fall of 1981 to ask for his support. It was my first meeting with the new president. Reagan liked the bill and related it to a James Cagney movie in which Cagney was sent "up the river" as a three-time loser.

In the fall of 1982, Congress passed a crime bill containing my career-criminal provision. When I heard that the president was considering a veto, I asked for a meeting. I was scheduled to go to South Africa to speak at a conference in late December 1982, but I got word that the president would see me shortly after New Year's Day. I canceled my trip and went to the White House. I sat down in the Oval

Office with the president, Vice President Bush, Attorney General William French Smith, Treasury Secretary Regan, Domestic Policy Counselor Ed Meese, and Senate Judiciary Committee leaders Thurmond and Joe Biden. Everybody just sat silently. Suddenly I realized it was my meeting, and everyone was waiting for me to begin. I made my argument, but my effort went nowhere because Attorney General Smith was dead set against the bill. The president's veto came a few days afterward.

Several months later, the president met with "The Sweet Sixteen," the sixteen senators who had been elected with him in 1980. Majority Leader Baker attended. When my turn came to speak, I took the podium and said, "I want to thank the president for all his help on my Armed Career Criminal Bill. He met with me. He encouraged me. He made thoughtful suggestions. He did everything to help me except for one thing: He vetoed the bill." The room broke up.

The bill finally passed in 1984. Former Attorney General William P. Barr called the act "one of the most effective tools we have in combating violent crime in the country." In 1985 I visited DAs in major cities throughout the country to promote the concept. In Miami I met a receptive DA, Janet Reno.

At the same time I introduced the Armed Career Criminal Bill in October 1981, I put in two other legislative proposals: to provide funding for literacy education and job training, and to provide federal prison space for defendants given life sentences under state habitual-offender statutes. In 1989 my legislation created the Office of Corrections Education, a federal focal point for prison learning programs. In 1994 grants were authorized to help paroled youths get equivalency diplomas and degrees. I supported Pell Grants for prisoners, which were eliminated and then reestablished in 1998.

The investment in educating offenders is a pittance compared with the social cost of fighting a generation of violent incorrigibles. And make no mistake: An illiterate without a trade or skill will probably return to a life of crime. Rehabilitation is important for humanitarian reasons, to bring the juvenile or first or second offender back into society as a contributing citizen. The public is more likely to support funding for rehabilitation when people realize that education and vocational training will reduce recidivism, protecting them against violent crime. If an offender, despite rehabilitation efforts, becomes a career criminal, then the only option is long incarceration.

I fought to restore the federal death penalty after it was declared unconstitutional in 1972. On the basis of my experience as DA, I believe that capital punishment is an effective deterrent to violent crime and murder. I saw many cases where professional burglars refused to carry weapons for fear they would use them and wind up charged with felony murder. One Philadelphia case illustrates capital punishment's deterrent value. Late in the 1950s, three young hoodlums—Williams, Cater, and Rivers—planned to rob a grocer. Cater and Rivers, who both had borderline IQs, refused to participate unless Williams left his gun home. Williams agreed, but then hid his pistol in his belt. The grocer resisted, and Williams shot him dead. All three got the death penalty. As an assistant DA, I argued the case in the Pennsylvania supreme court, which upheld the three sentences of death. Several years later, as DA, I agreed to commutation of the death sentences for Cater and Rivers because they, unlike Williams, had not shown the requisite malice, although as co-conspirators, they were equally responsible as a matter of law.

When I was district attorney, the commonwealth never asked for the death penalty in any of the five hundred homicides in Philadelphia each year unless I personally approved the request after reviewing the quality of the evidence and the aggravating circumstances. The recent advent of DNA technology has added an extra measure of proof in death-penalty cases.

The endless death-penalty appeals process is unfair to victims, their families, and the condemned prisoners. A European court refused to extradite a condemned man to Virginia several years ago, ruling that staying on death row for years was inhumane punishment. Punishment must be swift and certain to be effective. My federal-court habeas corpus reform bill, passed as part of the 1996 antiterrorism law, essentially cut the federal appeals process to two and a half years. Previously, cases had languished as long as fifteen years.

CONFRONTING ASSAD, ARAFAT, SADDAM, AND FIDEL

I immersed myself in international matters immediately after coming to the Senate. My keen interest in foreign policy began long before I took my first oath of office. At my father's knee I followed World War II closely. My father was especially anguished when Germany invaded Russia and the Nazis swept over Ukraine and Batchkurina, his birthplace. He knew that the Germans left nothing in their wake, especially no Jews. He surmised that the worst had happened to his family and later found that he was right. He predicted that Hitler would stumble and freeze in Russia, just as Napoleon did. He gave a long interview to that effect, which was published in the Wichita newspaper, and history proved him right.

When my brother, Morton, after graduating from Wichita University, enrolled in Navy Officers Training School in 1941, our family worried about where he would be stationed and what risks he would face. After my sister Hilda traveled to San Francisco on an April weekend in 1943 to marry Arthur Morgenstern, then an artillery officer, we followed Arthur's travels to the South Pacific and fretted about the risks this young lieutenant faced. So the globe was under constant surveillance by the Specter family. Although only fifteen, I fully agreed with President Truman's decision to use the atomic bomb to end the war. Like everyone else, I hated to see that kind of destruction rained down upon so many innocent people. But the alternative was an estimated 250,000 dead and 500,000 wounded U.S. soldiers if we invaded Japan.

While my mother toiled to care for the family and provide for all of our needs, my father was glued to the radio, which brought hourly news bulletins. The Franklin Delano Roosevelt Memorial has a reproduction of key scenes from FDR's administration, including the long breadlines. In one corner of the memorial a man sits hunched over on a chair, listening to an old-fashioned radio. Seeing that scene, I envisioned my father sitting there, and I almost heard Graham Fletcher of Wichita's KFH Radio News updating the German invasion of Russia.

I wrote my 1951 college senior thesis on U.S.-Soviet relations. While serving on the National Advisory Council of the Peace Corps in 1972, I was asked to travel to Micronesia to try to resolve a dispute between a young Peace Corps lawyer representing the Micronesians, who were drafting a new constitution and wanted the U.S. air bases out, and the commanding U.S. Air Force general, who wanted them in. The general objected to the American Peace Corps lawyer's taking a position contrary to U.S. interests, especially since the U.S. government was paying the lawyer's salary. "We have a Peace Corps lawyer who is fulfilling his duty to his client, Micronesia, regardless of the fact that the United States is paying his compensation," I told the general. "I prosecuted first-degree murderers who were defended by people paid by the taxpayers of Philadelphia. Those defense lawyers' duty was not to the taxpayers but to the defendants, just as this Peace Corps lawyer's duty is to his clients." The general understood and withdrew his objection.

As a senator I have traveled to many countries on a variety of missions, beginning in 1981 as a member of the Senate delegation to Venice for the North Atlantic Assembly. Much of my foreign travel involved fact-finding in my roles on the Intelligence Committee and the Appropriations Foreign Operations Subcommittee. I have focused on the Mideast tinderbox, but I've also pressed causes with leaders in Asia, South America, Africa, and Europe, on such issues as creating an international criminal court, increasing NATO's and South Korea's share of the burden of defense, cracking down on international narcotics trafficking, and investigating the murders of American citizens overseas, including the nineteen airmen killed by a terrorist bomb in 1995 at the Khobar Towers Air Force base in Dhahran, Saudi Arabia.

In September 1982 I persuaded Senator Mark Hatfield, chairman of the Appropriations Committee, to authorize a trip to Lebanon, which was under consideration for a U.S. grant. It was complicated to get there because of the intermittent fighting. I took a helicopter from an aircraft carrier off Cyprus and landed in Beirut on one of the few days of cease-fire. I stayed overnight in a ramshackle hotel pockmarked by bullet holes.

The next day, Saturday, September 11, I met with Bashir Gemayel, Lebanon's thirty-four-year-old president-elect. We discussed Israel's invasion of Lebanon and the agreement the Lebanese and Israelis had signed. Gemayel, who had been commander of the Christians' Lebanese Forces militia, was a handsome young man, elegantly dressed right out of Paris's finest men's shops. That may have been Gemayel's last official visit, because two days later he was assassinated by a bomb in his office, where we had met.

Later on that Saturday afternoon I was able to observe war-torn Lebanon on a car trip south into Israel. En route, near Sidon, I picked a piece of paper off the ground. My escort officer scolded me, warning me that the landscape was filled with explosives, some appearing to be innocent-looking paper. The following day I visited with Prime Minister Menachem Begin, whom I had met a few months earlier in Washington, D.C., when he invited a group of senators to his hotel suite. In Washington the prime minister was very disarming, telling us of a meeting that day in which he and President Reagan had a little argument over how Begin would address Reagan. "Call me Ron," the president had insisted. "No," Begin replied, "it would be inappropriate for me to address you, the head of state of a superpower, by your first name." "Well," admonished Reagan, "if you won't call me Ron, I won't call you Menachem." The senators broke up laughing, but it told us something significant about both men. The prime minister was self-effacing and diplomatically correct. The president was a regular guy who succeeded with friendly informality.

When I met Prime Minister Begin that September Sunday night, he was under doctor's orders to take it easy, because he was just recovering from a heart attack. A television crew from Pittsburgh-based KDKA-TV was following me and asked if they could at least come in just to get still shots of my meeting with Begin. I told Begin that the TV people had asked me to make the request, but we would certainly understand if he declined. Begin said, "Look, as one politician to another, I understand the situation. Of course, bring them in." The TV crew came in, not expecting much. Begin graciously gave a full interview, and the station got an exclusive.

Begin was very troubled that Sunday night by President Reagan's criticism over the killings at Sabra and Shatila, with the suggestion that Ariel Sharon, the Israeli general in command, let it happen. Although Begin didn't say so directly, there was the implication that Israel could have killed Yassir Arafat, who was close to the fighting in Lebanon. Perhaps that was deference to Arafat's position as the de facto leader of the Arab world. Heads of state have historically been given a kind of immunity, in part so there is someone from the enemy to negotiate with. Begin also said that Israel's heavy guns could have taken a huge toll on Damascus. It was left unsaid, but obviously implied, that Israel did not want to expand the war into Syria.

When I returned from Israel to Washington to the Senate to vote the following Tuesday afternoon, I was interviewed live on the NBC evening news about my trip. Waiting for the interview to begin, I looked down at the monitor and saw a picture of Princess Grace of Monaco with a notation "1929–1982." I was almost speechless after that signal of her death. Her brother, Jack Kelly, Jr., and I had been college friends at Penn. I had a unique experience with her father, John B. Kelly, Sr., when I sought to interview him as a character reference during my OSI days. I'd waited outside his office for more than an hour without gaining admission and then conducted a twenty-second interview, which was the best I could get, as I walked hurriedly alongside him en route to his car curbside at his Race Street office.

In the Mideast, terrorism has replaced open warfare as a means of obtaining political objectives. After losing the wars of 1948, 1956, 1967, and 1973, the Arab world has not directly confronted Israel militarily. The exception was the Persian Gulf War of 1991, when Saddam Hussein launched Scud missiles into Israel in retaliation for U.S. military action against Iraq, and in an attempt to draw Israel into the conflict. Former American Israel Public Affairs Committee director Morris Amitay alerted me on the second day of Operation Desert Storm that Israel wanted to send planes to take out Saddam's Scud launchers but did not have the Allied friend/foe codes. Without the codes, which allow fighter pilots to distinguish Allied from enemy planes, Israeli and U.S. planes might wind up shooting each other down. I phoned President Bush and explained the situation. He said he would "check it out and weigh in." And he did. The administration cleared the Israeli aircraft into western Iraq, accomplishing the same purpose as furnishing the Israelis with the codes.

Generally, though, enemies of Israel have followed the PLO's pattern of seeking their objectives by killing women, children, and any other available civilians by sneak attacks in restaurants, at shopping centers, and on street corners. September 13, 1993, when Arafat was honored at the White House, was a tough day for me and for many others. I had long thought that Arafat should have been prosecuted for his complicity in the murder of our ambassador to the Sudan, Cleo A. Noel, Jr., and our chargé d'affaires, George C. Moore, in Khartoum in 1973; for the murders of eleven Israeli athletes at the Summer Olympics in Munich in 1972; and for orchestrating the hijacking of the cruise ship *Achille Lauro* in 1985 that led to the murder of Leon Klinghoffer, who was pushed off the deck in his wheelchair. But on that warm sunny September day, at President Clinton's prompting, Israeli Prime Minister Rabin and Minster Peres shook Chairman Arafat's hand. Since the Israelis had been the principal victims of PLO terrorism and now signaled reconciliation, I decided that I, too, would shake Arafat's hand.

A few months later in December 1993, Arafat had a long discussion with our congressional delegation when he met with us in Cairo. In person, Arafat was friendly, even charming. He professed a desire to pursue peace with Israel, immediately asking for U.S. financial aid. As our group moved on and visited Jericho, we saw Palestinian flags flying. The PLO wasted no time in assuming the existence of a Palestinian state.

When PLO terrorism continued after the 1995 Oslo Accords were signed, Senator Richard Shelby and I introduced the Specter-Shelby Amendment, which became law as part of the 1995 Foreign Operations Bill. That amendment provided for a cutoff of U.S. aid if the PLO did not change its charter calling for the destruction of Israel and the Palestinian Authority did not make a 100 percent effort to stop terrorism.

I have visited Arafat in Gaza and met with him in Washington on a number of occasions. In 1995 I challenged Arafat at a meeting in Gaza on why he made speeches condemning terrorism in English but not in Arabic. Arafat contended that he had made the same speeches in Arabic, which we knew was not the case. When pressed as to why he did not do more to control Hamas, Arafat explained that he himself was under threat of assassination from Hamas, which was in part directed from Syria. But Arafat also told me that Syria's President Hafez al-Assad was his good friend. That led to the obvious question: How could threats of terror and assassination come from the Hamas in Syria, when Assad was a good friend? Arafat, trying to smile, said, "Well, that's his style."

On one trip to Gaza, Arafat served a sumptuous lunch. We exchanged token gifts and he handed Joan a box, proclaiming it a jewel box. Turning to me, he said, "And now it's up to you to fill it with jewels." I asked if Mrs. Arafat had a similar box filled with jewels. Arafat only laughed. When I asked to use his washroom, I was ushered into Arafat's living quarters. I saw a small bedroom with twin beds and a bathroom with only the essential inexpensive fixtures. Arafat's modest quarters offered a striking contrast to those of the other national leaders we visited.

I had the chance to talk at some length to Arafat in December 1998, when I accompanied President Clinton to Israel. In Bethlehem, House and Senate members were feted at a lavish lunch. I picked up a large souvenir poster, about three by four feet, showing President Clinton giving a thumbs-up gesture and Arafat standing next to him raising his hand in a peace symbol. Although the separate photos had obviously been placed together, the poster looked like a campaign photo. I had it framed and hung in my Senate hideaway, my small office in the Capitol.

In March 1999, Arafat visited me in my hideaway and was delighted to find the poster hanging just inside the door. He insisted on having his picture taken in front of his picture.

In my hideaway meeting with Arafat, I urged him not to unilaterally declare a Palestinian state. Statehood is a matter, I said, to be decided by negotiation with Israel. Widespread speculation held that Arafat would make that declaration May 4, over dissatisfaction with the Oslo Accords. Arafat said the decision was not his but the Palestinian Council's. I said, "I have a suspicion, however slight, that you might have some influence with your council." Arafat smiled and said, "Senator, when you urged us to change the charter on the PLO's intent to destroy Israel, we did so. I didn't hear one word of praise for our action in doing that."

"I have to say, Mr. Chairman, you're right about that," I said. "I should have."

Arafat asked if there would be praise if he did not unilaterally declare statehood on May 4. I said, "If you don't do it on May 4, on the first day the Senate is in session thereafter, I will go to the Senate floor and I will make a statement praising you."

"Would you put that in writing?" he asked me.

I said, "Sure." I promptly sent Arafat a letter to that effect on March 31, 1999, and promptly put it in the *Congressional Record*. As promised, I praised the Palestinian Authority on May 5 for its decision not to make a unilateral declaration of statehood on May 4.

I made my first trip to Syria in August 1984, not long after U.S.-Syria hostilities in Lebanon had ended. My request to see President Assad was not granted. Joan and I were having a buffet dinner at the home of chargé d'affaires April Gillespie at about 7:30 P.M. when a call came from Foreign Minister Farouk al-Shara with a request, more like a demand, to come right over to his offices. I was glad to oblige, since I'd come to Syria to get to know the Syrians.

The meeting was short, testy, even vituperative. Minister Shara, whom I have since come to know and respect, complained bitterly about U.S. policy in the Mideast. I defended our nation's acts and policies. I had the impression, perhaps unfair, that Shara felt all Jews belonged at the bottom of the Mediterranean, whether they came from Tel Aviv or Philadelphia.

My next opportunity to travel to Syria came in December 1988. On this occasion Foreign Minister Shara was genial and hospitable. With the new leadership of Mikhail Gorbachev in the Kremlin, the U.S.S.R. was no longer giving Syria much attention or military assistance. President Assad and I met for four hours and thirty-five minutes. We talked about U.S.-Syrian and Israeli-Syrian relations, the Iran-Iraq war, nuclear proliferation, and the U.S.-U.S.S.R. superpower struggle. On a number of occasions I said that the Syrian president had already been more than generous with his time, but Assad responded by asking if I had any more questions, which I always did.

Shortly after Pan Am 103 was blown up by terrorists over Lockerbie, Scotland, I confronted Assad with the U.S. speculation that a terrorist named Jabril, headquartered in Damascus, had been responsible for the explosion. Assad challenged me to provide proof, saying that he would take action if it was warranted by the facts. Returning to my office in Washington and my position on the Senate Intelligence Committee, I asked U.S. investigators for the complete story. One day, in the Senate Intelligence hearing room, the investigators laid out a good bit of the Pan Am 103 wreckage and brought me up to date on the investigation. Neither Jabril nor Syria was implicated. I candidly reported that to Assad at our next meeting.

Assad and I frequently talked about the plight of young Jewish women in Syria, where there were no Jewish men to marry. Assad made what appeared to be a spontaneous offer, saying that he would not stop any Jewish woman from leaving Syria if a suitor from another country arrived to marry her and take her away. I relayed that message to the

American-Syrian Jewish community, but there were apparently no takers to that proposal. Assad chided me on my next visit to Damascus about my failure to take him up on his offer.

From time to time I urged Assad to meet with Israeli Prime Minister Yitzhak Shamir, saying that if they sat side by side as Assad and I were, the picture would appear not only on the front page of the Damascus newspapers but all over the world. When Rabin, Peres, and Arafat received the Nobel Peace Prize for the Oslo Accord, I suggested that if Assad made peace with Israel, he, too, would be honored with a Nobel Peace Prize. Assad laughed and said that he might be well received in Stockholm but probably wouldn't be permitted to return to Damascus.

In August 1996 I served as an unofficial intermediary between Benjamin Netanyahu and Assad. Shortly after taking office, Netanyahu made bellicose statements that Israel would hold Syria liable for the violence instigated in southern Lebanon by the Hezbollah. Apparently in response, the Syrian Army engaged in ominous maneuvers near the Israeli border. Knowing I was on my way to Damascus, Netanyahu asked me to carry a message to Assad that Israel wanted peace and that Netanyahu would be willing to participate personally in such negotiations with Assad or his designee. The following day in Damascus, I passed those messages on to Assad and Shara. Neither appeared very interested, but I was later told by Syrian Ambassador Walid al-Moualem that my message was important to the Syrian leaders. The ambassador said that the Syrians didn't know what to make of the newly elected Netanyahu and found my message reassuring.

Shortly into my January 1998 meeting with Assad, Syrian television crews came in for the customary video shots. On camera I told Assad that I was up for reelection and would find these pictures very helpful. Assad asked a few questions about the election. To my surprise and delight, he then gave us the TV footage and still shots of our banter. I didn't use the pictures in my campaign, but the episode was an interesting commentary on the camaraderie of politicians from backgrounds as diverse as Damascus and Philadelphia.

Over the past several years, I've had repeated conversations with Netanyahu, Assad, and President Clinton over Israeli-Syrian peace negotiations. Apparently shortly before his assassination, Prime Minister Yitzhak Rabin made at least preliminary overtures to President Clinton that he would settle on terms acceptable to Assad, including return of the Golan Heights if Israel's conditions were met. Some have suggested that Assad wouldn't take yes for an answer. Israeli Prime Minister Ehud Barak campaigned on a promise to continue the peace process along the Rabin-Peres lines. At a July 1999 White House state dinner, shortly after his election, Barak spoke fervently about his desire to complete the peace process. In the receiving line, with President Clinton at his side, he asked for my help on the Appropriations Committee to fund the Wye River Accord. I agreed.

Whatever the status of the Rabin-Clinton discussions, the issue of the Golan Heights remained unsettled. President Clinton told me he was ready to get personally involved again when the time was right. Assad insisted that any renewed talks begin at the point where Rabin had left off. Netanyahu countered that the talks should begin anew. An atmosphere of distrust between the Israeli and Syrian leaders appeared more problematic than a precise starting point of new discussions. While those complex, controversial issues can be decided only by the parties involved, I believe that the prospects for a settlement are bright if an American president can get the leaders to the bargaining table.

By returning to Syria almost every year, I developed an easy rapport with President Assad and Foreign Minister Shara. My experience with those Syrian leaders has confirmed my view that members of Congress can promote better relations with other nations, even those who are thought to be unfriendly, like Iraq or Iran, with visits and discussions on issues of mutual concern. I have had many long talks with Walid al-Moualem, Syria's former longtime ambassador to the United States. He commented that I had "gained the trust and confidence and personal relationship with President Assad" because I was "objective" even though "nobody could question your support of Israel."

A major role in the Mideast peace process can also be played by Egyptian President Hosni Mubarak, who has been a solid ally of the United States and a supporter of the peace process since he took over after the assassination of Anwar Sadat in October 1981. Mubarak travels to the United States frequently, and I have visited him in Cairo frequently since the early 1980s. When Egypt sought forgiveness for a $7 billion debt that was carried on the U.S. books at a few hundred million dollars, I took his call and agreed to support forgiveness at a time when he faced severe internal pressures. In our visits I consistently urge him to develop a "warm peace" with Israel, encouraging trade, cultural exchanges, and tourism. Aside from this one issue where I feel he could do more, Mubarak has been a solid partner for peace in the region, justifying the approximately $2 billion in annual U.S. aid to his country.

I met Mubarak for the first time in early 1982, when he came to the Mansfield Room and made a terrific speech to some sixty senators. When he was done, the Egyptian president threw back his shoulders, thrust out his chest, and roared, "Ask me any question, any question." We did. And he answered them adroitly.

I was sitting next to a major general in the Egyptian Army, and I asked him, "General, I read in the paper that President Mubarak plays squash. Is that true?"

"Yeah, he plays squash," the general replied.

"Does he have a game today?" I asked.

"Why you don't you ask him?" the general said, clearly not wanting to be bothered. So I walked up to the head table, where Mubarak was sitting between Majority Leader Baker and Senator Charles Percy, chairman of the Foreign Relations Committee. I leaned over as we do in the Senate and interrupted the conversation. "I understand you're a squash player," I said to the Egyptian president.

"Oh, yes, yes!" Mubarak said. "You want to play squash? Yes!"

I said, "Yes, I'd like to play squash."

"Well, if I win, do I get an extra hundred million dollars?" The laughter was so loud that I couldn't ask Mubarak the counterquestion: "If you lose, do you take a hundred million less?" The conversation ended with Mubarak telling me, "If you come to Egypt, we'll play squash." On my next trip to Egypt I brought Mubarak a T-shirt from the Capitol Hill Squash Club, where I play in Washington. I checked into a Marriott hotel and was soon approached by a *Time-Life* photographer. "Nice to see you, Senator," the photographer said. "I'm all set for seven A.M."

I said, "What?"

"Yeah," he said, "I'm going to be taking pictures of your squash game with President Mubarak."

I said, "I'm delighted to hear that."

He said, "Yup, seven A.M."

But that night we were having dinner at Ambassador Alfred Atherton's house when word came through: No squash, come for breakfast at 7:45 A.M. Mubarak and I still have not played squash. Whenever the matter comes up, he says, "Come to Egypt and we'll play."

Like Sadat and Mubarak, King Hussein of Jordan bucked the Arab trend in pursuing peace with Israel. Hussein had been criticized by many, including me, for failing to cooperate fully with the United States and our allies during the Gulf War. I first met King Hussein, who made frequent visits to Washington, in the early 1980s when he addressed more than half the Senate in the Mansfield Room. Clearly sincere and determined, Hussein tried to expand his role in the Mideast peace process. On one of my visits to Amman, while waiting in a reception area to meet the king, I studied a large map of the Mideast. On the area customarily denominated "Israel" on every map I had recently seen, the name "Palestine" appeared. I asked King Hussein about that, drawing a smile and a reply that the name on the map was not as important as his de facto recognition of Israel and his efforts to bring peace to the region.

With the Iran-Iraq war winding down in the late 1980s, I wanted to visit both of those nations. I persist in trying to travel to Tehran every year, but to no avail. However, in 1989, I did secure a visa to Baghdad. In August I met with lower-level functionaries because President Saddam Hussein rejected my request for a meeting.

Senator Richard Shelby and I traveled to Iraq in January 1990, and this time Saddam Hussein agreed to meet with us. As I entered the palace, Iraqi security personnel took my camera. I found my pocket camera indispensable to help me remember the many brief visits we made on those whirlwind foreign trips. Persistently, I asked for my camera back, and I got it shortly before I was ushered in to meet with Saddam. My camera in my left hand, I shook the Iraqi president's hand with my right and noticed his intense gaze. Saddam stared at me for what seemed an unusually long time, and then said through a translator, "Well, well, aren't you going to take my picture?" Of course, I did.

Throughout our meeting of about an hour and a quarter, Saddam was professional and businesslike, except for one detail: He carried a revolver in his belt. I began by noting Iraq's recent launching of a three-stage rocket and asked Saddam if it would not be wise to negotiate a peace treaty with Israel, to prevent Israel from destroying Iraq's new rocket as Israel had destroyed Iraq's nuclear reactor at Osiraq in 1981. He finessed the question, saying there was no need to negotiate, because Israel and Iraq were not bordering states. Shortly into our talk Saddam asked me why the United States insisted on forcing all Russian Jews to emigrate to Israel instead of America. I could see that Saddam had my résumé before him and knew I was Jewish. I wanted him to know that I knew he knew I was Jewish, so I answered his question by referring to my father, a Russian Jew who had immigrated to the United States in 1911. I told Saddam that Russian Jews did come to the United States but faced a quota of 50,000, which I considered too low. I added that Russian Jews should be able to go to the United States or Israel or anywhere else they chose. Our discussion then ranged widely over Iran-Iraq relations, peace with Israel, and U.S.-U.S.S.R. arms-control discussions. Saddam said he was trying to raise the quality of life for the average Iraqi.

When we got back to our hotel later that night, we found a set of eight-by-ten glossy color photos of our meeting, taken by Saddam's palace photographers. When I returned to the United States, I discussed my trip with a number of senators, including Bob Dole, and urged them to travel to Iraq. The Dole delegation did visit Iraq in April 1990 and caused a furor when Saddam released tapes of Senator Howard Metzenbaum calling Saddam "a man of peace" and Senator Alan Simpson saying he sympathized with Saddam because Simpson also got a lot of bad press.

Dialogue in the United States and the president's bully pulpit can be a powerful force not only in the Mideast but around the globe, and especially on the Indian subcontinent, which has become a tinderbox. When Senator Hank Brown and I visited India and Pakistan in August 1995, we were amazed that the leaders of those two powers did not speak to each other even though their nations' interests so urgently demanded negotiations. Indian Prime Minister Narasimha Rao volunteered to us that he would very much like to see a nuclear-free subcontinent within ten or fifteen years. When we asked what Pakistani Prime Minister Benazir Bhutto thought about that, he said he didn't know because he never talked to her. The next day Hank Brown and I were in Islamabad and told Mrs. Bhutto about Mr. Rao's statement. She responded by asking if we had it in writing.

I asked her, in response, when she had last talked to the Indian prime minister, knowing that they didn't talk. With apparent embarrassment, Mrs. Bhutto confirmed the India-Pakistan estrangement, which to me seemed irresponsible, since those two nuclear powers appear continually on the brink of war.

The next day from Damascus, Brown and I wrote to President Clinton, reciting the Rao-Bhutto conversations and urging him to invite them to the Oval Office. It seemed to me then, as it does now, that those leaders wouldn't reject an invitation from the president of the United

States. When I followed up the letter in a meeting with the president after our return, he agreed that it was a good idea but said he was deferring it until after the 1996 elections. After the 1996 elections I brought the matter up again, and the president said he still thought it was a good idea.

Left to their own devices, India and Pakistan detonated nuclear devices during 1998, and the subcontinent was off and running on an arms race, with the rest of the world holding its breath. Finally, in March 2000, the president traveled to Pakistan and India in an effort to defuse the confrontation. Had the president followed Hank Brown's and my suggestion five years earlier, history might have been changed. By bringing together the leaders, each of whom was too proud to call the other, he might have brokered some dialogue, understanding, and agreement.

My longest session with any world leader took place on the night of June 2 and into early morning of June 3, 1999, with Cuban President Fidel Castro, at the end of a three-day trip to Havana. Those who are waiting for Fidel Castro to die before the United States normalizes relations with Cuba may wait a long time. I can attest that in June 1999 Castro was a vigorous seventy-three-year-old, as well as garrulous, humorous, and engaging. He looked fit in his trademark green military uniform with modest insignia. We had been advised that Castro enjoyed lengthy talks. We knew we were in for a long night when the Cuban president said he had worked until 5:45 A.M. the night before but had then slept eight hours, waking at 2:00 P.M.—just six hours before our meeting. We didn't even move from the president's conference room to his dining room until midnight.

Naturally, we talked politics. I urged him to run in a contested election. He laughed and replied that he ran against the United States. It may be that the United States is the only opponent less popular with the Cuban people than Fidel. Castro didn't complain about the U.S. embargo or urge its removal. When I broached the subject, he said its end might actually make him weaker, because it could no longer be blamed for Cuba's economic problems. The U.S.-Cuban situation has changed enormously in the nearly thirty-seven years since we imposed the embargo. Castro no longer threatens to instigate revolutions throughout Latin America, and Cuba is no longer an outpost for Soviet expansion.

I questioned Castro closely about his allowing the U.S.S.R. to base nuclear missiles ninety miles from Florida in 1962 and within striking distance of Washington, Pittsburgh, Philadelphia, and New York. He replied that he had first tried to buy weapons from Belgium, a NATO nation, to defend himself against attacks like the Bay of Pigs. When those efforts were sabotaged, he turned to the Soviet Union.

Castro then brought out a handwritten copy of the agreement to allow the U.S.S.R. to position its missiles in Cuba. He described how he had personally redrafted the legal papers. He told of going hunting with Nikita Khrushchev near Moscow when the Soviet leader read to him President Kennedy's letter promising to remove U.S. missiles from Turkey and Italy and to leave Cuba alone. Castro said he then knew that Khrushchev had decided unilaterally to remove the Soviet missiles, which Castro regarded as a breach of their deal. In the end, Castro said, the Russian withdrawal also served Cuba's purpose. "We preferred the risk of invasion to the presence of Soviet troops, because it would have established an image [of Cuba] as a Soviet base."

When our conversation reached its fifth hour, I brought up the CIA attempts on Castro's life, as documented by a Senate committee in the 1970s. Plans were launched to poison Castro's milk shake and to plant an exploding cigar. "Some of them were childish," he said. Castro said he had survived largely "as a matter of luck."

I asked him how he felt about being the target of so many assassination attempts. *"Muy bien,"* he replied—very well. I repeated the question. He gave essentially the same answer. I pressed, asking how he *really* felt. Castro replied, "Do you play any sports?"

I said, "I play squash every day."

"This is my sport," he said. A truly remarkable answer. Castro claims he has escaped 637 attempts on his life. The CIA cites a much smaller number.

I gingerly asked about the early rumors that he had conspired with Lee Harvey Oswald to assassinate President Kennedy. Castro said neither he nor anyone else in Cuba had anything to do with Oswald. "I'm a Marxist, not a crazy man," he said. I asked if he had been concerned about the early international speculation that he was involved in JFK's murder. He said, *"Sí,"* given that the United States, by his reckoning, was looking for a provocation or pretense to invade Cuba.

My contacts with foreign leaders have helped me press my causes, including a recent crusade against religious persecution. Around the world—and especially in Asia, Africa, and the Middle East—Christians, Jews, Buddhists, and members of other religious groups are raped, tortured, enslaved, imprisoned, and even murdered because of their beliefs. To crack down on countries that persecute religious minorities and to offer those persecuted easier access to asylum, I introduced the Freedom from Religious Persecution Act of 1997.

The White House resisted the bill mostly because of the sanctions, including bans on imports and a cutoff of all nonhumanitarian aid to offending nations. The bill was ultimately enacted with only some of the sanctions intact, and continuing Senate oversight will be required to ensure enforcement.

I have also pursued foreign policy issues on the Senate Intelligence Committee, which I chaired in 1995 and 1996, and the Veterans Affairs Committee, which I have chaired since 1997. In several investigations, we found that U.S. military and administration officials concealed information or deliberately misled Congress and then tried to obstruct our inquiries. In an extreme case, the CIA inspector general turned up information that a longtime CIA operative had passed Soviet material that he knew was tainted to the highest levels of government, including the president, without telling them it was planted by Soviet agents. Establishment of the office of CIA inspector general, which would later uncover Soviet mole Aldrich Ames, was the only legislative reform to come out of the Iran-Contra scandal, through legislation I introduced.

To confirm the allegation about passing tainted material to the president, I personally went to the Virginia home of the agent, who was then retired with a heart ailment, to take his deposition. One of his tainted bits of information, we learned, came on January 13, 1993, and went to both President Bush and president-elect Clinton. In contentious secret hearings, the Intelligence Committee admonished the former agent's supervisors, who should have known, or could have known, about the tainted material.

The Intelligence Committee conducted an important oversight hearing on Iran's sale of arms to Bosnia, which may have involved a covert action without the requisite finding and notice to Congress. The State Department and National Security Council took highly irregular steps to keep the action secret, even from the CIA and the Department of Defense. When Croatian President Franjo Tudjman asked the U.S. government for its response if Croatia resumed shipping arms to Bosnia, which U.S. officials knew would come primarily from Iran, Ambassador Peter Galbraith told Tudjman that he had "no instructions" as to how the United States would respond.

National Security Adviser Anthony Lake told the Intelligence Committee that the reply was crafted to encourage Croatia to go ahead with the shipments. U.S. officials were fully aware that such arms flows would violate UN Security Council resolutions that the United States had voted for and was bound by. The "no instructions" decision effectively changed U.S. policy from supporting the UN arms embargo to looking the other way as arms flowed. It was certainly not traditional diplomatic activity to give a response to a foreign head of state that effectively contradicted stated U.S. policy.

While Congress was sympathetic to administration concerns about Bosnia, without a clear understanding of what the United States was actually doing in the region, Congress came perilously close to passing precisely the legislation the administration wanted to avoid. The committee decided to give Assistant Secretary of State Richard Holbrooke, General Wesley Clark, and the others extra latitude because of their hard work and good intentions. I agreed with Senator Robert Kerrey, the Democratic Committee vice chairman, that we would not publish our critical report until after the 1996 election because of its potential political overtones.

After a year-long study of Gulf War syndrome in 1998, the Veterans Affairs Committee found that nerve gas contributed to the mysterious and debilitating malady that plagued nearly 100,000 American soldiers returning from the Persian Gulf War in 1990 and 1991. The committee also found that the Pentagon had concealed troops' exposure for five years. Initially, the Pentagon insisted that no U.S. troops had been exposed to nerve gas. Then, amid our investigation, Pentagon officials disclosed in May 1996 that they'd discovered that U.S. troops had been exposed to nerve gas when U.S. engineers blew up an Iraqi weapons depot in Kamisiyah in March 1991. Defense officials eventually estimated that some 110,000 U.S. troops had been exposed to chemical fallout, out of the 490,000 who served in the war theater. That estimate may have been excessive because of inaccurate data, but there was no doubt U.S. troops had been exposed to harmful chemicals.

Our 310-page report criticized both the Department of Defense and

305

the Department of Veterans Affairs for negligence in keeping poor records on troops' health and exposure and for not preparing for chemical war. The Veterans Administration, we found, showed "chronic and pervasive inability to generate valid and reliable data about the Gulf War veterans it serves."

"Troops need to be prepared to detect reliably the presence of chemical and biological weapons and to conduct effective military operations in an environment where chemical or biological weapons may be used," our report read. "This investigation confirmed that U.S. forces did not have those capabilities at the time of the Gulf War, a shortcoming that has not been fully remedied today."

Our report was worded cautiously, noting that poor agency record-keeping kept the committee from making a definitive link between chemical weapons and Gulf War syndrome. I declared at a news conference, "My judgment is that nerve gas is a factor contributing to Gulf War illness."

In the wake of our report, Senator Jay Rockefeller, the ranking Democrat on the Veterans Affairs Committee, and I introduced legislation requiring the military to improve troop readiness for unconventional warfare and requiring the government to provide health care to all Gulf War veterans who complained of ailments that may have been related to the war.

The 1996 Khobar Towers bombing was among our most explosive investigations, on several levels. On June 25, 1996, a fuel tanker truck carrying an estimated three thousand to five thousand pounds of explosives blew up at the Khobar Towers housing compound at the U.S. Air Force base in Dhahran, Saudi Arabia, killing nineteen airmen, injuring more than two hundred Americans and hundreds of other civilians, and destroying an eight-story building.

Our investigation found that the Pentagon had taken inadequate precautions to protect our troops, despite warnings and known threats. Top Pentagon and Air Force officials obfuscated the facts, did not cooperate with our investigation, and prevented others from cooperating.

I traveled to the Saudi desert in August 1996 to inspect the complex, interview U.S. personnel, and meet with Mideast leaders with insight into regional terrorism. Khobar Towers Building 131 was a horrible sight, more ghastly than the television and still photographs could convey. The building's front wall had been sheared off by the blast, exposing twisted wreckage and bloodstained walls. The wire fence was only sixty feet from the front of the building, substantially less than the distance officially reported. I met with twenty officers and airmen who had been at Khobar Towers when the bomb exploded, including many who were injured. They described, calmly and precisely, how the blast blew out their windows, lacerating them with glass shards and propelling them across their living rooms. I followed up with seven public hearings on terrorism, Saudi Arabia, and support to the military in the region. We took testimony from, among others, Defense Secretary William Perry, CIA Director Deutch, and FBI Director Louis Freeh.

I wrote Air Force Secretary Sheila Widnall five letters about Khobar Towers and got no response. Widnall had demonstrated gross impropriety in ordering Air Force personnel not to speak to our committee. By chance I ran into Widnall in June 1997 in a Capitol corridor. As *Roll Call* reported:

> Sources say Specter literally bumped into Air Force Secretary Sheila Widnall in a corridor last week and reminded her that senators are supposed to get a response to oversight inquiries. Sources say Widnall turned to a two-star general and said, "Will you make a note of that?"
> Specter snapped, "If he needs to make a note of that, he'll never be a three-star general."[1]

I experienced similar frustration with Perry, prompting me to send him a letter on November 5, 1996, that began, "Dear Secretary Perry: This letter constitutes a formal complaint on the obstruction by you, others and the Department of Defense on the inquiry by the Intelligence Committee to determine whether there was an intelligence failure relating to the terrorist attack in Dhahran on June 25, 1996, on the following: Prohibiting key witnesses from being interviewed by this Committee . . ."

In September 1996, a forty-member presidential commission run by retired Army General Wayne Downing, former head of the Special Forces, found that U.S. commanders failed to heed warnings of potential terrorist attacks. The Downing Commission placed blame as high as the Joint Chiefs of Staff. Perry prohibited Downing from testifying before the Intelligence Committee except on Perry's terms in closed session. Perry also refused to give our committee access to an Air Force report that, the *Washington Post* reported, contradicted a major conclusion of the Downing Report.

The Intelligence Committee report found that the Khobar bombing was not a result of an intelligence failure, but that officials should have taken greater precautions to safeguard our troops. It turned out that the Defense Intelligence Agency had issued an alert about Khobar Towers eight days before the blast, urging improved security. Incidents from April through June 1996 indicated possible terrorist surveillance of the facility. Trying to excuse DOD's inaction, Perry said the three thousand to five thousand pounds of explosives were a surprise and a level beyond any previously used bomb. That assertion was conclusively contradicted by the twelve-thousand-pound bomb used in the 1983 terrorist blast that killed 283 Marines in Lebanon.

I said publicly that Perry's blaming the attack on poor intelligence was "preposterous." In the past year, there had been more than a hundred intelligence reports on general security risks and on specific risks at Khobar Towers. We discovered that military commanders apparently never asked the Saudis to move the fence back four hundred feet, as the Defense Department had previously claimed. The request was to move the fence back ten feet, which the Saudis correctly deemed a minor cosmetic action and did not take seriously.

The Pentagon singled out the former base commander, Brigadier General Terry Schwalier, for blame. Schwalier's promotion to major general was canceled, and he retired. In my judgment the blame should have gone much higher. I suggested that Perry resign. He responded that he would resign if he had not done his job. Perry laid out a series of standards for protecting U.S. troops that the defense secretary should meet. When I posed those standards to General Downing, he found Perry derelict in two of his own standards: Perry had not set policies and standards, including those for force protection, for our commanders; and he had not structured the Department of Defense in such a way as to make force protection optimal. Perry made the perfunctory statement on September 16, 1996, that he took personal responsibility for the Khobar Towers tragedy, but he didn't resign. Perhaps his decision to leave in January, at the end of the president's first term, was his de facto resignation. Perry's interest in continuing governmental service was demonstrated by his taking on the tough job of negotiating with North Korea on the nuclear issue. From all indications he did a good job on that assignment.

General John Shalikashvili, chairman of the Joint Chiefs of Staff, was also criticized for failing to act on the obvious danger at Khobar Towers. He visited the base a few weeks before the attack, observed the situation, but was oblivious of the potential terrorist problem, notwithstanding two warnings from OSI in January and a car bombing in Riyadh in 1995 that killed four Americans.

Dissatisfied with the administration's response to the Khobar Towers tragedy, I pointedly questioned the Air Force chief of staff, General Fogelman, during the Defense Appropriations Subcommittee hearing on the Air Force budget in 1997. It was an argumentative exchange, with General Fogelman insisting that blame should not be attached to any individual, while I pressed the facts that should have alerted top Pentagon officials. I was impressed that Fogelman, as a matter of principle, took early retirement to protest singling out Schwalier for blame. I didn't disagree with his strong objection on that.

I firmly believed at the time, and in retrospect I still believe, that the top Pentagon officials should have been officially found at fault, with appropriate punitive action. With nineteen killed and four hundred wounded, DOD should not have treated it as "business as usual." Top officials must be held accountable to exert sufficient pressure and to be extra alert when they were on notice about the terrorist danger.

CIA Inspector General Frederick Hitz may have gone a little far in insisting that former directors William Webster, Robert Gates, and James Woolsey should be held personally responsible for not uncovering the spy Aldrich Ames, even though there were no facts to suggest they should have known about him. Absolute liability or responsibility under the "captain of the ship" doctrine may go too far, but where officials like Perry and Shalikashvili should have known, didn't, and didn't act to prevent a patent danger, the system should not "wink at" or condone that conduct.

My work in the Senate involves balancing national and world issues with Pennsylvania's concerns. After the 1980 election, Bob Kunzig, Senator Scott's former chief of staff, urged John Heinz and me to work closely together. John and I still had vivid memories of our bruising 1976 primary fight four years earlier. I also remembered his failure to take my calls early in the 1980 Republican primary and his ultimate support for my opponent, Bud Haabestad. But I also remembered and appreciated John's strong support for me in the 1980 general election. It was a new day, and in politics, perhaps more than other arenas, you have to forgive even if you don't forget. So we accepted Kunzig's counsel that we would be four times as strong working together rather than separately. We eventually developed a close working relationship and friendship.

John and I both had places in Georgetown. I used to drive John home after our frequent late-night Senate sessions, and we discussed the gamut of issues. We brought different views to our debate about a proposed constitutional amendment to balance the budget. In a long discussion the night before the vote, I told him why I opposed the amendment, and he gave me his reasons for favoring it. The following day I voted aye; he voted nay. We'd each persuaded the other to change his position!

Just as I had hit all sixty-seven Pennsylvania counties on the campaign trail as a candidate, I held town meetings or major events in each county almost every year. One Heinz staffer said, "Arlen Specter has visited counties John Heinz hasn't even flown over." When a flood hit Pittsburgh, I chartered a plane within a few hours. A Pittsburgh political writer said that I got to the flood before the rain stopped. *Pittsburgh Press* columnist Shirley Uhl wrote in one Thanksgiving piece, "We have something to be thankful for: Arlen Specter's not in town today."

Eight days before the 1986 primary, I found myself at 6:30 A.M. on a Philadelphia Airport gangway with Ed Rendell boarding the 7 A.M. flight for Pittsburgh. Rendell, who was running for governor in the Democratic primary, and I lived five doors apart. "What are you doing on this early flight to Pittsburgh?" Rendell asked me. I had only token opposition, but Rendell was in a tough fight. "Eddie," I told my onetime assistant, "I've been on this flight to Pittsburgh every two or three weeks for the last ten years." Now it's been every few weeks for more than two decades.

Whenever the occasion presented itself in my travels around Pennsylvania, I would compliment Heinz. I found there was no better way to cement our relationship than to say something good about John behind his back. My compliments were always sincere and never patronizing. In my relationship with John Heinz, I frequently thought about my father's advice: When you're in a partnership, you should give 60 percent, because it will look to the other guy like 50 percent. It you give 50, it will look like 40. Always give more.

In perhaps the ultimate in service to my constituents, I fought plans by the Department of Defense to close the Philadelphia Naval Shipyard. Officials often declare, "I'm going to take that to the Supreme Court!" Well, I did, arguing the case personally. Going into the argument on March 2, 1994, I knew I had a tough case. It was obviously difficult to get the Court to overturn some three hundred base closings, but we had twice persuaded the distinguished Court of Appeals for the Third Circuit that we were right.

I contended that the Navy's criteria for closing the yard were faulty and that its case was riddled with deliberate omissions, amounting to fraud. For example, reports from two admirals that the yard should be kept open were fraudulently concealed from the GAO and the Congress.

Under rules of the 1990 base closure law, Congress and the president, in turn, had been forced to either approve or reject the entire closure list. Citing the fundamental principle of judicial review, I argued it would not be cherry-picking for the Supreme Court to review the Philadelphia Navy Yard decision. "The Congress and the president may not make a pact which is unconstitutional," I said. "That why we have *Marbury* v. *Madison* and this Court." Further, I stressed, "We are not asking that the yard be kept open. We are asking that we have a fair day in court." I wanted the Navy Yard decision deferred to the 1995 batch of bases the closure commission was scheduled to consider.

I got about a minute into my argument before the justices began peppering me with counterarguments. I had questioned seven of those nine justices when they came before the Senate for confirmation, and there was an element of payback. My appearance before the Supreme Court, as a sitting senator, inevitably carried political overtones. But I brought the passion of the people to my argument. And this was my case. I had organized, nurtured, and developed it. I was the lead plaintiff and had participated in the legal preparation and court arguments at every stage.

At one point I got into a heated exchange with Chief Justice Rehnquist. "Senator Specter," Rehnquist began, referring to one of the primary precedents I had cited, "I think your reliance on *Panama Refining* may be rather strained . . ."

"Chief Justice Rehnquist," I replied, "I respectfully disagree with you categorically," and then told the court why. The chief justice had the last word when he cut off my argument in midsyllable when the red light went on. During senators' closing arguments in the 1999 Clinton impeachment trial, I noted that Chief Justice Rehnquist didn't hold us to the precise time limits, as he did in the Supreme Court. Rehnquist

311

only smiled when my closing argument in the impeachment proceeding went a little beyond the fifteen-minute allotment.

Three months after the oral argument, on May 23, 1994, the Court ruled against us 9–0. The ruling, written by Rehnquist, was and was not the last word. In a sense the final word comes from commentators. *The Harvard Law Review*, discussing *Specter* v. *Dalton*, claimed that the Supreme Court had taken the safe and politic course in upholding the commission rather than canceling three hundred base closings. The *Review* concluded:

> Though the result reached by the Court in *Specter* may be unobjectionable, the same cannot be said of the argument by which the Court reached that result. The Court relied on a dubious distinction between action in excess of statutory authority and action without statutory authority to conclude that an officer of the executive branch does not transgress the constitutional principle of separation of powers as long as he merely exceeds his *statutory* authority. . . . There are a variety of things the Court might have meant, ranging from the outrageous to the merely mildly disturbing and unprincipled. None is particularly attractive . . . .[2]

Despite the Court's ruling, our lawsuit was a qualified success. Our fight kept the yard open longer, maintained more jobs, and brought attention in Congress and the country to how Philadelphia had been unfairly treated. In the end the yard was sold to a Norwegian shipping conglomerate, Kvaerner ASA, Europe's largest shipbuilder. Kvaerner promised under the contract to hire hundreds of local workers.

The Senate's most important function, except for resolutions authorizing the use of military force, involves confirmation of Supreme Court nominees. The Supreme Court is the ultimate arbiter determining what the law will be. The Court, in the last few sessions, has handed down monumental, historic decisions on dying, religion, speech, due process, states' rights, and congressional power, among other areas. We talk a great deal about the legislature having the power to make the laws and the courts having the limited power to interpret the laws. But the reality is that the Supreme Court defines the horizons of the law.

Senator Robert Byrd and I have collaborated on an effort to allow the

Senate to exercise its constitutional "advice" function under the "advice and consent" clause by establishing a panel of possible Supreme Court nominees for consideration by the president when a vacancy occurs.

Many Court decisions are issued by 5–4 votes, which means that a single justice made the difference. While public hearings on Court nominees draw great public attention, the Court's 5–4 decisions do not, even though they are of enormous importance. Watershed 5–4 decisions include: *Lochner* v. *New York* (1905), in which the court struck down an early attempt at labor regulation by holding that a law limiting bakers to a sixty-hour workweek violated the liberty of contract secured by the due-process clause of the Fourteenth Amendment; *Furman* v. *Georgia* (1972), in which the Court struck down the death penalty under the cruel-and-unusual-punishment clause of the Eighth Amendment; *Webster* v. *Reproductive Health Services* (1989), widely viewed as a retreat from *Roe* v. *Wade*, in which the Court upheld various restrictions on the availability of abortion, including a ban on the use of public funds and facilities for abortions, and required viability testing after twenty weeks; *United States* v. *Eichman* (1990), in which the Court invalidated state and federal laws prohibiting flag desecration on the ground that they violated the First Amendment; and *U.S. Term Limits* v. *Thornton* (1995), in which the Court struck down a state law imposing term limits on members of Congress on the grounds that states have no authority to change, add to, or diminish the age, citizenship, and residency requirements for congressional service enumerated in the Constitution. During the past five years there have been seventy-three Supreme Court decisions decided by a single justice on a 5–4 vote.

In mid-1999, the Court issued three absurd 5–4 decisions on state sovereign immunity, holding that states may not be sued in federal court for infringing on intellectual-property rights. The decisions gave states—which participate in the intellectual-property marketplace through their universities and hospitals—an enormous advantage over their private-sector competitors. Under the Fourteenth Amendment, Congress has the power to void state sovereign immunity in certain lawsuits and had done so on intellectual property. In addition to treating Congress with disdain, the Court showed political activism and a political agenda. Laurence Tribe, the distinguished Harvard constitutional-law expert, said, "In the absence of even a textual hint in the Constitution, the court discerned from the constitutional 'ether' that states are immune from individual lawsuits."

313

There has been no doubt about the Supreme Court's great power since the Court itself decided in 1803 in *Marbury* v. *Madison* that it had the last word on the relative powers of Congress, the executive branch, and the states and on any disputes involving a constitutional ruling. The late Chief Justice Charles Evans Hughes accurately noted that the Constitution is what the Supreme Court says it is.

There is enormous legal talent in America, but very little of it is called to the president's attention when a vacancy occurs. From time to time, word spreads that a person has been considered for a vacancy, and the next time a vacancy occurs, that person is almost automatically nominated. We can and must create a better process. For the Supreme Court especially, we should seek the best and the brightest. In modern times the Senate has been diligent in exercising its consent function, in Judiciary Committee confirmation hearings. We should join the process earlier, as soon as the vacancy occurs.

When Justice Potter Stewart left the bench in 1987, Chief of Staff Howard Baker, the former Senate majority leader, told President Reagan, "I'll prepare a list of possible replacements for the Supreme Court of the United States." According to Baker, Reagan responded, "Do you think you could put Judge [Robert] Bork on the list?" An interesting remark, coming from the president of the United States.

In establishing a pool of possible Supreme Court nominees, the Senate would ask for suggestions from top judges at the various federal and state levels, from bar associations, and from the public at large. Obviously, the president can take or leave our advice.

JUDGE BORK

I was once introduced at a political event as a senator who had managed in two Supreme Court confirmations to alienate the entire electorate: half by questioning and voting against Judge Robert Bork and the other half by questioning Professor Anita Hill and voting for Justice Clarence Thomas. Each of those confirmation battles, in a different way, had a profound effect on American culture and social policy.

The Senate's constitutional "advice-and-consent" role involves truth-finding through investigation and interrogation. I have participated in confirmation hearings on eight of the nine sitting justices—all but Justice John Paul Stevens. The process formally begins when the president nominates a candidate to fill a vacancy on the high court. The Senate Judiciary Committee investigates the nominee and holds hearings to delve further into his or her legal views and background. Some nominees are more cooperative than others. From my experience participating in Supreme Court nomination hearings, I have found that the better a nominee thinks his chances are, the less he will say at the hearing to minimize his risk.

Chief Justice William Rehnquist, at his 1986 confirmation hearing, would not answer basic constitutional questions. Rehnquist, an associate justice since 1971, didn't believe he should have to go before the Senate a second time for promotion to chief, according to Tom Korologos, a premier Washington lobbyist who has specialized in shepherding nominees, including the chief justice, through the confirmation process. Rehnquist cited to Korologos the case of former Senator Sherman Minton, whom President Truman nominated to the Supreme Court and who refused to go before the Senate for a hearing. Minton argued that the legislative branch had no right to question a court nominee. The

Senate confirmed Minton without a hearing. "What do you think of that?" Rehnquist asked Korologos. "Why do I have to testify?"[1] he demanded. Rehnquist's record was there; his opinions were public. He would not expand on them or defend them. Rehnquist insisted that Korologos try to get him through without a hearing.

"I said, 'Fine, Bill,' and dismissed it out of hand," Korologos recalled. Tom Korologos had handled some 250 confirmation matters, including Gerald Ford and Nelson Rockefeller for vice president, and several Supreme Court justices. "What am I going to do, tell the leadership we're not going to have a hearing on Rehnquist? Anyway, it died before it got off the ground." Rehnquist relented and agreed to go before the Senate.

At his confirmation hearing for chief justice, I particularly wanted to ask Rehnquist whether Congress had the authority to strip the Supreme Court of its power to decide First Amendment and other constitutional issues. Some believed that Congress could pass a law saying the Supreme Court had no jurisdiction over constitutional issues generally, which would strip the courts of their power of judicial review. That is exactly what Congress did during the Civil War, leading to the *McCardle* case: Congress repealed the Habeas Corpus Act provision allowing appeals to the Supreme Court, and the Supreme Court upheld that act.

The fact is, there is no constitutional provision that gives the Supreme Court authority to review an act of Congress to see if it is constitutional. The Supreme Court asserted that power in *Marbury* v. *Madison* in 1803, and today not only can the Supreme Court invalidate an act of Congress, but so may lower federal courts. The precedent of *McCardle* has led many to contend that Congress does have the authority to take away the Court's jurisdiction, even on constitutional issues. As a matter of logic and practicality, congressional power to take away the federal courts' jurisdiction to decide constitutional issues directly conflicts with the Supreme Court's *Marbury* v. *Madison* decision, whereby the Supreme Court has had the last word for almost two hundred years.

Rehnquist refused to answer my question about stripping the federal courts' jurisdiction. "I feel I cannot go any further than that, for fear that that sort of issue will come before the Court," he said, deflecting one of my questions. When I pressed him, Rehnquist insisted, "I honestly feel I must adhere to my view that it would be improper for a sitting justice to try to advance an answer to that question."

During an overnight recess, when the hearing continued, a staffer brought me an article from the *Harvard Law Record* that Rehnquist had written in 1959, when he was a practicing lawyer, criticizing Charles Whittaker's nomination to the Supreme Court. Whittaker had essentially told the Senate only that he was the son of two states, that he had been born in Missouri and practiced law in Kansas. Rehnquist, in his Harvard article, expressed outrage that the Senate had endorsed Whittaker without asking him any substantive questions. The young lawyer had written, "Until the Senate restores its practice of thoroughly informing itself on the judicial philosophy of a Supreme Court nominee before voting to confirm him, it will have a hard time convincing doubters that it could make effective use of any additional part in the selection process." The next day I confronted Justice Rehnquist with his article and his own words twenty-seven years later. "Did I say that?" Rehnquist asked.

I replied, "Yes."

"That the nominee ought to respond?"

I said, "Yes, that's the import of it."

Well, Rehnquist said, he'd been wrong. "I don't think I appreciated, at the time I wrote that, the difficult position the nominee is in."

I pressed Rehnquist on jurisdiction. I withheld my own view, that Congress cannot dictate what the Supreme Court can review on constitutional issues. If that happens, the Supreme Court is no longer supreme. Finally Rehnquist answered my question. Congress cannot take away jurisdiction from the Supreme Court on the First Amendment, he said.

Okay, I said; now, how about the Fourth Amendment—search and seizure? Rehnquist wouldn't answer. Well, how about the Fifth Amendment—privilege against self-incrimination? No answer. How about the Sixth Amendment? No answer. How about the Eighth Amendment—cruel and unusual—"I won't answer that."

I asked Rehnquist, Why will you answer on the First Amendment but not the others? He wouldn't answer that either. Korologos recalled, "It might have been the day he said to me, 'I'm through answering, I'm through with that guy, finished with that guy's questions, I've had it with Specter. No more answers for him.' Snarl."[2]

Chief Justice Rehnquist answered barely enough questions to get my vote. In all, sixty-five senators supported him, but thirty-three others voted against his nomination.

Justice Antonin Scalia, a D.C. circuit court judge at the time of his nomination to the Supreme Court, was justifiably confident that he could get away with answering practically nothing. When captured in combat, U.S. military personnel should give only their name, rank, and serial number. Scalia gave his name and rank, but not his serial number. Feisty and combative by nature, he refused to answer even the most basic questions. Asked whether he agreed with the bedrock decision in *Marbury* v. *Madison*, which established the supremacy of judicial review, Scalia acknowledged that the decision was indeed a pillar of our jurisprudence. Beyond that, he said, "I do not want to be in a position of saying as to any case that I wouldn't overrule it."

When Scalia paid me one of the customary courtesy calls to members of the Judiciary Committee before his hearing, I asked if it was true that he would not discuss his judicial philosophy. He replied that this was correct. I then said, "You've been a distinguished professor, I hear first in your class at Harvard. Will you answer a substantive question on a legal issue?"

"Sure," Scalia said.

"Okay," I said, "this is on future interests, property law. What's the difference between a shifting use and a springing use?" Maybe one lawyer out of a hundred thousand could answer that esoteric question, unless he practiced in that field or was taking the bar exam the next day.

"Well, I'll tell you, Senator," Scalia began. "It's like these two guys who were riding in taxicabs that had a collision in midtown Manhattan. And while the drivers were exchanging information, the passengers started to talk. And one said, 'What do you do?' And the other guy said, 'I'm a lawyer.' The first passenger said, 'Hey, that's interesting. So am I. Where do you work?' 'I work on Wall Street.' 'Hey, you know, I do, too. Which firm?' Scalia quoted one passenger as naming a firm, maybe White and Case. The other passenger rejoined, 'Oh, I work at White and Case also. What branch are you in?' 'I'm in property law section.' 'I'm in property, too. What do you do?' 'Shifting uses.' 'Well, that's why I don't know you: I'm in springing uses.' " By the time Scalia had finished his answer, I had almost forgotten my question.

The Senate takes the Supreme Court confirmation process very seriously. It has rejected more nominees for the high court, proportionately, than for any of the almost 600 other positions that require confirmation. In the past two hundred years the Senate has rejected 29 of the 112 Supreme Court nominees, or 26 percent. By contrast, the

Senate has rejected only 15 of the 565 cabinet officers nominated, less than 3 percent.

The Senate's advice-and-consent process has grown more formal over time. It was not until 1939, with Justice Felix Frankfurter, that nominees began testifying before the Judiciary Committee. Before that, the Judiciary Committee considered nominees' records but did not hear from them.

In confirmation hearings the nominee faces a massive mahogany dais lined with Judiciary Committee members seated in order of seniority. Mounted lights bathe the would-be justice while cameras roll and click. When the questions end, the committee votes. The nominee is either passed to the Senate floor, with or without recommendation, or rejected. A majority "aye" vote from the full Senate makes the nominee a Supreme Court justice.

On July 1, 1987, President Ronald Reagan nominated D.C. federal appeals court judge Robert Heron Bork to the Supreme Court, to replace retiring Justice Lewis Powell. Powell had been the key vote on many critical issues. In a sense Reagan's social agenda was at stake. Bork might be the decisive vote or, even more important, the most persuasive voice during deliberations on abortion, race relations, women's rights, privacy rights, free speech, and other core issues. Bork's ascension to the court could set a course in American law and social policy.

No one suggested that Bork, sixty, lacked either the brains or the experience to do the job. He'd been on the federal bench since 1982. He'd earned a bachelor's degree and a law degree from the University of Chicago, while serving two stints in the Marine Corps. Early in his career he'd practiced law at major firms in New York and Chicago, then joined the faculty at Yale Law School, where he was a full professor from 1965 to 1973. At Yale, Bork had emerged as a conservative constitutional scholar, advising, among others, Republican presidential candidates Barry Goldwater and Richard Nixon.

In 1973 Bork was named solicitor general, a post he held until 1977. He was most famous for firing Watergate Special Prosecutor Archibald Cox during the Saturday Night Massacre in October 1973. The job had fallen to Bork after Attorney General Elliot Richardson and his deputy, William Ruckelshaus, had resigned rather than obey Nixon's order to fire Cox. As a result, Bork also found himself acting attorney general from 1973 to 1974. I didn't consider Bork's role in firing Cox especially weighty, in terms of his Supreme Court confirmation hearings.

Bork explained that if he didn't carry out the president's order and fire the special prosecutor, somebody else along the Department of Justice hierarchy was going to fire Cox. Maybe Bork's strong views on executive authority led him to give broader sway to carrying out an express presidential order, despite his own view of the fairness or justice behind it.

In 1977 Bork left the federal government to return to Yale, where he served as a professor until 1981. He then returned to private practice in Washington as a partner at Kirkland and Ellis. In 1982 he was appointed to the U.S. Court of Appeals for the District of Columbia Circuit.

The day that Bork was nominated, the Judiciary Committee was busy investigating another member of Reagan's legal team. The committee was holding a hearing on voting-rights cases that involved William Bradford Reynolds, the assistant attorney general for civil rights. The Democrats controlled the Senate in 1987, and Edward Kennedy of Massachusetts chaired the Subcommittee on Constitutional Law. Kennedy had asked me to join in questioning Reynolds, and I had agreed. Kennedy wanted me present because I'd played a key role in defeating Reynolds's bid to be associate attorney general in 1985. Kennedy had listed the Reynolds hearing for the afternoon specifically to accommodate my schedule.

Reynolds had once been heir apparent to become attorney general. I had opposed him in June 1985, when Reagan had nominated him for associate attorney general, the Justice Department's number-three post. I had joined the Judiciary Committee's eight Democrats and Republican moderate Charles Mathias in rejecting Reynolds 10–8. I thought Reynolds had been lax in enforcing civil rights laws and had misled the committee in sworn testimony. "It was a stunning rejection of the chief architect of the Reagan administration's civil rights policies, and a stinging political slap at President Reagan," the *Washington Post* reported. "Specter justified his vote on the grounds that Reynolds had 'placed himself above the law' by ignoring court rulings on affirmative action and school desegregation and seriously misled the committee in his testimony by implying that he had opposed discriminatory election laws in Georgia."[3]

My 1985 rejection of Reynolds, whose confirmation had seemed a certainty, had moved Governor Dick Thornburgh to consider for six months running against me for Senate in 1986. It would have been a tough fight to defeat a sitting governor in a Pennsylvania Republican primary. But Thornburgh ultimately stayed out. When he announced he wasn't going to run in mid-December 1985, he gave no reason but was probably motivated by Senator Heinz's repeated public statements opposing his candidacy and concern that he might be blamed for losing a Republican seat as a result of a primary fight.

On July 1, 1987, Ted Kennedy missed the Reynolds hearing that he was chairing, after having gone to all the trouble of reshuffling the schedule to enlist me. I flipped on the television. There was Kennedy on the Senate floor. It was 2:38 P.M., eight minutes after Bork's nomination was announced, and Kennedy was reading a prepared text laced with venom, charging that Robert Bork would have Rosa Parks ride in the back of the bus. "[In] Bork's America," Kennedy railed, "rogue police could break down citizens' doors in midnight raids."

Kennedy crusaded against Bork. He rallied African-American ministers and leaders in the South. Hundreds of liberal organizations enlisted in the anti-Bork cause. Bork's opponents launched a massive public relations campaign, replete with polling; television, newspaper, and radio ads; direct mail; advocacy phone calls; and assiduous lobbying of journalists. The idea was to poison public opinion against Bork, to influence and pressure senators. Bork's opponents painted him as an extreme conservative and inflexible ideologue who wanted to turn back the clock, especially on civil rights.

The anti-Bork coalition included civil rights groups, such as the NAACP; women's groups, including the National Organization for Women and the Women's Legal Defense Fund; organized labor, including the National Education Association and the American Federation of State, County, and Municipal Employees; and Hollywood celebrities. People for the American Way, a group founded in 1980 by television producer Norman Lear, was in the forefront of the Bork opposition. The day after Reagan nominated Bork, People for the American Way sent alerts to some twelve hundred editors and reporters. The group kept up the barrage several times a week, eventually expanding its list to nearly two thousand journalists. The group reportedly assigned five or six staff members to fight Bork's nomination full-time. In all, by most estimates, Bork's opponents spent a few million dollars in their crusade. In direct-mail pieces they called the judge "an autocratic radical" whose "legal philosophy is a sham."

Bork's supporters, including conservative groups such as the American Conservative Union, the 500,000-member Concerned Women for America, the National Conservative Political Action Committee, the Conservative Caucus, and the Reverend Jerry Falwell and his Moral Majority, fired back. But the Bork camp was at a disadvantage in the public relations war. While Bork's supporters praised the judge's intelligence and ability to make sound rulings, his opponents lashed out at him as an extremist, often distorting cases to make their points. Even if Bork could rebut a charge, the accusation was far more exciting—and played better in the media—than the Bork team's technical judicial defense. The battle over Bork was so high-profile that it became almost compulsory for interest groups to join. Ralph Nader, the consumer advocate, pleaded with Biden to make him a witness at the proceedings. Such testimony would help any group's fund-raising efforts. I didn't follow the public relations war at the time it raged. My position on Bork had a very different genesis.

I found myself at the center of the storm. "Both groups will be focusing on the same middle group of Senators—first the swing votes on the Judiciary Committee, primarily Dennis DeConcini (D-Ariz.), Howell Heflin (D-Ala.) and Arlen Specter (R-Pa.), and later the Southern Democrats and moderate Republicans whose votes will be crucial in the full Senate,"[4] the *Washington Post* reported on July 7, a week after Bork's nomination. I got many lobbying visits, including three from Bork and one emotional presentation from a Philadelphia lawyer who was afraid Bork would take away the right to a jury trial.

I also received an oblique message in support of Bork from President Reagan on a trip I made with the president to Philadelphia. Thursday, September 17, 1987, commemorating the two hundredth anniversary of the Constitution, happened to fall right in the middle of the Bork hearings. The president's itinerary included a ceremony at Philadelphia's Independence Hall, and he invited Senator Heinz and me to come with him. Heinz declined, but I joined the president on the trip to my hometown for the historic event.

At a lunch that day, a little African-American girl, eight or nine years old, came up and talked to Reagan. She asked him about Bork. "Will he be bad for black people?" Reagan was sitting on an eye level with the girl. He held her shoulders in a kind and grandfatherly way and said, "No, no, I know Judge Bork, and he will be good for black people. Don't worry." Reagan then looked back at me and said, "Did you hear that, Arlen?" With so much focus on Bork at that time and my vote publicly regarded as so important, I was surprised that Reagan didn't lobby me vigorously on Bork.

In many ways Ronald Reagan was hard to figure out and not an easy man to get to know. He didn't seem to know many of the people who surrounded him. There is a legendary encounter at a meeting of U.S. mayors at which Reagan greeted his secretary of housing and urban development, Sam Pierce, as "Mr. Mayor." At one bill-signing ceremony which I attended, members of the House and Senate clustered around the president, who turned when he had finished and handed his pen to John Heinz, the only person whose name he apparently knew. And that was probably more from Heinz Ketchup than from John's participation in the bill.

President Reagan showed total focus and command of the facts on issues that concerned him, such as national defense, Communists in Central America, and taxes. On those subjects he scored impressive victories. He was dogged and determined, as with his pressure on me in 1985 to support the MX missile. At an early meeting with Republican senators, as Reagan's knuckles tightened around the lectern, he reflected about taxes during World War II, which left only, as he put it, "a dime on the dollar." The marginal tax rate at the time was 94 percent.

In August 1986 the Senate scheduled two votes on aid to the Contras, which I generally opposed. After a discussion with Majority Leader Howard Baker, I agreed to support the president's position on the first amendment, which would earmark $450,000 for the Nicaraguan newspaper *La Prensa*. But I still opposed President Reagan's position on the other amendment. I believed the United States should terminate aid to the Contras if Nicaragua and four other Central American nations signed an agreement to provide democratic pluralism, freeze arms imports, and withdraw all Soviet-bloc advisers.

After the first vote, in which I supported the president, I got a phone call from Reagan. Encouraged by my first vote, which he viewed as a weakening of my overall position, the president gave me a tough sell on why I should support the Contras on the second vote, which was supposed to be razor-thin. When I told him I intended to vote against his recommendation, Reagan became agitated, raised his voice, and told me there would be glee in Managua, Moscow, and Havana if his opponents won. Nonetheless, I voted against the president. But Reagan's position was upheld anyway.

On other subjects that didn't keenly interest President Reagan, he was indifferent or changed the subject, sometimes with an irrelevant anecdote or misdirected humor, such as his remark that my Armed Career Criminal Act was like what happened in a James Cagney movie where Cagney was sent "up the river" as a three-time loser. Similarly, when I attended a small White House meeting to honor a Pennsylvania epileptic who had walked across America, Reagan told the man that he understood his illness from playing Grover Cleveland Alexander, an epileptic.

One of Reagan's stories offered an insight on his approach with humor that was right on target. At a 1985 luncheon for the "Sweet Sixteen." Senator Mack Mattingly of Georgia leaned across the table and asked, "Mr. President, why is it that you never change and all the rest of us are getting older?"

"Well, I'll tell you what it's like," Reagan replied. "It's like these two psychiatrists. Every day they came to work at the same time, in the same building, both immaculately dressed, and every day they left at the same time. And one was still immaculately dressed and the other was totally disheveled.

"And this went on day after day, week after week, month after month, year after year, until finally the disheveled doctor asked the other, 'Why is it that you and I come to work at the same time day after day, week after week, month after month, year after year, both immaculately dressed, and day after day, week after week, month after month, year after year, we leave at the same time, and I'm always disheveled and you're always immaculately dressed?'

"And the immaculately dressed psychiatrist looked at him," Reagan said, "and replied, 'Who listens?' "

At another Sweet Sixteen lunch early in President Reagan's first term, I broached the subject of trying to expand the Republican Party to include more African-Americans and said that minorities needed more housing and jobs in Philadelphia. The president immediately launched into a story about his high school football days, when the team's lone African-American player was barred from a hotel, prompting the whole team to stay at his hotel. That was his way of reacting to the issue of race, rather than responding to my suggestion that his administration should help African-Americans by providing more jobs and improving housing, which would broaden our party's base.

On our September 1987 trip to Philadelphia, Reagan and I found ourselves in a small holding room with a large wheel listing the names of all the presidents, beginning with Washington, followed by John Adams, then Thomas Jefferson, and ending with Reagan next to the father of our country. I was moved to ask, "Mr. President, how does it feel to be on this wheel right next to George Washington?" Reagan walked away without answering.

I had used our ride from the Philadelphia Airport to Independence Hall to discuss a variety of issues, and I broached another subject that brought an unusual response. I had heard Reagan say on several occasions, including a 1984 presidential debate with Democratic nominee Walter Mondale, that the United States would give the Soviet Union the technology from the Strategic Defense Initiative once it was developed.

"Mr. President," I said, "there are a couple of problems with that proposal: One, you won't be president by the time we develop SDI. And two, the president can't do that unilaterally. It's the property of the country, and only Congress can do that, with the president's approval or override." Reagan gave me a blank stare and changed the subject.

President Reagan was a strong and effective chief executive on matters he considered important but oblivious of subjects which didn't concern him. Or perhaps that was his way of showing he did not "suffer fools gladly," even if they were senators. Some people have speculated that Reagan was suffering from Alzheimer's disease long before September 1987. While not an expert, I didn't see any evidence of that in my contacts with the president.

During the fight over Bork's nomination, the rhetoric was far more fiery on the public airwaves than in lobbying visits to the Senate. The key anti-Bork ad of the campaign was a sixty-second television spot produced by Lear's group and narrated by actor Gregory Peck. As a family stood on the Supreme Court steps and gazed up at the engraved motto EQUAL JUSTICE UNDER LAW, Peck lashed Bork in a voice-over. "He defended poll taxes and literacy tests which kept many Americans from voting," Peck intoned. "He opposed the civil rights law that ended 'whites only' signs at lunch counters. He doesn't believe the Constitution protects your right to privacy . . . Robert Bork could have the last word on your rights as citizens, but the Senate has the last word on him. Please urge your senators to vote against the Bork nomination, because if Robert Bork wins a seat on the Supreme Court, it will be for life—his life and yours."

Ironically, the ad attracted little attention during its sparse and relatively brief run. It was only after Reagan's press secretary Marlin Fitzwater attacked the ad that it drew attention, running continually on TV news segments. "And that killed us. Gregory Peck," said Korologos, the veteran confirmation strategist who also handled Bork's nomination. Korologos said conservatives pressured him to let them raise money to buy billboards and ads for Bork. "And I kept saying that puts us in the same gutter as they are. If the Founding Fathers wanted a political campaign for Supreme Court nominees, they'd have had the electorate choose."

CLEAR AND PRESENT DANGER

In the Bork camp, I heard later, my support was considered vital. The battle plan that Tom Korologos sketched on yellow writing tablets was filled with directives on me. Over breakfast in the Senate dining room September 4, 1998, Korologos showed us the notes. "Gotta Keep Specter," read one entry. "Get Ken Davis to talk to Specter." "Get Heinz to talk to Specter." "Howard Baker go see Specter?"

One Korologos note read, "White House: Got to beat up Specter." How was the White House going to do that? I asked Korologos in September 1998, as we discussed the Bork nomination over breakfast. The lobbyist said he didn't know. "The point is . . . you were the most sought-after guy we needed," Korologos said. "Because we figured if we lose you, then we lose Heflin, we were dead."[1]

The first question I asked Bork, when he paid a mid-July courtesy call, was whether he thought judicial ideology was appropriate for our discussion. Bork replied that he didn't like the term "ideology" because it had political implications. Bork, at the time, was being branded an ideologue. He said he thought "judicial philosophy" was a fair subject.

Bork was willing, even eager, to discuss his views. At his hearing he engaged many senators in wide-ranging dialogues. Bork's 80 speeches, 30 law review articles, and 145 circuit court opinions had placed on the public record more material than was provided by perhaps any other nominee in Supreme Court history. An article in the *Indiana Law Review* outlined Bork's judicial philosophy. Considering the context and controversy, Bork concluded—correctly, I think—that he would have to answer questions on judicial philosophy to have a chance at confirmation.

And answer questions he did. Bork's hearings ran over the course of twelve days between September 15 and 30, 1987. Bork personally testified for thirty hours over four and a half days, including a marathon ninety-minute final session with me. The committee heard from 112 witnesses in all, including distinguished law school deans and professors, former Chief Justice Warren Burger, President Ford, and five former attorneys general.

Others submitted critiques and recommendations. The Senate Judiciary Committee received letters from 1,925 law professors opposing Bork, representing nearly 40 percent of the full-time faculty at accredited law schools, an unprecedented opposition. Bork's views had moved several members of the American Bar Association's Federal Judiciary Committee, for the first time in bar association history, to find a Supreme Court nominee "not qualified." Even so, most ABA members found Bork "well qualified."

The Bork nomination became a major national event. Even before special-interest groups had a chance to mobilize their troops, public interest flared. On the two days immediately following Bork's nomination, I held open-house town meetings in Pennsylvania and found attendance and emotions running high. At one meeting, two shouting foes had to be restrained from throwing punches. Others weighed in with me privately. I got 140,000 letters, cards, and calls on Bork. Norman Redlich, my former colleague on the Warren Commission and a brilliant legal scholar in his own right, contacted me to inveigh against the judge.

Bork and I had three long talks in my office, more than five hours in all. The first meeting was the nominee's customary call on a Judiciary Committee member. The second and third meetings came at Bork's request.

I had spent two weeks reading cases and reviewing constitutional law. Among other issues, Bork and I discussed *Oil, Chemical and Atomic Workers International Union* v. *American Cyanamid Company*, a 1984 case in which Bork supported a factory's policy of sterilizing its female workers of child-bearing age. To avoid exposure to lead, American Cyanamid had excluded women between ages sixteen and fifty from a plant unless they offered proof of surgical sterilization. Bork upheld a review commission's decision that the sterilization policy was not covered by the Occupational Safety and Health Act, leaving the workers with no ground to fight the policy. Bork viewed the case purely as an issue of the court's scope of review of an administrative agency's decision.

Bork would testify at his hearing, "I suppose the five women who chose to stay on that job with higher pay and chose sterilization—I suppose that they were glad to have the choice—they apparently were—that the company gave them." One of those women wrote in a telegram to two Judiciary Committee members, "I cannot believe that Judge Bork thinks we were glad to have the choice of getting sterilized or getting fired." Even with the women's consent, I found the sterilization policy shocking and unconscionable. Bork was out of touch with the basic humanitarianism of the law. Asked why he wanted to be a Supreme Court justice, Bork had replied that it would be "an intellectual feast." Senator Joseph Biden of Delaware, the Judiciary Committee chairman, found this response the "capstone" of Bork's arrogance, and the remark that made much of America realize, "Oh, my God, I don't want this guy." "What fun—play with your lives," Biden said over a November 1998 lunch in Wilmington, Delaware, recalling the hearings. "This is like a Rubik's Cube, and I'm one of the pieces? . . . I think Bork's arrogance was his undoing."[2]

When we were discussing the *American Cyanamid* case in my office, I told Bork about a 1967 Philadelphia murder case to make the point that justice must supersede technicalities. Agnes Malatratt, a police department medical expert, testified that fifteen "points of comparison" proved that a man had strangled a fifty-eight-year-old female neighbor. Under cross-examination by a veteran criminal defense lawyer, Malatratt broke down on the stand. She admitted she had falsified her credentials to get her job. This shocked the courtroom and much of the Philadelphia criminal bar, which for years had considered Malatratt eminently qualified.

My homicide division chief, who presented the case for the commonwealth, asked trial judge Edmund Spaeth to excuse Malatratt from further cross-examination. Spaeth agreed on the condition that all of Malatratt's testimony would be stricken, and that she not be recalled as a witness in any respect. Then it turned out that Malatratt was necessary to establish the technical chain of evidence. Without her testimony, the case would be dismissed. My assistant asked Spaeth to let Malatratt testify for that limited purpose. Spaeth refused. The assistant came to me.

I went to Judge Spaeth's courtroom. I told Spaeth it was true that my assistant DA, my homicide division chief, had the authority to bind our office to an agreement in court. But I said that even if I, the elected district attorney, had made the commitment, it should not prejudice my client, the commonwealth of Pennsylvania, where unconscionable injustice would result. The judge's paramount duty was to see that justice was done. Without Malatratt's testimony about the chain of possession, our case would fall and an accused killer would go free. Spaeth granted my request because he concluded it was necessary to avoid a gross miscarriage of justice. That required a broader view than the technical rules. Bork barely listened politely, not interested in the Malatratt case or the principle it illustrated.

Bork walked into his hearing confident that no one could touch him. His handlers were also confident. Overconfident, it turned out. "What Bork did is, he fooled us and he intimidated us," said Korologos, his chief handler. "We thought he was going to do infinitely better in the hearing because he was so smart that it showed in the murder boards." Murder boards were the simulated questions and answers in mock hearings that Bork's handlers used as training.

"In fact," Korologos said at our September 1998 breakfast, shaking his head, "[Howard] Baker said publicly something like, 'You wait until Bork gets up there. You'll see how good and smart he is.' Well, that's the regret: He wasn't that prepared. He wasn't that good."

A cadre of top Justice Department lawyers, including William Bradford Reynolds, and top political hands, including Baker and Korologos, tried to put Bork through the paces. "We'd go to his house, and they'd do these interminable sessions on cases," recalled Korologos, a journalist by training. "And my eyes glazed over, and they went on and on and on, and finally I would take over and ask the questions." Korologos read his handwritten notes from a bound composition book: "'What are the qualities of a justice? To what extent, if at all, can an individual justice influence the philosophy and direction of the Court? What are your views about an intercircuit panel to assist the Supreme Court in solving cases involving a conflict among judicial circuits?' These are things that I picked up in my readings. 'What are your views regarding constitutional interpretation by the judiciary?'

"See, I didn't give a damn about USC 35 and the *Brandenburg* case," Korologos said, referring to what he considered Bork's tendency toward dry and legalistic responses. "'We have seen since 1950 an alarming trend at ignoring precedent. What do you think about that, Mr. Bork?' Well, he was very flippant. You see, when he got the politicians in there, me and Howard Baker and [Kenneth] Duberstein and the

White House legislative liaison people, Will Ball and Pam Turner, he'd kiss these off.

"There was one that I'll never forget: Will Ball asked him, I don't remember the question, but his answer was, 'Well, do I give my Fourth of July speech now?' And everybody laughed, and we went on to something else. In other words, he intimidated us. He didn't answer these kinds of questions for us."

Korologos also threw personal questions at Bork at the prep sessions. Have you ever been cautioned by a doctor about alcohol excess? Have you ever been a member of a restrictive club that didn't allow blacks, Jews, Greeks, or women? Have you ever read the covenants of the deed to your house? Are there any restrictions? Have you ever had your income taxes audited? "He wouldn't answer those kind of things," Korologos said.

At Bork's hearings, senators covered the sweep of legal and background issues, as Korologos had anticipated. Even Bork's beard became an issue. "And then he had his weird beard," Korologos recalled. "That was a story in itself. Senator after senator told me before the hearing, 'Change that ugly beard.' There were meetings about shaving his beard. And I said, 'They're already after us—Leahy coined the phrase "confirmation conversion"; suddenly this guy who had written all these things, now you're going to tell me he's this way—if you go in and shave your beard Tuesday night and the hearing is Wednesday morning, what are they going to say about that?' I said, 'Hell, no, you're not going to shave your beard. You're going to stick to it.' So that was a factor, if you can imagine. Senators voting because of a guy's beard."

Bork had made a name for himself with his philosophy of "original intent." He maintained that judges must base their opinions on the Framers' original intentions. "This is my basic philosophy of judging— the original-intention philosophy . . ." Bork told me minutes into our first exchange at his hearing. Bork routinely described his constitutional theory as "intentionalist," which means he looked to the intent of the Founding Fathers on the Constitution and of the authors of its amendments.

Apparently Bork knew what the drafters and ratifiers of the Constitution had been thinking, or could find out. If so, that gave him unique insight. Bork's theory essentially held that judges should not make law but should merely follow what was originally intended. In pure philosophical terms, Bork's view that the Constitution should be interpreted as it was originally intended appeared to make sense, at least superficially. But the Constitution has turned out to be much more dynamic than that: a living, growing document, responsive to the needs of the nation.

Bork's narrow approach is dangerous for constitutional government in America. Without adherence to original intent, Bork said, there was no legitimacy for judicial decisions. And without such legitimacy, there could be no judicial review. He said our system could function without judicial review.

That was too much. The supremacy of judicial review—the authority of courts to annul laws and executive acts they find unconstitutional—is a fundamental principle of constitutional law. Although Bork retreated at his hearing and denied questioning judicial review, his earlier expressed views posed a real risk. As I said on the Senate floor before we voted on Bork, "If *Marbury* v. *Madison* does not govern and the Supreme Court does not have the final word, then I suggest that we have become a lawless nation." A nominee is entitled to wide latitude. But threatening judicial review exceeds all bounds.

Perhaps Bork launched his original-intent theory searching for a way to be unique and to publish. Perhaps he came to believe it. And it carried him a long way—but not to the Supreme Court. In his confirmation hearings, Bork's original-intent model failed him on several issues, including equal protection, free speech, and privacy. Original intent, Bork acknowledged, was often difficult to discern.

"It seems to me," I told Bork at the hearing, "that there was no question that at the time the equal-protection clause of the Fourteenth Amendment was adopted, the Framers, or ratifiers, didn't intend, in the remotest way, to cover desegregation. They expected to have segregated schools." Enacted right after the Civil War, the Thirteenth Amendment abolished slavery and the Fourteenth Amendment, among other things, guaranteed equal protection and due process. At the time, many states had segregation, I reminded Bork. "The District of Columbia schools were segregated. The Senate gallery was segregated." Separate sections in the upper chamber were reserved for whites and "coloreds."

"So that interpretation which you have advanced, that 'separate but equal,' in the absence of equality through separation must lead to integration, seems to me to be at very sharp variance with what the Framers had intended," I said. How could Bork argue that Congress, which had ratified the Thirteenth and Fourteenth amendments by two-thirds votes, wanted to integrate the country when it segregated its own balcony? Where Bork was looking for the Framers' intent, it was obvious they didn't think equal protection required abolishing separation, since they wrote the equal-protection clause at a time when segregation was rampant in every phase of society, including the House and Senate galleries.

"So that if you take a consistent interpretation," I continued, "you cannot come to the result that the Supreme Court did in *Brown* v. *Board of Education.*" *Brown* was the Warren Court's landmark 1954 decision ending segregation in the schools. Segregation had been the law of the land since the court approved "separate but equal" facilities in 1896 in *Plessy* v. *Ferguson*.

Bork made a strained argument that the Court had been able to end segregation and still remain true to original intent by choosing between two ideals of the Framers that had come into conflict: equal protection and separation. "By 1954 it was perfectly apparent that you couldn't have both equality and separation," Bork said. "Now the Court has to violate one aspect or the other of that clause, as I have framed it hypothetically. It seems to me that the way the actual amendment was written, it was natural to choose the equality segment, and the court did so. I think it was proper constitutional law, and I think we are all better off for it."

"Judge Bork, I think we are better off for it, too," I said. "But I do not think that that is a logical conclusion if you are looking at the Framers' intent."

During our debate in the hearings on segregation, we steered toward a case that posed a potential trap for Bork's approach. But I laid out the issue in advance for the judge, to avoid any suggestion that I was trying to trap him. In *Bolling* v. *Sharpe*, a Washington, D.C., companion case to *Brown*, the Supreme Court had been forced to come up with another rationale to end segregation, because the equal-protection clause of the Fourteenth Amendment applied only to the states, not to the District of Columbia. The Court based its ruling on the due-process clause of the Fifth Amendment, which did apply to the District of Columbia. Bork, in his testimony, expressed qualms about the *Bolling* decision, saying, "I think that, constitutionally, that is a troublesome case."

Bork, noted my chief of staff, Neal Manne, had argued strenuously that there was nothing left of the due-process clause, which conservatives had used in the 1930s to strike down New Deal legislation. Bork didn't believe it was valid to base a decision on the due-process clause, it seemed, unless there was a specifically enumerated right. Bork had missed the fact that the Fourteenth Amendment's equal-protection clause didn't apply to the District of Columbia; it applied only to the states. Under Bork's original-intent theory, then, there was no basis to end segregation in Washington, D.C.

Bork had taken a lot of criticism—some of it legitimate—for insisting over the years that equal protection applied only to race, as the Framers originally intended. "We know that, historically, the Fourteenth Amendment was meant to protect former slaves," Bork said in a 1982 speech at Catholic University. He argued in a June 1987 speech that equal protection should have been limited to race and ethnicity, disagreeing with more than a century of Supreme Court decisions that applied equal protection to women, aliens, illegitimates, indigents, and others. But at his confirmation hearing, Bork said publicly that the equal-protection clause should extend to "men, women, everybody." Considering the many subtle and discretionary judgments involved, I felt it would be unfair to people who sought equal protection in the Supreme Court to have their cases decided by someone who had for so long thought their claims were unprotected by the Constitution under standards that were so elusive to apply.

I was troubled by Bork's writings and testimony that expanding rights to minorities reduced the rights of majorities. By that thinking, giving a criminal defendant Miranda warnings deprives the police of a confession, which might put a criminal back on the street to harm the majority. While perhaps arithmetically sound, it seemed morally wrong. The majority in a democracy can take care of itself, while individuals and minorities often cannot. Moreover, our history has demonstrated that the majority benefits when equality helps minorities become a part of the majority.

Bork also questioned the authority of the Supreme Court as the final arbiter of the Constitution, a seminal principle established in 1803 in *Marbury* v. *Madison*. "It is emphatically the province and duty of the judicial department to say what the law is," Chief Justice John Marshall wrote in that landmark case. I had asked Bork about *Marbury* v. *Madison* minutes into our first meeting at my office. "You know, Senator," Bork had said, "*Marbury* v. *Madison* was not very well reasoned."

"No, Judge Bork," I replied, "I didn't know that."

Bork had also insisted on "Madisonian majoritarianism," the idea that, in the absence of explicit constitutional limits, state legislatures should be free to act as they please. On this point Bork broke with even conservative justices, who had traditionally protected individual and minority rights, even without a specifically enumerated right or proof of original intent.

Around the time of Bork's nomination, U.S. Attorney General Edwin Meese and then–presidential candidate Pat Robertson had also questioned the Supreme Court's supremacy. Meese said in a 1986 speech at Tulane University, essentially, that the president and Congress had as much authority as the Supreme Court to interpret the Constitution. Robertson told the *Washington Post* editorial board that "a Supreme Court ruling is not the law" and that neither Congress nor the president has a duty to obey judicial rulings with which it or he disagrees.[3] I had gone to the same law school as Pat Robertson at the same time. We had taken the same course in constitutional law with the same professor and the same casebook. But apparently we had studied different constitutions. The Meese and Robertson approach—with which I strongly disagreed—might have become the law of the land if an intellect of Bork's stature pressed that position in the Court's deliberations.

The decisive point in Bork's hearing, for me, was his discussion of two free-speech cases. Bork tried to assure the Judiciary Committee that he would apply the Court's current constitutional doctrines on free speech, even though he disagreed with those decisions. The hearing showed the difficulty, if not impossibility, of Bork's applying the "clear and present danger" standard to free-speech cases. That standard, articulated by Justices Oliver Wendell Holmes and Louis Brandeis in famous dissents in the early part of the century, held that speech criticizing the government was punishable only when it presented a "clear and present danger." Justice Holmes's famous dictum that "time has upset many fighting faiths" expressed the core American value of listening to others and permitting the best ideas to triumph in the marketplace of free speech, short of a clear risk of imminent violence.

Holmes, in a now-famous line from his 1919 *Schenck* opinion, wrote, "The most stringent protection of free speech would not protect a man in falsely shouting fire in a theater and causing a panic." The high court adopted the Holmes-Brandeis standard in the 1950s. The Court restated its "clear and present danger" standard in 1969 in *Brandenburg* v. *Ohio,* ruling unanimously that political speech could be prohibited only if it called for and would probably produce "imminent lawless action." Four years later the Court affirmed that standard in *Hess* v.

335

Indiana, in which a college student demonstrating against the Vietnam War had shouted, "We're going to take back the f—king streets." On its face, that statement is not unlawful unless the surrounding circumstances demonstrate that it would incite a riot, which was not the circumstance in the *Hess* decision.

Bork, in a 1979 speech at the University of Michigan, had called the *Brandenburg* decision a "fundamentally wrong interpretation of the First Amendment." He maintained that no speech advocating violation of the law should be protected, even if it didn't threaten danger of violence or lawbreaking. By the time of his confirmation hearings, Bork had committed to accepting the *Brandenburg* ruling. "On *Brandenburg*, I didn't say my mind had changed," he told me. "I think *Brandenburg* may have gone too—went too far, but I accept *Brandenburg* as a judge and I have no desire to overturn it. I am not changing my criticism of the case. I just accept it as settled law." But Bork insisted, in this exchange with me, that he was not committed to *Hess* because *Hess* was an "obscenity" case.

Hess was not an obscenity case. It was a "clear and present danger" case. The demonstrator's use of profanity was incidental. Bork himself had identified *Hess* as a "clear and present danger" case in previous writings. When Bork argued that Hess was not a speech case, he cast doubt on his ability to apply constitutional doctrine which he had so long opposed.

"A concern I have," I told Bork at the hearing, "is that when the next set of facts comes up—and they aren't going to be exactly like *Brandenburg* because no two cases are exactly alike on the facts—if you disagree with the philosophy, how will you decide the case?

"It just seems surprising to me," I told him, "that in the context where you characterize [the clear and present danger] doctrine as 'fundamentally wrong' and attack the rationale as 'frivolous,' that you can, at the same time, say that you now accept the current Supreme Court interpretation." The Judiciary Committee report, critical of Bork throughout, emphasized that point:

> Senator Specter then identified the difficulty with Judge Bork's views: ". . . One, the next case will have a shading and a nuance and I am concerned about your philosophy and your approach. And, secondly, I am concerned about your acceptance of these cases. If you say you

accept this one, so be it. But you have written and spoken, ostensibly as an original interpretationist, of the importance of originalists not allowing the mistakes of the past to stand."

In other words, Bork's grudging acceptance of the *Brandenburg* decision gave no assurance that he would rule the same way on a similar case that might arise in the future, especially given his dubious objections to *Hess*. Bork seemed inclined to ignore precedent he didn't like in favor of "original intent" and to find grounds, such as treating a speech case as an obscenity case, to justify doing so.

That tendency was troubling generally, and particularly troubling with constitutional law that established and protected liberties. Some protections become part of our notion of due process, whether or not they are spelled out in state law, as Justice Benjamin Cardozo articulated in 1937: Such protections are "the very essence of a scheme of ordered liberty . . . principles of justice so rooted in the traditions and conscience of our people as to be ranked fundamental."

Constitutional law has evolved through seminal civil liberties cases like *Brown* v. *Board of Education*, *Gideon* v. *Wainwright*, *Miranda* v. *Arizona*, and *Mapp* v. *Ohio*. I lived with many of those cases as a prosecutor, and I came to appreciate them even though they made my job more difficult. The story of America is the story of decency and fairness, with the Supreme Court as guarantor. Robert Bork displayed little grasp of that. After *Brown* v. *Board of Education*, nobody could argue in favor of segregated schools. But you don't get to *Brown* via original intent. You get there via evolving notions of decency and fairness.

At the hearings Biden also locked in on Bork's disregard for precedent. "Why did I spend so much time asking him whether or not he thought he was, as a Supreme Court Justice, bound by precedent? Why was that important? Well, it became clear to people that he thought he was not bound. And he couldn't define the confines within which he would operate, based on 'settled law.' Then all of the things he said he wanted to change became real possibilities."

Bork's handlers urged him to avoid lengthy exchanges with me. "Here are these two guys sitting there," recalled Korologos, "I could get a law degree based on watching these guys at these hearings. And Specter

337

would give this fifteen-minute thing, and say to Bork, 'What do you think of that?' And Bork would give this twenty-five-minute theory . . . and it wasn't going well.

"I said to Bork, 'Bob, for heaven's sake, quit arguing with Specter. First of all, he owns the bat and the ball. He votes no, you're going to lose. And he's just as smart as you are, so quit arguing with him.' He said, 'Well, what have I got to do?' I said, 'Here's what you do: The next time he gives you one of those long, bull—— things, you say to him the following: "Senator, that is a fascinating point you have made. That is very interesting." You have not agreed with anything. It's just fascinating and it's interesting. And, "Gosh, I'd like to talk to you more about that. I find that fascinating. Yes, I can't argue with that." You're not agreeing with it!' He said, 'Okay, okay.'

"So he comes back, and Specter starts down this thing again, see, and Bork says, 'I can't argue with that. That is a fascinating and interesting point you made.' And I poke the guy next to me and I say, 'God, he finally listened.' And then Bork says, 'But!' And there we were again, back in the soup."

In fact, whenever Bork said he was following precedent, there was always a but. Those buts indicated that in the crunch, Bork would revert to his long-held views.

We tried to finish Bork's testimony by Friday evening, September 18, but could not. We would have to hold a final session on Saturday, September 19. Tom Korologos's horoscope in that morning's paper read, "Finally, the votes are in. You could win by a surprisingly large majority." Chairman Biden walked over to me late Friday afternoon and asked me how much time I wanted. He identified one senator as wanting five more minutes, and another as wanting ten minutes.

"Joe," I said, "I don't like the idea of a time limit."

"Oh, come on!" Biden said. "How much do you want?" After waiting a few seconds for me to answer, he asked, "Okay, do you want a half hour?" Again I didn't respond immediately. Biden waited a short interval and said, "Okay, do you want an hour?" Again I didn't respond. "Okay, how about an hour and a half?"

"Okay," I said. "I'll take an hour and a half." Strom Thurmond, the committee's senior Republican, heard that Biden had given me an hour and a half and didn't like it. Strom came over and barked, "Arlen, what's this I hear, you want an hour and a half?!"

"Strom," I said, "I do not want an hour and a half. I don't want any time limit. I just want to question him until I finish questioning him."

"Okay, you can have your hour and a half," Strom conceded.

My colleagues were eager to finish the hearing by noon on Saturday. Only Leahy, Heflin, and I had asked for more time. Biden had a prior commitment and skipped the Saturday session. In his absence, Kennedy presided. I took all my time and still was not done. My questioning stretched over nearly two hours, including Bork's twenty-minute men's-room break two-thirds of the way through. The purpose of my questioning was to pin Bork down, particularly on judicial ideology, including original intent. I was trying to project what kind of Supreme Court justice he would make.

Ultimately, my view was that original intent cannot guide constitutional law very much. I suggested another standard, quoting Frankfurter, whom Bork had characterized as one of the stars of the Supreme Court. Frankfurter had quoted Cardozo on fundamental values and used the phrase "tradition and conscience" in his opinion in *Rochin* v. *California*, in which the Supreme Court suppressed evidence pumped from the defendant's stomach. Again the story of America and constitutional law is the story of decency. Original intent and legislative intent, I told Bork, "only take you so far, and beyond that you can rely on Cardozo or Frankfurter to effectuate the values and the tradition of the people without being able to pull out a specific constitutional right."

Tom Korologos told the *Washington Post*, "Specter hit the game-winning RBI."[4]

After long dialogues it remained unclear where Bork stood. In the hearing, his significant and sundry shifts from prior positions looked like a "confirmation conversion." They raised questions about Bork's motives and the depth of his convictions. A person is entitled to change his mind, and certainly to explain his new views, but Bork kept reverting to earlier stands. No sooner did we get involved in discussing a case than Bork returned to his old positions.

"It is not a matter of questioning his credibility or integrity, or his sincerity in insisting he will not be disgraced in history by acting contrary to his sworn testimony," I said on the Senate floor, but a question of Bork's "judicial disposition in applying principles of law which he has so long decried." Bork tried to ride two horses and fell from both. He left me with substantial doubt about what he would do on major constitutional cases.

Robert Bork could have been a great justice or a great disaster. He could have tipped the Court's balance. At the time, three aging justices were sitting: Blackmun, Brennan, and Marshall. I feared we might awaken one morning and find three vacancies. A Court dominated by Bork's intellect with three similarly disposed new appointees plus Rehnquist and Scalia could adopt original intent and weaken or even reject judicial review. I concluded that the country couldn't take the risk.

Before voting against Bork, I phoned the White House. I got Howard Baker, President Reagan's chief of staff, and told him I would vote no. Baker asked if I wanted to speak to the president. No, I said. Baker didn't press me. Then I phoned, in order, Minority Leader Robert Dole, Thurmond, and Bork, to inform them of my decision.

"I thought I'd addressed all your concerns," Bork told me.

"You did," I said. "But, although you addressed my concerns, you didn't satisfy them." Bork didn't try to change my mind. I then went to the floor and made my speech.

"Mr. President," I began, "I shall vote against Judge Bork on confirmation to the U.S. Supreme Court because I believe there is substantial doubt as to how he would apply fundamental principles of constitutional law. This is a difficult vote, since I will be opposing my president, my party, and a man of powerful intellect whom I respect and like." In my judgment, Judge Bork was simply outside the historical constitutional continuum.

"Specter delivered his verdict," the *Washington Post* wrote in a postmortem. "His decision to oppose Bork was a turning point in the bitter struggle over the nomination that produced another defeat for the battered Reagan administration."[5] On October 6, 1987, the Judiciary Committee voted 9–5 to report Bork's nomination with a negative recommendation. The vote ran along party lines, except for me. Bork didn't withdraw, despite reported pressure from the White House. He said he would stick out the battle so his attackers would not be encouraged to wage similar assaults against future nominees. "The process of confirming justices for our nation's highest court has been transformed in a way that should not and indeed must not be permitted to occur again," Bork said at a news conference. "The tactics and techniques of national political campaigns have been unleashed on the process of confirming judges. That is not simply disturbing. It is dangerous."

Bork had a point. While I gave no weight to the public relations campaigns in making my decision, and I'd like to believe my colleagues did the same, the campaigns had skewed and inflamed the debate. As the *New York Times* reported, "Some Senators who oppose the judge's nomination said they respected his decision to continue the fight. Senator Arlen Specter, the Pennsylvania Republican whose decision to vote against him was seen as a critical loss, said: 'I agree with him that unfair charges have been made against him. I hope the voices will be lowered, as he requested.' "[6] Bork's nomination went to the full Senate, where it was rejected 58–42 on October 23.

In his 1990 book, *The Tempting of America*, Bork was openly disdainful of senators in confirmation hearings. He wrote, "The hearings also illustrated the point that most senators would do well not to attempt to judge a nominee by engaging in a detailed discussion of legal doctrine." He then singled me out for criticism:

> The only senator who engaged in that enterprise at the hearing was Senator Arlen Specter, who questioned me on the subject of the first amendment's guarantee of freedom of speech. . . .
>
> I spent almost seven hours all told with Senator Specter, at the hearings and in his offices, discussing constitutional law, all of it at his request. To the end, he couldn't comprehend what I was saying about the first amendment, the equal-protection clause. . . . Because I was, out of necessity, patient with him, a lot of people not versed in constitutional law got the impression that this was a serious constitutional discussion.[7]

Many observers of our dialogue, especially the long Saturday session, evaluated it differently. The *Philadelphia Inquirer*, no fan of mine, ran an editorial titled, "Arlen Specter's Finest Hour." A. M. Rosenthal of the *New York Times* wrote that my questioning of Bork won "the respect of the nation." In Pennsylvania my party was not happy. Some Republicans remained sore for a decade or more.

Robert Bork did an enormous service to the Supreme Court confirmation process and to the country by discussing his judicial philosophy with the Judiciary Committee. Bork transformed the process, even if subsequent nominees have been less forthcoming. Bork's approach, not Rehnquist's and Scalia's, should be the precedent. In my judgment, the Senate should resist, if not refuse, to confirm Supreme Court nominees who refuse to answer questions on fundamental issues.

In voting on whether to confirm a nominee, senators should not have to gamble or guess about a candidate's philosophy but should be able to judge on the basis of the candidate's expressed views. In Robert Bork's case, perhaps more than any other, the Senate was able to make an informed decision.

HILL VERSUS THOMAS

A̲t the start, the Senate Judiciary Committee didn't "get it" about Judge Clarence Thomas's nomination to the U.S. Supreme Court. According to our critics, we just didn't understand. But in the end, the committee got it: a national avalanche of criticism. In retrospect it's hard to understand why the Judiciary Committee didn't focus on Professor Anita Hill's known complaint before reporting Thomas's nomination to the full Senate.

On July 8, 1991, President George Bush nominated Judge Clarence Thomas of the D.C. circuit court to the Supreme Court, to fill the seat vacated by Justice Thurgood Marshall. Marshall, who resigned after twenty-four years on the bench, had been the only African-American in the Court's history. As head of the NAACP's legal defense fund, Marshall had successfully argued *Brown* v. *Board of Education* in 1954; he was a civil rights crusader and a solid liberal voter. Marshall's successor would be the sixth justice appointed by Reagan and Bush, on an increasingly conservative Court.

Clarence Thomas, also African-American, had made his name as a conservative Republican. A devotee of conservative African-American thinkers like Thomas Sowell and J. A. Parker, Thomas opposed affirmative action, which he called a crutch that trapped minorities in dependency; opposed welfare; and was believed to oppose a woman's right to an abortion, though he had not taken a public stance on that issue. Thomas expressed his views in writings and speeches, which he was required, like all nominees, to provide to senators. I did not like a number of Thomas's views, but I thought there should be considerable latitude for the president's appointment. I disagreed with Thomas about affirmative action, but there was some basis for what he was saying. I had fought hard for pro-choice candidates on the ground that there should not be a litmus test, so how could I act differently toward a nominee on the other side of the issue?

Thomas, forty-three, had been on the bench less than a year when Bush nominated him for the Supreme Court. He had never argued a case before a jury and had not practiced law in a decade. But he had a compelling personal story, an impressive résumé, and the political outlook the White House was looking for. Thomas would come before the Senate a year before the 1992 elections. The far right was key to Bush's coalition, and getting a conservative like Thomas on the Court would make important inroads.

Broad-shouldered, muscular, and meticulously groomed, Thomas projected a scholar-athlete look, his close-cropped hair receding into a slight widow's peak above horn-rimmed glasses and just beginning to gray. Born out of wedlock in 1948 in a wooden shack in rural, segregated Pin Point, Georgia, Thomas had been raised by a strict grandfather in Savannah. He went on to graduate from Holy Cross College and Yale Law School. A protégé of Senator John Danforth (R-Mo.), Thomas had served as his assistant when Danforth was Missouri's attorney general; as an attorney for Monsanto Chemical Corporation; as a legislative assistant to Senator Danforth in Washington; as assistant secretary for civil rights at the U.S. Department of Education; and as chairman of the Equal Employment Opportunity Commission, before Bush appointed him to the U.S. court of appeals in early 1990, to fill the seat vacated by Judge Robert Bork.

Bush announced that Thomas was the "best qualified" nominee he could find for the high court, and that "the fact that he is black and a minority had nothing to do with this." Immediately I said publicly that Thomas certainly was *not* the best-qualified nominee available and that race *was* a factor—and properly so. I did not object to Thomas's nomination, because I thought he was entitled to a hearing and because on the record, with his degrees from Holy Cross and Yale Law School plus his tenure on the court of appeals, he appeared at least marginally qualified.

The American Bar Association wasn't impressed with Thomas. None of the fifteen members of the association's Standing Committee on the Federal Judiciary found him "well qualified," the association's highest rating. Twelve found Thomas "qualified," and two found him "not qualified." One member abstained.

Again, as in the battle over Bork's confirmation in 1987, special interests mobilized and sprang into action. Thomas's opponents, led by such interest groups as Norman Lear's People for the American Way, painted Thomas as hostile and dangerous to minorities and women and as intellectually lacking. Supporters, a host of conservative operatives led by Kenneth Duberstein, who had been Reagan's chief of staff, organized a campaign to trumpet Thomas's American success story and his credentials. Duberstein, by then a Washington lobbyist, would manage Thomas's Senate confirmation hearings, as he had managed Justice David Souter's hearings in 1990.

"From the start, the Thomas fight was the natural consequence of the Bork fight, conceived by people determined never to let another nominee be 'Borked,' " Jane Mayer and Jill Abramson wrote in their controversial book *Strange Justice*. "The liberal activist Tony Podesta, formerly president of People for the American Way (one of the main groups opposing Bork), later admitted that when the Thomas fight grew irredeemably nasty, liberal interest groups such as his own had chiefly themselves to blame."[1]

After Bork's defeat, which followed his extensive dialogues on his judicial philosophy, Duberstein and company didn't want Thomas to say any more than necessary to win fifty-one votes. Thomas refused to comment, for example, on abortion.

The afternoon before the Judiciary Committee was scheduled to vote on Thomas, Thursday, September 26, Dennis DeConcini and I were standing on the Senate floor during a vote, discussing the nomination. *The Legal Times* had reported a potential snag, that Thomas may have delayed publishing an opinion that he was supposedly writing on affirmative action, to avoid discussing that subject at his hearing. DeConcini expressed some concern about the judge's prospects. "I think it's going to be okay," I said. There were so many reasons for a judge to withhold filing an opinion, perhaps even to give other judges time to consider it for a possible dissent.

"No, that's not what I'm talking about," DeConcini said. "I'm talking about Anita Hill." I'd never heard of Anita Hill. But it was a name that would soon be linked with mine, and certainly Thomas's, perhaps indelibly. DeConcini told me that Hill, a law professor at the University of Oklahoma, claimed that ten years earlier, when she had worked for Thomas, he had pressed her for dates and made crude remarks. Biden

345

had told DeConcini about Hill, but nobody had told me or anybody else on the Republican side of the aisle. That night we were voting late, and I found Biden in the Senate dining room. "What's going on?" I asked.

"Well, didn't Strom tell you?" Biden said.

"No," I said. "What's going on?"

Biden was surprised that I didn't know about Anita Hill. "I had personally briefed every Democratic senator on the committee, assuming that Strom would brief every Republican senator on the committee," Biden recalled over lunch in November 1998. Thurmond told me in early 1999 that he had briefed only Senate leadership, and not Judiciary Committee Republicans. Thurmond and his staff felt that Hill's charges didn't rise to the level that required flagging committee members. To Thurmond, Hill's charges belonged among the many unsubstantiated accusations that pour into the committee against every nominee. Hill's charges were uncorroborated, concerned incidents that allegedly took place ten years earlier, were made by a woman who would not publicly identify herself, and were vehemently denied by Thomas. It would be unfair to circulate such unsubstantiated charges and risk having them exploited by Thomas's enemies, Thurmond reasoned.

"Let me get my staffer," Biden said in the Senate dining room the night before the committee vote, when I asked him about Hill's charges. The chairman's aide came over and gave me some files. I sat on a bench in the reception room, around the corner from the dining room, outside the Senate chamber and read. Hill's allegations to that point, in statements she had given to the FBI on September 23, were mild compared to what would come later. She hadn't even characterized her charges as sexual harassment. "Unwelcome conduct," as Biden put it. There was no mention in the FBI report of pubic hair on a Coke can, porn star Long Dong Silver, or Thomas's boasts about his own size and prowess, all of which would become notorious later.

Hill had spoken to investigators only after she was contacted, and reluctantly, she said. After Thomas was nominated for the Supreme Court, Hill had apparently complained to friends about Thomas's conduct years earlier, when she had worked for him. Tips about Hill's charges were passed to Metzenbaum's Labor Committee staff, perhaps because Metzenbaum, who had dealt with Thomas as chairman of the EEOC, was seen as most hostile to him. Hill wound up speaking at length to James Brudney, a senior aide at the Labor Committee, who had been a year ahead of her at law school. Brudney eventually turned the matter over to Biden's Judiciary Committee staff. The committee called in the FBI to take Hill's statement. Hill was dragged into the nomination fight an inch at a time, ambushed by Senate staffers and bounced between committees.

Despite the lower-key tone of Hill's initial statements, Biden insisted that he had immediately recognized her charges as important and explosive.[2] By the time I approached Biden outside the Senate dining room on September 26, he had spoken to Hill repeatedly and had already met with Senate leaders on the issue. "We were well into the hearings. We were about to close down the hearings on Thomas," Biden recalled, "and I got a phone call in the back room of the hearing, where the staff worked, saying that a woman called saying that she had a complaint against Clarence Thomas, sexual harassment."

Initially, the woman refused to identify herself, and Biden refused to take the call. But Hill gradually yielded on her conditions, Biden said. "She went from wouldn't identify herself to identifying herself but unwilling to allow her name to be used, unwilling to testify, to willing to allow her name to be used, to writing a letter to senators on condition that I could guarantee that her comments would not become known."

Biden said he pointed out to Hill that the Judiciary Committee hearings were not a Star Chamber, meaning there wouldn't be any issues discussed with the nominee behind closed doors without the public's knowing what was going on. Hill continued to yield on her terms, Biden said, "saying, okay, I could tell Thomas, but I couldn't have the FBI look into this, to finally agreeing the FBI could look at this, but I couldn't use her comments in letters to the committee, but that she wanted the committee to consider this not in a hearing; 'I want you to be aware of this before you vote.'"

"We had a unanimous consent agreement to vote on Thomas's nomination within the next number of days, while all this stuff was dribbling out." In other words, the Judiciary Committee was about to pass judgment on Thomas and forward his nomination to the full Senate. Biden asked for a meeting with Senate Majority Leader George Mitchell, Senate Minority Leader Bob Dole, and the Judiciary Committee's ranking Republican, Thurmond. "Gentlemen," Biden recalled saying, "here's our situation: And I laid out the facts, that she didn't want to go public.

"And I'll never forget George Mitchell saying, 'This is very serious.' A former federal judge said there appeared to be contemporaneous corroboration." Hill had referred Biden's staff to Susan Hoerchner, a law school classmate and workers' compensation judge in Norwalk, California, who said that Hill told her of Thomas's conduct at the time it allegedly took place. "That takes it out of he said/she said," Biden recalled Mitchell saying.

"We appeared to have, at first blush, a credible witness corroborating," Biden said. "I then walked onto the floor, grabbed every single Democratic senator [on the committee], and laid out where we were—with, at that point, the unwillingness of Anita Hill to go forward. None of my colleagues said, based on what little was in the file and her unwillingness to go forward, 'How do we vitiate this vote? How do we say we're not going to vote on this, without ruining his reputation and never having anything come of it?' "[3]

I asked Biden whether other Judiciary Committee members who knew about Hill's charges were concerned about them. I was told that no senator had seemed troubled, except for Mitchell, who was not on the committee. Only one other senator, I found out, had read the FBI report. Another unnamed senator had said that Hill's charges didn't seem like a big deal—after all, Thomas had never touched her. The Senate Judiciary Committee was utterly uninitiated regarding the concept of a hostile workplace, even though the Supreme Court had issued a decision on sexual harassment in 1986, five years earlier.

The committee was scheduled to vote on Thomas the next morning. That night John Danforth phoned me at my Washington apartment a little past eleven. Danforth, who was both a lawyer and a minister, was Thomas's mentor and champion. "I just wanted to be sure that you don't have a problem," he said.

"No, Jack," I said, "I don't think he's a Brandeis, but he passes the standard for basic qualifications, and I'm going to support him." Then I slept on it. I went to play squash the next morning at seven, and the whole situation bothered me. A little after seven, from the squash court, I phoned Danforth at home. "I want to talk to Thomas before the vote," I said.

I was due to speak on the House side of the Capitol at 9:00 A.M. at a symposium on the proposed International Criminal Court. The Judiciary Committee hearing and vote were at ten. I spoke at the House early and quickly, then dashed across the Capitol to the Russell Building, where I met Thomas in Danforth's office at 9:30 A.M.

I asked Thomas about the opinion on affirmative action that he was reportedly keeping secret. Thomas said that he couldn't talk about a matter pending in his court, but that, as a general matter, there was no truth to any charge that he'd withheld an opinion on any matter to avoid potential embarrassment at his confirmation hearings. I then confronted Thomas with Anita Hill's charges. "No, sir, with God as my witness," Thomas insisted. He was emphatic and upset. "It just didn't happen. . . . I wouldn't do that. . . . Black men are always accused of that. . . . Never happened, absolutely not." Thomas told me that African-American men are often described sexually, in terms of prowess and size, and as predators. He told me how painful it was for him to hear Hill's charges, and how untrue and extraordinary they were.

When I finished talking to Thomas, I hurried to the second floor of the Dirksen Building for the Judiciary Committee meeting. Looking back, I should have spoken to Anita Hill, under ideal circumstances. But there was no way I could have meaningfully talked to her before the Friday-morning Judiciary Committee vote. As it turned out, I had to be on the Senate floor during much of the meeting to argue with then-Senator Lloyd Bentsen about steel issues. At the committee meeting, as senators in turn stated their positions on Thomas and voted, I thought, Why doesn't some Democrat hold this thing over for a week? Biden and DeConcini certainly knew about Hill's charges. So must the others, I thought. And now I know that they knew. Every senator had an absolute right to carry over any nomination for a week. Holdovers often come at the drop of a hat. Granted, it was already September 27, and the Supreme Court would convene for its new term on October 5. But I doubt that senators were weighing an extra week of a justice's absence in their calculus.

Biden was unwilling either to compel Anita Hill to testify or to hold over Thomas without Hill's testimony. The Judiciary Committee voted, as scheduled, on Clarence Thomas's nomination to the Supreme Court. In our first ballot we voted 7–7 to report Thomas to the full Senate with a favorable recommendation—a failing score. The vote ran along party lines, with one Democrat, DeConcini, crossing over to support the judge. We then voted 13–1 to send Thomas to the full Senate without recommendation. Only Simon voted no. The matter passed to the full Senate.

Biden told me recently, "My role, I decided—and I had great debates with my staff about it—was I was going to be a judge, and I was going to apply the rules that were not required to be applied." The Judiciary

Committee was not a court of law and was not bound by courtroom procedure, Biden stressed. "But out of a sense of fairness, that's what I was going to do. And I wasn't about, with my view of civil liberties, to attack a guy I was already against. I was against him from day one. I announced I was against him. I voted against him. I led the hearing against him on the substance of his view on natural law. . . . And notwithstanding that, I couldn't bring myself, without her willing to confront it fairly, to bring this thing out in the open.

"I spent hours and hours and hours pursuing her, pushing her, cajoling her," Biden said. "My staff cajoled her. To come forward, come forward. And some think I should have done just what one of her friends did: just out her. Hey, this is it. But what would have happened had she not come forward? We'd look like fools. I said, 'What happens if she comes forward, and I subpoena her, and she says, Well, it wasn't much. He did do that, he did do this. . . . Yes, I was offended, but I didn't feel threatened, it didn't affect my job'—Now we look like fools."[4]

Other Democrats made the same argument at the time. Senator Paul Simon said during exchanges with me on *Nightline* and *The MacNeil/Lehrer NewsHour* that the committee didn't use Hill's charges at first because she would not come forward publicly. I can understand that Joe Biden didn't want to force Anita Hill to come forward, just as he explained it to me. But the committee should have considered subpoenaing her. It is a fundamental proposition that the public is entitled to everyone's evidence. Thomas's confirmation hearing was a public matter in which we had an obligation to find the facts for an important public purpose. Those facts are not a witness's personal preserve. The public has a right to know. That's why every criminal case is listed as the state versus the defendant, not as the victim versus the defendant. The state is a party to the case. And the confirmation carried much higher stakes than a routine criminal trial. The committee should do its best to accommodate Anita Hill, but not at the expense of omitting key evidence on a Supreme Court nominee. As a prosecutor I had often compelled witnesses to come in against their will. I had no personal stake in what they said once they took the stand.

By twenty-twenty hindsight, perhaps I should have carried Thomas's nomination over for a week, even though that would have brought the wrath of Republicans—especially after I had opposed Bork and William Bradford Reynolds. But it seemed to me that if the Democrats, who were out to defeat Thomas, wouldn't pursue Hill for another week, I shouldn't hold over the nomination.

The Democrats considered Thomas a bad choice and wanted to kill his nomination but didn't think Hill's charges offered much ammunition. This group of aging white males in 1991, like me, didn't understand the explosive nature of the issue. Later—probably when the Senate Democrats saw the issue's political capital, its mileage with women, and its potential utility in defeating Thomas—they began to use it.

A big argument erupted over when the full Senate should vote on Thomas. At the time most senators didn't understand all the ramifications. The Senate was scheduled to recess during the week of October 7. Danforth was pushing for a vote before we broke for the recess, which meant by Friday, October 4. Metzenbaum, among others, was pushing for a delay, perhaps trying to get Professor Hill to come forward. But the pressure was on to vote before October 14, the day we returned from recess. I was in Dole's conference room when two Republican senators from the other side of the continent, Mark Hatfield and Frank Murkowski, objected to coming back early. Hatfield had commitments in Oregon, and Murkowski had to go to Alaska.

A compromise was finally struck by unanimous consent for a vote on Tuesday, October 8. At the time I didn't understand why the vote couldn't wait until we got back from the week's recess.

THE SENATE ON TRIAL

I was watching the Philadelphia–Tampa Bay football game on television at my Philadelphia home on Sunday, October 5, when someone from the Associated Press phoned. Hill's allegations had reached the media, through a leaked copy of the FBI report. I turned down the sound on the game, which turned out to be a 14–13 thriller-loser for the Eagles. The AP reporter asked me questions, and I told him what I knew: that the Judiciary Committee had two statements from Hill, one given to committee personnel and one given to the FBI, but the committee had not acted on them. I didn't know at that time the details of Biden's discussions with Hill about her reluctance to step forward as a witness.

I don't know who leaked Hill's charges. I was later questioned by a tall, polished lawyer from New York who was investigating for the Senate. I didn't like being questioned about whether I was the leak, even though I wasn't. I'd been interrogated only once before, by the FBI during the Warren Commission about the leak of Jack Ruby's transcript to Dorothy Kilgallen, and it was no fun.

The leak sparked infighting among Judiciary Committee members. Metzenbaum and Hatch sparred on live national television. Metzenbaum said on PBS's *MacNeil/Lehrer NewsHour* on October 8, "One of my colleagues, whom I considered a friend, on the other side of the aisle, with absolutely no evidence is telling reporters that I am responsible for leaking Anita Hill's story to the press. That is wrong; that is untrue. . . . He owes me a public apology. . . ." Metzenbaum had a long record of opposing Thomas, going back to 1990, when he'd voted against Thomas's confirmation to the court of appeals.

"I know that my distinguished friend from Ohio feels that I named him as the person who leaked the information with regard to the FBI report," Hatch responded on the show. "And that is not true. . . . I have my suspicions who did, and I don't believe it was any senator who leaked the report. I do believe it was staff."

Senate investigators never identified the leak. Suspicion clearly pointed to somebody opposed to Thomas who wanted to force Hill's charges out to the public. Emotions were running high on Capitol Hill. On *Nightline* I told Ted Koppel that the leak was so outrageous that we should investigate and take action, though we would probably wind up in a wild-goose chase. Some have suggested that there was no deliberate leak, that Anita Hill had simply told enough people about her complaints to the Senate, and they had told enough people, that the press—initially National Public Radio's Nina Totenberg and *Newsday*'s Timothy Phelps—got wind of her charges, tracked Hill down, and ran with the story.

On Monday, the day after the AP reporter's call, I was scheduled to be in Reading for a full day of events, but I cut the trip short and returned to Philadelphia to talk about Thomas's nomination on *The MacNeil/Lehrer NewsHour* in the evening and on two more shows early the next morning. On the *Today* show, I called for a delay of the full Senate vote.

Even Mayer and Abramson, whose book mischaracterized my reaction to Hill's charges and my motives, at least credited me with early action. "Surprisingly," they wrote, "one of the first to get the message was Arlen Specter, a Republican supporter of Thomas who knew of Hill's charges early and initially dismissed them. Specter, who drew much of his financial support from women who appreciated his pro-choice record, appeared on the *Today* show on Tuesday morning and urged a delay."[1]

On *MacNeil/Lehrer* I got into a tiff with Paul Simon over what I viewed as a failure by Simon and other Judiciary Committee members who had known about Hill's charges for weeks to say anything about them.

"Well, the reason it was not raised publicly is she was unwilling to have her name used publicly," Simon said. He insisted that Hill's material had been labeled confidential and that it "was very clear . . . her name was not to be used publicly. It was not used publicly until she came forward this past weekend. These are the facts." Not quite, but we had to leave it at that on the program. After the morning talk shows, I cut Tuesday's schedule and hurried to Washington. The full Senate was scheduled to vote on Thomas that evening.

I went to Bob Dole's office. Several senators were gathered in the minority leader's suite, counting to see if they had fifty votes plus Vice President Dan Quayle for confirmation.

"We cannot do that," I said. "We cannot do that for many reasons." The Senate could not—or should not—rush a nominee through with such heavy charges hanging over him, I told the others. We could not bull Thomas through because of the integrity of the Supreme Court. If confirmed, Thomas would doubtless cast the key vote on many 5–4 decisions, which would put a cloud over the high court. Second, we couldn't do it because of the integrity of the Senate. And third, a charge had been made that had to be investigated out of fairness to both Thomas and Hill. Then I went out and made a speech on the Senate floor along the same lines, urging hearings on Hill's charges.

"I think the series of events has in a sense put the Senate on trial, and in a sense would send to the Supreme Court a cloud, and that it is in the public interest to have these questions resolved in, as Senator Danforth has suggested, an additional hearing," I said on the floor. "I think it is very appropriate that we not vote to confirm at a time when the cloud hangs over a nominee—and would for a long period of time—because of the tremendous importance of the decisions to be made by the Supreme Court of the United States, and judgments by that nominee if as and when confirmed."

I returned to *MacNeil/Lehrer* Tuesday evening to press my case. "Most important of all," I said, "we have the Supreme Court, which has to make very monumental decisions. And anybody who's confirmed there shouldn't go there with a cloud." I said I wished I'd known about Hill's charges earlier, and that those senators who had known had taken action earlier. "I came to the conclusion that whatever the motivation may be, the charges are there now and there are a lot of people in this country who were very uneasy about what the Senate has done, very uneasy about the whole situation, and I think we can take a little more time, hear Professor Hill, hear Judge Thomas's response, make a judgment. . . . I think that there ought to be a public hearing. The American people ought to be privy to it."

As the day wore on and the public furor grew, it became clear that the Republican leadership didn't have the fifty votes needed to confirm Thomas. Dole backed off. After a lot of wrangling, the Senate decided to delay its vote for a week, until Tuesday, October 15, to give the Judiciary Committee time to investigate Hill's charges. A hearing on her charges would begin Friday, October 11.

The next day, Wednesday, October 9, I drove to New York City on business. On the way, my car phone rang.

"Arlen," Strom Thurmond piped, "we want you to handle the questioning of Professor Hill." Then Dole got on the phone. Dole, Danforth, and Thurmond, and maybe some others, were in Dole's office. "Arlen, this is an assignment I want you to take," Dole said.

"Listen, Bob," I said, "I'm on the committee, and I'm prepared to participate."

Then Danforth chimed in. "Arlen, we need you to be Clarence's advocate."

"Jack, I'm not going to be anybody's advocate," I said. "I don't represent Clarence Thomas. I represent the commonwealth of Pennsylvania. I'm not about to be Clarence Thomas's advocate."

As Danforth wrote in his book on the Thomas nomination, *Resurrection*:

> Clarence needed an advocate. He needed what any party to a lawsuit is entitled to as a matter of right: a lawyer who would give full allegiance to him. Those present in Senator Dole's office were concerned that Arlen Specter would see himself not as an advocate but as an independent seeker of truth, and for that reason we decided that the designated Republican questioner of Clarence Thomas would not be Arlen Specter. Rather, we chose Clarence's strong supporter, Orrin Hatch.
>
> We decided that I should phone Arlen and ask him to question Anita Hill and any other witnesses except Clarence Thomas. At Senator Hatch's suggestion, the basic message we gave him was, "We are really counting on you, Arlen."[2]

Critics have charged that I was gung ho for Thomas. I wasn't. The early Judiciary Committee hearings show my views as I questioned Thomas—far more aggressively than I later questioned Hill—about affirmative action, about Thomas's respect for a defendant's individual rights, about his apparently disdainful view of Congress, about the tension between the president's authority as commander in chief and Congress's authority to declare war, and about Thomas's handling of a big labor case that seemed to show disregard for discrimination against minorities.

Even Mayer and Abramson noted that "only Specter questioned the judge about his controversial views on civil rights."[3] They added that "the inquiries were gentle," but the transcript shows that I wasn't gentle with Thomas on civil rights or other subjects. I took him to task at length over his position in the sheet-metal workers discrimination case, which ultimately reached the U.S. Supreme Court. The New York City Human Relations Commission had cited the Sheetworkers Local 28 in 1964 for discriminatory practices. The EEOC finally brought a lawsuit in 1971, which was followed by a finding of discrimination in 1975 and a court order to correct that discrimination. The union was cited for contempt in 1977 and again in 1982 over the court order.

I criticized Thomas bluntly for being soft on discrimination. "You have written you are astounded that there is more of a penalty for breaking into a mailbox than for discriminating against a minority or African-Americans, and you have advocated jail sentences and heavy fines for those who are in contempt of court, and [here] you have this kind of outrageous conduct that spans a twenty-year period, and then EEOC comes in at the latter stages of this litigation in the 1980s and takes a different position and argues against the court orders to stop the flagrant discriminatory practices . . . and you criticize the Supreme Court's decision in trying to do something to deal with proved discrimination. . . . That seems to me to come right within the purview of what you say ought to be done to remedy active discrimination, and yet you take the other side." Thomas replied that in cases such as the sheet-metal workers, he favored fines and penalties rather than court-imposed quotas or preferential treatment.

"Your writings and your answers are at loggerheads. They are inconsistent with what has been said," I told Thomas at one point, regarding affirmative action. "You had written earlier in your career that you thought flexible goals and timetables were appropriate, and you changed that. Judge Thomas, isn't it entirely possible that you could change your mind again and find that timetables and goals are the preferable course?"

At another point in my questioning, citing Thomas's written criticisms of Congress in speeches, I said, "The problem I have, Judge Thomas, is that if you take a large body of your writings, where you disagree with these cases and you disagree to the core with the congressional function, what assurances will we have that you will respect Congressional intent?"

I also took Thomas to task for supporting what I considered the Supreme Court's growing revisionist tendency to make law rather than to interpret it. We had a showdown over the Court's 1989 5–4 decision in *Ward's Cove* to overturn a 1971 federal regulation approved by the Supreme Court in *Griggs*. The cases dealt with the fundamental issue of proving race discrimination in labor cases. *Griggs* put the burden of proof on the employer, which meant the employer had to prove by preponderance of the evidence that there was no discrimination. Normally the plaintiff has the burden of proof. But in cases where the proof lies within the defendant's control, it is common for the burden to shift to the defendant. Establishing discrimination would require an analysis of what had happened with other similarly situated employees, which the employee could not provide. But the employer could go to all the other similarly situated employees and show that there had not been discrimination. I found it appropriate to put the burden of proof on the employer. And Congress made no effort to change the *Griggs* standard, which strongly implied that Congress was satisfied with it. Then, eighteen years later, *Ward's Cove* changed the law, putting the burden of proof on the employee.

"It seems to me that when a unanimous Supreme Court decision stands for eighteen years, that is long enough," I told Thomas at the hearing. "Or if it is not, I would like to know what is long enough." Thomas replied, "When Congress doesn't act, I think it is more difficult to determine precisely why Congress doesn't act." Thomas added that Congress's inaction for eighteen years was indeed "an important consideration in determining whether or not the prior ruling or the prior interpretation was the correct interpretation."

On the same matter, I expressed other qualms to Thomas: "I have a grave concern about a shift in regulation based on political considerations which you appear to sanction in your Creighton speech. And I have a very deep concern about the Supreme Court upholding a change in regulation because they [regulations] accord with a shift in attitude."

Later, when Thomas said he had not watched Hill's testimony, I told him—in a public session, with the cameras rolling—that I found this very disappointing. In fact, my interrogation of Thomas irked my finance chairman, Herb Barness, enough that he phoned me. "You're painting yourself into a corner, so that you'll have to vote against this guy," said Barness, who was also Pennsylvania's National Republican committeeman. I replied, "Well, if his answers are unsatisfactory, I *will* break party ranks again and vote against him."

In any case, Thurmond recently told me that he picked me to lead the questioning of Hill because he thought I would do the best job. That was nice to hear. But Dole, Thurmond, and Danforth also wanted my credibility.

"Orrin Hatch thought that the best person to question Anita Hill would be Arlen Specter," Danforth wrote in *Resurrection*. Among other reasons, Danforth wrote, "In Orrin's mind, Arlen was both low key and tenacious, with an ability to burrow in as a questioner and persist without raising his voice. Orrin reasoned that Arlen was the most liberal Republican on the committee, and he had excellent credentials with women's groups as a supporter of choice in abortion."[4]

My record on women's issues went back to my days as district attorney, when I had hired women and prosecuted many cases involving mistreatment of women, which was unusual at the time. In the Senate I had helped boost funding for research and treatment of breast, cervical, and ovarian cancer and for family planning, and I have always maintained that abortion is not a matter for the government to control.

I had also established a record for independence in my votes on Bork, Reynolds, and the MX missile. For that reason, the questioning of Hill was not the first time the Republican leadership had tapped me to play a prominent role. In July 1988, during the presidential race, Vice President Bush asked me to critique Massachusetts Governor Michael Dukakis's prison-furlough program. Dukakis was the Democratic nominee facing the vice president. I favored furloughs and halfway houses and reintegration of prisoners into the community. I had been a party to furloughs as Philadelphia DA. But I researched the Dukakis plan and found it was unsound, releasing dangerous criminals promiscuously. I decided to hold a news conference in Boston at the Massachusetts statehouse, right under Dukakis's window.

I took a 7:00 A.M. flight to Boston on July 6 and found Senator John Kerry, the Massachusetts Democrat, on the plane. I wondered, could there be some connection? Neither of us said a word beyond a perfunctory greeting. When I arrived at the statehouse, Kerry was standing with about two dozen law-enforcement officers, many in uniform, and the Massachusetts attorney general, a combative former congressman named James Shannon. I had only Dan McKenna, my press secretary, with me.

The *Orange County* (Calif.) *Register* reported, in a story that drew national attention:

> Massachusetts Democrats loyal to Governor Michael S. Dukakis ambushed a Republican 'truth squad' outside the Statehouse here Wednesday, touching off a sidewalk debate on crime between two Senators. Vice-President George Bush had dispatched Senator Arlen Specter, R-Pa., to attack Dukakis's record on crime. . . . But with the benefit of a day's notice, the Dukakis campaign assembled 20 law-enforcement officials—including district attorneys, several sheriffs and two uniformed police chiefs—and Senator John F. Kerry, D-Mass., to meet Specter.[5]

We wound up arguing over rights to the microphone, along the lines of Ronald Reagan's famous line regarding George Bush, "I paid for this microphone, Mr. Green," when they argued at a 1980 New Hampshire presidential debate over excluding other candidates. McKenna, burly and short-tempered, was furious. He wanted to fight Shannon, the equally large and pugnacious Massachusetts attorney general. We were able to avoid a fistfight, and I made my statement.

"My view is that there are a great many questions that are raised by this furlough program, which Governor Dukakis has yet to answer," I said. "I believe it raises a question as to his overall judgment." Kerry got in a few lines about the Reagan administration's record on combating illegal drugs. The conference was a hit. George Bush phoned me at home, and he and Barbara Bush both thanked me. I repeated the same theme at a news conference in Denver a few days later in advance of Dukakis's appearance at a forum on environmental issues.

Jim Baker made another request of me later in the campaign. In late October, Baker tracked me down on a Sunday when I was in California. "We need you in Washington tomorrow morning at a press conference," he said. Senator John Tower would speak on defense, former New Hampshire governor John Sununu would speak on the environment, and they wanted me to speak again on crime and furloughs.

"I'm sorry, Jim," I said. "I'd like to, but I can't." My schedule was packed, with a speech at an AIPAC [American Israel Public Affairs Committee] dinner that Sunday night and a host of other events on Monday. We went over my schedule, and every time I listed a commitment, Baker said, Well, we've taken care of that; X is going to speak in your place. Well, we've covered you on this; Y is going to do this.

I said, "Have you taken care of my wife?" Baker was stumped, but he didn't give up. I said, "I just can't do it."

"Look, Arlen," Baker said, raising his voice a bit, "we need you. You're the only guy who has the credibility. You voted against Bork, you're an independent, people trust you, we need you to do this news conference."

So I did. I crossed the continent on the red-eye and made Baker's news conference. Sununu spoke about Boston Harbor and the environment, Tower about defense and veterans. But because furloughs had become a major issue, the only speech anybody seemed interested in was mine. Sununu phoned my chief of staff immediately after the news conference to say my speech was the best presentation he "had ever heard from a podium"—whatever that meant.

Inevitably, my votes on Bork, Reynolds, and others brought grousing from my colleagues in the Republican cloakroom, so I was glad to find occasions when my reputation for independence would help the party. When Dole and Thurmond made a special request, I was glad to respond where I could do so consistently with my own views. After they asked me to take the lead role in questioning Anita Hill, I had just one day to prepare, which meant getting through a mound of papers. Meanwhile, the phone was ringing constantly. Then Thurmond scheduled a late-evening session for Judiciary Committee Republicans, and I went to the caucus room to find my colleagues arguing about minutiae. "Hey, I've got to leave," I said. "I've got to go prepare. I'm questioning Professor Hill tomorrow."

I went to my apartment, sat down at my desk, and again immersed myself in the paperwork. The phone rang. It was my aunt Rose from Wichita. Rose had lived with my family in Wichita when I was growing up, having come from St. Joseph for a secretarial job. When my parents announced they would name me Abraham after my paternal grandfather, Avram, my aunt, then eighteen, protested. "Oh, you're not going to do that to this poor little baby." She suggested "Arlen," after her favorite movie actor, Richard Arlen. And so it was.

Rose had been my mentor and champion from the time she arranged my first job delivering bills of lading by bicycle in Wichita. She had given me sound advice on the 1986 tax bill and on many other subjects. They say you can poll Peoria and get an accurate idea of what America thinks. I've found I could just ask Aunt Rose. Over the years she became my political adviser as well as surrogate mother.

On Senator Bill Bradley's 1986 tax bill, Rose counseled that she didn't like one tax rate on everybody—on herself and on the millionaires. I confronted Bradley on the Senate floor, quoting Aunt Rose's objection. Bill didn't have a good answer.

"Boozy Boy," Rose said, using my childhood nickname, her voice heavy with concern, "the TV says you're going to be the questioner of Anita Hill tomorrow. I don't like that. Don't do it, that's a bad thing to do."

"Why do you say that, Rosie?"

"Well, because you just shouldn't do that." Questioning Hill would get me into trouble, she warned. A burst of wisdom from the prairie.

I thanked Rose for her advice but told her I was already committed. Aunt Rose was not the only one who urged me not to question Hill. Biden, a good friend despite our political differences, warned me not to do it. "The reason why I pleaded with him not to do this," he said later, "is that I knew he couldn't put a governor on himself. I knew he could not do it. . . . He said, 'I've got to do it. I can control it.' I said, 'No, Arlen, there's no possibility of controlling it.' "

I was on the committee, and it was a role I had to undertake. I think I did control it. But that didn't stop me from being criticized. Joe Biden, along with many other senators and, for that matter, the entire Senate, also got plenty of criticism.

FLAT-OUT PERJURY

The Senate Judiciary Committee assembled in the Russell Caucus Room on the morning of Friday, October 11, to open hearings on Professor Anita Hill's complaint against Judge Clarence Thomas. The session began with an appearance by Thomas, who was escorted to the caucus room after a pep talk from Danforth in the senator's lavatory, during which Danforth played a recording of "Onward, Christian Soldiers" and they prayed together.

Thomas, in a brief statement, denied Hill's charges categorically. "I cannot imagine anything I said or did that could have been mistaken for sexual harassment," he said. If she had misinterpreted him, Thomas said, he was sorry. "But I have not said or done the things that Anita Hill has alleged."

Thomas offered a set of facts that he said undercut Hill's credibility: She had moved with him from the Department of Education to the EEOC, had voluntarily accompanied him to a speech he made at Oral Roberts Law School, and had contacted him repeatedly to ask for guidance and assistance. Thomas finished in less than an hour.

At that point I had seen only Hill's September 23 statements to the FBI and the Judiciary Committee. Hill had begun those statements with a brief career summary, explaining that she had worked with Thomas for two years, beginning at the Department of Education and continuing at the EEOC.

From the beginning, our working relationship was relaxed and open. . . . I, initially, believed that our common experiences in terms of background and legal education were the reasons he hired me.

. . . After approximately three months of working together, he asked me to go out with him socially. I declined and explained to him that I thought that it would . . . jeopardize what, at the time, I considered to be a very good, working relationship. . . . I was very uncomfortable with the idea and told him so.

. . . In the following few weeks he asked me out on two or three occasions indicating that my reasons for refusing were not sufficient. He pressured me to justify my reasons for saying "no" to him.

. . . The working relationship became even more strained when he began to use work situations to discuss sex. . . . After a brief conversation about work, he would turn the conversations to discussions about his sexual interests. His conversations were very vivid. He spoke about acts that he had seen in pornographic films involving such things as women having sex with animals and films involving group sex or rape scenes. He talked about pornographic materials depicting individuals with large penises or breasts involved in various sex acts. . . . I sensed that my discomfort with his discussion only urged him on, as though my reaction of feeling ill at ease and vulnerable was what he wanted.

. . . He would comment on what I was wearing in terms of whether it made me more or less sexually appealing and he commented on my appearance in terms of sexual attractiveness. All of this occurred in the Office of the EEOC, usually in his inner office. . . . I was sure that he felt he could pressure me to the point at which I could no longer refuse his advances.

. . . In February of 1983, I was hospitalized for five days on an emergency basis for acute stomach pain. Though the cause of the illness was not determined by my physicians, I am convinced the illness was in reaction to the stress I felt at work.

. . . On, as I recall, the last day of my employment at the EEOC in the summer of 1983, Clarence Thomas and I went out to dinner. . . . Finally, he made a comment the content of which that I will always remember. He said that if I ever told anyone about his behavior toward me that it could ruin his career.[1]

I thought it might be possible to reconcile what Professor Hill said with what Thomas was saying, a chance to bring the parties together. Sometimes, on further reflection, a witness modifies the things he or she said. Maybe recollection was faulty on a couple of points. Maybe Thomas would find he wasn't sure he had not said some of those things. Maybe he'd forgotten an incident or two. If Thomas had conceded any of the incidents Hill alleged, that conduct would have raised a firestorm and, depending on the specifics, might have derailed his nomination.

Formal questioning should seek to find if there really is a significant dispute on a material question. As soon as Thomas finished, Biden called Anita Hill. Professor Hill took her seat at the witness table. We waited a few minutes while Biden, noticing a large contingent of Hill's relatives and friends at the back of the chamber, tried to seat them in the front spectator row. Eventually bodies settled, and Biden asked Hill to begin.

The lasting image of the hearings is a TV close-up of Hill alone against a phalanx of senators. The shot looked like something out of the Star Chamber, with fourteen older white men in blue suits glaring down at a young African-American woman at the witness table. But, in fact, it was a more even setting. At the felt-covered witness table, in addition to her relatives, Hill sat flanked by several lawyers, advisers, and public relations aides, including several Washington pros who had helped prepare her testimony. But these handlers didn't make the television frame.

Hill brought an interesting background of her own, one similar to Thomas's. Born in 1956, the youngest of thirteen children, she was raised on a family farm without indoor plumbing in rural Lone Tree, Oklahoma, which was largely segregated. She graduated from Oklahoma University and went on to Yale Law School. After eleven months as an associate at a major Washington, D.C., law firm, she left in 1981 to work as assistant to Thomas, then newly appointed to his civil rights job at the Department of Education. When Thomas moved to the EEOC in 1982, Hill went with him. She left Thomas in 1983, taking a position as a professor at the new O. W. Coburn School of Law at Oral Roberts University in Tulsa, and moving in 1986, when the Coburn School folded, to Oklahoma University Law School in Norman.

Attractive, professional, and proper, Hill seemed to radiate credibility. She wore a turquoise suit and light jewelry; her wavy hair was cut shoulder-length. The caucus room seemed like a Yale Law School reunion. In fact, Joan and I had planned to travel to New Haven that weekend to attend my thirty-fifth law school class reunion. But the Senate gathering was almost as extensive. Thomas, a Yale Law graduate, was introduced by alumnus Danforth; alumna Hill was questioned by me and would be followed by a host of alumni witnesses, including Susan Hoerchner for Hill and John Doggett for Thomas. In New Haven the

364

alumni at the reunion were glued to the television watching their class-mates in the Senate Caucus Room.

If I had questioned Hill in a court case, I'd have had lots of help and lots of time to prepare. In the Senate all I had had were a few hours, working alone. At the outset I thought we might reconcile Hill's version with Thomas's version, on the basis of Hill's initial statement to the FBI and the Judiciary Committee that I had read the night before. That hope vanished shortly after Biden gaveled the hearing to order.

At 10:00 A.M., Anita Hill passed out a statement and began to read it. As it progressed, it was explosive—substantially expanded and different from her earlier statement to the Judiciary Committee and the FBI. When I read and listened to Hill's October 10 statement, I knew any chance of reconciliation was gone.

In her October 10 testimony, Hill expanded her earlier passage on Thomas's alleged remarks about pornography. Now Thomas was portrayed as more than a mere watcher. Hill read, "On several occasions, Thomas told me graphically of his own sexual prowess."

Later in her statement Hill added an allegation about a bizarre episode, along with more allegations about Thomas's boasts: "One of the oddest episodes I remember was an occasion in which Thomas was drinking a Coke in his office. He got up from the table at which we were working, went over to his desk to get the Coke, looked at the can and asked, 'Who has put pubic hair on my Coke?' On other occasions, he referred to the size of his own penis as being larger than normal, and he also spoke on some occasions of the pleasures he had given to women with oral sex."

"I may have used poor judgment early on in my relationship with this issue," Hill said, concluding. "I was aware, however, that telling at any point in my career could adversely affect my future career. And I did not want early on to burn all the bridges to the EEOC." Initially, as I read Hill's statement as she testified, I was very surprised at how different this was from what she had described earlier. The sweep and details of her testimony went far beyond the September 23 report I had seen.

Special FBI Agent Jolene Smith Jameson, one of the two agents who took Hill's September 23 statement, swore out an affidavit the day after Hill's October 10 testimony outlining "contradictions" between Hill's two accounts: In Hill's Senate testimony, Agent Jameson wrote:

Professor Hill made comments that were in contradiction with statements she had made to SAs Jameson and John B. Luton. . . . Professor Hill stated she could only recall specifics regarding the pornographic incidents involving people in sex acts with each other and with animals. Ms. Hill never mentioned Judge Thomas saying how well endowed he was. Hill never mentioned or referred to a person named "Long Dong Silver" or any incident involving a Coke can, all of which she testified to before the Senate Judiciary Committee.[2]

At a trial, two statements so much at variance from the same witness could impair or even destroy her credibility. Why did Hill give one set of facts on September 23 and then a different set on October 10? In a trial context, a cross-examiner would have hammered the differences.

Hill's account, on its face, had inconsistencies beyond those Thomas had listed in his morning testimony. When Thomas was named chairman of the EEOC, he had asked Hill to accompany him to the commission and continue as his assistant. Hill said she agreed to go because Thomas had stopped making sexual overtures and because she feared she would lose her job at the Department of Education if she stayed. But Hill had a protected employee status—she would not have lost her job. She claimed she didn't know she was a protected-class employee.

Hill had made no notes about Thomas's abuses, even while she was documenting her every assignment. She had moved with Thomas from the Department of Education to the EEOC after his alleged advances. And Hill had made efforts to stay on good terms with Thomas for years after she'd stopped working for him. She had phoned Thomas eleven times at his office over eight years, according to logs Hill didn't dispute. Once she said, "Just called to say hello. Sorry I didn't get to see you last week," according to the phone logs. Another time she left the message, "In town till 8/15," along with a hotel phone number. And those were only the calls that had not gotten through to Thomas immediately, causing Hill to leave messages. Thomas told me that more often Hill phoned his office, found he was unavailable, and told Thomas's secretary not to bother leaving a message. When Thomas had spoken at Oral Roberts University while Hill was teaching there, she'd driven him to the airport after the program. Hill and Thomas appeared to be on the best of terms.

After Hill finished her statement, Biden turned to me for questioning. I'd thought that I would begin with personal references to the similarity in our backgrounds. Hill and I were both "Sooners," in a sense,

366

since we had both spent time at the University of Oklahoma. The school had adopted the nickname Sooners from the nineteenth-century races in covered wagons, in which those who arrived first claimed the land. Hill was a real Sooner, having been born and raised in Oklahoma, while I was more of a "Later," having spent my college freshman year at the University of Oklahoma. I gave some thought to reminiscing a little, talking to her a little about Norman, Oklahoma, and how the campus had changed.

The thought crossed my mind, although I didn't consider bringing it up, how different it was having this polished, attractive African-American woman on Oklahoma University's law school faculty, contrasted with my day at the school, when an African-American woman was kept outside the classroom door.

In 1947, when I was a freshman at the University of Oklahoma, an African-American woman, Ada Lois Sipuel, wanted to attend the university's law school. This was seven years before *Brown* v. *Board of Education*. There had been a law school for African-Americans in Oklahoma City, but it closed, so the university system brought Sipuel to Norman and put her in a chair outside the classroom door. That way, they reasoned, she could see and hear the professor but would not be in the same room with the white students. When the hallway arrangement proved impractical, officials moved Sipuel inside the classroom, but put her in a playpen-type fence. Eventually, when everyone realized the playpen was ridiculous, it came down.

While I didn't consider recounting the Sipuel story to Hill, I did think about noting that she and I were both graduates of Yale Law School, as were so many others involved in the hearing. I thought about pointing out that I'd expected to be in New Haven on that very morning attending my thirty-fifth law school reunion. I contemplated asking Hill if her reunion was that year. I didn't know offhand whether she was a graduate of a class ending in either 1 or 6, which were the reunion classes that year.

But after rolling these thoughts through my mind, I decided not to mention them. The time was limited, and once I'd heard Hill's testimony, I knew it wasn't going to be easy. Also, I didn't want to appear casual or patronizing. I decided to keep the discussion at a very serious, professional level.

In retrospect, I think my approach was a mistake. It would have established a little rapport and perhaps eased some of the tension if someone in my position had been friendlier and less formal. Still, I was painstakingly polite. David Gergen of *U.S. News & World Report* said that evening on *The MacNeil/Lehrer NewsHour* that I had been "very respectful" to Professor Hill.

I was conscious of Marshall McLuhan's admonition about television being a "hot medium" that requires the subject to be cool. I wasn't going to sacrifice substance, but I did try to be low-key, considerate, and courteous to Professor Hill and to all witnesses. I was aware from prior hearings and C-SPAN repeats that television cameras are very strong, and the sound systems pick up every nuance. And I was aware of David Garth's admonition that sometimes when I say "Good morning," I sound tough.

Nobody, during the hearing or afterward on videotape, has found an abrasive or offensive moment in my questioning of Hill. Even my 1992 campaign opponent, Lynn Yeakel, who based her campaign on the Hill-Thomas hearings, simply showed footage of Hill and me in her TV spots without any voices. If Yeakel had found any question or comment by me harsh, she surely would have shown it in her campaign commercials.

I wasn't averse to Hill. I didn't want to embarrass her. I didn't plan to impugn her credibility. I wanted to find out what had happened. I began by asking Hill about the various differences among her accounts, such as her earlier public and private praise of Thomas, contrasted with her portrait of Thomas in her recent complaints, and the new material that she hadn't told the FBI on September 23. "You referred to the 'oddest episode I remember,' then talked about the Coke incident," I said. "Why, if this was such an odd episode, was it not included when you talked to the FBI?"

"I do not know," Hill said. She said the FBI agents had told her it was regular procedure to come back for more specifics, if necessary. That answer was insufficient. The FBI may have said something like that to her, but that didn't mean they wanted a partial statement. FBI Special Agent Jameson, in her affidavit following Hill's October 10 testimony, would write:

Professor Hill stated she didn't discuss specific incidents in detail because the interviewing Special Agent had advised her that, if the subject was too embarrassing, she didn't have to answer. In fact, SA Luton apologized for the sensitivity of the matter, but advised Professor Hill that she should be as specific as possible and give details. She was further advised if the questions were too embarrassing SA Luton [who was male] would leave the room and she could discuss the matter with SA Jameson [who was female]. . . . Professor Hill stated she had been advised early in the interview that SA Luton would recontact her at a later time to obtain more specific details. In fact, SA Luton advised Professor Hill, only at the termination of the interview, that a follow-up interview might be necessary if further questions arose.[3]

I asked Hill about some inferences she had made. "Professor Hill, you said you took it to mean that Judge Thomas wanted to have sex with you, but in fact he never did ask you to have sex, correct?"

"No, he didn't ask me to have sex," Hill said. "He did continually pressure me to go out with him, continually, and he would not accept my explanation as being valid."

"So that when you took it to mean 'We ought to have sex,' that was an inference that you drew?" I asked.

"Yes, yes," Hill said.

I decided to ask Hill about a *USA Today* story that asserted Hill had been told that if she made a complaint, Thomas would withdraw and she would not have to come forward. I asked her about this contention literally nine different times, nine different ways. Hill maintained that the suggestion had never been made.

"Professor Hill," I said, "*USA Today* reported on October ninth, 'Anita Hill was told by Senate staffers her signed affidavit alleging sexual harassment by Clarence Thomas would be the instrument that "quietly and behind the scenes" would force him to withdraw his name.' Was *USA Today* correct on that, attributing it to a man named Mr. Keith Henderson, a ten-year friend of Hill and former Senate Judiciary Committee staffer?"

"I do not recall," Hill said. "I guess— Did I say that? I don't understand who said what in the quotation."

"Well, let me go on," I said. "He said, 'Keith Henderson, a ten-year friend of Hill and a former Senate Judiciary Committee staffer, says Hill was advised by Senate staffers that her charge would be kept secret and her name kept from public scrutiny.' Apparently referring again to Mr. Henderson's statement, 'they would approach Judge Thomas with this information and he would withdraw and not turn this into a big story, Henderson says.'"

In other words, according to the *USA Today* story, Senate staffers were trying to enlist Hill in a plan to scare Thomas out of the confirmation battle. As David Brock wrote in his book *The Real Anita Hill*, staffers used a carrot-and-stick approach: "Hill had to be convinced that coming forward *then* was the only course that would allow her to avoid publicity. If she moved first, she could control the process, maintain anonymity, and prompt Thomas's quick withdrawal—or so she was led to expect."[4]

"Did anybody ever tell you that, by providing the statement, that there would be a move to press Judge Thomas to withdraw his nomination?" I asked.

"I don't recall any story about pressing, using this to press anyone," Hill replied.

"Well, do you recall anything at all about anything related to that?" I asked.

"I think that I was told that my statement would be shown to Judge Thomas, and I agreed to that."

"But was there any suggestion, however slight, that the statement with these serious charges would result in a withdrawal," I asked, "so that it wouldn't have to be necessary for your identity to be known, or for you to come forward under circumstances like these?"

"There was— No, not that I recall," Hill said. "I don't recall anything being said about him being pressed to resign."

"Well, this would only have happened in the course of the past month or so, because all this started just in early September," I said.

"I understand," Hill said.

"So that when you say you don't recall, I would ask you to search your memory on this point. . . . I would just ask you once again, and you say you don't recollect, whether there was anything at all said to you by anyone that, as *USA Today* reports, just by having the allegations of sexual harassment by Clarence Thomas, it would be the instrument that 'quietly and behind the scenes' would force him to withdraw his name. Is there anything related to that in any way whatsoever?"

"The only thing I can think of, and if you will check, there were a lot of phone conversations," Hill said. "We were discussing this matter very carefully, and at some point there might have been a conversation about what might happen."

"Might have been?" I asked.

"There might have been," she continued, "but that wasn't— I don't remember this specific kind of comment about 'quietly and behind the scenes' pressing him to withdraw."

"Well, aside from 'quietly and behind the scenes' pressing him to withdraw, any suggestion that just the charges themselves, in writing, would result in Judge Thomas withdrawing, going away?"

"No, no," Hill said. "I don't recall that at all, no."

I gave Hill another chance, asking her to tell me about the conversation she said might have occurred. "Well, I can't really tell you any more than what I have said," she replied. "I discussed what the alternatives were, what might happen with this affidavit that I submitted. We talked about the possibility of the Senate committee coming back for more information. We talked about the possibility of the FBI, asking, going to the FBI and getting more information; some questions from individual senators. I just— The statement that you are referring to, I really can't verify."

I gave Hill yet another chance. "When you testified a few moments ago that there might possibly have been a conversation, in response to my question about a possible withdrawal, I would press you on that, Professor Hill, in this context: You have testified with some specificity about what happened ten years ago. I would ask you to press your recollection as to what happened within the last month."

"And I have done that, Senator," Hill told me, "and I don't recall that comment. . . . To be honest with you, I cannot verify the statement that you are asking me to verify. There is not really more that I can tell you on that."

I tried a different approach. ". . . But when you talk about the withdrawal of a Supreme Court nominee, you are talking about something that is very, very vivid, stark, and you are talking about something that occurred within the past four or five weeks, and my question goes to a very dramatic and important event. If a mere allegation would pressure a nominee to withdraw from the Supreme Court, I would suggest to you that it is not something that wouldn't stick in a mind for four or five weeks, if it happened."

My time running out, I tried one last time. "Would you not consider it a matter of real importance if someone said to you, 'Professor, you won't have to go public. Your name won't have to be disclosed. You won't have to do anything. Just sign the affidavit on this,' as the *USA*

Today report would be the instrument that 'quietly and behind the scenes' would force him to withdraw his name. Now, I am not asking you whether it happened. I am asking you now only, if it did happen, whether that would be the kind of a statement to you which would be important and impressed upon you, that you would remember in the course of four or five weeks."

"I don't recall any specific statement," Hill said again, "and I cannot say whether that comment would have stuck in my mind. I really cannot say that."

"Over the luncheon break, I would ask you to think about it further," I said, "if there is any way you can shed any further light on that question, because I think it is an important one."[5]

After this exchange Biden recessed the committee. Biden told me in November 1998, "It was clear to me from the way she was answering the questions, she was lying."

"At that point I truncated the hearing and recessed it early for lunch," Biden said. "I turned to my chief of staff and said, 'Go down and tell her lawyers that if her recollection is not refreshed by the time she gets back, I will be compelled to pursue the same line of questioning the senator [Specter] did. Because it seems to me, she did what he said.' "[6]

Biden, as the committee's chairman and top Democrat, would have carried great sway if he had suggested publicly that Hill was lying when she repeatedly answered questions about Thomas's potential withdrawal by saying she didn't remember. The underlying point was that Hill wanted to do the minimum necessary to get Thomas rejected. Her position was the converse of a nominee who wants to answer only as many questions as he must to get confirmed. At first Hill wanted her allegations about Thomas circulated without senators even knowing where they came from. When Biden insisted that Hill make a formal statement, she gave a statement to the Judiciary Committee and the FBI, which went a certain distance. When Thomas didn't withdraw and Hill had to testify, she added substantially to her statement. Her pattern of wanting to say as little as possible to get Thomas rejected, and saying more when she had to, raised these questions: How far would she go to defeat him? What were the facts? Why not "the truth and the whole truth" from the outset? There is also a principle in the law, *Falsus in uno, falsus in omnibus,* meaning if a witness lies about one material issue, he or she is suspect of lying about everything. That principle wasn't conclusive, but it wasn't irrelevant either.

After the lunch recess, Hill returned to the witness table. "When my time expired," I said to her, "we were up to the contact you had with Mr. Brudney on September 9. If you could proceed from there to recount who called you and what those conversations consisted of as it led to your coming forward to the committee?" Brudney, a Labor Subcommittee staff director who worked for Metzenbaum, had been one of the first staffers to talk to Hill about her complaint. Brudney and Hill had attended law school together.

"Well, we discussed a number of different issues," Hill said. ". . . We talked about the process for going forward. What might happen if I did bring information to the committee. That included that an investigation might take place, that I might be questioned by the committee in closed session."

Hill added, "It even included something to the effect that the information might be presented to the candidate and to the White House. There was some indication that the candidate—excuse me—the nominee might not wish to continue the process."

I looked at Hill, surprised. "Mr. Brudney said to you that the nominee, Judge Thomas, might not wish to continue the process if you came forward with a statement on the factors which you have testified about?" I asked.

"I am not sure that is exactly what he said," Hill said. "I think what he said was, depending on an investigation . . . whether the Senate went into closed session and so forth, it might be that he might not wish to continue the process."

"So Mr. Brudney did tell you that Judge Thomas might not wish to continue to go forward with his nomination, if you came forward?" I asked.

"Yes," Hill said.

"Isn't that somewhat different from your testimony this morning?"

". . . I guess, Senator, the difference in what you are saying and what I am saying is that that quote seems to indicate that there would be no intermediate steps in the process. What we were talking about was process. What could happen along the way. What were the possibilities? Would there be a full hearing? Would there be questioning from the FBI? Would there be questioning by some individual members of the Senate? We were not talking about or even speculating that simply alleging this would cause someone to withdraw."

"Well, if your answer now turns on process," I said, "all I can say is that it would have been much shorter had you said, at the outset, that Mr. Brudney told you that if you came forward, Judge Thomas might withdraw."

After an interruption by Senator Ted Kennedy and some back-and-forth with Hill, I asked, "Is that what you meant, when you responded earlier to Senator Biden, that the situation would be controlled 'so that it would not get to this point in the hearings'?"

"Of the public hearing," Hill said. "In entering into these conversations with the staff members, what I was trying to do was control this information, yes, so that it would not get to this point."[7]

Biden's statement to Hill that he would pick up on my questioning after lunch undoubtedly concerned Hill and her advisers. Skepticism or worse from the Democratic chairman could have been disastrous for Hill. Hill's afternoon modification of her morning testimony, therefore, was not only deliberate but calculated to avoid greater erosion to her credibility.

Questioning of any witness should try to find the facts and test credibility. If Professor Hill would falsely state what had happened a few days before, what was the quality of her testimony on everything else she said, about events that allegedly took place ten years earlier?

In cross-examination a lawyer would say, "When you tell us you didn't know something that you now concede you did know, why should we believe you on other matters covered in your testimony?" That's what happens in a trial. You go through the evidence, the statements she's made, and challenge her on the basis of her false or inconsistent statements.

That Friday afternoon I questioned Hill on the various inconsistencies in her account. During Hill's morning testimony, immediately after she denied being advised that her charges might prompt Thomas to withdraw, I had said, "Professor Hill, the next subject I want to take up with you involves the kind of strong language which you say Judge Thomas used in a very unique setting, where there you have the chairman of the EEOC, the nation's chief law enforcement officer on sexual harassment, and here you have a lawyer who's an expert in this field, later goes on to teach civil rights, and has a dedication to making sure that women are not discriminated against."

I continued, ". . . What went through your mind, if anything, on whether you ought to come forward at that stage—because if you had, you'd stop this man from being head of the EEOC perhaps for another decade. What went through your mind? I know you decided not to make a complaint, but did you give that any consideration, and if so, how could you allow this kind of reprehensible conduct to go on right in the headquarters without doing something about it?"

"Well, it was a very trying and difficult decision for me not to say anything further," Hill replied. "I can only say that when I made the decision to just withdraw from the situation and not press a claim or charge against him, that I may have shirked a duty, a responsibility that I had, and to that extent I confess that I am very sorry that I didn't do something or say something. But at the time, that was my best judgment. Maybe it was a poor judgment, but it wasn't a dishonest and it wasn't a completely unreasonable choice that I made, given the circumstances."

In the afternoon I took up other weaknesses in Hill's account. "Did you ever maintain any notes or written memoranda of the comments that Judge Thomas had made to you?" I asked.

"No, I didn't," Hill said.

"As an experienced attorney and as someone who was in the field of handling sexual harassment cases, didn't it cross your mind that if you needed to defend yourself from what you anticipated he might do, that your evidentiary position would be much stronger if you had made some notes?"

"No, it did not," Hill said. ". . . Well, it might have been a good choice to make the notes. I didn't do it, though." Hill said she had documented her work, making notes of every assignment. She said she had done so to show a new employer how quickly she turned around assignments. I suggested the finished product alone should be ample for any prospective employer.

Turning to the timing of Hill's complaint, I asked her about the six-month statute of limitations on sexual harassment cases, which is shorter than every major criminal statute. "In the context of the federal law limiting a sexual harassment claim to six months because of the grave difficulty of someone defending themselves in the context, what is your view of the fairness of asking Judge Thomas to reply eight, nine, ten years after the fact?"

"I do not believe it is unfair," Hill said. "I think that it is something that you have to take into account in evaluating his comments."

Indeed, the time frame was something that we had to take very heavily into account. In the law a prompt complaint is a critical element in any she said/he said, one-on-one dispute, especially one that involves sex. If the woman does not make a prompt complaint on a rape charge, the case is materially weakened. That is because, if the incident really happened and the woman was outraged, the odds are there would be a prompt complaint. That is not always so. But the absence of a prompt complaint generally weighs heavily in jurors' minds.

Granted, a woman has a lot of reasons not to complain promptly: She's shocked, she doesn't know what to do, she doesn't want to be derided, she doesn't want the publicity and the problems. Perhaps the law imposes too much of a burden on a woman who has just undergone a horror. But traditionally the doctrine of prompt complaint is a cornerstone of the law governing sexual offenses.

"You have added, during the course of your testimony today, two new witnesses whom you made this complaint to," I said to Hill. "When you talked to the FBI, there was one witness and you are testifying today that you are now 'recalling more,' that you had 'repressed a lot.' And the question which I have for you is, how reliable is your testimony in October 1991 on events that occurred eight, ten years ago, when you are adding new factors, explaining them by saying you have repressed a lot?"

"Well, I think if you start to look at each individual problem with this statement, then you're not going to be satisfied that it's true," Hill said, "but I think the statement has to be taken as a whole."

Needless to say, I continued to look at each individual problem with her statement. I asked her about her decision to move with Thomas from the Department of Education to the EEOC, after he had allegedly harassed her. "Professor Hill," I asked, "did you know that, as a class-A attorney, you could have stayed at the Department of Education?"

"No, I did not know that at the time," she said.

"Did you make any effort to find out that, as a class-A attorney, you could have stayed on at the Department of Education?"

"No . . . I relied on what I was told by Clarence Thomas. I did not make further inquiry."

I asked Hill about phoning Thomas eleven times after she had stopped working for him, an issue she had told the *Washington Post* was "garbage."

"I do not deny the accuracy of those logs," she said in response to my questions. "I cannot deny that they are accurate, and I will concede that those phone calls were made, yes."

"Each of those calls were made in a professional context," Hill said. "Those calls that were made, I have attempted to explain, none of them were personal in nature; they involved instances where I passed along casual messages or instances where I called to either find out whether or not the chairman was available for a speech, acting on behalf of someone else."

"You say that they were all professional," I said, "and you have accounted for a number of them in your statement, but a number of them have not been accounted for. For example, the log on January 30, 1984, 'Just called to say hello, sorry she didn't see you last week.' May 9, 1984, 'Please call.' October 8, 1986, 'Please call.' "

The log indicated a message from Hill to Thomas on August 4, 1987, in which Hill left her phone number and indicated she would be in town until August 15. Hill said her recollection was that Thomas's secretary had asked her how long she would be in town, that Hill had not volunteered that information. Even confronted with the phone logs, Hill gave no ground. "No, they have very little, if any, relevance at all to the incidents that happened before those phone calls were made," she said.

"Very little relevance, but perhaps some?" I asked.

"I believe they have none," she replied. "We may differ on that."

Indeed, we did.

Hill finished testifying at 7:40 P.M. Thomas returned to the caucus room to testify again. He vehemently and categorically denied Hill's allegations, as he had been doing since they surfaced. Thomas said he had never asked Hill out socially, had never discussed sex with her, and had never made crude remarks. He testified that he had always made sure not to "commingle" his professional and personal lives.

Becoming animated, Thomas went further, saying Hill's charges played into sexual stereotypes of black men, the same point he'd made when I questioned him in Danforth's office just before the morning committee vote. "This is something that not only supports but plays into the worst stereotypes about black men in this society," he said, his voice rising. "And I have no way of changing it, and no way of refuting these charges!" Later Thomas would call the hearings "a high-tech lynching for uppity blacks."

The news accounts varied, but most credited Hill with weathering rigorous examination. On the *MacNeil/Lehrer NewsHour* Friday night,

Roger Mudd said, "Although Senator Specter had made several dents in her account, Anita Hill was still holding her own as the day ended."

David Gergen, the *U.S. News & World Report* editor and future Clinton adviser, was asked on the *MacNeil/Lehrer* show whether I'd been able to avoid coming off as badgering Professor Hill, who was seen as a sympathetic witness. "I think he has done a superb job so far," Gergen replied. "He's been very respectful of her, but at the same time, from his colleagues' point of view, from his Republican colleagues' point of view, he is gradually building up on the edges of the story, a number of instances in which she is disagreeing with other people about a perception of what happened or what she said. . . . I think he's gradually building up a case that the Republicans can say this woman is very sincere but she's fantasizing; she's somehow made something up in her own mind, for whatever reason; we don't understand it."

Mark Shields of the *Washington Post*, who often plays counterpoint to Gergen, agreed with him. "I think Arlen Specter did a super job today," he said, given the difficulty of exploring holes in the story of a sympathetic witness.

Not all the comments were complimentary. Tom Shales wrote in the *Washington Post,* "Under merciless, snide, supercilious interrogation from Senator Arlen Specter, Hill had an answer for every question, never losing her cool, never losing her composure." Calvin Trillin featured my questioning of Hill in a syndicated column headlined WHO WAS MOST REVOLTING?

The night of Friday, October 10, after Hill finished testifying, I took the hearing transcript home but didn't read it. It had been a very tiring day. I had a drink and went to bed. I woke up in the middle of the night and could not get back to sleep. I went through the transcript line by line, underlining and rereading Hill's statement and growing dismayed at Hill's repeated, categorical denials to me that she'd ever had a conversation about Thomas's withdrawing, followed by her change in testimony.

I thought, here was a witness who would bob and weave: You went with him to EEOC from Education. Well, I had to keep my job. You phoned Thomas eleven times, including to "just say hello." The calls were professional. She had an excuse for everything.

Later, while questioning Thomas on Saturday, I said, "It is my legal judgment, having had some experience in perjury prosecutions, that the testimony of Professor Hill in the morning was flat-out perjury, and that she specifically changed it in the afternoon, when confronted with the possibility of being contradicted, and if you recant during the course of a proceeding, it is not perjury . . ."

My charge about Hill's veracity was not unfair or inappropriate, and it was legally correct. The precedents are conclusive that a person can be convicted of perjury for an "I don't know" answer. The following Tuesday, when the Thomas nomination was debated on the Senate floor, no one challenged my legal conclusion that Professor Hill had committed "flat-out perjury." Many senators, including a former federal judge, former prosecutors, and many lawyers, opposed Thomas and my arguments, but no one disputed my legal conclusion of perjury.

But my remark about perjury was impolitic. "I didn't know quite how to put it," I told the *Washington Post* a few days later. "What do you do when you realize that someone has committed perjury? When I reached that conclusion, I expressed it. I think I was legally correct, emotionally perhaps too hard, and, as it turns out, politically unwise." Across America my remark sparked outrage among women and some men.

I was a lightning rod for criticism. In the caucus room and on the Senate floor, Ted Kennedy took me on. Kennedy interrupted me at a crucial point in my questioning, trying to throw me off track, when I was trying to resolve with Hill the question of whether Senate aides had told her Thomas might withdraw in the face of her charges. "Mr. Chairman," Kennedy broke in, "could we let the witness speak in her own words rather than having words put in her mouth?"

"Mr. Chairman," I said, "I object to that. I object to that vociferously. I'm asking questions here. If Senator Kennedy has anything to say, let him participate in this hearing." Kennedy, contending with some personal scandals, had been practically invisible during the proceedings.

Later, while we were both on the Senate floor, Kennedy said, "There is no proof that Anita Hill has perjured herself, and shame on anyone who suggests that she has." Aside from that assertion, Kennedy made no effort to contradict my analysis on perjury.

"We do not need characterizations like shame in this chamber from the senator from Massachusetts," I said.

"I reiterate, Mr. President," Kennedy railed, "I reiterate to the senator from Pennsylvania and to others, that the way that Professor Hill was treated was shameful." Kennedy's generalizations didn't deal with Hill's specific testimony or the perjury issue.

Later Hatch joined the fray. "The fact of the matter is, anybody believes that, I know a bridge up in Massachusetts that I'll be happy to sell them, with the help of Senator Kennedy." Hatch said later he meant no reference to Chappaquiddick.

I summarized Hill's perjury in a floor statement October 15:

> But the substance here is what did she say? In the morning, nine questions responding to the way she answered, but always seeking the critical fact as to whether a Senate staffer said Judge Thomas might withdraw, and she said no. Then in the afternoon . . . she says in response to my question, "So Mr. Brudney did tell you that Judge Thomas might not wish to continue to go forward with his nomination if you came forward?" Professor Hill said, "Yes."
>
> . . . In rereading this testimony it seemed to me that there was an intentional misstatement of fact.

While I do not doubt the accuracy of my assessment of Hill's testimony as flat-out perjury, a more difficult question is whether I should have kept my conclusion to myself. My father used to say, "Know what you say, don't say what you know." My statement on "flat-out perjury" is probably the only well-remembered specific of my role in the hearings, and was at the center of fierce criticism of me.

If Hill *had* committed flat-out perjury, that was certainly important to the outcome of the hearing, which turned on credibility. I was the one to whom Hill had directed her false testimony. Perhaps, then, I was in the best position to say it was false. All that is true, but incomplete. If I had concluded that she was lying and Joe Biden had, too, my Senate colleagues and the public might have been trusted to reach their own conclusions. It might not have been necessary for me to say what I thought. Every witness to those hearings poured the testimony through the colander of his or her own personal experience. People didn't necessarily need me or anyone else to tell them what to think. Minimally useful as my conclusion was, it instantly identified me as a "bad guy" with most people who believed Anita Hill.

In the cauldron of the hurried hearings where the committee was directed by the Senate to finish by the close of business on Sunday (we actually concluded in the middle of the night), I decided to express my legal judgment because I thought it necessary for those not as deeply involved to understand what was happening.

During breaks in the hearings, the national media blanketed the caucus room. Correspondents stalked the halls for senators to put on national television. I'd never seen anything like it. Andrea Mitchell was sending direct feeds to NBC in New York, where Tom Brokaw was anchoring. Peter Jennings was doing the same for ABC. On Friday, October 11, *MacNeil/Lehrer* gave its entire sixty-minute show to the Hill-Thomas conflict and billed the program "Moment of Truth." When we held executive committee meetings, it was hard to get senators to attend. They were out giving interviews.

The hearing had caught everybody by surprise. My press secretary was home in Philadelphia, my chief of staff had gone away for the weekend, and nobody was in the office. The Senate dining room was closed for the weekend, along with the various take-out shops. I'd been giving interviews in the corridors and had a limited time before I had to return to the hearing. I wound up walking to Union Station, a few blocks away, to get sandwiches for Joan and myself. Neither the Senate nor the senators were prepared for the weekend media circus.

GETTING IT

Clarence Thomas finished testifying in the evening of Saturday, October 12. The next day the Judiciary Committee heard from expert witnesses and from panels of witnesses who supported Thomas and Hill.

Hill's original corroborator was her friend and law school classmate Susan Hoerchner, then a workers' compensation judge in California. Hoerchner proved a poor witness, offering only a vague recollection of events, botching dates, and seeming nervous. Hill's three other witnesses included her friend and onetime romantic interest John Carr; American University professor Joel Paul, who had once recruited her for a teaching job; and her friend Ellen Wells. They all said Hill had told them about Thomas's behavior shortly after it had allegedly occurred. But none could recall Hill mentioning any graphic sexual terms, and Carr and Paul couldn't be sure Hill had been talking about Thomas.

When I questioned Hoerchner, I began with her October 10 statement to Senate staff that she was the only one Anita Hill had told about Clarence Thomas's conduct. For several minutes we tried to sort through what Hoerchner had told the staffers, what she had concluded from earlier conversations with the FBI, what mistakes Hoerchner had made in her accounts, and which mistakes she had formally corrected. Finally I said, "Well, let me ask you this: Did you say anywhere in this interview that when you had said Professor Hill told you that you were the only one she had told this about, that you were incorrect on that?"

"I don't think that I explicitly retracted that," Hoerchner replied. "I do believe that was incorrect."

Soon afterward I asked Hoerchner, "Well, did she tell you about the sexual harassment after she moved from the Department of Education to the EEOC?"

"I have made clear to the FBI and in the staff interview that I simply cannot pin down the date with certainty," Hoerchner said.

David Brock wrote in *The Real Anita Hill* that Justice Department lawyers knew—but did not tell me—that Hoerchner had said in a previous statement that her conversation with Hill had taken place in the spring of 1981. "They had been reluctant to pass the tip on to the Senator, who prided himself on his independence, not to mention his reputation as a prosecutor. . . . Had Specter hit the target, it would have been apparent to all—including a national television audience—that Hill's conversation with Hoerchner, if it had taken place at all, could only have been an allegation about sexual harassment at Wald, Harkrader & Ross, the law firm where she was working prior to September 1981, and before Hill ever met Clarence Thomas."[1] In fact, Thomas would tell me in July 1999 that Hill had told him, when she first applied for a job with him, that she left the Wald, Harkrader law firm because her boss pressed her for dates and the unwanted sexual attention hurt her work.

I asked John Carr and Joel Paul, Hill's other corroborating witnesses, whether Hill had identified Thomas by name as her boss who had been making sexual advances. Carr said, "I don't recall that she did, no." Paul eventually said, "I don't know, Senator."

On the other side, two independent written statements suggested that Hill had fantasized Thomas's harassment. One came from Charles Kothe, dean of the Oral Roberts Law School, who knew both Thomas and Hill, and the other from John Doggett III, a lawyer and international management consultant from Austin who had met Hill at a Washington social gathering. Doggett said that years earlier Hill had fantasized his own romantic interest in her, to the point that she lectured him for leading her on.

Doggett wasn't scheduled to be a witness. I woke up in the middle of the night again Saturday night and decided I wanted his testimony. Doggett's response about fantasizing, which was nearly identical to Kothe's, warranted hearing from him. I phoned Doggett around five-thirty Sunday morning, Texas time, to urge him to come to Washington. He caught a plane and testified that night, as did Kothe. When Doggett turned out to be unhelpful to Thomas's case, that was okay with me; I wasn't trying to prove anything.

On Sunday afternoon the Judiciary Committee had a fascinating discussion in executive session about whether we should close off the witness list. Assembling a complete panoply of witnesses was just like making the ballistics tests and other simulations that the staff had to fight for during the Warren Commission—without them the investigation would be incomplete. We just weren't doing our job here.

I urged that we extend the hearings, do more investigation, and call more witnesses. There were outstanding matters we should have gone into, such as an allegation that Hill had complained of sexual harassment at a law firm where she had worked; some potential evidence, including Hill's hospitalization records, that might have clarified whether she'd complained about sexual harassment at the time of Thomas's alleged acts; and, according to Senator Alan Simpson, a purported affidavit from University of Oklahoma students that Hill had sprinkled term papers with pubic hair.

Simpson, the rangy Wyoming Republican, remarked about a deluge of allegations against Hill, "And now I really am getting stuff over the transom about Professor Hill. I've got letters hanging out of my pocket. I've got faxes. I've got statements from her former law professors, statements from people that know her, statements from Tulsa, Oklahoma, saying, 'Watch out for this woman.' "

The caucus felt like a locker room at halftime of the Super Bowl, with both teams present. And nobody could quite figure out what to do. We had more problems than senators. Late on Sunday afternoon I suddenly inherited another big problem assignment. I was handed a transcript of Angela Wright's October 9 telephone deposition, sixty-nine pages long, which I was seeing for the first time. Strom Thurmond then told me it was my job to question Wright later during the Sunday session. Adequate preparation would take hours. I barely had minutes.

One witness we certainly should have called was Angela Wright, who also claimed that Clarence Thomas had pressed her for dates and made unwelcome sexual remarks. Wright would have been the second woman to make such charges against Thomas. All of Hill's other witnesses had simply corroborated her account that she had complained about Thomas's conduct, or had vouched for her character. Wright's account could have been powerful, because sexual harassment is generally habitual behavior, and Hill had so far been the only one ever to accuse Thomas of it.

Angela Wright, thirty-seven, an assistant metro editor at the *Charlotte Observer* in North Carolina, had been Thomas's press secretary at the EEOC from March 1984 until May 1985. She was considered attractive but tough and combative. She said that Thomas made crude remarks to her, including asking her the size of her breasts.

Wright had given her lengthy deposition during a telephone interview to Senate staffers of both parties. "You know you need to be dating me," Wright quoted Thomas as telling her. "You're one of the finest women I have on my staff. You know we're going to be going out eventually." Wright had been subpoenaed and scheduled to testify Sunday, and had flown to Washington for the occasion.

We should have called Wright, I thought, just as the commonwealth has an obligation to produce all eyewitnesses at a murder trial, whether they will help or hurt the prosecution. Good, bad, or indifferent, Angela Wright belonged at the witness table. Her allegations suggested a common motive, plan, scheme, or design, and thus would have been admissible in a court of law.

Angela Wright was the sole additional witness that some of my Republican colleagues wanted to call. But they did not want her testimony out of a sense of legal thoroughness. They wanted her testimony because they thought she would make a lousy witness. Thomas had fired Wright in April 1985 because, Thomas testified, she had called a co-worker a "faggot."

Some thought Wright's firing would give her a motive for revenge against Thomas and that this could be used to discredit her. Thomas wasn't the first boss to fire Wright. Before joining the EEOC, Wright had been fired from a job with former Congressman Charlie Rose (D-N.C.). About to be fired from a job at the Agency for International Development for poor work performance, Wright had resigned flamboyantly, accusing her supervisor, Kate Semerad, of racism. Wright sent her written complaint about Semerad to the Senate, where Semerad was up for a confirmation as assistant administrator for External Affairs. The Senate found Wright's charges without merit and confirmed Semerad.

Some Republican senators insisted that we call Wright. Her credibility was so poor that it would tar Hill and help Thomas, they said. Another school of thought held that any additional witness—no matter how weak—who accused Thomas of harassment could sink the judge's nomination.

Then there was some discussion about Anita Hill's having been hospitalized for stomach pain. Could we get the records? Did we have to have her consent? Should we subpoena them? And there was Hill's alleged sexual complaint at a law firm, and how were we going to find out about that? Somebody brought up porn star Long Dong Silver, suggesting Hill had concocted her account based on his exploits.

The caucus was bedlam. Hill's charges had become an international hot potato. Here it was 5:00 P.M., we had many witnesses to put on, and Joe Biden was determined to finish on Sunday, or early Monday morning. The Judiciary chairman wanted to complete the record and give senators a day to prepare for Tuesday's floor debate and vote.

I reiterated, "We've got to do this right; we need time." The only senator at that executive session who agreed with me that we should extend the hearings was Hank Brown from Colorado. When we returned to open session, I made a formal motion that we seek more time.

Most senators didn't say anything. Biden said no, we had to finish, we had a charge from the Senate to come back and finish it, and finish it we would. Biden was under orders from Majority Leader Mitchell to get it done. The general sentiment was to wrap up. Senators didn't like working on Sunday, especially when we had worked all day Saturday. We were tired. Sometimes our work isn't good even when we *are* well rested. We certainly were exhausted by these final caucuses on Thomas's nomination.

I had made my motion to extend the time because I didn't feel we should be bound by the majority leader's schedule, especially under significantly changed circumstances. We had a lot of work to do. We were dealing with a Supreme Court nomination, and an extra day or two would be warranted.

Danforth, who opposed extending the hearings, wrote in *Resurrection* that he had changed his mind:

Arlen Specter, in contrast, thought we were moving too fast. . . . All those matters deserved attention. There was a second reason for Arlen's concern: fatigue. The committee was moving too quickly and its members were too fatigued to do an adequate job. I did not agree with Arlen at the time. I do now. Then I wanted the end to come. Now I believe that a more deliberate process would have been more orderly, fairer, and more comprehensive in developing the case for Clarence.[2]

My formal motion to take more time for the hearing failed 12–2, with only Brown and me in favor. The Democrats apparently felt that Angela Wright's reliability would invite much doubt, and the skepticism would rub off on Hill. Senators on both sides of the aisle opposed calling Wright but didn't want the appearance that the Senate had refused to hear her. They wanted the appearance that Angela Wright didn't want to testify. There was some talk about seeing if Wright would withdraw or state her unwillingness to testify, to make her absence at the witness table mutually agreed upon.

"So why didn't Angela Wright testify?" asked the *Washington Post* in an October 1994 profile of the would-be witness. "It's a simple question that should have a simple answer. But interviews with dozens of participants in the hearings produce no clear explanation, and several disparate theories."[3]

The panels of witnesses ran past midnight. Late in the evening Biden interrupted the proceedings to announce that Angela Wright had decided not to testify. He read us an excerpt from a letter he faxed her. Biden's letter, on Judiciary Committee letterhead, read in full:

Dear Ms. Wright:

It is my preference that you testify before the Judiciary Committee in connection with the nomination of Judge Clarence Thomas. But, in light of the time constraints under which the committee is operating, and the willingness of all the members of the committee to have placed in the record of the hearing the transcripts of the interviews of you and your corroborating witness, Ms. Rose Jordain, conducted by majority and minority staff, I am prepared to accede to the mutual agreement of you, and the members of this committee, both Republican and Democrat, that the subpoena be vitiated. Thus, the transcribed interviews of you and Ms. Rose Jordain will be placed in the record without rebuttal at the hearing.

I wish to make clear, however, that if you want to testify at the hearing in person, I will honor that request.[4]

Ultimately, Wright's statement was placed in the record in lieu of her testimony. "By bipartisan agreement, the 37-page [in smaller type] transcript of her interview with Senate staffers was released to the press in the wee hours of the morning, and was effectively buried in the avalanche of more spellbinding telegenic events,"[5] the 1994 *Washington Post* retrospective said. In the *Post* the following day, it was mentioned on page A17. To this day, few people outside the Beltway recall that there ever was another woman, that the great he said/she said showdown was at one point shaping up as he said/they said. I don't think Wright's testimony would have changed the outcome, but she should have been called.

Biden gaveled the hearing closed at 2:03 A.M. that Monday. We hadn't reached a conclusion as to whether Hill's charges were true.

On the Senate floor during Tuesday's debate, I squeezed thirty minutes out of Thurmond, who controlled time for the Republicans, to lay out the case against Hill's testimony. Nobody challenged my legal analysis.

Who was telling the truth? Anita Hill? Clarence Thomas? I don't think anyone will ever know for sure. The weight of the evidence supported confirming Thomas, I said. Whatever had happened between them, it wasn't so bad as to stop Hill from following Thomas from the Department of Education to the EEOC. Whatever had happened between them, it wasn't so bad as to stop Hill from trying to maintain their relationship well after that. Whatever had happened between them, it wasn't so bad as to stop Hill from writing to Thomas to invite him to give a lecture, and then driving him to the airport.

Granted, it was very difficult for the fourteen men on the Judiciary Committee to understand the attitude of a woman in Hill's circumstance. But her charges had to be seen in the context of waiting until the last minute to come in and then drastically expanding her story.

My net assessment was that I didn't know what had happened between those two people ten years earlier, but whatever it was, it wasn't bad enough to disqualify Thomas in Hill's mind until ten years later, and therefore it should not disqualify Thomas to us.

The full Senate voted October 15 on Clarence Thomas's nomination to become the 106th Justice of the U.S. Supreme Court. The tally was 52–48, the narrowest margin by any successful nominee in the Court's history. I voted for Thomas and would vote the same way today. The president is entitled to some deference. There wasn't enough evidence to disqualify Thomas.

"I believe that he is intellectually, educationally, professionally qualified," I said on the Senate floor. I had stated my reservations about Thomas at great length in three earlier floor statements. Even one of Thomas's fiercest opponents, Professor Drew Days of Yale Law School, had conceded that Thomas was intellectually qualified.

I remained concerned about several issues from Thomas's testimony. I worried that Thomas would further an alarming Supreme Court trend of making law instead of interpreting it, in violation of the oaths that justices swear when they take office. Congress—and not the Court—

has the responsibility for making law. I was concerned that a revisionist Court was trampling on congressional intent.

Thomas had shown disdain for Congress, saying in an April 1988 speech, "Congress is no longer primarily a deliberative or even a law-making body. . . . There is little deliberation and even less wisdom in the manner in which the legislative branch conducts its business." I had asked Thomas head-on if he would pursue an agenda on the bench to overrule congressional intent, as his writings suggested. Thomas insisted, under oath, that he would follow congressional intent and that he had no agenda. I accepted his statement. In any case, Thomas did not pose anywhere near the threat to the constitutional process that Robert Bork had posed.

On the positive side, I was impressed by Thomas's account of watching criminals outside his window when he was a judge and thinking, There but for the grace of God go I. He understood the challenges of an underprivileged background. My reading of Thomas's opinions led me to believe that he was a solid judicial craftsman with a healthy streak of independence. I also thought he brought needed diversity to the Court and could serve as a role model for African-Americans and other minority group members. Thomas's background, beginning fatherless in segregated Pin Point, Georgia, would bring a unique perspective to the high Court. I believed that Thomas could be a positive role model for African-Americans even though he opposed affirmative action and other mainstays of the establishment African-American community. In fact, Thomas opposed affirmative action vehemently, arguing that it hurts the intended beneficiary, whom it brands as inadequate and traps in dependency.

Many in the Democratic hierarchy, along with the mainstream African-American leadership, opposed Thomas because of his different perspective. I didn't like that, even though I disagreed with Thomas on affirmative action and other issues. I don't believe in litmus tests, either for or against conservatives, or for or against pro-life or pro-choice nominees.

"I know that in Pennsylvania, in Philadelphia, we have a one-party system and have had for more than forty years," I said on the Senate floor. "And the possibility of having a role model or a conservative Republican who shows great success in climbing the ladder of success is something that is worthwhile in our society—not a reason to nominate a man, but a by-product worth noting."

The Thomas hearings, to say the least, were flawed. The Senate should never hold a confirmation hearing without adequate preparation. Notice, a right to be heard, and enough time to prepare are all constitutional requirements. In Thomas's case, they were not met. Also, we should hold closed executive sessions on such sensitive subjects as sexual harassment. The Intelligence Committee and the Ethics Committee both hold closed hearings on sensitive matters.

I was invited to Thomas's house for a victory celebration the night he was confirmed. I declined. I didn't consider Thomas's confirmation a victory. It wasn't a defeat either. It was just another tough day on the job. I thought I had done my job, and my duty.

Before his confirmation hearing, I'd met Clarence Thomas twice. The first time came immediately after the 1984 presidential election, when Bill Coleman, Thomas, and I met in the Senate dining room to talk about opening the Republican Party to more African-Americans. I had known Coleman since the late 1950s, when we worked for competing Philadelphia law firms in the antitrust field, and we'd served together as Warren Commission lawyers before he became secretary of transportation in the Ford administration.

Over the years Coleman and I had lamented our party's failure to encourage women and minorities to join our ranks. Bill called me in early 1985 and said Clarence Thomas was an up-and-coming African-American and we should get together to talk. Over bean soup we laid out a comprehensive battle plan. Thomas would have to do most of the work, Coleman some. After a year, when nothing had been done, I reconvened the group and began by asking the two of them to pay their shares of last year's lunch because they hadn't performed as promised. They laughed, and I picked up the lunch check again. We made more big plans, and again nothing was done to recruit African-Americans to the Republican Party. I next saw Thomas during his confirmation hearings for the court of appeals for the D.C. circuit. He was watched closely, not so much for that seat, important as it is, but for his potential to move up to the Supreme Court.

For years after his confirmation hearing, I saw Thomas only occasionally, exchanging greetings at Supreme Court–Senate functions. Our first extended conversation occurred in the Senate dining room in June 1999, when I saw Thomas having breakfast with Senator Chuck Grassley. I joined them and jokingly told Thomas that I had to talk Grassley into voting for him, which brought hearty laughs from both men. They laughed louder when I added that Grassley had fed me all the questions I'd asked Professor Hill. We then talked about Thomas's confirmation hearing, leading me to suggest a more extended discussion—if Thomas was so inclined. I told him I was writing a book that included his Supreme Court confirmation fight. We agreed to meet the following Friday morning when both the Court and Senate would be out of session.

Walking back to my own table in the Senate dining room, I passed a large round table about twenty feet from Thomas, where Senator Barbara Boxer was presiding over a meeting of Democratic congresswomen. Boxer, along with then–Congresswoman Pat Schroeder, had led the famous Congresswoman Charge up the Senate steps in October 1991 against Thomas's confirmation. Barbara and I had since been on the same side of a number of issues, and we enjoyed an easy, friendly rapport, prompting me to quip that she could renew her protest against Thomas that morning without walking too far. My suggestion drew laughs from most—but not all—of the group.

At 9:30 A.M. three days later, on July 2, 1999, Thomas and I met in my Hart Building Senate office. I was on my way to his chambers when I found that Thomas wanted to come to my office instead. My seventh-floor office faces the shorter Supreme Court building, leading some to say we look down on the Court. The Senate and the Supreme Court, with appropriate symbolism, are separated by Constitution Avenue.

When Thomas entered my office, he immediately focused on an NBC-TV artist's drawing of my March 1994 argument before the Supreme Court in which I had unsuccessfully challenged the decision to close the Philadelphia Navy Yard. Thomas asked me what I thought of the experience. I said it was the fastest thirty minutes of my life, with seven of the nine justices interrupting each other as well as me with questions. "Only Justice Blackmun and you didn't enter the fray," I reminded him. Thomas smiled and gave a short, well-reasoned rationale for his notorious silence on the bench during oral argument. Thomas said lawyers should have the opportunity in their limited time allotted to develop their arguments as they see fit. Interrupting questions always change the substantive flow, and in any event, the questioning justice could probably find the answer in the briefs.

Thomas opened our discussion on his confirmation hearing by saying this was the first time he'd discussed the matter, except for a brief talk with former Senator Jack Danforth. Thomas said he'd never wanted to be a judge but agreed to give it a try when asked to serve on the D.C. circuit, a position he came to like very much. He emphasized he had no interest in rising to the Supreme Court when Justice Marshall resigned. He was surprised and his "heart sank" when President Bush nominated him to the high Court at their very brief July 1991 meeting in Kennebunkport, Maine. Thomas said Bush requested only that he "call them as he saw them" and asked just one question: whether Thomas and his family felt comfortable about going through the confirmation process.

I asked Thomas about my personal view that, in retrospect, he would prefer not to have become a justice, considering what he had to go through to be confirmed. He was ambivalent. He suggested that the position wasn't worth the travail, lamenting his loss of anonymity and all the criticism. But Thomas also said he liked being on the Court and thanked God every morning that he could serve with eight such wonderful colleagues.

Justice Thomas thanked me for, as he put it, "standing in the breech" to question Hill's charges. He said he was surprised I had done so, because he and I were not ideologically close. I said it was a matter of fundamental fairness to question Hill closely, especially when her testimony expanded so materially from the statements she gave the Senate and FBI shortly before. Although almost eight years had passed, Thomas was obviously still pained by the hearing, which, he contended, should never have occurred so long after the allegations and with no corroboration.

We had a spirited exchange in my office on Thomas's failure to watch Hill's testimony. He insisted there was no point in watching it, since he knew it was all false. I countered that he should have watched Hill testify to know what to refute. Thomas, who during our talk steadfastly declined to comment on senators' questions, did disagree with Senator Howell Heflin's criticism of him for not watching Hill testify. I reminded the justice that I had made the same point at the hearing.

We reminisced about our brief meeting in Danforth's office the day of the committee vote. Thomas said I was the only senator who asked him questions about Hill before the matter was publicly disclosed. When I asked about his "high-tech lynching" remark, he said it was not a spur-of-the-moment comment, but that he had written it down earlier, noting that he had studied the real lynchings of African-Americans in the South.

Our two-hour conversation moved to recent Supreme Court decisions limiting the power of Congress and striking a different balance on state-federal relations. Taking care not to intrude into confidential matters, I asked about alliances among Court voting blocs and the "activism" of the five-justice majority: Rehnquist, O'Connor, Scalia, Kennedy, and Thomas. The justice spoke forcefully, in depth, and intellectually on the issues.

Over the years I've often been asked my views of Thomas's performance on the Court. In the early 1990s I expressed disappointment with his voting record and opinions, while noting that many justices take time to bloom. More recently I've praised some of his opinions, saying they reflected scholarship beyond the work of even excellent clerks. In our two-hour discussion I developed a new respect for Thomas's intellect and potential. During his confirmation hearing I questioned him closely on many substantive matters and constitutional issues. His 1999 responses differ materially from the 1991 answers. In addition, Thomas's 1999 spirited rebuttal of Hill's charges was much more compelling than the 1991 Thomas, who would not even watch Hill on television. If Thomas had projected the same intellect and passion in the 1991 hearings that he did during our 1999 meeting, I think more than fifty-two senators would have voted to confirm him.

Thomas has complained—and rightly so—that many holier-than-thou critics go after him out of racism, because he is an African-American conservative who opposes affirmative action. Thomas espouses a "pull yourself up by your bootstraps" approach. I don't think he is hypocritical because he took advantage of the system as he found it and, after experiencing the system, thinks that others would be better off if they had to compete without any preferential treatment by affirmative action. While I don't agree with him, I can see his point of view. Thomas has become more outspoken in recent years, blasting liberal groups for boycotting his speeches and condemning generally what he calls "the new intolerance." I think Thomas has a right to speak out against people who criticize him. Freedom of speech is a two-way street.

The special-interest battles and cultural wars that engulf Washington can be vicious when big-stakes issues come to town. No contests are more important than Supreme Court confirmations. That fifth vote in 5–4 decisions determines who will be born (abortion), who will die (the death penalty), and numerous important questions in between. When Judge Bork was selected, the knives were out of their sheaths the moment the nomination was out of President Reagan's mouth. The 2:30 P.M. presidential announcement was followed just eight minutes later by Senator Ted Kennedy's battle cry against Bork on the Senate floor. Although I opposed Bork because I thought his views threatened decades of sound constitutional construction, I abhorred the Madison Avenue tactics used against him. That battle was winnable on the merits, without the smears.

Similarly, Thomas's confirmation process was immediately sullied by devious tactics. Such stuff has become a part of our political process, including the politics of Supreme Court nominations and confirmations. Negative ads routinely smear, defile, and defeat honorable and decent candidates for elective offices. Soft money soils elections. Campaign finance reform is stymied by big money, trying to keep its cohorts in office, and by misguided arguments that freedom of speech entitles the rich to spend all they want for their own candidates or to hide behind fraudulent, so-called independent expenditures.

Clarence Thomas was subjected to one of the toughest public pummelings in history—if not *the* toughest. While his confirmation battle raged, I said feelings were intensified because the forty-three-year-old nominee might serve for forty years. I reminded Thomas of that during our meeting. He corrected me. He said he intended to serve until he was a hundred. I replied that I would tell Strom.

Justice Thomas shows potential for more growth. Justice William O. Douglas voted to uphold eavesdropping and invasion of privacy in his early days on the Supreme Court in *U.S.* v. *Goldman* in 1940. He later became a great civil libertarian. In his early fifties, Justice Thomas has decades to prove his critics wrong. He has a sign in his chambers that reads PATIENCE IS AN HONEST MAN'S REVENGE. He may have the last laugh, and he has a very hearty laugh.

After spending the two hours with Justice Thomas, I wrote to Professor Hill seeking comments on the hearings from her perspective eight years later. As of this writing, she has not replied.

To many people I am the senator who grilled Anita Hill. Would I prefer to have avoided the ordeal? Absolutely not. The hearing on Thomas's nomination was an important moment in American history for many reasons, not least of which were the tremendous advances that women have made from it. I was glad to play a part.

But I felt a backlash immediately. "In the past week, the Pennsylvania Republican with a strong voting record on women's issues has been castigated by women's groups, called Public Enemy No. 2 by feminist Betty Friedan (President Bush was No. 1) and become the object of fury from women all over the country for his surgical questioning of Prof. Anita Hill,"[6] the *Washington Post* reported. " 'I did not realize the extent of the anger,' says Specter, shaking his head as he tries to make sense of the past few days. 'I walked out of the Senate chamber yesterday and a woman said, "God should strike you dead." I got an obscene gesture from the staffer of a prominent woman politician. I really felt sort of betrayed. I've been with them 999 times out of a thousand. I'm doing a job fairly and properly, and they're responding like this. It's just not basic civility.' "

As David Brock wrote, "Hill's credibility was not tested, but simply asserted to enhance the 'he said, she said' melodrama. . . . But when one GOP senator, Pennsylvania's Arlen Specter, attempted to probe deeper, he was vilified in the media as if asking reasoned questions of an accuser were a crime."[7] Brock added later, "Much of the outrage, in fact, seemed to be directed at Specter's highly skeptical, plodding manner in grilling the witness. In addition, as the only senator on either side of the aisle who moved the hearings onto the grounds of fact, he did more than anyone to highlight Hill's credibility problems."[8]

That outrage was widespread and long-lasting. On inauguration day, January 20, 1993, I was riding down in the senators' elevator in the Hart Office Building when the car stopped on three. An enormous man walked into the elevator followed by a petite woman, whom I recognized as Barbra Streisand, the singer and movie star. I never stop anybody from entering the senators-only elevator, least of all such a major taxpayer. I said, "Hello, Ms. Streisand, I'm Arlen Specter."

She said, "Yes, I know who you are, and I don't like the way you treated Anita Hill."

I asked, "What took you so long to bring that up?"

She countered, "And it's Strei-sand, not Strei-zand."

I was perceived as too harsh. Biden said my prosecutorial approach makes me win the battle but lose the war. In the case of Anita Hill, he said, I established weaknesses in her account but came across as unfairly ferocious in doing it. "I believe strongly that this was about the single most significant social debate of the nineties," Biden said in our November 1998 postmortem. "Harassment and the relationship between men and women . . . it is deep. It is like a volcano. And you were sitting on top of it, pouring hot water into the volcano. You know, it doesn't really get you very far."

The day after the vote on Thomas, I appeared on *Nightline*. I hadn't wanted to do the show, for a lot of good reasons, but Ted Koppel pressed, and I finally relented. Koppel said *Nightline* would do an hour show on the hearings, from 11:00 P.M. to midnight, instead of its usual half hour beginning at 11:30 P.M. ABC did the show from 216 Hart, an auditorium in the modern Senate building. Once we were under way, the network further extended the show from midnight to 12:30 A.M., then to 1:00, to 1:30, then to 2:00 A.M. The show finally finished at 2:17.

Toward the end of the marathon, Harriet Woods of the National Women's Political Caucus, said:

> Well, all I have to say is, you still don't get it, do you, Senators? You still don't get it. . . . Women were not part of this process. The country would have been saved a lot if there had been somebody who had been alert to and sensitive to the importance of this issue. . . . I can assure you that there are a lot of us who are going to try to make sure that there are some women Senators there and will try to plug into this interest that's going around the country. But in terms of the process, it was disconnected, it seems to me, from the life experience of the person whose allegations you were trying to examine.

There is merit to what Woods and other critics said. Women on the Judiciary Committee would have given us a different point of view. The Senate—and the committee—would soon have them. One angry woman, in fact, would soon be running against me.

After the vote, I immediately scheduled open-house town meetings throughout the state, to face Pennsylvanians. The meetings were packed, and the crowds were furious. I explained why I had done what I had. Clearly, I had an enormous problem. Principally, it was women who were irate, but some men, too. In fact, some of the men had also been sexually harassed. I learned a lot about sexual harassment in those meetings.

I convened a group of four women, including members of prominent women's groups and Joan, to hold a strategy session with me at my house one Sunday. The tough part, politically, was finding something to say that would express my feelings without retreating.

I wound up saying that the hearings were a learning experience for me and, for that matter, for America, too; that I had not known how painful it was for women who were watching the questioning, so many of whom had been victims of sexual harassment and saw themselves, almost through transference, in Hill's position. When Hill was said to have lied, they felt that they, too, were not believed. And they knew they were telling the truth. It was only after the hearings had ended and I talked to many women that I found out how painful it had been for them to watch the questioning, and how painful the entire proceeding had been.

I wasn't going to apologize, because I'd done nothing wrong. I wouldn't apologize, even if it cost me my seat, just as my refusal to endorse Frank Rizzo for police commissioner cost me the 1967 mayor's election.

In October 1997, in the Oklahoma City airport, Joan's luggage cart became entangled with another woman's purse strap as we were preparing to board a flight for Houston. Untangling the bags, I looked up and saw Anita Hill. Quite surprised, I said, "Hello, Professor Hill." Hill looked at me and said, "Senator, Senator," either not remembering my name, which I doubt, or not wanting to utter it. We exchanged brief greetings and headed for our seats on the plane to Houston.

For some time I'd thought there should be a rapprochement between the antagonistic sides in the 1991 hearings. I knew that Hill and Thomas could never have a rapprochement, but I thought that she and I might. I'd sounded out some people who knew us both, but I decided to do nothing before my 1998 election, lest any overture seem politically motivated. I thought Anita Hill and I could find some common ground where we could collaborate, such as women's health, where I've supported increased federal funding as chairman of the Appropriations Subcommittee on Health and Human Services.

Shortly after takeoff I walked to Hill's aisle seat and suggested that there were some funding measures in my subcommittee where she might be able to provide helpful testimony. She said she would be glad to consider that. When I asked for her telephone number, she said she was listed in the Norman, Oklahoma, directory, and I should call her.

Early the following week, after returning to Washington, I got a phone call from a reporter for the *Washington Post*'s style section, who mentioned the flight. The reporter said that Hill had commented that I hadn't apologized. I said that was true and added that there was no reason for an apology.

I was then a little surprised to see the following item in the *Post* style section on October 24, 1997:

Last Sunday, Specter "spoke to me as if the bad thing that happened at his hand didn't really happen. It was sort of chitchat. It was bizarre," Hill told The Source yesterday.

"At first I was shocked and I was thinking, 'Am I mistaken or aren't you the person who accused me of flat-out perjury?' His reaction to me said that it had been part of his political game and it wasn't personal," noted Hill, who was in town hyping her book, "Speaking Truth to Power."

She called herself a "captive audience" when she found herself on an Oklahoma City–Houston flight with Specter, who was returning from a college reunion. They chatted briefly. "He did mention something to the effect that he would like to be in touch with me about women's issues. What is this? Some political bone I am supposed to appreciate? . . . An apology would be a good start."[9]

THE SHRIEK LEVEL

My questioning of Anita Hill almost cost me my Senate seat. The Thomas hearing had spawned "The Year of the Woman," in which an unprecedented number of women would run for, and win, seats in the Senate and House. My role in that hearing thrust me into the most complicated race of my career, and certainly my toughest Senate fight.

David Garth, my political consultant, mused recently, "I think that God has decided that Arlen's never going to have it easy. A lot of that problem is imposed on him, and a lot of those problems he makes for himself. I mean, if I ever dreamed of ever running for public office, looking at Arlen convinced me not to."

In my first Senate victory in 1980, the primary and general campaigns had both been tough. In 1986, in my first Senate reelection bid, I had faced Congressman Bob Edgar, an ordained Methodist minister and six-term House veteran from suburban Philadelphia. Smart, skilled, and good-looking, Edgar was, in George Will's words, "an unreconstructed, undiluted liberal."[1] Edgar's campaign, as the *New York Times* put it, "appears more like a social movement than a conventional electoral contest."[2]

In 1985, with the campaign heating up, a *New York Times* reporter informed me that the White House said if I did not vote for the MX missile, President Reagan would not come to Pennsylvania to raise $1 million for my campaign. I told the reporter, "He's not invited." The *New York Times* reported March 15, 1985:

> White House officials said Thursday that Republican senators up for re-election in 1986 are being informed that President Reagan's involvement in their campaigns will be limited unless they support administra-

tion programs. . . . The official added, ". . . The truth of the matter is going up and raising a million bucks for Arlen Specter in April this year goes a long way towards him having an easier time raising money. If he's not there with us, let him raise the money by himself." Informed of the comment, Senator Specter, a Pennsylvania Republican who is up for re-election in two years, said: "I'm prepared to raise my money by myself if somebody's talking about a quid pro quo. I have been told an early fund-raiser by the President was set for me this spring, and nobody raised any question with me about a quid pro quo."[3]

Shortly afterward, Reagan came to a Tuesday Republican senators' lunch, as he did from time to time. After the president spoke, I sought recognition. With about fifty senators in the room, I told Reagan that the administration's pressure meant I could not vote for the MX missile even if I wanted to, because an "aye" vote would look like a sellout. I was furious about the challenge to my integrity—the implication that I could be bought. The *Washington Post* reported on March 20, 1985:

> Specter was furious. At a meeting Friday night in Philadelphia with a coalition of MX activists, he denounced White House aides and said he was so mad he had to "go to the steam room to cool off."
>
> Yesterday, when Reagan came to lobby senators at the Capitol, Specter questioned him about it directly. "I told him I thought it was very destructive and very debilitating for senators to have that happen," Specter said.[4]

Vice President Bush called me the afternoon the *Times* story ran. Bush urged me to ignore the anonymous White House aide's comment and to do whatever I wanted to do on the MX vote but not to use the *Times* story as a reason to vote against the missile. I decided to vote for the MX, which I had been inclined to do, but I announced I would not have the president raise money for me. As the *New York Times* reported in June 1986, "Commitments are often costly in politics, but rarely as costly as the stand taken last year by Senator Arlen Specter. . . . 'I made the commitment that I would not call upon the President for fund-raising in order to avoid any misunderstanding on the independence of my vote on the MX,' he said. . . . And he is abiding by it, although he said he realized the cost. 'In comparable situations, the President has raised in excess of a million dollars,' the Senator said. 'But I'm not complaining.' "[5]

After I voted for the MX, former Secretary of State Henry Kissinger called to congratulate me for putting aside the insult and voting for the missile. Then he asked if there was anything he could do for me. I said, "Mr. Secretary, perhaps a fund-raiser would not produce a million dollars, but how about coming in?" And he did. Kissinger proved a big draw, although nowhere near as big as President Reagan would have been. He also had a profitable evening. He left the fund-raiser with four of Joan's pies in his arms.

On October 1, 1986, five weeks before the election, Edgar came within one point of me in our tracking polls. The congressman said he could go to sleep and get 45 percent of the vote. He campaigned hard and got 43 percent of the vote. But Republicans lost seven Senate seats and control of the Senate. Republican senators had been pressed to walk the plank and vote the party line on many unpopular votes, such as opposing a motion to add $7 million for children's inoculations and cutting Social Security. The 1985 vote against the Social Security COLA was an exercise in futility, because Reagan ultimately agreed to the increase.

Five years later, in October 1991, the clouds cleared the morning after the Clarence Thomas vote to reveal the size of the mountain I would have to climb to win reelection in 1992. Dirt from that mountain fell on Joan, who was running for reelection to the Philadelphia City Council. Although she was ultimately reelected to her fourth four-year term, many people opposed her to send a message to me. When she turned to helping on my women's outreach, she felt the fury, characterized by an early encounter she related:

We got these buttons made, "Another Woman for Arlen Specter." When they first came out, I wore one. And I don't usually wear buttons, even mine or Arlen's. I just don't wear buttons. But, anyway, we had just gotten them. So I put it on and I was having lunch with [former city solicitor] Charisse Lillie. There was a table of three women next to us and one woman, particularly, kept staring at me.

So, finally, she leans over to me and she says, "How can you be for him?"

Charisse said, "She's married to him."

Well, the woman, I thought she would fall through the floor. And she was so apologetic. She ruined my entire lunch, because she wouldn't stop apologizing. So I said her, "Well, what do you know about Arlen?"

Well, she only knew Anita Hill.

That's how it was. I mean, how many people lean over in a lunch and make a comment like that? But that is the level we were at.

Joan formed a team of women to fight for me. They made speeches, held meetings, wrote letters to the editor. She helped me understand where I stood with women and the feelings that were out there. Joan found that we were not going to win many converts to our position on Anita Hill. "It became clear to me that I was really going to neutralize people more than anything else," she said. "I wanted to get that shriek level down." My daughter-in-law Tracey pitched in, especially in the Philadelphia suburbs, where every household was targeted and bombarded by both sides.

In the 1992 Republican primary, I beat State Representative Steve Freind 65–35. Freind, a social conservative, had written Pennsylvania's restrictive abortion law. The primary had grown heated at times, including a fistfight between my press secretary, Dan McKenna, and Freind's aide. After the primary, Freind supported me.

In the Democratic primary, Lynn Yeakel, a suburban Philadelphia millionaire and head of Women's Way, a women's fund-raising agency, won a surprise victory in a five-way contest. From the time Yeakel announced her candidacy, she had been running against me. "Did this make you as angry as it made me?" she asked in a TV ad showing silent footage of my questioning Anita Hill. Yeakel, though a congressman's daughter, was essentially a political neophyte. And a one-issue neophyte, hammering my questioning of Hill. Her theme was "I want to retire Arlen Specter." Second only to the presidential contest, my race drew the most national attention in 1992. "For women in Pennsylvania and around the country," wrote the *St. Louis Post-Dispatch*, "the Specter-Yeakel race has become something of a referendum on the Thomas hearings."[6]

Yeakel wasn't my only obstacle. Oliver Stone's movie *JFK* came out in December 1991 and called me a liar by name. I had no time to fight a lawsuit against Stone, but I wanted to attack *JFK*, partly through TV spots. Garth and Shanin talked me out of it. Ignore it, they counseled wisely.

In 1992 I urged President Bush to take initiatives on stimulating the economy and reforming health care for a confluence of reasons: good public policy and to elect Republicans like him and me. The economy needed a boost, but there was gridlock between the White House and Capitol Hill.

In proposing legislation, the High-Value Economic Growth Act of 1992 with Senator Pete Domenici (R-N.M.), I noted in an April 9 Senate floor speech, "The president submitted an economic recovery package to the Congress which was rejected. And the Congress in turn submitted an economic recovery package to the president which was vetoed."

Domenici and I then extracted five common proposals from both plans for our compromise legislation: a $5,000 tax credit for first-time home buyers, the Specter-Domenici proposal for penalty-free withdrawals from IRAs, the president's proposal for a 15 percent investment tax credit, passive loss liberalization for real estate professionals, and modification of the debt-finances income rules. We omitted a cut in the capital-gains tax, even though fifty-six senators had voted for it, because that was short of the sixty votes needed to invoke cloture (cut off Senate debate), and the vast majority of Democrats opposed that provision.

On a plane trip to Pennsylvania that spring, I had a chance to lobby President Bush and his chief of staff, Sam Skinner, for about thirty minutes on our economic growth plan but was unsuccessful because the president insisted on including his capital-gains cut, which killed a possible compromise. As is often the case on legislative matters, the perfect was the enemy of the good.

Efforts to persuade Bush to act on health care also failed. Republican leader Bob Dole was very helpful to Bush in 1992, just as he had been in the 1988 presidential campaign after Dole lost the nomination to Bush. Dole would convene all the Republican senators, who would make suggestions to Bush from soundings in their own states.

At one such caucus in the summer of 1992, I pressed the president hard on health care. The issue had been spotted by Senator Bill Cohen of Maine early in his 1990 reelection campaign. After Democrat Harris Wofford's victory on this issue over Republican Dick Thornburgh in the special 1991 election to fill John Heinz's unexpired term, it was a no-brainer to address health care.

I had pressed Majority Leader George Mitchell (D-Maine) to take up my legislation, S 1995, on a specified date. On the Senate floor on July 29, 1992, I challenged Mitchell, noting that he had given a date certain to product liability the day after Labor Day, and pressed him to give a date certain for health-care legislation. But Mitchell declined. Despite my efforts and the efforts of many others, we simply could not get President Bush to act on these critical issues.

My relationship with George Bush had always been very friendly. I first met him in the summer of 1978, when he was relaxing playing tennis at the home of a mutual friend in the Philadelphia suburbs, Hal Haskell, a former mayor of Wilmington, Delaware. Shanin was his driver for that day. During his eight years as vice president, on occasions when he presided over the Senate, he would signal various senators, including me, to come up to the chair for friendly chats. Several times he invited me to the vice president's office, off the Senate floor, to discuss some issue, followed by a photograph that turned up on my desk a few weeks later with a cordial inscription. Bush was an inveterate note-writer, penning warm, chatty comments on five-by-seven cards. Like many others, I picked up this habit.

Our friendly relationship was strained by a speech Bush made in Philadelphia's Congress Hall on April 3, 1992 to limit senators to two terms. It seemed strange and out of line to me that he would choose to address that topic in my hometown with me in the audience when I was running for a third term. On our plane ride from Washington to Philadelphia, I came close to breaching protocol and bringing up the term-limits issue with Bush personally. I had already raised hell with his staff, to no avail. But I decided not to confront the president head-on because the issue was the centerpiece of his speech, and I surmised that advance copies had already been distributed, so a change would focus even more attention on the issue.

I felt very uncomfortable sitting in the audience while he recommended term limits and spoke against the proposition of a third Senate term. I felt that all eyes and cameras were on me, but they really weren't. Fortunately for me, the press paid little attention to the speech. I didn't get a single media query about the president's remarks.

The only time President Bush forcefully complained to me was when I refused to vote to sustain his veto on the cable bill. Through Senator Dole's legislative mastery, all thirty-five of the president's vetoes had been sustained until October 1992. I had voted in favor of the telecommunications bill because I thought it was good legislation. No special point had been made prior to the vote that Republican senators should rally to support the president's position. After Congress passed the legislation and the president vetoed it, it became a cause célèbre, with a White House full-court press.

At my one-on-one meeting with the president at 8:30 A.M. on September 25, 1992, Bush sat at his desk and I sat in a chair by his side. The photograph of the session looks cordial, but the conversation was not.

"Mr. President," I said, "if I were to have supported your position, I would have to have voted against the bill. But how can you bring me in after I voted in favor of the bill, and you veto it and ask me to support your veto? I just cannot do that. I'm up for reelection, too. But this is just the wrong thing to do."

"This is really a bad bill," President Bush said. "I really need you to do this, Arlen."

"I'd like to help you, but I can't," I replied. "If you had this position, the least you should have done was to ask me not to vote for the bill, to support you on a position you were going to take." I voted against the president's veto. That was the first override of a Bush veto, and the bill passed.

President Bush's loss in 1992 was a personal disappointment to me and a loss to the country. Votes around the nation mirrored the Pennsylvania tally, where Governor Bill Clinton of Arkansas drew 45 percent, George Bush 36 percent, and Ross Perot 18 percent. The Philadelphia suburbs were especially disappointing for the president. Traditionally, a Republican must carry Philadelphia's four bedroom counties—Montgomery, Delaware, Bucks, and Chester—by about 100,000 votes to carry the state. My majority in 1992 was 92,000. Surprisingly, the president lost those counties to Clinton.

The early attributes of George Bush the tough battler, the scrappy Yale first baseman, and the fighter pilot seemed lacking in his 1992 campaign. He was always truly decent, but a presidential campaign also requires toughness and occasional boldness. Bush didn't seem to be focused on carrying out some of the basics.

Meanwhile, a close friend of mine had died: John Heinz was killed in April 1991, at fifty-two, when his plane collided with a helicopter over a schoolyard in suburban Philadelphia. With John's passing, the country lost a statesman and a precious voice for centrism and pragmatism, Pennsylvania lost a powerful advocate and skilled senator, and I lost an ally whose counsel I had valued.

Early on, Shanin sized up the challenge precisely: The only way we could win was to run a perfect campaign while Yeakel made significant mistakes. Yeakel did make mistakes. She held a waffle breakfast to highlight what she considered my waffles in the Senate but couldn't name a single waffle when asked in a television interview with Pittsburgh's ABC affiliate, WTAE. "I think, let's see," she stammered. "Hang on a minute, let me think about that. Do you mind? Just for a second." We ran a devastating TV spot showing her fumble. "If she can't get her facts straight now, what's she going to do in Washington?" our voice-over asked.

Yeakel had also failed to pay Philadelphia income taxes for eleven years. She wrote the city a check for $17,856 the day before she announced her candidacy. She endorsed two candidates for the same office. She held a news conference in front of a shut-down store in Erie to blast me and Republican economics, but it turned out the store had folded under Jimmy Carter, before I was first elected. Yeakel also belonged to a country club with no African-American members.

One Yeakel ad called me "the most obnoxious man in the Senate." The Pennsylvania Citizens Jury, formed by the League of Women Voters, found that spot "very objectionable," the Associated Press reported. In the second of our two debates, we had an exchange that the *New York Times* saw fit to print in its entirety. The *Times* described our voices "rising and choking with anger" in a key flurry:

> YEAKEL: You know, Arlen Specter is in the mud pile with George Bush. He has been attacking my character since the day I won the primary.
> SPECTER: That's not true.
> YEAKEL: He has been diverting attention from the real issues of this campaign, and I want to tell you something. He is not running for prosecutor, he is running for the United States Senate. And he is not going to sit here and humiliate me the way he humiliated Anita Hill.
> SPECTER: I've been waiting for that for a long time.
> YEAKEL: I know you have.
> SPECTER: Here we are, back to the single issue.

"Political professionals said it was a campaign milestone because it was the first time Mr. Specter had attacked his opponent so strongly," the *Times* concluded.[7] I thought my comments were mild.

The *Philadelphia Inquirer*, even in endorsing Lynn Yeakel, questioned her competence. Yeakel's campaign "has at times left our confidence shaken," the paper wrote.[8] I picked up an unusual endorsement, from fabled Penn State football coach Joe Paterno. Paterno, who had caught flak for endorsing George Bush, attended one of my speeches on the Penn campus. Afterward reporters asked Paterno whether he was endorsing me for reelection. The Nittany Lion pawed the ground, as was his habit. Finally he said, "Well, if I've got a running back in there, and he's making yardage, and he's not tired, I leave him in. I'd leave Arlen Specter in."

The race, in the end, played out according to Shanin's no mistakes/mistakes formula. "Lynn Yeakel, arguably the least experienced major party candidate for national office this year, has made costly mistakes during her quest to become a U.S. Senator," wrote the *Boston Globe*. "Her Republican rival, Sen. Arlen Specter, has had far more funding and has run a nearly flawless race."[9] The *St. Louis Post-Dispatch* wrote in a summary piece, " 'He's run a textbook kind of campaign' says G. Terry Madonna, the respected pollster and political scientist at Millersville State University near Lancaster. 'She's run a very mediocre one.' "[10]

Garth lined up Teresa Heinz, John's widow, to endorse me in TV spots. In our ads Teresa said she differed with me over Anita Hill but supported me for my overall record.

In the end, I beat Yeakel 49–46 percent, with the remaining 4.6 percent going to Libertarian candidate John Perry. The victory boosted not only my Senate career but Shanin's avocation: volunteer political consulting. In 1994, when Rick Santorum ran for Senate and Tom Ridge for governor, both sought Shanin's counsel. Each campaign trusted Shanin to review its top-secret overnight tracking, so he could help direct strategy. Both candidates won. In the 1999 Philadelphia mayoral primary, Shanin advised both Republican Sam Katz and Democrat Marty Weinberg, with each knowing he was advising the other. Shanin's very successful law practice allows a little time for politics.

The 1992 race was my first campaign that Frank Rizzo did not see. Rizzo had run his own final race in 1991, a fifth campaign for mayor. The Cisco Kid had been on the verge of a comeback, after twelve years in the wilderness. Rizzo pulled off a miracle 34–33 percent victory in the primary over my former assistant Ron Castille, who had resigned as DA to run for mayor. Rizzo had dominated mayoral elections for twenty-five years. He ran and won in 1971 and 1975. In 1979 he tried to change the charter's two-term limit and run for a third straight term but could not.

In 1983 Rizzo ran in the Democratic primary and lost badly to Wilson Goode. Goode, a former probation officer with a Wharton M.B.A., became Philadelphia's first African-American mayor. Goode began with a lot of promise but soon proved a disappointment and then a disaster. On May 13, 1985, he gave police the green light to use explosives to evict members of the radical group MOVE from a West Philadelphia row house. A police helicopter dropped a bomb on the house, setting off a fire that killed eleven and destroyed sixty-one other houses.

Rizzo was back again for the 1987 mayor's race, this time as a Republican. He brought throngs of "Rizzocrats" with him when he switched parties. Right after my reelection victory in November 1986, I was asked by the Philadelphia ABC-TV affiliate about supporting Rizzo's candidacy. I said no. "Who are you for?" the reporter asked. "Hand me a phone book," I replied.

Frank Rizzo then got the Republican nomination. I wound up endorsing him. The media played the tape of me asking for a phone book. "How can you be for Rizzo?" they wanted to know. "Well," I said, "the Democrats nominated the one person, Wilson Goode, who is worse than Rizzo." The Republicans, in turn, nominated the only person who could lose to Goode. It was relatively close, but Rizzo lost the 1987 election by 17,000 votes, his second straight loss to Wilson Goode.

In 1991 Rizzo was back again, still a Republican. Goode had served two terms and couldn't run again. After upsetting Castille in the GOP primary, Rizzo faced Ed Rendell, the former DA and my former assistant, in the general election. He was the underdog, but Rizzo had made a career of doing the unpredictable. He always ran ahead of the polls, drawing votes from people who didn't like to admit their support.

By 1991 I saw Rizzo from time to time, and we talked occasionally. The old antagonism had cooled. On a Friday night in July 1991, I went out campaigning with Joan, who was running for reelection to city council. We ran into Rizzo at 52nd and Market streets, in the heart of the African-American community. He was prancing up and down 52nd Street, thundering, "I'm going to win this one, going to win it."

In campaigning, as in so many other things, finding an element of humor and making people laugh takes off much of the edge. I would go into delicatessens, sometimes taking the public-address microphone, and announce, "May I have your attention: I'm Arlen Specter. I'm here campaigning for my wife, Joan." Some startled customers might initially think the store was being robbed. Then they would recognize me. "She's running for reelection," I would say. "Done an outstanding job, and I want to thank you all for coming to this political rally." At Veterans Stadium at the October Eagles games, I campaigned for Joan using a bullhorn. Most people had never seen a sitting U.S. Senator working the stadium aisles. "Joan Specter for city council," I called. "Support Joan Specter. I do."

On 52nd Street that evening in July 1991, Rizzo called to Joan and me, "See, see how they love me? See how I'm going to win this?" They did love him. People swarmed around him. Frank Rizzo was larger than life, a legend in his own time. But I wondered if that show of adulation would translate into votes. Rizzo promised to hire fifteen hundred more cops, put the crooks in jail, and make the streets safe. Wherever Frank Rizzo went, he brought excitement. He radiated charisma.

That Friday night together in July 1991 ended on a high note. It turned out to be the final chord. The Tuesday after Joan and I campaigned with him on 52nd Street, Frank Rizzo suffered a massive heart attack and died. I was shocked. The indomitable, surreal giant was gone. An era had ended. I was glad Frank Rizzo and I had shared a last evening laughing together.

RUBY RIDGE

Ruby Ridge," the bloody 1992 federal raid on a mountain cabin in Idaho, has taken its place in American history with Kent State, Wounded Knee, and Waco—wrongful federal uses of deadly force. The raid weakened Americans' trust in law enforcement and incited militia groups to arm themselves against our government. Our Senate investigation of Ruby Ridge worked hard to find the truth, to hold officials at all levels accountable, and to restore faith in government. Our investigation led to the FBI's changing its rules on use of deadly force and the way it uses its Hostage Rescue Team.

The Ruby Ridge saga began in 1986, when a confidential informant for the Bureau of Alcohol, Tobacco and Firearms met and befriended Randall Weaver, a thirty-eight-year-old former Army Green Beret, at a white-supremacist Aryan Nations Congress. Three years later, in 1989, Weaver sold two illegally sawed-off shotguns to the informant. The ATF confronted Weaver about the gun sale and pressed him to inform on the Aryan Nations. He refused. The U.S. Attorney's office in Idaho indicted Weaver on a weapons charge. He was released on bail and given a court date. Weaver received a notice erroneously listing his court date as a month later than the actual date, and he failed to appear for trial. A bench warrant and later a grand jury indictment were issued. The U.S. Marshal's Service launched a seventeen-month investigation and surveillance of Weaver.

On the morning of August 21, 1992, while the Marshal's Service was watching Weaver's property, a firefight broke out between three deputy marshals and Kevin Harris, a twenty-four-year-old who was living with the Weavers, and Weaver's fourteen-year-old son, Samuel. When the shooting stopped, Deputy U.S. Marshal William Degan, a highly decorated officer, and Sammy Weaver were dead. Who fired the first shot would remain hotly contested.

The fight may have begun when a deputy shot Weaver's yellow Labrador, Striker. The Judiciary Subcommittee on Terrorism, which I chaired, concluded:

> It seems plausible that a 14-year-old boy, on seeing his dog shot, would have opened fire at the person who shot his dog. At that point, it was likely that the Marshals would shoot back at the two people who were firing on them. In the course of the gunfire, Marshal Degan was shot by Harris, and Sammy Weaver was shot in the arm and in the back.[1]

After the firefight, the Marshal's Service asked the FBI for help. The bureau rushed its elite Hostage Rescue Team to Ruby Ridge. Hundreds of federal, state, and local law enforcement officers descended on Weaver's property. On the first day of the siege an FBI sniper fired two shots. The first hit Randy Weaver in the shoulder. The second hit Weaver's wife, Vicki, in the head, killing her as she stood in the doorway of her house holding her ten-month-old daughter. That second bullet passed through Vicki Weaver's head, tore through Harris's arm, and lodged in Harris's chest, where it broke two ribs and damaged a lung. (Yes, another Single Bullet.) A week later Randy Weaver surrendered.

Weaver and Harris, who both recovered from their wounds, were tried in federal court in 1993 on charges ranging from conspiracy to murder. They were acquitted on all the major counts, including the original firearms charge. Weaver was convicted of failing to appear at his trial, even though his initial notice listed the wrong trial date, and for carrying a gun while on pretrial release.

The Department of Justice appointed a task force to investigate Ruby Ridge. The task force filed an internal report—which has never been made public—with the department's Office of Professional Responsibility. In January 1995 FBI Director Louis Freeh announced that he had either disciplined or recommended discipline for twelve FBI agents over their conduct at Ruby Ridge, including Larry Potts, then the FBI's acting deputy director. In May 1995 the FBI's on-scene commander at Ruby Ridge, Eugene Glenn, complained in a letter to the Justice Department that he was being made a scapegoat for misconduct by higher-ranking FBI officials.

Clearly, the matter had not been settled. I thought my Judiciary subcommittee had jurisdiction to investigate. I met with Randy Weaver in May 1995 at the Des Moines airport. He now lived nearby in Iowa, and I was in the area for a series of events in my presidential campaign. Weaver, wearing a black T-shirt and jeans, was trim and energetic. He was now forty-seven, and his full head of wavy brown hair was graying. Joining us were Weaver's lawyer and three young daughters, Sara, Rachel, and Elisheba. We sat at a Formica conference table that filled most of the windowless cubicle at the airport's charter-service office.

I asked Weaver for his account, from the beginning. He began by telling me about overtures by an undercover ATF agent. "He befriended me over a three-year period," Weaver said. "Over that period, he tried to get me to do things that weren't legal over and over and over. . . . It all sounded kind of crazy to me for a long time, but I got to the point where I needed to keep up, and he told me what he wanted and I went for it."[2] The agent wanted two sawed-off shotguns, which Weaver got for him.

Weaver said he was soon approached by the head of the Spokane ATF office and another agent. "What it came down to was they told me they were going to bring six or seven different federal firearms violations against me if I didn't join their team." Weaver refused. Six or eight months later, Weaver said, federal agents lured him and his wife out of their vehicle on a rural road using a ruse—an apparently disabled truck. The agents arrested the Weavers and held them in jail overnight. The next morning Weaver signed a bond and was given a court date.

When he failed to appear in court, Weaver became a fugitive. He holed up on Ruby Ridge listening to radio reports. "I'm thinking, what am I going to get if I go down there now? I'm going to lose my property, I'm going to lose my family, everything anyway, see? We talked it over, and my family is a loyal family. They weren't going to desert Dad. They didn't want Dad to go. . . . It was a year and a half we stayed on that hill. We never went anywhere. Nowhere." Attempts to negotiate failed, Weaver said, when officials refused his demands for the ATF to admit they had set him up, to apologize, and to return his gun.

Then, on Friday morning, August 21, 1992, the Weavers' Lab, Striker, "started raising a wild ruckus, and he was so excited," Weaver recalled. The dog was excited, it would soon turn out, because federal officials were on Weaver's property. Shooting soon erupted.

Weaver broke down several times in Des Moines as he described how his son and his wife were shot and killed. The former Green Beret was stoic in describing his own wounds from a bullet in the upper back. His two older daughters wept throughout the rest of our talk. Elisheba, who had been in her mother's arms when Vicki Weaver was shot dead, remained silent.

"I'm not going to tell you how he looked when I found him, because I've never told anyone before," Weaver said of his son, Sam.

"I can understand how emotional you are, Mr. Weaver," I said. "I can understand that. Just take your time."

"A little kid, he was a little kid who hadn't matured yet," Weaver continued. "He was four-eleven and weighed eighty pounds. A skinny little runt like I once was. His voice hadn't even changed. . . . He was going up the hill and that bullet went up and took his heart out and came right out this nipple. He'd been shot one time before that, I guess, in this elbow, I guess, about tore him off at the elbow and Kevin said when that happened, he yelled, 'Oh, come on, Kevin,' and he was standing there in the road. This kid was, he was in plain sight. So close to them guys. They didn't have to do that, Senator. They didn't have to do that. The kid was protecting his dog."[3]

Weaver described how he carried his son's body up the hill to a shed, where he undressed and bathed the boy and wrapped him in a sheet. The next day Weaver tried to enter the shed. "I come around this edge of the shed and I say I'm gonna go in and see Sam again, I want to be with Sam again, I want to be with Sam again. I come around and switch my rifle to this hand and reach up and turn the latch, POW! . . . I got shot in the back."

On August 31, after negotiations with more trusted intermediaries and talk of hiring a top lawyer, Weaver finally came out. Weaver's account at the Des Moines airport revealed a number of apparent serious violations by law enforcement. As we ended our talk, I told him, "I think this is something that ought to be seen and heard by the Senate, and the American people ought to know what is going on."

As chairman of the Judiciary Subcommittee on Terrorism, I launched an investigation. The subcommittee acted out of deep concern and outrage, especially because of the executive branch's failure to do justice and in the context of a burgeoning militia movement. We were trying to find whether several federal agencies had committed professional misconduct, broken criminal law, and violated the Constitution in investigating, capturing, and prosecuting Weaver and his friend Harris.

At its crux Ruby Ridge was a police brutality case. Instead of challenging Police Commissioner Frank Rizzo, the subcommittee was taking on the FBI, the attorney general, and the Bureau of Alcohol, Tobacco and Firearms. "The core issue is the use of deadly force," I told the press. "Hundreds of times, perhaps thousands of times a day, law enforcement is using deadly force. This will be a watershed focus on what may be constitutionally done. . . . The overarching issue is accountability at the highest levels of government."

In early May 1995 I announced that I would hold hearings on May 18 on Ruby Ridge and on the 1993 fatal federal raid of the Branch Davidian compound in Waco, Texas. I had been pushing the Judiciary Committee for two years to investigate the Waco fiasco, in which seventy-one people had died. Senator Orrin Hatch exercised his authority as Judiciary Committee chairman to preemptively cancel my hearings. He said hearings would be held "in the near future" by the full committee under his direction, not by my subcommittee.

Robert Novak, the political columnist, called Hatch's move an "extraordinary performance . . . in the tradition of Senate grandees, self-assured and answering to no higher authority than their own conscience. But they also display a nasty edge that I seldom found when I began covering Congress 38 years ago this month."[4]

I tried to force scheduling a hearing on Ruby Ridge by introducing a Sense of the Senate resolution, a measure expressing a philosophical or public policy view of the Senate without turning the issue into binding law. Although my resolution did not pass, sufficient pressure was exerted so that the subcommittee was authorized to proceed with hearings.

We held fourteen days of hearings in September and October 1995, heard testimony from sixty-two witnesses, interviewed many others, and reviewed thousands of documents. We held most of the sessions in 216 Hart, a cavernous amphitheater in the modern Senate office building. Every senator on the subcommittee attended almost every minute of every session, which is a rarity on Capitol Hill. I also invited two senators not on the subcommittee to participate: Charles Grassley of Iowa (where Randy Weaver was then living) and Larry Craig of Idaho (where Randy Weaver had lived).

The hearings were also unusual in that, by all accounts, the majority and minority worked together closely, rather than jockeying for partisan advantage. We all wanted to find the truth, not simply assign blame.

As a measure of our unity, the Democrats did not hire their own counsel or file a separate minority report. Senator Herb Kohl of Wisconsin, the ranking Democrat, helped set the tone.

On the first day of hearings, Randy Weaver told his story to America, much as he had told it to me at the Des Moines airport four months earlier. Weaver again wept as he told of the deaths of his wife and son and how Kevin Harris, severely wounded, had begged Weaver to shoot him and end his misery. We had to take several breaks as Weaver composed himself. The Ruby Ridge hearings were thorough and professional, limited only by lack of some evidence and the refusal of some witnesses to testify. We brought in the actual door from the Weaver cabin to try to determine whether the FBI sniper could have seen Vicki Weaver through its curtained window. We used the FBI's detailed scale model of the Weaver compound, which occupied two tables.

Security was tight at 216 Hart. We had received a stack of threatening letters from people who thought our hearings were designed to denigrate Randy Weaver. We posted security guards at every entrance to the hearing room and brought in bomb-sniffing dogs before each session. Even though he took the Fifth Amendment, we held a closed session for Lon Horiuchi, the FBI sniper who had fired the shot that killed Vicki Weaver, because Horiuchi was concerned that his recognizable face would draw the ire of militia groups. We let the ATF informant who had pressed Weaver testify from behind a translucent screen, his voice disguised by a scrambler.

Several themes emerged during our hearings. One was a disturbing lack of leadership from a variety of law enforcement officers, who were unwilling to take charge, make difficult decisions, and accept responsibility. Some high-ranking officials in every agency were unwilling to hold themselves accountable for their actions and those of their subordinates. As our report stated:

> Accountability is essential to public confidence; unfortunately, many law enforcement officers who appeared before us attempted to lay the blame on others for what went wrong at Ruby Ridge. For example, we still have not satisfactorily determined the individual responsible for the Rules of Engagement that encouraged HRT snipers to shoot on sight: during our oversight hearings, no individual acknowledged ultimate responsibility for those clearly unconstitutional rules.

FBI Agent Glenn, the on-scene commander at Ruby Ridge, maintained again before our subcommittee that he had been made a scapegoat. "We could say that the ship saw some hungry sharks swimming close by and they decided that they would put a few tuna out there and see if they could satisfy them," Glenn testified. A second theme that emerged from our hearings was that intelligence data used by every agency involved in Weaver's case, and passed among agencies, was deeply flawed. As FBI Director Freeh testified, "[O]ne misstatement of fact exaggerated to another one, into a huge pile of information that was just dead wrong."

Inaccurate information was passed along that Randy Weaver was a convicted felon, when he had in fact never even been arrested before the ATF informant contacted him. Inaccurate information also circulated that Weaver was a suspect in several bank robberies. During our hearings, ATF agents admitted fabricating Weaver's criminal record and his alleged involvement in bank robberies. This kind of false information may have moved federal agencies to go after Weaver on the gun charges in the first place and may have caused U.S. marshals and the FBI to overreact at Ruby Ridge.

A third theme involved the ability of law enforcement agencies to investigate themselves fully and impartially. The FBI's Shooting Incident Review Team, for example, found that in the case of Vicki Weaver, who was shot while holding open a door and carrying an infant, "the use of deadly force was justified in that she willfully placed herself in harm's way by attempting to assist Harris, and in so doing, overtly contributed to the immediate threat which continued to exist against the helicopter crew and approaching HRT personnel." There was no basis to conclude that holding a door open for a retreating man contributes to an immediate threat. And the team's conclusion that an innocent party who "place[s] herself in harm's way" can be the subject of deadly force is frighteningly wrong.

As we stated in our report, with a couple of exceptions, "it appeared to the Subcommittee that the authors of every report we read were looking more to justify agency conduct than to follow the facts wherever they led." The FBI Inspection Division, despite instructions to refrain from drawing conclusions, did just that in its report, finding that the shots fired by FBI sniper Horiuchi were lawful.

ATF Director John Magaw testified that ATF "agents' conduct was lawful and proper in every respect," despite evidence and sworn testimony to the contrary. Magaw's blanket insistence was so irksome that I summoned him for a private meeting in my office, along with Treasury Secretary Robert Rubin, whose department has authority over the ATF. Magaw again, in private, insisted that his agents had done nothing wrong. Rubin, more diplomatic, said he understood my point but ultimately sided with Magaw, unwilling to buck the bureaucracy he headed.

FBI Director Freeh, who candidly admitted the FBI's shortcomings in the Ruby Ridge case, was a notable exception to the accountability gap. Freeh testified that the FBI's use of a robot vehicle—with a shotgun attached—to deliver a telephone to the Weaver cabin was the "stupidest thing I ever heard of." Obviously, the equipment would frighten the Weavers, not encourage them to negotiate a surrender.

Many questions were raised about ATF's conduct in pursuing Randy Weaver for a relatively minor weapons offense. ATF's pursuit was the first in a string of events that ended in the bloody raid. Weaver and others suggested the ATF had "targeted" him for prosecution because of his religious and political beliefs, specifically his affiliation with the Aryan Nations. We concluded that Weaver was targeted not so much for his beliefs but for his association with violent people. Clearly, the ATF was not so much interested in prosecuting Weaver as in using its case against him to force him to inform against those in extremist groups who may have been engaged in major crimes involving weapons. But the distinction—between targeting people with offensive beliefs and targeting those who use their offensive beliefs to promote criminal violence—can easily collapse. The ATF should have handled Weaver's case with more sensitivity and monitored it from headquarters. The undercover ATF agent who approached Weaver should have had more training. His conduct led a jury to acquit Weaver, apparently believing the defense claim of entrapment.

We also recommended that all federal agencies review their practices of paying informants, to avoid even the appearance of impropriety when an informant thinks he will get paid only if he helps get a conviction. From the outset, we found, law enforcement agencies made a series of mistakes. They failed to check their information on Weaver, issued a bench warrant for Weaver instead of alerting him that they had sent him an erroneous court date, and rushed into confrontation without exhausting other avenues of negotiation.

Among the most serious flaws were the unconstitutional rules of engagement drawn for Ruby Ridge. Those rules began: "If any adult male in the compound is observed with a weapon prior to the [surrender] announcement, deadly force can and should be employed, if the shot can be taken without endangering any children." For Randy Weaver and Kevin Harris, these were virtual shoot-on-sight orders. The Ruby Ridge rules conflicted with the FBI's policy that agents not use deadly force except in self-defense or defense of another. At our hearings, Freeh and Deputy Attorney General Jamie Gorelick essentially conceded that the Ruby Ridge rules were constitutionally infirm.

Our hearings focused on the two shots fired by FBI sniper Lon Horiuchi on the evening of August 22, 1992. Horiuchi, a West Point graduate and thirteen-year FBI veteran, was one of nine snipers posted at four different positions around the Weaver compound. Horiuchi fired his first shot when he saw Randy Weaver appear at the side of the shed. Weaver, wounded in the shoulder, his daughter Sara, and Kevin Harris dashed back to the cabin. Vicki Weaver held open the cabin door. Weaver and Sara ran inside. As Harris, who was trailing slightly, reached the door, Horiuchi fired his second shot, killing Vicki Weaver and severely wounding Harris.

At Weaver and Harris's criminal trial, Horiuchi testified that he shot Weaver because he thought Weaver was trying to aim a gun at a government helicopter. Horiuchi said he never intended to hit Vicki Weaver and did not know at the time that he had.

The hearings didn't produce enough evidence to conclude that Horiuchi's first shot was unconstitutional. But we found reasonable basis to conclude that the rules of engagement—not fear for safety of the helicopter, which Horiuchi probably knew was out of rifle range—prompted him to take the first shot. As Horiuchi testified at Weaver and Harris's trial:

Q: You were waiting to kill the people that came out of the house, weren't you?

A: If they came out of the house and provided a threat, yes, sir, we were.

Q: You were waiting to kill them irrespective of a threat, weren't you?

A: Based on the Rules of Engagement, sir, we could.

Q: Based on the Rules of Engagement the decision had already been made that he was a threat?

A: Yes, sir, a Marshal had been shot, sir.

We concluded that Horiuchi's second, deadly shot was unconstitutional. The three people Horiuchi shot at were running toward the cabin and did not pose a threat to Horiuchi or anybody else. The second shot was even inconsistent with the Ruby Ridge rules of engagement, which permitted deadly force "only if the shot can be taken without endangering any children." Accepting Horiuchi's trial testimony that he couldn't see into the cabin when he fired the second shot, he knew or should have known that by firing blind through the cabin door, he could hit Vicki Weaver or the Weaver children. As we found, "We fail to see any reasonable basis for a judgment that a high-powered rifle shot through an opaque door into an area that could hold a mother and several children, including an infant, could have been taken without endangering the children."

At our hearing we questioned Freeh at length about the second shot. Initially, the FBI director resisted criticizing Horiuchi. Later Freeh, a former federal judge, acknowledged that the second shot should not have been taken "for policy and for constitutional reasons." Our subcommittee wanted to make sure that under similar circumstances in the future, inappropriate and unconstitutional deadly force like the second Ruby Ridge shot would not be used.

On October 16, 1995, Freeh proposed a unified policy that deadly force may be used only when an officer has a reasonable belief that a person poses an imminent danger of death or serious physical injury to the officer or to another person. Attorney General Reno approved Freeh's resolution the next day. The Treasury Department also has adopted this policy. The new deadly-force policy adds the element of imminence.

Our subcommittee also concluded that the FBI's Hostage Rescue Team should have been deployed only with permission from the top levels of both the FBI and the Department of Justice. Reno approved a new joint policy in September 1995 that the FBI will take charge of hostage and barricade situations whenever the agency's help is sought. The Hostage Rescue Team will be deployed only with approval from the FBI director. The team will be headed by an agent experienced in crisis management who reports directly to the director. Negotiators will always deploy with the team.

Our subcommittee investigation found that ultimate responsibility for Ruby Ridge must be shared by many people, beginning with Randall Weaver. If Weaver had not sold illegal weapons, his wife, his son, and Deputy Marshal Degan would still be alive. Instead Weaver holed up in his cabin, rebuffed all efforts to negotiate his surrender, and stated that he would use violence to defend himself. Weaver and his wife sent letters to federal authorities vowing not to obey "your lawless government." Vicki Weaver sent a letter to the U.S. Attorney for Idaho addressed to "Queen of Babylon" that quoted a former violent fugitive's warning: "War is upon the land. The tyrant's blood will flow." Weaver candidly acknowledged his errors to us and to the American people on the first day of the hearings.

But while Randy Weaver made mistakes, so did every federal law enforcement agency involved at Ruby Ridge. And federal law enforcement professionals must be held to higher standards. The events at Ruby Ridge weakened the vital bond of trust between ordinary Americans and our law enforcement agencies. The only way to strengthen that bond is through an honest accounting.

After our subcommittee issued its report, investigations of Ruby Ridge continued. A two-year federal investigation ended in August 1997 with no charges brought against federal officials. A week later, Denise Woodbury, prosecutor for Boundary County, Idaho, filed involuntary manslaughter charges against Horiuchi, alleging that the sniper had fired recklessly at Kevin Harris when he didn't know who else was standing behind the cabin door.

I told the press I believed that Woodbury filed charges against Horiuchi in part because she lacked confidence in the Justice Department's review of Ruby Ridge. "I believe the Justice Department is in total disarray on this case," the *St. Louis Post-Dispatch* quoted me as saying. "I am heartsick with the way this case has been handled because it leaves the public with no confidence in the Justice Department." In the end, on May 14, 1998, U.S. District Judge Edward Lodge cleared Horiuchi, ruling, "Mr. Horiuchi did no more than what was 'necessary and proper' for him to do to carry out his duties under the totality of circumstances." Perhaps.

Ruby Ridge represents a tragic chapter in the history of American law enforcement. The death of U.S. Deputy Marshal William Degan must not be forgotten. In September 1995 I introduced the "Degan Bill" to provide children of slain federal law enforcement officers the same educational benefits made available to the children of U.S. armed forces personnel killed in the line of duty. President Clinton signed the bill into law in October 1996. As a result, a child of a slain federal law enforcement officer can receive up to four hundred dollars a month for as long as forty-five months for education. In October 1998 Congress approved my legislation to expand those benefits to the children of slain state and local public safety officers, such as police and firefighters, killed in the line of duty.

The subcommittee's investigation and the reforms by the FBI and ATF have reduced the understandable public anger and cynicism over Ruby Ridge. But the incident at Waco still smolders, especially after revelations in August 1999 that officials did indeed fire incendiary rounds into the compound. If the public is to have confidence in government generally, and in law enforcement specifically, such incidents must be promptly investigated and appropriate reforms initiated.

A HUNDRED-MILE-AN-HOUR GAME

In 1995 I ran for the Republican nomination for president of the United States. I ran because I didn't like what was happening at either end of Pennsylvania Avenue.

I didn't like President Clinton's Economic Recovery Act of 1993, which carried a big tax hike. I did not like Clinton's Health Security Act, a 1,364-page bill to redraw the nation's health-care system. I was amazed at the complex bureaucracy and its structure. My office produced a chart that looked like a microchip circuit diagram showing 105 new federal agencies in red and 47 existing agencies, boards, and commissions that were given new responsibilities in green. Bob Woodward of the *Washington Post* called that chart the decisive factor in defeating the Clinton health-care plan.

When the president gave his State of the Union speech in February 1994, his health-care legislation received top advance billing. As the speech approached, I got calls from all the networks asking about my chart. Preparing for what I thought would be my TV presentation, I decided what shirt, suit, and tie I would wear that evening. Then I learned the networks didn't want me. They wanted my chart. Bob Dole used it for his reply to the president's speech. Later in the 1996 presidential campaign, when Dole was the nominee, he asked permission to use a giant blow-up of my chart. Dole's enlargement was a perfect replica except for one detail: My name was omitted. The fifty-square-foot chart now hangs in my conference room.

In 1995 I also didn't like what was happening in our Senate Republican caucus. I was the only Republican to speak in favor of the 1994 crime bill on the Senate floor. While the bill included some ill-advised measures, it had crucial provisions on the death penalty and rehabilitation. Opponents made a mockery of the bill over midnight basketball. Republicans didn't like rehabilitation. They wanted to put all the emphasis on tough sentencing. Ultimately, six Republicans voted for the bill, suffering severe criticism within the Republican caucus. Unhappy with Clinton's health-care plan, six of us Senate Republicans had worked every Thursday morning in 1993 and 1994 to craft a health bill. Dole, then the Republican leader, had encouraged us. But Dole opposed our plan, saying he wanted to be the leader of thirty-seven Republicans, not six.

I had no illusions about winning the nomination. It was more than a long shot. But there were policies and principles that needed to be expressed. I went to see Dole in April 1994, after I'd been invited to speak in Iowa before a group called We Are Republicans. Dole was the top GOP prospect, the Senate minority leader, and a friend since long before I had come to the Senate. Our families had grown up together in Russell, Kansas. My father had weighed his scrap metal on Dole's father's industrial scales. I wasn't going to have Bob learn from a newspaper that I'd gone to Iowa, which suggests a possible candidacy. "I'm considering running for president," I told him.

"You'll meet a lot of interesting people and a lot of nice people," Dole said. "At least our party will know who the real liberal is." He seemed to welcome my candidacy, perhaps to divert charges that he wasn't conservative enough. At the end of our meeting, I didn't know whether Dole was running. Later I found he was undecided; he didn't make a decision to run until early 1995. I figured that Dole would be the front-runner and probably the nominee, but somewhere along the line, he might stumble. And if Dole stumbled, it would be a jump ball. Damn the torpedoes, full speed ahead, I was going to run. I was going to travel the country and road-test my ideas.

In Des Moines on June 24, 1994, I talked about the constitutional doctrine of separation of church and state, and I was booed. I decided at that moment that I would not sit still in an America where people hiss at the doctrine of separation of church and state. That wasn't Arlen Specter's doctrine. It was Thomas Jefferson's. I would run, even if it was Mission Impossible.

I'd faced stiff challenges and tough situations before. But just to utter the words "I'm running for president of the United States of America" proved difficult. Who is up to being president of the United States—the most powerful and important person in the world? Who can say that he or she is worthy? I was not a Johnny-come-lately. I'd been in the Senate for three terms. But it was very hard to stand up and make that statement.

I didn't like what Clinton was doing on health care, on crime, in Haiti, in Bosnia, and on other issues. I didn't think he was up to the job. We needed a centrist Republican to replace him. A right-wing Republican had no chance to win. As I said in my announcement speech, a candidate from the intolerant right would only produce a president from the incompetent left. I thought I might, just possibly, catch fire and get the people off the sidelines and onto the playing field. It was worth a try. You only live once, and I was sixty-four.

I'd been encouraged by several meetings with women's groups, who saw me as their best—perhaps only—chance for a pro-choice Republican nominee. The only other pro-choice Republican candidate, Pete Wilson, joined the race late and left early. Although many women hadn't forgiven me for what they considered my tough questioning of Anita Hill, they knew about my strong record on women's issues. It was a new day, they wanted to protect choice, and I was their only horse.

The architect of my run and my campaign chairman was Roger Stone, a flamboyant political consultant and Nixon confidant. I had joined a Stone-sponsored group, along with Senators Warren Rudman and Nancy Kassebaum, dedicated to "taking the party back." Stone's campaign strategy called for me to win enough votes, as the lone centrist in a field of staunch conservatives, to advance beyond the early primaries. The arithmetic was tricky, riding largely on constantly recycled direct mail to raise the necessary millions.

Running for president is different from, not just bigger than, running for any other office. The pace, the scope, the scrutiny, the intensity all involve another order of magnitude. I began exploratory travels throughout the country on November 14, 1994, and announced my candidacy in front of the Lincoln Memorial on March 30, 1995. C-SPAN and CNN covered the announcement live, while other media spilled off a platform we'd built.

Timing is everything in politics, and I knew, on top of my other challenges, that my timing could have been better. November 1994, when I announced my exploratory travels, was about the worst time to take on the Republican apparatus. Republicans had just won control of the House and the Senate and most of the nation's governorships. But it was then or probably never. Notwithstanding Dole's candidacy at the age of seventy-three, I didn't think it likely that I would run for president in 2000 at the age of seventy.

We gave it our best shot. We opened offices in Des Moines and Manchester, New Hampshire, and ran campaigns in those two key early caucus/primary states with large staffs and big budgets. We lined up campaign chairmen in key states, including Congressman Tom Campbell in California, former Lieutenant Governor Art Neu in Iowa, Concord District Attorney Michael Johnson in New Hampshire, and a host of state legislature leaders.

I jetted at least once a week to either New Hampshire or Iowa, often staying for several days at a stretch. I made regular side trips to the six New England states, which had pooled into an early regional primary, and to Illinois, Colorado, South Dakota, Missouri, Nebraska, Kansas, and other Midwestern and Western states. I also made several trips to California; Arizona and Delaware, which were battling for rights to the first post-Iowa primary; and Texas, New York, and Florida. In all, I campaigned in twenty-eight states.

My daily schedules often ran to two densely typed pages. A typical day began with the alarm clock ringing at 4:30 A.M.; "wheels up" before 6:00 A.M.; fourteen to sixteen hours of meetings with editorial boards, party leaders, and interest groups; news conferences; fund-raising receptions; events ranging from state-fair barbecues to Memorial Day parades; and television and radio shows. We often checked out of hotels with the same clerk who had checked us in six or seven hours earlier.

Running for president was a hundred-mile-an-hour game, played on rough turf. We hit the roughest patch at Ames on August 19, 1995, at the state's first candidate forum, the Iowa straw poll. The event, it turned out, was a referendum by the right wing, not by Hawkeye State Republicans. The Iowa State University parking lot was packed with buses from all over the country. A bus with Alabama tags bore a BUCHANAN FOR PRESIDENT sign. The campaigns had hired the buses, bought enough twenty-five-dollar straw poll tickets to fill them, and brought people from all over the country. That night Chuck Grassley, Iowa's senior senator, told me he had 97 percent name recognition in the state, but nobody in the arena knew him because nearly everybody at the Iowa straw poll came from out of state.

The boos began when I was introduced. "Go back where you came from!" some shouted. "Baby killer!" When I made my speech, neither I nor anybody in the audience could hear a word I said over the jeers and catcalls. I went on, knowing C-SPAN's microphones would pick up my speech. I announced I was speaking not to the imported, partisan arena crowd but to Iowa and really to America.

Ralph Reed, Jr., then executive director of the Christian Coalition, excluded me alone among Republican candidates from the coalition's September 1995 "Road to Victory" conference because of my pro-choice views. While the Christian Coalition met in a Washington hotel ballroom, I held my own meeting with Thomas Jefferson, the champion of separation of church and state, at the Jefferson Memorial. I communed with the third president at 8:00 A.M. and invited the press to join us for a news conference at 9 A.M. I said:

> While Thomas Jefferson stands in that memorial, and while Thomas Jefferson's principles have been the lodestone of America on the Jeffersonian wall of separation of church and state, and the Constitution is what has guided this country and made it great, there's a small, select group downtown behind closed doors who want to pick the next President of the United States, and who are afraid to let Arlen Specter come to their meeting and speak to their membership because they're afraid of my ideas, which are the ideas of Jefferson and the ideas of the United States Constitution.

So much for the Republican "Big Tent."

There were other Republican candidates near the party's core, but they veered right on the campaign trail in their pursuit of the nomination. Former Tennessee governor and education secretary Lamar Alexander was the closest to a centrist in that GOP field. But Alexander got snarled, among other issues, on abortion. For a while he ran between the raindrops, never saying whether he was pro-choice or pro-life, leaving different impressions with different people.

I was debating Alexander and Senator Phil Gramm on a blustery February night in North Conway, New Hampshire, when the subject of Henry Foster, the embattled pro-choice nominee for surgeon general, came up in the question-and-answer session. Gramm spoke first, deriding Foster as unqualified and dangerous. I leaned over and asked Alexander, "Lamar, do you mind if I go next?" Okay, Alexander said. I rose and stood up for Foster, drawing so much applause that the *Boston Globe* called it a standing ovation. I closed by saying, "Well, you've

426

had two speakers. Phil says he's pro-life, I'm pro-choice, now Lamar can break the tie. Lamar, you have been quoted on both sides of the fence, but Lamar can clarify the record. Lamar, as I leave this podium, are you pro-choice or are you pro-life?" Alexander stood, obviously pained. Finally he said he was pro-life. Running the political rapids, it's very hard to be both principled and nominated.

I couldn't get the centrists off the sidelines and onto the playing field. Most of the moderate women, who had the most to gain, weren't willing to join the fight. The 1996 race sent a warning of clear and present danger to any pro-choice centrist who set foot into the wilds of Republican primary presidential politics. The primary campaign was not a shot across the bow for potential centrist Republican presidential candidates; it was a shot into the bow, below the waterline and below the belt.

Former chairman of the Joint Chiefs Colin Powell dangled the prospect of a candidacy for several months into September, sucking up the oxygen from my already-wheezing fund-raising. Many of my fund-raising letters came back marked "Waiting for Powell" or some similar message. Rather than go into debt, I suspended my presidential campaign in Philadelphia on November 22, 1995.

Responding to press questions after my announcement, I said I expected to run for another term in the Senate. I would be seeking an unprecedented fourth popularly elected Senate term from Pennsylvania. I began the 1998 Senate race with pundits and politicians widely questioning my viability, in the wake of my failed presidential bid. The vultures were circling. By the Republican National Convention in San Diego in August 1996, they were circling low. Tom Corbett, Pennsylvania's Republican attorney general, was traveling the state, making no secret that he was preparing for the Republican Senate primary. State Senator Melissa Hart, an able and intelligent lawmaker, was also traveling the state, mulling a primary bid against me.

But I knew, despite the polls and the pundits, that I had a lot of residual strength from all my years of work and travel throughout Pennsylvania. Shortly after Thanksgiving 1995, I continued making my way across the counties. The pros may have thought I was vulnerable and wounded, but different soundings came from the people in my county-by-county open-house town meetings.

Then, just as I was building and showing strength, I found that a benign brain tumor, which had been surgically removed in June 1993, had come back. While my operation had been performed by one of the finest surgeons at one of the best hospitals, I was among the approximately 15 percent of cases in which cells at the margin regrew. Now, almost all the doctors I consulted advised another operation. A minority suggested the gamma knife, a new technique in which doctors converge radiation beams to destroy small tumors.

Since there was no urgency, I took some time to study the alternatives. Most doctors, even some with extensive experience with the gamma knife, recommended conventional surgery. Why? Because that was the traditional approach, because there were more long-term follow-up data on surgery, and because the tumor was in a good location for surgery. The gamma knife, they argued, should be reserved for locations the surgeon's knife couldn't reach.

But my tumor was also in a good spot for gamma-knife radiation. My inquiries among some two dozen doctors in Sweden, where the gamma knife was invented, and the United States found almost universal agreement that the gamma knife, even if unsuccessful, would not make the tumor more difficult to treat. Surgery could always be performed later. After extensive research, I opted for the gamma-knife procedure, which is noninvasive and eliminates the risk of anesthesia and infection from surgery. I found that Dr. Dade Lunsford at the University of Pittsburgh Presbyterian Hospital had about the most experience in the United States with the gamma knife, and I arranged to have him perform the procedure.

Another brain procedure was not only a medical concern but a political concern, coming in an election cycle. We pressed the doctors to let me check into the hospital early in the morning on the day of the procedure, rather than the night before, which is conventional. Joan and I arrived at Presbyterian Hospital at 5:30 A.M. on October 11, 1996. I checked in, had a brace attached to my head, and took another MRI. All I needed was a local anesthetic before pins were pressed to my head to secure the brace. At about 9:30 A.M. my head was inserted into a 500-pound helmet with 201 holes, which directed cobalt beams from all directions to focus on the tumor. There were seven bombardments of radiation for no more than three minutes each. In midmorning, when the procedure was apparently going well, Shanin notified the media that I would hold a news conference at 2:30 P.M. at the hospital.

At 10:50 A.M. the radiation was completed and a head compress was applied. The hospital director was in the process of organizing a news conference when I came out of the procedure. After lunch and a brief conversation with Dr. Lunsford, we met the media.

I wore a brown glen-plaid sport coat, rather than the standard dark blue suit and white shirt, to set a casual tone. The gathered reporters didn't know what to expect. I walked out, shook hands with everybody, kidded around a bit, and showed them how sturdily I walked. I began, "We brought you here to tell you about the gamma-knife procedure because we knew you'd be interested." I didn't call it an "operation." "And we thought you'd be less interested if we told you about it than if you found out about it collaterally—understanding the rules of your profession, and ours." I proceeded to tell them what had happened, and that the procedure had been a complete success. One paper reported that I looked as though I were coming from a picnic.

That evening I had a roast beef dinner and a martini, and Joan and I watched a Demi Moore movie in our hotel room. The doctors insisted I remain in Pittsburgh overnight in case any problem developed, though I felt fine. The next day Joan and I flew to Philadelphia and held a news conference at Famous Delicatessen in Queens Village, where a newspaper photo showed me healthy, hardy, and happy, holding my two granddaughters, one in each arm. The politicians were amazed that I'd had brain surgery in the morning and held a news conference the same afternoon. Some were upset that I hadn't told them about my situation, especially since I'd attended a big dinner the night before the operation with Pennsylvania Republican National Committeewoman Elsie Hillman.

The Democrats sounded out other potential candidates but found little interest in view of my burgeoning political strength and campaign war chest. Former Lieutenant Governor Mark Singel and Linda Colvin Rhodes, a former state party chairwoman and Secretary for Aging, considered the race and ultimately demurred. Then State Representative Bill Lloyd, a Somerset County Democrat, stepped up to the plate. Lloyd was at risk of losing his seat in the state house of representatives, as he almost had in 1996. And, some said, he was positioning himself for a run in 2000 against Senator Rick Santorum. On paper Lloyd was formidable. He had been in the state legislature eighteen years, developing expertise in environmental and financial areas and acquiring a reputation for scrutinizing every bill that came up for vote. Lloyd was also a Navy veteran and had a Harvard law degree. He had a taste of statewide campaigning in a failed primary bid for auditor general in 1996, and he came out of the contest with quite a few editorial endorsements.

But Lloyd's campaign never got off the ground. He never raised enough money to air radio or television ads, and his statewide name recognition barely hit double digits. By the time I filed for reelection, we had preempted or were in the process of preempting almost every issue. One of my top aides, Steve Dunkel, described the strategy as "cross-pressure": When we couldn't win a group over, we found an issue that its members liked, which built a cross-pressure for them to support us, or at least not to oppose us.

Key Democrats at all levels came out for me. State Senator Vince Fumo, the South Philadelphia Democratic leader whom I'd once arrested, publicly urged the Democratic State Committee to endorse me, until he found it was prohibited by the committee's charter. U.S. Senator Bob Kerrey of Nebraska, then chairman of the Democratic Senate Campaign Committee, spoke at my annual issues forum in Washington, Citizens for Arlen Specter Day. At a podium at the Capitol Hyatt, the head of the Democrats' Senate political arm lauded my Senate record before a gathering of Pennsylvania political players and media. Compelling as he was, Kerrey did not draw as big a response as Clinton adviser James Carville did at my 1993 CAS Day. The new president had carpeted his bathroom in Little Rock, Carville said, and was so pleased he was going to run the carpet all the way to the house.

I had heavy Jewish support, which I've always enjoyed, even from those who don't support Republicans generally. Religious conservatives, some of whom were put off by my criticisms of Ralph Reed, Pat Buchanan, and Pat Robertson during my presidential bid, found common cause in my crusade to fight religious persecution worldwide. Then the issue of "partial-birth abortion" hit the Senate floor. I concluded that aborting a child halfway out of its mother's womb was not abortion but infanticide. Two strong pro-choice senators, Pat Moynihan and Pat Leahy, reached the same conclusion. I voted to ban the procedure. That vote, based on conscience and public policy, reduced the stridency of pro-life opposition to my candidacy.

Organized labor came out for me for a variety of reasons, from my health-care push to my stand against replacement of strikers to my support for prevailing wages under Davis-Bacon, which establishes the wage rate to be paid to labor in federal contracts. As chairman of the Appropriations Subcommittee on Labor, I had added critical funding for workers' safety and training to replace jobs lost to dumped imports. Labor realized it would be useful to have an ally in the majority party. As I said during my presidential campaign, I was a Republican who could walk into a union hall and come out unscathed. I had supported many labor positions.

I had enough momentum to survive, both physically and politically, another health scare five months before the election. After shaking numerous hands at an Israeli rally at Penn's Landing in Philadelphia one Sunday in late May, I suffered chest pains and checked into Thomas Jefferson Hospital. It turned out I needed a double bypass. Complications resulted in pneumonia and fluid around my heart and lungs, requiring two more operative procedures. I wound up spending two and a half weeks in a hospital bed. But the campaign marched on, and I was reelected with more than 61 percent of the vote, after spending less than $2 million on radio and television.

My head and heart procedures in 1996 and 1998 weren't my first medical emergencies. They were, in a sense, the third and fourth strikes against me. Ordinarily, three strikes and you're out, but I'm still in the batter's box. Twice before, doctors told me I had terminal ailments. The first time was in early 1979. I had traveled to Hawaii on a law case and returned with a sore left arm, the result, I thought, of carrying a heavy briefcase. I consulted a specialist in Philadelphia, who ordered an electroencephalogram. The results led him to diagnose amyotrophic lateral sclerosis, better known as Lou Gehrig's disease.

I sat in my room at the University of Pennsylvania Hospital tower, which overlooked Franklin Field, where I'd watched Penn football games as a student, and stared at my hand. In my mind's eye I saw my hand quivering, a sign of a nerve problem. I read all about amyotrophic lateral sclerosis. I learned that life expectancy with ALS was two to seven years. I also learned all the symptoms of the disease and immediately saw them in myself.

I was released from the hospital to await further developments. There was nothing more they could do for me. By May, when I had no further developments, the doctor told me, "Well, you must not have ALS, because if you had, you'd certainly know it by now." The only other explanation, he said, was that I had a mild case of poliomyelitis as a child.

I told that story to my colleague Senator Paul Tsongas in 1984, when he was deciding whether to run for reelection after being diagnosed

431

with cancer. Tsongas worried that he wouldn't be able to complete the term. I tried to persuade him to run and told him of my ALS scare. "You don't owe the voters a commitment to finish your term, Paul—just to disclose your medical condition and do your best." I tried to lighten the conversation by telling the gag about the eighty-year-old man convicted of a serious crime. The judge gives him twenty to forty years. The man says, "I can't serve that sentence. I'm eighty years old." The judge looks at him and says, "Just do the best you can."

I said, "Paul, just do the best you can." Tsongas didn't run for reelection to the Senate in 1984. But he survived and ran for president in 1992, making a surprisingly strong showing. Tsongas, it turned out, could have served a full Senate term from 1985 to 1991. If he'd done so, he might have built a record that would have catapulted him to the presidency. The country might be a different place today.

I was also diagnosed with a terminal ailment in June 1993. My shirt collars had felt tight, and light pains had been running up each side of my head. All tests proved negative, but the symptoms persisted. The Senate was not in session on Friday, June 11, 1993, so I decided to get a complete physical. Joan was scheduled to come to Washington later that day, and we planned to drive to a Virginia resort to celebrate our fortieth wedding anniversary, which was the following Monday, June 14. I wanted an MRI, but the doctors said I didn't need one. Since the procedure was risk-free and noninvasive, I insisted.

Around noon, the chief neurosurgeon at Bethesda Naval Hospital looked at the MRI films and told me I had a malignant brain tumor and had three to six weeks to live. Stunned, I said, "My wife is coming down today. We planned to go to Virginia to celebrate our fortieth anniversary." The neurosurgeon replied, "Go and have a good time." When he said that, I instantly doubted his judgment on all counts.

"Give me the MRI films," I said. "I'm going to Philadelphia." I called Joan and told her I had a medical problem and that I would be on the 2:00 P.M. train. It was the longest train ride in my life. I went straight from 30th Street Station to see another neurosurgeon. He looked at the films, said they were inconclusive, and said tentatively that the tumor was more likely benign than malignant. I consulted Dr. Eugene Flamm, a renowned neurosurgeon, who postponed a planned trip to Europe to operate on me the following Monday.

Late that Sunday night I checked into University of Pennsylvania Hospital. I had an innocuous statement prepared in case there were any media inquiries. At seven the next morning, they wheeled me into the operating room, shaved the top of my head, used a power saw to remove a two-by-two-inch section of my skull, and cut out the tumor. I was wheeled up to the recovery room at 10:30 A.M., then to my own room an hour later. When I had left my office on Friday for the weekend, there were several pressing items to be taken up Monday morning. At 11:45 A.M. I called my office to talk to my chief of staff about those items. Dr. Flamm walked in and saw me on the phone. He looked amazed. I speculated that he was thinking, What's this guy doing on the phone? Dr. Flamm's expression changed instantly, and I figured he was thinking, Great, if he can make a phone call, he must be okay.

On the same day as my operation, Pennsylvania's governor, Robert Casey, had a double-organ transplant in Pittsburgh. The *Philadelphia Daily News* ran the headline ANGUISH, above photos of Casey and me, juxtaposed so that each of us was looking at the other. The legislative and executive branches of state government in Harrisburg closed for the day for the stated purpose of expressing respect for two ranking officials who had undergone life-threatening operations. Some thought the Harrisburg crowd was busy figuring out who would replace the lieutenant governor, who would replace Casey, and who would replace me and who would replace him, and so forth.

But Casey and I recovered. After my operation the tumor still had to be examined by pathologists, who gave me a clean bill of health the next day. I received some excellent medical advice from my son Steve: "Listen to your body, Dad," he advised. My daily squash regimen has put me in tune with my body and has made me sensitive to its signals. My internal gauges sometimes seem more accurate than doctors' interpretations of high-tech readouts.

I'm madder than hell about the erroneous diagnoses from medical experts who told me I had ALS in 1979 and a malignant brain tumor in 1993. Such experts should be trained to handle such situations with better judgment and a modicum of tact and restraint. What's the point of shocking someone by saying he or she is terminally ill, when that conclusion may be wrong, as it was in my case? Doctors can alert patients to serious potential consequences without categorical pronouncements. For example, a doctor could say, "I'm concerned that your condition could turn out to be very serious, but we have to await tests or see how your condition develops in order to be sure." That would discharge the doctor's duty of candor without unduly alarming the patient. This subject is important enough to be covered in medical school and by hospital administrators or medical supervisors.

The bypass operation improved my fitness, and the 1998 election returned me to the Senate for another six years. I had an ambitious agenda, but I would soon have to suspend much of it as the House voted to impeach President William Jefferson Clinton and the Senate prepared to try him.

PART FIVE

IMPEACHMENT

At the start I stated publicly that the 1999 impeachment trial of President William Jefferson Clinton would be the most important trial in the history of Anglo-Saxon jurisprudence. At the end I wasn't so sure. The Senate paid only lip service to the constitutional requirement to conduct a trial.

The Clinton impeachment trial bears some resemblance to the Warren Commission: Both involved months-long investigations into the end of a presidency, or the potential end of a presidency, by top federal officials under the chief justice's supervision. Both will be scrutinized and second-guessed for decades, maybe even centuries. And both, perhaps forever, will be shrouded in cynicism. As the Kennedy assassination has been the most studied investigation in history, so, too, the Clinton impeachment will probably be the most studied trial in history.

But the parallels go only so far. While the Warren Commission labored to find the facts, the Senate conducted a pseudo trial, a sham trial. We senators had taken oaths to do "impartial justice." Instead we did "partial justice." We did only partial justice in the sense of unduly restricting the House prosecutors in presenting their case, thus denying all impartial justice, and in the sense of hearing only part of the evidence.

The United States Senate, after a four-week trial, acquitted President Clinton on February 12, 1999, of the two articles of impeachment voted by the House of Representatives: perjury and obstruction of justice. The charges arose over what Clinton termed his "inappropriate" sixteen-month relationship with Monica S. Lewinsky, a White House intern in her early twenties, and his efforts to hide their affair.

The case was doomed, perhaps, from the start when Attorney General Janet Reno made a major mistake in giving the Lewinsky investigation to Independent Counsel Kenneth W. Starr. Starr, a former federal judge and solicitor general, had been investigating Clinton for a variety of matters for several years when the Lewinsky affair hit his radar screen. Starr's original charge was "Whitewater," an allegedly fraudulent Arkansas land deal during the 1980s that involved the president and first lady when Clinton was governor of Arkansas. Starr secured several indictments and convictions of friends and business associates of the Clintons, including Associate Attorney General Webster Hubbell, a former colleague of Hillary Clinton's at Little Rock's Rose law firm; and Jim Guy Tucker, Clinton's successor as governor. But Starr hadn't produced evidence strong enough to indict the Clintons.

Starr, a sober presence in steel-rimmed glasses, was running an essentially unsupervised, open-ended probe. The independent-counsel statute, an outgrowth of Watergate, gave the prosecutor great leeway and autonomy. Starr got his jurisdiction expanded three times for additional investigations of Clinton: "Travelgate," the firing of seven White House travel office employees and their replacement by Clinton's cousin and her firm; "Filegate," the White House's apparent use of FBI records to investigate Republican operatives; and finally the Lewinsky affair. Clinton and Starr shared honors in 1998 as *Time* magazine's Men of the Year.

From my position on the Senate Judiciary Committee, which has oversight over the Department of Justice and the independent counsel, I occasionally discussed with Judge Starr specific issues that were in the public domain and required an answer. For example, on January 27, 1998, the first day the Senate reconvened for the second session of the 105th Congress, Senator Patrick Leahy took the Senate floor to criticize Starr. Leahy, a Judiciary Committee member and former prosecutor from Vermont, accused Starr of conducting a partisan investigation, making leaks to the press, coordinating his investigation with Paula Jones's civil case against the president, and running a "sting" operation by secretly taping conversations. "Have we sunk this low . . . that we would do things like this?" Leahy asked, calling the independent counsel's investigation "the most partisan, ends-justify-the-means investigation I can remember in my life." I phoned Starr to find out the facts. Then I went to the Senate floor, where Leahy had made his charges earlier that day, and responded.

During my discussion with Starr, I said, the independent counsel told me he had monitored a conversation between Monica Lewinsky and her friend Linda Tripp, with Tripp's consent:

> Mr. Starr said it was an appropriate exercise of his existing jurisdiction in his investigation involving [former associate attorney general] Mr. Webster Hubbell. Mr. Hubbell's situation involved a matter where an individual was involved in providing job arrangements for Mr. Hubbell outside the District of Columbia with a certain prospective employer. Mr. Starr said that the same person was involved in providing a job opportunity for Ms. Monica Lewinsky outside the District of Columbia with the same prospective employer and that this connection was sufficient for Mr. Starr to proceed with this consensual monitoring.

I didn't name the individual involved in arranging both jobs. The press identified him as presidential confidant Vernon E. Jordan, Jr. As the *New York Times* reported, "The jobs, some at Justice suspected, were simply vehicles for hush money."[1] In any case, Starr "emphatically denied" the leaks and all of Leahy's other accusations, I said on the Senate floor. "The facts as Mr. Starr outlined them to me justify the steps that he took. It would be my hope that as this matter proceeds, that there would be a toning down of the decibel level and a real effort made to find out what the facts are before accusations are made against anybody. I think that applies to President Clinton . . . and applies to Mr. Starr."

I was the only one to defend Starr on the Senate floor that day. At the time Republicans maintained silence about the entire investigation, to avoid politicizing it. But it seemed to me that Starr's probes concerned government matters that deserved comment from elected officials.

More than once, Starr took steps to resign his independent-counsel post before his investigation was complete. In February 1997 he announced plans to quit the Clinton investigation and move to California to take a position as dean of Pepperdine University's schools of law and public policy, a post that had been created for him. I faxed Starr a letter saying he should stay and finish the job: "Your departure will have a very serious, if not devastating, effect on the investigation. . . . There are many witnesses or potential witnesses who will be dissuaded by your departure as a sign that the issues will not be pursued with the same diligence. I share that concern."

Starr held a news conference to announce that he would stay to finish his investigation. As Bob Woodward wrote in *Shadow*, "Pennsylvania Republican Senator Arlen Specter, a former prosecutor, sent Starr an angry letter. . . . After four days of withering rebukes . . . he promised to stay until the investigation was completed. He cited Specter's letter as influential in that reversal."[2] The *New York Times* editorialized, "There is the further problem that Mr. Starr's temporary status will encourage some potentially valuable witnesses to withhold their cooperation in the expectation, created by Mr. Starr's announcement, that the case is winding down. Senator Arlen Specter of Pennsylvania made precisely this point when he noted that 'leadership and momentum' are crucial to any successful investigation."[3]

Judge Starr's investigation muddled along for months. Then, on January 12, 1998, Starr got word from Linda Tripp, a disgruntled Pentagon employee, that she had secretly tape-recorded her friend Monica Lewinsky while the two discussed Lewinsky's sexual affair with Clinton.

To Starr, Tripp's ammunition held promise of the magic bullet he had so desperately sought. Monica Lewinsky, recorded talking about an affair with Clinton that she was prepared to deny under oath, had been targeted as a potential witness in Paula Jones's sexual harassment suit against Clinton. Paula Corbin Jones, a former Arkansas government clerk, had sued Clinton in May 1994 for sexual harassment back in Clinton's days as governor of Arkansas. Jones said Clinton had summoned her to his room at a Little Rock hotel, exposed himself, and asked for oral sex. For three years Clinton tried to avoid Jones's suit by arguing that a sitting president should be immune from lawsuits.

Paula Jones, meanwhile, had become a darling of the political right. Her benefactors bankrolled her lawsuit and called the media and the women's movement hypocrites. The left, Jones's supporters said, had shunned Jones, whom they viewed as trailer trash out to destroy a liberal president, while embracing Anita Hill, a refined law professor who had targeted an outspoken conservative. Jones became a favorite media target and a cartoonist's delight. The press lampooned her big hair and large nose until Jones eventually got a professional makeover and plastic surgery. Then they lampooned her makeover and surgery.

In May 1997 the U.S. Supreme Court unanimously rejected Clinton's argument for immunity. Jones's lawyers immediately pressed for information about Clinton's sexual relationships with other women. The president's lawyers refused. In December 1997 Judge Susan Webber Wright ruled that Clinton had to supply information about all women who were state or federal employees with whom he had or had tried to have sexual relations.

Monica Lewinsky was on the Jones team's list and faced a deposition when her friend Linda Tripp contacted the independent counsel's office. Lewinsky planned to submit a false affidavit claiming that she had never had sexual contact with Clinton, to avoid having to testify. She confided all this and more in rambling conversations, e-mails, and letters filled with girl talk about diet, fashion, and men, to her friend Tripp.

Starr's office arranged for Tripp to wear an FBI recording device when she met with Lewinsky. Tripp came through, getting Lewinsky to say unwittingly on tape that she planned to lie about her affair with Clinton when she was deposed in the Jones case. On Friday, January 16, 1998, Tripp again wore a wire when she met Lewinsky for lunch at the Ritz-Carlton Hotel in Pentagon City, just across the river from downtown Washington. Starr's deputies listened in as Tripp prodded Lewinsky for details.

Starr's deputies got a rich recording. They grabbed Lewinsky after she left her table and spent the rest of the day and evening with her in Pentagon City, pressing the former intern to make statements and warning about criminal prosecution for perjury. In her authorized biography, *Monica's Story*, Lewinsky said Starr's deputies threatened her with twenty-seven years' imprisonment. Lewinsky, alternately tearful and resolved, waited for her mother and confidante, Marcia Lewis, to arrive by train from New York. She filled the hours by shopping and dining at the Pentagon City mall with Starr's deputies.

When I heard about the matter, I wondered about the specifics. Starr's deputies had no authority to detain Lewinsky. Their conduct has drawn public outrage and apparently a Department of Justice investigation. There was nothing, of course, to prevent Lewinsky from staying voluntarily with the independent counsel's deputies, nor was there anything to prevent her from leaving. The procedure on the record was lawful—with Starr's investigators marching right up to the line. But it is better practice not to stretch that line, especially when dealing with a young woman naive about criminal prosecution.

The day after Lewinsky's session with Starr's deputies, January 17, 1998, Clinton gave a deposition in the Jones case at which he was asked about Monica Lewinsky. The president denied that he'd had "sexual relations" with Lewinsky and said he had no specific memory of having been alone with her. During Clinton's deposition the president's lawyer, Robert Bennett, said Lewinsky had "absolutely no sex of any kind in any manner, shape or form, with President Clinton." Clinton sat quietly as Bennett made this statement.

The president's denials only fanned the media firestorm. TV producers found footage of Clinton at a receiving line embracing a beaming Lewinsky in red lipstick and a black beret. The beret became an international symbol for Monica. Reporters found other friends in whom Lewinsky had confided about Clinton, along with stories about Lewinsky's past adulterous affair with a high school music teacher. An image of Lewinsky emerged as a promiscuous, privileged Valley Girl, the troubled daughter of divorced professional parents.

Unable to escape barrages of questions about Lewinsky, even at news conferences with heads of state, Clinton turned and faced a pack of reporters January 26, 1998, at the White House. His jaw set, his eyes narrowed, his finger pointing at the cameras, the president said in barely controlled rage, "I did not have sexual relations with that woman, Miss Lewinsky. I never told anybody to lie, not one single time. Never. These allegations are false, and I need to go back to work for the American people." That statement would be replayed countless times in the coming months, often juxtaposed with Clinton's later televised regrets about his "inappropriate relationship" with Lewinsky.

In April 1988 Judge Wright threw out the Jones case on summary judgment. Even if Clinton had done everything Jones accused him of doing, Wright ruled, the president was guilty only of "boorish and offensive" behavior, not violation of the law. Clinton seemed to have won. Later, after charges were leveled that Lewinsky and Clinton had lied to cover up their affair, Jones's lawyers pushed to reopen the case, arguing that they had been denied all the evidence. Before the court ruled, Clinton settled with Jones for $800,000.

Ironically, if the president had settled the Jones case months earlier, as he had been urged to do, Lewinsky's name might never have reached Ken Starr, and Clinton might have avoided exposure of his affair and impeachment. Clinton had the option of not answering deposition questions or simply not defending the Paula Jones lawsuit. A nondefense would have led to a default judgment against Clinton. The worst that could have happened would have been an assessment of damages against him. But the worst thing to do—which should have been apparent at the time as well as later—was to give false answers under oath.

Starr's investigation rolled on. Days after the Ritz-Carlton recording, Attorney General Reno expanded Starr's jurisdiction to investigate the

Lewinsky matter. That was a major mistake. I said at the time that the public would suspect a vendetta on Starr's part, because there had been so many unproductive investigations going on for so long. I wasn't criticizing Starr. I was noting an inevitable public reaction. The Associated Press, in a story headlined STARR CHOICE QUESTIONED BY SPECTER, quoted me as saying that "the Monica Lewinsky investigation should have been handled by someone other than Kenneth Starr because too many Americans think he's out to get the President. . . . I think it would have been smarter had the Attorney General, looking at the many years of Starr's involvement and the public perception, which is adverse to Starr . . . let someone else come in."

" 'I don't think Ken Starr did anything wrong in taking over the investigation,' " the AP quoted me further. " 'He did what Attorney General Reno asked him to do, and what the court authorized him to do.' But Specter said that has led to a 'really curious turn of events here, where all the focus is on what did Starr do' and asked, 'How about a focus on what the President did?' "

I questioned the attorney general in a Judiciary Committee oversight hearing on July 15, 1998, about why she acted to expand Starr's authority, rather than assign the case to another independent counsel. Reno refused to answer the question, saying only, "The application speaks for itself, Senator." The application said nothing, but my time had expired and I could ask no more questions.

No matter what questions were asked, no matter how gentle the tone, no matter how deferential, Reno had long mastered the technique at hearings of charming the questioning senators and appearing far more reasonable than they. Perhaps the attorney general accomplished that feat because no senator is ever reasonable. No matter what we said or asked, she always smiled reassuringly, made some vague statement about what a good question or good comment it was, and said she would take it under advisement. Always calm, cool, and collected, Reno appears to answer questions. In reality she provides little information, usually deferring a substantive answer to a future that never comes. Her demeanor and approach matched that recommended to Robert Bork by Tom Korologos—if Bork had taken Reno's approach, he might have been confirmed.

At the July 15, 1998, oversight hearing, the attorney general was at her best. I had returned to the Senate eight days earlier, after open-heart surgery June 2. I usually rested in my hideaway when I wasn't taking the few steps to the Senate floor to record my votes. At the end of the hearing and my not-so-subtle questioning, Reno asked me, "Could I make a personal point?" I replied, "Sure." She said, "It's very nice to see you here." Totally disarming and as fine a finishing flourish as I have heard from any witness at any Senate hearing.

Starr was outgunned in the public relations war with the president, who was a real pro. The independent counsel's inexperience showed in two ways: He didn't tell the public the valid reasons for long delays in some of his prosecutions, and he responded excessively when criticized. Starr did master a perpetual smile that he could wear whenever he emerged from his Arlington home, but it was a thin veneer for a thinner skin.

Starr's worst mistake, perhaps, was subpoenaing top White House aide Sidney Blumenthal and two Little Rock private investigators in February 1998 to answer questions before his grand jury about whether there was a campaign to hinder his probe. Starr was vexed by investigations of some of his deputies. His suggestion that Blumenthal and his cohorts had somehow obstructed justice had no merit, and I said so on national television the weekend after he made his charges. I also put in a call to Sam Dash to discuss the matter. I thought it was inappropriate and dumb if Clinton's team had hired an investigator to look into Starr's prosecutors' personal lives with an eye toward embarrassing and distracting them. But it was not obstruction of justice. The detectives didn't suborn perjury, hinder a witness, or interfere with an investigation or prosecution of a case. The national news media seized on my criticism of Starr's obstruction-of-justice charges. Here was a chance to pit a Republican against Starr.

Starr was repeatedly thwarted by the Clinton defense, which was so good it was offensive. But a prosecutor must keep his bearings, no matter what. Starr was letting Clinton get to him.

Morton Witkin, who defended the Philadelphia Teamsters in our 1963 trial, once told me, "Never let your face show how hard your ass is being kicked." I didn't fully understand or appreciate that advice when I heard it in the late 1960s, but it has since grown on me. Witkin's advice has helped me over the years, and it helped more than one of my Senate colleagues with whom I shared it.

Shortly after the Persian Gulf War ended in 1991, Wyoming Senator Alan Simpson, then the Republican whip, got into a tiff with a CNN reporter, prompting Simpson to make a floor statement featuring a great deal of self-criticism. Alan had a remarkable facility for denouncing himself. He ranted on C-SPAN that people said he was obstreperous and obnoxious and cantankerous and argumentative and obtuse, dense, mean, and so on.

I walked up behind Simpson, interrupted him, and suggested the absence of a quorum, which put the Senate into a brief recess, stopping Simpson's tirade. Then I sat the whip down in the Senate chamber. "Simpson," I said, in a friendly tone, "you are dumber than hell. Why do you repeat all of those criticisms against yourself?" And then I gave him Morton Witkin's advice.

Simpson stopped his verbal self-flagellation. He would repeat the Witkin story to me often when we met, and would pass on Witkin's advice to others. I only wish I'd shared Witkin's dictum with Simpson earlier. It might have changed history. In the summer of 1988, before the August Republican convention but after Vice President Bush had wrapped up the presidential nomination, Alan Simpson walked into the nearly empty Senate chamber, sat down beside me, and began talking in a stream of consciousness. "I told Bush he shouldn't even consider me for the vice presidential nomination because so many groups would be against me," Simpson said.

"The veterans would be against me." Simpson, as chairman of the Senate Veterans Affairs Committee in the early 1980s, had consistently voted against veterans' interests. When I disagreed with him at committee meetings, citing my father's experiences to argue for more benefits, he would hold his bald head and groan, "Oh, no, not Harry Specter again." Simpson continued, "And the seniors are against me." That certainly was true, because Simpson voted against every measure the seniors favored. Simpson added, "And then there's the immigrant vote," referring to immigrants who had become citizens and could vote. He was right again, because as chairman of the Immigration subcommittee, the Wyoming senator had shown little sympathy for immigrants. That, too, was hard for me to understand. Wyoming had even more room for immigrants than Kansas, where my parents had settled because, as we jokingly said, that's where the wheel came off the wagon.

Simpson had given the same litany to George Bush, suggesting that Bush not pick him as a running mate. Bush's selection of Dan Quayle surprised his Senate colleagues. If the Republican senators had made book in early August between Dan and Alan, Simpson would have won overwhelmingly. Had Simpson expressed to Bush more self-confidence and less self-criticism, he might have been chosen. Who knows, a

Bush-Simpson ticket might have beaten Clinton-Gore in 1992. Simpson had his share of enemies, but he would have made an impressive VP candidate.

A few years later, in 1994, Texas Senator Kay Bailey Hutchison was indicted on charges that she had abused her state treasurer's office to further her Senate campaign. After the charges were dismissed, Hutchison approached me and said, "Arlen, I want you to know that Alan Simpson told me the story about never letting your face show, etcetera, and I credit that with helping me to be exonerated. When I was on trial, I thought about that story and tried to look as confident as I could. And when the case against me was dismissed, jurors approached me and said, 'Senator Hutchison, we thought you must have been innocent because you seemed so confident.' "

I thought about telling Ken Starr Witkin's dictum. But our relationship wasn't close, and I was concerned that Starr was too staid to take the advice in the right spirit. As the months passed, I occasionally spoke to Starr. Questions and complaints about the length of his investigation and the lack of tangible results were pounding like a drumbeat. I urged him to explain that legal technicalities, not lack of diligence, caused the delays.

I asked Starr in one phone call for specifics on the prosecution of former Arkansas Governor Jim Guy Tucker. The Tucker case, it turned out, offered a compelling example of the delays forced on the independent counsel. Starr indicted Tucker in June 1995 on charges of fraudulently obtaining hundreds of thousands of dollars in federal loans backed by the Small Business Administration. In September 1995 Arkansas Federal Judge Henry Woods dismissed the case, accusing Starr of overstepping his jurisdiction. In March 1996 the Eighth Circuit Court of Appeals ruled that Judge Woods, a friend of the Clintons', should not have dismissed the charges. The appeals court reinstated the indictments against Tucker and took the case away from Judge Woods.

In a separate indictment brought by Starr, Tucker was convicted in 1996 of bank fraud, along with James and Susan McDougal, for trying to get $3 million in illegal loans from federally backed lenders. The McDougals were the Clintons' former partners in the Whitewater development deal and the former owners of the failed Madison Guaranty Savings and Loan. Then prosecutions halted as Tucker's health failed and he underwent a liver transplant in 1997. In February 1998, during jury selection for Tucker's trial on tax fraud charges, the former governor pleaded guilty to conspiracy in the fraud case and agreed to pay a fine and cooperate with Starr's office.

Starr went through the chronology, which explained why the case had dragged on for so long. After a March 1998 phone call, Starr wanted to follow up but had to go to Little Rock, so he sent his top deputy, Jackie Bennett, to see me. I suggested to Bennett that the independent counsel do a better job of informing the public about the reasons for delays in the Tucker case and other cases. The general view among prosecutors and investigators is that you do not talk about your investigations until they are finished and you have a conclusion. But there is an exception if you're attacked.

The criticism about the length and cost of Starr's probe was in many ways unfair. If a different special prosecutor had been appointed to investigate the Lewinsky matter, there wouldn't have been a clamor six weeks later for that prosecutor to wrap up. And Clinton's lawyers were indeed dragging the process out with their objections and challenges.

The Sunday after my talk with Starr, I was asked on *Fox Morning News* what I thought about Majority Leader Trent Lott's suggestion that Congress censure President Clinton for his conduct. Censure, I said, was not worth a "tinker's dam." My remark set off both a political and an etymological dispute. Pundits balked at or applauded my bucking the majority leader's suggestion. And literati, including *New York Times* columnist William Safire, traced the derivation and correct spelling of the term "tinker's dam" to try to settle the centuries-old controversy over whether the "dam" had a final "n." Lott called me the next day to say that his comment had been taken out of context, and he actually opposed censure. I accepted what Lott said. Often, television news shows extract a phrase or clause that makes a good sound bite.

After months of delay, Lewinsky made a deal with Starr, on July 28, 1998, for her cooperation and testimony in return for immunity from criminal prosecution. She turned over to Starr's office gifts the president had given her, answering machine tapes containing the president's messages, and a blue dress that was stained with what Lewinsky claimed was the president's semen. The FBI lab eventually confirmed her claim. Lewinsky gave the independent counsel and his grand jury extensive testimony, including detailed accounts of ten sexual encounters with Clinton. Without the blue dress, the president would probably never have admitted a relationship. As with Clarence Thomas, it would have been just he said/she said.

On August 17, from the White House Map Room, the president testified under questioning by Starr's deputies before a grand jury by video hookup. Clinton's lawyers had fought an appearance by the president at the federal courthouse where the grand jury was gathered a mile from the White House. The lawyers wanted to avoid photos of the president on the courthouse steps. That decision would later prove ironic, when Clinton's entire three-hour grand jury testimony was aired on national television. Doubly ironic was that once it aired, the president's poll ratings climbed even higher.

Clinton acknowledged "inappropriate intimate contact" with Lewinsky but insisted that he'd been telling the truth when he testified in January in the Jones case that he had not had sex or sexual relations with Lewinsky. As for his lawyer Bob Bennett's statement at that January deposition that the president "had not had sex with Lewinsky in any manner, shape or form," Clinton said he hadn't been paying attention to Bennett.

The case got bogged down in semantics—what constituted sex? Clinton maintained that sexual relations meant intercourse and that all other acts, even oral sex, did not qualify. He also maintained that whether one was having sexual relations depended on whether one was touching his partner or being touched. As the Starr Report put it, "If Ms. Lewinsky performed oral sex on the President, then—under this interpretation—she engaged in sexual relations but he did not." Clinton tried to defend this reasoning on the ground that it was not his definition but his interpretation of Judge Wright's definition.

At 9:00 P.M. August 17, hours after his testimony ended, Clinton gave a nationally televised address from the White House Map Room, the same chamber where he had sparred with Starr's deputies hours earlier. While acknowledging an inappropriate relationship with Lewinsky, Clinton never apologized and spent much of his four-minute address lambasting the independent counsel.

The speech was considered by many to be a disaster. Judiciary Committee chairman Orrin Hatch was overheard by broadcasters saying, "Wasn't that pathetic? I tell you, what a jerk." The president's nationally televised speech drew enormous public attention. The networks not only carried it live but devoted extensive air time to commentary. If President Clinton had waited at least a day after his grand jury testimony before addressing the nation, he would certainly have been better composed and might have avoided a public relations disaster. It's a tough decision whether to address a hot topic immediately or to wait until heads cool. In retrospect, the lesson is: Wait. I think President Clinton would agree on this one, after the fact.

In conversations with Ken Starr in early August, I urged the independent counsel to finish his investigation as soon as possible and file his report by the end of the month, if at all possible. I suggested that he ought to have his paperwork all set to go before President Clinton's deposition, scheduled for August 17, so that Starr would be positioned to incorporate the deposition and conclude the matter. Starr didn't say yes. He didn't say no. He didn't say anything. Starr was circumspect in our conversations, limiting what he told me, frequently citing the limitations of Rule (e), which protects grand jury secrecy, and staying noncommittal on my suggestions. I admired Starr's reticence but gave him my reasoning that it would be useful to have a report in Congress's hands at the earliest moment allowed by a thorough investigation.

On September 9 Starr issued his report to the House of Representatives, offering eleven "acts that may constitute grounds for an impeachment of the President." Starr's report charged that Clinton lied about his sexual affair with Lewinsky as a defendant in *Jones* v. *Clinton* before Starr's grand jury and in a civil deposition; and that he had obstructed justice by concealing evidence, including gifts he had given Lewinsky, by suggesting that Lewinsky file a false affidavit to avoid being deposed in the Jones case, by enlisting Vernon Jordan to help Lewinsky obtain a job in New York in return for her silence, and by lying to potential grand jury witnesses, knowing they would relay falsehoods to the grand jury.

The Starr Report, written in a fluid narrative style that read to many like soft-core pornography, became an overnight international bestseller. Two publishers rushed out bound volumes. The entire text was posted on the Internet. Newspapers reprinted the report as a whole or in part. The report further churned the stomachs of an already-queasy public. Children across America were asking their parents and teachers what oral sex was. Parents agonized about how they could tell their children not to lie and not to engage in casual sex when the president apparently did both. I was bombarded with these questions when I held open-house town meetings throughout Pennsylvania. I think Starr could have toned down his report substantially and still made his points. More important, I think the report should not have been released publicly the way it was. It should have been given to the House Committee and gone through the regular procedures on dissemination. If brought up at a hearing, it would have been made a part of the record and available for publication by the media.

On November 11, I wrote an op-ed piece published in the *New York Times* calling for a criminal trial of Clinton instead of impeachment. The piece concluded:

> If Congress deliberately avoided impeachment to leave the President open to criminal prosecution, I believe Mr. Clinton would face the distinct possibility of conviction and a jail sentence. My experience as District Attorney of Philadelphia convinces me that the issues of character, lying to the American people and putting the country through hell for months would weigh heavily in the sentencing phase after any conviction.
>
> This course—no impeachment proceeding, which the President would be certain to win, and a criminal prosecution, which the President might well lose with a jail sentence—might even induce the President to consider resignation. If so, I could conceive of a Congressionally approved plea bargain in which the President would promptly exit from the White House with his liberty, his pension and our recommendation that he keep his law license. In exchange for giving up the last two years of his Presidency, he would avoid criminal prosecution.
>
> I concede this President seems unlikely to pursue such a course. But if he did, that would be the very best of the undesirable alternatives.

By chance, my article ran on Veterans' Day. The president held a White House breakfast commemorating the national holiday, which I attended as chairman of the Senate Veterans Affairs Committee. When I approached the president in the receiving line, I wondered what his reaction would be. I figured he'd seen the op-ed piece, given his extensive staff and all the talk about impeachment. When we shook hands, the president didn't show a glimmer of anger or even concern.

Maybe he liked my idea, I thought, since it would spare him an impeachment trial. I could not know that two months later the president's lawyers would use my article as a basis for arguing against conviction in his impeachment trial. Sitting in the Senate chamber during the trial, thumbing through the exhibits prepared by the president's counsel, I was surprised and amused to see my *New York Times* op-ed. A few minutes later, presidential counsel Gregory Craig began to argue the president's defense, armed with a large blowup of my op-ed. Craig suggested voting against impeachment in deference to a later criminal trial. I'm not sure if my Senate colleagues shared my amusement that Clinton's lawyers thought my op-ed might help their case.

In any case, as chance would have it, I returned to the White House on November 12, the day after my op-ed ran, for a presidential statement on education. I was listed as a speaker because of work I had done as chairman of the subcommittee that appropriated for the Department of Education. Customarily, speakers assemble with the president and others in a room adjacent to the White House ballroom. On this occasion we gathered in the Red Room with the president, Mrs. Clinton, and several other members of Congress. When the time came to begin the program, the Marine Band played. It was all very heady to walk into the ballroom to the strains of "Hail to the Chief." The president and Mrs. Clinton led the parade, but even walking a few steps behind them, I enjoyed the music.

Unlike his predecessors, President Clinton leaves the presidential seal on the podium throughout a White House program instead of having it affixed when he begins to speak, so the seal was there when my turn came. Despite a bit of tension from my op-ed piece the previous day, I began lightly, saying how much I enjoyed walking into the room to the strains of "Hail to the Chief." The president laughed robustly. I said that I had tried to win the podium on my own in 1996, and noted that I had friends among the battery of photographers and hoped to get a photo of myself speaking behind the presidential seal.

Despite our differences, I've always found Bill Clinton easy to talk to. We first met in early 1993, when he came to address the Republican caucus shortly after becoming president. After he spoke, the new chief executive walked around the small room in the Capitol and chatted with senators individually. Clinton has a great manner of not being in a hurry, even when he is harried. "Senator," he told me, "you ran a really fine campaign." I had just edged Lynn Yeakel to win a third term in the wake of the Hill-Thomas hearings.

"So did you, Mr. President," I said.

"Well, yeah," Clinton said. "We got a lot of the same votes."

Some months later he invited Pennsylvania's Democratic senator, Harris Wofford, and me to travel with him to Ambridge, Pennsylvania, for a health-care forum. As I sat in Marine One with Clinton and the first lady on the White House lawn, waiting to lift off for Andrews Air Force Base, I said, "This helicopter, and then Air Force One—I think the transportation is the best part of your job, Mr. President."

"It's mighty fine, but it's not the best part," Clinton replied. I didn't ask him what the best part was.

Sometimes President Clinton took my advice. I was sitting in my den one night in December 1995 when I got a call from the White House. The president said, "Senator, I got your letter." I had just nearly finished a martini, and I had to focus on which letter. Then I recalled that my general counsel, Mark Klugheit, had written to President Clinton urging him to veto a securities bill. I had told Klugheit after reading his letter, "Mark, we have a limited amount of stationery, which makes me reluctant to do letters like this, since they're obviously so futile. But since it's already prepared, I'll sign it." I put a little note on the bottom: "Going back to my roots on studying this issue at the Yale Law School, I think that my Federal procedure professor—Judge Charles Clark— would roll over in his grave to see the specific pleading standard in this bill. . . ." Clark had been dean of Yale Law School in the late 1930s and became a distinguished judge on the Second Circuit Court of Appeals. I'd had Clark for Procedure 1 in his last days, but I doubted Clinton would know anything about him. Tossing the letter into the out basket, I knew that was the last I would hear of it. Wrong.

The president said, "I've decided to veto the securities bill based on a letter you sent me." I nearly choked on the last sip of the martini. Before I could respond, he said, "Do you have time for me to read you part of my veto message? I refer to you a couple of times." While we were talking, the call waiting rang on my phone, but I ignored it. When I hung up, the phone promptly rang. It was Roger Stone, my campaign manager, who had just gotten a call from the president's political adviser, Dick Morris. Morris told Stone, "The president's about to call your boss to tell him that he's vetoing the securities bill based on the senator's letter." I don't doubt the president's motives, but since Morris knew about it, there was at least a slight political overtone to the matter.

Unlike his response to my letter on the securities bill, the president's reaction to my op-ed column about avoiding impeachment was not to take my advice. Nor did the House of Representatives take it. The House Judiciary Committee reviewed Starr's referral for several weeks and held two days of hearings at which the independent counsel and several panels of experts testified.

Led by Judiciary Committee Chairman Henry Hyde, a massive, silver-haired solon, the House decided in a series of party-line votes to release not only the Starr Report but the complete videotape of Clinton's August 17 grand jury testimony.

The videotape, while containing embarrassing moments for Clinton, backfired on House Republicans, as the president drew wide sympathy. For three hours Clinton sat in a wooden chair under harsh lights answering questions about his intimate sexual acts from the disembodied voices of Starr's deputies. It looked like an interrogation scene from a Fascist documentary. One Republican political consultant was quoted in the next day's papers as saying, "Even I felt for the guy."

Perhaps the most memorable moment of Clinton's testimony was his response to a question about whether he was engaged in an intimate relationship with Lewinsky. "It depends on what your definition of the word 'is' is," Clinton replied. Later, asked whether he had ever been alone with Lewinsky, he said that depended on how one defined "alone." This was familiar wordplay. Asked during his first presidential campaign about his past drug use, Clinton replied that he'd never broken the laws of his country, neatly sidestepping his pot-smoking in England while a student. Clinton, for his part, maintained that his minimal responses to questions about his private conduct satisfied his requirements as a witness while volunteering nothing that might help his vindictive adversaries.

With the country growing increasingly restless over the impeachment investigation, Republicans lost five House seats in the November 1998 election, bucking a decades-old trend that the party out of the White House would win seats in midterm elections. House Speaker Gingrich, newly reelected, resigned his seat. Gingrich, who had led the Republican Revolution that captured control of the House for the first time in forty years, had faced an uncertain battle for reelection as speaker in the wake of the election debacle.

On December 10 the morning press reported that House Republican Whip Tom DeLay was trying to persuade Republicans not to push for censure as an alternative to impeachment. I agreed, and called DeLay to make sure he knew the key language in the Constitution: "Judgment in Cases of Impeachment shall not extend further than to removal from Office, and disqualification to hold and enjoy any Office of honor, Trust or Profit under the United States." DeLay, who wasn't a lawyer, seemed surprised. He hadn't noted the provision, and his legal staff hadn't called it to his attention. In the next several days DeLay was able to avoid a censure vote. Shortly thereafter, speaker-designate Bob Livingston took a position opposing censure. During a brief conversation months later, DeLay told me that my point about the Constitution had persuaded a number of wavering Republicans against censure. It may also have influenced Livingston.

On December 12, as the House neared its impeachment vote, I traveled with the president to Israel while he furthered the Mideast peace process. I heard objections from Republicans about going with the president while he was facing an impeachment vote in the House. But I thought it was important to make a bipartisan showing on a vital international mission. Only two senators were there—Minnesota Democrat Paul Wellstone and I—along with a dozen House members, including Republicans Jon Fox of Pennsylvania and Rick Lazio of New York.

Flying with the president on Air Force One from Washington to Jerusalem was surreal. We talked about Iraq, Netanyahu, Arafat, steel imports, stem-cell research, football, and a variety of other subjects—everything except what everyone was thinking about: impeachment. A day earlier the House Judiciary Committee had finished its hearings. The full House vote, scheduled for the next week, promised to be razor-thin. Yet the president didn't say a word about impeachment on the ten-hour flight or during our three days in Israel. He appeared focused on the Israeli-Palestinian peace process. His speeches were on target.

The president had come to the Holy Land to persuade Netanyahu and Arafat to carry out terms of the Wye River Accord, reached weeks earlier in Maryland. Privately, both Democrats and Republicans in our congressional delegation wondered whether he would have spent so much time on this issue, serious as it was, if it were not for his personal difficulties. I myself doubt that he would have made the long trip to Israel if he hadn't needed a public relations coup and, as a by-product, a chance to lobby some jurors. In effect, the House members were grand jurors, and senators would turn out to be jurors. That was before Senator Byrd's warning to the president: "Don't tamper with the jury."

In Israel, Likud Knesset members inveighed against Netanyahu's decisions at Wye. Palestinians stoned the home of Arafat's chief negotiator. There seemed to be more disagreements within each side's ranks than between the parties. Compelled to look tough and defiant, facing an imminent vote to bring down his government, and perhaps genuinely dissatisfied with Palestinian compliance, Netanyahu postponed the withdrawal schedule.

So, despite his herculean efforts, President Clinton flew back to Washington to face the House impeachment vote a day later without the foreign policy victory he so desperately wanted. Arriving in Washington past midnight on Thursday, December 17, the president ordered missile strikes on Baghdad at seven-thirty that morning. Iraq had repeatedly flouted UN resolutions calling for inspections of Iraq's weapons, especially efforts to check Iraq's chemical, biological, and nuclear efforts.

I think the president should be better rested when he makes such momentous decisions. In his job he bounces from one historic event to another. That was one reason I argued that Clinton's accountability on the perjury and obstruction-of-justice charges should be handled in the criminal courts after his term ended, so that he could concentrate on the country's problems while in office.

When the American missiles began landing in the early morning of December 17, I was sleeping in the Sheraton Hotel in Damascus. The day before, I had met with President Assad of Syria, who emphatically opposed Saddam Hussein and his policies but also strongly opposed an Allied attack against Iraq. I was awakened at 12:20 A.M., turned on CNN, and saw the missile strike. I could not get back to sleep. I had previously arranged to meet the press the next morning at six-thirty, and I issued a guarded statement. I thought it inappropriate to disagree with President Clinton's action. But I did say I thought the Constitution required prior congressional authorization for such military action.

I left Damascus one step ahead of a mob that broke into the U.S. ambassador's home. The ambassador's wife had retreated to the safe haven of a steel-walled closet, where she remained, terrified, until Syrian security forces arrived to rescue her. The United States strongly protested the incident, and Syria ultimately paid $500,000 in damages.

Flying on to Cairo, I met later that morning with President Mubarak. We discussed a wide range of subjects, including the Mideast peace process and the possibility of reinvigorating the Israeli-Syria peace track, but most of all the U.S. attack on Iraq. Mubarak spoke at length about Saddam's false promises to the Arab League before his 1990 attack on Kuwait, but he also expressed concern about the U.S. military action. Before I left, Mubarak could not resist a question about Monica Lewinsky. What was she like? the Egyptian president wanted to know. I replied, obviously in jest, that the House of Representatives was considering an additional article of impeachment: bad taste.

Saturday, December 19, proved perhaps the biggest news day in decades. In my London hotel room I watched CNN as the network showed a split screen with the Baghdad bombing on one side and the House impeachment vote on the other. The House, largely along party lines, approved two of four proposed articles, one on perjury and the other on obstruction of justice. President William Jefferson Clinton had been impeached.

On the other side of the Capitol, for the first time in 131 years and only the second time in history, the Senate would try the president of the United States. The only other president tried by the Senate was Andrew Johnson, who was impeached in 1868 on charges that he fired his secretary of war without Congress's permission. Johnson was acquitted by one vote. In December I wrote a fifteen-page memo to Trent Lott on how I thought the Senate should handle the Clinton impeachment trial. This memo, which I faxed Lott from Ankara, Turkey, on December 29, supplemented a nine-page December 10 memo and a December 22 phone call in which I gave the majority leader my thinking on some of the legal issues. The later, longer memo suggested procedures to deal with the Senate trial in light of public dissatisfaction with the House proceedings, public impatience with impeachment generally, and the need to achieve a judicious, nonpartisan Senate trial.

My second memo outlined procedures for shortening the trial to a few weeks, structuring presentation of the evidence through a small bipartisan group working with the House managers and the president's lawyers, and holding long trial sessions six days a week. I also urged that we call live witnesses. I wrote:

> I think it is fair and accurate to say that no trial in history to date has been or will be so closely watched. We have some gauge as to how closely this trial will be watched from the Warren Commission, which has been the most closely dissected investigation in history. Notwithstanding constant pressure from Chief Justice Warren, who wanted the inquiry concluded at an early date, the staff lawyers insisted on extended tests and extensive interrogation, knowing the record would be closely examined. At that time, we couldn't conceive of the extent of the scrutiny, but we had some inkling of what was coming. At this time, the Senate should be on notice to cross every "t" and dot every "i" twice.

I suggested calling at least three witnesses: Monica Lewinsky, Vernon Jordan, and the president's secretary, Betty Currie. In listing the witnesses, I did not intend to rule out latitude for the House prosecutors to try their case as they saw fit. I also advised in my memo that I believed the Senate had the authority to compel the president to testify, but that many considerations came into play and the decision could be postponed until the situation arose, if it did arise.

I ended my memo by reiterating my preference for holding the president accountable in the criminal courts after his term ended, rather than impeaching him in 1999. But I warned that censure was no solution. "A rush-to-judgment censure plea bargain would complete the trifecta of inappropriate action by the Senate as well as the House and President. If the Senate is going to do an impeachment trial, let's do it right."

THE SENATE'S FINEST HOUR?

Senator Lott moved quickly. The trial began on Thursday, January 7, 1999, the day after the 106th Congress was convened. The media spotlight was intense. It was like the hearings on Clarence Thomas's nomination again, but seven times as bright, as every senator, not just the fourteen Judiciary Committee members, was targeted, stalked, and interviewed. In the Senate, sentiment favored conducting the trial as quickly as possible. Joseph Lieberman, the Connecticut Democrat, and Slade Gorton, the Washington Republican, collaborated on a plan for each side to outline its case in opening arguments and then to move immediately to a Senate vote. If more than thirty-four senators voted for acquittal—and with forty-five Democrats, that was almost certain—the whole proceeding would be over in a few days.

Other senators, including me, insisted on fulfilling the constitutional mandate to conduct a trial. Once the House voted the articles, I argued we had an obligation to complete the process. The constitutional requirement for a Senate trial is plain in Article I, Section 3, Clause 6: "The Senate shall have the sole Power to try all impeachments." The same clause refers to conviction and the next clause to judgment.

Majority Leader Lott made several references to my two memos on trial procedure in our Republican caucus, but the format remained undetermined. The trial of Andrew Johnson offered some precedent, but much of that proceeding had been conducted in secret closed session. A dozen Republican senators, mostly lawyers, drafted procedures, beginning on January 5 and continuing after the trial was under way. Our meetings were spirited, emotional, legal, and political, all at once. A number of senators were fiercely proud of what we were doing, calling it our finest hour, which it might have been—at least to that point, but not for long.

With procedures still undecided, the Senate convened as a court of impeachment on Thursday, January 7. Shortly before 1:00 P.M. I walked out of the Mansfield Room, where Republicans had gathered for our luncheon caucus, and headed for the Senate chamber only a few steps away to take the impeachment trial oath. I started to turn left, heading for the main Senate doors linking the chamber to the corridor that led to the Rotunda and ultimately to the House chamber. I saw a phalanx of cameras larger than I had ever seen, perhaps as many as a hundred television and still cameras. The cameramen and -women were two and three deep the length of the corridor. I turned away, taking another hallway to the Senate chamber.

The army of cameras rolled and clicked as Chief Justice William Rehnquist walked down the hallway into the chamber. Rehnquist was wearing his black robe with four gold stripes on each arm that he had modeled on the Lord Chancellor's costume in Gilbert and Sullivan's *Iolanthe*. I thought the stripes were a good idea. They livened up his robe a little and him a lot. There was an aura of solemnity as the chief justice marched to the dais of the chamber. Senator Strom Thurmond, at ninety-six the oldest senator ever, administered the oath to Rehnquist, twenty-two years his junior. "Hear ye, hear ye," intoned the sergeant at arms. "All persons are commanded to keep silent, on pain of imprisonment."

The thirteen "House managers" then entered the Senate chamber, the last to arrive. The congressmen took their places on newly constructed tables immediately in front of the Senate Democrats. An identical table accommodated the president's counsel, who sat immediately in front of the Senate Republicans. The advocates faced those senators most likely to oppose their position.

Hyde, his baritone carrying through the still Senate chamber, read the articles of impeachment. The House of Representatives had charged William Jefferson Clinton with high crimes and misdemeanors. Senator Mitch McConnell of Kentucky, who sits next to me in the Senate, leaned over and asked, "Who would've ever thought it would come to this? That we'd be sitting here in a court of impeachment?"

I wondered what was on the president's mind when he strayed so far from the truth in his testimony before the grand jury and at his deposition in the Paula Jones case that had led to all this. What were his lawyers doing? How could the president have given such testimony?

The charges read, the chief justice then directed all senators to rise.

459

Each senator was given a commemorative pen, which he or she would use to sign the oath. The pens, as though by providence, had a typographical error in their inscriptions: "*Untied* States Senate." Speculation immediately arose that these mementos would be even more valuable because of the typo, just as postage stamps with misprints command higher prices among collectors.

Contrary to rumors, senators were not asked to return the "Untied" pens. I actually wound up with two of them: one from the opening of the trial and one from the day before, when newly elected or reelected senators were issued pens to sign their oaths of office for the 106th Congress.

Just before noon on that first day of the trial, we had discussed the ceremony protocol in a caucus and had decided that we should take the oath individually, rather than collectively. The moment was full of history, sentiment, and pageantry as we raised our right hands and said "I do" when our names were called. Many moist eyes gazed from the Senate floor. My eyes were not moist, but I did have a profound sense that history was in the making. So much so that I asked the chief justice and every one of my ninety-nine colleagues to sign the impeachment resolution, HR 611, and then had separate copies signed by all thirteen members of the House of Representatives who served as managers and eleven members of the White House counsel's office who participated in the defense. This one-of-a-kind historical memento, together with the "United States Senate" pen and the pin given to me by the sergeant at arms, number twenty-three by my seniority, hang in my Senate office.

The pens distributed, the chief justice administered the oath to the senators. We swore to do "impartial justice." In turn, each of us signed the registry in the well of the Senate. The oaths taken, the next formal occasion, the opening of the trial, was scheduled to begin a week later, Thursday, January 14. But there was a great deal of work to do in the interim to set the trial procedures. The first Senate caucus began spontaneously on the Senate floor minutes after we took our oaths.

We had planned to vote later that afternoon on competing Democratic and Republican trial plans. Majority Leader Lott and Minority Leader Tom Daschle started to confer as soon as the chief justice left the chamber. While the leaders were talking, senators gradually walked over to listen in, until about forty of us were gathered at the center of the floor. Senate practice holds that unless senators walk to the side of the chamber to signify they want a private conversation, other senators are welcome to join in. There is a camaraderie among senators, and we feel comfortable joining our colleagues' discussions. Joining the conversation is even more common practice when the caucus leaders discuss Senate procedure and a senator may influence the outcome.

As the *Baltimore Sun* reported:

> The scrum grew to more than 40 Senators in all—nearly half the Senate—as leading negotiators from both parties took their back-room dealing out in the open. For nearly a half hour, they went back and forth, seemingly oblivious to a cluster of reporters eavesdropping from a nearby balcony. "Can y'all hear?" Sen. John Breaux shouted up to the journalists, who could only catch snatches of conversation.[1]

During the course of the impromptu caucus, Lott suggested that a small group of senators, three from each party, meet to draw the trial road map. That was the approach I had recommended in my memos. There was a strong feeling among Republican senators that we ought to proceed on a bipartisan basis. We had more to gain from bipartisanship than Democrats because we wanted to avoid the House partisanship that had moved much of the public to dismiss the impeachment as a vendetta.

Daschle didn't like Lott's idea of a small bipartisan working group. Drafting procedures should not be limited to a small group of senators, Daschle said, because many, perhaps all, senators wanted to play a part in those decisions. Senator Don Nickles, the majority whip from Oklahoma, then suggested a joint caucus, all one hundred senators. My distinct impression was that Daschle agreed, along with every other Democrat and Republican who spoke up in that rump, impromptu session. No senator voiced an objection to the joint caucus.

At this point there were high hopes of a rare full-Senate meeting. But as the afternoon evolved, the press reported that Daschle had denied agreeing to a joint caucus. Republicans retired to the Mansfield Room for our own caucus. The Mansfield Room, named for the former Democratic senator Mike Mansfield of Montana, who served as majority leader from 1961 to 1976, occupied by the majority party for its meetings, is the Senate's premier meeting room.

As Republicans settled into the Mansfield Room, the word was that Daschle was reneging on the joint caucus. Rumors were flying fast. I heard that Daschle had walked into Lott's office later that afternoon and

461

saw John Kyl on television saying that the Democrats had reneged on their commitment to have a joint caucus. Daschle reportedly expressed surprise that someone had accused him of reneging, rather than characterizing the disagreement as a miscommunication, and then reportedly suggested that he'd never agreed to the caucus in the first place. Either way, the joint caucus seemed off.

I suspect that when other members of Daschle's caucus talked to him, they objected to a joint caucus because the president's position was weakened by bipartisan agreement and strengthened by partisan bickering. It is likely Daschle felt there may have been enough ambiguity for him to get away with denying that he had agreed to a caucus. Decisions on matters such as caucuses are up to the leaders. This unique situation evolved into a spontaneous preconference caucus on the Senate floor. Whatever his reasons, Daschle backed down and the joint caucus was held.

From the beginning I had urged a bipartisan trial. "It is only through bipartisanship that the Senate can succeed in having a judicious, nonpartisan trial which can gain public acceptance," I had written Lott on December 29. "So, all significant procedures must have the concurrence of most Senators from both parties." I also urged Lott that we avoid separate, partisan caucuses. That idea had sprung from a comment by Lieberman on *Face the Nation* on December 20, when we appeared jointly, he from the United States and I from London. Lieberman suggested that the Senate should hold joint, not separate, caucuses during the trial. When I returned from my travels, I called Lieberman and told him that we really ought not to have separate party caucuses.

"You know," the Connecticut Democrat said, "I think that's a good idea."

"I thought you would, because I got it from you on *Face the Nation*," I said. Lieberman laughed appreciatively.

With the joint caucus apparently canceled, we seemed to be heading for two votes that Thursday evening: one on the Democratic plan, which called for no witnesses and very brief arguments from each side, and the other on the Republican plan for five days of presentation from each side, followed by a determination on witnesses and then a debate and vote on both articles of impeachment. The Gorton-Lieberman proposal, which called for outlines from each side followed by an early vote on the charges, had been rejected.

It was obvious that the votes on the competing party plans would go by the party line. Lott pressed us to adopt the Republican position even if it meant a partisan vote. But Olympia Snowe, a moderate from Maine, made an impassioned speech to our caucus that we ought not to hold those votes on the competing plans and get our Republican way through sheer force of numbers. "We ought to exhaust every opportunity for bipartisanship," she pleaded.

When Snowe paused for breath at one point, I shouted, "She's right, Trent."

Ted Stevens, the crusty Appropriations chairman from Alaska, stood up and made his own impassioned speech echoing Snowe, urging us to take our time and seek bipartisanship. Stevens said that he didn't like hearing talk about protecting the House managers, that we weren't Republican senators in this trial, we were jurors. Lott had better be careful, Stevens warned, because he wouldn't have Stevens's vote for long the way the process was moving. The forty-five Democrats, if they voted as a bloc, would need only six Republican crossovers to end the trial by majority vote, so Stevens's threat was potent.

The momentum reversed, the evening votes were canceled, and Lott went to talk to Daschle. Lott told the minority leader about the Republicans' change in position and invited Daschle and the Democrats to a joint caucus at nine-thirty the next morning, Friday, January 8. Daschle, facing unflattering news reports accusing him of reneging on the joint meeting, reversed his field and accepted Lott's invitation.

The bipartisan caucus Friday morning was an extraordinary session. As the *Washington Post* reported, "Although private sessions are held occasionally on national security or other matters, no one could remember such a joint meeting of the Republican and Democratic caucuses before."[2] We met in the Old Senate chamber, near the Rotunda, which the Senate had used until 1859, where Daniel Webster and Henry Clay had held forth. The private session began a little after nine-thirty. Daschle and Lott stood together at the front of the packed room. I sought recognition but didn't get a chance to speak. The next two hours provided time for only a small number of senators to be heard.

Robert Byrd, the former majority leader and courtly self-appointed guardian of Senate tradition, took the floor as the first speaker after brief comments by the leaders. Byrd, his hand occasionally resting in his vest pocket below the copy of the Constitution he always carries in front of his heart, spoke for roughly forty minutes. "We look very bad," Byrd told us. "We appear to be dithering and posturing and slowly disintegrating into the political quicksand." Byrd recounted "The Pardoner's Tale" from Geoffrey Chaucer's *Canterbury Tales*, about three men who all wind up dead in their attempts to cheat each other. Byrd said he told the tale to illustrate the folly of greed. Also, clearly, he had told it to call on Republicans and Democrats to cooperate, rather than sabotage each other for partisan advantage or personal greed. In a sense we got off easy. Byrd is known for his hours-long orations on the history of the Senate, going back to ancient Rome. Byrd, eighty-one, made a point of his seniority, noting that he'd been in Congress longer than anybody else, even ninety-six-year-old Strom Thurmond.

After a few other speakers, Senator Phil Gramm made a short presentation, noting that the Democratic and Republican proposals contained no real differences, because the Senate could, by majority vote, decide to call witnesses under either plan. Both partisan plans addressed only preliminary procedures, leaving the tough issues such as witnesses until later. Gramm invoked Daniel Webster, the famous nineteenth-century orator who had said in the Old Senate chamber during the debate over the Compromise of 1850 that he was speaking "not as a Massachusetts man but as an American."

Senator Ted Kennedy, who later called the day "probably the most dramatic" in his thirty-seven years in the Senate, was moved to jump up. "I think his reference to Webster sort of caught me a little bit,"[3] Kennedy told his hometown *Boston Herald*. Agreeing with Gramm, Kennedy urged the joint caucus to go to first and second base together, and then to a discussion on how to get to third base and beyond.

Kennedy caught the caucus by surprise, and shouts of "Here, here, here! Let's do it!" sealed the plan in an instant, with Republicans especially jumping at it. Trent Lott seized the moment, declaring, "You've got an agreement from Kennedy and Gramm, so let's proceed on that basis." Ted Kennedy, the liberal Democrat, and Phil Gramm, the conservative Texan, had found little common ground in the past. As Senator John McCain told the *Washington Post*, "Stranger things have happened in politics, but the Kennedy-Gramm alignment is one of the strangest."[4]

A number of Democrats, I was told later, were angry at Kennedy because they didn't like the deal. But with Kennedy and Gramm agreeing, they had little room to argue. Some Democrats opposed the compromise because they thought the interests of the White House and Democrats would be best served by the same party-line votes that had poisoned the House proceedings. As the afternoon evolved, I was told, the White House and Kennedy's staff counsel raised a number of objections in an apparent effort to rescind the agreement. But it was too late.

The bipartisan caucus broke shortly before noon, after a little more than two hours. I walked into a Republican lunch-caucus around 1:00 P.M. Trent Lott asked me what we should do next with the House managers. I said we ought to bring them up to date on the bipartisan caucus and on the specifics of what was resolved and left unresolved. Beyond that, I told Lott that we should determine from the House and the president's counsel what witnesses they felt they needed, to prepare for deciding procedures beyond what had been agreed to.

Throughout the trial the principal bone of contention was the issue of witnesses. Lott tried desperately to accommodate the very different views of three groups: the House managers, who wanted a full-blown trial with as many as fifteen or even twenty-five witnesses; many Republicans, who wanted to give the House managers relatively free rein, but with fewer witnesses; and the Democrats, who wanted no witnesses at all—and no trial at all, for that matter. Whenever the witness issue arose, the Democrats recoiled. The 100–0 vote on Thursday to establish the procedure for the initial phase of the trial came off only because this issue was excluded.

On top of solid Democratic opposition to live witnesses, it was clear that a number of Republican senators—more than the six needed to swing a vote—were skittish about having live witnesses or even many depositions, and were teetering. I suggested that we discuss with the House managers where witnesses were necessary, such as where important accounts conflicted. Lott agreed and asked me to take up the matter with Chairman Hyde promptly. Others chimed in, offering to help. Saying, "You, you, and you," Lott designated John Kyl of Arizona, Jim Inhofe of Oklahoma, Jim Bunning of Kentucky, and me, later joined by Jeff Sessions of Alabama.

I left the lunch and called Henry Hyde. We arranged a 2:00 P.M. meeting at Hyde's office. It was already 1:20 P.M. Bunning, Kyl, and I met briefly in my hideaway office in the Capitol, tracked down Inhofe in the cloakroom, and headed across the Capitol. We crossed the "crypt," the first-floor Rotunda, took the House subway, and ascended to Hyde's office in the Rayburn Building.

I carefully avoided giving the House managers advice on how to handle the trial as we briefed them on the morning joint caucus and other developments. The oath about "impartial justice" stuck in my mind. We were on a mission to try to determine the standards for calling witnesses. Shortly into the meeting, the telephone rang. It was Phil Gramm reporting to Henry Hyde about what had been worked out during Gramm's own talks with some House people. Gramm wanted the Senate to agree to call the witnesses whom the House managers wanted. The Congressmen put Gramm on the speakerphone. The Texas senator noted that this was the best that could be done with the "moderates."

Near the end of the meeting there was some talk about how we were going to get this president, how we were going to convict Bill Clinton. That line of conversation made me uncomfortable. I stood up to draw the meeting to a close, or at least leave the room. We had accomplished our purpose of briefing the House managers. But we hadn't settled the question about witnesses. I learned long ago always to arrange the next meeting before leaving the current one. We set our next meeting, in which the managers would detail the witnesses they needed, for 2:00 P.M. Monday in my hideaway.

We went back to the Senate, and I reported briefly to Lott. "Would you like me to follow up?" I asked.

"Yeah," he said. "Who do you think ought to help you?"

"Well, Jeff [Sessions] and Jon [Kyl] are both lawyers," I said. "Either one would be fine."

Lott replied, "The conference would feel more comfortable with both of them on." In other words, the Republican caucus, which was predominantly conservative, would prefer to have two conservatives along with me. It's always a balancing act. The conservatives find me useful to lend credibility to their proposals, as on Thursday afternoon, when it looked as though we were heading for party-line votes on our competing plans.

Slade Gorton and Phil Gramm had been assigned to put finishing touches on the Republican proposal for the Senate trial procedures. Gramm walked into the caucus late in the afternoon and handed me a copy of his draft. I read it and told him I thought it was satisfactory. When I stood to leave, Gramm asked me to wait until the other copies had arrived and the rest of the caucus had a chance to read them. "Before you go, would you mind telling people that you liked this?" Gramm asked. He was eager for me to speak up, less for my expertise than for the imprimatur of a centrist.

I asked Gramm how long it would take for the copies to arrive. I was scheduled to appear on *Larry King Live* that night. Not long, Gramm assured me. A few minutes later the copies of the draft arrived. While some twenty-five caucus members were reading, Gramm asked me for my views. I responded with a two-word speech: "Looks good!" That brought a round of applause and laughs. My colleagues had never heard a two-word speech.

Just after 4:00 P.M. on Friday, January 8, the Senate voted 100–0 to approve initial procedures for the trial, riding the momentum of the Gramm-Kennedy agreement in the joint morning caucus. Each side would have twenty-four hours to make opening arguments. Senators would then have sixteen hours to submit questions in writing to the chief justice, who would propound the queries. The White House would then be allowed to offer a motion to dismiss.

The adopted resolution also outlined deadlines for filing briefs and beginning arguments, allowed a motion to subpoena witnesses, and allowed for a final vote if the trial was not dismissed. The House managers would have to request all their witnesses for depositions at one time, in a block. This posed a dilemma for them. If they asked for too many witnesses, they might get none.

By late Friday, conversations were going in all directions: Republican senators talking to House managers, Democratic senators talking to the White House and White House counsel. We were not bound by limitations on ex parte contacts as we would have been if the case had been in a civil or criminal courtroom. But the partisan currents bothered me.

Outside the Senate chamber and the caucus rooms, the media were insatiable. Television bookers clogged my press office phones. On top of Thursday's *Larry King Live*, I appeared that Sunday on NBC's *Meet the Press* along with five other senators. Early the next week, I would appear on CNN's *Late Edition*, *The NewsHour with Jim Lehrer*, *CBS Evening News*, ABC's *Good Morning America, Crossfire*, and a CNBC news show. On any given weekend during the trial, twenty senators—a fifth of the Senate—hit the network talking-head shows. Almost every senator was catapulted into being a virtual national celebrity. The impeachment case was being tried not in the Senate chamber but in the Senate corridors, on the evening TV interview shows, and on the Sunday talk shows.

Over the weekend I decided that my first order of business Monday morning would be to include Democratic senators in the 2:00 P.M.

meeting with the House managers. When I got into the office on Monday morning, I called Lott. He was out, and I called Jon Kyl, who was also unavailable. Then I called Sessions and told him I thought we should do the meeting on a bipartisan basis.

Technically, we were not precluded from talking to the house managers, because we were acting in our capacity as trial managers, not as jurors, in trying to set standards for witnesses. The situation was dicey. It was preferable not to talk to one side's lawyers without having the other side's lawyers present. Even though the impeachment trial was not a judicial proceeding, I decided we would be wise to bring in the Democrats.

Sessions agreed. We recognized that having Democrats along would constrain what we could say, but it was worth the price. I called Hyde and told him we wanted the process to be bipartisan. "Whatever you want to do, go ahead," the House chairman said.

I called Joe Lieberman, who had criticized Clinton over the Lewinsky matter in an early Senate floor speech. That speech elevated Lieberman's public reputation. I had always found him easy to deal with and as close to a nonpartisan as there was on that side of the aisle or, for that matter, in the entire Senate. I told Lieberman about the 2:00 P.M. meeting and asked him to attend. Lieberman said he'd better check with Daschle, and he called back a few minutes later. "Daschle is not willing to do this, because he thinks our caucus would not like it. And although it really is a pretty good idea, it's premature. We could have this meeting when we get to the witness issue." I said, "Joe, that really isn't true. We're going to be really busy, and if we're going to get standards for witnesses, we're going to have to do it now. But listen, I understand."

Later I phoned White House counsel Charles Ruff, the tough and talented head of the president's legal team. "Chuck," I said, "Senator Lott asked Senators Sessions and Kyl and me to try to structure some standards for calling witnesses. I invited Senator Lieberman to join us in talking to the House managers, but he declined after checking with Senator Daschle. We'd like to have your views on standards for calling witnesses if you care to do so."

"Senator," Ruff said, "I really appreciate you calling me, but this is more political than legal. I'd like to get back to you if I may."

I had gone quite a few rounds with Chuck Ruff on federal judges from Pennsylvania, and we had a good relationship. Ruff and the White House especially appreciated my fighting for Judge Frederica Massiah-Jackson in early 1998 when no Democrat would fight for her. Massiah-Jackson was, in my opinion, unfairly denied a seat on the federal district court in Philadelphia, where she would have been the first African-American woman. She was pelted by allegations that she was soft on crime and temperamentally unfit for the bench. The Philadelphia Bar Association, among others, found those charges "unfair" and "unbalanced." But Massiah-Jackson did not get a fair chance to rebut them. As the *New York Times* editorialized, "She had been subjected to what Senator Arlen Specter called 'water torture' in an unfair process that is bound to have a chilling effect on judicial independence."[5]

Ruff called me back to say he thought it best not to participate, since the Senate Democrats weren't ready to proceed on a bipartisan basis. The Democrats didn't want bipartisanship. They wanted a party-line 55–45 vote to make the Senate trial—like the House impeachment—look like a Republican crusade. I had talked to one Democratic House member who was adamant that bipartisanship ran counter to the president's and Democrats' interest. That House member told the president after the Friday joint caucus was called, "This bipartisanship is trouble for you, Mr. President."

So we went ahead with our Republicans-only meeting on Monday afternoon, January 11. Kyl, Sessions, and I met with three House managers and continued reviewing the list of witnesses. We senators, careful to stay within what we considered proper bounds, made no specific recommendations about how many witnesses the House managers should call, either at that meeting or at later ones. It was a battle to balance establishing the trial procedures, including getting all the material witnesses to testify and avoiding or minimizing contact with the trial managers, which might suggest some bias. We were in largely uncharted waters. I felt uncomfortable because the ex parte contacts might give the appearance of bias, but we had to talk to the people involved to set the trial procedures.

The House managers wanted to call Lewinsky because she had conflicts with Betty Currie over returning the president's gifts, the timing of phone calls, and other matters. They wanted to call Vernon Jordan because he had arranged a job for Lewinsky. There were conflicts between what Jordan and Lewinsky had said. The managers also wanted to call expert witnesses to testify about what legally constituted obstruction. I said it was doubtful that the Senate would vote to hear such testimony, because it could be effectively covered in lawyers' arguments.

I raised the issue of the president as a potential witness. I said I had researched the issue and thought the Senate had the power to call the president, but that the politics were delicate. If the managers had any intention to call the president, I advised, they ought to consider listing him among the potential witnesses. They were apprehensive.

"Listen," I said, "I don't know whether the president should testify or not. It's obviously going to be very, very delicate. Who knows what's going to happen in this trial? If he weren't the president, then he'd certainly be called upon to testify as to what happened."

One manager said, "Well, maybe the Senate should call him."

I said, "You're the managers, and you have to decide what witnesses to call." The Senate would then vote on whether to allow those witnesses to testify. But I did concede that the Senate had the authority to compel the president's appearance even without a request from the House managers.

The House managers pressed for the Senate to call the president. No, I said, at this stage it was the House's call. I told the managers it would be tough enough to get fifty-one votes to call the president, but tougher if they didn't list him among the witnesses they wanted. Further, I said, if the House managers didn't list the president initially and then tried to call him later, somebody would certainly object, saying they had waived their right. I advised that as a precautionary measure the House managers say, "We're going to list the president. We don't know if we're going to call him. We don't want to waive the right. And, depending on how the trial's going, we may call him."

In the end they didn't have the chutzpah to list the president. I thought he should be called, but I was the only one willing to put his name behind that position, in my early memos to Lott and in my comments in the Republican caucus.

The same morning we met with the House managers, I also met with a group of twelve Republican senators on a broader range of issues, including witnesses, whether our sessions would be public, and what questions senators would submit to the chief justice. My colleagues were leaning toward keeping the Senate doors closed during our next orders of business: debating the motion to dismiss and the motion to take depositions. Mitch McConnell, the Republican Senate campaign chairman, was opposed to open sessions for political reasons. "I don't want to emphasize the next election too much here, but that's a factor, and we're going to look just like the House," McConnell said.

I argued for an open session. "We'll conduct ourselves well. I believe the public has a right to know how the issues will be discussed." I thought the public and posterity should know the reasons for our votes as a guide for today and the future. The informal, seat-of-the pants, corridor comments may be found in the CNN or MSNBC files, but there would be no Senate videotape to record what could be important views expressed on the floor.

I added that senators' speeches might affect public opinion. There was always the sense that senators did little important speaking in the nearly empty chamber. But now the public was tuning in as senators expressed their views in corridors, by the subway, and on talk shows. They would certainly listen to speeches on the Senate floor.

Surprises were always possible when senators spoke publicly, I said. For example, I quipped, I was surprised when Phil Gramm made a good speech in the joint caucus, producing the bipartisan compromise. I said I was even more surprised when the Democrats agreed with Phil. Then, I said, I was most surprised when Kennedy jumped up and sealed the deal. "You never know what will happen when someone speaks up."

"Arlen," Gramm drawled, "if you listened to me more often, you'd be better off."

Still, a number of Republican senators continued to fight open sessions, arguing that opening the doors would prolong the trial, as virtually every senator would feel compelled to speak, and that the debate would degenerate into bitter partisanship, which would hurt Republicans in the 2000 elections. Ending my call for open sessions, I said, "I think we ought to reflect on this. We don't have to decide this right now. Let's see what happens in the course of the next several days."

The caucus reached no decision about an open session, deferring the matter. Every time we tried to make a decision, we ran into objections and problems, so we deferred as many decisions as we could to try to come to as much agreement as we could on narrower issues. In any case, with or without bipartisanship, with or without procedures set, with or without a decision to open the doors, the impeachment trial would begin the following Thursday.

HOSTILE WITNESSES

As the trial was about to begin, I asked Senator Robert Byrd if he had ever thought he would sit on an impeachment court. "Not of the president, I didn't," the West Virginian said. During the trial I often talked to Byrd before the chief justice arrived and during the breaks. Our bordering states had many overlapping interests, especially the steel and coal industries, and we had worked together on a great deal of legislation.

Our contacts had not always been congenial. When Byrd chaired the Senate Appropriations Committee in 1989, I challenged the allocations he'd made for the various subcommittees. It was unheard of to challenge the chairman, but I thought it important, because Byrd had changed the numbers set by the full Senate in the Budget Resolution. He had established, by himself, the Senate's position on how to spend all discretionary federal dollars.

I began that showdown on July 15, 1989, by noting that Byrd had reduced the allocation to the subcommittee on Labor, Health and Human Services, and Education, on which I was then the ranking member. I made a motion to restore the funding for that subcommittee and other subcommittees. Byrd brushed off my concerns, saying the budget resolution was based on staff work, not on senators' wills.

"I believe there is a little more strength in the congressional budget resolution than just staff work," I said. "We have a Budget Resolution which has been passed. It is very hard to say what is staff and what is senators. . . . But we have very exacting figures which are being very markedly changed by what is being proposed here today."

Byrd pressed for a vote on his numbers, and got it. Two other senators joined me: Bob Kasten of Wisconsin, who was upset over Byrd's allocation to his Foreign Operations Subcommittee; and Alfonse

D'Amato of New York, who sat next to me and joined me when I told him some younger, independent senators ought to stand up to the autocracy of the old guard. The vote was 26–3 for Byrd.

Two years later, on June 5, 1991, I again sparred with Byrd over his allocations. He gave a lengthy response, essentially saying he would run the Appropriations Committee his way. Then he told me, "But I can only say this, Senator Specter: that when you become chairman of this committee, you will run it your way, and you won't find me grumbling." I remind Byrd of that remark from time to time, now that I am only two seats from that lofty position.

In the decade that has passed since that debate, Byrd and I have become better friends. I especially valued his views on impeachment, and he often referred to me as his "attorney general."

The trial of the millennium began slowly. Over the first three days, from January 14 to 16, the thirteen House managers each made opening statements, some laced with grand rhetoric and Shakespearean, biblical, and historical references.

The austere scene in the Senate chamber was almost surreal. All one hundred senators sat silently in their chairs for hours. Despite the high stakes and higher oratory, heavy eyelids fell and heads nodded. But the one senator who was constantly under surveillance—Senator Strom Thurmond—remained upright and alert throughout the proceeding. I fought off the tendency to doze, recalling an admonition Senator Paul Laxalt had given me when I attended my first State of the Union speech in 1981. Laxalt, who sat next to me, leaned over and said, "Be careful not to doze off. Last year Senator Sam Hayakawa fell asleep, and the national television camera was on him for three minutes."

There were some bright spots during those first days of the impeachment trial. Asa Hutchinson, a former prosecutor from Arkansas, was terrific, using charts that were as easy to follow as his argument. Congressman Jim Rogan, a former judge, made an intense, compelling presentation, even if he grew overly caustic at times, as when he likened the president of the United States to a murder defendant who claimed he had not been at the scene of the crime and, alternatively, if he was at the scene, he'd acted in self-defense. Congressman Lindsey Graham of South Carolina, although not as pointed legally, used his drawl and Southern charm to great effect.

I joshed Tom Harkin, the populist Iowa Democrat, about his outlandish public statement that the trial was "a pile of dung." "You get away with murder," I told him.

The drama picked up on January 15, the second day of the trial, as Congressman Bob Barr concluded his opening speech: "We urge you, the distinguished jurors in this case, not to be fooled." Tom Harkin of Iowa shouted, "Objection!" Rising from his seat, he said that senators were not jurors and should not be referred to as jurors. Senators were more like judges, he said. Harkin cited the Constitution and *The Federalist Papers*.

Harkin's objection was out of line. It was also wrong, on the basis of his citation of *The Federalist Papers*. And it violated the rules, which, on pain of imprisonment, barred any senator from speaking during the trial. If there was anything a senator needed to say to the chief justice, he or she must hand him a note and keep quiet. Rehnquist eventually told Harkin just to state his reason, not "argue ad infinitum." Harkin said he was just stating his reason.

Then Chief Justice William Rehnquist issued his first official ruling of the Clinton impeachment trial: He sided with Harkin. "The Senate sits as a court and not a jury, and therefore counsel shall refrain from referring to senators as jurors," Rehnquist ruled. Counsel could call us senators "triers of fact."

I think Rehnquist made the wrong ruling. We *were* jurors. We happened to be many other things, including, in effect, judges, but we were also jurors. We were jurors because we would render a verdict. We were fact finders. We applied the law to the facts. We gave a verdict as to whether the president's conduct constituted guilt under the articles of impeachment. You can be a juror while you're still a judge, just as you can be a fact finder while you sit as a judge in a court of impeachment.

Whether I was officially a juror or not, one role I decided I would not play during the trial was media commentator. I declined TV interviews once the trial began. I felt that giving interviews on the day's proceedings might conflict with my juror's role and jeopardize my sworn oath to do "impartial justice."

Beyond question, we set a new endurance record for senators sitting still. When Dale Bumpers, who had retired from the Senate earlier in the month, addressed the Senate on behalf of the president, the Arkansan struck the funniest chord of the trial. Bumpers was legendary for addressing an empty Senate chamber. Any senator present at the start of a Bumpers speech, unless presiding, soon left. Bumpers spoke too long and too loudly, and he spoke repeatedly on the same subjects. His recurrent themes resounded in the vacant chamber as his extra-long lapel microphone cord let him pace far down the aisle.

When Bumpers took the Senate floor at 4:10 P.M. on January 21, the first day of defense arguments, he received a warm response from all his old Senate colleagues and from the new senators sworn in two weeks earlier. It was his first time back, it was nice to see one of our brethren undertake an important assignment, and Bumpers made a good speech. Looking at his audience, he said, "It is a great joy to see you. And it is especially pleasant to see an audience which represents about the size of the cumulative audience I had over a period of twenty-four years."

In those early days some spectators, and even some senators, complained that the proceedings were boring. Lindsey Graham, the sharp young congressman, noted how extraordinary it was to call the proceedings boring when control of the country was at stake. That led me to muse that the trial was really a revolution—a peaceable, civilized, constitutional effort to overthrow the head of state.

During opening arguments I was struck by how far apart the Democrats and Republicans were in their views of the case. This became clear when I talked to Joe Biden, the Delaware Democrat who had chaired the Judiciary Committee during Bork's and Thomas's confirmation hearings. Biden and I are very good friends. We talk for hours on the Metroliner from Washington to Wilmington, where he gets off, while I stay on to Philadelphia. Biden, elected to the Senate at the age of twenty-nine, has been in Washington longer than I. But my first executive assistant, Sylvia Nolde, was a Capitol Hill veteran who had developed the contacts and clout to hold a Metroliner for as long as five minutes when I needed to get from a vote to the platform. Biden recalls racing through Union Station after a vote one evening in early 1981, nearly clipping passersby with his bags, trying to make the train he took twice a day, when a porter told him, "Relax, buddy, we're holding this train for a senator."

After a House manager argued that Clinton could not govern with the scandal hanging over him, Biden railed, "How could you say that this president can't govern, since he's so popular? And look how he took the Congress to the cleaners in establishing the budget last year, and when he walks into the United Nations, he gets a standing ovation."

476

A pretty good argument, but the president did have problems. When Clinton traveled to Africa during the scandal, a newspaper cartoon there showed Air Force One as a huge phallic symbol. The president did get a standing ovation from members of Congress, including Republicans, at the State of the Union address, but that was hollow symbolism. The Republicans, even those who were openly disdainful and contemptuous of the president, rose out of respect for the office. He was the president, it was the State of the Union speech, and perhaps most important, they were on national television.

I thought it was smart of the president to give the speech in January, as the trial was running full steam, to try to carry on the country's business. I thought he was impressive that night. He did a superb job on the podium at the House of Representatives, when earlier in the day he'd been in the Senate dock across the Capitol Rotunda. I marveled at how the president could attend public meetings with a confident air, not blanching, at the same time the television stations were repeating his statements, "I did not have sexual relations with that woman, Miss Lewinsky," juxtaposed with his later statement acknowledging his "inappropriate relationship" with Lewinsky. I was amazed but impressed that he could carry it off without showing the shame he must have felt. Or maybe he didn't.

Clinton's two bold-faced, contradictory declarations about Monica Lewinsky, permanently recorded on videotape, perhaps as much as the impeachment itself mar what might otherwise have been heralded as an extraordinary presidency. On TV Bill Clinton has no peer, with the possible exception of Ronald Reagan. Before large audiences he is superb. I attended his speech on health care in Ambrose, Pennsylvania, in the fall of 1993, and he had the audience of about two thousand in the palm of his hand.

In small groups I found President Clinton extraordinarily effective. During his series of meetings in March 1999 with about forty representatives and senators on the bombing of Yugoslavia, he listened and exchanged ideas, demonstrating depth, patience, and flexibility. Although members drifted out for votes or committee meetings, he stayed for two hours, until the stragglers had concluded their questions and comments. One-on-one he was even more effective, with a compelling personal touch.

I accepted many of President Clinton's invitations to the White House for events on education and health care, matters related to my

Appropriations subcommittee chairmanship. While it was always interesting to observe the president and the presidency, these events were not the best use of his time. Had he been less devoted to media events, photo ops, and transitory poll ratings, his historical presidential rating might have soared.

Biden and I usually agree, but our views differed strikingly on almost all aspects of the impeachment trial. Joe told me, "Even with your skill as a prosecutor, Arlen, you couldn't get a conviction on this case."

"I disagree," I said with a smile. "I could—unless you were defense counsel."

It was good to hear Biden laugh. "That's a hell of an answer, Arlen," he said.

I considered it best to discuss the trial further with Biden on one of our train rides. It was clear to me that our sharp differences stemmed from the influence of our party caucuses. It wasn't exactly brainwashing, but we were both heavily preconditioned.

As John Kennedy said, "Sometimes party asks too much." I was concerned that both parties were always asking too much in this case. Inevitably, prior contacts, especially with the president, had an impact and an influence. Democratic senators would naturally feel loyalty toward a president who had campaigned with them. Republicans would resent a president who had come into their states to campaign against them.

For my part, I had always found Bill Clinton personable and likable in our many contacts over the past six years. I had often crossed party lines to work with him on education and health-care issues, although I had fought his massive 1993 bill to transform America's health-care system.

The controversy over Clinton's health-care plan, loud as it was, was minuscule compared with the impeachment fight. The trial under way, the media barrage raged. Reporters surrounded senators every time we took a break or left a meeting or passed down a corridor. At the Senate subway at day's end, senators were accosted by as many as a dozen reporters. I fell back on my standard "No comment." I walked out of the trial after sitting silently next to John Chafee on the Senate floor, came back to the office, and there was John being interviewed on CNN, with a long line of senators waiting to follow him. The tube is a senator's natural habitat.

Joe Lieberman approached me on the Senate floor and said, "You and I have come to the same conclusion again. I've decided to go off television myself." Byrd announced he would say nothing at all about the trial. The *Washington Post* reported that the former majority leader was not talking even to his staff.

As the opening presentations played out, the House managers did a good job in presenting their case, but were no match for the president's lawyers. In caucus I said we ought to anticipate a Democratic effort to make it look as though the trial would become long and drawn out. We should try to get a bipartisan agreement on the rules, but if we couldn't, we had to set procedures for handling depositions and witnesses without letting the process run interminably. There was a sense of unease in our caucus as media criticism mounted that the trial was a waste of time and a serious distraction from the country's more important business.

I noted that Democrats were beginning to talk as if the case were over, trying to seize on momentum favoring the president to wrap it up quickly. I cited a *Philadelphia Inquirer* about the president's momentum and a page-one story in the *New York Times* quoting evangelist and former Republican presidential candidate Pat Robertson that the trial was essentially over and we should move on. I said we ought to stay the course, complete the process, and not be stampeded.

In caucus I heard too many comments about structuring our questions to help the House managers make their case. It becomes tough to discharge our oath to do "impartial justice" when we talk about the Republican point of view and throwing softballs to the House managers. John Ashcroft, the conservative Missourian, was on the right track when he made a speech about the necessity of appearing neutral. I added, "We have to really *be* neutral if we want to be successful in appearing neutral."

On the morning of Thursday, January 21, when I arrived at the office at 8:30 A.M., I saw a notice that Senator Lott had scheduled a 10 A.M. caucus, which required me to rush a subcommittee hearing. I was trying to do regular Senate business in the mornings before the impeachment court convened and sometimes in the evenings. I held one hearing on stem-cell research, which promises cures for Parkinson's disease and a variety of other illnesses but has become mired in dispute over the use of live embryos. Little attention was paid. As Senator John McCain had predicted the preceding fall, impeachment was sucking all the oxygen out of every room in Washington.

A *Time* magazine reporter pressed me for an interview. The only thing I agreed to talk about was my decision not to be interviewed. Why was I not talking when most of my colleagues were, she wanted to know. "I'm not talking because I'm a juror and there's no way you answer a question without signifying what you might have in mind," I said. *Time* ran a story likening my stance to a monk's vow of silence.

B yrd, the self-appointed parliamentary expert, announced on Friday, January 22, that he would make a motion to dismiss the case. If Byrd's motion won a majority, the trial would be over. In the Republican caucus, Trent Lott tried to perk everybody up. "When you make your statements this weekend, don't look down in the dumps," he counseled. "Stand up and be firm and confident. We're not going to have a caucus decision, but I would be very disappointed if we didn't stick together on defeating this motion to dismiss."

The second day of questions, Saturday, January 23, I got three of my own questions and one joint question asked by Rehnquist, which drew little in the way of substantive response. One of my questions for the Clinton team read, "You have argued that when the president made his famous statements to Betty Currie on January 18, he was not seeking to coach a potential witness but was merely seeking to refresh his memory and get information in preparation for a media barrage. Yet if the president was truly seeking information, why would he ask Ms. Currie questions to which she could not possibly know the answer, such as, 'Monica came on to me, and I never touched her, right?' and 'You were always there when she was, right?' "

National Public Radio, at least, liked my question. "Well, there wasn't a lot of crackle in the questioning, I thought today . . . except for Senator Specter," Ken Bode, who doubles as dean of Northwestern's journalism school, said during an NPR broadcast. "His was my favorite question of the day," Mara Liasson added. "He asked . . . how could the president be refreshing his recollection when he had that extraordinary conversation with Betty Currie, where he said, 'Monica came on to me, right?' . . . How could he be refreshing his recollection by telling Betty Currie a lot of false statements? I mean, that was a good question."[1]

In caucus we were still trying to work out a procedure for witnesses, how to handle Byrd's motion to dismiss, and whether to close the proceedings. I said Byrd's motion had the advantage, if handled right, of leaving open the option to prosecute Clinton later. If the Senate folded its trial without reaching a verdict—rather than by acquitting the president—a criminal prosecution would stand a greater chance of success.

Against my arguments, and against a petition circulated by Kay Bailey Hutchison that I signed, the Senate voted to close the proceedings to the public. Many senators reasoned that without the cameras rolling, senators would not feel compelled to perform and the trial would move faster.

On January 25, Senate Republicans began our caucus at 10:00 A.M. For two hours we discussed Byrd's motion to dismiss. Shortly after noon I took my lunch to my Capitol hideaway office to do some work. No sooner had I arrived than Jon Kyl called me and said, "Lott wants us to go talk to the House managers."

I said, "I'd be glad to do that, but only after we invite the Democrats."

Kyl said, "Would you mind coming upstairs right now? He wants us to do this right away."

I went upstairs to our second-floor caucus room and walked over to the majority leader. "I'd be glad to do this, Trent, but I want to invite the Democrats in," I said.

"I've already checked with Daschle, and he says absolutely not." So we again had no choice but to bring a Republican-only team to meet with the House managers. At 1:30 P.M. Kyl and I met with Congressmen Ed Bryant, Asa Hutchinson, and Lindsey Graham to go over the proposed list of witnesses.

After introductory remarks by Kyl, we got down to the bottom line. "You could ask for all of them," I said, "but how many you're going to get is another proposition. What is it that you want Blumenthal for?" Sidney Blumenthal, a journalist turned presidential adviser, had testified that Clinton told him Lewinsky had been stalking him. Starr, during his ill-advised 1998 obstruction-of-justice query, had dragged

Blumenthal before the independent counsel's grand jury over investigations of Starr's deputies. I tried to derive what the House managers were really looking for from these prospective witnesses. We ended the meeting without a final list.

For the rest of the day, until nearly 10:00 P.M., we took up Byrd's motion to dismiss. I cannot comment on senators' arguments, even my own, in that closed session because of Senate rules that carry a sanction up to expulsion. The next day, January 26, the morning Republican caucus began with Lott saying he had heard of discussions between senators and House managers about witnesses. "Arlen, do you know anything about them?"

"I do because you instructed me to participate," I said. I gave my report, and we discussed what the conference would be willing to do. The sentiment ran toward giving the House managers some latitude, but a number of Republican senators expressed reluctance to go much above the three principal witnesses. I had argued in several caucuses that we should press hard to bring Monica Lewinsky to the floor, because I thought her presence indispensable to our fact-finding and because she could change the dynamics of the case. I didn't see much prospect of getting testimony from Kathleen Willey, the Richmond socialite who had complained that the president had groped her in the Oval Office. But I thought the Democrats feared that Lewinsky's testimony might somehow lead to Willey.

In retrospect, I think the White House also feared that Monica Lewinsky's testimony, especially if given on the Senate floor, could spark a chain reaction that would eventually lead to Juanita Broaddrick, known as Jane Doe #5. Broaddrick, an operator of a nursing home in Arkansas, charged that Clinton had raped her twenty-one years earlier. The "Jane Doe" designation came from the potential-witness subpoena list from the Paula Jones case, with the names redacted. While the outline of Juanita Broaddrick's story was generally known, the details had never been presented to Republican senators, even in our closed caucuses.

Apparently, details had been presented to wavering House Republicans by the majority whip, Congressman Tom Delay, who used Broaddrick's story to press Republicans to vote for the articles of impeachment. As *Newsweek* reported, "One GOP House member says the sealed Broaddrick material was decisive for 'a few' of his colleagues. With the obstruction count carrying in the House on Dec. 19 by only five votes, that may have been enough to change history." What was completely unknown was the impact that Juanita Broaddrick's testimony would have on the public. When Broaddrick told her story on NBC's *Dateline* on February 24, twelve days after the trial ended, she made a compelling presentation.

Broaddrick said she met then–Arkansas Attorney General Clinton in 1978 at the nursing home she ran in Van Buren, Arkansas. When Broaddrick visited Little Rock, she phoned Clinton, as he had asked, she said. Clinton told her the Camelot Hotel lobby was too crowded and suggested meeting in her room. After some coffee and small talk, Broaddrick said, Clinton pinned her on the hotel bed, bit her lip, and raped her. She said he told her to fix her swollen lip and left. Alternately tearful and resolute, Broaddrick seemed convincing. As *Newsweek*'s Jonathan Alter put it, "She would have to be Meryl Streep to be faking it."[2]

Broaddrick's charges were not provable in court in 1999. The statute of limitations had expired. Even if it hadn't, after twenty-one years any evidence was long gone. Also, there were mixed signals: Broaddrick had filed an affidavit in the Jones case denying the incident. She had attended a Clinton fund-raiser weeks after the alleged assault and even accepted a volunteer appointment on a state advisory board in Governor Clinton's administration. And Broaddrick's corroborating witnesses, the people she had told of the alleged attack at the time, were biased against Clinton.

On television Broaddrick tried to explain the inconsistencies, saying that she had been in denial. She also pleaded "stupidity." The immediate question was why Juanita Broaddrick had not surfaced in the public view before the trial ended. NBC-TV, which had Broaddrick's story ready for airing for three weeks, will be answering that question for a long time. The network says it needed time to corroborate the charges and the details. *The Wall Street Journal* and the *Washington Post* had also both interviewed Broaddrick, but didn't mention her charges until February 19 and 20, days after the president's acquittal.

Immediately after the NBC story ran, the president's personal lawyer, David Kendall, denied it, but only in generalized terms. When the president refused to issue even a general denial himself, the media started a drumbeat demanding a personal explanation.

The determination about witnesses—and perhaps the decision not even to mention Broaddrick—was badly prejudiced by the preordained conclusion that there was no way to get sixty-seven votes for conviction. Senator Pete Domenici was quoted as telling the House managers early on, "Let's be honest about this. Nobody in the Senate thinks there are sixty-seven votes for conviction, so let's talk practically about how we're going to wrap this matter up." Senator Stevens of Alaska added, "You know as well as we do that there aren't the votes to convict."

At our morning caucus on Tuesday, January 26, I again raised the question of getting the president's testimony. Why shouldn't we get the president's testimony? I asked. If Paula Jones can get his testimony in a civil lawsuit, does Paula Jones have more standing than the United States Senate? If the grand jury can get his testimony, why not the Senate? Do we have less standing than the grand jury? If he is, in effect, asking us to leave him in his job, why shouldn't we get his testimony?

I had a discussion with Kyl and devised a format: Lott should go to Daschle with a suggestion that the Senate issue a joint, bipartisan invitation to the president to testify, knowing that the minority leader would refuse. When Daschle refused, Lott should then issue an invitation on behalf of the Republican Caucus for Clinton to testify. If we had to, we could issue a subpoena.

At the caucus, John Chafee leaned over to me and said, "Why are they calling all hostile witnesses?" I said, "John, they don't have any friendly witnesses. They're all hostile."

Senator Ben Campbell of Colorado had a different complaint about the proposed witnesses. He said he couldn't see despoiling the Senate chamber once occupied by Daniel Webster and John F. Kennedy with Monica Lewinsky. Many Republican senators agreed. I found that argument inadequate. If a president were on trial for treason, we would probably have alleged traitors testifying on the Senate floor.

At midmorning on January 26, with the Democrats still unwilling to participate, Kyl and I left the Republican caucus and went to my hideaway to continue our witness discussions with the House managers. They told us they had narrowed their list to three witnesses: Monica Lewinsky, Sidney Blumenthal, and Vernon Jordan. They omitted Betty Currie because they figured they had as much as they were going to get from the president's secretary from her grand jury testimony. I told the managers I thought they would be likely to get approval for that short list and probably could get more.

Kyl and I had talked in advance about suggesting that the managers ask for depositions from five or six witnesses and then choose the three best to testify live before the Senate. We suggested that approach. The managers said they were too far along to change, that all thirteen managers had come up with the three-witness plan.

We had a discussion about political consultant Dick Morris, a one-time ally of Clinton's who had apparently soured on the president after being fired over a toe-sucking fiasco with a prostitute. Morris, who was tweaking the president regularly in media interviews, was apparently willing to testify about Clinton's state of mind on concealing his gifts to Lewinsky.

"What did Morris say that Clinton said about concealing the gifts?" I asked. The congressmen didn't know. Only their staffs had talked to Morris.

I asked Asa Hutchinson if he had talked to Jordan. "No," he said. "We only talked to Jordan's lawyer."

"Why didn't you talk to Jordan?" I asked.

He said, "Well, he was out of town."

Since they were in charge of prosecuting the case, I decided not to ask why they hadn't pressed to talk to Morris and Jordan personally. But there is nothing like a personal interview to flesh out testimony and get at the truth.

I did make a suggestion. "You don't have it in your written motion, but you can move to amend your motion" to include Morris. That couldn't be done, we were told, because it would require clearance from the thirteen-manager team, and they didn't want to go back and fight out the issue again. The congressmen decided to stick with their three witnesses—Lewinsky, Jordan, and Blumenthal.

The absence of Betty Currie as a trial witness made it impossible to clear up her earlier conflicting statements. In late January 1998, Currie testified before the grand jury that she thought the president was trying to influence her testimony through his famous series of questions ending in "right?" But when Currie testified before the grand jury in July 1998, she said she had felt free to disagree with the president's statements. Ultimately, many senators noted Currie's absence as a factor in their vote to acquit the president.

Senator Richard Durbin's floor statement is illustrative: "Betty Currie was critical to the most credible charges against the president. . . . Is there anyone in this chamber who believes that Sidney Blumenthal was a more valuable witness to this case than Betty Currie?" Durbin cited the rule relating to instructions to jurors in federal criminal cases to suggest that the House managers' failure to call Currie raised the inference that Currie's testimony would have hurt the prosecution. To this day I think Betty Currie was a crucial witness, certainly more important than Sidney Blumenthal, and arguably more important than Vernon Jordan.

On January 26, the House managers began their arguments for their motion to issue subpoenas to Lewinsky, Jordan, and Blumenthal. Their motion also asked that the Senate request the appearance of president Clinton at a deposition. The arguments, by the House managers and president's counsel, continued until almost 4:00 P.M. Then we went into closed session and debated the issue until 8:00 P.M.

Carl Levin, a Michigan Democrat, approached me on the Senate floor after the closed session ended and asked, "Do you see any way we can get out of this morass and shortcut the process?" After an extended talk in the otherwise empty well of the Senate, we decided to continue our talk the next morning at seven at the Washington Sports Club, where we both played squash.

Levin and I had been in the Senate together a long time. We were about the same age and both Jewish. We had played squash together often in 1981 and 1982, my first two years in the Senate. But then Carl's brother Sander was elected to the House in the fall of 1982, and the brothers Levin became exclusive squash partners. Graying, balding, and heavy, Carl Levin did not look like an athlete, but he was a talented squash player. One of his 1984 reelection campaign pieces called him a "mensch," which I thought was accurate. I liked and respected Carl.

At seven the next morning he and I sat on the small couch in front of a glass-walled squash court. We talked for nearly an hour. Levin had written down some ideas following our conversation the night before. He said he'd tried to reach Daschle that night, but the minority leader's phone had been busy for an hour.

Levin outlined a procedure that I found problematic in a number of respects. His plan provided that the depositions of the three witnesses would be seen only by senators and senior staff, not by the public. At an absolute minimum, I said, we ought to videotape the depositions for use at the trial, or at least leave open the option of using the videotaped depositions after we saw them. I refrained from pressing for live witnesses, because it seemed plain that the Republican caucus would not provide fifty-one votes for live witnesses. I thought our discussion and Levin's draft would at least offer a starting point that might lead to a bipartisan agreement.

Levin's plan featured some unduly tight restrictions on the scope of testimony. Only subjects that had been in the record by a certain date could be brought up. Levin also had some provisions about access by the president's counsel to files of the independent counsel and House managers. I offered some counterproposals and told Levin I thought the plan was a starting point. I promptly called Lott and told him that Levin and I had a proposal. Levin was going to go back to his office and put it in writing.

The majority leader was interested. Levin brought a document labeled "Levin-Specter Proposal." The heading was inaccurate, because I'd not had a chance to read it, let alone approve it. Meanwhile, I talked to Jon Kyl by phone. Jon was skeptical but wanted to know more. I outlined the proposal to the Republican caucus.

When Kyl spoke at the caucus, he said he disagreed with major points in Levin's proposal. I said I, too, disagreed with some of what Carl had suggested but considered it a good beginning point. John Chafee and Olympia Snowe agreed that the plan should be considered. Snowe was particularly eager for bipartisanship. But Phil Gramm stood and said, "I think we really ought not to make any concessions on the issue of live witnesses at this point." After an extended discussion, a consensus emerged that we should not make any of the concessions suggested by Levin.

I called Levin and told him the reaction of the Republican caucus. He said the Democratic caucus hadn't cared for the plan either. At that stage neither caucus was willing to expend the time and energy to find a bipartisan solution. I think it would have been worth the effort, and Levin and I would have been able to work through the differences.

We had done so in mid-1997 while serving together on the Governmental Affairs Committee, which was conducting hearings on campaign finance reform. "The June 17 meeting between Sens. Arlen Specter (R-Pa) and Carl Levin (D-Mich) on the Capitol lawn was part of an ongoing series of secret peace talks between the senators, according to sources, which has produced a tentative deal that may get the probe back on track," *Roll Call*, the Capitol Hill newspaper, reported in a front-page story.[3] But on impeachment our joint effort died when the party caucuses adjourned around noon on January 27.

The first order of business at the trial that day was to vote on Byrd's motion to dismiss. Shortly before 1:00 P.M., I walked into the Senate chamber and sought out the former majority leader. Byrd, who always wore a vest, was wearing a bright red one that day. "Perjury is just terrible," Byrd told me. "It just strikes at the foundation of our judicial system."

"Well, what are going to do with this guy, Bob? You've made a motion to dismiss and end this thing now. Why'd you do that?"

"Well, I think he is bad," Byrd said, going on about Clinton's alleged perjury. But as for a trial, he said, "It just mires the Senate."

"Yes," I said, "but the Senate has to deal with it."

"It seems so political," Byrd added. We then talked about options for voting separately on guilt and removal. Reaching for his vest-pocket copy of the Constitution, Byrd said removal was automatic without a separate vote after conviction. I replied, "Bob, you don't have to pull out the Constitution. I know you're right." By this time most of the hundred senators knew the relevant text, Article II, Section 4: "The president shall be removed from office on impeachment and conviction."

Despite this, I pointed out to Byrd that there were three precedents for taking two separate impeachment votes, one for conviction and the second for removal: The 1803 trial of Justice John Pickering, the 1862 trial of Judge West Humphreys, and the 1912 trial of Judge Robert Archibald. The two-vote practice ended with the 1936 impeachment trial of District Judge Halsted L. Ritter. After senators voted guilty 56–28, the chair ruled that under the Constitution a second vote was unnecessary to expel Ritter.

Our conversation was interrupted by the entry of the chief justice and the chaplain. After the chaplain finished, Byrd walked the few paces to my seat on the Senate floor and said we should finish our conversation later. He was clearly troubled. All of his statements pointed toward a "guilty" verdict. The former majority leader seemed dissatisfied with his own motion to dismiss, which was emblematic of the Senate's confusion.

Minutes after the opening gavel on January 27, we voted on the motion to dismiss. It failed, 44–56. Then we voted on a motion to subpoena Lewinsky, Jordan, and Blumenthal. That passed 56–44. The trial would continue, and the subpoenas would go out. I thought it would have been far more important to subpoena Betty Currie than Blumenthal, but his testimony was still important.

The battle lines were drawn. The Democrats wanted to limit the trial as much as possible—first, to get it over with as soon as possible and, second, to expose the president to as little risk as possible. They wanted no live witnesses, not even video presentations, so that the case would have to be decided on the record in the House of Representatives. That record was already public, so it could not do the president any more damage. They pressed that agenda every time a procedural issue came up. They thought they could get away with it, because the American people opposed the impeachment and wanted it concluded.

A significant group of Republicans who thought the president was guilty wanted to put as much on the record as possible. Then there were a number of senators who thought the proceedings should be limited for a variety of reasons, like Campbell, who didn't want want to sully the Senate floor with someone like Monica Lewinsky. Other Republican senators thought it was enough already, feeling pressure from their home states and from the general public view that the impeachment never should have been brought.

My view was that we should have deferred the matter until after Clinton's term ended, as I stated in my *New York Times* op-ed, but that once we had a trial, we should put on all the witnesses, including the president. But the only way to draw support for my view, even among Republicans, was to build public sentiment that the charges were serious and that understanding the case demanded hearing from Monica Lewinsky and Betty Currie in the witness chair. That testimony could have set the stage for calling the president—which would not happen unless the Republican caucus could produce fifty-one votes and was prepared to withstand the prospective public backlash.

All the long, often dull hours, all the stress and fatigue and the shared sense of crisis, created a bond among senators who usually spent little time together. The closed sessions brought us together, with the television lights off. There was no public-address system, although a microphone was installed on the second night of closed session. The most remarkable element was that the senators were all there—and listening. You could feel the communication. We spent long hours together at our desks, in caucus, at lunch. I spent more time with Phil Gramm, John Ashcroft, and Jeff Sessions in the few weeks of the impeachment trial than I'd spent with them in the preceding few years. There was also some bonding across the aisle, when we tried to work things out with the other side.

I found myself in extended, amiable conversations with Gramm, whom I had disagreed with on so many Senate votes. I had long admired Phil's intellect and told him so. His country drawl and wry comments camouflaged a powerful mind. And Gramm wasn't shy. In terms of time of possession, he controlled a significant amount of the debate in the caucus.

"I just love it being in there with all you lawyers," said Gramm, an economics professor by background. "I've never done this before, asking all those questions."

I said, "Phil, you don't ask many questions. But you do make plenty of declaratory statements."

He smiled. Gramm had been very complimentary to me after the hearings on Clarence Thomas. His nonlegal background helped cut through technicalities to practical answers. Phil had come over and told me, "If I ever need a criminal lawyer or I ever have a legal problem, Arlen, I want you to represent me."

Perhaps I strained the relationship during our brief competition for the 1996 Republican presidential nomination when I said I didn't like what was happening at either end of Pennsylvania Avenue. I objected to president Clinton's policies at one end and was concerned with Phil Gramm's influence over the Republican caucus at the other end. Obviously, Gramm's conservative views were much closer to the caucus majority than my moderate positions.

Listening to all the speeches on the Senate floor, one couldn't help noting the power of the party line. The forty-five Democrats voted in a solid phalanx. Only Russ Feingold broke ranks on one issue: He voted against Byrd's motion to dismiss. One Democrat after another came down on the side of his party. The Republican side was almost as bad. Among fifty-five Republican senators, only five would vote "not guilty" on both articles of impeachment, with five others joining to vote "not guilty" on the perjury article. The reality was that the caucuses had driven almost everyone to his or her respective party's position.

Lott did an outstanding job in compromising diverse views and maintaining his composure. Usually calm and cool, Lott occasionally grew agitated. On one occasion he snapped at his staff, "When I went in to see Daschle last night, Daschle told me that 'even your own lawyers don't agree with you.' " One of Lott's top staffers interjected, "That's not right, Senator." I quipped that we ought to take Daschle's deposition. Not necessarily videotape it, but at least take his deposition.

One principal difference between the two parties was that the Democrats didn't want to have the depositions videotaped, and if they were, the Democrats wanted a strict rule that they could be seen by only senators and senior staff. Republicans, on the other hand, wanted videotaped depositions without any commitment as to what we would do with them. The GOP line was that we could substitute the tapes for live testimony at the trial or we could still insist on live testimony.

A controversy also remained about the scope of the questioning at the depositions. The Democrats wanted the questions limited to what was in the record. But if that was the case, why bother to take depositions? We compromised, restricting questions to material relevant to the record.

Gramm said that the caucus would fracture if we couldn't agree. I read his warning as a euphemism for "The moderates won't back us up here." Gramm was saying he wanted the moderates to stay with the majority. If they didn't keep the moderates, they didn't have a majority, even on the procedural issues. But if the Republican majority faced opposition from forty-five Democrats and five moderate Republicans, they wouldn't have a majority vote for the procedural issues. I thought that on these procedural issues, Gramm was right.

Orrin Hatch said, "We've got to be partisan. We've got to get used to being partisan here."

I stood up and said, "I don't mind that. I tried hard to avoid the two partisan votes yesterday on the motion to dismiss and depositions. But I don't mind a partisan vote when we're right. The business about not having the videos available for public view is just beyond the pale. I think everyone should at least be for videotaping the depositions, deferring the decision on how to use them. I don't think the caucus will splinter, Phil.

"We've got the high ground here," I said. "Let's go out and vote." And we did. Republicans, in party-line votes on January 28, got our way about videotaping the depositions. The House managers would take three depositions: Lewinsky, Jordan, and Blumenthal. The depositions would be videotaped. One senator from each party would preside at each deposition, and two others would attend.

After the January 28 votes on the videotapes, I decided to break my self-imposed silence and talk to reporters, who had been clamoring for comment, about the trial procedures. I would still say nothing about fact-finding. I met with journalists at the press gallery in the Capitol for about half an hour and discussed the deposition procedures.

FRAUD ON THE SENATE

W hen Senator Lott asked me on Friday, January 29, to be the Republican Senate-presider at Sidney Blumenthal's deposition, I had no idea I would wind up in a showdown over alleged perjury that would draw a retaliatory threat to expel me from the Senate. I looked forward to presiding at Blumenthal's deposition and to being one of the two additional Republican Senate-observers at the depositions of Monica Lewinsky and Vernon Jordan. The sessions would enable me to evaluate these witnesses' testimony and gain additional insight into the importance of live witnesses before the full Senate.

President Clinton had reportedly trashed Monica Lewinsky in a private conversation with Blumenthal, who would be the last of the three witnesses to give videotaped depositions. Lewinsky would open the process, flying in from California to testify on Monday, February 1, followed by Vernon Jordan on Tuesday and Blumenthal on Wednesday.

Lewinsky's deposition, when excerpts were played at the Senate trial, would let America for the first time hear the president's paramour's voice. Only snippets of Lewinsky's deposition were played at the impeachment trial, so the public has been exposed to relatively little of her testimony. The transcript of her deposition will be a treasure trove for journalists and historians, who will dissect her words for insights into her relationship with Clinton. For my part, I was interested to hear from this woman who had transfixed the nation and nearly derailed the government.

The trial had recessed until the depositions were completed, so I returned late Friday afternoon to Philadelphia for my first full weekend home in a month. On Sunday afternoon I had a headache and slight chills. I thought I was just tired from the night before. I had gone to the Academy of Music Ball Saturday night and had not gotten to bed until 1:00 A.M., which was unusual for me. The next morning I went to play squash, my daily exercise, and could barely move. I got home, checked a thermometer, and found my temperature was 102. I kicked myself. With all that was going on, I should have been home and in bed Saturday night long before 1:00 A.M. and should have skipped Sunday squash.

On Monday morning Joan awakened me shortly after her 5:00 A.M. "beep-beep" alarm sounded too softly for me to hear. I still could barely move. I checked my temperature—101. I called my doctor, who prescribed a whole medicine chest of remedies. I had to scurry around to find a drugstore open that early in the morning. Instead of taking a train and standing on the drafty platform, I climbed into my car for the ride from Philadelphia to Washington. With my aide at the wheel, we left at 7:45 A.M. When we approached the Mayflower Hotel a few hours later, Connecticut Avenue looked like television city. "Monica Watch" was at full throttle, with reporters and cameras jamming the sidewalks and street. It was 10:25 A.M. and the Lewinsky deposition was under way, but the cameras focused on anyone from the Senate who approached the hotel.

When I stepped out of my car, photographers snapped away. Bob Franken from CNN rushed up and wanted an interview. I said "No comment." I went into the hotel and up to the presidential suite, where I saw a small opening at one end of the long table. Then I spotted an empty chair and squeezed in.

There, at the other end of the conference table, was Monica Lewinsky—a celebrity, a star, a woman known the world over by just her first name. People who had never heard of Antony and Cleopatra or Anita Hill and Clarence Thomas had all heard of Bill and Monica. She was exquisite. I had heard that Lewinsky had grown heavy and despondent, but she did not look that way to me. Her fair, pretty face and red lips were framed by a full, thick head of black hair. The world has since seen snippets of her testimony as it would be played at the Senate trial, but Monica Lewinsky was far more compelling live and up close.

Shortly after I settled into my chair, Tom Griffith, the Senate legal counsel, walked up and said to me, "Senator, I hate to tell you this, but the senators who are not presiding have to sit back in our section of the room." The majority and minority leaders wanted to limit the number of participants at the table.

So I walked to the back of the hotel suite, where I saw Senators Chris Dodd, Fred Thompson, and John Edwards. Edwards, the newly elected Democrat from North Carolina, was scheduled to preside with me on Wednesday at Blumenthal's deposition. This back section of the suite, through a small archway, was actually a separate, adjoining room. The bedroom and living room had been converted into a sprawling court chamber. My seat wasn't ringside, but it was much better than watching the videotapes.

I saw most of Lewinsky's deposition, far more than the video snippets shown during the trial. Monica Lewinsky was obviously well prepared and very well coached. She was young and brash, but she was by now experienced in depositions and seemed at home answering questions. When Congressman Ed Bryant asked her two questions at once, she replied, "Uh, can I separate that—that into two questions?" She knew that any answer she gave could be attributed, perhaps erroneously, to either question.

When Bryant asked Lewinsky whether her cover story about her relationship with Clinton would be misleading if told to Paula Jones's attorneys, Lewinsky replied with a carefully tailored statement: "They were literally true, but they would be misleading, so incomplete." She gave the same answer—"true but incomplete, therefore misleading"— to other questions, such as her statement to the grand jury that she was not alone with the president.

At other times Lewinsky sounded like a schoolgirl. She said the president's tone had become friendlier during a phone conversation. "I mean, we made up." When Bryant told her, "I want to refer you to the first so-called salacious occasion," Lewinsky cut him off. "Can we— can you call it something else?" she asked. "I mean, this is my relationship. . . . It was my first encounter with the president, so I don't really see it as salacious—that's not what this was." At another point Bryant asked her, "And what did you do after you accepted service of the subpoena?" Lewinsky replied, "I started crying."[1]

Bryant asked Lewinsky a question, then added, "I guess that was wrong," and withdrew his query. Lewinsky said "Sustained," to laughter in the room. After twenty-two previous depositions, beyond having the legal lingo down, she was an accomplished witness. This is not to say that Monica Lewinsky set the tone or avoided all disclosures. Bryant did establish some key points. He asked the former intern, "And prior to being on the witness list [for Paula Jones's case], you both spoke about denying this relationship if asked?"

"Yes," Lewinsky said. "That was discussed."

Bryant asked, "Well, if I ask you today the same question that was asked in your grand jury, is your statement, quote, 'I have never had a sexual relationship with the president,' unquote, is that a true statement?" She replied, "No."[2]

Seeing Monica Lewinsky up close confirmed my speculation about why the White House and so many Democratic senators had fought to keep her off the Senate floor. If Lewinsky testified live, America would be glued to the television. That was confirmed when she appeared in March 1999 on ABC-TV with Barbara Walters. America was fascinated. If Lewinsky had told her whole story in the well of the Senate, a rapt national audience would have been watching, and the dynamics of the proceeding might have dramatically changed.

I think the nation would have watched Monica testify even though it was fed up with the trial and disgusted with the coverage. The day after Lewinsky testified, the *Philadelphia Daily News* published an open letter to me on its op-ed page headlined, LET'S GET THIS DAMN THING OVER WITH. The country was disgusted, but wherever Monica Lewinsky went, she was the biggest celebrity since Princess Di. She was phenomenal, and you could see it. She was young and beautiful and sexy and the president's consort.

Watching Lewinsky, and later Vernon Jordan and Sidney Blumenthal, confirmed my sense that the full Senate should have seen and heard their testimony in the traditional way trials are conducted. While a videotape is informative, there is no substitute for the more precise evaluation of demeanor and its many nuances that come across fully only through live testimony. When the videotapes were played in the Senate chamber the following Thursday, they contrasted starkly with the live testimony I'd seen and heard earlier that week. In several places the sound was inaudible, and the tape couldn't be rewound. There was a far better chance in person to observe the witnesses' facial responses, their reactions, and their general demeanor. In addition, only a portion of their videos would be played. Although senators had a chance for full private viewings, many busy senator-jurors did not utilize that opportunity.

At least the Senate was wise enough not to release Lewinsky's entire deposition as the House had dumped the video of the president's grand jury testimony. Appropriately, only those excerpts introduced into evidence were played publicly. If the whole deposition had been released, I think the Democrats would have cried foul, but I don't think the full release would have changed the verdict.

In all, I saw an hour and a half of Monica Lewinsky's six-hour deposition. When I arrived at the Mayflower at 10:25 A.M., I was running a fever of 103. At noon the thermometer read 104. Since I was entering the fever danger zone and I had the flavor of Lewinsky's testimony, I left.

I got to my condominium at 12:30 P.M., took some medicine, and collapsed into bed. I woke at 4:45 to take more medicine and went back to sleep until 9:00 P.M. The night before, I fell asleep at 8:30, missing much of the Super Bowl. Tuesday morning my temperature read 101, so I saw the doctor at the Capitol and then took the elevator to S407, where secret briefings are held and where Jordan and Blumenthal would testify. When I arrived, at 10:30 A.M., a twenty-minute power outage had just hit, and Jordan's deposition was on hold.

I had met Jordan several times and knew him slightly. Vernon Jordan is a striking man, tall, perhaps six two and a half, and powerfully built. He was poised, polished, and smooth as silk. He was also intimidating, or at least he tried to be. As I watched him testify, Jordan reminded me of my high school football coach, who told our nose guard to smash into the opposing center on every play, just to make the center worry about being hit rather than concentrate on snapping the ball.

Jordan was questioned by House Manager Asa Hutchinson, the able former prosecutor from Arkansas. Tall, good-looking, and affable himself, Hutchinson had a charming and easy manner. *Time* magazine ran a squib on Hutchinson in a posttrial wrap-up: "If the other 12 House prosecutions were half this good, they might have convicted." That was an overstatement, but Hutchinson was perhaps the best of the House team, which had several excellent prosecutors.[3]

Jordan gave no quarter from the beginning. Hutchinson said, "I've looked forward to this opportunity to meet you. Now, you have—"

The superlawyer cut him off. "I can't say that the feeling is mutual."

"I certainly understand," Hutchinson said, maintaining his calm. A few moments later, still on the preliminaries of establishing Jordan's background, Hutchinson asked, "When you say 'making rain,' that's the terminology of being a rainmaker?"

"I think even in Arkansas, you understand what rainmaking is," Jordan replied. Jordan showed no shortage of self-confidence. He no longer billed by the hour, he said. "I graduated." His last billable rate, he said, was between $450 and $500 an hour. "Not bad for a Georgia boy." Jordan explained that he had referred Lewinsky to Frank Carter, a Washington lawyer, to draft her affidavit. "I don't do affidavits," Jordan said in a line already famous in legal circles.

Jordan discussed his friendship with the president. "President Clinton has been a friend of mine since approximately 1973, when I came to your state, Arkansas, to make a speech as president of the National Urban League about race and equal opportunity in our nation, and we met then and there, and our friendship has grown and developed and matured, and he is my friend and will continue to be my friend." He added, "Every year since his presidency, the Jordan family has been privileged to entertain the Clinton family on Christmas eve."

"And have you vacationed together with the Clinton family?" Hutchinson asked.

"Yes. I think you have seen reels of us playing golf and having fun at Martha's Vineyard."

At one point in the deposition, Hutchinson asked Jordan whether the president had given him any instruction other than to find Lewinsky a job. Jordan corrected the congressman. "The president is a friend of mine, and I don't believe friends instruct friends. Our friendship is one of parity and equality."

At another point Hutchinson asked Jordan what led him to ask the president of the United States the "extraordinary" question of whether he'd had a sexual relationship with Monica Lewinsky. "Well, first of all," Jordan said, "I'm asking the question of my friend, who happens to be the president of the United States."[4]

Although he showed no sign of concern, Vernon Jordan was in a hot spot, at the center of an impeachment trial that involved his role in alleged obstruction of justice, considered the stronger of the two charges against the president. At the president's request, Jordan in December 1997 and January 1998 had helped find Monica Lewinsky a job in New York City.

On Friday, December 5, 1997, the president's attorneys received a witness list for the Paula Jones case. Lewinsky was included on that list. On December 11, 1997, Judge Susan Webber Wright issued an order stating that Paula Jones was entitled to "information regarding any individuals with whom the president had sexual relations or proposed or sought to have sexual relations and who were during the relevant time frame state or federal employees." Jones would be able to subpoena Monica Lewinsky.

Also on December 11, 1997, Jordan and Lewinsky met, and Jordan took concrete actions to help Lewinsky find a job. He placed calls on her behalf to three business contacts. Jordan also told her to send letters to three additional firms. This meeting and the phone calls took place hours before Judge Wright issued her order. By filing an affidavit that she'd not had sex with President Clinton, Lewinsky could avoid being deposed in the Jones case.

Jordan, by his account and hers, asked Lewinsky if she'd had sex with the president, and she denied it. Jordan then went to the White House, passed the downstairs security detail, and walked up to the residential quarters, where he asked the president if he'd ever had sex with Lewinsky. Clinton said he had not.

On January 7, Lewinsky signed Carter's affidavit. On January 8, Lewinsky had an interview with McAndrews & Forbes Holdings Inc. in New York. Afterward she phoned Jordan to report that the interview had gone poorly. Jordan immediately phoned Ron Perelman, the CEO of McAndrews & Forbes, and asked for his help. The next day Lewinsky was given another interview and offered a job at Revlon, a subsidiary of McAndrews & Forbes. Jordan phoned Clinton to report, "Mission accomplished."

At the deposition, Hutchinson asked Jordan, "It comes to your attention from Ms. Lewinsky that she has a subpoena in a civil rights case against the president. And did this make you consider whether it was appropriate for you to continue seeking a job for Ms. Lewinsky?"

"Never gave it a thought," Jordan replied. For that matter, Jordan told Hutchinson, even after Lewinsky had been subpoenaed and even if Jordan believed she had sexual relations with the president, "I do not think it would have affected my decision" to help Lewinsky find a job.

Jordan defended his efforts to help Lewinsky get a job as payback for assistance he had received when he was as a young lawyer victimized by racial discrimination. Jordan testified that he told no one at Revlon that Monica Lewinsky was a witness in a case involving the president and that Revlon offered Lewinsky a job because she was qualified. If the Revlon job offer was part of a plan or conspiracy to obstruct justice, then Jordan's conduct warranted scrutiny. The House managers raised no such contention.

Smooth and powerful as he was, Jordan faltered a couple of times during his deposition. He became evasive on the subject of whether he had told Revlon executives that he was acting on President Clinton's behalf in trying to find a job for Lewinsky. At first Jordan said, "I don't think so. I may have." Later he said, "I'm certain I did not say that" to one of the executives.[5]

Like Lewinsky's testimony, only a small part of Jordan's videotape was seen at the Senate trial, and there has as yet been little focus on his testimony. Legal scholars and historians will probably analyze his words closely, along with the other evidence, to evaluate whether there was an obstruction of justice and, if so, whether Jordan was a co-conspirator. I think it would have been warranted to question Jordan in much greater detail about his participation and to bring in the people he talked to at Revlon, to get a fuller picture as to what he did. But on this date of the record, it would be unfair or premature to classify him as a co-conspirator.

On the quid pro quo question, an important piece of evidence was Lewinsky's uncontradicted testimony that she intended to deny her relationship with the president from the outset—before she was sub-poenaed or Clinton coached her or Jordan helped her get a job. Her testimony raised a reasonable doubt and supported Jordan's testimony that there was no quid pro quo of a job for the affidavit. That would be an exonerating factor if anyone got around to questioning Jordan's role. The Revlon executives would not be implicated in the obstruction issue unless someone contradicted Jordan's testimony that the corporate hierarchy did not know the job search was designed to buy Lewinsky's silence.

Some have argued that Jordan was saying, or at least implying, that the president wanted Lewinsky hired. That could be determined only by questioning Jordan in greater detail and by talking to the people at Revlon. And, of course, there was another key witness who was party to the conversations and knew exactly whether Jordan was complicit—and that was the president.

Jordan, presumably, did not relish this widespread publicity, including a *Saturday Night Live* skit, about how he made his money.

As the *Washington Post* put it in a satirical transcript of Jordan's deposition:

> My name is Vernon E. Jordan Jr. I am an attorney who does not actually appear in court or represent clients or engage in litigation or answer interrogatories or draft briefs, but who earns $73 million a minute because I am not entirely without personal influence; I am privileged to number among my friends and colleagues many persons of stature; accordingly, individuals in need of assistance might occasionally find my intervention of some small benefit, such as when, by placing a phone call from the fourth green at Avanel, I can obtain for an individual the dismissal of a charge of extortion and his simultaneous appointment as ambassador to Sweden. . . . [6]

During the power failure at the beginning of his deposition, Jordan, Fred Thompson, and I were chatting. "I've got a good Bill Hundley story," Jordan said. William G. Hundley, then representing Jordan, had represented former Attorney General John Mitchell on the day of Mitchell's sentencing before Judge John Sirica. Jordan recounted the vignette: When Mitchell and John Ehrlichman, a top Nixon aide, were in court for sentencing, Ehrlichman made a long plea about his contrition and how he was going to work with the Navajos. He would do extensive community service, which would help the Navajo Indians help him, seeing God again and helping his fellow man. He went on and on and on. John Mitchell leaned over to Hundley and said, "If they offer me the Indians, turn them down."

Questioning Jordan, Hutchinson ran an effective deposition, professionally posing a logical stream of questions. Hutchinson didn't argue with Jordan, who trumped him with rhetorical flourishes every time Hutchinson pressed him. Throughout the deposition, Jordan sat motionless in his chair, maintaining an intense gaze despite the lights and camera fixed on him.

During a series of questions about Lewinsky's relationship with the president, Jordan told Hutchinson, "I think it's safe to say she was not happy."

Hutchinson asked, "You're speaking of Ms. Lewinsky?"

"That's the only person we're talking about, Congressman," Jordan retorted. In fact, they had also been talking about First Lady Hillary Rodham Clinton.

At another point, Jordan said, Lewinsky told him she hoped the president would leave the first lady after his term ended and marry Monica. "And that was alarming and stunning to me," Jordan said.[7]

Around 12:30 P.M. the Jordan deposition broke for lunch. I'd had enough. My temperature was 102, so I went home to bed.

The next day, Wednesday, February 3, was Blumenthal's deposition and my turn to preside. The lead House managers putting the questions were James Rogan and Lindsey Graham. Sidney Blumenthal was a match for the combative Graham. Blumenthal had been described as brilliant and arrogant, a journalist who built a career on intellectual dueling and had brought the same zeal to the White House, where he mixed it with fierce partisan loyalty. Blumenthal was prominent in the Washington elite that moved too easily between media and government. The *New York Times* described him as "the opinionated journalist turned White House adviser. . . . Mr. Blumenthal is long despised by Republicans as fostering theories that conservatives have engaged in various conspiracies to undermine the President."[8] Thin and youthful at fifty, in a well-tailored suit, his dark hair styled above his glasses, Blumenthal was polite, restrained, and very smooth.

The House managers moved quickly to the main question: What had President Clinton told Blumenthal about Monica Lewinsky on January 21, 1998, the day the Lewinsky story broke in the *Washington Post*? Blumenthal at first gave less than a vivid account of the conversation. He said he could not remember how he happened to discuss the *Post* story with the president. While Rogan asked pointed questions, Graham was more general, drawing repeated objections from White House lawyer Lanny Breuer.

I tried to rule on the objections with a light touch. On one occasion I said, "Senator Edwards and I have conferred, and he thinks it's an objectionable question. I disagree with him, but in the interest of comity and brevity, I'm going to join him in sustaining the objection because it's easier for you to rephrase the question." People laughed, and the deposition proceeded much more quickly than if we had labored over the legalities of objections.

At another point Rogan made a statement, Blumenthal's lawyer William McDaniel objected, I overruled the objection, and Rogan, even with the objection overruled, said, "Let me restate the question, if I may."

"We withdraw the ruling," I quipped. Still, this was serous business. Consistent with his February 1998 grand jury testimony, Blumenthal

502

stated that Clinton "said that she [Lewinsky] had come on to him and made a demand for sex, that he had rebuffed her, turned her down, and that she, uh, threatened him. And he said that she said to him that she was called 'the stalker' by her peers and that she hated the term, and that she would claim that they had had an affair whether they had or they hadn't, and that she would tell people."

"Do you remember him also saying that the reason Monica Lewinsky would tell people that is because then she wouldn't be known as 'the stalker' anymore?" Rogan asked.

"Yes, that's right," Blumenthal said.

"Can you describe the president's demeanor when he shared this information with you?" Rogan asked.

"Yes. He was very upset. I thought he was a man in anguish."[9]

Blumenthal insisted he had never shared any of that information with reporters. Graham asked him, "When you talked to Mr. Lyons [a newspaper columnist], you never mentioned what time at all that Ms. Lewinsky was making demands on the president and he had to rebuff her?"

"Absolutely not," Blumenthal said. ". . . I've been asked, and answered that, and I haven't told anyone else."

About forty minutes into Blumenthal's testimony, Graham asked him, "Knowing what you know now, do you believe the president lied to you about his relationship with Ms. Lewinsky?"

"I do," Blumenthal replied.[10] Whatever the context, that was a striking statement from a top aide.

Blumenthal's deposition lasted an hour and fifteen minutes. Graham wanted to ask Blumenthal about Kathleen Willey, the former White House volunteer who had testified before the grand jury in Paula Jones's case and then appeared on CBS's *60 Minutes* to describe how the president had groped her in the Oval Office against her will. President Clinton had denied her charge.

Lanny Breuer, the White House lawyer, objected to Graham's question about Willey. Generally, the prosecuting attorney would have the right to ask about matters showing the same method, pattern, or design, which I noted. During the ensuing argument, the Democrats made a suggestion. "Well, if you're going to let him ask him, do it at the end of the tape so we can slice that part off [if the objection is ultimately sustained] and that doesn't become in the public domain." That seemed to make sense. Senator Edwards and I conferred, agreed, and then returned and gave the lawyers that ruling.

Then, after all that argument, Lindsey Graham finished questioning Sidney Blumenthal without asking him the questions about Kathleen Willey. We took a five-minute break, during which I approached Graham. "Hey, Lindsey," I said, "you reserved the question about Willey until the end."

"I don't know, Senator," Graham said. "I didn't think that would be honored." I replied, "We agreed to let you do it at the end of your interrogation, but it's up to you."

When we returned to the deposition, Breuer said, "Senators, the White House has no questions for Mr. Blumenthal."

I then said, "We had deferred one line of questions which had been subject [to] objection and considerable conference, and we put it at the end of the transcript so it could be excised. Do you wish to—"

"Yes," Graham said. The White House lawyers, obviously exercised, asked to go "off the record," which Edwards and I agreed to.

"If we don't cross, they can't have any redirect," the White House team said.

I said, "Well, that certainly is true under the general rule, but not when we had reserved that question for the end of the tape so that if this was not upheld it wouldn't foul up the tape."

Edwards, my Democratic counterpart, paused and said, "Well, Senator Specter has been so reasonable on all these things. I think I'll go along with him on that."

Graham asked Blumenthal a series of questions about Willey, interrupted by frequent objections by Blumenthal's lawyers, who wanted the record to reflect that they objected to the entire line of questioning. Graham asked, among other questions, "Did anybody ever discuss the fact that Ms. Willey may have had a checkered past?"

"No, absolutely not," Blumenthal replied.[11] After all the controversy, Blumenthal essentially said he knew nothing about Kathleen Willey.

Sidney Blumenthal was not as billed. He was restrained throughout the proceeding. Rogan said, "I found him to be a gentleman, and I hope he felt the same way about us." When parts of Blumenthal's deposition were played in the Senate, I got some good-natured ribbing from my colleagues. Ted Stevens said, "You did a good job, Judge. Looks like you're heading for the bench, Senator."

The following morning, Thursday, I was working in my Senate hideaway when my secretary, Patricia Haag, called shortly after 9:00 A.M.: "Congressmen Graham and Rogan called and have something important they want to talk to you about." I said, "Put them through."

Lindsey Graham's Southern baritone floated through the receiver. "We have information, Senator, that when we asked a question about whether Blumenthal had ever passed on any derogatory information to anyone, he had told [Arkansas author and columnist] Gene Lyons. Lyons talked about it all around Arkansas and is supposed to have talked to a man who is now in England.

"We didn't want to do anything about this because it was in the Senate proceeding," Graham continued. "We thought we'd better report it to you."

I said, "Well, I think it is very important. Let me just give you a thought off the top of my head. If you can get an affidavit or affidavits specifying that Mr. Blumenthal told other people derogatory information about Ms. Lewinsky, then what you might want to do is file a petition with the Senate for leave to reopen and continue the deposition of Blumenthal."

"Well, we'll pursue that," Rogan said. "Thanks for the suggestion."

Later that morning I attended the Republican caucus. I spoke up again in favor of live witnesses, although I knew the prospect was highly unlikely. I said that Monica Lewinsky would make a compelling witness and ought to be seen in person. I again made the point that if the stage was set properly, we might yet see the president testify, either on his own volition or through a subpoena if the trial developed in a way that emboldened the Senate and made it politically palatable to compel the president's testimony.

I said I was against findings of fact, a nascent effort to go on record finding that President Clinton committed perjury and obstruction of justice without actually finding him guilty. The findings were a cop-out on conviction, I said, and a violation of the Constitution, which says judgment in cases of impeachment shall not extend beyond ouster and prohibition from future office. The findings of fact were also a public relations gimmick, something to wave so the president couldn't claim victory. Republicans were irate when the president, joined by throngs of Democrats, held a "victory celebration" in the Rose Garden after the House voted out articles of impeachment. Presidential spokesman Joe Lockhart promised a "gloat-free zone" if and when the Senate acquitted the president.

As for suggestions that the Senate censure the president for his behavior, a move gaining steam in the Democratic cloakroom, I remained vehemently opposed. I had denounced censure on national

TV as "not worth a tinker's dam." Censure was beyond the Constitution's express remedies.

I was awaiting lunch in the first-floor Senate dining room on Thursday, February 4, when a telephone call came in from my secretary, Patricia. "Congressmen Rogan and Graham want to talk to you. It's very important." The congressmen were calling back after our morning phone tag.

Graham asked if they could see me right away, and I told them to come to the Senate dining room. They arrived shortly. "We got the telephone number of this guy in Arkansas, Lyons, who is supposed to have been told by Blumenthal all this derogatory information about Monica being a stalker, and of course he'd denied in his deposition that he had ever done that," Graham said. "We got this guy in London who says that Lyons told him that Blumenthal told him about it, and he also told a lot of other people. What do you think we should do?"

I said, "I think you ought to pursue it."

Rogan said, "We can't really do that, Senator. We talked to Chairman Hyde, who said that he didn't want us to do that. This was now in the Senate, and he's tired of being criticized for trying to run the Senate proceedings." Henry Hyde was growing angrier as the trial progressed and acquittal seemed more and more likely. Hyde would be quoted at the trial's end as saying of us senators, "It's a good thing they weren't at Valley Forge or the Alamo."

Graham showed me Gene Lyons's phone number but said they couldn't make the call because of their chairman's instructions. By this time the trial was scheduled to reconvene in ten minutes. Abandoning my lunch, I invited Rogan and Graham to accompany me to my hideaway in the corridor adjacent to the dining room.

The Senate was scheduled to hear arguments on presentation of evidence that afternoon, view the video presentations on Saturday, and then move to closing arguments on Monday, so there wasn't much time to find out whether Blumenthal had talked to Lyons, the *Arkansas Gazette* columnist, or others. Since I had presided at Blumenthal's deposition, I felt it appropriate to call Lyons directly. In view of the limited time, I decided to do so immediately.

Lyons answered the phone. I said I had presided at a deposition of Sidney Blumenthal and asked Lyons if Blumenthal had ever made derogatory statements about Monica Lewinsky. Lyons flatly denied that this had ever happened, saying, "I've known him for a long time. He didn't do that. As a matter of fact, he said they were protecting Monica Lewinsky and that it was a firing offense if anybody tried to do anything. He didn't do that."

Lindsey Graham prompted me to ask about Kathleen Willey. I asked Lyons whether Blumenthal ever made any comments to him about Kathleen Willey.

"Oh, no. He didn't say anything about Kathleen Willey either."

Congressmen Graham and Rogan looked mystified. I cut the conversation short so I could run up the flight of stairs to get to the Senate chamber before the chief justice arrived. I took my seat and settled in. I'd been seated only a few minutes when a young man walked down the aisle next to Senator Jesse Helms's seat and whispered to me, "There's a telephone call from London in the Marble Room."

The House managers had been given the Senate Marble Room, our reading room, for their working quarters during the trial. I walked out of the Senate chamber, through the cloakroom, and around the back way to the Marble Room. I was directed to Lindsey Graham, who put down the telephone and said he was talking to Michael Mewshaw, a London-based writer who identified himself as an acquaintance of Gene Lyons.

Mewshaw told me, "Senator, it's a great pleasure to talk to you. If I may just take a minute, we met about ten years ago in Morocco." Apparently we had both been at the La Mamounia, a fabulous art deco hotel.

Mewshaw told me what Lyons had told him: that Blumenthal had told Lyons that Lewinsky stalked the president; that she was unstable and fantasized; that there was no substance to Willey's charges; and that Willey was interested in the president, and if the president had groped her, she would have welcomed it.

I asked, "Are you sure Lyons said all that?"

Mewshaw replied, "That's what Lyons told me Blumenthal said to him."

Mewshaw said he had received a fax on January 29 telling him that Lyons's source was Sidney Blumenthal. I hurriedly finished the call in order to get back to the trial. Graham said he was going to get an affidavit attesting to what Mewshaw had said. If the House managers got an affidavit and filed a petition with the Senate to reopen the Blumenthal hearing, it could affect the trial.

But Henry Hyde would not take action. He said he didn't want to step on the Senate's toes. I told Lott about the latest developments that afternoon when I found a minute to talk to the majority leader on the floor.

That day was taken up hearing arguments and voting on what evidence to admit. In the end the Senate voted to allow the House managers to present all or portions of the three videotaped depositions at the trial. On the question of live witnesses, we lost badly, 70–30. Out of our fifty-five-member caucus, twenty-five Republicans voted against live witnesses, including several senators who had spoken forcefully in caucus in favor of a full trial. The Republicans who changed their positions yielded to the mounting public pressure to get the trial done. Nothing of substance was happening. The Democrats were in lockstep, and the president was going to be acquitted, so why tarry? Using the video testimony carried 68–32, with the help of fourteen Democrats. Only one Republican, Olympia Snowe of Maine, voted against having the videotapes seen by senators. She seemed to feel that the case had gone on long enough, that it was pointless.

The next night, Friday, February 5, Lindsey Graham phoned me at my Washington condo around 10 o'clock. He said he wanted to send over an affidavit on the Blumenthal matter the next morning. In view of the time, I suggested he send it over that night. He did.

I took the opportunity during our phone call to raise several points with Graham. The next day, Saturday, February 6, was slated for video presentations by the House managers and would be Graham's last chance to make his points and introduce evidence. I brought up Kathleen Willey. A serious charge was floating around about an attempt to scare Willey into silence. Scant details had been reported in the press. Allegedly, two days before Willey's deposition in the Jones case, a jogger had bumped into Willey, who ran daily. The jogger identified Willey's cat, which had been missing, by name, along with the names of her children and her lawyer's children. The next morning Willey found her cat's severed head on her front doorstep.

Investigators were developing more evidence, I had been told. They thought they'd identified the jogger and thought they had some link to someone in the White House, although no specific proofs have yet been presented on either point. However, it was public record that Independent Counsel Starr was pursuing the Willey matter by indicting a woman who had allegedly changed her testimony on one aspect of that matter.

I told Graham that if they wanted to preserve the point for later use in the trial, they would have to establish a record Saturday morning at the trial, which was rapidly coming to a close. I said I was advising the congressman in my capacity as presiding senator at Blumenthal's deposition. I told Graham he would need evidence. He could not just drop something so prejudicial and significant as the encounter between Willey and the jogger onto the U.S. Senate without tangible evidence.

Late Friday night, after talking to Graham, I tried to phone Senator John Edwards, my Democratic counterpart at the Blumenthal deposition, but I couldn't make contact. A House staffer delivered Graham's package after 11:00 P.M.

Graham had enclosed an affidavit from Christopher Hitchens, a "social friend and journalistic acquaintance" of Sidney Blumenthal. This affidavit, dated that day, February 5, 1999, read in part:

> 8. During lunch on March 19, 1998, in the presence of myself and Carol Blue, Blumenthal stated that Monica Lewinsky had been a "stalker" and that the president was "the victim" of a predatory and unstable sexually demanding young woman. Referring to Lewinsky, Blumenthal used the word "stalker" several times. Blumenthal advised us that this version of the facts was not generally understood.
>
> 9. Also during that lunch, Blumenthal stated that Kathleen Willey's poll numbers were high but would fall and would not look so good in a few days.
>
> 10. I have knowledge that Blumenthal recounted to other people in the journalistic community the same story about Monica Lewinsky that he told to me and Carol Blue.

Graham included in his package a two-page document captioned "Sidney Blumenthal Perjured Himself Before the United States Senate When He Testified That He Was Not Involved in Disseminating Negative Stories About Monica Lewinsky." The document's summary section read, "In response to questions from Manager Graham, Sidney Blumenthal testified that he 'certainly never mentioned [his conversation with the president regarding Monica Lewinsky] to any reporter.' "

Early Saturday morning I again unsuccessfully tried to reach Senator Edwards by phone. Then I called Lott, who was eager to see the affidavits. When I arrived at Lott's office at about 9:40 A.M., Henry Hyde and Graham were already there. We discussed how to handle the matter. During a brief break in the trial, I finally found Edwards and told him I wanted to talk to him later that day to discuss developments from Blumenthal's deposition. During the lunch break on Saturday, Lott and I briefed Daschle and Edwards and showed them the affidavits. Daschle downplayed that matter, saying it was tangential to the trial and should not divert us in our move to finish the case on the established schedule.

Meanwhile, Graham handed me a memorandum from Gene Lyons. The memo was addressed to Mewshaw, with a copy to journalist Joe Conason. It read, in part, "For Specter to tell me the contents of Blumenthal's depo was every bit as illegal as anything they claim Clinton did. For him then to discuss it with you only compounds the matter. . . . Specter's calling me could put him into a world of s—t, and possibly result in his being forced to leave the Senate. . . ." Lyons's baseless threats were never taken seriously by anyone.

At midday on Saturday it was decided to wait on Blumenthal's and Willey's allegations until Monday, when it was hoped the House managers would have affidavits to flesh out a motion. Senator Lott would need Senator Daschle's concurrence to introduce the motion, according to the rules the Senate had set for the impeachment trial.

I spent Sunday at my desk in my Philadelphia home drafting a closing statement. Monday morning I caught an early train for Washington and was at my desk at 8:45 A.M. working on my statement. Our caucus commenced at 10:25. I spoke early on the Blumenthal situation. We now had a second affidavit about Blumenthal's conversations about Lewinsky, this one from Christopher Hitchens's wife, Carol Blue. Blue's affidavit was almost identical to Hitchens's.

The Blumenthal story had already made headlines around the country and the globe. Many of the articles focused on the falling-out among Blumenthal and his friends. Others, some critical, some neutral, focused on my efforts at fact-finding. The *Washington Post* ran *Philadelphia Inquirer* reporter Steve Goldstein's story under the headline, SPECTER STARTED PROBE OF BLUMENTHAL'S ACCOUNT. Goldstein's piece began, "The day after he presided over the impeachment trial deposition of White House aide Sidney Blumenthal, Senator Arlen Specter (R-Pa.) began his own behind-the-scenes investigation into whether Blumenthal was lying when he denied spreading damaging information last year about Monica S. Lewinsky."[12] The *Post* ran its own piece days later, writing, "The increasingly bitter dispute between White House aide Sidney Blumenthal and British writer Christopher Hitchens is a *cause célèbre* that has grabbed plenty of inside-the-Beltway media attention."[13]

I told the caucus that we should consider trying to reopen Blumenthal's deposition. In a civil or criminal trial, perjury is a fraud on the court and a very serious matter. If the affidavits were true, we might be looking at a fraud on the Senate.

On Tuesday, February 9, I took the floor to make a unanimous consent request on behalf of Majority Leader Lott and in my capacity as co-presider for the Senate at Blumenthal's deposition. "I ask unanimous consent that the parties be allowed to take additional discovery, including testimony and oral deposition of Mr. Christopher Hitchens, Ms. Carol Blue, Mr. R. Scott Armstrong [another journalist in Hitchens's circle], and Mr. Sidney Blumenthal with regard to possible fraud on the Senate by alleged perjury in the deposition testimony of Mr. Sidney Blumenthal with respect to allegations that he, Mr. Sidney Blumenthal, was involved with the dissemination beyond the White House of information detrimental to the credibility of Ms. Monica Lewinsky. . . ."

"Is there objection?" Chief Justice Rehnquist asked. Minority Leader Daschle objected.

By the rules, an application could be considered only if it were jointly agreed to by the two leaders. As *USA Today* reported, "Republicans, who are eager to wrap up the trial, dropped the matter rather than demand a vote by the full Senate." In retrospect it would have been wiser for Republicans to have retained our procedural rights including the right to reopen Blumenthal's deposition on a majority of fifty-one votes.

Lott had made an agreement with Daschle that any further proceeding would have to have the two party leaders' joint agreement. I don't know why Lott made that deal. Still, we could have controlled the procedure if we had been unified, but we were not. We might have been unified to plow ahead if Blumenthal's testimony had led to revelations about Kathleen Willey's allegations, but Graham did not press the question at Blumenthal's deposition. I thought we should have proceeded, as I thought we should have taken many other steps on this trial.

We also voted February 9 on a motion to open deliberations, so that senators' floor statements could be televised, which I supported. The media had been lambasting the Senate for closing earlier deliberations on Byrd's motion to dismiss and on the question of which witnesses to depose. Reporters jumped on Harkin's line, in arguing to keep the doors open, that "the Senate is not a private club."

Along with Senators Collins and Hutchison, I was one of three Republicans who voted to keep those earlier sessions open. Under pressure from the media, fourteen Republicans voted on February 9 to open final deliberations to the public. The tally was 59–41, short of the two-thirds majority needed to change the rules. The Senate's final deliberations would be closed.

By this time most senators seemed not to care very much about Sidney Blumenthal, or about anything else in the impeachment trial, except finishing it.

NOT PROVEN

G od almighty, take the vote and get it over with!" spectator Richard Llamas shouted from the Senate balcony February 4. Llamas was arrested and removed, but he spoke for millions. From the time the Senate reconvened on January 6, the public pressure to conclude the trial promptly was palpable. The rancor that pervaded the process helped shape the public view that it was all politics without substance.

The Senate turned to closing arguments from the House managers and the president's lawyers on Monday, February 8, finishing a long day after 6:00 P.M. The senators' final speeches and deliberations would follow. A final vote would come by Friday, February 12. The press churned out stories about exit strategies, predicting various scenarios.

Public opinion hung heavily over the Senate chamber. On the Democratic side of the aisle, public support for the president gave aid and comfort, promising only praise and no political retribution for an acquittal. On the Republican side, storm clouds threatened a downpour if the trial did not end quickly. As Senator Connie Mack of Florida put it, "We should not deceive ourselves into believing that public opinion did not impact this process."

Byrd said, "The American people deeply believe in fairness, and they have come to view the president as having 'been put upon' for politically partisan reasons." While it takes two to tango, somehow the House Republicans caught most of the public disdain on the partisanship charge, although the House Democrats were equally partisan. It was more than the party-line votes. The Senate struggled to achieve bipartisanship, with limited success, and we did avoid the bitterness that dominated the House side.

Despite the serious charges of perjury and obstruction of justice,

Democratic senators argued—and many Americans agreed—that a private sexual liaison should not have set off a multiyear, multimillion-dollar investigation. If the independent counsel could establish no wrongdoing in Whitewater, Travelgate, and Filegate, they argued, why elevate a charge based on sex to an impeachable offense? Clinton had made the privacy argument, saying publicly, "This matter is between me, my wife, and our daughter. It's nobody's business but ours."

The impeachment and trial were taking a heavy toll on everybody involved. First Lady Hillary Rodham Clinton had drawn considerable public support from her charge that the whole thing was a "vast right-wing conspiracy." That statement would produce substantial Republican fund-raising when she later got involved in the New York Senate race. Arguably, the process had already cost five House Republicans their seats in the November elections—seven, counting Speaker Newt Gingrich, who resigned in the wake of the electoral debacle, and Speaker-designate Bob Livingston, who resigned in the face of reports about his own extramarital affairs. Within days after the trial ended, Democratic Senators Frank Lautenberg of New Jersey and Richard Bryan of Nevada announced they would not stand for reelection in 2000.

Bryan said he'd made up his mind the previous weekend, after soul-searching with his wife. The Nevadan didn't attribute his decision to the impeachment trial, but I sensed that the trial's wear and tear played a role. Lautenberg said he didn't want to spend hours every day raising money. Vigorous as Frank Lautenberg was at seventy-five, I thought he might be exhausted. Within a month after the trial ended, two Republicans, John Chafee of Rhode Island and Connie Mack of Florida, also announced they would not stand for reelection.

The week after the trial ended, Senator Jay Rockefeller, a West Virginia Democrat, and I commiserated about its heavy toll when we held a public hearing in Pittsburgh on steel imports. I told Rockefeller how much I had slept in the few days after the trial ended, over the President's Day recess. He told me how hard it had been for him to sleep nights during the trial. Rockefeller joked that I could sleep because I was a trial lawyer. I countered that I could sleep because it was over.

As the final vote neared, Byrd, still uncomfortable with his choices, agonized both publicly and privately. "I have no doubt that he [President Clinton] has given false testimony under oath, that he has misled the American people, and there are indications that he did, indeed, obstruct justice," Byrd said in a widely quoted television interview. The former majority leader seemed headed for a "guilty" vote until the very instant he uttered his verdict. In the end, he voted "not guilty" on both counts. In a published interview, he said:

> In my view, Mr. Clinton has abused the powers vested in him by the people. His offenses do constitute an "abuse or violation of some public trust." . . . [He] broke the law by lying under oath. . . . The president lied to the American people, and, while a great majority of the people believe, as I do, that the president made false and misleading statements under oath . . . [t]he basic question for me is this: Having reached a judgment in my own mind that President Clinton's offenses constitute at least "high misdemeanors," should I vote "guilty" when my name is called, and, thus, vote to remove him from office? Some critics may ask: If you believe he is guilty, how can you not vote to remove him from office? There is some logic to the question. But simple logic can point one way, while wisdom may lie in quite a different direction.

A number of senators apparently found the legalisms a bit excessive. Republican James Inhofe of Oklahoma said, "I have often said that one of the qualifications I have for the U.S. Senate is that I am not an attorney. So, when I read the Constitution, I know what it says. When I read the law, I know what it says. When I look at the evidence and apply common sense from a nonlawyer perspective, I know what it says. In this case, it says—without question—the president is guilty as charged." Republican Connie Mack of Florida made the same point with a little more panache: "I approached this process unencumbered by a law degree."

The trial had been flavored by calls for bipartisanship, especially by Republicans. Republicans were more eager for bipartisanship for several reasons. Some hoped to pick up a few Democratic votes. Some of us were following the tradition of the centrist Wednesday Lunch Group formed by former Senator Jacob Javits, the New York moderate. The lunch group roster had shrunk to five senators: Chafee, Snowe, Collins, Jeffords, and me. Other Republican senators had reservations about the impeachment charges. Within the caucus there was a general sense that the perjury charge was weaker than the obstruction charge.

Richard Shelby of Alabama, a former Democrat who had turned Republican in early 1995 after a public feud with Clinton, expressed so much displeasure in the Republican caucus at the process and the charges that he would have surprised few by voting "not guilty" on both articles. As it turned out, Shelby voted "not guilty" on perjury and "guilty" on obstruction of justice.

Ted Stevens, the Appropriations Committee chairman from Alaska, had complained that he was unhappy with such a strong focus on impeachment when we faced international crises from Kosovo to North Korea to the Mideast. Like Shelby, Stevens wound up voting "not guilty" on perjury and "guilty" on obstruction.

Republican courtship of Democratic support and cooperation went unrequited. Except for a brief and transitory opening when Senator Russell Feingold of Wisconsin voted against Byrd's motion to dismiss, there was no rightward movement across the aisle. The Democrats had a popular president and plenty of political cover to fight the charges and the trial.

As we prepared for final deliberations, the timing and the protocol were tricky. The Senate was still setting the trial rules as we went along. And we were getting dire warnings to obey what rules existed, such as the announcement at each day's session that senators would remain silent on pain of imprisonment. The combination had senators constantly running to the parliamentarian and the rules book.

The issue of whether we could disclose our final statements turned on interpretation of Rule 29.5, which prohibited us from repeating publicly anything said in the Senate chamber during closed session. That led Senator Bob Smith, chairman of the Ethics Committee, to interpret the rule to mean that a senator stayed within Rule 29 if he first gave a public version of his statement and later made the same speech in closed-session final deliberations. It was not so clear whether the senator could make a public statement identical to his earlier remarks in a closed session.

A decision came down that senators would eventually be able to release transcripts of their Senate floor statements. But until then we could not disclose what had been discussed in closed session. As the *Washington Post* reported, that left us free to announce what we thought but not what we had said. Because of doubt about how the Senate rules would ultimately be interpreted, I decided to make my public statement announcing my vote on Wednesday, February 10, before I made my floor statement in closed session. I held a news conference at 2:00 P.M. in the Capitol's third-floor radio/TV gallery.

Journalists jammed the gallery. My impeachment statement was the only activity in town at that hour, since the rest of the Senate was sequestered behind closed doors. CNN and CNBC carried my statement live. The gallery can fit seven or eight television cameras behind about forty reporters seated in rows of chairs, with room for about twenty more standees on either side. That is ordinarily enough room to accommodate every reporter interested in covering a senator's announcement. But the gallery was packed.

"Under Scottish law there are three possible verdicts: 'guilty,' 'not guilty,' and 'not proven,' " I began. "And I intend to vote 'not proven' as to both articles. That is not to say that the president is not guilty, but to specifically say that the charges, in my judgment, have not been proved."

Citing the senators' oath to do "impartial justice," I concluded that the Senate had done only "partial" justice, because we had cut the process short and not given the House managers a chance to prove their case. The Senate had declined to hear live witnesses, which is the essence of a trial. The Constitution is explicit that the Senate has an obligation to try the case. I intended to vote "not proven," because there had been no trial and therefore no foundation for a finding of "guilty" or "not guilty."

My news conference followed the outline of my twenty-seven-page floor statement: Given the absence of live witnesses and the limitations on depositions, the House managers had to rely on transcripts of questioning by the independent counsel in grand jury proceedings. Those transcripts left many key issues unresolved. The president's version was limited to his deposition in the Paula Jones case on January 17, 1998, and his grand jury testimony on August 17, 1998. In their totality, those two cameo appearances raised far more questions than they answered. As expected, the president was exceptionally well prepared on the law and exceptionally adroit and manipulative on the facts or, more accurately, on evading the facts.

On the issue of perjury, President Clinton was artful in dodging the legal requirements for conviction, set out in the 1973 Supreme Court case *Bronston* v. *United States*. For example, the president said he had told his aides some things that were true about his relationship with Monica Lewinsky. The president had apparently also told his aides some things that were false. But the questioner failed to pursue the inquiry to pin down Clinton on the things he told his aides that were not true.

Similarly, Clinton dodged the perjury charges in his testimony on being alone with Monica Lewinsky by giving vague, unresponsive replies. When the president said, "I don't believe we were alone in the hallway, no," there was then no pursuit as to whether they had been alone in other places. The president avoided and misled, but he did not make the unequivocal false statement required by *Bronston* to constitute perjury.

When the president testified, he was treated very differently from other grand jury witnesses. He was allowed to read a prepared statement and was not pursued on the specifics. When he was asked specific questions, he referred to his statement. The key portion of his one-page statement read:

> When I was alone with Ms. Lewinsky on certain occasions in early 1996 and once in early 1997, I engaged in conduct that was wrong. These encounters did not consist of sexual intercourse; they did not constitute "sexual relations" as I understood that term to be defined at my January 17, 1998, deposition; but they did involve inappropriate intimate contact. These inappropriate encounters ended, at my insistence, in early 1997. I also had occasional telephone conversations with Ms. Lewinsky that included inappropriate sexual banter. . . .
>
> While I will provide the grand jury whatever other information I can, because of privacy considerations affecting my family, myself, and others, and in an effort to preserve the dignity of the office I hold, this is all I will say about the specifics of these particular matters.

The Senate was schizophrenic: Some senators wanted to avoid what they considered a pointless trial, including the forty-four Democrats who voted for Byrd's motion to dismiss. Others, including me, considered it our constitutional duty to hold a trial once the House had voted impeachment articles.

If the full weight of the evidence, including Juanita Broaddrick's complaint, had been presented with live witnesses instead of bits and pieces of cold transcript, perhaps the Senate and the American people would have demanded the president's appearance in the well of the Senate. Under firm examination, the president might have shown the low character denounced even by his defenders in their proposed censure petitions. That sequence might conceivably have led to his removal.

Senator Christopher Bond, a Missouri Republican who ultimately voted "guilty" on both counts, also recognized the Senate's failure in not calling witnesses. "The Senate made a serious mistake in beginning the proceedings by limiting the ability of the House managers to call witnesses," he said. "The absence of witnesses to testify to the acts alleged as the basis of impeachment charges significantly impeded the progress toward resolving the allegations against the president."

The Senate had stumbled through a pseudo trial, a sham trial, really no trial at all. In the end, letting the House managers put on their case with a full White House defense would have taken less time than the helter-skelter procedures adopted by the Senate. The president had dodged perjury by calculated evasion and poor interrogation. Obstruction of justice had failed by gaps in the proofs. The case had not been proved.

I would vote "not proven," I told the reporters.

What did that vote mean? the press wanted to know.

"There is precedent for a senator in an impeachment case to vote other than 'guilty' or 'not guilty' by voting 'present,' " I answered. "And I think that I can vote 'not proven' without being incarcerated by the sergeant at arms. At least I'm going to try."

Pressed for details, I said, "I have discussed my conclusions with some of my colleagues, and they've been respectful of them. And when you say some people are going to be in disagreement with what I have done here, I fully expect that. I do not know how you could do anything in a case like this without having a lot of people in disagreement."

"So did you anger both sides by doing it this way?" one reporter asked.

"I've had some experience at that," I replied. The room broke out in laughter.

The Senate trial may not—and should not—end the Clinton-Lewinsky matter. Perjury and obstruction of justice are serious offenses that must not be tolerated. President Clinton could still be prosecuted in the federal criminal courts when his term ends. His lawyers, in effect, invited that prosecution when they cited it as preferable to impeachment and hoisted my op-ed piece as an exhibit to boost their argument.

Before and after the verdicts, many senators pushed for findings of fact or censure, to express their displeasure with the president's conduct. Many Democrats wanted to officially condemn Clinton's conduct so they would have some political cover when they faced angry constituents.

I rejected both findings of fact and censure. The Constitution says that judgment in cases of impeachment shall not extend beyond removal and disqualification from future office. Under the separation-of-powers doctrine, Congress is not and should not be in the business of censuring any president. We are properly in the business of examining our own conduct as senators. On that score, on the record of this "pseudo trial," the Senate failed to fulfill its Constitutional mandate to "try" this case.

Before I had even left the radio/TV gallery, the phone lines exploded at my offices in Washington and throughout Pennsylvania. Many callers identified themselves as Republicans who were livid because I hadn't voted to convict the president. Other callers didn't understand "not proven."

I was one of three Republicans that Wednesday who announced we would oppose conviction on both charges. The other two were fellow centrists John Chafee and James Jeffords. Senators Stevens and Gorton announced they would vote "not guilty" on the perjury charge but "guilty" on obstruction.

The sixty-seven "guilty" votes needed to expel the president seemed beyond reach, by any count. But many who favored conviction had lowered the bar to a majority of fifty-one guilty votes as a symbolic victory. My vote jeopardized that margin.

In my closing floor statement, I told my colleagues that I intended to vote "not proven" because of my deep-seated disagreement with the way the trial had been run without witnesses. My fifteen minutes on the floor Thursday afternoon, as the third speaker after lunch, did not let me cover as much detail as I had at my news conference. I based both my announcements on the twenty-seven-page statement I'd spent most of the week writing and rewriting.

I cited precedent from previous impeachment trials for senators to vote other than "guilty" or "not guilty," generally by voting "present." During the break after I made my final argument on February 11, I consulted with the deputy parliamentarian, Alan Frumin, who advised me that by voting "not proven," I risked being recorded "present." Later that afternoon I consulted Chief Parliamentarian Bob Dove, who told me that the Senate rules and precedent held that I could be compelled to cast a conventional vote if challenged by any senator.

I then researched the Senate precedent. In the early 1950s senators had twice demanded roll-call votes to force colleagues voting "present" to change their votes to "aye" or "nay." Senator Herbert Lehman was forced to change his "present" vote in 1951 on a complex banking bill he would rather have seen pulled from the floor and redrawn. Senator Mansfield was forced by a roll-call vote in 1954 to change his "present" vote on a bill he regarded as a private matter between two Republican senators. "The chair rules that the senator from Montana is required to vote," the presiding senator ordered.

On the basis of those precedents, I didn't want to risk having someone challenge my "not proven" vote in the middle of a roll call on impeachment and then have a separate vote taken to try to force me to vote "guilty" or "not guilty." But I still wanted to stand by my announcement of "not proven." I resolved to vote "not proven and therefore not guilty."

A major argument for closed sessions was that they would shorten the process, since television lights invariably expand senators' speeches. But even with the doors shut, most senators presented closing statements, using all or most of their allotted fifteen minutes. Still, the Senate debate was a big improvement over the arguments by the president's lawyers and the House managers, which had become painfully repetitious. We heard the same rhetoric and reasoning again and again, in opening statements, the motion to dismiss, the motions on depositions, and closing arguments by the House managers and presidential counsel.

Another supposed advantage of closed sessions was that they would spur exchanges of ideas in so-called deliberations. That did not happen either, as senators asked few questions and mostly made party-line speeches. Trent Lott wanted to finish the debate and vote Thursday evening, February 11. But by Thursday afternoon it became clear we would run out of time. The vote was set for noon on Friday, February 12.

Friday happened to be my birthday. A staffer greeted me that morning by saying, "Happy Birthday, Senator."

"Who says so?" I asked. That stumped him. It was my birthday, but that was the furthest thing from my mind.

At noon the clerk called the roll for the first charge, perjury. In alphabetical order, senators announced their votes. After each vote the clerk repeated what the senator had said, either "guilty" or "not guilty." When the clerk called my name, I stood and said, "Not proven and therefore not guilty." The clerk said nothing. He paused and then simply went on to the next senator.

I checked the tabulation. When it came up 55–45, I knew my vote had been counted as "not guilty." If my vote had been counted as "present," I was prepared to seek recognition and ask the chief justice to order my vote recorded as "not guilty" because that was much closer to my view than "present."

Ten Republicans, including me, had crossed over to vote against conviction on the first article. The president had escaped the perjury charge. After the first vote, Senator Lott left the majority leader's seat, walked two rows back, and leaned over to talk to me. I rose from my chair and leaned forward to hear his whispered comment.

Lott asked me whether I planned to vote differently on the second article, on obstruction of justice, so that my vote would be recorded as "present." No, I said. I would vote the same way as on the first article: "not proven and therefore not guilty." After that brief exchange, Lott returned to his seat.

NBC Washington bureau chief Tim Russert, who was broadcasting live, speculated that Lott was trying to press me to vote differently on the second article. In fact, the majority leader did want me to vote in a way that would be tabulated as "present" so that Republicans might claim a symbolic victory if the vote turned out 50 "guilty," 49 "not guilty," and 1 "present." Apparently, the Republican leadership had speculated that the final tally would narrowly favor conviction, 50–49–1.

On the second article, obstruction of justice, I again called out, "Not proven and therefore not guilty," when my name was called. The clerk then said, "Not guilty." This time, the tally was 50–50.

I submitted an addendum to the *Congressional Record* days after the vote, to have my vote recorded precisely. The *Record* had simply listed my name among senators who had voted "not guilty." I consulted with the parliamentarian because I wanted my words recorded exactly: "not proven and therefore not guilty." The precise entry, just as I had articulated my vote on the Senate floor, was entered in the *Congressional Record*.

I was one of five Republicans who voted to acquit on the obstruction charge. The Democrats had voted solidly to acquit on both articles.

The Wall Street Journal ran a page-one news brief headed SURPRISING SPECTER: "The GOP expected a 50–49 majority for the obstruction count against Clinton, assuming Pennsylvania Senator Specter's 'not proved' vote would be tallied as 'present.' But Specter angered some GOP colleagues by adding, 'therefore not guilty,' making the count 50–50. He says he wanted to take a 'firm position.' "[1]

In fact, Lott was not angry, or at least he expressed no anger toward me. When the proceedings were over, I walked to the leader's desk, congratulated him for his energetic leadership on the trial, and shook his hand. I told him I had added the words "therefore not guilty" to avoid the possibility that some senator could challenge my vote as the votes of Senators Lehman and Mansfield had been challenged and to avoid any doubt about my verdict. Lott appeared to accept my reasoning, saying only that he should have stayed in closer touch. I don't think he expected that he would have changed my mind, but at least he would have known what I would do.

The president had escaped conviction. The impeachment process was over. Fully half the United States Senate had voted to expel the president, but that was not enough to convict. Bill Clinton retained his office, but he hadn't really won. There were no winners. William Jefferson Clinton will go down in history as the first elected president to be impeached.

As presidential historian Arthur Schlesinger, Jr., wrote in *Time* magazine:

> For a president uncommonly sensitive about his place in history, this must be a staggering blow. There are some who fear that Clinton is getting off, as they say, scot-free. Scot-free? He is already a man hopelessly damaged in the eyes of his wife, his daughter, his friends, his supporters and the nation itself, as well as in the judgment of history. However much he may pride himself on supernatural skills as an escape artist, he can never escape the stain of presidential misbehavior and personal betrayal.[2]

Senators were visibly affected, if not shaken, by the enormous weight of having to decide whether a president should be removed from office. The only comfort was that the verdict was a foregone conclusion which would not rest on a single vote.

Senator Ted Stevens correctly called his impeachment verdict "the most important vote I will ever cast as a senator." Strom Thurmond, the longest-serving senator at forty-five years, said, "The vote I cast on the articles of impeachment was one of the hardest votes that I have had to make in all my years."

I felt the strain, too. The charges were serious, and the evidence appeared overwhelming from news accounts, though not from the Senate trial record. It was hard to deny that charges like perjury and obstruction of justice constituted impeachable offenses. And the Constitution made removal from office automatic upon conviction: "The President, Vice President and all civil officers of the United States shall be removed from office on impeachment for and conviction of Treason, Bribery or other High Crimes and Misdemeanors."

Despite the constitutional provisions, many senators expressed the sense that something more was needed for removal. For a criminal conviction of perjury and obstruction of justice, the proof must be beyond a reasonable doubt. Even beyond that, the House managers needed an extra measure of certainty to persuade the Senate that the national interest mandated the extraordinary step of removing the president. The national interest may include whether there is a clear and present danger to the integrity or stability of the national government, or whether the president's conduct is so vile or reprehensible as to establish unfitness for office, or whether the electorate has lost confidence in the president to the extent that he cannot govern.

Senators, on the basis of precedent and commentary, had a lot of room to set their own standards for conviction. Defining an impeachable offense may ultimately be analogous to Associate Justice Potter Stewart's struggle to define obscenity. Stewart concluded that "perhaps I could never succeed in intelligibly doing so. But I know it when I see it."

Senator Gorton looked for some additional "gravity" to warrant conviction, if removal must follow. Senator Susan Collins, even after finding the evidence sufficient to establish obstruction of justice, voted to acquit because she felt that another element was needed to justify a guilty verdict: that the president's conduct "poses a threat toward governmental institutions." Senator Larry Craig adopted a two-step standard: whether the acts committed were the kind of "high crimes or misdemeanors warranting removal from office" and "whether the interests of the nation are served by removal." Senator Bryan said, "The president's conduct is boorish, indefensible, even reprehensible. It does not threaten the republic."

Like so many other senators, Ted Stevens struggled to reach his verdicts. He noted that if he were sitting as a juror in a criminal case, he would find the accused guilty of perjury. But he voted to acquit the president on that article, reasoning, "I do not believe his criminal activity rises to the level of 'high crimes and misdemeanors' which requires his removal from office by this Senate." Stevens did vote to convict on the obstruction charge. But even there, he said, "If I knew my vote would be the deciding vote here, I would not vote to remove this president despite his unlawful acts. He has not brought that level of danger to the nation which, in my judgment, is necessary to justify [removal]. . . ."

Even senators who voted to acquit had harsh words for the president. Olympia Snowe voted "not guilty" on both articles because she said the president's conduct did not constitute "an egregious and immediate threat to the very structure of our government." Still, she lambasted Clinton, saying:

> If I were a supporter, I would abandon him. If I were a newspaper editor, I would denounce him. If I were an historian, I would condemn him. If I were a criminal prosecutor, I would charge him. If I were a grand juror, I would indict him. And if I were a juror in a standard criminal case, I would convict him of attempting to unlawfully influence a potential witness. . . .

Those who voted to convict were even harsher. Senator Richard Lugar voted guilty on both articles, emphasizing the danger to the country from the president's loss of leadership in international affairs. Lugar identified that vital leadership quality: "In times of war or national emergency, it is often necessary for the president to call upon the nation to make great economic and personal sacrifices."

When the vote tally was concluded, Senators Lott and Daschle presented a plaque to Chief Justice Rehnquist expressing appreciation for his service. As the chief justice and two senators smiled for the camera in that brief presentation ceremony, it was an almost bizarre ending to such a serious chapter in our nation's history. Or maybe it reflected the casual approach to the trial: No one expected anything to happen, and we were all going through the motions.

That congenial ending was good for the Senate. Republicans and Democrats could at least join together in thanking Rehnquist. It was Lott's final stroke in keeping the Senate together so we could go forward with the nation's business. The majority leader had done an excellent job in keeping Republicans pretty much united in numerous party caucuses, with all senators having full opportunity to express themselves. And he had moved through some treacherous currents and concluded the proceeding in relatively short order. Senator Lott's leadership had preserved the frequently cited Senate motto that the next vote is the most important vote.

Shortly after the Senate vote, the president stepped outside the Oval Office to make a brief, contrite statement, offering his regrets for visiting the spectacle and pain of an impeachment trial on the American people.

In the end Bill Clinton's popularity—helped by a public perception that the entire impeachment matter was driven by politics—tipped the scales to allow the president to serve out the remaining twenty-two months of his term.

It did not take the president long to articulate his real defense. Clinton said in a CBS interview on March 31 that his impeachment was "no great badge of shame," because it was brought by partisans "furious that the country was doing so well." Comparing himself to South African freedom fighter Nelson Mandela, Clinton said he was "honored" by the chance to defend the Constitution. My judgment is that history will solidly reject Clinton's vacuous rationalization.

The trial carried costs for all sides. Chris Dodd, outgoing chairman of the Senate Democrats' campaign arm, politely observed that "the passion for conviction of ten of the thirteen House managers may not have been tempered by the voices of dissent within their own congressional districts." In other words, those managers were going against their constituents' wishes in pressing for conviction.

Several of the House managers, most notably Jim Rogan, have been targeted for defeat for their unpopular actions. The managers have formed a PAC to raise funds to defend themselves. The House managers, for their part, felt they were denied the chance to present their case. Rogan reportedly said, "I believe that every manager believes that we could have gotten the twelve Democratic votes if we had the opportunity to present our case."

House Judiciary Chairman Hyde, in his postmortem, said, "It's essential, for impeachment to prevail, to have bipartisan support. We never had it." Hyde tried to mask his disdain for the Senate's decision to preclude live witnesses and hamstring the House managers. "It fell short of an adequate trial," he told *The Wall Street Journal*.

After the vote I appeared on CNN's *Inside Politics in Washington*, held a news conference in Philadelphia, and gave interviews to a host of reporters Friday to amplify my view and my vote. "Some of your colleagues say you were just trying to be different," CNN anchor Bernard Shaw told me shortly into the *Inside Politics* segment, a few hours after the roll calls on the verdicts. I replied, "Different in the sense of disagreeing with the Senate conclusion on not having witnesses."

My vote set off "a pause of hushed murmuring on the Senate floor," the *Philadelphia Daily News* and other papers reported. "But the response since then from residents of Pennsylvania and around the nation has been deafening."[3] Letters, cards, and calls flooded my offices from across Pennsylvania and the nation. On any controversial vote a senator will hear more and more loudly from those who oppose his position. On the impeachment votes I heard mostly—and often at full volume—from those who favored convicting the president. Many of those who objected to my "not guilty" vote latched on to the "not proven" element. One card that arrived at my Washington office read, "Senator Specter, look out your window. Do you see any sheep? No! Because you're not in Scotland!"

The Monroe County (Pennsylvania) Republican Committee censured me. "We find Senator Specter's disregard of the facts, his blatant devaluation of the House's findings, and his use of the glare of the mass media pre-emptively—before the Senate vote—to be reprehensible and regrettable," the committee wrote in a handwritten letter signed by thirty-two of its thirty-three members.

I found it odd that at the end of the impeachment trial, I—and not the president—should be censured. In retrospect it was also curious that while President Clinton remained in office, Speaker Newt Gingrich and Speaker-designate Bob Livingston resigned their posts over fallout from the scandal.

Clinton's impeachment provides perspective on another aspect of the hearings: Senator Hatch raised the point that Anita Hill's charges against Clarence Thomas were mild compared with the conduct proved against the president. Nobody argued. Rightly or wrongly, the impeachment saga shows that the American public was prepared to accept boorish behavior, perhaps simply because the economy was so strong and the government was otherwise running so smoothly. Looking back, it probably is no coincidence that those who were against Thomas from the start believed Hill and vice versa. In President Clinton's case, admitted behavior clearly more repugnant than that denied by Judge Thomas still did not outrage the American public or switch many congressional minds. Had Thomas admitted Hill's charges, his nomination could not have survived. Perhaps today it would be different.

The alleged conduct of Clinton and Thomas was obviously distinguishable because Lewinsky had consented where Hill had not. But the gravamen of the charges against the president concerned not his sexual involvement with Lewinsky but his later conduct involving potential perjury and obstruction of justice.

When I went to Wilkes-Barre on Tuesday, February 16, the first business day after the trial ended, reporters were far more interested in my impeachment votes than in the $47 million in federal funds we were lining up for a local veterans' hospital. That afternoon, near Harrisburg, I spoke at a dairy farm on my bill to reauthorize milk compacts, an issue of economic life or death for area farmers. The *Harrisburg Patriot* ran a picture of me in front of some cows with a story about impeachment.

Two days later in Pittsburgh, at my hearing on steeldumping, impeachment had already begun to subside. In a taping on Thursday, February 18, of KDKA-TV's *Sunday Edition*, John Craig of the *Pittsburgh Post-Gazette* and Stacy Smith of KDKA questioned me about steel dumping for the program's first extended segment and then segued from foreign steel dumping to foreign policy on Scotland, which was their transition to impeachment questions.

Unlike the mail and faxes, the comments I got on the street, on trains, at supermarkets, and at movie theaters were favorable. From experience I know that not everyone who makes supportive comments in my presence necessarily agrees with me. But face-to-face, people were positive.

James Q. Wilson, a distinguished professor emeritus at UCLA, wrote in a *New York Times* column on February 15, "I am struck by the fact that President Clinton never had to face a knowledgeable personal accuser. Senator Arlen Specter has said that what he witnessed was a sham trial, and in one sense he is right. No one close to Mr. Clinton told the public that the president lied or worked to keep the truth secret. . . . By contrast, when Richard Nixon was impeached, John Dean, a man close to and often in the Oval Office, talked at length."[4]

Following the trial, former Republican presidential candidate Pat Buchanan said, "It was a sham and a farce of a trial, and Senator Specter is right." Television commentator John McLaughlin fretted that the "sham" trial would give us "no closure" on the Clinton-Lewinsky matter.

Nancy Eshelman, columnist and assistant city editor of the *Harrisburg Patriot-News*, began a piece:

Say what you want about U.S. Senator Arlen Specter—and believe me, I've muttered a few things over the years—what he did this time deserves admiration. After all the evidence had been presented, he did what he had asked of juries when he played a starring role in the courtroom. He made a decision based on the evidence presented. . . . For that, I say congratulations. Scottish common law aside, it was the honorable thing to do.[5]

Those comments gave some balance, but the real point was that the Senate should never have set rules that precluded witnesses and led to a "pseudo" or "sham" trial. As I told Bernard Shaw on *Inside Politics*, "Institutionally, if we ever have to face this nightmare again, we ought to be sure that there are live witnesses, and I intend to take the lead to try to revise the Senate rules." Maybe the next time "impartial justice" will be done.

With some perspective, more than a year after I wrote in a *New York Times* op-ed article in November 1998 that President Clinton should be prosecuted criminally after his term ended instead of impeached, it is now conclusive that Congress took the wrong course in conducting impeachment proceedings. The American people believed that the president was doing an adequate job, so that at a minimum he should not be removed from office.

Even Republicans who vociferously denounced him, like Senator Olympia Snowe ("If I were a supporter, I would abandon him," etc.), voted to acquit. One Republican, Senator Ted Stevens, who voted to convict, said that if his vote was crucial for ouster, he would have voted "not guilty," and others also felt this way. Even a self-proclaimed guardian of the Constitution like Senator Robert Byrd ended up supporting the president in a syllogistic snarl. Byrd said: (1) Perjury and obstruction of justice were high crimes and misdemeanors; (2) if a president was guilty of a high crime or misdemeanor, then removal from office was automatic; (3) President Clinton was guilty of perjury and obstruction of justice; (4) nonetheless, the president should remain in office, so Senator Byrd voted "not guilty" on both articles.

The Senate Democrats found sufficient cover in President Clinton's favorable public-opinion polls to support him at every turn. Unlike Barry Goldwater, Hugh Scott, and other Republican senators in 1974, when the revelations of President Nixon's tapes made support impossible in the face of rising public opposition, Senate Democrats felt impregnable behind their circled wagons.

House Republicans, shaken by their narrow victory in November 1998, rushed to bring articles of impeachment before the year's end without calling any fact witnesses, thereby handing the Senate a vacuous record. The Senate, in turn, searched for an early exit through a vote that would show that more than one-third of the body opposed conviction. While that early vote was rejected by enough Republican senators to move forward with what was initially thought to be a semblance of a trial, a decisive majority ultimately settled on a proceeding without the testimony of a single witness on the Senate floor.

And so it came to pass that the impeachment of Clinton established the political standard that a president, however errant, would remain in office unless he had lost the confidence of the American people that he could perform his official duties. History will not say the president was not guilty, although he was entitled to acquittal because the charges were not proved in a Senate trial, but historians will reject William Jefferson Clinton's brazen contention that it was all Republican politics and a right-wing conspiracy.

For me it was just one more investigation. As I had argued to question Jacqueline Kennedy and Lyndon Johnson, so, too, I sought the testimony of the key witnesses and Bill Clinton. As I had thoroughly questioned Robert Bork and Anita Hill, so, too, I sought more thorough examinations of Sidney Blumenthal and others. I was as disappointed in the Senate's failure to the American people in the trial as my father was in not receiving his war bonus from the Congress. I had not forgotten why I went to Washington—to get my father's bonus and to complain loudly when our government failed. A thorough investigation is a partial remedy. Without a thorough investigation, no full remedy is possible.

LOOKING FORWARD

Sometimes, returning alone on the Friday-night Metroliner from Washington to Philadelphia, I focus my attention on those issues that are certain to profoundly affect the lives of a very special constituency—my grandchildren. This is particularly true when I turn my attention to our nation's struggle to control the spread of weapons of mass destruction. The stakes may well be survival. The consequences of failure are beyond our wildest imagination. It is no longer classified information that one Trident nuclear submarine carries warheads with a total destructive power two thousand times greater than that of the Hiroshima bomb.

Simply stated, nuclear, biological, and chemical weapons of mass destruction pose the greatest single threat to the United States and the world. Some twenty-five nations today have such weapons. North Korea has developed long-range missiles that could reach Alaska and Hawaii. Some weapons capable of decimating continents can cross international borders in a suitcase. The knowledge needed to turn common industrial materials into a death cloud is no longer the province of just a few scientists. Even the Internet carries how-to guides.

At the federal level we are simply not properly organized to address this issue. As chairman of the Senate Intelligence Committee in 1995, I was surprised to learn that ninety-six uncoordinated federal agencies shared some responsibilities on this issue. Our committee chart demonstrated a bureaucratic maze almost as bad as the proposed governmental structure of the Clinton health-care legislation. In 1996 I introduced legislation creating a commission to reorganize that bureaucracy. After extensive hearings in 1998 and 1999, this commission, chaired by former CIA Director John Deutch (I served as vice chairman) published a 176-page report specifying a reorganization plan.

Noting that a problem of this magnitude required the personal attention of the president, we urged him to assign the vice president day-to-day operational command to arbitrate the many turf battles involving the departments of State, Defense, Justice, Energy, Health and Human Services, and others. The commission recommended staffing within the National Security Agency headed by a special assistant to chair a working group of Senate-confirmed departmental deputies.

The disarray is discouraging, the inertia frightening. Yet the consequences of failure call into question our survival as a nation and perhaps even as a species. International control and reduction of weapons of mass destruction are more than a priority; they are a passion. The consequences of failure are unthinkable and unacceptable. To the extent that one United States senator can make a difference, on this issue I intend to do so—not just for my grandchildren, but for every child and grandchild both here and abroad.

In this same category—issues in which our survival is at stake—are terrorism, missile defense, and arms control. Congress must pass legislation preventing attacks on our population centers by developing a national missile-defense system and combating terrorism more aggressively. As we begin the twenty-first century, terrorism has replaced classic warfare as the means of achieving political objectives. Soon after the terrorist murders at the airports in Rome and Vienna in 1985, my Terrorist Protection Act gave U.S. courts extraterritorial jurisdiction when Americans were attacked, maimed, or murdered anywhere in the world. As the world becomes smaller, American law must reach beyond our boundaries to provide a protective shield around our citizens no matter where they travel. Increased funding for CIA human intelligence, FBI counterterrorist activities, and the 1997 Anti-Terrorist Act have strengthened law enforcement without trampling on civil rights.

Cooperation among the intelligence services of our allies—including Israel, Egypt, and Jordan—has promoted preventive action. An ounce of prevention in this field is worth much more than a pound of cure. It could mean preventing a megaton catastrophe from reducing an American city to rubble. Additional congressional action is necessary to supplement 1999 legislation on missile defense. We need a strategic system to intercept missiles, but destroying such weapons before possible launches is even more effective. The $2.7 billion spent under Nunn-

Lugar legislation to destroy former U.S.S.R. missiles has been highly effective. Agreements by Ukraine, Belarus, and Kazakhstan to transfer all nuclear weapons to Russia have reduced the threat of accidental launches or deliberate strikes by a rogue nation.

I am increasingly persuaded that for the sake of our future we must now give careful consideration to revising the 1972 ABM (Anti-Ballistic Missile) Treaty, which sharply limited possible defenses to missile attack under the MAD (Mutual Assured Destruction) doctrine, which assumed that both the United States and the U.S.S.R. would be deterred from initiating nuclear strikes for fear of massive retaliation. While the United States should avoid unilateral action to rekindle the arms race, I believe it is possible to revise the ABM Treaty in negotiations with Russia that are tied into SALT III (Strategic Arms Limitations Talks).

After long delays the Senate finally ratified the Chemical Weapons Treaty in 1998. A year later the Comprehensive Test Ban Treaty (CTBT) did not fare so well. In the face of demands, mostly from Democrats, for Senate action, Majority Leader Trent Lott scheduled a ratification vote under a unanimous consent agreement that is binding under Senate rules unless all senators agree to change the time set for the final vote.

When it became apparent that the treaty would be decisively rejected, President Clinton sought a delay in negotiations with Senator Lott, which disintegrated into partisan bickering. Senator Lott wanted written assurances that Democrats would not seek ratification in 2000. He wanted to avoid an unpopular Senate vote that could hurt Republicans' chances to maintain control of the Senate and win the White House. With both sides playing Russian roulette, the president resisted that commitment until it was too late, even though sixty-two senators signed a letter urging delay of the vote. By a vote of 48–51, far less than the two-thirds constitutionally necessary, the Senate rejected ratification, causing an international furor.

What better legacy could the next Senate offer posterity than ratifying the CTBT and thereby writing a proud chapter in the arms-control book the Senate has been working on since rejection of the Treaty of Versailles and the League of Nations in 1919? A victory in this arena will be achieved only by persistent, persuasive, and wise senators who recognize that sometimes it is more important to succeed in the Senate cloakroom than in floor debate. Even the former Soviet premier Nikita Khrushchev understood what was at stake when he observed that after a nuclear exchange "the living would envy the dead." We agree on that. We can therefore reach agreement on even more.

I accept as a cardinal principle the view expressed by the Greek philosopher Diogenes: "The foundation of every state is the education of its youth." One thing is clear to me. The information age requires educated, computer-literate citizens who can fully participate in the new global economy. Every man, woman, and child in our society must be given the opportunity to participate in this new era, and the federal government must do even more to make this happen.

I take a special pride in my stewardship of medical research. The National Institutes of Health are the crown jewels of the federal government, and I am committed to their growth and fiscal stability. In assessing the priorities on our $1.85 trillion federal budget, we have sufficient resources to fund all the meritorious research projects that hold a realistic potential to save and extend lives. NIH has advanced medical research to the threshold of conquering dreaded ailments, including cancer, heart disease, Alzheimer's, and Parkinson's disease. Since January 1989 the Appropriations Subcommittee on Health and Human Services has taken the lead in increasing NIH funding from $7.57 billion to $17.9 billion. I oppose earmarking money for specific diseases, because the best judgment can be made by NIH research scientists, not by members of Congress responding to pressures from groups who favor one ailment or another.

As long as I can breathe, I will fight crime. It is that much a part of me. Propelled by forty years of effort from my early days as an assistant district attorney in 1959 to my current work on the Senate Judiciary Committee, I continue to push for a criminal justice system that will impose tough sentences on tough criminals to get them off the streets and will provide realistic rehabilitation—beginning with job and literacy training—for those, especially juveniles, who will be released from prison. The investment in rehabilitating offenders is a pittance compared with the social cost of fighting a generation of violent incorrigibles.

For federal funding for 2000, the Subcommittee on Labor, Health, Human Services and Education, which I chair, reallocated almost $900 million for an initiative to prevent violence among young people. This program responded to the wave of shootings at schools and the estimated 3 million crimes committed in or near the nation's 85,000 public schools. Rejecting one frequently cited cause, movies and TV—or any other single factor—the subcommittee called for governmental leadership to "enlist the energies and resources of private organizations, businesses, families, and children themselves." In 1982 then–Surgeon General C. Everett Koop identified youth violence as a public-health problem. The subcommittee directed the surgeon general to lead this federal initiative, which reprograms or adds funding to teacher grants, early intervention, character education, mental health, drug and alcohol counseling, parental instruction, literacy programs, and job training— all in coordination with crime-prevention programs with the Department of Justice, and to report on the effects of movies, TV, the Internet, and video games on violent behavior.

It is often said that war is much too serious a matter to be entrusted to the military. Permit me to add the president. It is also too often overlooked that the Constitution grants only to Congress the authority to declare war. Presidents have historically eroded that authority by unilaterally exercising their power as commanders in chief to involve the United States in war. During my tenure of almost two decades, I have repeatedly argued on the Senate floor, usually unsuccessfully, that the president should not order our military forces to initiate acts of war. Vietnam demonstrated the impracticality, if not the impossibility, of a war unauthorized by the Congress and lacking the support of the American people.

Four congressional-presidential confrontations—Lebanon in 1983, the Gulf War in 1991, missile strikes against Iraq in 1998, and air attacks against Yugoslavia in 1999—illustrate the continuing constitutional conflict. In 1983 Senate debate on the applicability of the War Powers Act to President Reagan's sending Marines into Lebanon, Senator Charles Percy, chairman of the Foreign Relations Committee, responding to my questions, conceded that U.S. military actions in Korea and Vietnam were wars that required congressional authorization. My efforts to structure a test case to determine the constitutionality of the War Powers Act were unsuccessful. After consulting with Majority Leader Howard Baker, I prepared an elaborate complaint and sought White House joinder to take the issue to the Supreme Court. The Reagan administration declined to join in the submission, preferring the existing ambiguities.

Congress was successful in 1991 in asserting its authority to determine U.S. participation in the Gulf War. Noting the unusual Senate debate, the *Washington Post* wrote on January 10, "There were moments that looked historic, as when Senator Sam Nunn (D-Ga.)

engaged in a polite, quietly fervent exchange with Sens. John W. Warner (R-Va.) and Arlen Specter (R-Pa.) about the costs and benefits of acting now." Although the vote was close, the Senate decided in favor of the resolution for the use of force, 52–47; the House provided a larger margin of approval, 250–183. That congressional support provided absolutely essential public as well as constitutional backing.

President Clinton acted unilaterally in ordering missile strikes against Iraq in December 1998. Since Iraq's noncompliance with commitments to the UN had come to a head as early as February 1998, Congress had ample time to authorize or vote against such strikes but chose through inaction to take no position, because many, if not most, members of Congress are not eager to assert the institution's constitutional authority. It is safer politically to sit back and let the president take the responsibility, then applaud if military action succeeds or criticize if it turns out badly. I opposed the missile strikes because I thought they would kill many innocent people and have no effect on Saddam Hussein's conduct.

The conflict between Congress and the president arose again in 1999 over air strikes against Yugoslavia. In four extraordinary meetings attended by about forty members of the House and Senate in late March, the president, the secretaries of state and defense, and the chairman of the Joint Chiefs of Staff, many members urged the president not to act without congressional authorization. The president finally made such a request after it was clear that he would act regardless. The Senate did approve air strikes by a 58–41 vote, but the House did not, on a 213–213 tie vote.

One disquieting note was the implication of partisanship in the votes, whether the commander in chief was Republican or Democrat. When President Bush was in office in January 1991, the Senate vote was 52–47, with forty-two Republicans and ten Democrats voting for the use of force. In 1999 the Senate vote was 58–41, with forty-one Democrats and seventeen Republicans voting for the air strikes. This is one area that must be "off-limits" to partisan politics. For the sake of our nation and the young men and women who will be asked to risk their lives, every effort should be made by the Congress both to end partisan politics at the water's edge and to stop any president from ordering acts of war without congressional authorization. We should never accept less courage from those in Congress than we expect from those we are sending into combat.

"Conscience," said Mark Twain, "is that little voice inside that says someone may be watching." The Constitution tells Congress to play this role for our people. Congressional responsibility to legislate and the Senate's role in confirmation are major duties leaving relatively little time for Congress to exercise its third principal function: oversight of the executive branch. Two-year budgets, now under consideration, would give the House and Senate more time to scrutinize departments and agencies under presidential control. How well we perform the oversight role often determines how confident our citizens are in the integrity of their government.

For instance, Ruby Ridge was a festering sore until our Senate Subcommittee on Terrorism exposed FBI and AFT excesses and forced reforms by those agencies. There has never been closure on the Waco tragedy, aggravated by the August 1999 revelation of a six-year cover-up on the FBI's use of incendiaries there. Following Ruby Ridge and Waco, militias sprang up in the United States as thousands of Americans doubted the integrity of the federal government and took up arms.

It took the Department of Defense six years to make full disclosure on the exposure of U.S. military personnel to chemical weapons in the Gulf War at Khamisiyah in March 1991. The Veterans Affairs Committee exposed that dereliction in an oversight investigation in 1997 and 1998. Notwithstanding an important investigation and report by the House Cox Committee, further intensive congressional oversight of the departments of Justice and Energy is necessary to determine the adequacy of security for U.S. nuclear secrets. The Department of Justice has effectively evaded oversight by delaying tactics and the reluctance of Congress to take strong action through subpoenas and contempt citations, which risk long-term litigation. I am persuaded that intense oversight is the only way to bring the critical facts to light. In September 1999 I was asked to lead a Senate Judiciary Subcommittee inquiry on Department of Justice activity on alleged Chinese espionage, plea bargaining in charges related to campaign financing, and a reinvestigation of Waco.

Over the years I have come to realize that no Senate action, with the possible exception of declaring war or equivalent resolutions authorizing the use of force, matches the high drama or importance of Supreme Court confirmation hearings. There is a special symbolism to the fact that the Roman columns of the Senate line up directly with those of the Supreme Court building across the Capitol green. Considering the determinative role of the Supreme Court in our national life, where a single justice on a 5–4 vote defines the legal standards from birth or abortion to death through capital punishment and everything in between, the Senate should focus more on its constitutional "advice and consent" function. With four sitting justices over seventy-five years of age, it appears that the next president will have a number of Supreme Court appointments to consider.

Before giving its "consent," the Senate should be much more exacting in insisting on answers in the confirmation hearings while not asking for commitments on matters that may come before the Court. We should press nominees for appropriate answers and reject those who are not candid and forthcoming. The Senate has shown that it has interest and tenacity regarding Supreme Court nominees by rejecting 29 of 112, or 26 percent, contrasted with negative votes on 15 of 565 cabinet candidates, or less than 3 percent.

While the history of the Court has arguably been filled with making rather than interpreting the law, recent decisions by the Rehnquist Court demonstrate an unusually activist agenda to reduce congressional power. In 1995 in *Lopez*, the Court reversed sixty years of Congress's use of the Commerce Clause by invalidating federal legislation creating gun-free school zones. In *Sable* v. *FCC* in 1989, the Court held legislation unconstitutional because "no Congressman or senator purported to present a considered judgment. . . ." What is the authority of even the Supreme Court to substitute its judgment because there was no "considered judgment" by members of Congress?

The same rationale was used by the Supreme Court to invalidate the Age Discrimination Act early in 2000, because "Congress had virtually no reason to believe that state and local governments were unconstitutionally discriminating against their employees on the basis of age." It is appropriate to question nominees on judicial philosophy or ideology and reject those with activist agendas where they would seek to be superlegislators.

Another area where the Supreme Court has complicated the landscape of our body politic is campaign finance reform. Momentum is building in Congress to reduce the influence of money in U.S. elections, but much remains to be done. I am co-sponsoring the McCain-Feingold campaign finance reform bill, which is still short of the sixty Senate votes needed to cut off debate and bring the legislation to final passage. Democrats and dissident Republicans in the House succeeded in 1998 and again in 1999 in passing reform legislation. If, however, the Supreme Court will not reverse *Buckley* v. *Valeo*, it will be necessary to pass a constitutional amendment, since the Court has justified unlimited campaign funding as free speech.

Senator Ernest Hollings and I have pressed for that amendment for more than a decade. The Court got it wrong in *Buckley*, and the nation has suffered ever since. Unlimited campaign funding and soft money are corrosive enough to warrant a constitutional amendment if the Court will not recognize the mischief its ruling has created. Overturning the opinions of the six justices who concurred in *Buckley* does not require amending the language of the First Amendment. I would strenuously oppose any effort to change that language. What is realistically involved is overruling some justices' interpretation of what that language means.

Although as a United States senator I must focus on national issues, I also never forget that I am, and am proud to be, a Pennsylvanian. My senior position on the Appropriations Committee helps ensure my state's fair share of federal funding for education, health care, housing, defense contracts, job training, environmental protection, and economic development. Special attention must be paid to maintaining and building infrastructure such as the state highway system, Pittsburgh's locks and dams, and Erie's Presque Isle; to deepening Philadelphia's port channel; and to flood control for Scranton, Wilkes-Barre, Harrisburg, and the Susquehanna River Basin generally. "Maglev," or magnetic-levitation trains, could revolutionize surface transportation for the nation and have unique potential for Pennsylvania. Our early federal grants could lead to a three-hundred-mile-per-hour rail line that would take passengers from Philadelphia to Pittsburgh in two hours and seven minutes, with stops in Lancaster, Harrisburg, Altoona, Johnstown, and Greenberg.

Since the early 1980s I have pressed for federal legislation for a private right of action to stop dumping, which is the practice of selling foreign products in the United States below cost. Dumping violates U.S. and international trade laws. Such a law not only would benefit Pennsylvania's steel industry but would also level the playing field for the producers of more than two hundred U.S. products who are victimized by dumping because the executive branch elevates defense and foreign policy considerations over fairness for domestic goods.

In addition to this partial list of legislative initiatives, my most important activity for Pennsylvania is the frequent visits I make to the state's sixty-seven counties. In an era that emphasizes access to senators and House members through fund-raisers, it is more important than ever to hold town meetings where constituents can question their senator. Similarly, there is enormous benefit to the senator who wants to stay in close touch with constituents' concerns—and to merit reelection. I live in Pennsylvania, not Washington, D.C. Most Mondays begin with my taking a plane ride to Pittsburgh or car trips to Harrisburg or the Wilkes-Barre/Scranton area, arriving in Washington late Monday afternoon for the week's first vote. Then, late on Friday, I'm on the Metroliner back to Pennsylvania for the weekend. Recesses are used for travel to the rural parts of the state.

TRUTH VANQUISHES DISTRUST

To combat distrust in America, senators—along with all others in government—must simply tell the people the truth. Sometimes this is tough. Sometimes it's embarrassing. There is never a time when the alternative is better. If there is cause to suspect a governmental cover-up, the Senate or the House, through prompt oversight, should ferret out the facts. Had congressional oversight on Waco been as effective as it was on Ruby Ridge, the militia movement would have been less motivated to mobilize. It is even conceivable the Oklahoma City bombing could have been avoided.

Congress should work to restore public trust by acting on key problems of public concern in a bipartisan way. People are sick of partisanship and politics as usual. President Kennedy said it best: "Sometimes party asks too much." I am thoroughly convinced that trust is the glue that holds a democracy together. Public trust must be earned, nurtured, and insulated from the effects of a sound-bite society that too often encourages the white lie or the whitewash. In my early days in the Senate I learned the importance of crossing party lines to enact important legislation. Senator Tom Harkin and I have put politics aside to work closely together for more than a decade, alternating as chairman and ranking member on the Appropriations Subcommittee on Education, Labor, and Health and Human Services. Together we have taken the lead on funding NIH research, Head Start, college grants, and many other targeted programs to help needy Americans lead better lives and promote the feeling that their government cares about them.

The abiding philosophy of Congress should be to legislate on common areas of agreement to provide at least incremental progress when more cannot be achieved. Too often that principle is shunted aside for the political "advantage" failure to legislate brings by creating a campaign issue demanding public support for "all or nothing." That strategy routinely fails. America yearns to be governed from the center. Generally, this nation wants something done—not everything, because Congress is rightly not trusted with radical approaches, but not nothing either. When Congress lets progress fail at the altar of partisanship, America sees through it, and the result is distrust. In the final analysis it is widespread distrust that destroys democracies more certainly than any foreign enemy. Our best work in Congress has always been done when party labels are put aside, answers vigorously sought, and thoughtful laws enacted.

The issues I've addressed are all tough, but I approach them with strength and vision inherited from my family. Despite the many difficulties faced by my father on his tortuous journey from the czar's Russia to the United States, back across the Atlantic to fight in World War I, and returning to Kansas to struggle through the Depression, he always had confidence in America. He would say, "In America there has to be a way for a man to make a living." He trusted America, as did my mother, and I have inherited that trust from them. That sense of trust and confidence was nurtured by the values my brother, my two sisters, and I observed in our parents' daily lives. Considering their sacrifices, their children would not even think of doing anything to embarrass their parents. Compared to the climb my parents faced, my life has been a gentle downhill ride all the way. My children and grandchildren are the inheritors of this legacy of optimism, tenacity, and service. As my parents did for me, I want to leave them a better world, a brighter future, and challenges worthy of their gifts.

Notwithstanding the current popularity of cynicism and distrust, I firmly believe that America is more troubled than in trouble. Our national institutions, established by the oldest and most inspired Constitution in history, have enabled us to survive and surmount wars, depressions, assassinations, and impeachments. We are still the shining symbol of human dignity that sparks the flame of hope in so many sad, frightened corners of the world. We are still the best hope on earth, and my abiding confidence that optimism will conquer cynicism comes from the roots of my courageous immigrant parents, who in the face of so many setbacks always believed in themselves and their adopted country.

FULL CIRCLE

In 1987 I had a chance to argue my father's case for leaving Russia and coming to America in an informal debate with Soviet Ambassador Victor Karpov in Geneva after a rigorous day of arms-control talks. Our conversation turned into a confrontation on the relative merits of the United States and the U.S.S.R. It wasn't too hard to demonstrate that Adam Smith's free-enterprise system had vastly outproduced Karl Marx's Communist cooperatives. Nor was it difficult to show that democracy had won out over totalitarianism in the titanic struggle of the twentieth century. Perhaps Karpov would have preferred my side of the argument, but he had no choice, since he did not have my great good fortune to be an American. His father had stayed in Russia. Losing the argument on the merits and perhaps inspired by several glasses of vodka, Karpov sought an end to the debate with an observation he was certain I would find difficult to challenge.

"If I lived in Pennsylvania, I'd never vote for you!"

"Fine," I replied, "but at least you'd have the right to vote."

Silence.

EPILOGUE

THE MIDNIGHT PARDONS

National affairs have turned so spectacular, astounding, and historic in the months following the initial publication of this book, through the court-decided presidential election, midnight pardons of billionaire fugitives, and Sen. Jim Jeffords's seismic leap from the Republican party, among other events, that it seemed natural to update this paperback edition with a chapter on some of the highlights.

It was thought impossible for Bill Clinton to surpass the reckless conduct that led to his impeachment, but he managed to do so by granting more than 140 midnight pardons for Marc Rich, the international fugitive; drug kingpin Carlos Vignali; Whitewater figure Susan McDougal; and the president's own half brother, Roger Clinton, among others. Sen. Trent Lott, the Republican Majority Leader, asked me to lead a Judiciary Committee inquiry into the pardons Clinton granted the morning he left office.

Even in that crowd, Marc Rich got the most attention, and for good cause. Indicted in 1983 for fraud, trading with the enemy by buying $200 million of Iranian oil and evading $48 million in income taxes, Rich had fled to Switzerland and renounced his U.S. citizenship. Department of Justice pardon attorney Roger Adams first heard of Rich's pardon at 1:00 A.M. on January 20 and immediately called the White House. Adams testified before the Judiciary Committee on February 14 that a presidential aide told him that little information was available on Rich because he was "traveling abroad." That brought the loudest outburst of laughter I'd heard in twenty years of Senate hearings.

In granting the pardons, Clinton said he relied on the representations of his former White House Counsel Jack Quinn, who got a $300,000 fee for his successful efforts. Quinn was free to set whatever fee he chose, but there was no doubt that the size turned on his ability to access Clinton and influence him. Quinn sought to buttress his case with an exonerating opinion letter from Harvard Professor Bernard Wolfman and Georgetown Professor Martin Ginsburg, husband of Supreme Court Justice Ruth Bader Ginsburg. Ginsburg told me that both relied solely on what Quinn had told them.

The prosecutors, including New York Mayor Rudy Giuliani, who as U.S. Attorney had indicted Rich, were outraged by the pardon, especially because they were never consulted. Instead, Clinton had listened to Rich's ex-wife, Denise, who contributed more than $1,000,000 to the Democratic party, $109,000 to Hillary Clinton's Senate campaign, and $450,000 to Clinton's Presidential Library and to Beth Dozoretz, a top Democratic National Committee fund-raiser. E-mails disclosed that Denise Rich, Quinn, Dozoretz, and others had made strenuous efforts to keep their lobbying secret. Even Israeli Prime Minister Ehud Barak had weighed in for Rich.

While the prosecutors and the Department of Justice pardon attorney were kept in the dark, Dozoretz called Clinton at 11:00 P.M. on January 19 to thank him for the Rich pardon. When it was disclosed that Sen. Hillary Clinton's brother Hugh Rodham had received $200,000 for his successful efforts on the Vignali pardon, Rodham returned the money.

Faced with an avalanche of criticism, Clinton wrote an op-ed piece on February 18 for the *New York Times,* raising more questions than he answered and further fanning the public outrage. The Rich pardon drew extensive media coverage away from the new administration's agenda, leading President George W. Bush to say it was time to "move on." Faced with that comment, Republican senators were reluctant to press Clinton to testify before the Judiciary Committee and the Democrats opposed all aspects of the inquiry.

I thought we should hear from Clinton. In hearings, like trials, the legal principle has been firmly established that the parties are entitled to hear every person's relevant testimony. That also applies to the president, as the Supreme Court ruled in compelling Nixon to produce his Oval Office tapes.

As assistant counsel, I had unsuccessfully urged the Warren Commission to call President Lyndon Johnson to testify. He was an eyewitness riding in the car immediately behind President Kennedy. Although Johnson was obviously not involved in the assassination, there was worldwide speculation since he had much to gain by succeeding to the presidency. In many countries around the world, assassinations of leaders are planned by people who want to succeed them. But when the evidence started to come in identifying Oswald as the assassin without a link to Johnson, the speculation subsided. Nonetheless, Johnson was an obvious witness because he succeeded to the presidency and was an eyewitness to Kennedy's murder.

In 1999, I had pushed to have Clinton testify in his impeachment trial. Since he had testified in the Paula Jones civil case and before the grand jury, why not in the Senate trial, which was so much more important than those proceedings? My Republican colleagues were so anxious to conclude the trial as soon as possible that no witnesses were called—not even Monica Lewinsky or Betty Currie.

When Republican Judiciary Committee members discussed calling Clinton as a witness on the pardons, I conceded it was risky. The former president was a superb communicator. Everyone had expected him to be embarrassed by his grand jury video testimony, but he emerged the victor. And senators with their long-winded speeches and meandering questions were not known to excel in hearings. It is practically a violation of the Senate code of ethics to listen to an answer.

Faced with my colleagues' reluctance to even "invite" Clinton, I used the Sunday talk shows to urge him to appear voluntarily on the model of President Ford's testimony before the House Judiciary Committee after his controversial Nixon pardon. Clinton declined, even though there was considerable editorial support for the idea.

So a different approach was adopted. After consulting with Senators Trent Lott and Orrin Hatch, the committee chairman, and other committee members, I wrote to Clinton on February 28, suggesting that he submit to questioning by a Democratic committee member and me in his office without the media present, with the transcript to be released to the public after he had a chance to review it.

I learned that Clinton wanted to accept my offer, but was discouraged by Democratic senators who were strenuously opposed. Fundraising had dropped off for the Democrats and they wanted to put the scandal behind them, so Clinton acquiesced. He never formally declined, but instead had a spokesperson say that he was not inclined to respond at that time.

As soon as the pardons became public, my staff asked key witnesses to testify. Denise Rich's lawyer said his client was "traumatized" by the media onslaught, but would consider our request when things calmed down. Later, she took the Fifth Amendment after the U.S. Attorney for the Southern District of New York initiated a grand jury investigation. Similarly, the attorney for Beth Dozoretz scheduled an appointment with my staff, but that meeting never occurred because Dozoretz changed lawyers and took the Fifth Amendment after the grand jury was impaneled. After Rich was granted immunity, she no longer had an excuse not to talk. Rich later gave extensive interviews to Larry King, Barbara Walters, and others, denying any improper conduct.

Inquiries by both the House of Representatives Governmental Operations Committee and the Senate Judiciary Committee were held in abeyance pending action by the grand jury.

Meanwhile, my staff and I were developing remedial legislation to close the gaps disclosed by the Rich pardon. For a time, I considered reviving a constitutional amendment proposed by then–Senator Walter Mondale after the Nixon pardon. Under Mondale's amendment, Congress could nullify a presidential pardon on a two-thirds vote by each body. That effort was abandoned in the face of a consensus that Clinton's conduct was so aberrational and he had paid such a high political price that it was unlikely to be repeated.

There was considerably more support for the legislative remedies I was proposing. The Rich pardon had succeeded because it had flown below the radar of public scrutiny. While existing federal law contained many registration requirements, none were triggered by the Quinn situation.

Similarly, there was no requirement for reporting contributions to Presidential Libraries during the recipient's term in office. I reasoned such donations should be treated like campaign fund-raising, with a similar form of disclosure, so the public could evaluate whether official decisions were being influenced.

In mid-March, during a private conversation with Sen. Hillary Clinton on the Senate floor, she volunteered that she thought I was right that contributions to Presidential Libraries should be reported. I replied there was another provision in my bill calling for lobbyists to register. Her immediate response included a reference to "Jack," obviously Quinn, and she said she agreed with that provision, too. Since senators are always looking for co-sponsors, I said the obvious: "Would you consider co-sponsoring?" She said to send her the bill and she'd think about it.

A few days later, she asked me how the bill would handle a situation where a person in a "ropeline," where the president greets people who are behind a restraining line, shouts out "pardon X," or when a friend casually urges a pardon. Those situations, I said, would be excluded because those people were not being paid to lobby. My bill would require registration of any person who was getting paid $5,000 or more in a year to lobby for pardons and who contacted certain officials including the president, vice president, staff at the Executive Office of the President, cabinet-level officials, or members of Congress.

The following week, after our staffs had talked, Senator Clinton joined four other Democrats and four Republicans in co-sponsoring Senate Bill 645. Editorial writers speculated that she had supported the legislation to separate herself from her husband's unpopular pardons, to separate herself from her husband generally, and to try to revive her favorable poll ratings, which had sunk after the pardons and the criticism the senator received for taking furniture and other gifts from the White House.

I thought her comment hit the mark when she told the press she supported my bill because it was "sensible bipartisan" legislation. In an article about Hillary Clinton's first few months in office in its April 13 edition, the *New York Times* said Senator Clinton was "forging alliances with some of the fiercest critics of the Clinton White House, like Senators Arlen Specter and Orrin Hatch."

The question comes up repeatedly: How does President Clinton get into such messes? The pardon fiasco is more of the same: a big, handsome, very bright, good-natured fellow whose overwhelming bravado makes him confident that he'll charm everybody in the end so that no matter what he does, they'll love and forgive him. He deludes himself. Like many public officials, he seeks to excel by proposing innovative ideas to help people and to advance his personal achievement for re-election and history's verdict.

I admire what Clinton did on welfare reform and education programs. He went too far on his proposal for a massive federal bureaucracy on health care, but he continually tried to improve the quality of life in America, especially for the poor.

Did Clinton pardon Marc Rich for money? I don't think so. Was the friendship of Denise Rich and Beth Dozoretz a factor weighing on his goodwill? Yes. Perhaps he favored Rich because he wouldn't pardon Jonathan Pollard, an American who is serving a life sentence for spying for Israel, when asked by many of the same people. Clinton faced a lot of pressure over Pollard, with CIA Director George Tenet threatening to resign if Clinton pardoned Pollard and with heavy opposition from the intelligence and military communities. And Clinton has a capacity for rationalization. I think he structured the Marc Rich pardon in a way he could talk himself into it, but no one else was persuaded.

THE PARTISAN DEPARTMENT OF JUSTICE

While Clinton's pardons drew more immediate censure, I believe history will be far more critical of the decision by the Supreme Court of the United States in favor of Governor George W. Bush over Vice President Al Gore. Many people were surprised to learn that a majority of the popular vote does not elect a president. It's the vote of the electoral college. Even more people were surprised that the electoral college vote was subordinated to the Supreme Court's vote. This truly was the election decided by a single vote: five to four.

The Bush/Gore election was arguably marked by partisanship on both sides. Attorney General Janet Reno appeared to favor Gore. The Supreme Court appeared to favor Bush, although, as it turned out, Bush would probably have won anyway had a full recount occurred, according to a comprehensive newspaper review.[1]

We pride ourselves on being a government of laws, not of men and women. The Department of Justice is charged with prosecuting without fear or favor. The Supreme Court is the ultimate symbol of blindfolded, impartial administration of justice. Perhaps it is too much to expect human beings not to reflect their own passions, prejudices, or predilections, but I found that the 2000 presidential election was influenced by discernible partisanship.

Gore dodged a bullet or perhaps a cannonball when Attorney General Reno refused to appoint independent counsel to investigate his alleged false statements and solicitation of campaign contributions on federal property. Reno's decision was hard to understand and legally unjustifiable in light of the evidence. And then there were the affirmative recommendations of FBI Director Louis Freeh, FBI General Counsel Larry Parkinson, and Department of Justice attorneys Charles LaBella and Robert Conrad.

Typical of the attorney general's refusal to consider the law and the hard evidence was her response to my questioning during Judiciary Committee oversight about notes made by David Strauss, Gore's deputy chief of staff, on a key meeting in the White House on November 21, 1995. Several participants, including the president's chief of staff, Leon Panetta, said discussions that day included the vice president's role on fund-raising for "hard money" as well as "soft money." Soliciting contributions for "hard money" would fall under the prohibitions of the campaign finance laws, and such funds could not be raised from the vice president's White House office.

Strauss's written notes of the meeting said "35% hard/65% soft." When asked, Strauss claimed he didn't remember that part of the meeting, but conceded those were his contemporaneous notes. Reno testified that she did not consider that evidence in deciding whether Gore raised "hard money" because Strauss didn't remember such a discussion.

Fundamental rules of evidence hold that witnesses' notes may be used to refresh his/her recollection and the testimony would be admissible as "recollection refreshed"; or if those notes did not refresh witnesses' recollections, the notes themselves would be admissible evidence as "prior recollection recorded" as long as they were made contemporaneously with the event, which was the case with Strauss's notes.

Attorney General Reno had no explanation as to why she did not consider that relevant, probative, admissible evidence.

While refusing to appoint independent counsel on Gore, Reno continued the Department of Justice campaign finance investigation into 2000. In June, the Judiciary Subcommittee I was chairing learned that her most recently appointed chief counsel on campaign finance, Robert Conrad, had joined Freeh, LaBella, and others in recommending independent counsel.

When I disclosed Conrad's recommendation in again urging Reno to act, Gore's press secretary inexplicably accused me of McCarthyism. I responded that the only possible McCarthyism was Charlie McCarthyism, with Clinton being Edgar Bergen and Gore the dummy—or maybe I said "puppet."

But it was no laughing matter and I demanded that Gore apologize for the affront. He declined. I looked for an opportunity to confront him directly in the Senate chamber, where he was occasionally required to appear to break a tie. That opportunity did not arise before his term expired.

There was a dynamite December 9, 1996, FBI memo on that issue of appointing independent counsel and reappointing Reno. It did not come to light until late April 2000 and then only in response to a subpoena that I finally got from the Judiciary Committee for the famous LaBella memorandum and other documents on independent counsel. It took the unusual form of a memo from Freeh to FBI Deputy Director William Esposito about a Reno/Freeh meeting on December 6, 1996:

> I also advised the Attorney General of Lee Radek's comment to you that there was a lot of "pressure" on him and PIS [the Public Integrity Section] regarding this case because the "Attorney General's job might hang in the balance" (or words to that effect). I stated that these comments would be enough for me to take him and the Criminal Division off the case completely.

It then recited that Freeh had suggested Reno pick a first-rate Department of Justice legal team from outside main justice because of Radek's comment.

Radek's comment to Esposito was explosive since it had been made at a time when President Clinton was reported to be undecided about retaining Reno for his second term. My immediate, firm reaction was that the Freeh memo and the underlying incident should have been disclosed to the Senate Judiciary Committee for oversight at that time. Had the matter been the subject of open hearings in early 1997, the public pressure might have compelled Reno to appoint independent counsel or had some other effect on Reno's tenure as attorney general. The Freeh memo offered evidence that the attorney general's top advisers were letting considerations other than the facts and the law influence their decision not to appoint independent counsel to investigate campaign finance allegations.

As soon as I saw the December 1996 memo in April 2000, I told Freeh that I strongly disagreed with his decision not to advise at least the Judiciary Committee chairman and ranking member of the Radek/Esposito meeting. He disagreed, saying such disclosure would have irreparably impaired his relationship with Reno.

I asked Freeh to testify alongside Reno. He refused. I thought it was important for Freeh to confront Reno in a public hearing on their meeting where he personally called her attention to Radek's statement and

conflict with the president and Reno was obviously enhanced by his ten-year term, though he could be removed for cause.

In retrospect, I think Freeh was on very thin ice if he did not, in fact, exceed his authority. Under the Constitution, the president has the authority to discharge his duties unless removed from office as a result of conviction by a two-thirds vote of the Senate after impeachment by the House. Although undecided by case law, it is generally viewed that a president cannot be prosecuted criminally while in office. If the evidence that led Freeh to say President Clinton was the subject of a criminal investigation had risen to the level of terminating the president's duties through impeachment, that would have been a matter for Congress.

Had we known about the December 9, 1996, memo when Freeh told us in February 1997 that he had foreclosed Clinton from obtaining national security data, I think we would have pressed for the underlying facts relating to why Clinton was under criminal investigation. We might even have gone to the federal judge presiding over the grand jury to have access to that information. Knowing the Justice Department's Public Integrity Section was influenced by Reno's job status in the face of specific information strong enough to lead Freeh to deny the president national security data, we would have been in a much stronger position to press for appointment of independent counsel.

THE RENO/FREEH COMBAT CONTINUES OVER WEN HO LEE

Even though the FBI is technically part of the Department of Justice, the bureau and the department (and also Freeh and Reno) had sharp conflicts over Dr. Wen Ho Lee's case, which is still pending in mid-2001, nineteen years after the file was opened. To this day it is not known whether Lee was a major spy who threatened U.S. nuclear superiority or a victim of U.S. governmental abuse.

As the FBI and Justice Department sparred over lie detector tests and issues of probable cause for fifteen years, Lee, a scientist at Los Alamos National Laboratory, was reportedly compromising precious U.S. nuclear secrets. No action was taken against Lee until December 1999, when he was arrested, manacled, and held in solitary confinement on Department of Justice/FBI allegations that he unlawfully tampered with, altered, concealed, removed, and retained restricted data and defense information. The importance of Dr. Lee's case was articulated at his bail hearing on December 13, 1999, when Dr. Stephen Younger, Associate Laboratory Director for Nuclear Weapons at Los Alamos, testified: "These codes and their associated databases and the input file, combined with someone that knew how to use them, could, in my opinion, in the wrong hands, change the global strategic balance."[2]

Ultimately, the prosecution accepted a bargain providing for Lee's immediate release for a guilty plea on one count of downloading weapons-design secrets to a nonsecure computer. I thought the evidence looked as though the department and the bureau held Lee under extraordinary detention conditions—manacles and solitary confinement—to coerce a guilty plea. How else could they justify leaving him at large for months and then treating him as being more dangerous than Public Enemy No. 1? In Judiciary Subcommittee oversight hearings on September 26, 2000, I said: "The manacles, the references to the Rosenbergs, the false testimony given by the FBI raise a possible inference—and I say only possible—that these were pressures to compel a guilty plea."

The Judiciary Subcommittee investigation and hearings on Wen Ho Lee did lead to significant remedial legislation. The Intelligence Authorization Act for 2000, among other provisions, requires the attorney general to personally review a Foreign Intelligence Surveillance Act application submitted by someone like FBI director Freeh and to issue a written declination of such a request, and then for someone like Freeh to personally follow up on the matter.

I believe Louis Freeh, who stepped down as FBI director at the end of June 2001, did an excellent job, notwithstanding some serious lapses under his watch, including the Wen Ho Lee case, deficiencies at the FBI crime lab, his delay in identifying Robert Hanssen as a spy, and failure to disclose documents on Waco and the Timothy McVeigh case in a timely manner. Freeh did an outstanding job on the Khobar Towers investigation, which involved numerous overseas trips, and on expanding the bureau's international activities to crack down on international organized crime.

The bureau's unpublicized investigations have foiled potential terrorist attacks and the convictions in the Kenya and Tanzania embassy bombings have undercut Osama bin Laden's terrorist operations.

Freeh showed courage in changing the FBI's rules of engagement and use of deadly force in the wake of our Ruby Ridge investigation, when other agency heads such as ATF Director John Magaw and Treasury Secretary Robert Rubin would not buck institutional resistance. Freeh was also forthcoming when asked for material, unlike many other federal agency heads. And he did his job at tremendous personal and financial sacrifice. I was personally impressed when I occasionally called Freeh at his home and found him busy caring for his six young sons.

Had Reno followed Freeh's recommendation to appoint independent counsel, and especially Conrad's recommendation in the spring of 2000, it is doubtful that Gore would have been chosen by the Democratic Convention in August. Gore was saved by a friendly Justice Department. He was almost saved by the Florida Supreme Court with a majority of Democrats; but his luck, or perhaps more accurately his constituency, ran out in the U.S. Supreme Court.

The campaign finance and Wen Ho Lee investigations are a minuscule part of the expanding responsibilities of the FBI director, with nearly 28,000 staff members and a budget of $3.29 billion, and the massive jurisdiction of the attorney general, with 125,000 employees and a budget of $24 billion. In the face of such duties, it is an open question whether their jobs are too big for one person, which brings us to the biggest job—the presidency.

THE COURT ELECTS THE PRESIDENT

I first met young George W. Bush in Sen. Bob Dole's office when Republican senators were rallying to help his father win re-election in 1992. I liked him immediately. His charisma and candor that all of America now knows were apparent in our first meeting. I watched his two election victories in 1994 and 1998, and admired his leadership in Texas.

In mid-1999, Governor Bush visited the Senate and spoke informally to some twenty-five Republican members standing in the Foreign Relations Room. He was a big hit. Sen. John Chafee, who hadn't said much about him until then, was so enthusiastic that he declared his endorsement at the end of the governor's short speech.

I campaigned for Governor Bush all over Pennsylvania in 2000, especially in the Philadelphia suburbs, which were key to a victory. The four bedroom counties, Montgomery, Delaware, Bucks, and Chester, ordinarily provided at least 100,000 Republican votes for a victory.

Bush lost them by 54,000 votes and ended up losing the state by more. I agonized until dawn on election night as the votes and moods swung back and forth. During the protracted recounts in the Florida courts, I continued to agonize.

On Saturday, November 25, I played squash in the morning so I could take our oldest granddaughters, Silvi and Perri, to the Children's Theater that evening to see *Jungle Book*. On my way out the door, the phone rang. It was Jim Baker.

I had worked closely with Baker when he was President Reagan's chief of staff and treasury secretary, and then President Bush's campaign manager and secretary of state. We were about the same vintage, fellow lawyers and dedicated politicos. I had always admired his intelligence and directness, and the way he got difficult things done leaving everyone smiling.

"The governor needs you in Tallahassee immediately," he said. I considered it irrelevant and obviously pointless to tell him about my packed schedule, so I said okay. Baker wanted me on the scene by early the next morning so I boarded a jet at 6:30 A.M. in Philadelphia and arrived about 9:00 A.M. with the Sunday morning crew at the Bush headquarters in Tallahassee.

The headquarters, which had been commandeered from the Florida Republican State Committee, was a beehive of activity. Baker was the commanding general and he had an army of some of the best legal talent in the country assembled there.

I immediately plunged into the facts on the chads, dimples, and butterfly ballots. I reviewed the applicable law including Article II, Section 1, of the Constitution, which provided for selection of states' presidential electors. Then I studied the confusing federal statute enacted in the Tilden-Hays era, which provided a safe haven for presidential electors if certain procedures were followed. Most of all, I got a feel for the politics of the local trial courts and the Florida State Supreme Court, which held its sessions close by in Tallahassee.

Baker wanted me to handle Governor Bush's major media briefing of the day, which was scheduled around noon. The briefing was held in a large state office building filled with TV cameras, radio microphones, and print media. There was almost as much media outside the building as inside. I commented on the evidence and the law, and concluded Bush had carried Florida and said the nation's interests would be best

mented, "The Court's majority has embarked on a venture as detached from any Constitutional moorings as was the liberal Warren Court of the 1960s in its most activist mood." In 1999 former Solicitor General Walter Dellinger, a leading constitutional scholar, described these cases as "one of the three or four major shifts in constitutionalism we have seen in the last three centuries."[6]

Following the patent/trademark cases, I made an extensive statement on the Senate floor in August 1999 concluding that those cases "drastically reduced the Constitutional power of Congress" and were a "usurpation of Congressional authority."

When the trend continued in 2000, Senator Joe Biden and I introduced Senate Bill 3086 on September 21, providing that the Supreme Court of the United States shall permit the telecast of all open sessions unless the Court decides by majority vote that such coverage of a particular case would constitute a violation of due process rights of a party. The Court would obviously have the last word on the constitutionality of such legislation under the doctrine of separation of powers. Since 1803, *Marbury* v. *Madison* had given the Court the power to decide what was a constitutional issue and when the Constitution was violated.

Notwithstanding the doctrine of separation of powers, I felt Congress had sufficient established authority over the Court's structure and procedures to make such legislation constitutionally sound. The Constitution provides for the Court's jurisdiction "under such regulations as the Congress shall make." Acts of Congress establish time limits for criminal trials and appellate habeas corpus proceedings, the number of justices, what constitutes a quorum, and the Court's calendar and procedures in the event of disability of the chief justice. I summarized my argument for televising the Supreme Court in a Senate floor statement:

> The purpose of this legislation is to open to public view what the Supreme Court of the United States does in rendering important decisions. It is grounded on the proposition that since the Supreme Court of the United States has assumed the power to decide the cutting-edge questions on public policy today and has in effect become virtually a "super legislature" . . . the public has a right to know what the Supreme Court is doing, and that right would be substantially enhanced by televising the oral arguments.

I had long before not only accepted but endorsed *Marbury* v. *Madison*. That was a contentious issue in Judge Bork's confirmation battle when he argued that absent original intent, there was no judicial legitimacy, and absent judicial legitimacy, there could be no judicial review. In 1986, then–Attorney General Meese and presidential candidate Pat Robertson agreed with Bork's arguments and publicly questioned the Supreme Court's supremacy.

I had also fought efforts to limit federal court jurisdiction under an 1868 Supreme Court decision in *Ex Parte McCardle,* which could have removed the Court's final authority to interpret the Constitution. As recently as 1982, the Senate passed an amendment to prohibit the Court from asserting jurisdiction to require busing as a remedy for racial discrimination. The House did not concur so the Senate action did not become a federal statute. While insisting on the Court's traditional role in interpreting the Constitution, I strongly believed the public should understand what the Court was doing.

THE CANDIDATES GO TO COURT

After the election in 2000, the candidates turned to the courts to decide the contest. The Florida recount, the ruling of the Florida Secretary of State, the trial court hearings, and the appellate decisions created a political and emotional roller-coaster ride. On Saturday, December 8, several thousand Pennsylvania politicos had assembled in New York City for the 101st Annual Pennsylvania Society Dinner. That morning, there was pervasive gloom at the Pennsylvania Manufacturers' Seminar, attended mostly by Republicans, because of Friday's 4–3 decision by the Florida Supreme Court endorsing massive recounts, which were thought to presage a Gore victory.

That afternoon, just before a 3:00 P.M. National Public Radio debate with Nevada Sen. Harry Reid, I learned that the U.S. Supreme Court had stayed the Florida Supreme Court order shortly after the recount had begun. I marveled at Justice Scalia's convoluted reasoning on "irreparable injury" to Bush: that the public would never accept a later Bush legal victory if Gore amassed the most votes in an erroneous intervening recount. Justice Scalia wrote:

> The counting of votes that are of questionable legality does in my view threaten irreparable harm to [Bush], and to the country, by casting a cloud upon what he claims to be the legitimacy of his election. . . . Per-

mitting the count to proceed on that erroneous basis will prevent an accurate recount from being conducted on a proper basis later . . . [7]

Although I was glad Scalia was on my side, that was, in my legal judgment, an untenable stretch of the equitable doctrine of "irreparable injury." In my squash discussion with Bruce Kassold I hadn't predicted the rationale, but I had foreseen the result.

When the Supreme Court scheduled oral arguments on *Bush* v. *Gore,* Senator Biden and I wrote to Chief Justice Rehnquist on November 29, 2000, urging television cameras be allowed in the chamber. Rehnquist declined in a curt note on December 1, 2000. Perhaps our request had some effect on the Court's unprecedented order to release a taped recording of the oral arguments as soon as the proceeding ended.

The day of the final argument, Monday, December 11, 2000, was filled with drama that no Hollywood script could match. Gary Cooper and *High Noon* were dull by comparison. The streets surrounding the Supreme Court building were overrun with television trucks and inter- viewers who intercepted arriving senators, House members, cabinet officers, academics, and columnists.

Inside the clerk's office, I talked to Don Evans, Bush's closest Texas confidant and later secretary of commerce, former Secretary of Trans- portation Bill Coleman, former White House Counsel Lloyd Cutler, and many past and present members of Congress. A special section had been reserved for so-called dignitaries immediately behind the aisle that separated the area reserved for members of the Supreme Court Bar. I was seated in the front row at the center aisle until I moved over to squeeze in Sen. John Warner, a late arrival. I thought it appropriate that, as usual, the front section had been reserved on a first-come, first-serve basis for those attorneys who were admitted to practice before the Court. They had begun arriving before 6:00 A.M. for the ten o'clock argument.

As the starting time approached, the courtroom was abuzz with ner- vous conversation. I sat next to Bill Daley, son and brother of Chicago's famous mayors, who had resigned as secretary of commerce to run Gore's campaign. David Boise, the lawyer famous for the Microsoft case and even more so for his many TV appearances in Florida's recount, came over to talk.

"Your best argument," I told Boise, "is that the institutional integrity of the Court depends on following the precedents and leaving the Florida state court decisions intact." Believing that the Court would not accept that or any other Gore argument, and knowing Boise wouldn't listen anyhow, I felt free to advise. Daley glared at me and said, "Don't listen to him, David. He's trying to trick you."

The two-hour session was lively with justices firing questions, except for Thomas, who retained his reputation for silence. As expected, Boise emphasized the precedents that state laws were interpreted with finality by the highest court of the state, without federal court intervention, especially in the context of the Constitution explicitly giving the state the authority to determine the manner of selecting presidential electors.

For Bush, Ted Olson argued that the Equal Protection Clause was violated because the Florida Supreme Court had not established uniform or equal standards for conducting the recount and there was not enough time for the court to do that and still have a recount. The federal "safe harbor" statute provided there could be no challenge to the designated electors if they were selected six days before the tabulation by the electoral college, which was set for December 18. Olson won the case and the solicitor general's job in the process.

Ruling for Bush in a per curiam opinion, a joint statement without a single author, Rehnquist, Scalia, Anthony Kennedy, Sandra Day O'Connor, and Thomas said, "The recount cannot be conducted in compliance with the requirements of equal protection and due process without substantial additional work." The opinion then cited the federal "safe harbor" statute that

> requires that any controversy or contest that is designed to lead to a conclusive selection of electors be completed by December 12. That date is upon us, and there is no recount procedure in place under the State Supreme Court's order that comports with minimal Constitutional standards.

In dissent, Justices Souter and Breyer agreed that the existing procedures violated the Equal Protection Clause but reasoned that there was enough time for a recount before December 18, the day the electoral college was scheduled to meet. Failing to qualify under the "safe harbor" statute, they said, was not determinative because the electors could qualify without that presumption.

From the reasoning of the per curiam opinion, the Court felt obliged to issue its decision with opinions by December 12, which it did at ten o'clock that night. It was obviously a prodigious job for the nine justices to issue six lengthy, complex opinions in only thirty-four hours after the oral argument, even if some drafts had been prepared in advance.

The dissents were biting. Justice Ginsburg violated the Court's custom of civility by curtly concluding her opinion with "I dissent" instead of the standard "I respectfully dissent." Although Justice Stevens, a Republican appointed by President Ford in 1975, included the word "respectfully," his opinion minced no words:

> What must underlie petitioners' entire federal assault on the Florida election procedures is an unstated lack of confidence in the impartiality and capacity of the state judges who would make the critical decisions if the vote count were to proceed. Otherwise, their position is wholly without merit. The endorsement of that position by the majority of this Court can only lend credence to the most cynical appraisal of the work of judges throughout the land. It is confidence in the men and women who administer the judicial system that is the true backbone of the rule of law. Time will one day heal the wound to that confidence that will be inflicted by today's decision. One thing, however, is certain. Although we may never know with complete certainty the identity of the winner of this year's Presidential election, the identity of the loser is perfectly clear. It is the Nation's confidence in the judge as an impartial guardian of the rule of law.

Many legal scholars were even less charitable. More than 660 of them signed an ad in the *New York Times* objecting to the *Bush* v. *Gore* decision on the ground that the justices acted "as political proponents for candidate Bush, not as judges."

"The three (or more) justices who bought into those [Bush's] arguments were, at the very least, guilty of hasty and careless constitutional decision making," wrote two leading constitutional law professors at California universities, Vikram David Amar of Hastings College of the Law and Alan Brownstein at the Davis School of Law.[8]

Views of the Court's decision often reflected the writers' politics. But even staunch Bush supporters stopped short of praising the decision on its merits. Richard A. Epstein, interim dean and professor at the University of Chicago Law School and a conservative, wrote an essay defending the *Bush* v. *Gore* decision: "If Constitutional law is politics by another name, then it makes no more sense to condemn the United States Supreme Court for its political predilections than to condemn the Florida Supreme Court for its."[9]

Although I liked the result because my team won, an impartial view could not overlook the weakness of the five-member per curiam opinion, which rested on the statute providing the electors' legitimacy could not be challenged if completed by December 12. There was arguably sufficient time until December 18 to complete the recount with the electors' legitimacy reasonably secure, although not inviolate under the "safe harbor" provision.

Even for the liberal publication *The Nation,* the language was especially strong: "The Court committed the unpardonable sin of being a knowing surrogate for the Republican party instead of being an impartial arbiter of the law. . . . That an election for an American President can be stolen by the highest court in the land under the deliberate pretext of an inapplicable constitutional provision has got to be one of the most frightening and dangerous events ever to have occurred in this country."[10]

As we awaited the court decisions, Dick Cheney, poised to ascend to the vice presidency, met with the five Senate Republican centrists in my Capitol office, where we talked about a wide variety of subjects. The Cheney meeting was portentous, drawing live coverage on CNN of Cheney striding down the aisle to my hideaway. There was some thinking that the centrists would hold the decisive balance of power in a 50–50 Senate.

We thoroughly enjoyed the lunch with Cheney, whom most of us had known since he served in the House and as defense secretary. We were impressed with his casual, down-to-earth approach. I worried a little when he ordered fried chicken, considering he had just suffered his fourth heart attack, but he devoured it with gusto.

With the election still in the courts, we turned to look after our "walking wounded"—defeated Republicans, as Senator Hugh Scott had once used the term. With a 50–50 split, no sitting Republican senator was going to get a cabinet appointment and tip control of the Senate to the Democrats, but senators who had lost in 2000 might be hot commodities.

We made recommendations. Slade Gorton, who had narrowly lost his Washington Senate seat, wanted a spot on the U.S. Supreme Court.

I thought at seventy-two the odds looked a little long, but there was no harm in trying. We recommended Spence Abraham, defeated for re-election in Michigan for a key position, which later evolved into secretary of energy. We urged the appointment of John Ashcroft, who lost his seat to Missouri Governor Mel Carnahan after Carnahan died in a plane crash, for attorney general.

The president-elect was concerned as to whether Ashcroft could be confirmed with a 50–50 split and the Republican moderates in doubt because of Ashcroft's extremely conservative record. Giving the traditional deference to the president on cabinet officers, contrasted with Supreme Court nominees, I felt Ashcroft should be confirmed. After all, he had won five elections, twice for state attorney general, twice for governor, and once for the Senate, in a moderate swing state. We had no idea that our input would prove pivotal in Ashcroft's appointment. But the administration was concerned about confirming him and without the centrists, Ashcroft might not have had the fifty votes plus Cheney he needed.

It was ironic that the thirty-five-day drama of hearings, trials, and appeals produced the same result that a recount apparently would have—a Bush victory. A comprehensive review of 64,248 ballots in all sixty-seven Florida counties found that George Bush's 537-vote margin would have increased to 1,665 under the counting standards advocated by Gore supporters.[11] As the *Washington Post* put it, "President Bush's victory in Florida, which gave him the White House, almost certainly would have endured even if a manual ballot recount stopped by the U.S. Supreme Court had been allowed to go forward."[12]

While the Supreme Court's opinion raised doubts in many minds as to whether Bush had really won the presidency, challenges to the new president's legitimacy in his administration's opening days were smothered by Clinton's outrageous conduct on the pardons. The converse of the dictum "With friends like these, who needs enemies?" would be "With enemies like Clinton, who needs friends on the Supreme Court?"

SENATOR JEFFORDS BLOWS UP WASHINGTON

The 2000 elections split the U.S. Senate 50–50, the first time the body was evenly divided in 120 years, except for a brief period in 1953. Similarly, the committees were evenly divided. But Republicans maintained control and Senator Trent Lott retained his title as majority leader because the GOP held a 51–50 advantage counting the vice president's tie-breaking vote. And Democratic Minority Leader Tom Daschle of South Dakota agreed to an arrangement where a bill or nomination would be reported to the full Senate on the application of the majority leader where a committee was evenly divided, such as a Judiciary split 9–9 on reporting out a judicial nomination.

The key concern was that control of the Senate could change hands with the loss of a single Republican Senator. Sen. Strom Thurmond was ninety-eight. Strom had been vigorous and in remarkably good health until the fall of 2000, when he began to show signs of decline. His handshake remained firm, he attended all the sessions and was alert, but he obviously grew tired as our sessions frequently went past 10:00 or 11:00 P.M., and even to midnight when we voted on the tax bill on May 21. We joked a little, saying that each morning forty-nine of us would walk in, shake Strom's hand, take his pulse, and tell him how much we admired and loved him.

It wasn't a problem with Senator Thurmond that ultimately tipped the balance. It turned out to be Senator Jim Jeffords of Vermont, one of the small band of remaining Republican moderates. The moderates, once a powerful group in the Senate with such stalwarts as Jacob Javits of New York, Clifford Case of New Jersey, Hugh Scott, Richard Schweicker and John Heinz of Pennsylvania, Ed Brook of Massachusetts, Chuck Percy of Illinois, Bob Stafford of Vermont, Charles Mathias of Maryland, Mark Hatfield and Bob Packwood of Oregon, John Danforth of Missouri, Bill Cohen of Maine, Warren Rudman of New Hampshire, David Durenberger of Minnesota, Nancy Kassebaum of Kansas, and John Sherman Cooper of Kentucky, had dwindled to a small clique under the leadership of John Chafee. Contrasted with the so-called Steering Committee, which had more than forty regular attendees, only five of us met each Wednesday for lunch: Jeffords, Olympia Snowe and Susan Collins of Maine, Lincoln Chafee of Rhode Island, and me.

Jim customarily did not say a great deal and his hearing was bad, so we had no clue of the depth of his dissatisfaction, or that he was even considering voting with the Democrats on organizational matters. We knew that the White House had snubbed Jim when a constituent from Vermont was honored as Teacher of the Year and Jeffords was not invited to the White House ceremony even though he was chairman of the Senate Education Committee. We did not know how badly that had rankled him.

Subordinates frequently do what they think the boss wants done. I am confident that President Bush did not seek to exclude Jeffords or even know about it. That incident was reminiscent of Alabama Sen. Richard Shelby's getting only one ticket to the White House when Alabama's national championship football team was honored there. Shortly thereafter, Shelby changed from Democrat to Republican, and many attribute that switch, at least in part, to that White House snub. It offers a good lesson that when something like that occurs, the president should acknowledge it and make amends.

We also knew that Jim's views, even though he was chairman, were in the distinct minority on the Education Committee and that Senator Lott and the White House sometimes circumvented him and dealt directly with Senator Judd Gregg of New Hampshire. Again, we did not know that Jim was so disturbed by that factor.

The first real insight occurred late on Monday, May 21. Senator Lott had scheduled votes to begin at 6:00 P.M. on the so-called votarama on the tax reconciliation bill, which is limited to twenty hours of debate. When that time expires, votes occur on all of the pending amendments. On that evening, we voted seventeen times, adjourning around midnight. Jim told Olympia Snowe near midnight that he was considering becoming an "independent Republican" and voting with the Democrats for organizational purposes. He and Olympia had been close friends since their days together in the House of Representatives in the 1970s. Olympia immediately called the White House but could not reach Chief of Staff Andrew Card until the following morning.

On Tuesday, May 22, the Senate corridors were abuzz with the rumor that Jim Jeffords was contemplating organizing with the Democrats. When I heard that, I simply didn't believe it and responded to media inquiries, "It shouldn't happen, it can't happen, it won't happen." Well, I was wrong. When I talked to Jim privately later that day, he told me the Democrats had offered him "the moon."

On Wednesday, May 23, I walked through the corridor adjacent to the Senate floor at about 10:00 A.M. when voting on the tax bill was resuming, and joined a conversation between Senators John Warner of Virginia and Chuck Hegel of Nebraska. When Olympia Snowe walked by, John motioned her to join the group and we talked about the potential of Jeffords's defection. Warner suggested that we meet with Jim that morning at 10:45.

When that small group disbanded, Olympia and I continued the conversation and decided to walk over to the majority leader's office, where a leadership meeting was in process involving Senators Lott, Nickles, Santorum, and Craig.

We talked about what we could do to try to keep Jim in the Republican caucus: waiving the term limits on his committee chairmanship, making a place for him in leadership, and providing more funding for education. In January 1995, the Senate Republican Conference adopted a rule of limiting chairmanships to six years so Jim's position would expire in January 2003. The leadership group agreed to go so far as to make federal funding for special education an entitlement, which would have added billions of dollars to the program without yearly appropriations. Lott and others quickly agreed to my suggestion that Jeffords be appointed to a leadership position and that the term limits be waived on his chairmanship of the Education Committee.

Shortly after 10:45 A.M., Senators Warner, Snowe, Hegel, Bob Bennett of Utah, Collins, and I met with Jeffords in the vice president's office adjacent to the Senate floor for the better part of an hour. We pleaded with, really begged, him to stay in the Republican caucus. Jeffords responded that he increasingly found himself at odds with the party and the White House, which he considered dominated by the far right. He strongly objected to their policies on funding for social programs, environmental protection, and missile defense. We urged him to stay with us moderates and fight, and enumerated the major concessions that we were authorized to make.

We thought he would be moved by the fact that some of his best friends would be badly hurt by losing their chairmanships. In a number of cases, the chairperson was facing a tough election fight, such as Susan Collins, who would lose a key subcommittee chairmanship on government affairs; John Warner, chairman of Armed Services; and Pete Domenici, chairman of the Budget Committee. And everyone knew that those chairmanships were influential in giving voters a strong reason to re-elect senators with enough seniority to hold those key assignments.

We argued that Jeffords's change would fundamentally alter the Senate's agenda and the nation's positions on key international matters, such as national defense, if Joe Biden became chairman of the Foreign Relations Committee and Senator Carl Levin of Michigan took over Armed Services. The Senate would no longer serve as the forum for Lott to present the president's agenda but for Daschle to present the

Democrats' platform on such issues as the Patient's Bill of Rights and campaign finance reform. Perhaps some of those arguments only strengthened his resolve. Jim appeared unmoved, I think, because he felt he had already given his commitment to the Democrats and was past the point of no return. He did, however, agree to meet with us again that afternoon.

Later that morning, I informed Senator Jon Kyl of Arizona of that meeting. Kyl, who had recently taken over the Steering Committee chairmanship from Senator Phil Gramm, invited me to the Steering Committee lunch that day to report on what had occurred. I was hesitant to accept because we had our regular Wednesday moderates lunch meeting. On that day, as chance would have it, Jeffords was host. When I went into the Senate dining room at about 12:45 P.M. looking for the moderates lunch, I found no one there, so I walked upstairs to the Mansfield Room, where the Steering Committee had convened, stepped inside, saw Snowe and Collins sitting at a table with Warner, and joined them. Chafee joined us a few moments later.

Jeffords was the day's obvious hot topic. Kyl first called on Warner, who had taken over as de facto chairman of our rump group since he had convened the first discussion in the Senate corridor and then led the morning meeting. Warner, Snowe, Bennett, and I gave brief reports. While no formal vote was taken, the Steering Committee seemed to approve our offers and efforts to persuade Jim Jeffords to remain in the Republican caucus.

At the 4:00 P.M. meeting with Jeffords, the group grew to eleven senators, with Pete Domenici, Ted Stevens, Lugar, Grassley, and Chafee joining. While not all were moderates, all were welcome.

I grew a little apprehensive when Jeffords did not arrive for twenty or twenty-five minutes, but he finally appeared after a call was made to his office. While covering the same ground as the morning meeting, this meeting was more emotional. As the newspapers reported, Senator Grassley wept and couldn't speak. There were few dry eyes in the room. Only Senator Chafee dissented when called upon and said, "Go, Jim, go!"

This time, unlike the morning meeting, Jim Jeffords seemed to be moved by our entreaties and said he would reconsider when he traveled to Vermont later that day. When the forty-five-minute meeting ended, I thought we had a significant chance to keep Jim in our Republican caucus. Hegel was quoted in the next day's newspapers saying that he would be very surprised if Jeffords announced that day he was leaving.

We all held our breath at 9:30 A.M. on Thursday, May 24, as Jim Jeffords strode to the microphone in his home state of Vermont before live television cameras. CBS and CNN had asked and received permission to come to my office and film me watching the Jeffords announcement.

I was deeply disappointed with what I heard and said so in brief comments to the TV cameras upon conclusion of Jeffords's announcement. He made his decision after discussions with his family and a few close advisers, he said, and based it on a belief that the Republican party had strayed from the principles of moderation, tolerance, and fiscal responsibility.

My feelings were summed up in my concluding statement: "It's like there's been a death in the family."

Thursday afternoon, a Republican caucus was convened to analyze the conference report on the reconciliation tax bill, but our discussion centered on Jeffords. After that meeting, Lott approached me and said he still wanted to bring a moderate to leadership even though Jeffords had turned down that offer.

The initial reaction among Republican senators was hurt, disappointment, confusion, and a lack of understanding about why he had done it. As it began to sink in, anger and resentment became the dominant mood. Word was all over the Senate chamber and, for that matter, all over Washington, that the Democrats had promised Jeffords the chairmanship of the Environment and Public Works Committee. The senior Democrat on the committee, Harry Reid, who was also assistant minority leader, was reported to have been key in persuading Jeffords to turn. One of the inducements attributed to Reid was his agreement to relinquish the chairmanship, which would have been his.

That Thursday evening, Senator Kay Bailey Hutchison and I appeared on PBS's *NewsHour with Jim Lehrer* along with Reid and Senator Byron Dorgan of North Dakota. While acknowledging Jim Jeffords to be a man of highest principle, I raised a concern over whether it was true that Jeffords had been promised the chairmanship of the Environment and Public Works Committee to have a shift in "party control" for a "special benefit." Reid then said, "There was no quid pro quo." I had not used the term "quid pro quo" and responded,

> But Senator Reid didn't quite deal with the specifics as to whether there is an arrangement for Senator Jeffords to become chairman of the Environment and Public Works Committee, which is a position which

570

would customarily go to Senator Reid, and the word is that Senator Reid is going to step aside. Senator Reid used the term "quid pro quo." I'm not saying that Senator Jeffords did switch because he is getting the chairmanship. . . . But one of the reasons may well be this chairmanship and we'll find out about that in due course if we don't this evening.

Friday morning, before another Republican caucus on the tax bill, scheduled for 10:30 a.m., I phoned Senator Snowe and went over to her office to discuss the Jeffords matter. We talked generally about what the moderates' response should be, and I told her I thought we should take Lott up on his offer for a leadership position very promptly. She agreed, and asked if I would like that position. I said I would. I had thought that among Snowe, Collins, Chafee, and me, I would be the logical choice since I was senior in the group and Snowe had already taken the co-chairmanship along with Democratic Senator Breaux of the moderates' coalition.

During the 10:30 A.M. caucus, I told Collins about my discussion with Snowe and she immediately concurred I should be the moderates' representative. When I talked to Chafee, he said it was all right with him, but he thought it was a waste of time. After the caucus, we met with Lott, told him of our discussions, and I was designated the moderate representative on the leadership panel.

In our meeting with Lott, Linc Chafee repeated his statement that he thought it was all a waste of time; the die was cast, and there was nothing that could be done. I urged Linc to withhold judgment on the subject, saying it was certainly better for the moderates to have a seat at the table than not, and that we were trying to work out concerns that had been on Jeffords's mind and were obviously on Chafee's mind. It was apparent that Linc had deep-seated objections that would have to be considered and satisfied to the maximum extent possible.

In a Friday filled with meetings, Lott scheduled a leadership conference for 3:30 P.M. and I attended. The hour-long meeting was concerned mostly with strategies on how we would deal with the Democrats on reorganization, and then Lott asked for my views. I told him that I thought we ought to be considering issues pending before the Senate that would make good public policy and be politically attractive to voters we had lost when Abraham, Ashcroft, and Gorton were defeated.

I used the Patient's Bill of Rights as an illustration. Two hundred years of common law experience had established the principle that when someone is injured as a result of another person's fault, the victim should be compensated without a cap or limitations. An accommodation or compromise could be reached, I said, by permitting such lawsuits only in federal court so that cases could not be instituted in state courts, which Senator Kennedy's bill allowed, where there was special concern about high verdicts. Others at the leadership table appeared to think that modification might be acceptable.

Our leadership meeting was followed by a news conference principally to update the press on the status of the tax bill. When Senators Nickles and Santorum had finished commenting on the tax bill, I was asked about my new seat at the leadership table. I learned later that at that point, CNN went live with my saying

> Senator Lott met this morning [with] Senator Snowe, Senator Collins, Senator Chafee, and myself, and we pursued the issues which Senator Jeffords had raised about greater participation from the moderates—for the moderates to have a place in leadership. And I have been selected by my colleagues to do that. And I just finished my first leadership meeting, and I found it very worthwhile and I found that I had some things to say which presented a somewhat different point of view.

Deeply troubled by the Jeffords events, I had a hard time sleeping Friday night. I awoke at 4:00 A.M. and went to my desk to write out a statement for delivery on the Senate floor Saturday morning while we waited for the conference report on the tax bill to come over from the House of Representatives. I had considered making an extemporaneous floor statement on Friday and decided against it because of concern that I might say something imprecise and later regret it. I was on the Senate floor at 9:55 A.M. and in a position to seek first recognition when the Senate convened. Shortly after 10:00 A.M., I read a brief floor statement, the only written speech I remember delivering in my twenty years in the U.S. Senate.

Stating that I took second place to no one on independence in voting, I said I thought the organizational vote belonged to the party that supported the senator's election. Without using Senator Reid's words, I then turned to the substance of the expression "quid pro quo" that he had used on the *NewsHour with Jim Lehrer* two days before. On the Senate floor that Saturday morning, I said,

Accepting [that] Senator Jeffords's decision was based on principle for the reasons he gave at his news conference on Thursday morning, a question still remains as to whether any such inducement was offered and whether it played any part in Senator Jeffords's decision.

Reid and Sen. Dick Durbin of Illinois then spoke, arguing that Jeffords acted properly.

While Republicans did offer substantial concessions to Jeffords, it was in the defensive context of fighting fire with fire. Notwithstanding the commonplace practice of political deals at the highest levels, like presidential candidate Dwight Eisenhower's alleged offer in 1952 to then–Governor Earl Warren to give him the first vacancy on the Supreme Court in exchange for his support for the Republican nomination, I questioned the propriety of such arrangements when the consequence was to turn over control of the U.S. Senate to the other party.

This change in party control, with new chairmen of Foreign Relations and Armed Services, significantly affected the administration's program on missile defense. No longer would President Bush's agenda be given priority on the Senate's legislative calendar. Aside from changing chairmanships, Thursday afternoon following Jeffords's announcement found Senate staffers shocked and in tears over fears of losing their jobs. As *Newsweek* blared in a June 4 cover story, MR. JEFFORDS BLOWS UP WASHINGTON.

In my Saturday morning floor statement, I announced that I would propose a new Senate rule precluding a repetition of the Jeffords shift. A senator would retain the right to change parties but could not change control of the Senate by voting to organize with his or her new party.

Roll Call, a semi-weekly newspaper distributed on Capitol Hill, editorialized against my proposed new rule on May 31. The most significant part of the editorial was the candid reference to the "B" word—a "bribe"—in referring to the Republicans' counteroffer to keep Jeffords in the party. If so, what was the arrangement between Jeffords and the Democrats?

Although it has been frustrating to be a "moderate Republican," I believe that once elected as a Republican, there is an obligation to fight it out within the party. Several years ago, I was urged to change parties by the Senate Democratic leadership. I rejected the suggestion out of hand. I have always believed my voice was much more important

573

within the Republican caucus to articulate a different point of view. Lincoln's principles of tolerance and inclusion are worth the fight.

The extraordinary events of the past year have again demonstrated the strength and resiliency of our institutions of constitutional government. No tanks were in the streets or shots were fired when the presidency hung on a single vote in the Court. While recognizing the need for reform, we moved on to the nation's business after the unpardonable pardons. We will take care of the people's business notwithstanding the seismic shift in control of the U.S. Senate on one senator changing his mind. The United States remains whole as a nation and a body politic.

The generally quoted English translation of a famous Chinese saying is "May you live in interesting times!" Some historians say the Chinese word "interesting" means "dangerous" or "turbulent," so the saying is a curse. Any of those interpretations would fit the American scene for the six-month period where Republicans took the White House and Democrats took the Senate.

NOTES

Part One

Leaving the Wall-to-Wall Life

1. Jeanne R. Lowe, *Cities in a Race with Time: Progress and Poverty in America's Renewing Cities* (New York: Random House, 1967), p. 319.

The Crusading Kennedy Brothers

1. United States Senate, *Final Report of the Select Committee on Improper Activities in the Labor or Management Field*, 86th Cong., 2d sess., 28 March 1960, Report No. 1139 Part 3, Washington, GPO, p. 724.
2. Walter Sheridan, *The Fall and Rise of Jimmy Hoffa* (New York: Saturday Review Press, 1972), p. 217.
3. John Rogers Carroll, interview with the author, 3 September 1996.
4. Bureau of National Affairs, *The McClellan Committee Hearings—1957* (Washington: BNA, 1958), p. 301–2.

The Tilting Courtroom

1. Brief for Appellee, *Commonwealth of Pennsylvania* v. *Raymond Cohen,* Superior Court of Pennsylvania, Philadelphia District, October Term 1963, No. 273, pp. 31–32.

Part Two

The Warren Commission

1. Lindy Boggs, interview with the author, 2 May 1999.
2. Gerald Ford, interview with the author. Tape recording. Washington. 4 June 1997.
3. J. Wesley Liebeler, interview with the author, 4 April 1996.
4. David W. Belin, *November 22, 1963: You Are the Jury* (New York: Quadrangle/New York Times, 1973), p. 15.

Truth Is the Client

1. Ford, interview
2. Burt Griffin, interview with the author, 6 March 1997.
3. Ford, interview.
4. Ibid.
5. David Belin, interview with the author. Tape recording. Washington. 7 June 1996.

Quick Reflexes

1. *Report of the President's Commission on the Assassination of President John F. Kennedy,* Washington: GPO, 1964, Commission Exhibit 1020.
2. Sam Stern, interview with the author. Tape recording. Washington. 7 June 1996.

Bullet 399

1. Joseph Ball, interview with the author. Tape recording. Los Angeles. 27 May 1996.
2. Dr. James Humes, interview with the author. Tape recording. Washington. 5 May 1998.

The Biggest Mistake

1. Belin, *November 22,* p. 345.
2. David Belin, interview with the author. Tape recording. Washington. 18 April 1996.
3. Belin, *November 22,* p. 348.

The Magic Bullet

1. Ford, interview.
2. Stern, interview.

Bedlam

1. Dr. Charles Carrico, interviews with the author. By telephone on 28 July 1997 and in Dallas on 20 October 1997.
2. Dr. Kemp Clark, interview with the author, 15 July 1997.
3. Dr. Malcolm Perry, interview with the author, 8 July 1997.

The Sheriff's Kitchen

1. Stern, interview.
2. Belin, interview 18 April 1996.

Truth and Lies

1. Ford, interview.
2. William Coleman, interview with the author. Tape recording. Washington. 5 February 1997.

The Nation's Worst Courts

1. Donald Goldberg, interview with the author, 3 October 1996.
2. "Philadelphia's Magisterial Mess," *Time*, 1 October 1965, p. 59.
3. Arlen Specter, Commonwealth of Pennsylvania Department of Justice, *Report of the Attorney General on the Investigation of the Magisterial System* (Philadelphia, 1965). (*Magisterial System Report*), pp. 513–14.
4. Ibid., p. 8.
5. Edward Becker, interview with the author, 20 March 1996.
6. William Scranton, interview with the author, 12 August 1996.

Peddling Cantaloupes and Candidacies

1. James Cavanaugh, interview with author, 7 August 1996.

Guardians at the Gates of Hell

1. Edward Rendell, interview with the author. Tape recording. Philadelphia. 30 July 1996.
2. H. Patrick Swygert, interview with the author, 24 July 1996.

The Sliding Scale of Justice

1. *Time*, 1 October 1965.
2. Paul F. Levy, "No Political Hurt Felt by Welsh in Bribe Role," *Philadelphia Bulletin*, 16 March 1966.
3. The account of the Hubert case is from Specter, *Magisterial System Report*.
4. Ibid.
5. Ibid.

The Keys to the Jail

1. Frank J. McDevitt, "Specter Accuses Judge of Interference," *Philadelphia Inquirer*, 16 February 1968.
2. Dave Racher and Nels Nelson, "Bonnelly Jails Freed Pair After Specter Visits Court," *Philadelphia Daily News*, 22 February 1966.

A National Model

1. Sydney Hoffman, interview with the author, 28 March 1996.
2. Nixon Project, National Archives, College Park, Md. *Oval Office Conversation No. 512–18*, June 4, 1971, 1:18–1:42 P.M.
3. "Crackdown on Criminals—How It Worked for One City," *U.S. News & World Report,* 11 November 1968, p. 14.
4. Harvey Steinberg, interview with the author, 23 May 1996.
5. Martin Weinberg, interview with the author, 5 March 1996.

Mayor

1. David Garth, interview with the author. Tape recording. New York. 19 September 1996.

Coffins on Wheels

1. Alan J. Davis, Philadelphia District Attorney's Office and Police Department, *Report on Sexual Assaults in the Philadelphia Prison System and Sheriff's Vans*, Philadelphia, 1968, p. 1.
2. Arlen Specter, *The 1968 Report to the People of Philadelphia from the Office of the District Attorney,* Philadelphia, 1968, pp. 61–2.
3. *60 Minutes,* CBS News, 10 December 1968, "Sexual Assaults in Prison."
4. "Prisons: Catalogue of Savagery," *Time*, 20 September 1968, p. 54.

South Philadelphia Tradition

1. Robert Nix, interview with the author. Tape recording. Philadelphia. 17 June 1996.

"They're Younger, They're Tougher, and Nobody Owns Them"

1. "Why the Democrats Sing Chorus of Big-City Blues," *The National Observer*, 22 December 1969.
2. Charles Peruto, interview with the author. Tape recording. Philadelphia. 8 May 1996.

Justice Specter?

1. H. R. Haldeman, *The Haldeman Diaries* (New York: G. P. Putnam's Sons, 1994), p. 355.
2. Oval Office tapes, Nixon Project, National Archives, College Park, Md. *Oval Office Conversation No. 512–16*, June 4, 1971, 12:22–1:15 P.M.
3. Don Haskin, "D.A. 'Would Take' U.S. Post," *Philadelphia Daily News*, 10 November 1971.

"Even Carmella Doesn't Like That"

1. Stephen J. Sansweet, "Philadelphia Story: Urban Renewal Beset by Delay and Scandal in Fourth Biggest City," *Wall Street Journal*, March 17, 1970.
2. Carroll, interview.
3. Sal Paolantonio, *Frank Rizzo, The Last Big Man in Big City Politics* (Philadelphia: Camino Books, 1993), p. 166.
4. Jon Katz, "The Wiretap Controversy: Many Officials Fear Bugging; Specter Plans a Probe," *Philadelphia Inquirer*, 19 December 1972.

A Dumb Mistake in a Class by Itself

1. Dan McKenna, interview with the author, 2 August 1996.
2. Editorial, "Since Specter Won't, Packel Must Probe Applegate," *Philadelphia Inquirer*, 9 April 1973.

"You Know You Can Trust Them. Doesn't It Make Sense to Keep Them?"

1. F. Emmett Fitzpatrick, interview with the author. Tape recording. Philadelphia. 17 June 1996.
2. Ibid.

PART FOUR

Running

1. Ward Sinclair, "Senate Race in Pa.: A Lackluster Story, Promising Suspense," *Washington Post*, 1 November 1980.

Confronting Assad, Arafat, Sadam, and Fidel

1. Ed Henry, "Specter, Levin Hold Secret Talks on Bipartisan Deal for '96 Money Probe," *Roll Call* (Washington), 26 June 1997.
2. "Judicial Review of Defense Base Closing," 108:139 *Harvard Law Review*, pp. 305–6 (1994).

Judge Bork

1. Tom Korologos, interview with the author, 4 September 1998.
2. Ibid.
3. James R. Dickenson, "Running Scared in Pennsylvania; Sen. Specter Aims to Survive in Democratic Territory," *Washington Post*, 6 July 1985, final edition.
4. Ruth Marcus and Gwen Ifill, "Lobbying Groups Gather Steam for Bork Confirmation Battle; Conservatives, Liberals Cultivate Grass-Roots Pressure on Senators," *Washington Post*, 7 July 1987, final edition.

Clear and Present Danger

1. Tom Korologos, interview with the author. Tape recording. Washington. 4 September 1998.
2. Joseph Biden, Jr., interview with the author. Tape recording. Wilmington, Del. 6 November 1998.
3. T. R. Reid, "Robertson's Bid Powered by Faith, Self-Assurance; 'Prophet' Struggles with Secular Role," *Washington Post*, 11 September 1987.
4. Edward Walsh, "In the End, Bork Himself Was His Own Worst Enemy, Intellectual Approach Lacked Appeal," *Washington Post*, 24 October 1987.
5. Ibid.
6. Joel Brinkley, "Angry Bork Says He Will Not Quit Nomination Fight," *New York Times*, 10 October 1987.
7. Robert Bork, *The Tempting of America* (Touchstone/Simon & Schuster: New York, 1990), pp. 301–2.

Hill versus Thomas

1.   Jane Mayer and Jill Abramson, *Strange Justice:The Selling of Clarence Thomas* (New York: Houghton Mifflin, 1994), p. 178.
2.   Biden, interview.
3.   Ibid.
4.   Ibid.

The Senate on Trial

1.   Mayer and Abramson, *Justice,* p. 269.
2.   John C. Danforth, *Resurrection: The Confirmation of Clarence Thomas* (New York: Viking Penguin, 1994), p. 93.
3.   Mayer and Abramson, p. 218.
4.   Danforth, *Resurrection*, p. 92
5.   Kenneth J. Cooper, Knight-Ridder Newspapers, "Supporters of Dukakis Crash Republicans' Pro-Bush Media Event," *Orange County* (Calif.) *Register*, 7 July 1988.

Flat-Out Perjury

1.   Senate Committee on the Judiciary, *Nomination of Clarence Thomas to Be an Associate Justice of the United States Supreme Court*, 102d Cong., 1st sess., 1991, Exec. Rept. 102–15, Washington, pp. 41–48.
2.   Ibid., p. 126.
3.   Ibid.
4.   David Brock, *The Real Anita Hill: The Untold Story* (New York: The Free Press, 1993), p. 117.
5.   Senate Judiciary Committee, *Nomination of Clarence Thomas*, pp. 64–67.
6.   Biden, interview.
7.   Senate Judiciary Committee, *Nomination of Clarence Thomas*, pp. 107–118.

Getting It

1.   Brock, *Hill*, p. 217.
2.   Danforth, *Resurrection*, p. 176.
3.   Florence George Graves, "The Other Woman; Remember Angela Wright? Neither Do Most People. Her Testimony Might Have Changed History. If It Had Happened. A Look at How Politics Works, and Sometimes Doesn't," *Washington Post*, 9 October 1994.
4.   Joseph R. Biden, Jr., to Angela Wright, 13 October 1991.
5.   Graves, *Washington Post*, "Other Woman."
6.   Judith Weinraub, "Arlen Specter's Rude Awakening; Women Have Sounded the Alarm for the Judiciary Committee 'Hit Man,' " *Washington Post*, 18 October 1991, final edition.
7.   Brock, *Hill*, p. 170.

8.   Ibid.
9.   Annie Groer and Ann Gerhart, "A Specter from the Past," *Washington Post*, 24 October 1997, final edition.

The Shriek Level
1.   George F. Will, "A 'Conviction Politician' vs. a Survivor," *Washington Post*, 30 October 1986.
2.   E. J. Dionne, Jr., "70's Mode for Pennsylvania Underdog," *New York Times*, 16 October 1986, late city final edition.
3.   Bernard Weinraub, "22 G.O.P. Senators Pressed to Back Reagan Programs," *New York Times*, 15 March 1985, late city final edition.
4.   Dan Balz, "One Senator's Hour of Reckoning; Anecdote Swayed Specter," *Washington Post*, 20 March 1985, final edition.
5.   Irvin Molotsky and Robin Toner, "Briefing; Specter's Stand," *New York Times*, 6 June 1986, late city final edition.
6.   Bob Adams, "Gender Gap in Pennsylvania Race," *St. Louis Post-Dispatch*, 1 November 1992, late five-star edition.
7.   Michael DeCourcy Hinds, "Tempers Flare as Pennsylvania Rivals Debate," *New York Times*, 21 October 1992, late edition—final.
8.   Editorial, "Yeakel for Senate," *Philadelphia Inquirer*, 18 October 1992.
9.   Adam Pertman, "Anita Hill's Pennsylvania Presence; Specter Has Funds and Polish, but Also Some Baggage from Thomas Hearings," *Boston Globe*, 20 October 1992, city edition.
10. Adams, *St. Louis Post-Dispatch*, 1 November 1992.

Ruby Ridge
1.   *Ruby Ridge: Report of the Subcommittee on Terrorism, Technology and Government Information of the Senate Committee on the Judiciary*, Washington, 1995, p. 46.
2.   Randall Weaver, official interview with the author. Tape recording. Des Moines. 13 May 1995.
3.   Ibid.
4.   Robert Novak, editorial, "Senators Should Recall Promises," *Chicago Sun-Times*, 15 May 1995, late sports final edition.

PART FIVE

Impeachment
1.   R. W. Apple, Jr., "The President Under Fire: The Power Broker; Jordan Trades Stories with Clinton, and Offers Counsel," *New York Times*, 25 January 1998, late edition—final.
2.   Bob Woodward, *Shadow: Five Presidents and the Legacy of Watergate* (New York: Simon & Schuster, 1999), p. 351.

581

3.   Editorial, "Topics of the Times," *New York Times*, 21 February 1997, late edition—final.

The Senate's Finest Hour?
1.   Paul West, "In the Senate, a Solemn Ritual; Chamber Now Enters Uncharted Waters," *Baltimore Sun*, 8 January 1999, final edition.
2.   Helen Dewar and Peter Baker, "Senate Votes Rules for President's Trial; Proceedings to Begin Next Week, Decision on Witnesses Deferred," *Washington Post*, 9 January 1999, final edition.
3.   Joe Battenfeld and Ellen J. Silberman, "President on Trial," *Boston Herald*, 9 January 1999.
4.   Dewar and Baker, "Senate Votes," 9 January 1999.
5.   Editorial, *New York Times*, 20 March 1998.

Hostile Witnesses
1.   National Public Radio, 22 January 1999.
2.   Jonathan Alter, "Disgraceful All Around," *Newsweek*, 8 March 1999, U.S. edition, p. 25.
3.   Henry, "Specter, Levin."

Fraud on the Senate
1.   Senate of the United States, Sitting for the Trial of the Impeachment of William Jefferson Clinton, President of the United States, *Video Deposition of Monica S. Lewinsky*, Washington, 1 February 1999.
2.   Ibid.
3.   Harriet Barovick, Tam Gray, et al., "Notebook," *Time*, 22 February 1999, p. 21.
4.   Senate of the United States, Sitting for the Trial of the Impeachment of William Jefferson Clinton, President of the United States, *Video Deposition of Vernon E. Jordan, Jr.,* Washington, 2 February 1999.
5.   Ibid.
6.   Gene Weingarten, "Attorney at Large," *Washington Post*, 3 February 1999, final edition.
7.   U.S. Senate impeachment trial, *Jordan deposition*.
8.   Lizette Alvarez, "The President's Trial: The Witness; In Breaking No New Ground, Blumenthal Blunts His Sharp Edges," *New York Times*, 4 February 1999, late edition—final.
9.   Senate of the United States, Sitting for the Trial of the Impeachment of William Jefferson Clinton, President of the United States, *Video Deposition of Sidney Blumenthal*, Washington, 3 February 1999.
10. Ibid.
11. Ibid.
12. Steve Goldstein, "Specter Started Probe of Blumenthal's Account," *Washington Post*, 11 February 1999.

13.   Howard Kurtz, "Experts Deflate Luncheon Disputer; No Legal Ramifi-
       cations Expected Unless Justice Probes Blumenthal," *Washington Post*,
       19 February 1999, final edition.

Not Proven

1.   "Washington Wire; Surprising Specter," *Wall Street Journal*, 19 Febru-
      ary 1999.
2.   Arthur Schlesinger, Jr., "How History Will Judge Him: Clinton could
      just coast to a finish now, but to make his mark he has to act boldly,"
      Time, 22 February 1999.
3.   Lisa Fine, States News Service, *Lancaster* (Pa.) *Intelligencer Journal*,
      18 February 1999, "Specter Blasted for Vote in Trial; Many Angered
      by 'Not Proven.' "
4.   James Q. Wilson, op-ed, "This Time There Was No John Dean," *New
      York Times*, 15 February 1999.
5.   Nancy Eshelman, editorial, *Harrisburg* (Pa.) *Patriot-News*, 18 Febru-
      ary 1999.

Epilogue

1.   Associated Press, "No Surprises in Florida Ballot Review," *Washington
      Post,* 11 May 2001, p. A11.
2.   Wen Ho Lee bail hearing, 13 December 1999.
3.   *Reno* v. *ACLU,* 521 US 844 1997.
4.   *Sable* v. *FCC,* 492 US 115 1989.
5.   *Kimel* v. *Florida Board of Regents,* 522 US 62 2000.
6.   "Supreme Court 1998–1999 Term Review," *Legal Times,* 12 July 1999,
      p. S23.
7.   Justice Antonin Scalia, Concurrent Opinion, *George W. Bush and
      Richard Cheney* v. *Albert Gore Jr. et al.* No. 00-949 (00A504), 121 S.
      Ct. 512; 2000.
8.   Vikram David Amar and Alan Brownstein, "*Bush* v. *Gore* and Article
      II: Pressured Judgment Makes Dubious Law," *The Federal Lawyer,*
      March/April 2001, pp. 27–33.
9.   Richard A. Epstein, "In Such Manner as the Legislature Thereof May
      Direct: The Outcome in Bush v. Gore Defended," in *The Vote: Bush,
      Gore and the Supreme Court,* edited by Cass R. Sunstein (Chicago:
      University of Chicago Press, 2001).
10.   Vincent Bugliosi, "None Dare Call It Treason," *The Nation,* 5 February
      2001, pp. 11–19.
11.   Martin Merzer, "In Ballot Audit, Bush Prevails," *Washington Post,* 4
      April 2001, p. A7.
12.   Ibid.

INDEX

Associated Press (AP), 352, 353, 406, 443
Atlantic City, N.J., Specter's law practice in, 268, 269

Baker, Howard, 163, 233, 274, 280, 281, 285, 299, 323, 535
  Bork nomination and, 314, 327, 330, 340
Baker, Jim, 359–60, 556–57
Ball, Joseph A., 51, 57, 60, 76, 77, 79, 86, 89, 90, 92, 112, 113, 115, 120
Ball, Will, 331
Barak, Ehud, 298, 544
Barbieri, Alexander, 220
Bardascino, Joseph, 173–75
Barkley, Alben, 277
Barnes, Dechert, Price, Myers and Rhoads, 12–13, 14, 129–30, 166, 262–64
Barness, Herb, 357
Barr, Bob, 475
Barr, William P., 288
Batchkurina, 8, 160, 290
Battisfore, Marjorie, 33–35
Bauer, Edward, 212
Baxter, Charles, 90
Bayh, Birch, 273
Baylson, Mike, 167, 168
Beasley, James, 121, 247
Becker, Ed, 136
Begin, Menachem, 292–93
Belin, David, 52, 60, 61, 76, 86–88, 90, 114–15, 120, 121, 124
Bell, Ed, 212
Bell, John, 185, 187, 211, 212
Bellevue-Stratford Hotel, 145–46, 149, 156, 250
Bellis, Isadore, 239
Bennett, Bill, 162
Bennett, Jackie, 447

Bennett, Joyce, 162
Bennett, Robert, 441–42, 448, 568
Bentsen, Lloyd, 349
Berger, David, 227–28, 252
Bethesda Naval Hospital, 77–83, 89
Bhutto, Benazir, 301–2
Biden, Joseph, 277, 288, 329, 337, 338–39, 476, 478, 559, 561, 568
  Thomas nomination and, 345–50, 352, 361, 364, 366, 372, 374, 380, 386, 387–88, 395–96
Blackmun, Harry A., 340, 391
blacks, *see* African-Americans
Blanc, Victor Hugo, 13–16, 132, 140, 158, 171
  Teamsters Union and, 13, 16, 20–24, 26, 32
Blue, Carol, 509, 510, 511
Blumenthal, Sidney, 444, 481–82, 484–86, 488–89
  deposition of, 491–92, 493, 495, 496, 497, 502–12, 530
Board of Judges, 249
Board of Magistrates, 183
Bode, Ken, 480
Boggs, Hale, 47
Boggs, Lindy, 47
Boise, David, 561–62
Bok, Curtis, 187
Bok, Derek, 187
Bolling v. *Sharpe,* 333
Bond, Christopher, 518–19
Bonnelly, Adrian, 185–87
Bonnelly, Mrs. Adrian, 186–87
Bonus Army (Bonus Expeditionary Force), 7–8, 10–11, 143

Bork, Robert Heron, 251, 281, 314, 319–23, 325–42, 344, 345, 350, 358, 360, 393–94, 443, 557
  original-intention philosophy of, 331–34, 340
Bosnia, 304–5
Boston Globe, 407, 426
Bosurgi (burglar), 191
Boswell, J. Thornton, 77, 78, 80, 88, 89
Bowron, Diana, 97
Boxer, Barbara, 161, 391
Boyle, John, 190–91
Bradley, Bill, 361
Branche, Gil, 209
Brandeis, Louis, 335
Brandenburg v. *Ohio,* 330, 335–37
Breaux, John, 461, 557, 571
Breuer, Lanny, 502, 503, 504
Breyer, Justice Stephen, 562
Britton, Nan, 280
Broaddrick, Juanita, 482–83, 518
Brock, David, 383, 395
Brokaw, Tom, 381
Bronston v. *United States,* 517, 518
Brook, Ed, 566
Brown, Dorothy, 269
Brown, Hank, 301, 386
Brown University, 163–64
Brown v. *Board of Education,* 55, 333, 337, 343, 367
Brownstein, Alan, 563
Brubaker, 218
Brudney, James, 346–47, 373, 374
Bryan, Richard, 514, 524
Bryant, Ed, 481, 495–96
Bucci, John, 210, 214, 251
Buchanan, Pat, 430, 528
Buckley v. *Valeo,* 265, 539
Bumpers, Dale, 278, 281, 475–76

David Brinkley's
   Journal, 31
Davis, Alan, 167, 168,
   170, 198–99
   prison violence
   investigated by, 217,
   220–21
Davis-Bacon Act, 430
Days, Drew, 388
Daytop Village, 204
Dean, John, 528
death penalty, 289, 313,
   422
Dechert, Bob, 13
DeConcini, Dennis, 322,
   345–46, 349
Defense Department,
   U.S. (DOD),
   284–85, 304–9, 311,
   532, 537
Defense Intelligence
   Agency, 308
defense issues, 271, 281,
   284–85, 291, 323,
   399–401, 531–34
   see also arms control;
   foreign policy, U.S.
Degan, William,
   410–11, 420–21
de Gaulle, Charles, 11
DeLay, Tom, 453–54,
   482
Dellinger, Walter, 559
DeLoach, Cartha D.
   (Deke), 94
Democratic City
   Committee,
   Philadelphia, 13, 21,
   24, 26, 136, 139,
   140
Democrats, Democratic
   party, 279–81, 346,
   350–51, 386, 403,
   407–8, 415
   Clinton impeachment
   trial and, 458–70,
   474–84, 486–92,
   495, 496, 502–11,
   513–19, 525–26,
   529–30
   contributions, 544
   elections 2000 and
   Jeffords's defection
   to, 565–73
   liberal vs.
   conservative, 62

in Philadelphia, 13,
   21, 24, 25, 26,
   44–45, 52, 136,
   139–41, 144,
   151–53, 155–57,
   160, 168, 179, 183
   Specter's switch from,
   140–46
   see also specific
   elections
Dennis, Magistrate, 186
Denton, Jeremiah, 275,
   276
Depression, Great, 7,
   143
DeSapio, Carmine, 26
desegregation, 37, 39,
   320, 333
Deutch, John, 532
Devlin, Bill, 145
Dewey, Thomas E., 29,
   151
DiBona, Fred, 188
Dilworth, Richardson,
   23, 139, 141, 146,
   151, 153, 158,
   159–60, 210, 211,
   236–37, 240–41
Diogenes, 534
District Attorney
   National Convention
   (1962), 25
District Attorney's
   office, Philadelphia,
   see Philadelphia
   District Attorney's
   office
Dobelle, Evan, 148
Dodd, Chris, 495, 526
Doggett, John, III, 364,
   383
Dole, Robert, 59, 215,
   269, 277, 283, 285,
   301, 340, 360, 403,
   404, 555
   COLA and, 280–81
   in election of 1996,
   422, 423, 424–25
   Thomas nomination
   and, 347, 354, 355,
   358
Domenici, Pete, 403,
   484, 568, 569
Donolow, Ben, 13, 136,
   223
Dorgan, Byron, 570

Douglas, William O.,
   193–94, 394
Dove, Bob, 520
Downing, Wayne, 307,
   308
Downing Commission,
   307–8
Dozoretz, Beth, 544,
   546, 547
drug rehabilitation,
   203–4
drug trafficking, 188,
   197, 203, 239, 291
Duberstein, Kenneth,
   330, 345
due process, 55, 190,
   194, 313, 333–34
Dukakis, Michael,
   358–59, 557
Dulles, Allen, 80, 83–84
dumping, in foreign
   trade, 539
Duncan, Thomas, 131
Dunkel, Steve, 430
Durbin, Richard, 486,
   573
Durenberger, David,
   162, 566
Durkin, John, 273

East, John, 273, 275,
   276
Economist, 558–59
Edgar, Bob, 399
education, 534
   desegregation and, 37,
   39, 320, 333
   of prisoners, 287, 288
   school prayer and,
   160–61
   see also specific
   schools
Education Department,
   U.S., 344, 362, 364,
   366, 376, 378, 382,
   388, 451
Edwards, John, 495,
   502, 503, 504, 509,
   510
Egypt, 298–99, 455, 532
Ehrlichman, John, 501
Eide, Julie, 74, 106
Eighth Amendment, 222,
   313, 317
Eilberg, Joshua, 267
Einhorn, Ira, 263–64

589

594

Specter, Tracey
(daughter-in-law),
402
Specter-Shelby
Amendment, 294
Specter v. *Dalton,* 312
Spencer Gifts, 263
Sprague, Dick, 159, 182,
186–87, 213,
243–47, 250
House Assassination
Committee and,
267–68
Stafford, Bob, 274, 283,
566
Stalberg, Hirsch, 165
Starr, Kenneth W.,
438–44, 446–49,
481–82, 508
inexperience of, 444
Lewinsky's deal with,
447
Specter's
conversations with,
438–39, 446, 449
Specter's
correspondence
with, 439–40
Tripp and, 439–41
Tucker case and, 438,
446–47
Starr Report, 448,
449–50, 453
Stassen, Harold, 214
State Department, U.S.,
304, 532
steel industry, in
Pennsylvania,
282–83, 539
Steffens, Lincoln, 131
Stein, Gil, 236
Stein, Louis, 32, 33
Steinberg, Frank, 237
Steinberg, Harvey, 203
Stern, Sam, 94, 107,
112, 123
Stevens, Justice John, 563
Stevens, Ted, 275–76,
277, 569
in Clinton
impeachment trial,
463, 484, 504, 516,
520, 523, 524–25,
529
Stevenson, Adlai, 26
Stewart, Potter, 314, 524

Stockman, David, 280
Stone, Oliver, 121–22,
402
Stone, Roger, 424, 452
Strange Justice (Mayer
and Abramson), 345,
353, 356
Strategic Defense
Initiative (SDI), 325
Strauss, David, 549
Streisand, Barbra, 395
Suckle, Bill, 22
*Sunday Philadelphia
Bulletin,* 48, 139, 171
Sununu, John, 359, 360
Supreme Court,
Pennsylvania, 21,
43, 131, 189
Supreme Court, U.S., 3,
53–54, 115–16, 166,
168, 182, 209, 213,
228, 243, 247, 269,
278, 311–23, 517,
537–39
Bill 3086 on
televising, 559–60
Bork nomination to,
281, 314, 319–23,
325–42, 350, 358,
559–60
Buckley v. *Valeo* and,
265
Bush v. *Gore,* 560–65
Clinton immunity
rejected by, 440
Commerce Clause
and, 558
defendants'-rights
cases and, 55–56,
190–95
Eisenhower's views
on, 154
Ex Parte McCardle,
560
Marbury v. *Madison*
and, 311, 314, 316,
318, 332, 334,
559–60
Nixon impeachment
proceedings and,
259–60
Nixon tapes and, 544
presidential elections
2000, 548, 557–58,
560–65
Rehnquist and, 558

revisionist tendency
of, 357, 388–89
segregation issue and,
55
Specter considered for
appointment to,
231–34, 262
states' rights
decisions, 558–59
televising sessions
and, 559–60, 561
Thomas appointment
to, 2, 261, 315,
343–97, 399
see also specific cases
Swygert, H. Patrick,
169
Symms, Steve, 273,
282
Syria, 293, 294, 296–98,
455

Taft, Robert, 274
Talmadge, Herman, 273
taprooms, nuisance,
202–3, 211
Tate, James H. J., 153,
158, 167, 210–14,
220, 234, 237
Rizzo wiretap charges
and, 240, 241
taxes, 323, 403, 422,
446–47
1982 bill on, 285–86
as 1992 Senate
campaign issue, 406
Taylor, Elizabeth, 286
Taylor, Paul, 272
Tayoun, Jimmy,
223–25
Teamsters, *see*
International
Brotherhood of
Teamsters;
Philadelphia
Teamsters;
Philadelphia
Teamsters trial
Teeter, Bob, 269–70
telecommunications bill,
404–5
Temple Law School, 167
*Tempting of America,
The* (Bork), 341
Tenet, George, 548
term limits, 404, 407